the Prisoner
& DANGER MAN

DAVE ROGERS

the Prisoner
1967 1992
&ITC 25

4

**A CHANNEL
FOUR BOOK**

BⒷXTREE

DANGER MAN

AND the Prisoner

First published in Great Britain in 1989
by Boxtree Limited
Published in association with ITC Entertainment Ltd

Reprinted in 1990, 1992

Edited by Charlotte Mortensson
Designed by Julia Lilauwala
Cover design by Dave Goodman
Typeset by Action Typesetters, Gloucester
Printed in Great Britain by
Redwood Press Ltd, Wiltshire

For Boxtree Limited
36 Tavistock Street
London WC2E 7PB

British Library Cataloguing in Publication Data
Rogers, Dave
   The prisoner and the Danger man.
   1. Television drama series in English, to 1983
   I. Title
   791.45'75
   ISBN 1–85283–260–6

CONTENTS

ACKNOWLEDGEMENTS

THE AUTHOR wishes to thank the following individuals and organisations for their invaluable help and support during the preparation of this work.

In no particular order of merit: Karen and Roger Langley; Dave Jones and Julie ('Snouty') Benson; Simon Coward and Jane Rawson; Howard Foy; Larry Hall; Roger Caton; Colin Bayley (who was forced to upset his regular viewing pattern – but 'gained' as a result); Andrew Pixley and Neil Alsop for their helpful advice.
The co-ordination team of the *Six Of One* Prisoner Appreciation Society, for their unselfish support in dotting the i's and crossing the t's. In particular Roger Langley for allowing me to use his masterful work *The Making of The Prisoner* as a building block in order to define the true story. The boys and girls of Brit TV Entertainment (Chicago, USA).
Don Mead, Peter Harrington and Sheila Morgan of ITC (Filmbond). The management and staff of Channel 5 Video.
And last but not least, my wife Celia and daughter Leah, who sweated it out and wined and dined the 'caged tiger'.

PREFACE

WHEN I first approached my publisher with the idea of doing a book based upon actor Patrick McGoohan's tour de force portrayal of John Drake (*Danger Man*) and the enigmatic Number 6 (*The Prisoner*), I had no concept of the task I would be setting myself. No comprehension of the ordeal that lay in store. Nor any notion of the fact that I, too, would soon become a prisoner of sorts – one chained to the television screen and the typewriter keyboard until the task was overcome. A book is a book is a book, I thought – whatever the subject matter. Perhaps that is true of most subjects, but when one is dealing with a series that has taxed the minds of greater scholars than myself, a series which has confused, confounded and resisted all attempts to categorise its unique (some would say bizarre) qualities, a series that has a fan following second to none (whose membership is so eagerly protective of the subject matter), one is not dealing with any old subject matter, but with the sacrosanct progeny of a television product held dear by millions.

My initial task then, was to ward off any criticism that I had not done my homework, by getting to grips with the *facts* surrounding the chronological history of the programmes. But what were they? How does one begin to approach a subject which, during the last 12 years or so, has been treated to acute investigation in an abundance of 'fan' magazines produced by the official *Danger Man/The Prisoner* society, *Six of One* (?) – magazines which tell the whole story in far greater detail than any one volume on the subject can hope to achieve. The answer. Go directly to the horse's mouth, the co-ordinators and production staff of the society itself – the inner domain of *Six of One*.

Their assistance assured, I was off and running – but in which direction? Wherever I turned for research matter, I found myself returning to the society's substantial outpourings. The facts were all there. All I now needed to do was to collate and shape the material into something resembling what I was aiming for – the *true* story behind the making of the programmes. Page after page of typed material was mailed to the society co-ordination team. Page after page was returned with their comments. Many weeks later, I finally had what I was looking for – as complete a comprehensive picture of the background history as I could hope to find. Armed with this, I picked up my pen and settled down to record the storyline of each and every episode of the *Danger Man/The Prisoner* ethos in their entirity. The results of my labour you hold in your hand. The *facts*, presented for the first time in one (long overdue) volume.

The chains are broken *I* am a free man.
Have a nice day. Be seeing you.

Dave Rogers 31 March 1989

Author's note: *The Prisoner*

Not wishing to confuse the issue I have, for the most part resisted the temptation to inject my own theories and observations as to what is taking place (and why) in each of the 17 Prisoner stories. These are written exactly as they appear on screen (as are the *Danger Man* synopses which, being straightforward thrillers, require little in the way of explanation). The clues as to what Number 6 is up to are all there, allowing you, the reader, to draw your own conclusions as to what is happening. But be warned. In the complex world of *The Prisoner*, nothing, absolutely *nothing* can be taken at face value. The path woven by Number 6 and his persecutors is, to use a non-intended pun, torturous in the extreme. Until you have viewed an episode many times, the nuances and mysteries that permeate each and every story will, I guarantee, throw you more than one red herring – and even then will leave you somewhat befuddled as to exactly *what* has taken place!

Incidentally, I make no apology for placing the story titles of the episodes entitled *Do Not Forsake Me Oh My Darling, Living In Harmony* and *Fall Out* in their rightful chronological order – a full few paragraphs *after* the synopsis begins. That is where they appear on screen; that is where they rightly belong.

Finally, whereas a great deal of argument and debate has been attributed to trying to discover the correct *production* order of the episodes, for the purpose of this work I have used documentary evidence (compiled by Prisoner aficionados Simon Coward, Andrew Pixley and myself) as a basis for the running order of the 17 stories as they appear in this book. It is my belief that this constitutes the correct order of production.

DANGER MAN

A TALL, ATHLETIC figure emerges from a federal building in Washington DC, crosses to his sleek white sports car, throws his mackintosh casually onto a seat and drives away at speed. Cue title music: *Introducing Patrick McGoohan*.

Throughout this sequence, McGoohan's voice-over narration informs the viewer that: 'Every government has its Secret Service branch. America, its CIA; France, Deuxième Bureau; England, MI5. NATO also has its own. A messy job? Well that's when they usually call on me. Or someone like me. Oh yes, my name is Drake, John Drake.'

This was how British television viewers were first introduced to the man whose job was 'of international importance' – John Drake – the latest in a long line of small screen super sleuths. The date, 12 September 1960. The programme, *Danger Man*, a series of 30-minute intrigue and espionage thrillers that were destined to make its star a household name across the world. Not that McGoohan needed or craved such adulation.

McGoohan had a heritage of meritorious film and stage appearances to his name, as well as two prestigious acting awards in his pocket. He had been nominated as the theatre's best actor of the year for his performance in *Brand* (BBC television, 1959) and, barely weeks before beginning his role as John Drake, had pocketed a second honour as television's best actor of the year for his role as the first man on the moon in *The Greatest Man in the World*. His stardom was already well assured. However, although McGoohan had notched up a string of live television appearances, *Danger Man* would be his first starring role in a major television *series*. A vast new public would now be able to see the man who several noted newspaper theatre critics had dubbed 'the most stimulating actor of the day.' Whether he knew it or not, McGoohan was plunging headlong into television's Hall of Fame and his newly-found role would eventually lead to him producing what is now regarded as a television classic – the enigmatic *The Prisoner*, a series that would have viewers and critics alike scratching their heads in an attempt to unravel its controversial mix of bizarre elements.

The role of John Drake, the Danger Man, was created in the fertile mind of Australian-born film director/producer, Ralph Smart. While working in England, Smart had heard that Lew Grade was looking for film technicians who were interested in creating British-produced television films for the export market. Smart took up the challenge. Offering his services to Sapphire Films (a company owned by American emigrate, Hannah Weinstein, and set up to produce television films for Lew Grade's infant ITC company), Smart turned his hand to television film writing and direction. After several years of working on such programmes as *The Adventures of Robin Hood*, *The Adventures of Sir Lancelot* and *The Buccaneers*, to name but three, he was asked to suggest a new subject for filming and, out of several ideas and outlines emerged

John Drake, the Danger Man. At this time, Smart had no particular actor in mind. Then he saw Patrick McGoohan in the television production of *The Big Knife*. McGoohan was offered the role. The rest is history.

Drake was to be a special undercover security operator for the North Atlantic Treaty Organisation (NATO). A man who worked alone and was free to go wherever duty called. A handsome, athletic, fearless figure he met danger every day of his life. He attracted beautiful women, detested physical violence (but had to fight his unscrupulous enemies by any means available to him) and had danger hurled at him from both sources. He was a man of ideals, with a passionate belief in the dignity of mankind, who risked his life in the cause of international peace and understanding.

The stories themselves depicted Drake as a lone wolf undercover man in a post-war world of international tension and intrigue, whose adventures were played out against a panoramic view of the world's trouble spots. Working only at top government level, he attempted to rid the world of subversive elements and to resolve any situation that jeopardised his objective. Drake took risks. But they were calculated risks in the cause of world peace.

A man who believed in the sanctity of human life, he was the only permanent character in the series. McGoohan saw him as 'A man who has done lots of jobs in his time. He doesn't come from a well-off family. He's had to struggle for an education, and has gained an interest in science, going on to university to study science and its effects on world affairs. He has seen a lot of the world and has studied people. He is also an athlete, who has reached the stage of wanting to do something exciting, but also something that will do good. When he comes into contact with international politics, he finds himself embarking on this new career.'

International in both outlook and setting, no two stories found Drake in the same location. One week he could be found in Rome; the next in Paris. A week later and he would be dropped by helicopter into the middle of a sun-drenched Arabian desert, or be gazing down from a cable car swinging high above the Austrian Alps. Or, perhaps, in a small village market, not far from Kashmir. Colourful backgrounds were used that provided the series with exciting locales. Authentic location shots were skilfully intercut with realistic studio reproductions. One such location, this time much closer to home, was used as the background for the story *View From the Villa* – Portmeirion, a quaint *Italiante* village situated near to Penrhyndeudraeth, in North Wales. Impressed by its remarkable architecture, McGoohan made a mental note to use the atmospheric locale again – one day! True to his belief, Drake travelled to wherever his own particular brand of justice could be used to best effect. Producer Ralph Smart said at the time, 'Our aim is to present pictorially interesting backgrounds as well as exciting stories. Today, television can bring the whole world into every viewer's home, and the popularity of travelogues proves how much interest there still is in faraway places. We have literally scoured the world in our search for *Danger Man* settings. Our hero is the most travelled character yet seen on television.'

McGoohan, a man respected for his integrity in refusing to appear in anything he considered second rate, swiftly brought his star status to bear by laying down ground rules for the character. While accepting the physical canvas painted for Drake by the producers, the actor, never a man to mince words, insisted that any 'rough stuff' the series contained had to be treated in the *Boy's Own* adventure comic fashion. Sadism was OUT. Good old fashioned fisticuffs was in. 'He is not a thick-ear specialist, a puppet muscle man,' he said at the time. 'There will be action, plenty of it. But no brutal violence. If a man dies, it is not just another cherry off the tree. When Drake fights, he fights clean. He abhors bloodshed. He carries a gun, but doesn't use it unless absolutely necessary – then he doesn't shoot to kill. He prefers to use his wits. He is a person with a sophisticated background and a philosophy. I want Drake to be in the heroic mould – like the classic Western hero – which means he has to be a good man.' Nevertheless, the fights, (at least one per story), remained exciting and full of suspense.

Having set Drake's attitude to violence, McGoohan, ever the perfectionist, turned his attention to the action sequences and insisted that they were planned in minute detail from the first swing of the hero's fist, to the coup de grâce. Peter Perkins, who served as fight arranger on the series, recalled that, 'Although there are clichés in screen fights, just as there are in dialogue and story action, McGoohan wouldn't have anything to do with them. Every single fight had to be scripted on paper first, then approved by McGoohan himself. He would never repeat anything and everything had to be *possible*. He wouldn't let doubles take the risks and did everything himself.' In McGoohan's words, 'Drake's fights had to be as virtuous as his cause.' Further concessions were gained when the star insisted that the hero should only win against overwhelming odds if he *deserved* to do so.

One thing the viewer did not find in the series, was slap-happy sex on the part of its husky hero. Believing that promiscuity should not be encouraged on television, McGoohan suggested further changes to the character's romantic interests. The producers acceded to the star's request. Drake's encounters with the fair sex were given a similar treatment to his involvement with his adversaries. The first script he received contained a romantic sequence between Drake and a beautiful girl in a hotel bedroom – McGoohan called for the scene to be exorcised and any further scenes of that nature to be eliminated from the scripts.

Although Drake was not prevented from having an appreciative eye for the ladies, not once during the entire series did he fall for, or find himself entangled with, an on-going love affair. The character could obviously appeal to women, but he carefully avoided any romantic entanglements and tempered his relations with the opposite sex with the knowledge that his career was far too perilous to allow him to let his heart rule his head. The handsome hero would not – could not – fall in love. Sex would not be introduced into the series just for its own sake. 'When the *character* logically indulges in torrid scenes,' said the star, 'then I'll play them. I don't believe for one moment, though, that Drake would chase any of the girls he meets. He is the sort of man who has a healthy enough respect for women to realise that it would not be fair on a girl to ask her to marry him while he is away on dangerous missions nearly all the time. His life is too full of risks, too insecure, too roving for Drake to ever fall in love. To do so would interfere with the life of adventure he has chosen. He would like to marry, and he has it at the back of his mind all the time – but it is something he has no intention of doing while risking his life so often. The fact that he *is* taking such risks is a vital element of the stories. With a wife in the background – and probably children as well – he would be tempted to cut down on the risks. Therefore it would affect his work. This doesn't mean that he avoids women. He enjoys the company of pretty girls. And there are plenty of stories in the series showing him closely involved – with women. But only when the *job* calls for him to do so.' The fact that John Drake was unattainable, he believed, made him, in a perverse sort of way, all the more popular with women viewers: a man who kept women at arm's length being a very different matter to a man who chased a girl, only to give her the cold shoulder when the going got tough.

Invariably, each story began with a pre-title credit crime (an assassination, a murder, someone suspected of selling secrets to the enemy fleeing the country, as examples) leading to the hero being assigned to the case by some highly-placed government official or, as seen in several of the episodes, by Drake's immediate superiors, Hardy and Keller. The undercover man would then board a plane in pursuit of the baddies, emerging – several fist-fights later – as the victor, to hand the culprits over to the authorities.

Bearing in mind the helter-skelter production schedule which dictated that studio sets were re-used time and again, and the four-day turn around which left little room for character development, the stories managed to pack in enough thrills and excitement to sate the appetite of the most ardent thrill-seeker. Possibly best described as 'the thinking man's hero', in the time honoured tradition of Richard Hannay and Bulldog Drummond, the stories remained logical and never insulted the viewer's intelligence.

A further distinction held by the series, was that Drake preceded the film/television spy craze for software/gadgets by several years – Sean Connery's gimmick-ridden attaché case used in *From Russia With Love* was still almost three years away. John Drake was possibly the first theatrical secret agent to be equipped with a plethora of gadgets. Tie-pins that doubled as cameras, cherries containing miniature microphones and an electric razor that served as a tape-recorder and transmitter were just a few of the many devices invented by the scriptwriters.

Together with McGoohan, the writing team left no stone unturned in their search for Drake's outrageous – but practical – spy kit. One of the series' scribes, Brian Clemens (himself on the verge of international acclaim with *The Avengers* production stable), dreamed up the following example for the story entitled *Time To Kill*:

Having parked his car in the forest clearing, Drake throws open its doors and lays a blanket on the ground. Reaching beneath the driving seat, he produces two innocent-looking French loaves. He breaks them apart and removes a small metal box. From this he takes out seven rifle bullets. The second loaf contains a rifle trigger mechanism. Reaching behind the car's steering column, he removes a thermos flask which, once its stopper has been removed, reveals a silencer. A tug beneath the dashboard and the undercover man holds an ammo-magazine. Placing this next to a rifle butt (secreted in a false door panel), Drake adds further pieces to the puzzle: a telescopic rifle sight, a rifle barrel (when you're a secret agent, a car's bonnet holds several secrets) until, neatly slotted together, Drake holds a death-wielding device.

As we will learn when the series adopted its hour-long format, the gadgets became more ingenious – and useful – than ever.

DANGER MAN

SEASON ONE

39 monochrome
30-minute episodes

THE KEY

Screenplay by Jack Whittingham

Original story by Ralph Smart

Logan	Robert Flemyng
Maria	Monique Ahrens
Ambassador	Charles Carson
Alex	Charles Gray
Joe	Peter Swanwick
Police Supt	Charles Lloyd Pack
Detective	Martin Sterndale

Directed by Seth Holt

JOHN DRAKE IS called in by the American Ambassador in Vienna to investigate leakages of information which point to the traitor being Logan – an American newspaperman who is also a secret agent – or to the Ambassador himself. Drake undertakes a dirty job to keep the Ambassador's name clean. Posing as Van Orn, a newspaperman, Drake loses no time in getting to know Logan and his attractive Continental wife, Maria. He tells Logan that he has been ordered to contact him with instructions to encode a message for cabling to Washington and then to come back to Logan for any further messages for coding and transmission. Days pass without the information leaking out and Drake becomes convinced that his contact is not the type of man to betray his country. He finds it equally hard to believe the Ambassador to be the guilty man. Calling on Logan, he finds Maria waiting for her husband to come home. They are planning their first wedding anniversary celebration and Drake is asked to stay. Maria tells him that she was born in Budapest, and escaped from the country with her husband's help. Drake's chances of learning more about her background are interrupted when Logan returns looking tense and bewildered, bearing the news that the information Drake gave to him is in the Eastern newspapers, word for word as Drake gave it to him. When Drake breaks his cover by telling his contact that there is a double agent working in Vienna, Logan accuses Drake of lying to him and orders him out of the house. Drake leaves, but arranges for Logan to be watched. Logan, shattered by the incident, questions Maria, asking if she is behind the leak. His wife denies any involvement. Drake returns to his hotel, aware that his taxi is being followed. The mystery deepens when he is attacked in his bedroom by a man posing as the hotel's detective. They fight, but the assailant escapes. Learning from the local police superintendent that his attacker was Alex, a thug well-known to the police as a man with a long record of violence, Drake requests that the man be left free and given enough rope to hang himself. Meanwhile, Logan has found a duplicate set of keys to his safe in Maria's belongings, and confronts his wife for an explanation. With a tear-stained face, Maria confesses her involvement, but swears she knows nothing further. Soon afterwards Logan reports to the Embassy where, in the presence of Drake and the Ambassador, he confesses to having betrayed his country. Drake, however, calls him a liar. He is informed by telephone that Maria has booked out of her room and is heading for a hotel in the city. The undercover man escorts Logan to a hotel bedroom. After several minutes, Maria arrives and enters the adjoining room. Via a bug placed in the room, they hear the woman confessing her love to Alex, the man seen earlier attacking Drake. Alarmed by Maria's scream, Drake races to the room in time to stop Alex strangling the woman. Both are then led away by the police, leaving Drake to comment, 'Other people's dirty work. *Someone* has to do it. Someone's got to – I suppose.'

VIEW FROM THE VILLA

Screenplay by Brian Clemens and Ralph Smart

Gina Scarlotti	Barbara Shelley
Stella Delroy	Delphi Laurence
Mayne	John Lee
Mego	Colin Douglas
Delroy	Philip Latham
Finch	Court Benson
Waiter	Andreas Malandrinos
Cafe Artist	Charles Houston
Housekeeper	Marie Burke
Taxi Driver	David Ritch
Maid	June Rodney

Directed by Terry Bishop

IN ROME, Frank Delroy, an American banker directly responsible for a large reserve of gold held in the city as part of the United States' NATO contributions, is beaten and tortured in an attempt to force him to share the secret of where he has hidden the five million dollars he has stolen. He is beaten with such force that he dies. The crime has been witnessed by a woman who, unseen by the thugs, escapes into the night. Drake is assigned to solve the murder mystery and to recover the missing millions. He discovers that Delroy, though married, had a feminine companion. Her clothes are found in his apartment. They possess a designer's tag: 'Scarlotti'. Scarlotti turns out to be the glamorous Gina Scarlotti, the owner of an exclusive gown shop. Identifying the clothes as being made by her, the woman can shed no light on the client's name, but recalls that she was a blonde. She has a note of the girl's address, but it proves to be false. Delroy's widow, Stella – totally unconcerned by her husband's death – is no more helpful. Drake leaves Stella's home, unknowingly passing Mayne, the man responsible for Delroy's death as he does so. He returns to Gina Scarlotti's shop to inform her that the address she gave him does not exist. Gina recalls that there was something odd about the girl Drake is searching for: no matter how large the bill, she always paid in cash, and all her orders were collected by a messenger – a man who never entered her establishment, but sat outside in his car. Showing her a photograph of Delroy, Gina says that it could be the same man. Drake's next step is to visit a restaurant frequented by Delroy. A waiter remembers the murdered man and describes his constant companion as a lovely brunette. An artist who sketches customers remembers her, too: the woman was an excellent artist herself. In fact, he has a sketch drawn by her, which he sells to Drake. Realising that a sketch he saw hanging in Delroy's apartment was obviously drawn by the same woman, Drake returns to the apartment with the police. The picture is of a small seaside resort, which Stella Delroy and her companion, Mayne, confirm as being similar to the one Delroy kept at his flat. Via ordnance maps, Drake identifies the location and finds his way to a villa owned by Gina Scarlotti: she is the artist, and the woman in Delroy's life. But she is innocent of his death and the theft of the gold. Before he died, she and Delroy were to marry. She confesses that she witnessed Delroy's death and has taken refuge at the resort to escape his killers. Her mention of a wooden crate that her lover had delivered to the villa, saying that it contained old books, leads Drake to a room – and the gold. At that moment Mayne and Stella Delroy arrive, together with Mego, a hired thug. Mego thrusts Gina Scarlotti aside and smacks Drake across the jaw with the barrel of his gun. In the ensuing fight Drake disarms the thug but ends up on the floor – facing Mayne's loaded automatic. As the killer's finger tightens on the trigger, Gina Scarlotti shoots Mayne with the gun Mego dropped during his fight with Drake. Confirming that she had no option but to shoot the man, Drake thanks Gina for saving his life.

In order to obtain information that will lead him to those responsible for Delroy's death, agent John Drake gives the waiter an extra large tip. A scene from View From The Villa

FIND AND RETURN

Screenplay by Jo Eisinger

Vanessa	**Moira Lister**
Nikolides	**Donald Pleasance**
Hardy	**Richard Wattis**
Ramfi	**Paul Stassino**
Mrs Ramfi	**Zena Marshall**
Shashig	**Warren Mitchell**
Detective	**Keith Rawlings**
Airport Official	**Frank Thornton**
Mrs Nikolides	**Nancy Seabrooke**

Directed by Seth Holt

AWAKENED IN THE middle of the night by a telephone call, Vanessa Stewart rises quickly and begins to pack her luggage. She has every reason to do so. She is wanted for espionage and the police are on their way to arrest her. When they arrive, the bird has flown. Drake is called in by Hardy and is sent to the Middle Eastern state of Beth Ja Brin. His mission is to confiscate the girl's passport and return her to London to face charges of treason to the Crown. (At first unwilling to accept his assignment, Drake demanded £10,000 sterling. To his chagrin, Hardy agreed.) Arriving at Beth Ja Brin, the undercover man visits the premises of Nikolides, a key and typewriter repairer – and Drake's contact. Learning from Nikolides that Vanessa Stewart is staying at a villa owned by a millionaire named Ramfi, and that both are occasional visitors to the casino, Drake visits the gambling establishment that night. Ramfi turns up, as do his wife and Vanessa Stewart. Drake takes direct action and tells Mrs Ramfi that her husband intends to marry Vanessa. If she will help him, he will get the Englishwoman out of her house and out of her life. He persuades her to invite him to her villa. Back at his hotel, Drake is dressing when a bullet hole appears in the tuxedo jacket he has selected for the evening. Shashig, an agent of another country, appears from outside Drake's bedroom window. Although the men were once friends, Shashig explains that they are now on opposite sides of the fence: his girlfriend is being held in custody and, if her life is to be saved, he must carry out his order to kill Drake. However, confessing that he has not got the heart to fulfil his mission, the man leaves. Moving fast, Drake assumes the identity of Mr Denton, an attorney, visiting Mrs Ramfi on family business. When Mr Ramfi asks the nature of his business, Drake is non-committal. During a moment alone with Vanessa, Drake tells here that he is a foreign agent, sent to get her out of the country before the British authorities do so. The woman falls for his deception and hands over her passport, agreeing to leave with Drake the following morning. Drake accepts Ramfi's offer to drive him to the airport, and shows no surprise when Nikolides hijacks the car. He allows his friend to drive Vanessa to the plane he has waiting. Back in London, Hardy accuses the woman of treason and asks Drake for her passport. Smelling a rat when Drake says she destroyed it, Hardy swears to make the charge stick in spite of the lost passport. Left alone with Drake, Vanessa confirms his suspicions that she had seen through his deception, but accompanied him to London anyway. Moved by her reasons for doing so – she no longer wishes to be the cause of men dying – Drake pulls her passport out of his jacket pocket and throws it into the embers in the office fireplace, thereby delivering the woman from an eight year prison sentence. Silently, Vanessa is taken away by Hardy's men.

Ordered to Find And Return *Vanessa Stewart to London, Drake seeks information from his contact Nikolides*

TIME TO KILL

Screenplay by Ian Stuart Black and Brian Clemens

Original story by Ralph Smart

Lisa Orin	**Sarah Lawson**
Colonel Keller	**Lionel Murton**
Vogeler	**Derren Nesbitt**
Professor Barkoff	**Carl Jaffe**
Sally Raymond	**Louise Collins**
Waiter	**Anthony Jacobs**
Patrolman	**Endre Muller**
Frontier Guards	**Edward Hardwicke**
	Harvey Hall

Directed by Ralph Smart

PROFESSOR BARKOFF, a famous Continental scientist, is about to sip a drink on a sunlit cafe veranda, when he suddenly slumps forward, dead. He has been shot by Hans Vogeler, a hired assassin. The pretty blonde girl at his side screams. Drake is instructed to sit at the corner table of the cafe in Paris at 6.15 precisely and await the arrival of 'the inevitable mysterious stranger' who will introduce himself with a password. He is not too surprised when his contact turns out to be Colonel Keller. Drake's assignment is to track down Vogeler, who has now extended his activities from Europe to America, and to bring him back – dead or alive. Drake is informed that when not killing people. Vogeler enjoys nothing better than big game hunting, and that the assassin will be attending a bear hunt in a few days. Drake determines to take him alive – despite Keller's insistence that Vogeler be eliminated. At a border frontier post, Drake meets Lisa Orin, an English girl holidaying abroad. Soon afterwards, she catches up with him when he is trying to hide his car in a wood to overcome curfew restrictions. Fortunately, Drake manages to conceal the weapon he is assembling before Lisa catches sight of it. The girl's well-meaning efforts soon lead to them being caught by a motorcycle patrolman who, arresting the couple, handcuffs the two together. When Drake knocks the patrolman unconscious, Lisa shows alarm but Drake explains that he is on a mission of international importance and, ignoring her comments, drags her along with him into the forest. Eventually they reach the hunting lodge in which Vogeler is expected to stay during the bear hunt. They are about to enter when a woodsman and his dog disturb them. Hidden in the trees, they watch the man depart and Vogeler arrive by helicopter. Training his gun sight on Vogeler's heart, Drake is about to fire when Lisa, confused as to what is going on, brings a rock smashing down on the weapon. Drake's mistimed shot draws Vogeler's attention to their presence. Signalling to his men to flush out the intruder. Vogeler, anticipates the thrill of a hunt and crouches behind a rock, his rifle primed and ready to fire. Drake and Lisa hurry to the safety of the trees and take refuge in a ditch, before doubling back on their pursuers to the hunting lodge. Attracted by their presence, the woodsman's dog lets out a yelp and Vogeler and his men close in for the kill. In the minutes left to them, Drake severs the handcuffs with a hammer found inside the cabin. He orders Lisa to run, while he searches the hunting lodge for a weapon. Finding a rifle, Drake is about to look for some shells when Vogeler, rifle at the ready, enters the room. Cautious at first, then recalling that he had left no rifle bullets in the room, the assassin calls Drake's bluff and the undercover man is forced to lay down the empty carbine. At that moment Lisa returns, allowing Drake the opportunity to leap at his quarry. A fight breaks out between the men, during which Vogeler is shot. Drake races outside to the assassin's helicopter and takes the controls. The machine rises above the trees and heads for home.

In Time To Kill, *Lisa Orin's well-meaning efforts lead to herself and Drake being handcuffed together*

UNDER THE LAKE

Screenplay by Jack Whittingham

Von Klaus	**Christopher Rhodes**
Mrs Grahame	**Hermione Baddeley**
Mitzi	**Moira Redmond**
Colonel Keller	**Lionel Murton**
Von Golling	**Roger Delgado**
Receptionist	**Walter Gotell**
Attendant	**Norman Florence**
Driver	**Jack Cunningham**
Porter	**Andrew Downie**
Cable Car Attendant	**Reginald Jessup**

Directed by Seth Holt

DRAKE IS employed by Colonel Keller of US Intelligence to track down a counterfeiting gang who have flooded the capitals of Europe with forged American banknotes to the value of $25 million. His only clue is that an ex-Nazi General named Gunther von Klaus is Keller's top suspect as the man distributing the counterfeit money. Drake gets to know von Klaus by forcing his attentions on the German's lovely daughter, Mitzi, who he meets on a train heading for Vienna. Von Klaus is angry at Drake's attempts to talk with Mitzi. The girl is obviously dominated by her father but, at the same time, she is attracted to Drake. Their friendship develops when they break their journey to visit a beautiful lakeside hotel in the mountains, the grounds of which, Drake discovers, were used to house a concentration camp during the war.

The hotel is now run by the aristocrat, von Golling. Coming across Mitzi and her father in the hotel's rest area, Drake reintroduces himself. Von Klaus, however, concerned by the man's unwanted attention, arranges a test with von Golling: the following morning, Mitzi will remain at the hotel while von Klaus takes a walk in the mountains. Should Drake ignore the girl and follow the German, it will confirm the suspicion that the Englishman is interested in von Klaus alone. Unwittingly, Drake chooses to sit with Mitzi, but she rebuffs him, stating that her father is concerned about their friendship. The undercover man leaves the girl sitting alone and follows von Klaus into the mountains – watched from the hotel by von Golling. Travelling in a cable car, Drake accuses the German of being involved in the distribution of the counterfeit dollars and tricks him into an admission of guilt by warning him that his daughter will suffer unless he gets out of the racket. It soon becomes obvious to Drake that von Klaus is just a pawn and that von Golling is the brains behind the operation. Von Golling realises that the game is nearly up and arranges to rid himself of both von Klaus and Drake. That night, while Drake is searching von Klaus' room, he hears footsteps in the hallway and hides in the bathroom. Accompanied by von Golling, von Klaus enters his room. Within seconds he lies dead, shot by von Golling. Hearing the sound of gunshots, Drake escapes through the bathroom window and telephones the police to report the murder. Concerned for Mitzi's safety, Drake races upstairs and convinces the girl that her father asked him to look after her. He asks her why her father regularly visited the hotel. The girl's reply gives Drake the final clue to the mystery: the money lies under the lake. Begging Mitzi to trust him, he escorts her to the pier, in time to witness the boat departing – and von Golling's henchmen guarding the quayside. Back at the hotel, he locks Mitzi in her room and sets out to play an amusing game of cat and mouse with their pursuers. He returns to his own room and, locking the door behind him, climbs onto the narrow ledge outside his window and edges his way to the girl's room. Watching with amusement as von Golling's men rap heavily on Drake's bedroom door, the couple await their chance to escape. The moment arrives when the men smash down the door and enter the empty hotel room – allowing Drake and Mitzi to race to the elevator. However, with the villains' henchmen guarding all exits, Drake is forced to rip out the elevator's mechanism and await the arrival of the police. When the lake is dragged later that day, it reveals millions of counterfeit dollar bills, each commissioned by Himmler during the war. His mission accomplished, Drake rejoins Mitzi to break the news of her father's death.

In the story Under The Lake, *stuntman Les Crawford finds himself on the wrong end of Drake's revolver*

THE JOURNEY ENDS HALFWAY

Screenplay by Ian Stuart Black

Dr Bakalter	**Paul Daneman**
McFadden	**Willoughby Goddard**
Miss Lee	**Anna May Wong**
Paterno	**Paul Hardtmuth**
Masseur	**Martin Boddey**
Tai	**Burt Kwouk**
Chang	**Anthony Chin**

Directed by Clive Donner

BELIEVING THAT he is being taken to freedom. Senor Paterno and his entourage willingly board a boat piloted by a man named Chang. Barely have they set sail when Paterno and his party are mown down with a machine-gun. In the guise of a Czech engineer. Drake travels to Mankow to meet McFadden, his Oriental contact. McFadden informs him that Senor Paterno is being held on the mainland. the pawn of a traitor in the local spy chain. McFadden can arrange for Drake to visit the mainland. but the agent will have to use his own ingenuity to make the return journey. Crossing into enemy territory. Drake's enquiries lead him to *The Lotus Leaf*. a hotel in Chan-Ling. where he receives a tip that he should visit a masseur who might be able to help him. While there. he also meets Miss Lee, a lovely Chinese girl. From the masseur he learns that the man who can help him follow the journey taken by Senor Paterno is a Dr Bakalter. On the pretext of suffering pains in his shoulder. Drake visits the doctor's surgery. where he again meets Miss Lee. but the woman refuses to acknowledge that they have met before. Pretending that it is vital for him to get out of the country. Drake pleads with Dr Bakalter to make arrangements to get him passage on the next boat out. After further questioning. the doctor agrees. but warns Drake that he must obey his instructions implicitly. The escape route is well organised. and Drake is told to be at the doctor's surgery at eight o'clock that night. As he leaves the surgery. Drake bumps into a squad of policemen searching the premises for Miss Lee. but the girl has vanished. Preparing to leave his hotel. he sees Miss Lee hiding from the police. who are questioning Tai. the hotel manager. He discovers that she. too. is trying to escape from the mainland and persuades the girl to trust him. Leaving her hidden in the shadows. he casually descends the hotel staircase and fools the policemen into believing that he is a colleague of their leader. General Chin. As they bow their apologies. the policemen fail to see the girl descend the staircase and race outside. to be joined by Drake. They walk. unnoticed. to Dr Bakalter's surgery. after which they are taken to the pier where Chang. the man seen earlier murdering Senor Paterno. waits with his boat. Barely have they sailed. when Chang signals to his henchmen to attack Drake. But the undercover man is ready. Drake disposes of Chang's men and is forced to shoot Chang when the man tries to throttle him. He returns to Dr Bakalter's surgery alone. and informs the doctor that his escape route is blown: the others were caught by a patrol boat. If the doctor is to escape with his life. he must do so immediately. Dr Bakalter packs his luggage and joins Drake on Chang's boat. Out at sea. Drake cuts off the engine. and demands that the doctor open his briefcase. The case contains jewels and money stolen from Chang's victims. Headed by Dr Bakalter the gang was running an escape route to death. Drake and Miss Lee set sail to freedom.

POSITION OF TRUST

Screenplay by Jo Eisinger

Original story by Ian Stuart Black

Aldrich	**Donald Pleasance**
Sandi Lewis	**Lois Maxwell**
Paul	**John Phillips**
Alison	**Gilbert Winfield**
Mrs Aldrich	**Irene Prador**
Fawzi	**Martin Benson**
Mrs Fawzi	**Madeleine Kasket**
Casino Manager	**Derek Godfrey**
Aly	**Derrick Sherwin**

Directed by Ralph Smart

ARRIVING AT THE home of his friend, Paul, Drake is taken aback when his friend shows him a photograph of his daughter, Cathy. Although alive, the girl might as well be dead. Her haggard looks, staring eyes and sunken cheeks give her the appearance of a worn-out, middle-aged woman. But Cathy is only 21 – a victim of narcotics. Paul blames himself for his daughter's plight, and turns to Drake for help. Because of their friendship, and because he feels that he must prevent the same thing happening to other young people, Drake visits a police officer friend, who tells him that the only way to smash the drug ring is to wipe out their base in ElDora. Drake is soon on his way to the Middle Eastern state, determined to crush the villains bringing misery and pain into their victims' lives. His contact there is a beautiful American girl, Sandi Lewis, an agent from Washington. Sandi has already tried, without success, to find the man responsible for selling raw opium to known smugglers. She is satisfied that a government official is behind it all and suggests that Drake's best approach is to get to know Thomas Aldrich, an ineffectual Englishman working as a clerk in one of the ministries. Using the pretext of having been educated at Aldrich's old school, Southminster, Drake strikes up an acquaintance with Aldrich and his Indian wife. Later, sharing drinks in Drake's hotel room, the clerk is offered a 'bribe' of £12,000 to give Drake the details behind Minister Fawzi's plans to profit from a tender being made for the building of a new hospital: Fawzi is planning to accept a high tender from a relative and to pocket the difference of a much lower bid. Aldrich, however, is reluctant to accept the money, stating that he wishes only to see justice done. Nevertheless, Drake shoves the money into the man's briefcase – which is then exchanged for a duplicate case by Sandi Lewis. That evening, when Aldrich loses his entire savings during a game of chance at a casino and finds himself presented with an IOU he cannot pay, Drake speaks to the casino manager, intimating that Aldrich has left some money in his hotel room. Accompanying Aldrich to his room, Drake opens the briefcase. It contains torn sheets of paper. Aldrich is aware that if the police are called in he would not be able to account for the missing money. Against his better judgement, he is persuaded by Drake to photocopy Fawzi's secret files which reveal the names of the opium wholesalers who are in the minister's pay. Informed that Aldrich has stolen the files, Fawzi orders Drake and the clerk to be taken into custody – his guards arrive at the very moment that Drake is photographing Fawzi's private papers. However, when the film from Drake's camera is processed, it reveals nothing more incriminating than snaps of Sandi Lewis and Aldrich walking through the streets – together with a picture showing Fawzi's guards arresting Drake, clear evidence that Fawzi is somehow involved. Fawzi has no wish to explain his actions to the police, or to anyone else, and orders Drake to leave the country within 24 hours. However, when Drake reveals his knowledge of the hospital tender fraud, from which Fawzi himself will pocket £140,000, Fawzi realises that the game is up and orders both men out of the country. Back at his hotel, Drake reveals how he switched the camera before Fawzi's guards arrived. Drake offers to find the trustworthy Aldrich a position with his colleagues in London and the grateful clerk departs with Drake for London.

THE SISTERS

Screenplay by Jo Eisinger

Original story by Brian Clemens

Nadia	**Mai Zetterling**
Gerda	**Barbara Murray**
Hardy	**Richard Wattis**
Radek	**Sydney Tafler**
Security Officer	**Anthony Dawson**
Nagor	**Martin Wyldeck**
Embassy Man	**Hedger Wallace**
Parsinski	**Michael Hunt**
Glazanov	**Michael Jacques**
Maria	**Antonia Gilpin**

Directed by Seth Holt

AT THE BRITISH EMBASSY in Slavosk, a young woman waits patiently for the arrival of the British Consul. She is informed by a junior minister that the consul has left the building and is told to return the following morning. In desperation, the woman explains that she is Gerda Sandor, the sister of Nadia Sandor, a political refugee and a brilliant scientist. Gerda, it appears, wishes to join her sister in England. Nevertheless, the junior minister insists that nothing can be done until the following morning, when she will be able to see the consul. The woman leaves and, as the man locks the Embassy doors behind him, he is too late to prevent her being thrust into a waiting car by two burly men who drive her away at speed. In London, Drake is called to the office of Hardy, his superior. Informed that Gerda has been arrested by the State Security Police, and that the British suspect Nadia Sandor of being a 'plant', he is asked to help decide if the scientist is genuine: her 'escape' could easily have been contrived. She could well be an impostor! However, before Drake can discover the truth, he must first get Gerda out of custody and bring her to London to confront her sister. Working in conjunction with Miguel Radek, a one-time comrade, Drake succeeds in freeing the girl. The following morning, the two women come face to face for the first time since they were little girls. At first everything points to the women being sisters. But discrepancies in their stories and memories lead Drake to suspect otherwise. Convinced that one of them is lying, he determines to get to the truth by tricking Gerda into telling her 'sister' a story about their pet spaniel. Nadia refutes having any knowledge of the dog and accuses Gerda of being an impostor. Digging further, Drake confronts Nadia with several names, but the girl has no knowledge of ever having met such people. Later, when Drake gives Gerda the names, she recalls having met one Professor Loutner – a friend of the family. A meeting is arranged, and Drake drives Gerda to the professor's hotel. When they arrive, Radek is waiting for them, his finger on the trigger of an automatic pistol. Aware now that Radek and Gerda have been working together in an attempt to have Nadia discredited and returned to the State Security Police, Drake enters the professor's room, and produces his trump card: Loutner does not exist. He was just a figment of Drake's imagination: a sprat to catch a mackerel. What's more, Drake has the hotel surrounded. Radek and Gerda are trapped in a web of their own making. Gerda's attempts to bribe Drake into letting them go fall upon deaf ears and the couple are deported. The game over, Drake greets Nadia with the news that, although he has no news of her real sister's whereabouts, he will move heaven and earth to locate her.

AN AFFAIR OF STATE

Screenplay by Oscar Brodny

Ortiz	Patrick Wymark
Alvarado	John Le Mesurier
Raquel	Dorothy White
Santiago	Warren Mitchell
Mr Hartley	Alan Gifford
Airport Official	Victor Baring
Barman	Michael Hitchman
Croupier	Andre Charise
Police Sgt	Anthony Viccars
Hostess	Fenella Fielding

Directed by Peter Graham Scott

DRAKE IS told that American economics expert, Arthur Winfield, has committed suicide in the Caribbean state of San Pablo. The American had been sent to San Pablo to investigate the country's finances and gold reserves, prior to the US agreeing to give the country a large loan. Drake flies to San Pablo where, posing as a treasury official, he is met by his contact Hartley and driven to Winfield's home. Their departure from the airport is witnessed by Esteban Ortiz, the Minister of Police. The circumstances of Winfield's death are suspicious. Winfield left a suicide note, but his body has disappeared. Drake is introduced to Jose Santiago, who was working with Winfield before his death. He questions the man about his dead colleague, but Santiago can shed no light as to why the American should have taken his own life. At police headquarters Drake learns that Ortiz personally investigated Winfield's death and that he has information which shows the American was living it up on his employer's money. While he is telling Drake about the case, they are interrupted by the arrival of an attractive local girl, Raquel, who demands to speak with Ortiz. She is hurriedly escorted from the room and the Minister of Police explains that she is impatient because he has been unable to trace her lover who has recently disappeared. Drake meets Raquel again when he is at Winfield's bungalow and learns that the man in her life was Winfield. After talking for several minutes, the girl is about to leave, when two burly thugs pounce upon her and Drake is forced to intervene. Drake overcomes the men and carries Raquel back to the bungalow. Raquel decides to place her trust in the stranger and explains that she and Winfield were secretly married. She disputes the stories of high living and says that her husband was murdered. In Winfield's office, Drake tricks Santiago into admitting that his colleague's suicide note was a forgery: Santiago was responsible for obtaining Winfield's signature on a blank piece of paper. The man had unwittingly signed his own death warrant! Pressed further, Santiago confirms Raquel's suspicions that her husband was silenced because of something he discovered while checking the gold reserves. Raquel herself disappears and Drake discovers that she has been secretly arrested by Ortiz's men. He tricks the Minister of Police into believing that Santiago has spilled the beans about Winfield's death. Reporting to Alvarado (the man seen earlier disposing of Winfield's body), Ortiz is instructed to eliminate Drake and Santiago. That night a bomb is

thrown through Drake's bedroom window but, having anticipated an attempt upon his life, Drake escapes and joins Hartley and Santiago in their car. Drake visits Alvarado and fools the man into believing that he has the proof needed to expose Winfield's killers. Seeking Alvarado's permission to visit the gold vaults, Drake joins Alvarado, who is the country's Finance Minister, as he descends to the bullion room where, joined by Ortiz, the two men watch as the agent carefully weighs selected gold bars. As he already suspected, Drake discovers that the 'bullion' is nothing more than gold-painted lead ingots. Covering Drake with a gun, Ortiz confesses that he and Alvarado are responsible for the fraud. The under-cover man spies his chance and breaks free, releasing a lever which brings a metal security door crashing down between himself and his would-be assassins. As he covers the men with Ortiz's gun, Drake sounds the alarm and waits for the police to arrive. Winfield's killers brought to book, Drake meets Raquel at the airport and boards a flight home.

Above: *Will Drake succumb to casino hostess Fenella Fielding's obvious charms? a scene from An Affair Of State*

Below: *In An Affair Of State, Drake plants a punch on the jaw Of Ortiz, the crooked Minister of Police*

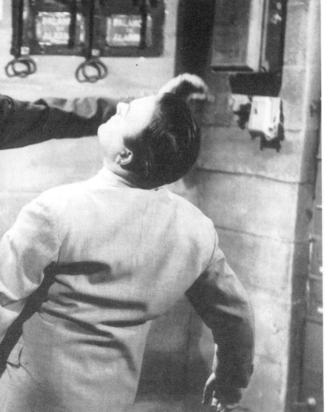

DEADLINE

Screenplay by Jo Eisinger
Original story by Ian Stuart Black

Khano	**William Marshall**
Thompson	**Edric Connor**
Mai	**Barbara Chilcott**
Ajali	**Christopher Carlos**
Professor Moma	**Earl Cameron**
Sir Moses Amadu	**Lionel Ngakane**
Sir Aaron Nelson	**Andre Dakar**
Daniels	**John Harrison**
Bartender	**Lloyd Reckord**
Officer	**Harcourt Curacao**
Native Woman	**Pearl Prescod**

Directed by Peter Graham Scott

DRAKE'S INSTRUCTIONS, received for once immediately after breakfast at a London hotel (his superiors, it seems, have the habit of rousing him from a warm bed at two or three o'clock in the morning!) are clear and simple. He is to call at 449 Wigmore Street. Arriving at the address, 'a genteel Victorian house, on a genteel Victorian street,' Drake is greeted by Sir Aaron Nelson, Sir Moses Amadu and Professor Moma, a doctor of medicine. He is shown some movie footage of an extremist group led by a man called Thompson, who is the mainspring in a web of violence, whipping the people of an African country into a ferment of tension and terrorism. Drake is told that Thompson, the agent of an exiled extremist called Khano, cannot be arrested in the prevailing climate and the gathered African dignitaries ask Drake to help them. Within hours he has arrived in Victoria, Bassaland. His first task is to unearth the facts surrounding the death of Ajali, a man who has devoted a lifetime to peace. His death is now being blamed on British agents. Drake must also find Mai Thompson, Ajali's niece and the wife of a terrorist leader who, by telling the truth about her uncle's death, can bring a halt to the fast-rising fever of revolt and bloodshed. Arriving at the Prince Albert Hotel, Drake immediately makes contact by handing a waiter one half of a torn pound note. The waiter produces the other half and advises Drake to visit a local hotel. Drake follows the instructions and finds Daniels lying ill in his room. Daniels gives him the information he requires to approach the terrorists. Posing as a gun-runner, Drake offers to sell Thompson as many weapons as he can buy. The African, however, cannot make such a purchase alone and Drake is driven to Saul Khano's home. There he meets Mai Thompson but, before they find an opportunity to talk, her husband ushers Khano into the room. The men ask Drake to supply wholesale quantities of arms and are taken aback when the Englishman asks for one hundred million US dollars in payment! They propose depositing half that sum in Drake's name at an African bank. Khano shows disapproval when Drake demands that the *entire* sum be deposited in an *English* bank. Aware that he has no option but to agree to the gun-runner's terms, Khano insists that Drake gives him some security to ensure that the consignment is delivered as charged: like it or not, Drake himself will act as security. He will be kept at Khano's home until the weapons are delivered. In the event that they do not arrive, Drake will pay with his life! Racing against time, Drake places Mai Thompson's loyalty to her husband and uncle against that of the extremists. Admitting that she may have been used as a dupe by her husband to lure Ajali to his death, the woman is forced to concede to Drake's terms when he escorts her to a forest burial mound where, lying stewn across each other, are the bodies of innocent people killed by her husband's followers in his quest for power. She agrees to accompany Drake to Victoria and to tell the authorities the true facts of Ajali's death. Mai is about to leave with Drake when they find themselves pursued into the forest by Khano and her husband. Hunted like animals they race from cover to cover until, discovered by Thompson, Drake is forced to dispense with the man – only to find himself face to face with the nozzle of Khano's gun. As the terrorist's finger tightens on the trigger, a shot rings out and Khano slumps to the ground, shot by Mai with her husband's revolver. Her testimony given, Mai joins Drake at the London home of Moses Amadu. Drake is offered payment in return for his services, but advises the African to put his fee towards peace and understanding amongst the African community.

In this scene from Deadline, *Mai Thompson is forced to shoot her own husband in order to save Drake's life*

BURY THE DEAD

Screenplay by Ralph Smart
Original story by Brian Clemens

Jo Harris	**Beverly Garland**
Hugo Delano	**Dermot Walsh**
Police Captain	**Paul Stassino**
Bart	**Patrick Troughton**
Bruno	**George Murcell**
Barman	**George Eugeniou**
Tony Costello	**Robert Shaw**

Directed by Clive Donner

IN SICILY, NATO undercover agent Tony Costello, lays a wager with Hugo Delano that he can outrace him in his car. He dies when the vehicle he is driving careers through a fence and explodes on a mountainside. Evidence points to an accident, but when a department agent dies in unusual circumstances, particularly an agent investigating a gun-running racket, it becomes a matter for official examination. Drake is not too surprised when he finds himself in Sicily investigating Costello's death. He is told by the local police captain that Costello is already buried and that he will need a court order to check the dead man's apartment. Drake has no wish to wait the three days it will take for the order to be processsed, so he takes matters into his own hands and breaks in. Someone else is there, too, someone who manages to slip away unseen as Drake climbs in through the window. However, in their haste to depart, the intruder has left behind a clue – Juno, a Great Dane. When released, the dog leads Drake to an adjoining apartment in which he finds Jo Harris, Costello's lovely fiancée. Masquerading as the dead man's attorney, Drake gains entrance and questions the woman about Costello's death. She is convinced that Tony was murdered, and explains how, days before his death, Costello changed, somehow – a change she finds it difficult to explain. They had met and got engaged while she was working at Hugo Delano's tuna-canning factory. Everything was going fine at work until, after Tony's death, she was dismissed for no reason. Since then, she believes that she is being watched. She is frightened because Delano controls the whole district. Asking the woman to take him to the scene of the accident, their arrival is greeted by someone taking a shot at Drake. They have run foul of Delano who states that as they are on his property they are fair game and orders them to leave. The couple return to their vehicle, to find Juno has disappeared – from a car with closed doors! Drake returns to Costello's apartment and finds it stripped bare. He reports this and the confrontation with Delano, to the police captain. Discovering Delano hiding behind a door, Drake now realises that the gloves are off. The cannery owner has the policeman in his pocket: Drake and the girl must watch their step. Parked outside police headquarters, waiting for Jo, Drake shows no alarm when a jeep parked in front of him deliberately reverses into his vehicle, and its occupants, Bart and Bruno, approach his

vehicle to lay the blame on Drake. Delano emerges from the police building to confirm the men's claim and orders the police captain to place Drake under arrest. Drake, however, produces proof that he could not have been responsible: the car belongs to Jo Harris who, watching the scene with amusement, produces the ignition key. Angry at being outfoxed, Delano sends his thugs after Drake with orders to get him involved in a brawl for which he can be arrested. Despite being harassed and slapped around by the men, Drake flatly refuses to be intimidated. When Delano and the policeman arrive, Drake and the girl calmly leave the scene. That night, Drake breaks into Delano's warehouse. Finding a cache of arms in a packing case containing tinned tuna, the undercover man is preparing to leave when Delano and the police officer arrive – their guns trained on Drake's chest. Seconds later, they are joined by Jo Harris, who is escorted into the room by Bart and Bruno. Told that they will be shot as trespassers, Drake's face shows no emotion until, at that very moment, Juno, the Great Dane, pads into the warehouse – followed by Tony Costello, looking remarkably healthy for a dead man! Taking command, Costello orders Delano to load the packing cases onto his boat. Then, turning to Drake, he explains why he sold out and arranged his own funeral. The money gained from gun-running proved irresistible, but tonight will be their last run. Costello pleads with Drake to put in a negative report in exchange for his own life. He wants Jo to join him abroad and becomes angry when his offer is refused. Spying his chance, Drake overturns a table and leaps into the fray. Cutting down Delano's thugs, the undercover agent turns to face Delano's gun, but Costello springs in front of him and takes the shot in the chest. Disarming the gunman, Drake escorts the policeman outside where, at gunpoint, the officer is forced to allow the couple to make good their escape. Speeding to safety, Drake remarks that the mission had begun with Costello and he being friends. What happened in between was an expensive experiment, which cost Costello his life.

Spying his chance, Drake overturns the table to dispense with Delano's thugs and thwarts their attempts to Bury The Dead

THE GIRL IN PINK PYJAMAS

Screenplay by Ian Stuart Black and Ralph Smart

Original story by Brian Clemens

The Girl	**Angela Browne**
Dr Keller	**John Crawford**
Major Minos	**Alan Tilvern**
Dr Stanifors	**Robert Raglan**
Hospital Director	**Richard Warner**
President	**Robert Cowdron**
Farmer's Wife	**Colette Wilde**
Country Doctor	**Frederick Schiller**
Captain Franz	**Harvey Hall**
Anaesthetist	**Richard Marner**
Nurse	**Janine Gray**
Telephone Operator	**Marian Diamond**

Directed by Peter Graham Scott

WHEN A strikingly lovely blonde, wearing only pink pyjamas, is found wandering in a dazed condition along some wasteland in a Balkan state, she will eventually provide Drake with a clue to the mystery surrounding the attempted assassination of the country's President – a man whose friendship is important to the Democracies. The man, President Varnold, is lying close to death in the hospital of a quiet little town, although his people have been led to believe that he is in the country's capital. An assassin's bullet lies lodged in his brain. His identity is not even known to the hospital director, and Minos – his Chief of Security – is on guard. Posing as Dr Drake, a specialist in infective diseases, Drake meets Minos and is shown to the President's bedside where an American surgeon, Dr Keller, is discussing the patient's condition with Dr Stanifors, the President's private surgeon. Dr Keller has been brought over to perform the delicate operation to remove the bullet from the patient's brain, bringing with him a nurse, Anna Wilson. They plan to operate later that night. As Drake prepares to leave for his hotel, he receives a message from the American Embassy, informing him of the girl in pink pyjamas who, though suffering from memory loss, appears to know the President's whereabouts and has full details of the planned operation. Drake must interview her and find out how she came to possess such knowledge. Save for a few minor bruises and the occasional lapses of memory, the girl is well and is being cared for by the wife of the farmer who found her wandering alone. A local doctor is in attendance. The girl, obviously an American, appears to be suffering from loss of memory, but from her incoherent mutterings Drake realises that she is fully informed of the President's plight. Visiting the location at which she was found, Drake reaches the conclusion that she fell – or was pushed – from a train. His persistent attempts to penetrate her consciousness result in Drake realising that she is the real Nurse Anna Wilson, the girl Dr Keller brought with him to attend the operation. That being the case, both Keller and the nurse are impostors, and the President's life is in danger! With minutes to spare before the operation begins, the real Anna Wilson is confronted with Captain Franz, the man who pushed her off the train. Her memory returns and Drake sees through the subterfuge: the man masquerading as Keller has been sent to kill the President. Drake must prevent the operation from taking place. Wearing a surgeon's smock, he enters the operating room and tricks Keller into confessing his guilt. A no-holds-barred fight breaks out between Drake and the impostors. Emerging victorious, Drake requests Dr Stanifors to perform the operation alone. He does so, and a grateful President offers thanks for his life.

SABOTAGE

Screenplay by Michael Pertwee and Ian Stuart Black

Peta Jason	Maggie Fitzgibbon
Giselle	Yvonne Romain
Meisener	Oliver Burt
Benson	Alex Scott
Chin Lee	R. Booby Naidoo
Ann	Lyn Ashley
Taxi Driver	Jimmy Fung
Pilot	John Sterland
Co-pilot	Peter Dolphin

Directed by Peter Graham Scott

A TRANSPORT plane on its way from Singapore to New Guinea makes radio contact with its base, then explodes, sending the plane and its pilot, Paul Jason, to their doom. It is not the first of the airline's planes to be wrecked in this manner. When Drake is called to the home of Jason's widow. Peta, who assures him that she will carry on running the business alone, he volunteers to investigate. Peta believes that an enemy of the republic is blowing up the planes to set world opinion against the government and its new regime. Drake joins the company in the guise of John Barnes, a hard-drinking, down-at-heel pilot. He moves into a dead pilot's apartment where his first visitor is Giselle, the girlfriend of the dead man. Saying she has been on leave, she is stunned when Drake tells her that her boyfriend has been killed. Drake pours her a drink and goes into his bedroom to straighten his tie. While doing so, he catches sight of the girl going through the dead man's belongings. Allowing her to leave, Drake carefully searches the rooms and finds evidence that the pilot had been a smuggler. Later, at his apartment, he disturbs an intruder who, escaping to the elevator, drops a key and lipstick. They belong to Giselle who, when questioned by Drake, confirms that her boyfriend had been smuggling contraband. As they talk, the local police chief, Lieutenant Chin Lee, enters Giselle's room, places Drake and the girl under arrest and attempts to take them in for questioning. Drake knocks him unconscious. Recovering, the Lieutenant shows his true colours by offering to pay Drake to take one of the airline's thermos carriers to Balcoa. He refuses to say what it contains and orders Drake not to tamper with it. Drake shows the flask to Peta Jason, who confirms that it is identical to the type her company uses to transport goods. Drake carefully opens the container's seal. As he suspected, it contains an ingot of gold. Unfortunately, Chin Lee is one step ahead. By sticking an undeveloped strip of film beneath the container's lid, he will now know that Drake has tampered with the flask. With no other option open to him. Drake delivers the container as ordered. That night, when he returns to his apartment, Chin Lee is waiting for him — accompanied by two burly henchmen. Drake is beaten within an inch of his life and left grovelling on the floor. He somehow manages to reach the street and hails a taxi cab to follow Chin Lee's car. Seeing Giselle arrive in the driveway of a mansion he is watching. Drake orders the cab driver to take him to Jason's Airline. Forcing aside Benson. the company's chief pilot, he races into Peta's office where, by checking the telephone directory, he learns that the mansion belongs to Meisener, the editor and owner of the local newspaper. It now becomes clear that Meisener, a man with no love for the new regime, is paying Chin Lee to smuggle bombs aboard the aircraft. Then, when the planes disappear without trace, he uses the front page to accuse the new republic of having shot them down. Hearing from Anna. Peta's secretary, that Giselle has changed shifts with the airline stewardess due to fly that night. Drake sees a way of smashing the saboteurs. That night, Peta welcomes Meisener aboard her plane and explains that he has been called in to help them investigate the reasons for her company's lost aircraft. Meisener shows concern when the plane taxies to the runway and takes off on, as Peta puts it, 'a joy ride' to New Guinea. He orders the woman to return to the airfield. Meisener becomes more alarmed when Drake appears. together with Giselle and Chin Lee. The sight of Drake producing one of the thermos containers and threatening to unscrew its lid. proves too much for Meisener who, screaming that it is a bomb, visibly pales when Drake informs him that it is nothing more harmful than a tea urn. Filling his tea cup from the 'bomb' he offers a toast to Peta's continued success.

When her freight airline is plagued by Sabotage, attractive Peta Jason seeks help from undercover man John Drake

THE TRAITOR

Screenplay by John Roddick

Noel Goddard	**Ronald Howard**
Louise Goddard	**Barbara Shelley**
Rollo Waters	**Jack Watling**
Banarji	**Warren Mitchell**
Panah	**Derek Sydney**
Blatta	**George A. Cooper**
Guard on Train	**Guy Deghy**

Directed by Terry Bishop

AFTER TRAVELLING fourteen hundred miles from Calcutta by way of New Delhi to Kashmir, Drake finally catches up with his prey on a train. His quarry, a traitor named Blatta, sits in the next carriage, and he is due to pass on his information very soon. Drake's job is to be there when he does so. Seeing Blatta leave the train, the secret agent attempts to follow him, but a ticket inspector blocks his way. By the time Drake reaches the platform Blatta has disappeared. The only person who can help Drake trace Blatta's whereabouts, is a man named Banarji – a letter writer in the town of Karaz, in Northern India. Banarji is not too surprised when Drake shows him a NATO warrant for Blatta's arrest. Drake advises his contact that he has been following Blatta, a man known to Banarji as 'The Cockroach' and asks the letter writer to trace him. Promising to send a courier when he has some news, Banarji arranges for Drake to be given transport from a garage owned by Rollo Waters. At the garage Drake meets Louise, the wife of Noel Goddard, whose car Waters is repairing. Before very long, Banarji's courier arrives and leads Drake to Blatta. Unseen by Blatta, Drake watches him slip a package into a shopping bag being carried by Louise Goddard. From information given to him by Rollo Waters, Drake traces the woman to a lonely mountainside bungalow, where he meets Noel Goddard. Introducing himself as John Allan, a tourist who has lost his way in the mountains, Drake accepts the man's

Having survived an attempt by Panah to kill him, Drake is ready to face all opposition in his bid to unmask The Traitor

invitation to share a drink. Louise is convinced that she has seen Drake before and, suspicious of the newcomer who has now accepted her husband's invitation to stay for a few days, persuades Noel to take a photograph of their guest. The photograph is sent via a microwave transmitter and, back across the Chinese border comes the terse identification and instruction: 'John Drake, NATO agent. Eliminate'! Fortunately, Drake, searching the bungalow, finds the reply first, but he is set upon by Goddard's Indian servant, Panah. He survives the encounter and Noel Goddard apologises for his servant's actions. Now that the cards are on the table, Noel has nothing to hide. He has no feeling of guilt and can live with the suffering and death he has brought to the people he betrayed. What he is doing, he believes, is for the benefit of mankind. Seven years earlier, when he was working as a senior executive for the Indian Government Service, he had been arrested and charged with subversive activities for which he received a five-year prison sentence. One day he was granted a free pardon by the State, but the stigma of being a traitor still sticks, and he has grown accustomed to accusations against him. Drake gives him an hour to make ready to leave. But Goddard is a dying man, kept alive by the drugs his wife is obtaining for him. Telling Drake that her husband has but one year to live, and that he was pardoned because of this knowledge, Louise adds that should Drake take Noel down to the valley, he will be signing her husband's death warrant: he can only survive in the mountains. When her pleas for clemency fail to shake Drake's resolve, the woman breaks down in tears. Joined by her husband, the couple depart in Drake's car. With the temperature in Karaz reaching over 100 degrees in the shade, and their flight delayed, Drake watches with concern as Goddard grows weaker. Ordering Banarji to travel to Goddard's home and destroy the transmitting equipment, Drake leaves to contact his headquarters with instructions to send a plane. Louise, meanwhile, concerned by her husband's worsening condition, races outside to fetch his hypodermic and drugs from Drake's car. As she does so, Panah enters the room with the intention of doing his duty by slaying his master with a dagger. But he is too late – seeing his servant, Goddard passes peacefully away. Joining Louise at her husband's bedside, Drake thinks to himself that although the woman will hate him for the rest of her life, her dead husband would have understood that Drake was only doing his job.

THE NURSE

Screenplay by Ralph Smart and Brian Clemens

Mary McPherson	**Eileen Moore**
Prior	**Jack MacGowran**
Innkeeper	**Eric Pohlmann**
Hamilton	**Robert Ayres**
Helen Hamilton	**Heather Chasen**
Moukta	**Harold Kasket**
Idris	**Harry Lockart**
Ahmed	**David Oxley**
General Khan	**Andrew Faulds**
Major Ghazi	**Maxwell Shaw**
Pilot	**Harold Siddons**

Directed by Peter Graham Scott

IN THE heart of an Arabian desert, American consulate Hamilton and his wife Helen weave their way through the sand dunes to await the arrival of a helicopter sent to get them safely out of the country. They are fleeing from rebel tribesmen who have assassinated King Salud. Sent to ensure the consul's safety, Drake descends from the helicopter and hustles the Americans aboard. Believing that they are the last Europeans to leave, Drake is surprised to learn that a Scottish girl is said to be hiding in a shepherd's hut close by. He tells the helicopter pilot to take the Hamiltons to safety and to return in one hour. Drake goes in search of the girl – Mary McPherson. He finds her with a baby in her care – King Salud's son who is now the new King. He also meets a young Arab boy who he knocks to the ground but allows to escape. Mary tells him that she ran from King Salud's palace when she heard the sound of gunshots, slipping away with the baby into the night. Explaining that his helicopter will return in 45 minutes and that the Arab boy may have told the rebels where they can be found, Drake tells her they must leave. Their attempts to do so are forestalled by the arrival of Ahmed, an outwardly charming Arab, who offers them a lift in his Land Rover. Swearing to protect the boy King with his life, he tells them that they will drive north and take refuge with his friends. But a slip on his part betrays him as a rebel and Drake has to use his wits to escape with the girl and baby. Pursued by rebels who fire at their vehicle, they finally reach the helicopter's pick up point and await its arrival. However, when the machine arrives, it is forced to fly away when Ahmed and his followers open fire at it with their rifles. Having finally given their pursuers the slip, Drake and the girl reach the town of Barak where they take refuge at an inn. They are greeted by the manager who, having heard radio reports that an English couple are travelling to Barak with a baby, races to inform Moukta, the town's ruler, of their presence. Moukta, whose allegiance swings easily to whichever side appears to be winning, sends Prior, his personal secretary, to the inn to ask Drake to visit him. Moukta informs Drake that he would not care to see the Englishman's 'family' come to harm and offers him the safety of his home. When Drake refuses the Arab's offer, the man tells him not to be foolish – the rebels are hot on their heels and only he can protect them. Adamant that he will not stay, Drake is offered a lift back to the inn in Moukta's car. Climbing into its rear seat, he finds himself held prisoner by Moukta's burly henchmen. Moukta, meanwhile, makes a deal with Major Ghazi, emissary of General Khan, leader of the dead King's troops, to return the baby – provided that he is given the General's own son as a hostage. While this is taking place, Drake is thrown from Moukta's car and left stranded in the desert. Unaware of these events, Mary receives a visit from Prior, and accepts his explanation that Drake has sent him to take her to a place of safety. She leaves with the baby in a car. Having made his way back to the inn and found Mary missing, Drake pays the innkeeper for his silence, then persuades him to take one of a series of forged documents he has printed to Moukta's home. Arriving there, Drake demands that his 'family' be released. Moukta sneers with confidence as he retorts that the woman can leave, but the child – no son of Drake's, but the dead King's heir – must stay. Drake insists that the boy is, in fact, the son of Baroud, a car dealer and that he has promised to take the baby to its grandmother. Ghazi, however, refuses to release the child until he is certain of its true identity. He smiles when Moukta says that identification is easy: he has in his possession a government leaflet (one of Drake's forgeries) which states that the royal child has a heart-shaped birthmark on its left leg. Needless to say, the boy King carries no such mark and Drake and Mary are permitted to leave. As they cross to the door, General Khan arrives with his troops. Major Ghazi is arrested as he attempts to escape and Moukta exchanges the General's son for his freedom. Mary refuses Drake's offer of a lift to England, preferring to remain with the young King, and Drake is given safe conduct to the coast.

If he is to get The Nurse *to safety, Drake must ward off the attempts of Moukta's henchmen to cleave his head in two*

THE BLUE VEIL

Screenplay by Don Ingalls and Ralph Smart

Spooner	Laurence Naismith
Clare	Lisa Gastoni
The Moukta	Ferdy Mayne
Hassan	Joseph Cuby
Pilot	Peter Thornton

Directed by Charles Frend

WORD REACHES the United Nations consul that the age-old bartering in human lives is flourishing behind the great wastes of the Arabian desert. People are being kidnapped from along the coast and sold to chieftains like cattle in a market. Danger Man John Drake flies to the desert to obtain close-up photographs of the enslaved coastal people. The photographs, showing their definitive facial characteristics, will be proof enough of the people's slavery. In the guise of a dead beat, hard-drinking desert rat, he arrives in the town of Medai, wondering how to get into the palace of The Moukta, a man reputed to be the master of many slaves. A meeting with Spooner – an Englishman who informs him that he cannot expect anything in the town except, perhaps, death – leads to a chance encounter with attractive European showgirl, Clare Nichole. She tells Drake that she has been stranded there after a long series of Spooner's broken promises and seeks the newcomer's help. After learning that she has received an invitation to visit The Moukta's palace, Drake promises to help her to escape. He asks the girl to introduce him as an old friend and returns to his hotel to pack. Entering his room he finds Hassan, a young Arab boy, rifling his luggage. The boy is obviously in awe of The Fat Man (Spooner), whom he says is dangerous and has many friends who could make trouble

for Drake. Drake pays the boy and joins Clare to travel to The Moukta's palace. He explains to The Moukta that he is interested in the ruler's diamond mine but, in spite of Clare's efforts to persuade the Arab to take them to the mine, he refuses to do so. Telling The Moukta that he is in a position to supply him with labour at very favourable rates, Drake is informed that they may be able to do business – eventually. Drake's talk of slavery disillusions Clare who, believing the Englishman to be nothing more than a sordid slave-peddlar, berates Drake and walks away. Drake is told by Spooner that he must take his warnings seriously. The Fat Man, believing Drake to be a loud-mouthed drunkard, pays scant attention when Drake whispers to Clare that she will be hearing from him soon. Returning to his hotel room and finding the door unlocked, Drake enters with caution. Hassan stands before him, proffering a message. Behind the door, however, hides an assassin, ready to plunge his dagger into Drake's back. Sensing danger, the undercover man throws back the door and pulls the intruder forward, eventually disarms him, then throws him in an untidy heap onto a bed. It is then that Hassan strikes. But Drake is too quick for him. Side stepping the boy's knife, Drake twists the weapon from his hands and points its blade at Hassan's throat. Retreating backwards, the young Arab looks astounded when Drake reverses the blade and hands the knife back to its owner. In return for his life, Hassan swears his allegiance to Drake and the two depart, locking the would-be assassin in Drake's room. The boy tells Drake that The Moukta's mine is surrounded by an electric fence. Drake gives Hassan a note addressed to Clare, then revisits Spooner, to wish him goodbye: heeding the man's warnings, Drake is leaving town. Driving only as far as The Moukta's diamond mine, the undercover man removes a pole he has stored on top of his vehicle and vaults over the electrified perimeter fence, recovering the pole with a length of cord tied to its base. He locates the mineworkers' sleeping quarters and slips inside. Removing a miniature camera he has strapped to his ankle, Drake photographs the sleeping slaves, using a flash-gun he had prepared earlier. Wakened from their slumber, The Moukta's guards flood into the room, but Drake escapes by setting off an incendiary device. Departing the same way as he arrived, the NATO agent drives to the rendezvous point he set out in the note Hassan took to Clare. Drake wishes his young friend adieu and he and the girl climb aboard a helicopter. They soar upwards with the evidence Drake needs to put an end to the slavery ring.

Believing Drake to be a loud-mouthed drunkard, fat man Spooner spills the beans about the mystery of The Blue Veil

THE LOVERS

Screenplay by Jo Eisinger and Doreen Montgomery

Maria	**Maxine Audley**
Stavros	**Martin Miller**
Miguel Torres	**Michael Ripper**
President Gomez	**Ewen Solon**
Leonido	**Carl Bernard**
Rosa	**Hermione Gregory**

Directed by Peter Graham Scott

SURPRISED TO BE summoned to the Boravian Embassy (its government had once sentenced him to death – in his absence, of course), Drake receives an even bigger surprise when, on his arrival, he is ushered into the office of Miguel Torres – a spy, undercover agent, provocateur, freelance saboteur – and an old enemy of Drake's. But this time, Torres is on the side of authority, employed by the President of Boravia. He requests that Drake work with him as a security agent during the visit of the President and his wife to London. Known to the world as 'The Lovers', because of their happy marriage, Torres has been handed the task of protecting the President and his wife Maria during their visit. Reports suggest that several of the men behind the latest rebellion in Boravia have secretly entered the country and Torres wants the top man to discourage any attempts on the President's life – the 'top man' being Drake. He will be paid $20,000 plus expenses; double that sum if he stops any attempt; treble if he 'stops a bullet'. Refusing to accept a fee, Drake nevertheless agrees to help, if only to prevent the rebels, some of whom he numbers as friends, from throwing their lives away on a man who Drake considers not worth the trouble. He is taken to meet Maria, the President's wife. The woman politely berates Drake for having friends among the rebels, but agrees to allow him to act as her bodyguard. Drake finds her attitude towards the men who have threatened her life puzzling: convinced that they have been persecuted enough, she asks him to leave them alone – unless, of course, they do make trouble. Told that he is answerable only to herself or her husband, Drake leaves to drive back to his hotel. He finds a message attached to the steering wheel of his car stating that a Mr Stavros wishes to meet him in a bar. Stavros, it transpires, makes bombs and such a device – a thermal bomb – has been delivered to someone associated with the President. For a fee of £10,000, the man agrees to telephone Drake later that day with details of who purchased the bomb and the time it is due to be detonated. Unfortunately, Stavros is gunned down in a railway station before he can deliver the information. Drake accompanies the wounded man to hospital in an ambulance and learns that the bomb is due to be detonated at 8.25 pm precisely, but Stavros dies before he can tell Drake its location. Concerned that Torres may have had him followed to the rail terminus, Drake accuses the man of complicity, but Torres denies telling anyone of the arrangements. Checking with the exiles appears to be the only logical step, so Drake visits several of his Boravian friends. None of them, save Leonido, whom Drake sees last, knows anything. Drake spots a bouquet of flowers handed to Rosa, Leonido's wife, by a caller and finds Maria, the President's wife, in the house. During their drive back to the Embassy, Drake learns from the woman of her affection for Rosa. Before marrying President Gomez, Rosa was her friend. Whatever she can do to help the girl and her sick husband she will do – despite her husband's position,'or objections to the contrary. Drake also learns that the reputation enjoyed by Gomez and his wife as being devoted to each other is a sham. There is obviously friction between them. With barely 36 minutes to go before the bomb is due to explode, its whereabouts are still unknown to Drake. A search of the Embassy proves fruitless. As zero hour draws nearer, 'The Lovers' decide to go off on a private visit to the ballet. The undercover man makes a last minute move to crack the mystery. He is informed that Maria had reserved the tickets for the ballet concert before arriving in England and decides to join the couple during their ride to the theatre – anticipating that one of the two would find an excuse to remain behind. The woman's husband receives a last minute telephone call and asks Drake to accompany his wife alone. Although he is suspicious of the man's excuse, Drake agrees to do so. However, checking his watch during the journey, Drake orders the driver to stop, forces Maria and the chauffeur out of the car, and drives it a short distance before leaping from the vehicle and rejoining the couple. Three minutes and 25 seconds early the bomb hidden in the car explodes, sending the vehicle skywards in a sheet of flame. Returning to the Embassy, Drake reports the explosion to President Gomez. He shows little concern for his wife's welfare and the man's face drains when, seconds later, Maria enters the room. Informing the President that should any further 'accidents' happen to his wife the world will learn the truth, Drake escorts 'The Lovers' from the building. As far as he knows, we are told, the two lived happily ever after.

At Leonido's home, Drake learns that all is not quite as it seems between **The Lovers**

THE SANCTUARY

Screenplay by John Roddick and Ralph Smart

Crawford	Kieron Moore
Kathy	Wendy Williams
Liamond	Barry Keegan
Anders	Charles Farrell
Brannigan	Shay Gorman
Neil	John Rae
Hamish	Ewen MacDuff
Mullins	Peter Murray

Directed by Charles Frend

DRAKE IS driven to a gaol to see a prisoner named Michael Liamond – an Irish-American who, seven years earlier had been found guilty of a violent bomb outrage in South London. Aware that the man's actions had been motivated by deeply felt political beliefs and aware that Liamond is due to be released in twenty-four hours, Drake offers Liamond a chance to redeem himself. By sheer coincidence, the prisoner bears a striking resemblance to the undercover man, and Drake persuades him, for his own good, to forget about a job he has been offered in the Western Highlands working for a man named Crawford, and to allow Drake to take his place. Having no wish to head back into trouble, Liamond allows Drake to accept the post. Arriving at a small Scottish railway station, Drake is met by the attractive Kathy, Crawford's wife, who tells him that he might as well be taking a job on a rock in the middle of the Atlantic. It is a lonely place and Drake notices that she is obviously a lonely woman. Her husband, she confesses, seems to spend most of his time bird watching at Ranoch Point, a bird sanctuary. Crawford is away from his home when they arrive, but soon returns and begins to question Drake about his time spent in prison, attempting to provoke the newcomer by saying that he is a tamed 'Mick', a man softened by the prison authorities. Retaliating, Drake tells Crawford that, far from being tamed, he will put one man under for every year he spent in his cell. Replying that he was simply testing the newcomer, Crawford throws a spanner in the works when he tells Drake that they are to be joined the next day by an old friend of his: Brannigan, a man who worked with Liamond on the London bombings. The undercover man soon discovers that Crawford's bird-watching activities are a blind. Ranoch Point is more than a sanctuary. It is a fort. The Army trained sabotage units there during the war and Crawford is using it for much the same purpose. It is a base for IRA commandos who make their sallies into Northern Ireland by sea; and while the police are searching the whole of Ireland for the bombing gang, they are safely back in Scotland. As 'Michael Liamond', Drake has been recruited because of his skill as a saboteur. When Brannigan arrives, Drake is concerned that his real identity will be exposed, and accuses the newcomer of being an impostor. Then, snatching Brannigan's travelling pack, he throws it into the newcomer's face, allowing himself the opportunity to race outside and escape in a Land Rover. In an attempt to throw his pursuers off the track, he parks the vehicle outside a country mansion and drives away in an estate car, much to the consternation of the chauffeur cleaning its windscreen. The chase is short-lived. His way is accidentally blocked by Kathy Crawford and within minutes he finds himself surrounded by his pursuers. Having no wish for his wife to discover the truth about Ranoch Point, Crawford plays along when Drake invites himself to dinner and carries Kathy's shopping into the house. Drake's attempt to telephone the police is forestalled by Crawford who, pulling his gun on the man, is about to take him outside when Kathy arrives to call them to dinner. Slipping the gun beneath his jacket, Crawford joins his 'guest' in the dining room where, using Kathy as bait, Drake turns the situation to his own advantage by telling Kathy a 'make-believe' story that her husband's bird watching activities are really a front for IRA activities. Kathy falls in with the 'game' and offers to drive Drake to 'freedom'. Adopting his role, Crawford agrees to join them. During the macabre car ride Drake, expecting Crawford to spring an attack, shows surprise when he allows the vehicle to reach the railway station. Joining Drake and Kathy on the platform Crawford indicates that he noticed that the car was low on fuel and sends the unsuspecting Kathy to the petrol station to fill its tank. The second she departs, one of Crawford's heavies appears and clubs Drake to the ground. Recovering consciousness, the undercover man finds himself hanging precariously over the railway line, his arms held firmly by the two men who mean to throw him under the wheels of an approaching express train. With split-second timing, Drake pulls himself free and scrambles to the opposite platform as the train speeds by, its wheels narrowly missing his body. The pursuit continues until, exhausted, Drake stumbles, only to be lifted aloft by Kathy. The Crawford's butler, Mullins, had telephoned the police. Crawford and his gang are taken into custody and Drake boards the next train home.

A dazed Drake prepares to meet his doom under the wheels of an approaching train. A tense scene from The Sanctuary

THE COYANNIS STORY

Screenplay by Jo Eisinger

Coyannis	John Phillips
Zameda	Charles Gray
Lorain Zameda	Heather Chasen
Captain Achard	Liam Gaffney
Marco	Stuart Hutchison
Salcito	Peter Welch
Medana	Julie Hopkins
Storch	Robert Raglan
Finance Minister	Leonard Sachs
Acardi	Bartlett Mullins

Directed by Peter Graham Scott

SENT TO A Balkan country to discover what has happened to rehabilitation money which does not seem to have been put to its intended use, Drake meets Deputy Coyannis, representative of the Peasant Land Party. Coyannis alleges that the money has been misappropriated by Minister Zameda, who he also accuses of the murder of his son and Salcito, his best friend. Drake meets Zameda and his attractive American wife, Lorain. She dismisses Coyannis' allegations as nonsense and maintains that the lack of improvement in the country's working conditions is because the peasants resist modernisation. Zameda also promises that the murderer of Coyannis' son will be found. During a meeting with the Finance Minister, Drake is introduced to Acardi, the minister's aide, who hands him a note stating that he wishes to talk to Drake. Drake is driven to the rendezvous by Medana, Coyannis' daughter-in-law. He asks her to wait while he meets Acardi, but a second car races into view and Acardi is riddled with bullets before he has the opportunity to speak. Drake is chased into the woods by the armed assailant, but doubles back to Medana's car and escapes without injury. Armed with the knowledge that Coyannis was the only person he told about the meeting, Drake accuses the man of setting him up, stating that he will be at his hotel should Coyannis have anything to tell him. Arriving there, he finds Madame Zameda waiting for him. She tells him that she wants her husband to be forced to flee the country and to go into exile. She explains that he has been pushed into diverting the money by someone powerful in the background. If Drake can do a deal with Coyannis, she will provide the necessary documents to give him all the evidence he needs. As she leaves she gives Drake a private telephone number where he can call her to arrange to see the documents. Coyannis is suspicious of the offer and warns Drake that he might be stepping into a trap. To test his theory, he arranges for Medana to telephone Madame Zameda in case Zameda himself should be at home, but earlier than was arranged between the woman and Drake. When Medana returns to say that the message has been delivered, Drake is suspicious of something the girl says and cross-examines her. Drake once again asks the girl if she is certain she spoke to Madame Zameda: did she ring the correct number? Quite certain she replies, trotting out the first five digits of the woman's telephone number. Removing the card given to him by Madame Zameda, Drake arrives at the truth. The girl has not dialled the private number. She has actually telephoned Minister Zameda, revealing the man to be her lover. She was responsible for telling Zameda where Coyannis' son and Salcito could be found on the night they were murdered. Aware that Lorain Zameda's life is in danger, Drake rings her and tells her that he is on his way; she should lock her door and await his arrival. Driving to her home, he accuses the woman of being the 'informer' who lured Marco Coyannis and Salcito to their deaths on the pretext of handing over documents that would incriminate and eventually break her husband. Just then, Zameda and Achard, the Minister of Police, arrive and Drake is forced to hide. Zameda breaks open his wife's door and attempts to throttle her, but Drake leaps from his hiding place and struggles with the men. Accidentally shot during the fight, the minister tumbles down the staircase, to be joined seconds later by Achard who is thrown over the balustrade by Drake. Joining Madame Zameda as she kneels at the side of her dead husband, Drake thinks aloud that Zameda had a fitting end. Who knows?

Having knocked out the opposition, Drake joins Madame Zameda to ponder the outcome of The Coyannis Story

THE BROTHERS

Screenplay by Ralph Smart

Lita Rossi	**Lisa Gastoni**
Police Comm.	**George Colouris**
Guiseppe	**Ronald Fraser**
Hugo	**Derren Nesbitt**
Luigi	**John Woodvine**
Housekeeper	**Nancy Beckh**
Policeman	**Gino Melvazzi**
1st Airman	**Rodney Burice**
2nd Airman	**Wesley Murphy**

Directed by Charles Frend

A PLANE CRASHES off the coast of Sicily. The airmen get safely to shore with their mailbags and a diplomatic satchel – only to be shot and robbed by Guiseppe and Hugo Morelli, two Sicilian bandits. Arriving in Sicily during a torrential downpour, Drake arouses the local Police Commissioner from his slumber and learns that a meeting with the Morelli brothers will not be that simple to arrange. Hidden in the wildest parts of the mountains, the brothers have, so far, defied all police efforts to find them. However, Drake learns that there is one person who might be able to lead him to his quarry – Lita, their accomplice, who at present resides in the local prison, having been arrested for selling stolen property. Drake is told by the Police Commissioner that he can visit the girl in the morning. With the Commissioner's co-operation, Drake plans an 'escape' for her and wins her confidence. She promises that she will take him to the brothers, in return for a large reward that he is willing to pay to get the vital diplomatic papers belonging to him. Warned by the policeman to keep his wits about him when he meets the Morellis, Drake leaves to arrange Lita's 'escape'. Having already primed the girl to ask to be allowed to visit the rest room at the court where she is to be tried that afternoon, Drake is waiting below the rest room window as Lita pops out the window bar (conveniently loosened by the Police Commissioner's men). She slides into the safety of Drake's waiting arms. The alarm bell sounds and they race away to a waiting car. Drake gives the girl one half of the agreed $1000 reward – the rest is to be paid when she leads him to the Morelli brothers. She keeps her word and takes him to their mountain hide-out. Lita asks Drake to wait in his car and gets out alone to prepare the brothers for his arrival. Unknown to the girl, Drake has secreted a portable receiver into her handbag and is able to overhear the conversation between Lita and Luigi, one of the Morelli brothers' confidants. He tells the girl that the men are out hunting. Returning to the vehicle, Lita asks Drake to drive her to a secluded spot in the forest which she knows that her brothers frequent. Once there, pretending to search for some water to brew some coffee, Drake leaves the girl behind and heads off into the trees. Hidden nearby, he sees the Morelli brothers arrive and overhears their conversation with Lita via his portable transmitter. The American, she tells them, will pay handsomely for the mailbags they stole, but there is a problem. Hugo, it appears, has burned the majority of the papers when

signalling Luigi. But the Englishman does not know this, so Drake hears them plan to take his money and kill him. Burying his receiver headpiece, he returns to where the girl is waiting with her accomplices. Alerted to their game, he tricks the brothers into believing that by simply looking into their eyes he can read their thoughts: for instance, didn't Hugo burn some of the papers recently, while making a signal to Luigi? Confused by Drake's behaviour, Guiseppe leaves to fetch the bag they stole – the diplomatic satchel that Drake has been sent to find. His ruse falls apart however when, messing around with Lita's handbag, Hugo stumbles across Drake's portable transmitter. Guiseppe returns and stops his brother from harming Drake – at least until he has handed over the money. Hugo leads Drake deep into the forest to the place where Drake says he has buried the money. He is about to shoot Drake in the back when he suddenly drops to the ground, a bullet from a gun Drake had hidden, lodged deep in his shoulder. Covering the men, Drake stows them, uncomfortably, in the boot of his car and returns to town to hand them over to a delighted Police Commissioner. Pausing only to request that the policeman drop all charges against Lita, Drake leaves, his assignment complete.

Unaware that Drake has arranged her escape in order that she can guide him to The Brothers, *Lita slides to the safety of the undercover man's arms*

COLONEL RODRIGUEZ

Screenplay by Ralph Smart

Colonel Rodriguez	Noel Willman
Martine	Maxine Audley
Joan Bernard	Honor Blackman
Walter Bernard	Ronald Allen
General Abeijon	Campbell Singer
Pietro	Cyril Shaps
Chloe	Pearl Prescod
Danny	Neville Becker
Barman	Lloyd Reckord
Policeman	Brian Jackson

Directed by Julian Amyes

MASQUERADING AS A journalist, Drake flies to Moutique, a Caribbean country, to help an American reporter, Walter Bernard, who has been arrested on espionage charges. His wife Joan is with him. It is a trumped-up charge for internal propaganda purposes – the new dictatorship needs scapegoats to divert attention from its failure to fulfil all its promises. Drake meets his old friend General Abeijon, who tells him that, drunk with success, the government is even flaunting Uncle Sam: the arrest of Bernard will keep the media's attention off things until another 'entertainment' can be devised. The police chief, Colonel Rodriguez, is responsible for the arrest and Abeijon warns his friend to be careful. The Colonel is a personal friend of the President. But he was also a close friend of the former President, Gomez, who is now dead: Rodriguez is obviously a skilful and ruthless man who will always be on the side of the winning team. Calling on Mrs Bernard, Drake learns that her husband works for the International Press Group. He was arrested when Rodriguez learned that the journalist had openly criticised him in an overseas press report. When Bernard refused to withdraw the report, Rodriguez had promised to make an example of him. One evening, the Colonel's men had arrived at their apartment, turned the place inside out and found documents incriminating her husband in espionage – planted, of course. As the woman is telling Drake her story, a note is pushed under the door advising Joan that if she goes to a certain club with $10,000, she will be handed information that could win her husband's release. Drake goes instead and very nearly walks into a trap. Lured outside the premises, he finds the nozzle of a gun, held by a man named Pietro, shoved into his chest. Pietro explains that he is a friend of someone with the proof Drake requires: a letter written and signed by Rodriguez, showing that Rodriguez was responsible for betraying President Gomez to his enemies. Pietro agrees to meet Drake later that evening to give him the letter. Drake returns to his hotel room and finds Rodriguez and his guards waiting for him. Told that his passport is being confiscated, Drake demands a receipt for the travel document. Rodriguez is confident of his ground and signs the receipt note written by Drake. Hearing that the visitor has arrived to cover Bernard's trial, Rodriguez informs Drake that he should not write anything before the hearing or he too, may be arrested. He tells Drake that both his passport and an air ticket will be waiting for him the following morning at the airport, and leaves. Pietro's

friend turns out to be glamorous nightclub singer, Martine. She was the former President's girlfriend and the letter she has is damning proof of the Colonel's treachery. But she is killed before she can hand over the note and Rodriguez attempts to frame Drake with her murder. Rodriguez finds a wad of money in the dead woman's handbag and assumes that Drake has taken receipt of the incriminating evidence. Drake appears to be about to hand the letter to Rodriguez, when he leaps through the window and returns to Joan Bernard's apartment. Drake advises the woman that he has arranged to meet General Abeijon there, after which she must leave and wait at the airport for her husband. The undercover man is forced to climb out onto the balcony when a knock on the door announces the arrival of Rodriguez and his men. Having searched the apartment and found nothing, the policemen leave, at which point Drake climbs down from his perch *above* Joan's bedroom window. Under cover of darkness, Drake breaks into the Colonel's home. Having planted a listening device in his bedroom, Drake deliberately knocks over an item of furniture, waking Rodriguez, who, in one

Seconds from now, the sleeping Colonel Rodriguez will face a fait accompli when Drake forces him to order Bernard's release

swift movement sits up in his bed and grabs a revolver from beneath his pillow. Drake informs the man that, should anything happen to him, the letter he seeks will be handed over to General Abeijon. Drake offers the letter in exchange for Bernard's freedom: the Colonel must pick up the phone and order the journalist's release. Rodriguez agrees. Within minutes Bernard is released and 'deported' to England. Having kept his side of the bargain, the Colonel asks Drake for the letter. He has not got it: Rodriguez had Martine killed before she could hand over the document. Forestalling the Colonel's threat to shoot him, Drake explains that he has planted a relay device in Rodriguez's bedroom – every word the man has said since Drake roused him has been heard and taped by General Abeijon, who arrives at that moment to take the Colonel into custody.

THE RELAXED INFORMER

Screenplay by Ralph Smart and Robert Stewart

Joseph Brenner	**Duncan Lamont**
Ruth	**Moira Redmond**
Colonel Doyle	**Paul Maxwell**
Frederick	**Brian Rawlinson**
Benedict	**Stanley Van Beers**
Captain Brandt	**Tom Gill**
Greta	**Pauline Letts**
French Delegate	**Henry Vidon**
Sergeant	**Charles Vance**

Directed by Anthony Bushell

IN AN EFFORT to unravel a security leak, Drake carries out an audacious hold-up. The man he robs is a courier known by the codename 'Frederick'. Drake catches up with him in a Bavarian town and robs him of his car and his shopping, which he immediately takes to Police Chief, Captain Brandt, for examination. The contents of the shopping bag are examined thoroughly. Anything broken is replaced. Frederick's car is given the heave-ho treatment by a heavy goods truck until it is dented and wrecked. A puppet is found, containing a coil of recording wire, which Drake substitutes with electrical fuse wire. When Frederick arrives he finds everything as it was, except for his wrecked car. Captain Brandt tells him that it was damaged by Drake, an American deserter who was arrested for speeding. Finding the puppet intact, Frederick leaves without his suspicions being roused. The intercepted recording leads Drake to the headquarters of SDCAL (Strategic Defence Control, Allied Liaison) where retired veterans relive some of their greatest battles. Playing back the recording wire to Colonel Doyle, the head of security at the establishment, Drake hears a Scottish voice revealing vital secrets. The voice is identified by Doyle as belonging to Ruth Mitchell, an interpreter whom he believes to be utterly reliable. The officer takes Drake into a games room where, seated around a table, military veterans of all nationalities are discussing that day's schedule. Their words are being interpreted by the girl Doyle has brought Drake to see. The undercover man meets Ruth in a nightclub later that evening. Pretending to be working for the people who should have received her last taped message, he is somewhat surprised when the girl invites him to continue their conversation in the privacy of her apartment. Before leaving, Ruth uses the telephone: to cancel an appointment she says. Drake knows otherwise. The girl is ringing for help. However, Ruth has actually reported their meeting to her boss and, instead of the heavy Drake was expecting, it is Doyle he finds waiting for them at Ruth's flat. But is the girl as innocent as she makes out, or is she just being clever? To test their theory, Doyle has the girl brought to his office, where Drake plays her the recording he took from Frederick. Astounded by what she hears, Ruth denies having made any such recording. She sticks to her story and tells Drake that she refuses to be questioned further. Aware that the girl has several friends on the island, Drake asks Ruth to take him to meet them and, in particular, a Joseph Brenner, a man whose photograph the girl keeps in her apartment. A Paxite, Brenner founded SDCAL. Drake's meeting with the man is delayed by Benedict, a man he had seen earlier handing over the puppet to Frederick. One of Brenner's employees, Benedict tells them that they must wait until the council meeting to meet their host. Bidding the couple welcome, Brenner introduces Drake to his wife Greta, before asking Drake to leave: he wants to talk to Ruth in private. Drake does so, leaving behind him a camera/transmitter. The conversation he overhears explains everything. Ruth has been tricked into becoming a traitor without her knowledge: by hypnotising the girl, Brenner learns everything he wishes to know. Before Drake can act, Frederick arrives to tell Brenner that the latest report fell into the hands of a man calling himself Drake. With Benedict in tow, Brenner races to Drake's room. Too late. Drake has managed to signal his position by releasing a rocket flare. Outside on the landing, the undercover man throws Benedict to his death and Brenner is soon defeated. The rest of the gang are rounded up by the police and Ruth is delighted to learn from Drake that, as she had insisted, she is not a traitor.

FIND AND DESTROY

Screenplay by Ralph Smart and John Roddick

Major Hassler	Peter Arne
Melina	Nadja Regin
Gordon	Peter Sallis
Helen	Helen Morton
Commander Ford	Ronald Leigh-Hunt
Enrico	Alec Mango
Fedor	Richard Clarke
Corto	Brad Dancy
Pia	Rebecca Dignam

Directed by Charles Frend

PACKING TO leave for a vacation, a telephone call delays Drake's departure. It is Gordon, his superior. A situation has cropped up in Korea: Gordon wonders if Drake would like to stop off there during his journey, it won't take very long. It is an order, not a request. Asking Helen, Gordon's secretary to cancel his reservation in Rio, Drake, having deliberately knocked back a large glass of Scotch before Gordon arrived, feigns being lethargic. Concerned by Drake's appearance, Gordon withdraws his order and the undercover man is allowed to board his original flight. Drake enters his hotel room, expecting to have a few days much needed rest, but finds the place a hive of activity. Three men are shuffling through his belongings and his bathroom contains a diver's air supply bottle, together with a scuba-masked Commander Ford. Producing a British Intelligence identity pass, Ford tells Drake that a KX35 miniature submarine has been wrecked off the shores of a South American country, after drifting helplessly inside the territorial waters. Drake is being hired by British Intelligence to blow her up. Still on the secret list, the submarine is a prototype and was being navigated by remote control from a mother ship. If the South American government gets a sniff of what is at stake, they will tie the operation up for days — allowing the enemy to learn every secret the submarine contains. Drake's assignment: to locate and destroy. Taken to the coastline by helicopter, Drake parachutes out with diving apparatus, collapsible canoe and explosives. Playing the role of fisherman, he hides his equipment and endeavours to locate the vessel. He is discovered on the beach by a beautiful girl who rides up on horseback and accuses him of trespassing on her land. They are joined by a second rider — Corto. The girl, Melina, takes Drake to her father, Enrico Piero, who betrays the fact that he knows about the submarine but admits that he has not informed the authorities. Drake offers to pay the man $10,000 for his co-operation in blowing up the vessel. Enrico accepts, but tells Drake that the job must be done swiftly. Drake soon discovers the reason for the man's urgency. Piero has already sold the secret to Major Hassler, a representative of a foreign power. Shortly afterwards, Hassler arrives, stating that he has come to take pictures of the submarine. Drake bluffs that he is too late and the submarine has gone. But the newcomer informs him that he saw the vessel only minutes earlier when he flew over the island. Introduced to Drake as Mendez, Melina's fiancé, Hassler believes that the couple are trying to trick him. He has his men hold the Piero family prisoner until he has taken his photographs. Drake and Melina cook up a story that a diver has been seen near to the submarine's location. They lead Hassler and his henchmen to the beach where, producing a map he has buried there earlier, Drake adds fuel to his story by producing the intruder's ammunition supply and canoe — but not before he has secreted some explosives under his shirt. Alarmed that the ammo box is almost empty, Hassler, fearful that the man they are searching for is already planting his explosives aboard the submarine, hurries with his men to the vessel's location. Planting his own explosives in the sand, Drake shouts at the men to take cover: the submarine might be mined. He tricks them into allowing him to unfasten the vessel's conning-tower. Before Hassler realises what he is really up to, Drake leaps into the submarine and slams the door shut behind him. As the men outside attempt to gain entrance, the undercover man attaches his thermo-fused charges to the vessel's secret guidance system, praying aloud that the explosives he planted on the beach as a diversionary tactic detonate on time. Shouting to Hassler that the submarine is due to explode in 30 seconds, Drake's prayers are answered when the beach charges erupt, sending Hassler and his men running for cover. Drake escapes to safety as the submarine follows suit in a sheet of flame. His prize lost, an affronted Major Hassler departs, praying that he meets Drake again, soon. Back in Rio, expecting a well-earned rest, Drake is lying on the beach when a hotel porter arrives with a telephone. It is Gordon. He has a job. No, not in Korea. This time it's closer to home. It appears that a prototype miniature submarine has been washed up on a beach . . . can Drake help? Smiling, the agent accepts the job.

Assigned to Find And Destroy *the KX35 submarine Drake, armed with explosives, hides behind a sand dune to escape Hassler's men*

Screenplay by Ralph Smart and Robert Stewart

James Carpenter	
Oscar Schumak	**William Sylvester**
Sue Carpenter	**June Thorburn**
Colonel Vasco	**William Lucas**
President	**Michael Peake**
Passport Officer	**Keith Goodman**
Policeman	**John Slavid**

Directed by Terry Bishop

JAMES CARPENTER, a prisoner in the American Embassy in Cabiba (a Caribbean city) turns to his wife Sue, then makes a bid for freedom. He gets no further than the corridor outside where, overcome by Embassy guards, he is knocked to the floor and taken back to his room under escort. Drake is given the job of finding a double for the prisoner. He finally locates Oscar Schumak, a noted concert pianist and a man with the qualities Drake is seeking: a man of integrity, a man willing to take risks, a man of quick decision and physical courage of a high degree and, most important of all, a man who bears an uncanny likeness to Carpenter. Cultivating a friendship with Schumak, Drake introduces him to Sue Carpenter. She is astonished by the pianist's rememblance to her husband. The woman listens as Drake tells Schumak that Carpenter is being held prisoner in the Embassy because his enemy, Colonel Vasco, cannot touch him there as it is, technically, on American soil. Vasco has sworn to kill Carpenter, so he must be rescued: will Schumak help? Sympathetic to the man's plight, the pianist agrees to do what he can. The problem now facing Drake is to convince everyone that Carpenter is in fact Schumak, and vice versa. This is arranged when, arriving at the Embassy with 'Mr Schumak, a noted concert pianist', Drake arranges for Carpenter, ashen-faced from being held indoors, to trade places with Schumak — after the pianist has had a false scar and make-up applied to his suntanned complexion. However, while attending an Embassy party, Colonel Vasco, invited as a guest, becomes suspicious when he notices the resemblance between the pianist (really Carpenter) and the man he is after. Baiting the pianist with questions that only a true musician could answer, Vasco appears satisfied and leaves — but promises to attend the pianist's concert to be given that evening. As Drake has predicted, Schumak is arrested just before the concert. Drake challenges Vasco to accompany Schumak to the concert hall to see for himself that the man he suspects of being Carpenter really can play. The policeman does so and finds, to his discomfort, that there is no doubt about the man being Schumak. He has been tricked, of course, by Drake, who smuggled the real pianist out of the Embassy and switched the men prior to the concert. The ruse works. After a successful recital, Schumak once again trades places with his lookalike and Colonel Vasco himself escorts the prisoner to the airport and freedom. Driven to the President's palace by the policeman, Vasco is somewhat bemused when, on entering the President's room, he finds the premier being entertained by Schumak who, sitting at the piano, is playing a selection of the President's favourite music. Vasco is told by Drake that the real Carpenter, the man whom Vasco had placed on the plane, has been instructed to tell the American media that he has been granted a free pardon by the President. Aware that his Chief of Police has been fooled, the President is forced to agree with Drake that it is, perhaps the best way out of a delicate situation. Telling Vasco that he will be dealt with the next morning, the President asks a favour of Schumak: would he play for him once more?

In The Prisoner, *Drake is ordered at gunpoint to drive Oscar Schumak to a piano recital*

THE LONELY CHAIR

Screenplay by John Roddick and Ralph Smart

Guest stars

Noelle Laurence	**Hazel Court**
Patrick Laurence	**Sam Wanamaker**
Hardy	**Richard Wattis**

with

Brenner	**Patrick Troughton**
Holst	**Howard Pays**
Caldwell	**Jack Melford**
Fordyce	**Alexander Melford**
Rolf	**Robert Harbin**
Mrs Hardy	**Dorothy Hersee**
Porter	**Clifford Earl**
Sally	**Liz Lanchbury**

Directed by Charles Frend

A S SALLY LAURENCE climbs out of her friend's custom-built racing car and mounts the steps leading to her home, a second car pulls up at the pavement. The driver jumps out and runs to Sally's side. His wife has been taken ill, would the girl take a look at her? Climbing into the vehicle's rear seat, Sally's face is smothered by a chloroform pad. The car speeds away, leaving behind the girl's racing helmet. Drake is roused from his bed at 1.30 in the morning by a telephone call from Hardy, his superior, who tells him to come to his home. The door is opened by Hardy's mother – odd really, as Drake had always believed that his superior had been found under a file in the Foreign Office! He learns that it is no ordinary kidnapping. Sally is the daughter of Patrick Laurence, an industrial designer specialising in thermodynamics. His company has vital government contracts and the kidnappers' terms are Sally's life in exchange for plans of a secret thermodynamic reactor. Only Drake, Hardy, Patrick Laurence and his wife Noelle are aware of the girl's kidnapping: the police have not been informed and will only be used as a last resort. From Hardy, Drake learns that Laurence is seen by few people. Once handsome, he is now badly scarred and crippled through an explosion. Tied to a wheelchair and locked away from the world, he controls his organisation from his penthouse apartment. He has been married twice, Sally being the daughter of his first marriage. Drake is introduced to Laurence as a security agent of inestimable experience. Drake ignores Laurence's protests that he does not require any help and that he would rather agree to the kidnappers' demands than risk his daughter's life. He tells Noelle that her husband is in no condition to protect either Sally or himself once the gang have got what they want and eventually convinces them that he can save both the plans and Sally. The kidnappers make contact and a date is set for Laurence to meet them in a deserted house. Drawings of the Columbia thermodynamic reactor project, supplied by Hardy's man, Fordyce, will then be handed over and Sally will be released. As the gang are unlikely to know what Laurence looks like since the accident, Drake persuades the worried father to let him take his place. Heavily muffled and wearing dark glasses, Drake is taken to the rendezvous by Noelle in Laurence's wheelchair. Sally is handed over

and brought home by her stepmother, leaving her 'husband' behind, who says he will draw the plans once he receives confirmation that Noelle and Sally are safe. Drake realises that Holst, the man he is talking to, is not the real brains behind the ransom plot, and insists on speaking to the head man. Holst telephones his chief and Drake tells the unseen caller that he will not play ball until he sees Sally and Noelle on the television hook-up he has arranged. The voice agrees, telling Holst that he is on his way to 'handle' Laurence himself. The kidnappers now discover that, instead of an invalid, they have a very physically active prisoner indeed. Ramming his wheelchair into Holst's legs, Drake rises from his seat, handcuffs the man and throws him into a cellar. A telephone call to Laurence confirms that Sally and Noelle are on their way home. Drake informs Hardy, who is sitting with the industrialist when the phone call arrives, that he is staying behind to meet the brains behind the kidnapping. Ignoring his superior's advice to leave while he still can, Drake reassumes his disguise and races to a spare room. When Brenner, the gang leader arrives, accompanied by Rolf, his henchman, they find 'Laurence' complaining about being locked up. Drake witnesses the safe arrival of his 'daughter and wife' and then refuses to keep his word and draw the plans. Beaten savagely about the face, he retaliates by rapping Brenner's aide over the head with his drawing board, before taking Brenner himself into custody. As Drake wishes the Laurences goodbye, he offers to drive Sally to the starting gate of her next race meeting.

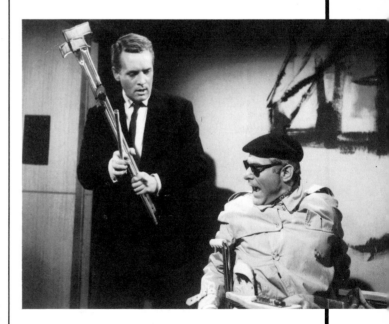

The kidnap gang are unlikely to recognise Laurence, so Drake convinces the wheelchair-bound father to allow him to occupy The Lonely Chair

DEAD MAN WALKS

Screenplay by Ralph Smart and Brian Clemens

Hardy	**Richard Wattis**
Sita Shapadi	**Marla Landi**
Natalie Smith	**Julia Arnall**
Keith Smith	**Richard Pearson**
Rangit Pal	**Michael Ripper**
Professor Hanbury	**Bryan Coleman**
Nawi	**Joanna Dunham**
Azad	**William Peacock**
Wasing	**Zia Moyheddin**

Directed by Charles Frend

CALLED TO Hardy's home early one morning, Drake finds his superior sipping a glass of hot milk. As always, Hardy has a challenge up his sleeve. It appears that all the members of Professor Stanley Radford's research team – a unit who were experimenting in tropical plant diseases – are believed to have met their deaths. Radford himself died in a laboratory fire, the others apparently committed suicide. Cooking Drake's breakfast, Hardy tells his man that he has discovered that, as a side product of their research, the team had hit on a bacteria of such virulence that if it were bred and used as a weapon of war it could be as devastating as the atom bomb, killing any vegetation it came into contact with in a matter of hours. Radford had called his team together to discuss the matter and it was decided by common consent that their appalling discovery should be kept a secret forever. Aware that his team were government employees and were, therefore, wrongly witholding information that really belonged to the government, Radford asked them to sign the minutes of the meeting, so that each man took individual responsibility for the decision. Every man who signed the document is believed to have died – but Hardy believes that one of the team is still alive. A scourge that has suddenly destroyed the harvest in Kashmir might be the result of Radford's bacteria. Drake must travel to India to see Sita Shapadi, the daughter of Professor Shapadi, who was the Indian member of the research team. If he is alive, Shapadi holds more potential power than any other man on earth. The undercover agent meets the girl and discovers that she is an orchid grower. Saying that he was a friend of her father's and worked with him as a member of Radford's research team, Sita invites him into her home. From Nawi, the girl's maid, he learns that Sita always goes alone to find her orchid seeds or, on occasion, with Azad, the only one she trusts with the knowledge of the secret location. The next morning, when Sita sets out on her journey, Drake follows her. He is caught doing so by Azad, who takes him to the girl at gunpoint. Confused by Drake's actions, the girl tells Azad to take Drake back to her home. When an attempt is made on Drake's life, his suspicions that the girl's father is still alive are further aroused. But a curious incident leads him to another trail: Sita tells Drake that she has discovered that he is an impostor and that no one named Drake ever worked with her father. He asks the girl where she obtained such information and Sita states that her friend Natalie Smith, whose husband Keith has been a member of the research team, told her. Later, Drake tricks Natalie by having a local photographer fake a photograph showing himself with her husband, then plays on her jealous nature by letting her come into possession of a forged letter which purports to be a love letter from her husband Keith to Sita Shapadi. Taking the bait, Natalie drives away and is followed by the undercover man in a truck driven by Rangit Pal, a contact of Drake's. He trails the woman to a hut in the jungle where, hidden in the bushes outside its window, Drake sees Natalie talking to her 'dead' husband. Entering the cabin, Drake accuses the man of murdering his colleagues, but Azad arrives and shoves the muzzle of his rifle into Drake's chest. The arrival of Rangit Pal saves Drake's life for, hidden in the back of the truck, are a squad of policemen. The trap has been sprung just in time: in hiding, Smith has tested and isolated the deadly bacteria and was about to sell it to the highest bidder. 'Nothing purifies like fire', says Drake, igniting his torch to burn Smith's jungle laboratory to the ground.

Called to Hardy's home, Drake listens as his superior cooks him breakfast and assigns him to the case classified as 'Dead Man Walks'

THE CONTESSA

Screenplay by John Roddick and Ralph Smart

Guest star

Francesca	**Hazel Court**

with

Julio	**John Wyse**
Keller	**Lionel Murton**
Minister	**Ralph Truman**
Mario	**Bill Nagy**
Rosa	**Jennifer Jayne**
Maria	**Irene Prador**
Giorgio	**Dudley Foster**
Rossi	**Edward Cast**
Lucia	**Jackie Collins**
Intern	**Glenn Beck**
Singer	**Terence Cooper**
Old Man	**Eddie Malin**

Directed by Terry Bishop

A LONGSHOREMAN IS injured when a heavy packing case falls from a crane while a ship is being unloaded in the New York docks. Taken to hospital, the man is found to be carrying cocaine, cleverly concealed in his jacket. The man is Angelo Rossi, a petty thief. Called in by Colonel Keller. Drake's theory is that the man was wearing an identical jacket which he exchanged with a member of the crew, using this as a method of smuggling drugs into the country. Keller believes that the racket is being run by one particular man, someone who is very high up in the social swim. But they cannot put a finger on the suspect without cast-iron proof so Drake is sent to see Rossi. Dressed as a doctor, he visits the man's bedside and is about to return Rossi's clothes when, noticing that the patient seems concerned about the jacket, Drake offers to get a message to Rossi's colleagues. He flies to an address in Genoa which the patient has given him and rents a room overlooking the berth where the *Capo Mera*, Rossi's ship is docked. Drake settles down to keep watch. At midnight, the crew begins to disembark and, at last, he spots a sailor wearing the jacket he is looking for. Following the man. Giorgio, to a waterside café, by pretending to offer Giorgio a watch he wishes to sell. Drake succeeds in making a mark on the back of the man's jacket. In this way he knows that the jacket has been switched when Giorgio visits the men's room. Drake trails the man as he leaves with Lucia, a girl Giorgio has met. and sees them enter an apartment block. He pays an old man he meets on the stairs to take a puppy to Giorgio's girlfriend and while Lucia is distracted. the undercover man creeps into the room and steals the jacket, returning with it to the café. Making conversation with the man he knows to be Giorgio's contact. Drake puts forward a business proposition, stating that he has good contacts in New York, for certain merchandise. This approach seems to lead him nowhere – until Drake collapses. His drink has been spiked. When he comes round, he is in the lounge of a luxurious villa and in the company of the bewitchingly lovely Contessa Francesca Scarafino. She tells him that he has been in a fight and that her husband

Drugged by Maria's coffee, Drake awakens in his hotel room to find Rosa standing at his bedside. A scene from The Contessa

41

has brought him home. The jacket, which she appears to know Drake has stolen, is missing, taken by the men who attacked him. Drake is served coffee by Maria, the Contessa's maid, and gradually regains his senses. Asked why he stole the jacket, he replies that he was tipsy, the skipper had paid him off and he was cold: perhaps her husband can find him a job? Her husband is not there, having left to visit colleagues in Rome. Before he can question her further, he collapses again, drugged by Maria's coffee. This time he awakens back in his hotel room. Rosa, a girl he saw at the cafe, is standing by his bedside, but she knows, or is saying, nothing. Dazed from the effects of the drug, Drake determines to find the Contessa. Three days and nights of searching for the woman lead nowhere until, while talking to Julio, a gossip columnist in a nightclub, he sees Francesca enter with a State Minister. He asks Julio to introduce him to the couple. Drake is surprised when the woman recalls having seen him before. He, however, thinks not, telling the Contessa that she must be mistaken. Drake invites the woman to dance and asks her to arrange for him to meet her husband. Why not immediately, the woman replies, offering to drive Drake to her home. There they find a message scribbled on a notepad: her husband, due to fly to Paris the following morning, has retired early. Suspicious, Drake follows Francesca to her bedroom. As he suspected, it is empty. She finally admits that her husband died four years earlier. In order to keep a throttle-hold on his business empire, she has led her make-believe life, perpetuating the legend that her husband is still giving the orders. He was feared by everyone when he was alive and his employees would never have accepted orders from a woman. By the time she had discovered that her husband was involved in a drugs racket, it was too late — she had grown accustomed to the high profits and gracious lifestyle the business afforded. Intimating that they are in the same business, Drake tricks her with his pipe dream of even higher profit margins if she throws in with him. At that moment Julio arrives, exposed as Francesca's partner. Told by his partner of Drake's plans, Julio becomes suspicious when he is notified by telephone that the customs have seized their latest drugs assignment. Aware that Drake alone can be responsible, the couple race upstairs. Drake has gone, escaped into the night — or so they believe. In reality, he is hiding in Francesca's bedroom. Creeping downstairs, he attacks Julio as the man and the Contessa return from the garden, having checked their drugs cache. Francesca receives a bullet through her heart when Julio's gun goes off during the fight. Drake telephones the police, informing them of the cocaine: the property of a Contessa from the gutters of Naples.

JOSETTA

Screenplay by Ralph Smart

Guest stars

Juan Cortez	**Kenneth Haig**
Josetta	**Julia Arnall**

with

Colonel Segur	**Campbell Singer**
Olot	**Randall Kinkead**
Sandra	**Claire Gordon**
Motril	**Glenn Beck**
Miguel	**Robert Bernal**
Policeman	**Anthony Viccars**

Directed by Michael Truman

JOSETTA INGRES, a blind girl, sits playing a piano in her South American home. A man calling himself Da Silva arrives, saying that he is there to meet her brother Senator Miguel. When Miguel enters the room, shots ring out and a horrified Josetta realises that her brother has been murdered. The assassin escapes. The murder attracts world-wide attention. Drake is called in when an insidious whispering campaign in San Pueblo lays the death of Miguel, a rising compatriot, at the door of American interests, stirring the people to besiege the American Embassy there. Drake's job: to track down the person who was really responsible for Miguel's death. He finds Josetta in the company of Colonel Segur, the local police chief, who advises him to keep out of the affair — he is quite capable of handling it himself. However, when Drake points out that his own government is being blamed for the Senator's death, which makes it his affair also, Segur offers no objection and allows him to talk to Josetta. The girl dismisses the rumours that the murderer was American. His voice was that of one of her own countrymen. Her only other clue is that he wore a distinctive scent which might have been shaving lotion or hair oil. The man gave a false name, which her brother failed to recognise, but when he entered the room Miguel obviously knew his killer. Although reluctant to help Drake, Segur confirms that the Army party has most to gain from the assassination, and that their agents are whipping up the people. If they can provoke sufficient trouble, the Army will step in to 'save' the country, and General Hargos will take over temporary power — temporary meaning forever. Segur has one particular suspect in mind: a young Army officer named Juan Cortez. The man has a talent for getting himself into trouble — gambling, women, nothing too enterprising. Posing as a simple-minded millionaire, Drake has no trouble in meeting Cortez at a gambling club. The more he loses, the more acceptable he becomes to the assassin. He obtains a tape recording of the man's voice, which Josetta identifies as the man who visited her brother. A sample of the man's hair oil clinches the matter — but the evidence of a blind girl would not be enough. Drake must pressurise the man into giving himself away: playing on his nerves, breaking him, forcing him into making a false move. With the help of one of Segur's men, an electronics expert, Drake sets out to achieve this. Before he can act, however, he is picked up by Cortez who orders him out of the country. To add strength to his argument, the assassin has Drake framed for the illegal possession of a firearm, abduction and attempted murder. Colonel Segur's hands are tied. However, having spoken to Drake's Ambassador, Segur arranges for the undercover man to be released on bail. Later that day, Drake explains to Josetta how he intends to trap Cortez. They will convince the assassin that she can see; that she saw him kill her brother. Drake places a small amplifier in the girl's ear. Its wire, concealed by Josetta's hair, is attached to a receiver hidden in the girl's dress. Drake can then give her directions in his minature transmitter. After a great deal of practice, she gives the impression that she can see, avoiding obstacles than an unsighted person would stumble over. Agreeing that Drake has performed a 'miracle', Segur agrees to allow one of his men to join Drake as he sets out to trap the assassin. That evening, Cortez accompanies Lieutenant Olot and his wife Sandra to a reserved table in a nightclub. Drake sits nearby, his eyes on the restaurant's entrance. Accompanied by Segur, Josetta arrives. Following Drake's instructions, she walks unescorted to her table and sits calmly in her seat. Bemused when the girl dips into her handbag and applies make-up to her face, Cortez is unable to take his eyes off her. He writhes in his seat as Josetta rises to her feet and, pausing only to stare him full in the face, leaves with her escort. Following the couple to Josetta's home, Drake sends Segur's man away and remains with the girl to see if Cortez takes the bait. He does so, arriving alone seconds later. He breaks into the house and fires at a figure standing at the window, emptying his bullets into the body. But the figure refuses to die. How could it? It is a dummy placed there by Drake who, entering the room with Colonel Segur, places the assassin under arrest.

THE ISLAND

Screenplay by Ralph Smart and Brian Clemens

Mr Wilson	**Allan Cuthbertson**
Mr Jones	**Peter Stephens**
Bobby	**Ann Firbank**
Kane	**Michael Ripper**
Pilot	**Ronan O'Casey**
Bobb	**Richard Thorp**
Airport Official	**Charles Irwin**
Stewardess	**Nyree Dawn Porter**

Directed by Pennington Richards

DRAKE HAS chartered an aircraft to take two assassins, Jones and Wilson, back to the mainland from an island off the North American Atlantic coast. He turns down a request from Bobby Palmer, daughter of the wealthy airline owner, for a lift in the chartered aeroplane. She has missed the scheduled flight. Telling the girl that he cannot oblige, Drake leaves to pack his luggage. However, Bobby changes places with a stewardess and Drake finds her on the aircraft. Although he protests, the plane takes off as planned. Bobby is warned by Drake that although the men look deceptively innocent, they are very dangerous. She is, nevertheless, flattered when Jones

On The Island, *Drake thwarts Wilson's attempt to steal the hermit's rifle*

turns on the charm. While Drake is in the cockpit informing the pilot that he wishes to be transferred to the plane that is waiting for him without going through customs, he is unaware of the commotion behind him. His prisoners have stolen a bottle of perfume from Bobby's handbag and flung its contents into the eyes of Bobb, a security guard accompanying Drake on the flight. They steal Bob's keys and release themselves from their handcuffs. The assassins make their bid for freedom by overpowering Drake and killing the pilot. The plane crashes into the sea. Drake and the girl succeed in reaching a tiny island and find that Jones and Wilson, the only other survivors, have managed to do so as well. Scouring the undergrowth, Drake and Bobby come across the murderers hiding in the forest. Warned that he has no allies and it is now two against one, Drake calls a truce, telling the men that he and the girl will stay on one side of the island, providing they agree to do the same. Wilson tells Drake that it is now a matter of survival and that they must all pull together towards a common aim, but Drake refuses to join them and they go their own ways. However, they are not alone. The island has one other occupant, a bearded hermit named Kane, who came to the island to escape the wickedness of the 'civilised' world. Drake and Bobby meet the man first – or so they believe, but when he escorts them to his home – a cave – Jones and Wilson are already there. Having arrived before Drake and the girl, they have made an astute move, telling the hermit that the couple are criminals who they were escorting back to the mainland. The unsuspecting Kane sides with them, mounting guard over the 'prisoners' while the real assassins wine and dine themselves from the hermit's larder. They tell Kane that Drake wishes to overpower them and leave with the girl when the next boat arrives. Jones is delighted when Kane, who needs little sleep, offers to watch the prisoners while his guests get some rest. As things transpire, Kane does fall asleep, but Wilson's attempt to steal the man's rifle is ruined when Drake sounds the alarm – and receives a sore head for his troubles. At dawn, believing Drake and the girl to be asleep, Wilson and Jones follow Kane out of the cave. On the pretext of fetching water, Wilson heads to the bushes. Within seconds, Kane lies unconscious at Jones' feet, flattened by the bucket Wilson was carrying. Grabbing the man's rifle, the assassins race back to the cave to deal with their prisoners. In the meantime, however, having witnessed the men attacking the hermit, Drake has found Kane's rifle cartridges and scatters them on the glowing embers of a fire built to cook breakfast. As the men enter the cave and order Drake and the girl to show themselves, the cartridges explode, sending bullets ricocheting in all directions. Racing outside, Drake and Bobby gather up Kane's body and make for the trees. Kane admits that a fisherman calls at the island almost daily and sends Drake to light a signal fire. Tricking the assassins into believing that he has taken refuge in a cave on the beach, Drake leaps onto his pursuers and quickly dispenses with them. The fisherman arrives and, thinking out loud how right he was to seek solitude from civilised society, Kane watches Drake and the girl leave his island for the mainland.

THE CONSPIRATORS

Screenplay by Ralph Smart and John Roddick

Lady Lindsay	**Patricia Driscoll**
Saunders	**Terence Longdon**
Sir Arthur Lindsay	**Hugh Moxey**
Craven	**Alfred Burke**
Innkeeper	**Percy Herbert**
Burke	**Rory McDermot**
Skipper	**Neil McCarthy**
George	**Michael Sands**
Kip	**Ian Ellis**
Tim	**Timothy Benke**

Directed by Michael Truman

THIS TIME, the call to action is as brief as it is explicit: 'Subject, Judith Lindsay, wife of the British diplomat Sir Arthur Lindsay, deceased. It is anticipated that an attempt will be made on her life while she is on the island of Franju. Move with extreme caution. Advise.' This dramatic message sends Drake to Franju, a remote island north of the Brittany coast. Sir Arthur has been murdered to prevent him giving evidence at an inquiry into an administration scandal in Africa, although the inquest verdict was suicide. His widow, Judith, has taken her two children with her to the island, where she is writing a book revealing the truth about the scandal. At the local inn, Drake is introduced by the innkeeper to George, the island's postman. Stating that he is on the island to visit the old castle, the innkeeper is delighted to hire Drake a pony and trap to transport him to the castle grounds. But his way into the castle is barred by a caretaker named Craven, who tells him that no one is allowed inside. Drake, however, succeeds in getting into the grounds by climbing over a wall. He makes himself known to Judith who scorns his warning that her life is in danger. Drake tells the woman that his government believes that her husband's death was organised by certain interested people who did not want him to appear at the inquiry, people to whom his evidence would have been damaging. Judith, nevertheless, remains determined that the world will learn the truth – her husband was not responsible for the riots which caused hundreds of deaths, and she refuses to leave. When a helicopter arrives, Drake hides. A stranger walks in and introduces himself to Judith as Saunders, a man sent to carry out restoration work on the castle. Convinced that the man is a spy, Drake attempts to ring his headquarters from the only telephone on the island, but the instrument is out of order. Told by Drake that he had been turned away from the castle by a caretaker, the innkeeper replies that he did not know that a man had been employed in that capacity. He is about to offer Drake a drink, when Saunders appears, intimating that the lady at the castle has two lovely children. Drake tells the man he would not know, he was not allowed inside. Pretending that he has to visit the mainland, Drake pays the ferry boat's skipper to drop him on the far side of the island. He arrives back at the castle to be told by Judith that her children have disappeared. While searching

Watched by their mother, Kip and Tim Lindsay join Drake as The Conspirators' *helicopter zooms overhead*

NAME, DATE AND PLACE

Screenplay by Ralph Smart and John Roddick

Nash	Cyril Raymond
Hardy	Richard Wattis
Deirdre	Kathleen Bryon
Rosemary	Patricia Marmont
Kim Russell	Jean Marsh
Nita	Susan Travers
Franky	Delena Kidd
Chambermaid	Olive McFarland
Vogel	Guy Deghy
Small Man	Frederick Piper
Butler	Beaufoy Milton
Det Insp Marks	Frank Sieman
Det Sgt Davis	Peter Hutton

Directed by Charles Frend

A SPANISH ROYALIST is killed in Edinburgh, a Communist diplomat in France, an Irish MP in Italy . . . and from other parts of the world come further unsolved mysteries, none connected with the others in any way, yet all the men were killed in an identical fashion – a shot in the back from close range. When a seventh victim is discovered in a seedy London hotel bedroom, Drake is handed the task of finding the link. Working on the theory that this might be the work of a Murder Incorporated organisation that kills for profit, he seeks a contact which might lead him to the gang. At Hardy's instigation, he meets Kim Russell, a girl from Soho who knows her way around. Drake puts it to her bluntly: 'I am trying to locate an organisation that makes murder its business. You pay, we kill 'em – no questions asked.' Their first port of call is a run-down Soho nightclub. For three days and nights Drake learns nothing, until he is introduced to Franky, a young girl with an obsessive gambling fever. Through her he goes to see a respected business man named Collingwood-Nash. It appears, however, that the girl has made a mistake. When Drake tells the man that he wants someone eliminated, Nash's reaction is a threat to call the police. Back at his hotel, a card is pushed under Drake's door: 'Cosmopolitan Services: Mayfair 0051. Our representative called but you were out. She will call again.' The girl, a Mrs Rosemary Hammond does so and explains that they can supply anything. Murder? It can be arranged, but they will require $50,000 in used bills. Once the fee is paid, Drake will be hearing from them. The money must be waiting for collection by four o'clock that afternoon. No contact arrives, just a small empty box containing a card requiring three details to be filled in: name, date and place. Having written 'Ivor Towers: 14 July: Hotel Gustave Leon, Paris', he is contacted by telephone and told to take the package with him and board a number 74 omnibus. During the journey he receives further instructions telling him to deposit the package on the ledge of a fence outside the entrance to a factory. He settles down to observe who collects the money. His vigil is fruitless: within minutes hundreds of workers walk through the factory gates – each carrying a luncheon box identical in size to the money package, which has now disappeared! None too pleased when Drake tells him that the money has been lost, Hardy's demeanour brightens when his junior

for them, an audacious attempt is made on the woman's life: a helicopter tries to sweep her over a cliff. She is saved by Drake and places her trust in him from that moment on. Back at the castle the boys are found safe, having been to see a smuggler's cave with Craven. Entering Judith's room alone, Drake finds Saunders reading the typescript for her book. Drake confirms that the book will tell the true story about the Naiamba riots, and badgers the intruder by suggesting that although he is a man who prefers to mind his own business, he will make an exception in Saunders' case. At that moment, Burke, the helicopter pilot enters the room. Drake tells the newcomer that he admired the manoeuvres the man made on the clifftop, pushing Judith 'right over the edge' so to speak. Drake is not too surprised when the man pulls a gun. He bluffs the men by telling them that Judith is still alive and is at that very moment on her way to the mainland; if he is shot she will know who killed him. But his ruse is spoiled when Judith chooses that moment to walk into the room. In the ensuing fight, Drake knocks the men unconscious. He then races past the startled woman to the castle's main gate where he disarms Craven, who has the ferry skipper and his mate at gunpoint (the men having arrived at the castle under orders Drake had given to them earlier). Incarcerating the conspirators in the castle dungeon, the first people to be imprisoned there since 1346, Drake takes the helicopter's controls and flies Judith and her sons to safety.

suggests that he masquerade as Towers, the intended victim: he will fly to Paris and await his own assassination, thereby ensuring that Hardy's money is put to its intended use. 14 July finds Drake ensconced in the Hotel Gustave Leon to keep an appointment with a stranger – one who will shoot him in the back with a .32 calibre pistol. After a short wait, a man calling himself Hans Vogel raps on the door of Drake's room. A false alarm. Vogel has mistaken Drake for another man named Towers with whom he has exchanged correspondence. Apologising for the error, the man leaves – bumping into a girl in the corridor as he does so. The girl, a beautiful brunette named Nita, pleads with Drake to take her out on the town, but the undercover man tells her he is expecting his girlfriend. Having pushed her way into the room, Nita calmly uncovers a gun hidden beneath her fur stole and shoots Drake in the chest, sending the agent spinning into the bedroom. Attempting to follow him and finding the door locked, the girl peeps through the keyhole. When she sees that her victim is prostrate on the floor, she leaves. Seconds later the 'dead' man recovers and telephones his contact who is waiting in the hotel lobby, giving him instructions not to let the woman out of his sight. Drake removes his bullet-proof vest and hastily packs his suitcase. The following morning, together with CID detectives Marks and Davis, the undercover man storms into Collingwood-Nash's home. He orders the man's wife and butler from the room and Drake angrily berates him for not keeping his side of the bargain: he has paid Nash's hamfisted organisation $50,000 to have one Ivor Towers wiped out, but Towers is still walking the streets of Paris! Because of Nash's foul up, Drake stands to lose a $200,000 deal he had planned: he is now unable to do so and he has come to collect. Believing the men who arrived with Drake to be his personal bodyguards, Nash proclaims his innocence and orders Charles, his butler to ring for the police. However, when Drake continues to charge him with negligence, he orders the butler to leave, and offers to prove that Towers has been dispensed with. A telephone call brings the murderous Nita to Nash's home. The girl confirms that she shot Towers through the heart – a statement confirmed by the 'dead' man who turns around to face the girl. Drake is not too surprised when the detectives find the murder weapon in her handbag. The murder for sale organisation smashed, Drake follows the detectives from the room.

In Name, Date and Place, *undercover man John Drake pays a $50,000 price tag to have himself murdered*

THE LEAK

Screenplay by Ralph Smart and Brian Clemens

Doctor Leclair	Zena Marshall
Doctor Bryant	Bernard Archard
Sheik Ahmed	Marne Maitland
Martin	Anthony Dawson
Finch	Lawrence Davidson
Colonel Perar	Walter Gotell
Secretary	William Peacock
Salah	Barry Shawzin
Mrs Parkes	Patsy Smart
Sadi	Joseph Cuby
Moham	Eric Pohlman

Directed by Anthony Bushell

WHEN ONE MAN after another falls ill with radiation sickness at an atomic energy plant in North Africa, agent John Drake arrives on the scene to investigate. Outside the plant he finds himself confronted by a number of natives carrying placards calling for the establishment to be closed. Having informed their spokesman that he is not an employee, Drake is allowed to pass. He is met by a man named Finch and is shown into the office of Martin, the head of the nuclear plant, whom he finds attempting to convince a protest committee that the establishment is not responsible for the deaths of natives. The statement is confirmed by Doctor Bryant, Martin's technical adviser. However, Corinne Leclair, a beautiful and efficient European doctor, is inclined to side with the powerful Sheik Ahmed who wants the plant closed down, believing that a leakage is responsible. She is certain that her diagnosis is correct and that the men did die of radiation sickness. Bryant shows anger, accusing the Sheik of only being concerned for selfish reasons: if the reactor succeeds, it will change the area's economy and Ahmed will lose all his labourers and face ruin. Saying that the Sheik has never spared himself to maintain the welfare of his people, Dr Leclair takes exception to Bryant's accusation, as does Colonel Perar, a representative of the government, who adds that the final decision will be taken tomorrow. After the Sheik and Leclair have left, Perar informs Martin that unless steps are taken to stop the leak, his superiors will almost certainly instruct him to close the plant down. A visit to Corinne Leclair's hospital leads Drake nowhere: she is adamant that the reactor is responsible. Drake is keeping an open mind, aware of the possibility that she may be wrong, in which case the sickness must originate from another source. A factor to bear in mind is that only natives have become infected, although several Europeans work at the reactor plant. Ahmed has a simple explanation for this. The natives are not so well fed and have less resistance than the whites who are healthy and have a better diet. But the next patient is a European – an aged professor named Jauncey, living in distressed circumstances and looked after by a native boy named Sadi and a friendly housekeeper, Mrs Parkes. From Sadi, Drake learns that all Jauncey has eaten during the past few weeks is bread which the boy obtained for him. Sadi refuses to say where the bread came from, but Drake discovers that it was stolen from a baker in the Arab quarter. Following up this clue, he interviews the baker,

Attempting to discover The Leak *Drake finds himself set upon by one of Ahmed's thugs*

Moham, who tells him that he has obtained his flour from Sheik Ahmed's mills. When a sample loaf proves to be radioactive, Martin and Bryant remain adamant that their plant cannot be responsible. Ahmed's estates are way up in the north. However, the nuclear waste has to be disposed of somewhere and, when shown the isolated dumping ground on a map, Drake is quick to point out that an underground stream may be responsible for feeding the contamination into the Sheik's water wells. A sample of water from each of Ahmed's water holes is brought to Dr Leclair's hospital. The Sheik, indignant when Drake suggests that he must be allowed to inspect the man's estate, flatly refuses to allow the foreigner to do so. As Drake and the doctor leave, Finch is ushered into Ahmed's tent, bearing the loaf of bread that Drake left at the reactor plant. A short time later, Drake learns from Martin that the loaf is missing. Salah, the Sheik's man-servant knocks on the agent's door: his master begs Drake's forgiveness and asks that he visit him immediately. It is a trap. Driven by Salah to Ahmed's mill, Drake is set upon by three Arabs. His training gets him out of trouble and the heavies are soon dispensed with, leaving Drake to race to Ahmed's home. Brushing Salah aside, he enters the Arab chieftain's tent and accuses the Sheik of knowing all along that his flour was contaminated. Ahmed denies Drake's accusation, failing to see his unwelcome guest pour the contents of a small phial into his teacup. Drake baits his host by suggesting that Ahmed himself may already have been exposed to the radiation. He takes great delight in subjecting the man to cross-examination about his health: the disease begins, says Drake with sweating palms, weariness of the limbs and headaches – symptoms which, as Drake takes his leave, Ahmed is beginning to show. The drug is beginning to take effect. Within minutes, Ahmed has collapsed into Salah's arms. Ahmed's manservant telephones Corinne Leclair for assistance. Reminding the girl to play it his way, Drake drives her to the Arab's home. As the woman prepares to treat the Sheik, Drake interrogates the man about his part in the affair. Believing he has but seconds to live, Ahmed confesses the truth, calling for his accomplice Finch to join them. Ahmed is staggered when Dr Leclair offers him water instead of the medicine he expected. Aware that he has been tricked, he orders his guards to prevent the couple leaving. But Drake has outwitted him and within seconds Ahmed and his thugs are arrested by Colonel Perar.

THE HONEYMOONERS

Screenplay by Ralph Smart and Lewis Davidson

Guest stars

Mr Chung Sun	**Lee Montague**
Ted Baker	**Ronald Allen**
Joan Baker	**Sally Bazely**

with

President	**Michael Peake**
Reporter	**Kerrigan Prescott**
Williams	**Sheldon Lawrence**
Mitchu	**Anthony Chin**
Police Lieut	**Eric Young**
Gate Keeper	**Myo Toon**
Maid	**Barbara Lee**
Receptionist	**Jimmy Fung**

Directed by Charles Frend

TRAGEDY STRIKES Captain Ted Baker and his wife Joan, a young couple who are honeymooning on the Far Eastern island of Banton. The husband is accused of the murder of a Chinese businessman who entered Baker's hotel bedroom while the bride was alone. One month later, with Ted Baker sitting in a death cell and his wife lying in bed wishing she could die, too, Drake is flown out to discover what really happened and to try to save the young man from execution. Drake is invited to meet Mr Chung Sun, the Minister of Justice to whom he introduces himself as a representative of the International Press group. He discovers that the man, running in opposition to the President in the forthcoming elections, considers that a gesture of standing up to the West would be a good vote catcher. Baker's victim had a wife and four children: what he did was barbaric and Chung Sun is determined to make him pay. Drake asks the Minister if he has any idea why the accused man put up no defence against the charge and is told the he does not know why but that the stranger is welcome to read the transcript of the trial, which is legally correct. Replying that he has done so, Drake asks if he might visit the condemned man. He calls at the gaol – a place with the appearance and amenities of a medieval dungeon. Under guard, Drake joins several journalists as Baker is escorted into the prison's visiting room. Sitting quietly at the back of the room, Drake listens as Baker (who he has met previously when working with the Signals Regiment) answers questions in monotone fashion: the prisoner has no complaints, other than for the trial which, though handled fairly, brought a sentence tougher than he had expected: he has registered an appeal and still has hopes of being pardoned. Informed by a reporter that his appeal has been quashed by Chung Sun, Baker admits that he expected nothing better. When Drake asks him why he pleaded guilty, a glimmer of hope crosses Baker's face as he recognises the 'journalist'. He answers that he had no defence: he shot the man. Back at Joan Baker's room, Drake is delighted to see that the woman is up and about and suggests that she repeat her evidence to him from say, the time her husband left the room. Joan does so, and Drake spots a hole in her story. He suggests that the dead man could have made a mistake – the numbers on his key ring were printed one above the other and, as Orientals read from the bottom to the top, the man could have mistaken room 42 for his own, room 24. Drake, suspecting that the woman is lying, tricks Baker's wife into admitting that she killed the man in a state of panic. That said, she does not need Drake's help, everything is going to be all right. Concerned that Chung Sun has made a deal with the woman, Drake is about to question her when he finds himself ushered from the room by one of the Minister's guards. Drake finds the President, who is aware of his true identity, in a state of dilemma, although he is anxious to save Baker's life. If the President were to reprieve and deport the prisoner his standing with the Western powers would soar, but it would put an end to his hopes in the election: he desperately needs another term of office to establish his people in a state of freedom and prosperity which they have not enjoyed for a thousand years. Supposing, says Drake, that Mrs Baker were to sign a full confession that it was she who did the killing, would that not solve both their problems? The President is delighted with the idea: if they could pull it off, Captain Baker would be the hero of the hour for his marital devotion and the popular Mr Chung Sun would come under severe censure for having attempted to bring about a miscarriage of justice. What is more, in such circumstances, the President could safely deport the woman. Having convinced Joan Baker that Chung Sun's words are just empty promises, the woman reluctantly falls in with Drake's plan and signs a confession. But they have fallen into a trap. Joan's room has been bugged. A police lieutenant races into the room and

Drake is thrown into a prison cell. Hours later when he is released, the confession signed by Joan has been 'mislaid'. The woman, too, is missing, forced by Chung Sun to flee the country. Out-manoeuvred, Drake proposes to the President that a desperate situation calls for desperate measures: he will attempt to break Baker out of jail. With the aid of a fellow journalist, he manages to join other newspaper men as they enter the prison's visiting room. As the journalists question Baker he positions himself near the prisoner. Drake slips open a satchel – supposedly containing camera flash equipment – and flings canisters of gas at the guards. Within seconds everyone in the room is gasping for breath – all save Drake who, wearing breathing apparatus, throws the prisoner a gas-mask. Shoving aside the guards, the men race to the safety of the corridor where Baker finds a change of attire hidden in a corner by the undercover man. One minute later, disguised as a journalist, the prisoner walks calmly to the freedom of a waiting car. After journeying to the mainland on a trading junk, the two men arrive safely in Hong Kong.

Posing as a journalist, Drake visits Chung Sun's medieval dungeon in order to engineer prisoner Ted Baker's release. A scene from The Honeymooners

THE GIRL WHO LIKED GI'S

Screenplay by Marc Brandel and Ralph Smart

Vicki	**Anna Gaylor**
Lotsbeyer	**Anthony Bushell**
Wetzel	**Nigel Green**
Doyle	**Paul Maxwell**
Krug	**Charles Farrell**
Sgt Ross	**Graydon Gould**
Sgt Poole	**Bill Edwards**
Manservant	**Rudolph Offenbach**
Receptionist	**Betty Le Beau**

Directed by Michael Truman

SCARCELY MINUTES after kissing his attractive date goodnight, Technical Sergeant Peter Ross is approached in his Munich hotel room by two well-dressed men. Seconds later, the American soldier lies dead, accidentally struck on the head by one of the men. Ross had planned to spend his weekend leave in Munich; Drake had planned to spend his on a beach, soaking up the sun. Now both holidays are spoiled. The soldier had worked on the Top Security missile section and his sudden violent death sees Drake hot-footing it to Munich to find out why the man was murdered. Booking into his hotel, the undercover man finds Colonel Wetzel of West German Intelligence waiting for him. Not wishing to have it known that Drake is in the city, Wetzel has arranged to meet the Englishman in private. It appears that the German has already made up his mind that the dead soldier was selling official secrets, but Drake is not convinced. From Ross' service pal, Sergeant Poole, Drake learns that Ross was fond of girls and was also a camera enthusiast. The last girl he saw was the attractive Vicki Lotsbeyer, who works in a camera shop. As the men are talking, the girl telephones the hotel and asks to speak to Ross. Masquerading as Poole, Drake talks to her and arranges to meet the girl at the Blue Barn restaurant that evening. Dressed as a GI sergeant, Drake spends the evening with her. She tells him that she likes GIs because they are fun to be with, they're free, they have no worries, no responsibilities. She met Ross when he came to her photographic shop to buy some film and she looks shocked when Drake tells her that Ross is dead. Having dropped the girl outside a young women's youth hostel, Drake is driving away when he chances to notice Vicki turn on her heel and walk away from the building. He trails the girl to a nearby house where, confronted about her actions, she explains that it is her home; she misled him because she did not want her father to know that she was seeing an American soldier. As they talk, her father arrives by taxi and orders Drake to leave. Debating the question of whether Lotsbeyer is really a respectable businessman or connected with an espionage ring, Drake hears a scream from Vicki's room. Racing to the building's front door, he is pushed aside by a man carrying a gun. Ordering Drake to go inside, the man hops into a car and escapes into the night. Lotsbeyer's manservant tells Drake the man was a thief, but Vicki's father refuses to speak, slamming the door in Drake's face. As he walks back to his hotel, Drake is attacked by the man with the gun. A car draws up and a second man assaults the agent from behind, throwing his tie around Drake's neck, and threatening to squeeze the life from his lungs. As fast as a cobra, the undercover man throws his would-be assassin headlong into his partner. Springing forward, Drake grabs the second man's gun and escorts them to Wetzel's headquarters. From Colonel Doyle, the dead soldier's Base Commander, he learns that the man with the gun is Stephen Krug, a courier for the West German Embassy at Bonn. Demanding to know why he has been brought to Doyle's headquarters, Lotsbeyer enters the room accompanied by Vicki. Drake acknowledges that the man is free to go, but he must talk to his daughter alone on a matter of security. The German waits in another room while Vicki's interrogation leads nowhere. She remembers nothing of use – other than the fact that she recognises the man in a photograph Drake shows her as Krug, the man who attacked her in her bedroom. Why he was there the girl does not know, unless he was searching for the roll of film Ross gave her to develop. Film? Has she still got it asks Drake? Yes. It is at the camera shop; she developed the negative and printed several photographs. Escorting Vicki there, one of the pictures holds a vital clue, a clue which links Krug with the head of West German Intelligence – Colonel Wetzel – who at that very moment enters the shop, his revolver trained on Drake's heart. Confessing that the killing of Ross was a blunder – Krug hit the man too hard – the German proposes to rectify his comrade's mistake. Drake and the girl must die. Drake, however has other ideas. As Wetzel closes in for the kill, the British agent snatches up a camera and depresses its flash control. Its glare momentarily blinds the German. A second is all Drake needs. Within the blink of an eye, Wetzel lies unconscious at his feet, his chin smarting from Drake's knock out blow. Apologising to the girl for doubting her story, Drake telephones Colonel Doyle to relate that Ross' killer has been brought to justice.

Drake dons the uniform of an American serviceman to interrogate the attractive Vicki, **The Girl Who Liked GI's**

HIRED ASSASSIN

Screenplay by Ralph Smart and John Roddick

Alexis	Alan Wheatley
Luis	Cyril Shaps
Edouardo	Nyall Florenz
Juanita	Judy Carne
Senor Lazar	Wensley Pithey
Fernandez	Bill Nagy
Pietro	Henry Lockhart
Viccenti	J. Leslie Erith
Kovac	Charles Hill
Pepe	Frank Thornton

Directed by Charles Frend

SEEKING PROTECTION from the police, Drake enters a nightclub. Without so much as a glance at the pretty girl entertaining the diners with her songs, he is ushered to his seat by Kovac, the nightclub manager. Barely minutes later, Colonel Fernandez, a policeman, enters the club with two of his men. Shown a prison record bearing Drake's photograph, Kovac denies having ever seen the man. Unconvinced, Fernandez orders his men to search the place. In the meantime, Drake has taken refuge in the singer's dressing-room and is waiting for the girl when she arrives there to change her dress. Hearing the policemen approaching, the undercover man orders her, at gunpoint, to remain quiet. As he hides in a wardrobe, he hears Fernandez telling the girl that the man they are searching for is a known assassin, wanted by the police in a dozen countries. In reality, the policeman is working with Drake. The British agent has been assigned to prevent an attempt on the life of President Valesco who will shortly be visiting the country. Although every security precaution has been taken, Drake is aware that extremists will attempt to kill the President. The girl, Juanita, is a member of the anti-Valesco group, and the undercover man hopes to trick her into helping him meet the would-be assassins.

The ruse works, but not before an attempt is made on Drake's life. Dining at Juanita's home, a man named Alexis creeps up behind him and threatens to shoot Drake. It is a test. On the condition that the assassin undertakes a simple mission for him, Alexis can get Drake out of the country. The mission? To kill President Valesco. Drake's plan has worked. Accompanied by Alexis and several other members of the action group, Drake is surprised when he discovers the whereabouts of their hideaway: 20 feet under the nightclub he had left earlier. It is here that he is introduced to Edouardo and Luis, two of Alexis' colleagues. Although Luis has heard of 'Bullinger's' reputation, Edouardo is suspicious of the newcomer. As an example to the others, and Drake in particular, Alexis has Pietro, an assassin who has bungled his last job, shot dead in the cellar. Before long, Drake has won the confidence of everyone but Edouardo, particularly when he outlines his plan for the assassination. Drake proposes that they wait until the end of the visit, when those in charge of the President's security will feel that everything has gone satisfactorily and will, therefore, be less alert. Then, as Valesco is on his way out of the city and his entourage passes over a narrow bridge, they will blow him up. Everyone except Edouardo, who wishes to shoot the President with a rifle, agrees and Alexis sends Drake and Juanita to scout around for a house from which they can proceed with the bomb attempt. The most likely place is the home of pottery collector, Viccenti, an eccentric who lives only for his collection of porcelain. On the pretext of selling the man an earthenware pot, Drake and the girl gain entrance to Viccenti's home, whereupon Drake threatens to smash the man's prized collection unless he allows them to 'borrow' his home for a few days. Joined by the others, after hours of digging, they reach an impenetrable barrier, a wall of rock. Seeing this as his chance to take over, Edouardo complains that all is lost, there is no way they can dig through the obstacle before morning, the chance to kill Valesco is lost. He then proposes a new plan: the house is close enough to the President's route to enable him to pick off Valesco with his rifle. Drake disagrees, stating that the car's windscreen will be bullet proof. It is then that Luis proposes that they burrow under the barrier and the spade work begins anew. At daylight the following morning, Drake and Luis lay the explosive charges – the undercover man ensures that the detonation will never take place by cutting the fuse wire. At the appointed time, Valesco's entourage appears on the street. Drake, meanwhile, has slipped into the bedroom and seen to Edouardo, who was waiting at the window determined to have a shot at the President's car. When Luis exclaims that the detonator will not work, Drake races to the tunnel to prevent the man from reconnecting the fuse wires – too late. Alexis sends a current shooting through the wires and Drake and Luis are buried as the roof above them caves in, the resulting explosion failing to penetrate to street level. Racing for his life, Drake extricates himself from the rubble and, running up the stairs, locks the cellar doors behind him. As he does so, alarmed that the explosion will smash his porcelain collection, Viccenti races down the stairs to state that, despite Drake's threats, he is going to telephone the police. 'Please do,' says the agent, rubbing his wounded arm.

Hired Assassin *Drake outlines his plan to assassinate the President*

THE GALLOWS TREE

Screenplay by Ralph Smart and Marc Brandel

Laing	Paul Rogers
Jean	Wendy Craig
Clements	Raymond Huntley

with

Craig	Ewan Roberts
Mackenzie	Andrew Crawford
Hamish	John Glyn-Jones
Shepherd	John Rae
Hawkes	Reginald Hearne
Duncan	Gareth Tandy
Conductor	Michael Bird
Jock	Finlay Currie

Directed by Michael Truman

IT IS AN UNUSUAL appointment. Boarding the 9.15 Glasgow-bound express from platform 4, at Euston Station, Drake is unable to comply with the railway porter's request to produce his ticket. He does not have one; he does not even know which sleeping berth he is travelling in! Perhaps the ticket inspector can help? He can. Showing Drake to carriage 14B, he tells the traveller that he is booked to go to Fort William. What is more, a Mr Clements is waiting to see him. High in the echelons of the British Secret Service, Clements has a story to tell. It appears that a car, stolen in the Scottish Highlands, bears two sets of fingerprints – one belonging to the thief, the other to a certain Hans Brechter, a master spy and terrorist who was believed to have died ten years earlier. Drake has been selected by Clements because he is one of the few men who knew Brechter. The undercover man must locate the man, who is obviously living under an assumed name, and keep him under surveillance until he finds out what he is up to. Drake is met at Fort William by Inspector Mackenzie and is soon introduced to Craig, the owner of the stolen car. Craig, however, can throw no light on the second set of fingerprints, stating that he only saw the thief, who is now in custody. Mackenzie asks Craig if he has given anyone a lift recently, a stranger perhaps? Pressed further, the man recalls having picked up a clean-shaven, grey-haired man in Castletown a week earlier. Working on the supposition that Brechter has shaved off his beard and is living somewhere on the headland, Drake persuades the policeman to take him there by rowing boat. Barely minutes after he steps ashore he bumps into

Alone at a table in The Gallows Tree Inn, *Drake dusts a drinking glass for Hans Brechter's fingerprints*

a poacher, Hamish, hiding in the trees. Seconds later, both men are running for their lives when a gamekeeper takes a shot at them. Aware that Drake has been dropped secretly on the headland by boat, Hamish tells him he will not let on if Drake stays silent about his own poaching activities. Content that the man is harmless, Drake agrees. Making his way to *The Gallows Tree*, the local inn, the newcomer is greeted by Jock, the local lobster fisherman, who offers to buy him a toddy but Jean, the innkeeper's daughter, has to refuse: it is after 9 pm and the law forbids the sale of alcohol. However, as Jock leaves, promising to supply the girl with a nice fat lobster the following morning, Jean succumbs to Drake's charm and serves him a whisky. Alone at a table, Drake dusts several glasses for fingerprints, finding at the bottom of each glass, Hans Brechter's tell-tale thumbprint. At that moment, Laing, the innkeeper, appears behind the bar and pours himself a drink. Watching the man, Drake cannot help but notice that he holds the glass in an unusual manner – with his index finger shading the glass, and his thumb supporting the base! Convinced now that the man is Brechter, Drake pretends that he has been sent by their mutual bosses to contact him and receive instructions. Laing, no longer denying that he is Brechter, says a mistake has been made: he gave up his spying activities many years ago, using his assumed death as an opportunity to do so. He has realised the waste and uselessness of his former life; trying to change the world by glorious revolution. Unconvinced by the man's claim, Drake is put on guard when interference breaks up a television picture – someone is transmitting messages by short-wave radio. Bidding Brechter goodnight, Drake races to his bedroom and listens in to the transmission via a miniature walkie-talkie device. He hears someone in the village ask questions about him, a message which seems to confirm that the inn is being used for illicit purposes. A knock on his door heralds the arrival of Laing. He has come to confirm that he has lost the gift for hatred – Drake must inform his employers that 'Brechter' has finished with the spy game. He will never work for them again. Jean arrives, and ushers Laing off to bed, apologising to Drake for her father's behaviour. As the door closes behind them, a note attached to a stone is thrown through the bedroom window. It reads 'Don't leave until we contact you – sometime tomorrow.' The following morning, Jean arrives with a breakfast tray bearing a letter addressed to the guest. 'They' have made contact: Drake is to meet someone called Ivan on top of Glen Bay. Climbing the tor, the agent is met by Craig, the owner of the stolen car. He offers Drake a lift – literally, by attempting to drive him headlong off the clifftop! Forced to run for his life, Drake eventually succeeds in mounting Craig's Land Rover and wrestles the controls from the driver's grasp, sending Craig tumbling through the vehicle's door. He throws Craig's unconscious body into the back of the vehicle, dons the man's hunting jacket and cap and drives back to the inn. Drake is met by Jean, who berates the man she believes to be Craig for bringing Drake's body back to the inn. Thanking the girl for being thoughtful enough to give him breakfast before sending him out to be killed, Drake accuses her of carrying on her father's work. Joined by a confused Laing, Jean confesses how, when her father's spy masters found out that he was still alive, she had made a bargain with them in order that Brechter might be left in peace; he had betrayed them, she had not. Both the girl and her father are taken away by Inspector Mackenzie, leaving Drake to pack his bags and leave for London.

VACATION

Screenplay by Ralph Smart

Amory	Hugh McDermott
Baron	Esmond Knight
Veronica	Jacqueline Ellis
Georges	Barrie Ingham
Gautier	Lawrence Davidson
Butler	John Wynyard
Ricki	Richard Clarke
Gunsmith	Charles Lloyd Pack

Directed by Patrick McGoohan

HE CAN HARDLY believe it. After four years without a break from the rigours of the spy game Drake has at last found time to take a vacation. He is off to the Mediterranean, to lie on the beach, to soak up the sun – to forget. Boarding his flight, he finds the seat he has reserved occupied by a man named Amory. However, the place beside him is vacant and Drake is quite happy to make conversation. 'East, west, wherever one travels home is best,' Amory tells him, handing Drake a photograph of himself and his pretty wife. The picture turns a cog in Drake's memory and he suggests that he has met Amory before – he is sure he has seen the man's face, somewhere. The other's reply that he has made a mistake fails to allay Drake's concern. He soon remembers that, although he has never met Amory before, he has seen his photograph – in a file marked A-017 in the Washington criminal records: the man sitting next to him is a professional killer, an assassin for hire! Arriving in Nice, Amory books into his hotel room where, unseen at the door, Drake watches the man make a telephone call. He also removes a package from his suitcase – a package containing a gun! Hearing the assassin speaking to someone named Georges, Drake slips into the corridor, pauses for a moment, then raps on Amory's door. Invited in, he confronts Amory with the fact that he is an American Intelligence agent. Drake accuses the man of being Andreas Amari, a killer for hire. Amory goes for his gun, but Drake is ready for him. Disarming the man, Drake arranges by telephone to have Amory safely ensconced in a police cell. Drake is waiting when Georges arrives. Bluffing his way through their meeting, the undercover man finds himself engaged to murder someone – he will not know who until he receives a photograph of the intended victim. Furthermore, the identity of the person who has hired him must remain a mystery. Georges alone knows who employed him, and he is not telling. Georges directs him to a sumptuous villa occupied by a Mr Baron and his beautiful young niece, Veronica. Meanwhile, Drake's policeman friends arrive to collect Amory, but the man has vanished. Having no idea why he has been taken to the villa, Drake soon learns from Baron's secretary, Gautier, that he is 'Harrison', a tennis coach employed to help Veronica with her game. He also meets Mr Baron, a man who collects guns. Drake's prowess with a rifle on the man's indoor shooting gallery is impressive enough for Baron to challenge him to a shooting contest. It soon becomes clear that Veronica and her uncle do not get on well together and that Baron has forbidden her boyfriend, Ricki Clement, to enter his home. Escorted to Baron's tennis court by the butler, Drake bluffs his way through the girl's tennis tutorial by studying Veronica's racket strokes, informing the girl that he has not been employed to 'knock the ball around' and prefers to improve her natural style. Amory, meanwhile has escaped detention and telephones Georges with the astonishing news that the man he escorted to the villa is an impostor. That evening, as Drake is taking drinks with Baron and Edwards, his gunsmith, Gautier arrives carrying a tray on which rest two envelopes. One is handed to the gunsmith, the other, addressed to 'Harrison', is given to Drake. The envelope contains a photograph – his victim is Veronica. Visiting the girl's room, he shows her his intelligence credentials and warns her that she is in danger. Does she know of anyone who would benefit from her death? Veronica explains that she is an heiress, and that her uncle is her trustee. Frightened by Drake's insistence that someone wishes to see her dead, she tells him that in the event of her death, her money and estates will go to her uncle. Aware that Baron has business troubles, she asks if they should ring the police. Confirming that she should, Drake shows concern when the butler tells her that the telephone line is out of order. In a state of panic, the girl asks Drake to telephone the authorities from the boathouse; the receiver there is an outside line. Locking Veronica in her room, Drake descends the stairs and confronts Baron with the charge of hiring him to kill his niece. The man need not worry; everything is going to plan, but the price they agreed is too low, he requires a higher fee for his services. Appearing to know nothing of the plot, Baron attempts to telephone the police, an action that leaves Drake unconvinced: as the man who arranged the killing, Baron would obviously be aware that the telephone wires have been cut. Why doesn't he use the boathouse telephone? Because, says Baron, the line there is connected to the exchange, a fact confirmed by Gautier. Drake smells a rat and races to the boathouse to find Georges, Amory and Ricki Clement waiting for him. Drake is thrown to his knees and interrogated. He tricks the boyfriend into confessing that he was responsible for sending him the photograph of Veronica instead of the intended victim – Mr Baron – whose death would leave Ricki free to marry the girl and become a wealthy man. In a flash of anger, Ricki also confirms that he and Veronica were working together. That is all that Drake was waiting to hear. Throwing the men off guard by convincing them that the police are waiting outside, he sets about teaching them a lesson. Just as the intelligence man is beginning to enjoy his work, Baron arrives, his finger on the trigger of a rifle. Watched by Drake, the would-be assassins are handed over to the authorities, leaving the undercover man free to pursue his well-earned vacation.

THE TRAP

Screenplay by Ralph Smart and John Roddick

Beth	Jeanne Moody
Gino	Noel Trevarthen
Carla	Marie Burke
Whitmore	Alan Gifford
Liz	Louise Collins
Miss Bishop	Georgina Cookson
Papa	Victor Rietti
Moma	Miki Iveria
Stashig	John Bonney
Officer	Patrick Maynard
Pilot	Graham Stewart

Directed by R. Pennington Richards

ATTRACTIVE BETH WARREN, who works in the cipher department at the American Embassy in London, has suddenly taken off to Italy with her boyfriend, Gino, without official permission. There is good reason for wondering whether she has really gone to see Gino's mother or if there is more to her vacation than meets the eye. John Drake finds himself at the home of Colonel Whitmore, an Embassy official, who introduces him to Miss Parish, Beth's room mate. The girl says that she is surprised by her friend's sudden departure. Whitmore is concerned that, should the trip be anything but coincidence, and should anything happen to Beth, it could prove disastrous: Beth had been given the new cipher index that very week and he does not want to take any chances. Drake is sent to Venice to investigate. At the hotel run by Gino's mother, Carla, he meets both Beth and her boyfriend. Gino says that he has just returned from telephoning the hospital to which his brother Alberto was taken after an accident. He tells his mother that Alberto has had a good night and is doing as well as can be expected. Later, however, when he shows Drake to his room, Gino confides that he is not hopeful about Alberto's chances of recovery. Speaking to Beth alone, Drake tells her why he is in Venice and asks her why she left England in such a hurry. She assures him that the only reason for her hasty departure was because of her boyfriend's family problems: Gino had heard of his brother's traffic accident in the Yugoslavian mountains and needed help with running the hotel, while he attended to his mother. The girl becomes angry when Drake suggests that she is 'running away to the other side.' Why Alberto should have been over the border when he crashed his car, she has no idea, but she is certain of one thing — Gino loves her, and they are to be married. Accepting Beth's story, Drake tells her that he will cable London and let them know the score: but the girl should not be too surprised if they order her back to London. That evening, Gino, confirms the girl's story and thanks the Englishman when Drake tells him that he has advised his superiors to allow Beth to remain in Venice, as long as she reports to the American consulate once a day. The following morning, however, Drake learns from two guests that Beth, Gino and his mother have gone — they are headed for the Yugoslavian border and the hospital to see the dying Alberto. The undercover man is soon on their trail. He finds Beth in a house bearing a wreath on its door: Alberto has died. The body is in a coffin, ready to be taken back to Venice. Drake warns Beth that she has been tricked and that Gino intends to take her over the border where her secrets will be forced from her. He is about to take the girl to his car, when Gino arrives with four men dressed as undertakers. Faced with the undercover man's accusations of treachery, Beth's boyfriend shows his true colours by producing a gun and ordering one of his henchmen to take Drake away. The 'undertakers' are Russian colleagues. Carla produces a hypodermic syringe — the coffin is empty, awaiting Beth's drugged body. Thrown into a cellar, Drake swiftly overpowers his guard. When Gino arrives, concerned that his colleague has not reappeared, the Italian soon joins his henchman, Stashig, in the cellar. Meanwhile, having placed 'Alberto' in the hearse, Gino's henchmen drive away in the direction of the border. Following the vehicle in a helicopter and seeing the hearse being stopped at the border, Drake orders the helicopter pilot to set down immediately in front of the hearse. He then leaps from the machine and, showing the border guards his credentials, rescues the unconscious cipher clerk from a fate worse than death.

THE ACTOR

Screenplay by Marc Brandel

Colonel Graves	**Rupert Davies**
Al Jason	**Gary Cockrell**
Suzan	**Julie Allan**
Mrs Harkness	**Patsy Rowlands**
Chen Tung	**Burt Kwouk**
General Chu Yee	**Andy Ho**
Mr Toy	**Eric Young**
Karibz	**Sam Chowdhary**
Receptionist	**Chin-Yu**
Secretary	**Soo-Bee Lee**

Directed by Michael Truman

FOR SOME TIME, the Chinese mainland has been sending information out of Hong Kong. The British authorities believe that it is being done by code during the daily English language conversation programme. Chen Tung, a sound technician had approached Colonel Bob Graves, Drake's immediate superior in Hong Kong, with the news that he had information to confirm this, but Chen Tung ended up dead, shot as he was leaving the studio. The murder was investigated, of course, but the killer has not been found. Since then, all the radio station's transmissions have been monitored and everything points to the dead man being right. The fact that the Chinese have never attempted to jam the English conversation lesson confirms this. Colonel Graves wants Drake to infiltrate the organisation and find out how the code works – but carefully. Graves suspects that there is an informer on his team and if the opposition suspects that Drake is working on the case, he won't get far – except perhaps to the bottom of Kowloon harbour, with his throat cut from ear to ear! Drake makes his entrance in an unusual manner. He asks Graves to find him a man on his staff who can put up a good fight. Hours later, the undercover man introduces himself to Sergeant Karibz in forceful fashion, by engaging the man in a no-holds-barred fight in the market place. His excuse for walloping Karibz is that he saw him steal the wallet of a man named Jason – a wallet which, when returned to its owner, allows Drake to strike up an acquaintanceship with Jason, a member of the English lesson radio team. He convinces the man that he is an out of work actor and, in return for Drake's assistance in recovering his wallet, Jason gets the undercover man a job with the broadcasting team. The English lesson proves interesting but leads Drake no-where, until he is handed the next day's script, which he studies with interest. Outside, while on his way to Colonel Graves' office, Drake once again meets Karibz, who wishes to be of further aid: Drake, says the foreigner, is treading on dangerous ground. Having dismissed the man's warning, Drake and Graves discuss their next move. Drake tells his friend that he intends to attend Mr Toy's garden party that evening and, while there, attempt to panic his fellow actors into making a counter move. The Colonel says that he is worried: he would feel a lot happier if Drake would allow him to appoint someone to watch over him. Believing that Graves had already appointed Karibz to act in this role, the Colonel's offer puts the undercover man on his guard: perhaps the foreigner is not all that he seems. Drake's fellow broadcaster, Mrs

Harkness, is the first to be told of Drake's suspicions that there is something odd going on in the English lesson, but she does not have the faintest idea of what her colleague is referring to. Neither has the pretty Oriental, Suzan Kep. Mr Toy appears to know nothing, stating that he can throw no light on the death of Tung, the sound technician. Only Jason takes the bait, leading him to make an unsuccessful attempt on Drake's life. Foiled by the undercover man, Jason freely admits that he is the one responsible for broadcasting the code. It appears that the actor was contacted by men he has never seen, but who pay him to leave his scripts behind in the studio. His attempt to silence Drake was made because 'they' don't like anyone interfering with their plans – or trying to get out: if they had heard Drake's wild talk at the party, Jason would have come under suspicion, because he was the one who introduced him to the team. Under the threat of being jailed for Tung's murder – a crime the broadcaster denies – Jason is tricked into playing the hand Drake has dealt him. Using the script that Jason will read during the next broadcast, and a tape-recording of the last English lesson, Drake discovers that the third letter of every word Jason speaks, spells out the message. With the code sequence cracked, the undercover man makes easy work of doctoring the actor's script for the following day, thereby ensuring that Jason will tell his unseen masters that he is getting scared: he wants out, or a letter he has written will be handed over to the Hong Kong police. Within minutes of the next lesson being broadcast, Drake, assuming Jason's identity, is contacted and told to report to a house in the country. Here he comes face to face with the mastermind behind the code programme – General Chu Yee. However, before Drake can act, Suzan arrives and blows his cover. Told that Drake is an impostor, Chu Yee gives orders for the Englishman's death. But having already taken care of the treacherous Karibz, who lies outside in the garden trussed up like a chicken, Drake is ready for them and it takes him but a few minutes to put an end to their tricks. Back at Colonel Graves' office, a bemused but delighted Jason asks Drake why he was not arrested? Told by the undercover man that he will be travelling back to America with him, pending an investigation into his part in the affair, the actor breaks into a smile. When Drake adds that he has handed over Jason's uncollected wages to the Actors' Benevolent Fund, Jason's smile breaks into a guffaw.

To trap **The Actor** *involved in giving secrets to the Chinese, Drake arranges to beat the living daylights out of Sergeant Karibz*

DANGER MAN

Return of the Super Agent

WHEN THE LAST OF the 30-minute *Danger Man* stories was transmitted in Britain on 20 January 1962, it seemed that viewers had seen the last of John Drake. Although the series had been a spectacular success in the UK, foreign sales and, in particular, the USA television deal had not been closed. Such sales were essential if the series' high production costs were to be recouped. ITC boss, Lew Grade, alert to the fact that the Americans needed a ready-made programme to fill a gap left in their schedules when a show they had expected to do well had flopped at the beginning of the season, flew to New York and offered them *Danger Man*. A brilliant salesman, he clinched the deal he was looking for. *Danger Man* was picked up as a replacement for the failed American product, and joined other ITC favourites such as *The Adventures of Robin Hood*, *William Tell* and *The Invisible Man* on the USA syndication circuit. Within weeks the programme had been picked up in almost every part of the world, and the show's success was assured.

The decision to produce a further series, this time in a one-hour format, was taken by Grade and after a hiatus of approximately three years, Patrick McGoohan stood in front of the cameras once again in the guise of John Drake, stepping back into a character that had brought him world-wide fame, and a salary reputed to be the highest ever paid to a television actor.

During the years that had elapsed between the completion of the first series and the start of the new one-hour programmes, McGoohan had played a wide variety of roles in feature films and television productions, ranging from a jazz-drummer in *All Night Long* to a memorable role as a prison officer in Brendan Behan's *The Quare Fellow*. In the rip-roaring *Dr Syn*, *Alias the Scarecrow*, he played the dual role of the respected, serene Vicar of Dymchurch, and the notorious and daring smuggler 'The Scarecrow'. Oddly enough, he also starred in a television play *The Prisoner* (BBC television, February 1962)! But to the public he remained 'Danger Man'. The impact he had made as John Drake was unshakeable – a fact that was brought home right at the beginning of the new series, when the film unit were on location in London. Lunching at a restaurant, the group were recognised by a waitress who, pointing to McGoohan as he and his companions left their table, turned to her companion and said, 'I'm right, aren't I? That *is* the Danger Man, isn't it?' Letters and cards from all parts of the world, many addressed simply to 'The Danger Man, London' turned up daily at the production company's office.

When the star arrived on the set for the first day's shooting on the new series, no one was surprised when McGoohan commented 'It's an odd feeling to return to a character after such a long break. I'm feeling quite nervous.' It was not long, however, before he found himself slipping naturally back into the character of a man he had played for a whole year of his life. The years had

treated McGoohan lightly. He had changed little, but confessed 'I had to trim off a bit of weight to get back to Drake's athletic figure! At the same time, in portraying him, I'm not forgetting that he is four years older, and this is reflected more in his mental attitude towards people and events than physically.' Pressed for his opinion as to why an actor who had always selected his roles because of the variation they provided should return to a character he had played before, McGoohan replied 'There is nothing monotonous in playing Drake week after week because each episode of Danger Man is quite different from the others. Each one has a different setting. And in each one, Drake has to assume a different identity in the course of his job. Therefore, though I am John Drake all the time, I am in actual fact portraying a wide variety of different characters, some of which call for Drake to don a physical disguise. In one of the earliest of the new stories, for instance, Drake assumes the identity of a schoolmaster, and for this, I wear glasses, walk with a bit of a shuffle and bow my shoulders. I find the role as stimulating as playing in repertory, with something fresh to tackle in every new production.'

When we met Drake again, he was four years older, but his idealism had remained undimmed. He had changed only in certain personal respects. As Patrick McGoohan explained: 'Drake now finds himself more emotionally involved with the other characters. Maturity has given him a greater depth of understanding. He now sometimes rebels against some of the assignments he's given. He doesn't want to do them because he sympathises with the under-dog. His views on marriage and family life have changed, too. He is beginning to feel that the time is fast approaching when he must consider this before it is too late. He intends, however, to give up his job before he takes this step. This development has made him change his attitude towards women. They are no longer deliberately out of his reach, potentially dangerous to his own happiness and way of life. He now regards them with more personal interest and understanding, because any one of them might be the woman who appeals to him strongly enough to make him break away from his job at last and settle down to a more secure way of living.' In the words of Ralph Smart, creator and producer of *Danger Man*, the format had been changed to show Drake as a more humane and less calculating character. 'Drake is now less cold, clinical and perfect. He is less infallible. He behaves more humanely. He makes mistakes. And he is altogether more likeable.'

The broadened concept of the character was matched by Drake's broader involvement with the job. The new series would take a sidelong look at the professional, rather than the political aspects of spying. They kept pace with a world that had changed and developed considerably, on almost every level, since the first series was produced. The new series had to reflect this.

Confident that they now had a winning forumla, ITC wasted no time in promoting the new series:

Danger Man is Back! One of the most popular characters ever introduced to television screens, the original Danger Man swept the world, bringing international fame to its talented and goodlooking star, Patrick McGoohan. Danger Man is now produced as one-hour programmes, with vivid new stories which take Special Security Agent John Drake into even more tensely dramatic adventures in every part of the globe. He is a man who jousts with danger, a man who takes calculated risks, a man dedicated to his ideals. He respects his adversaries and he respects the beautiful women who come into his life. Excitement and suspense are the keynote of stories which live up to the title. The emphasis is on Danger!

One thing, however, remained unchanged: the action. To back up their claim, the production company spared no expense to inject each story with a liberal sprinkling of action and nail-biting suspense. As before, Drake's assignments took him to remote corners of the world. This time, however, he was contracted to his assignments only by individuals at the highest level — by Ministers of State, heads of the various Intelligence Services, by Interpol, Scotland Yard or, on occasion, by Hobbs, his London-based superior. The world Drake operated in was one of intrigue. The issues at stake were vital to the world's welfare with, more often than not, an international prize at stake. Adventure and danger were Drake's bread and butter.

The previous series had shown him assigned as a special investigator to an undesignated NATO department based, we were led to believe, in Washington DC. This time around Drake found himself a member of Her Majesty's Secret Service, working as a Special Security Agent for a British government department known as M9, whose headquarters were situated somewhere in London. The changes in format aside, however, Drake had hardly changed at all. It is true that he was (slightly) less clinical in his investigative approach, but *perfection* was still a byword in the agent's dictionary. He entered into each new adventure with as much zeal and determination to succeed as he had shown in the previous stories. Still a loner, a ruthless hunter who gave and expected no quarter, he continued to tackle his assignments without the added distraction of having to worry about a colleague's welfare. A man of the world, Drake was at home anywhere he unpacked his suitcase. Although the things he had to do sometimes nauseated him, he nevertheless carried his mission through to its logical conclusion — regardless of how tough or distasteful it was. In a word, Drake was the complete PROFESSIONAL.

McGoohan's ongoing refusal to portray 'violence for its own sake', was demonstrated by his insistence that, as Drake, he would remain a gentleman. As Drake, the star disowned any comparison or on screen association with the Bond-type hero. Although the two operated under the auspices of the British government, they were as dissimilar as chalk and cheese. Bond was surrounded by beautiful women. Drake always played down romantic interests and tempered his relations with the opposite sex with the knowledge that should he ever become 'involved', the lady in question might get hurt, or used as a hostage to impair Drake's reasoning. 'Drake is a moral fellow,' McGoohan said. 'He is all business. Ladies might show an interest, but he doesn't reciprocate. He's basically good, seldom carries a side-arm, never kills and never has promiscuous relationships. Bond, I really think is a sort of cartoon strip fantasy with morals that I find questionable. On our show, good guys are really good and villains are really villains. We have straight plots and legitimate villains. Let's put it this way. Bond is a not-so-good-guy and Drake is a really good guy. And that's why, if you can imagine it, Drake would always beat Bond in a fight. Another thing, Drake is as down to earth as good English mutton. He has none of this expertise with a menu. Unlike Bond, whose cars are fantastic engines of adolescent wish-fulfillment, Drake makes the scene in a proper English mini-car.' At McGoohan's insistence, the John Drake character drove a Mini-Cooper, instead of the trappings one usually associates with a super-cool spy: a flashy sleek sports car. 'The sort of car,' the star pointed out, 'that can get Drake anywhere at high speeds, can get in and out of places where a larger car couldn't possibly take him — and is unostentatious.'

One thing the two characters did share, was their love of gadgets — although McGoohan took a resolute stand against any suggestions that the series should try to compete with the more fanciful science-fiction stories which introduced colourful but *improbable* creations. Anthing approaching 'the realms of fantasy' was therefore out. The challenge was to provide Drake with a variety of unique secret weapons, that *had* to work; gadgets that looked like ordinary objects which would not arouse suspicion if found on Drake's person. A useful cigarette lighter which was, in reality, a miniature camera. A watch which, though it looked ordinary enough, served a dual purpose. Lift the winder, and it became a weapon that enabled Drake to paralyse his opponent. A cigar that shot out a cloud of tear gas the moment it was lighted. A pipe that received radio signals. Pens which contained tiny microphones and a radio transmitter. Skeleton keys safely tucked away in a shaving brush. The writers dreamed up dozens of highly unusual gadgets every time a new episode went into production. 'It's getting this way now,' said McGoohan, 'that I look at the most everyday objects and find myself wondering if they could be adapted for my secret agent's spy kit!' The star, in fact, invented several of the gadgets used by Drake. One of the most unlikely of these was an ordinary fishing rod, which became a high-velocity rifle working by compressed air — not, however, to fire bullets, but to project capsules containing miniature radio transmitters. One day McGoohan was looking at an everyday double-headed razor. The next day, studio technicians had adapted it into a miniature tape-recorder!

Every time a scriptwriter evolved a new thrill-a-minute hazard for Drake to face, he was providing Danger Man's stunt arranger, Frank Maher, with another face-to-face encounter with real life danger. Maher, a 6ft 2in Londoner of American-Irish extraction, not only arranged the fights and high-speed thrills, but took part in them as well. One thing he did not have to do, however, (except occasionally when on second unit work while the star was busy in the studios) was to double for Patrick McGoohan. Television's John Drake did his own stunts. But Maher did double for other artists in some exacting jousts with the star – actors are seldom experienced in screen fights and could be a menace to their co-player. An ex-paratrooper, Maher had grown acustomed to the assortment of cuts, grazes and bruises of his profession. As a stuntman/actor, it was an exception for him to get through any role he was playing without meeting a nasty 'death', ranging from being shot and strangled or stabbed and drowned. Nevertheless, he came close to breaking his neck while on location with the series in Wales. The script called for him to make a spectacular leap from a mountain ledge. But the rocks were damp from the spray off a nearby waterfall. Maher skidded, fell 21 feet and dislocated his neck. He spent the next three weeks working in a plaster cast. On another location, he had his nose smashed – when he wasn't even before the camera! Standing off-set, while the actor who was *supposed* to be attacking Maher with a bottle went through his moves, the stuntman got the bottle full in the face when the object broke in the actor's hand and the bottle shot past the camera. Mind you, not all the stunts were dangerous, and Maher found amusement in some of the odd things he was asked to do: doubling for a sack of potatoes, for instance! The sack of spuds was supposed to be in a runaway car which had to speed across a mountain field, shoot straight past the camera and between a hut and a slab of rock, before coming to an halt by a hedge. So Maher was done up in a sack to look like potatoes, propped up in the driving seat, given a couple of small eye-holes to see through, and had to drive with his arms inside the sack, with only a few inches of manoeuvrability to steer the vehicle! From straight fisticuffs, to driving a go-kart while disguised as a bale of straw, to leaping through glass and pole-vaulting through a window, Maher mastered them all.

Working on a show that chewed up new story scripts at the rate of one every ten days, it was fortunate that McGoohan had a good memory for dialogue, though, as he was once heard to say, 'After months without a break, your memory gets like a sponge.' A perfectionist, the actor found it difficult to learn what he termed as 'bad' scripts. Faced with a poor line of dialogue, it was his custom to deliver the line slowly, each word delivered separately, to give the script more meaning. A firm believer in the discipline of acting, he considered it unforgiveable when an actor arrived on the set not knowing his lines. He also detested people arriving late for a scene. To McGoohan, acting was a job, just like any other job. He refused to believe that it was a high-flown work of art, and insisted that he was *not* a star. 'A star,' he said, 'is a personality whose name is enough to draw people into the cinema, a theatre, or in front of a television screen. My name alone will not do this. After all, what is an actor? An entertainer. A rogue. A vagabond, a clown – a man who plays at living and gets paid for it. I enjoy the work I'm doing now. I make a good living. I'm lucky to be working at all!' This down-to-earth attitude made him easy to work with in some ways, difficult in others. 'I've sometimes been accused of being difficult and edgy and complicated,' he told Mike Tomkies, during an interview, 'but only because I want the end product to be as perfect as possible. I haven't always endeared myself to some people perhaps. But we all work very hard on *Danger Man* and it became the first ever British made series to break through into the American market. It paved the way for many other British shows that have since followed.' As Jimmy Millar, McGoohan's stand-in and personal assistant since 1952 recalled, 'Patrick McGoohan is a man in a million. A *man*. A real man, both on and off the screen. The last thing you could call him is temperamental. I've never known him to lose his temper on the set. If anything gets out of order, he retires into himself. All the time I've known him, he has tried hard not to upset those he is working with. But he hates people who are rude or snobbish. He can't stand the sort of person who is self-important. And he can't see that there is any excuse for rudeness.'

Little wonder, then, that many people in the industry had learned from experience that McGoohan was not exploitable – as a group of American television executives discovered to their cost. Flown to England by the network screening *Danger Man* in the USA, the men attempted to wine and dine the star and achieve the impossible: to get McGoohan to loosen up his character and change Drake's attitude towards the women he encountered during the series more into keeping with the accepted view of what (they believed) the American viewing public required form their television heroes. 'They said I had to have more contact with women in the series.' said the star. 'I told them that I wouldn't have sex dragged into *Danger Man*, and sent them packing with their tails beneath their legs.'

As the production progressed, McGoohan became more personally involved with the scripting and production side of the series. 'I was able to bring onto the show, film directors who had worked for the old fashioned Ealing Studios,' he said, 'they'd held aloof from television, which was considered second rate, but eventually I was able to persuade them.' As a consequence, he gained effective control of the production and star names from the acting profession queued up to take part in the proceedings. Thespians such as Mervyn Johns, Donald Houston, Moira Redmond and Virginia Maskell, to name but four of many, dotted the supporting cast.

The show was picked up by America – under the title of *Secret Agent* – and the American viewers went wild over Drake's exploits (almost, it seems, to the degree of adopting Drake as their own creation – changing not just the programme's title, but adding brand new title credits, which bore little, if any resemblance to the regular *Danger Man* theme.) The show gained favour all across the globe – being transmitted in French-speaking Europe under yet another title: *Destination Danger*. Danger Man John Drake's career looked set to run and run. But for how long?

Outgoing agent, John Drake, and superspy, Sean Connery meet on the set of the final series of Dangerman.

DANGER MAN

(Secret Agent USA)

SEASON TWO

32 monochrome
60-minute episodes

FISH ON THE HOOK

Teleplay by John Roddick and Michael Pertwee

Guest star

Gerdi   **Dawn Addams**

with

Nadia	**Zena Marshall**
Rowland	**Terence Longdon**
Dr Zoren	**Martin Miller**
Gamal	**Peter Bowles**
Tewflick	**Vladek Sheybal**
Abdul	**Michael Godfrey**
Maxwell	**Harvey Hall**
Albert	**Robert Henderson**
G's Secretary	**Clive Russell**
Cockney Soldier	**Walter Randall**
Arab Girl	**Durra**
Captain	**Prem Bakshi**
Dr Zoren's Nurse	**Karen Clare**

Directed by Robert Day

THE TELEPHONE message is short and to the point. Drake is wanted – immediately. He parks his Mini Cooper S (registration number 731 HOP) outside the offices of World Travel (the front for M9, the hush-hush department he works for) and races into his superior's office where he finds the man in a state of anxiety. A mayday signal has been received from Station ME7. Together with its Controller, Fish, the entire Middle Eastern spy network of British agents could be blown, unless Drake goes in and brings Fish to safety. If the opposition gets their hands on the Controller, it will result in a spy trial in open court, with the Fish in the dock and Drake's Department on the spit, in danger of being burnt to a crisp. There is just one problem: no one, not even Drake's superior, knows the Controller's real identity. 'Fish' appeared, out of the blue, in 1961 and has been feeding the Department signals ever since; all top secret, all confirmed authentic. To protect his/her identity, the Controller had made it quite clear that should the Department try to unmask him, it would be the last they ever heard from him. Handed a passport made out in the name of Maxwell Ryder, a public relations man, Drake visits his first contact, Albert Ryder, father of the man whose identity he has adopted. Drake need not worry, Ryder tells him. His son takes no interest in his father's business empire and is well out of the way in New York, where he devotes his time to chasing pretty women. He is told to contact Gerdi, the woman who runs Ryder's business in his absence. Drake finds the woman suspicious of his motives believing that he has been sent by her employer to check upon her business abilities. Nevertheless, Drake soon allays her fears and the two become good friends. Drake is told by Gerdi that Kassen, the Minister of the Interior, has left a message indicating he would like to meet the newcomer, so he promises to call at the man's home. However, before doing so, he meets Rowland, the final link in the network's espionage chain before the messages from 'Fish' are delivered. Rowland is getting ready to leave, but security officer Gamal is already on to him and the M9 agent is arrested – but not before he has been able to give Drake the name and identification sign of his next contact, Tewflick, a camera shop owner. However, when Rowland breaks under interrogation, one of Gamal's men beats Drake to Tewflick's shop. When Drake contacts Tewflick with the password, he believes Drake to be an impostor and orders him out of the premises. Later, at Kassen's home, Drake is introduced to his host's beautiful wife, Nadia. Gerdi is there, too, as is Gamal who, when introduced to Drake by Gerdi, intimates that he is aware that 'Ryder' is up to something. Thereafter, wherever Drake goes, one of

Believing Drake to be an imposter, camera shop owner Tewflick orders the undercover man out of his establishment. A scene from Fish On The Hook

Gamal's men is always close to his side — making it doubly difficult for the M9 man to return to Tewflick's camera shop. Managing to accomplish this in secret, Drake convinces the contact of his bona fides and Tewflick passes on the name of Drake's next contact, a Doctor Zoren. But once again Drake's identity is treated with suspicion and, before he is accepted, he is drugged by the doctor. Having recovered, Drake is concerned when Zoren, the only man who knows who the 'Fish' really is, refuses to reveal the Controller's name, or to arrange for Drake to meet 'Fish' until the Controller authorises him to do so. Matters now take a turn for the worse. Told by Gerdi that 'his' father has died suddenly, Drake is about to move into top gear when the real Maxwell Ryder arrives to inspect his inheritance. Fortunately, he reports to Drake, believing him to be his father's personnel manager. Drake installs Ryder in a hotel to rest after his long journey, promising to return for him soon. As requested by Doctor Zoren, Drake races to Kassen's home. Seconds after his arrival, Gamal ushers Kassen away, saying that he has news which his friend will find of great interest. As the men are talking, Drake takes the opportunity to tell Nadia — revealed now by Dr Zoren as 'Fish' — that he has planned an escape route: the girl must join him at a rendezvous set by Dr Zoren. Unknown to Drake, immediately he leaves, Gamal has the doctor arrested. Under interrogation, the man coughs up the truth: Nadia Kassen is the woman the policeman is looking for. Back at the Ryder building Drake and Gerdi find themselves confronted by the real Maxwell Ryder, whose charge that Drake has duped them both brings surprising results: Drake knocks the man cold and, apologising to Gerdi, drags them both into a room and binds them securely with a rope. Having packed her luggage, Nadia is about to depart when her husband and Gamal enter her room. Accused by Kassen of betraying his trust, her husband tells the policeman to take her away. It is then that Drake arrives. Creeping up behind the unsuspecting Kassen, he knocks the man unconscious and races outside to join Nadia, the doctor and Gamal, who now sits erect at the wheel of his car, the Controller's pistol jammed in the nape of his neck. He is driven by Drake to a secluded beach where he sees a group of Arabs rise from behind the sand dunes. Gamal, believing them to be his own men, orders them to arrest Drake and the girl. A Cockney voice confirms the policeman's mistake, and Gamal is held at gunpoint while Drake and Nadia depart aboard a British naval freighter.

DON'T NAIL HIM YET

Teleplay by Philip Broadley

Guest stars

Rawson	**John Fraser**
Dian	**Sheila Allen**

with

Lucus	**Anthony Dawson**
Gorton	**Raymond Adamson**
Mumford	**Edwin Apps**
Sir Ralph	**Edward Chapman**
Bennett	**Edward Cast**
Sue	**Wendy Richard**
Lennie	**Leonard Monaghan**
Bill	**Keith Bell**
Jeannie	**Jackie Pearce**
Waiter	**Nicholas Hawtrey**
Pub Landlord	**Ian Collin**

Directed by Michael Truman

THE OBJECT OF M9's attention is a minor naval official named Peter Rawson, who has been under surveillance for some time. Leakage of information has coincided with an upsurge in Rawson's standard of living. He is also a compulsive drinker. There is, in fact, very little that Drake's superior, Gorton, has not been able to find out about him — except the final proof of his guilt, which is where Drake comes in. When the M9 man strikes up a friendship with Rawson in a seedy back street public house, Drake does not look much like his usual forceful self. In the guise of John Kieron, a teacher of modern languages, his shoulders droop, he walks with a shambling gait, and he wears spectacles. Before Drake can corner Rawson, however, he has to undergo some teasing about his appearance and, in particular, his love of classical music records, from three young tearaways, Sue, Bill and Lennie, who, after smashing one of Drake's classical record albums, find themselves thrown out into the street by the pub landlord. It is Drake's interest in the works of classical composers that brings Rawson and his observer together. Drake now has the opportunity to visit his new friend's home — a luxurious apartment which is well beyond the reach of a minor naval official. It does not take long for Drake to find the evidence he requires to prove that Rawson is smuggling copies of secret documents to someone. Gorton is all for pulling the man in, but Drake resists the idea of an early arrest, stating that he does not want to nail Rawson until he has learnt who his contact is and how the information is being sent out of the country. Introduced by his superior to Sir Ralph, a government minister, the official overrules Gorton's request and agrees to allow Drake to run with the case until he has evidence that will put the traitor and his contacts away. As a safeguard, another agent, Bennett, is drafted in to keep a watch on Rawson while Drake 'accidentally' bumps into the traitor at various places, including the local football ground. Watched by the two agents, Rawson makes no apparent move to contact anyone. At the same time, however, he becomes increasingly annoyed with the schoolmaster's persistent efforts to be with him so often. An examination of dozens of photographs Bennett took at the football match reveals one suspicious point. A woman in a photograph taken by Drake in a restaurant at which he bumped into Rawson, bears a strong resemblance to a woman among the crowd at the football match. But she is not in a second picture taken ten minutes later in the soccer stadium. Watched by Bennett and Mumford, Gorton's second-in-command, Drake once again forces his attentions on the now somewhat bewildered and rebellious Rawson. This time, however, Drake is given the cold shoulder, his friend saying that he has an important meeting to attend. For five days Rawson makes no move until, while keeping the man's apartment under scrutiny, Drake and Bennett see Rawson make a dash for it. Racing off in pursuit, Drake sees his quarry about to enter a bookshop but, spotting Drake behind him, Rawson races away and gives Drake the slip. Drake doubles back to the bookshop and, on the excuse of looking for a book for his aunt, meets Lucus, its proprietor. But the man is unable to help him. Told by Drake that Rawson has given him the slip, Gorton calls in Special Branch to find and arrest the naval man. In the meantime, however, Drake has broken into the flat above the bookshop. In hiding, he sees Rawson arrive to be greeted by the girl in the photographs. She is Dian, Rawson's contact. Pushing his way past the woman as she attempts to close the door, Drake confronts the couple with his evidence. Drake picks up the book of poetry Rawson has brought with him and demands that Dian hands over the microdots. Claiming to know nothing of photography, or of Drake's claims that they are up to something, the girl says that she and Rawson are simply friends, the poetry book being a gift. Rawson, however, realises that the game is up and, as Dian turns her back on him, he races to a mirror on the wall of the woman's lounge and smashes it into fragments, revealing a radio transmitter. It appears that Drake's task is now complete, but the girl proves cleverer than he anticipated. While his attention was distracted, she has signalled to Lucus, who now enters the room to confront Drake with the barrel of an automatic pistol. The girl has everything planned: Drake will be taken with them as hostage and Rawson will answer for his behaviour later. Taken to an airport at gunpoint, Drake and Rawson are installed aboard Dian's getaway plane. But the naval man makes a bid for freedom and Drake follows him through the door. Grabbing the wheel of Lucus' car, Drake motors at speed down the runway. Overtaking the aircraft, he swings the vehicle into the oncoming plane and leaps to safety as, unable to take evasive action, Dian and her passenger are blown away in a deafening explosion. Injured by his leap from the aircraft, Drake ends up in hospital. He receives two visitors: Sir Ralph, who brings a gift for the hero, and Gorton who, spurred on by his superior, adds his own congratulations for a job well done.

In Don't Nail Him Yet, *Drake makes his bid for freedom by leaping from a moving aircraft*

To ensure a Fair Exchange, *Drake prepares to cut an escape route through the Danzig border perimeter fence*

FAIR EXCHANGE

Teleplay by Wilfred Greatorex and Marc Brandel

Guest star

Lisa   **Lelia Goldoni**

with

Pieter	**James Maxwell**
Wilhelm Berg	**George Mikell**
Otto Berg	**Andre Van Gyseghem**
Foster	**Barry Linehan**
Mumford	**Edwin Apps**
Gorton	**Raymond Adamson**
Dr McKenna	**Noel Howlett**
Sustri	**Kenneth Adams**
German Farmer	**Thomas Gallagher**
German Guard	**John Kirby**
Servant	**Hugo De Vernier**
East German Guard	**Jerry Tunnicliffe**
German Taxi Driver	**Bernard Davies**
Pohlman	**Ernest Lindsay**
English Taxi Driver	**Bruce Whightman**

Directed by Charles Crichton

LISA LANZIC, an old colleague of Drake's, arrives at his basement flat in London in a state of terror, seeking his protection because she is being followed. The M9 man finds an excuse to slip outside and telephone his chief, Gorton. Alarmed to learn that Lisa is at Drake's home, Gorton tells him not to let the girl out of his sight. But Lisa, suspicious that Drake is playing for time, succeeds in giving her colleague the slip, jumping out of his car as they drive into town together for a meal. Racing after the girl, Drake loses her amongst the crowd. Lisa, who has taken refuge in a health food shop, manages to remain out of sight when Drake enters the premises on the pretext of buying a slimming powder. As soon as the M9 man leaves, she hands the shop's owner, Mr Sustri, £50 and demands to be given the packet she ordered earlier. Alarmed when the girl tells him that if he does not do as she asks she will squeal what she knows from the highest building, Sustri hands the girl an envelope and she leaves. Catching sight of Lisa as she steps out onto the pavement, Drake races towards her, but Lisa makes good her escape in a taxi. Drake's attempts at pursuit are shortlived when Foster, a Special Branch man who has been tailing Lisa, leaps onto Drake's back and impedes his progress. Gorton is furious when he hears that Drake has lost the girl, particularly when he learns that Special Branch have entered the scene. Ordering his aide Mumford to have Foster brought to his office immediately, Gorton tells Drake why the Department is so interested in the girl. The story is a tragic one: as a special agent operating in East Germany, Lisa was caught and tortured by the Chief of Secret Police, Pohlman. But, versatile though Pohlman was, the girl did not break. Lisa was exchanged last year for Guttman, but her treatment at Pohlman's hands had affected her so badly that she could no longer work for the Department. For sometime now, she has been a patient at a mental hospital but Dr McKenna, her physician, believing the time was right to put her back into the swim, released her without notifying Gorton. Now, because of the doctor's ill-advised diagnosis, Drake's superior believes that Lisa will attempt to kill Pohlman again: she tried once before, and had nearly pulled it off, getting into the heart of East Germany unknown to either side. If Pohlman, now an important minister, is killed, it would lead to serious repercussions. Informed by Foster that Special Branch know that Sustri is dealing in forged passports, Gorton orders Drake and Foster to pay Sustri a visit. Confronted with several forged passports, the health food supplier confirms Drake's fears: he has handed Lisa a passport to East Germany made out in the name of Elizabeth Shearing. Instructed by his superior to stop the girl at all costs – including, if she will not return, handing her over to the German authorities, Drake assumes the identity of John Shearing, described as Lisa's husband and a travel agent. Contacts lead him to Lisa when she visits an old friend, Pieter, hoping for help in finding Pohlman. Pieter refuses to help her destroy herself, but his words of caution fall on deaf ears. Drake's efforts to persuade her to return meet with the same result, so the M9 man's only alternative is to go to the Security Chief, Otto Berg. Introducing himself as Lisa's husband, he explains that his 'wife' is determined to kill Pohlman. When Drake asks for the girl to be detained and sent out of the country, Berg hands the matter over to his son Willi. But, far from co-operating in the way Drake had hoped, Willi makes no effort to interfere with Lisa's movements. He has Drake arrested on a charge of entering the country under false pretences, claiming that his father Otto signed the papers for Drake's arrest. Drake succeeds in getting away and, with Pieter's help, makes his way to Pohlman's home in the country. Lisa is already there, hiding in the bushes, waiting for the moment when Pohlman will come out onto the terrace for his lunch. Willi is there, too, watching the girl's every movement. When Lisa's attempt to kill the German is thwarted by Drake, it is Willi who shoots Pohlman in the chest, killing the man. Realising now that Berg and Pohlman have been at each other's throats for years and nothing could suit Willi better than for a British agent to kill the man he hates, Pieter explains how Lisa was allowed to run free in the hope that her attempt would succeed. Having killed Pohlman, she would have been treated to a staged trial, leaving Berg to cry crocodile tears. Hearing that Pieter could cross the border checkpoint with forged papers, Drake acts quickly. Determined to get Lisa out of the country, he arranges for one of his contacts, a farmer, to telephone Berg with the news that an escape route has been planned and that Lisa will be crossing the border to Danzig at dusk. Tricked, Willi follows a girl dressed as Lisa across into the Federal Republic where Pieter is waiting with several West German guards. Returning to Otto Berg's office, Drake then proposes an exchange: Willi for the girl's freedom. Aware that Willi might crack and confess his part in the Pohlman killing, Berg has no option but to agree to Drake's terms, and the following morning the M9 agent and Lisa cross the border to freedom.

THE PROFESSIONALS

Teleplay by Wilfred Greatorex and Louis Marks

Starring

Mrs Pearson	**Helen Cherry**
Ira	**Nadja Regin**
Desmond Pearson	**Jerry Stovin**
Milos Kaldor	**Alex Scott**

with

Rhodes	**John Welsh**
Ambassador	**Noel Johnson**
Miss Burnham	**Joan Young**
Interrogator	**Steve Plytas**
Czech Receptionist	**Hana Pravda**
Landlord	**Jan Conrad**
Nadia	**Stella Courtney**
Czech Policeman	**John G.Heller**
Secretary	**Brenda Dunrich**
Police Motorcyclist	**Charles Laszlo**

Directed by Michael Truman

MRS PEARSON, the wife of Desmond Pearson – ostensibly a businessman, but in reality an agent for M9 – calls at the British Embassy in Prague to tell senior minister Rhodes that her husband has not been home for two weeks. Rhodes advises her not to worry: Desmond will turn up – he always does. The Ambassador, however, aware of Pearson's real identity, sends a coded message to London, a mayday that brings John Drake to Prague. He arrives in the guise of an unreliable, hard-drinking diplomat named Terry Stuart, appointed to the Embassy staff as Third Secretary. Drake wastes no time in reporting to Rhodes, who tells him that his reputation has preceded him: the man's drinking activities will not be tolerated by his new masters. At a party given at the Embassy that evening, Drake learns from Pearson's wife that her husband had no apparent money problems, but had never been the same since he met the exotic Ira Frankel, a close friend of a leading minister named Josef Redl. According to Drake's information, Redl is the man from whom Pearson obtained the secrets he filed to London. Mrs Pearson blames Milos Kaldor: it was he who introduced her husband to Ira. Ira, she believes, is one of the 'women' working for Kaldor, who has something to do with cultural relations. Invited to Kaldor's home, Drake soon learns that the man has great wealth. His luxurious home stands in its own grounds and dozens of guests, mainly beautiful women, sunbathe around the swimming pool. Drake meets Ira and, in keeping with the character he has assumed, allows himself to be persuaded to down one too many drinks. Too late, he realises that he has been tricked. His drinks were doped. Regaining consciousness, he finds himself in the hands of the police, accused of drunken driving and the death of a pedestrian: the police have a witness, and Drake has no alibi. It is the suave Kaldor who gets him out of his difficulties. Arriving at the police station with Ira, the man makes a telephone call and within minutes Drake is released. Dropping a hint to 'Stuart' that tomorrow is another day, and that he has very important friends, one of whom could prove very helpful to Drake, Kaldor tells him that he will be in touch.

However, when Drake says that he must report his arrest to the Ambassador, Kaldor becomes angry and tells him he must report to no one: he will tidy things up. During a visit to Mrs Pearson's home, Drake learns more about his benefactor. Kaldor, it seems, is always trying to ingratiate himself with everyone. Since her husband was introduced to Ira, Desmond had gone steadily downhill and had started to hit the bottle, making him difficult to live with. At Kaldor's home, Drake explains that Mrs Pearson is a very nice woman and that he would like to help her – if he could. He is told by Kaldor that he would be delighted to assist. Then, dropping a hint that he knows how little the Embassy pays its employees, he suggests that he and 'Stuart' should go into business. Drake also learns that Desmond Pearson is installed in a clinic, having treatment for a nervous breakdown. Kaldor, who has arranged the treatment, takes his newly-found friend to see him. Pearson greets the newcomer with suspicion. Told by Kaldor that his friend has heard about him from his wife, Pearson fears that the newcomer will relay his findings to the Ambassador. His doubts are allayed when Kaldor explains that Drake will remain silent: he, too, has 'certain problems', ones that Kaldor alone can help him solve. The meeting with Pearson decides Drake's course of action. Aware now that the man is being pumped full of drugs in order to keep him out of the way, he determines to call on Ira. As he arrives outside her flat, he catches sight of minister Redl driving away. The man is just a friend, pleads Ira, showing Drake the pair of earrings Redl has brought for her. He tricks the girl into believing that Pearson has spilled the beans and told him all about the 'arrangement' Ira shares with Kaldor and the minister. She is confused when Drake asks her if Redl talks about his job at the ministry when they are 'playing games', and orders Drake to leave. Proceeding with his plan, the M9 agent returns to Pearson's wife and tells her that she must leave: her husband will soon be safe in London, where she and the children must join him. This achieved, he sets about getting Pearson out of the clinic. He tells Pearson that in two hours' time his friends will be informed that the Embassy knows that Pearson is working for them. His life, therefore will not mean a thing. Drake tells him that his wife has returned to London, and Pearson agrees to fall in with Drake's plan. As fate would have it, Kaldor chooses that very moment to visit the clinic. Alarmed to see Drake escorting Pearson to the elevator, the man's attempts to stop them leaving leads to him being trussed up by Drake and locked into the room vacated by the patient. Making their escape from the clinic unseen, Drake and Pearson's attempts to drive to the airport are hampered by Pearson's craving for drugs and the arrival of a police motorcyclist. Eventually, however, they give the policeman the slip and pull into a roadside inn. Asked for their passports by a policeman who has been playing a game of cards with the locals, the men are told to wait while the constable telephones his headquarters. They try to drive off, but their vehicle's rotor arm has been removed, the men race into the trees on foot, pursued on all sides by policemen with sniffer dogs. Hot-wiring a parked police car, they leap inside and speed away. But still they cannot escape: their progress has been observed by another group of law officers. In desperation, Drake drives the car into the forest where, seeing their pursuers being observed by men patrolling the border crossing, Drake eventually tricks the lawmen into chasing after a driverless car. Drake and Pearson cross the border to the safety of foreign soil.

THE COLONEL'S DAUGHTER

Teleplay by David Weir

Starring

Joanna	Virginia Maskell
Colonel Blakeley	Michael Trubshawe
Chopra	Warren Mitchell
Khan	Zia Mohyeddin
Minister	John Bennett
Petel	George Pastell

with

Interrogator	Kenneth Adams
Plainclothes Man	Frank Olegario
Picton Jones	Michael Nightingale
Gumta	Kumar Ranji
Personal Asst to Minister	Balu Patel
Barman	Dean Francis
Margaret	Zoe Zephyr
Subra	Jaron Yaltan

Directed by Philip Leacock

DRAGGED FROM his room at two o'clock in the morning, Drake is 'arrested' by two men and taken outside to a car. Chief of Police, Major Khan waits for him. The policeman is offended that Drake, who has been in Delhi for three days, has not looked him up. They are, after all, good friends and have spent some happy times together in London. Asking if Drake is in the country on 'business', the M9 man replies that, policeman or not, he should know better than to ask such questions. To relieve his friend's embarrassment, Khan tells Drake why he is in Delhi! The M9 man is looking for a certain Indian national – a man who, for now at least, will remain nameless. Drake has not been able to find him and Khan offers to help, in an unofficial capacity, of course. In return, Drake can help him. Khan is investigating an Englishman named Blakeley; an ex-Colonel in the British army, who now subsidises his pension by collecting and selling butterflies.

Colonel Blakeley had an assistant, an Indian who has just been found dead in suspicious circumstances – cyanide poisoning. An apparent accident, Khan's suspicions have been aroused because, before his death, the assistant seemed to have quite a lot of money. A discreet check of the Colonel's bank account has revealed a series of unexplained withdrawals. It could have been blackmail, but perhaps not. However, Blakeley is now in Khan's security files. As a fellow Englishman, Drake can check on the ex-soldier without drawing too much suspicion to himself. Khan, meanwhile, will attempt to find Drake's man; each of them doing each other's job better than they could do alone. Agreeing to the proposal, Drake learns from Zen, Khan's colleague, that the Colonel lives in a jungle bungalow with his unmarried daughter, Joanna. Drake devises a means of getting to know the girl and being invited to Blakeley's home: he steals the rotor arm from Joanna's Land Rover. The car will not start at which point Drake, conveniently at hand, offers to drive the girl home. The Colonel makes him welcome, and the M9 man agrees to meet the man and his daughter for dinner that evening at the Colonel's club. Arriving there early, Drake meets colonial Picton Jones, a fellow countryman, who tells him that Blakeley's wife ran off with another fellow; the Colonel, he feels, has a conscience about this, believing that he has ruined Joanna's chances of finding a wealthy spouse. Over dinner, Drake soon learns that Blakeley would like to see his daughter married and Drake, being an eligible bachelor, would make a fine catch. This situation is dangerous but useful. Drake's first evidence that something strange is afoot comes when he follows the Colonel into the jungle when Blakeley is, ostensibly, looking for butterflies. He sees the man approach a tree trunk, and take out a waterproof package containing papers. A long vigil lies ahead for Drake. Saying that he has got to go away for a day or two, he goes into the jungle and builds a platform for himself from where he can see the tree trunk that the package was hidden in. His lonely watch is rewarded, at last, when Petel, a European-clothed Indian approaches the spot and places some documents into the hole in the tree. Drake photographs him as he does so, and later photographs the papers, which prove to have come from the Defence Ministry. They are arms specifications for a new British weapon.

In Delhi on 'business', Drake finds himself cajoled into helping police chief Khan to expose The Colonel's Daughter

To investigate The Colonel's Daughter, *Drake erects a lookout platform in the jungle*

Shown the papers, Khan promptly informs a Senior Civil Servant named Chopra that he has proof that military information is being stolen from his ministry and that it is being passed on to Colonel Blakeley. Chopra, however, waves the matter aside, with the explanation: 'This is a top security matter. Sometimes we have to pass out information deliberately to mislead our enemies.' The policeman is to say nothing about his discovery, to Drake or anyone else. Khan is deflated, and tries to persuade Drake to drop the whole matter. The M9 man, however, is by no means satisfied: the arms are, after all, British. A further watch in the jungle leads to an attempt on Drake's life when two Indian men attempt to give him a close shave with their machetes. But Drake overpowers them easily enough. He visits Joanna, where he succeeds in being left alone in her father's butterfly workroom. The Colonel returns home unexpectedly, looking shaken – and becomes even more perplexed when he finds Drake at his home. Another attempt is made on Drake's life – and Khan is found murdered. Determined to press home his advantage, the M9 man decides to go straight to the Minister, who immediately calls for Chopra. Drake recognises the secretary as the man who placed the package in the tree. When he is shown the photographs of Petel, Chopra says that, following an order by Khan for him to be arrested, the man was warned and has since disappeared. Drake tells the Minister that he is convinced that Chopra is lying and Petel is brought in for questioning. The man admits to nothing, beyond saying that he was leaving for Calcutta on the first available train. To forge a link in the chain between Chopra, Petel and the Colonel, Drake dupes Petel into telephoning Chopra and telling him that they must meet before he departs. Arriving at Petel's hotel bedroom, Chopra, alarmed to find Drake waiting for him, attempts to explain how they have only been passing on false information to the enemy, but neither Drake nor the Minister believe him and the civil servant is taken into custody. Blakeley, meanwhile, hands Joanna a package that he insists must be mailed that evening. However, when the girl arrives at the post office, she, too, is placed under arrest – but not before she has secreted her handbag under the seat of her vehicle. When opened, the package appears to contain nothing more incriminating than butterfly specimens, until, on closer inspection, Drake finds the evidence he is looking for: a microdot carefully placed inside one of the insect's wings. When magnified, the film reveals the plans for a top secret British rifle. Blakeley, meanwhile, aware that the game is up, stows his belongings into a bag and races into the forest. Arriving seconds later, Drake convinces Joanna that it would be better for her father if he is found. The girl leads him to Blakeley's hiding place. But in attempting to place the Colonel under arrest, Drake finds himself staring down the barrel of a revolver held by Joanna. Her father urges her to shoot him. As Drake had found and removed the bullets from her gun which she had left in her handbag earlier, the girl is unable to do so. The Colonel and his daughter are placed under arrest and Drake escapes with his life.

Teleplay by Philip Broadley

Original story by John Roddick

Starring

Paula	**Sylvia Syms**
Charles	**Robert Urquhart**
Nicos	**Maxwell Shaw**
Hobbs	**Peter Madden**
Paula's Mother	**Vera Cook**
Mimiko	**Harry Tardios**
Customs Man	**Meadows White**

with

Secretary	**Sarah Brackett**
Greek Policeman	**Andreas Lysandrou**
Greek Boy	**George Zenios**
British Agent	**Anthony Baird**
Plainclothes Man	**John Bryans**
Truck Driver	**William Hurndell**
Girl	**Sally Douglas**

Directed by Michael Truman

CALLED TO THE office of World Travel by Hobbs, his superior, Drake finds the holiday he had planned cancelled and a new assignment waiting for him. Charles Glover, a Whitehall official, has suddenly left the country. He has been known as a security risk for some time, and his defection leads to Drake being ordered to try to bring him back before he reaches his destination. The quickest way to achieve this is through Glover's wife Paula, who has been left at home with two children on her hands. According to information gleaned by M9, she will either abandon her children to follow her husband, or try to persuade him to give up his political ideals and return home. Hobbs gives his word that if Drake manages to get Glover to return immediately, the man will be left alone; no charges will be brought against him. Drake determines to make full use of Paula. He overhears her telling her mother that she intends to follow Charles to Greece; Drake is waiting at the airport when Paula books in for her flight. With the co-operation of a customs officer, Drake plants a transmitter in her suitcase, which makes it possible for him to hear any conversations she may have. In this way he is able to discover that the next stage of her journey to join her husband will take her to a village on the Albanian border. Drake gets there first, booking in at the only hotel in the village. It is not long before a young man named Nicos strikes up a conversation with him. An incorrigible rogue, who enjoys doing playing card tricks, Drake finds Nicos hard to shake off, particularly when the attractive Paula arrives and the Greek takes a shine to her. As the only two English people in the village, it is easy for Drake to get to know the woman; she can hardly snub a fellow guest from the same country. Introducing himself as a man who has decided to settle on the island, Drake offers to buy Paula supper. Nicos soon shows his true colours, and Drake is not surprised when he hears the young man talking to Paula in her bedroom. He tells her that he has instructions to take her to her husband, who is not too far away. It will mean but a short boat journey. Unfortunately, Nicos spots the listening bug Drake has placed in Paula's luggage and, realising that Drake is listening to their every word, races to the beach. Drake is already there, interfering with the outboard engine of the Greek's motorboat. Only quick action on Drake's part saves him from being shot. Deflated but not broken, Nicos regains his reserve and tells the Englishman that, despite his attempts to stop him, he intends to take Paula to see Glover. Turning this situation to his own advantage, the M9 man now comes clean with the woman. Telling her his true identity, he informs her that Nicos is an agent who intends to deceive her: in reality he plans to take her and Charles across the border to Albania, and then to China. He wants her husband to settle in China where he will be used for propaganda purposes. He, however, can help her, if she lets him. He has the full authority of the British government behind him and, if she can talk Charles into returning to London before the news of his defection breaks in the newspapers, Drake gives her his word that her husband will be left in peace; he will not be prosecuted. Nicos, of course, attempts to influence her in the opposite direction. But when he fails to crack Paula's resolve that Charles should return to England, he agrees to take a message to Glover: if Charles refuses to come to her, she will think again about going to join him. Disappointed by his failure to win the woman's confidence, Nicos attempts to buy off Drake, offering him a $50,000 'bonus': beware of Greeks bearing gifts Drake tells him, adding that it is up to the lady who wins. With some time to wait until Nicos returns with Glover's answer, Drake takes Paula into the mountains for a picnic to the place he has selected being an ideal spot for the woman to talk to her husband without being observed by Nicos' prying eyes. Back at the hotel, when the Greek and Glover arrive, Drake asks the defector to trust him implicitly. Drake takes the man to meet his wife. Glover explains to Paula that he has burned his boats and is unable to return to England for fear of arrest. Paula's reply that Drake has given his word that he will retain his freedom, clinches the matter in Drake's favour: Glover agrees to return to London. Surprisingly, Nicos appears not to mind that he has lost the game. Departing with a smile, the Greek wishes Glover to have a nice time – in Dartmoor, and leaves. Drake is concerned that Nicos will attempt to stop them leaving, and brings forward their time of departure to sunrise the following morning. But something goes wrong: the boat from the mainland fails to arrive, and the M9 man's attempts to hire a boat almost cost him his life when Nicos overturns the dinghy Drake has hired for the purpose of reaching a yacht moored some distance off shore. Believing that Drake has drowned, Nicos throttles his motor launch back to the beach where, armed with several newspapers bearing the headline that Glover has defected, he convinces the couple to join him on a trip to the border. In a car stolen by Nicos, the Glovers are soon speeding off into the countryside. Far from being dead, Drake races after them in a stolen delivery truck. He catches up with his quarry when Nicos' stolen car breaks down and he and his passengers are forced to continue their flight on foot. Halfway up a mountain, Nicos spots Drake in pursuit. He signals to his friends to collect the couple, while he waits in ambush. As the M9 man appears into view, Nicos fires his revolver at Drake. The bullet hits Drake's shoulder throwing him to the ground. Paula hears the sound of the shot. She realises that Nicos intends to finish the job and races down with her husband to offer Drake assistance. But Glover is thrown aside by the Greek who attempts to strangle Drake. At that moment, several

policemen, sent in pursuit of the car thieves arrive on the scene, as do Nicos' comrades. Conceding defeat, Nicos is taken away by the police. After a short flight to England, the English trio arrive in the customs hall at London airport. However, despite Drake's assurances to the contrary, Glover is placed under arrest. Unable to stop the authorities from taking the man away, Drake telephones Hobbs. 'You gave me your word that Glover would remain free!' he roars into the receiver. 'Did I Drake?' comes the ominous reply. 'You gave me your *word*, you hypocritical . . .' screams Drake as the line goes dead. Leaving the kiosk, Drake looks across to a knowing but saddened Paula, who turns on her heels and departs.

To protect Drake from further injury, runaways Paula and Charles Glover race to the undercover man's assistance. A scene from It's Up To The Lady

THAT'S TWO OF US SORRY

Teleplay by Jan Read

Guest stars

Sheila	Francesca Annis
Landlord	Finlay Currie
Magnus Sutherland	Nigel Green
Angus McKinnon	Duncan Lamont
Donald McKinnon	Brian Phelan

with

Braithwaite	Graham Crowden
Mrs Braithwaite	Barbara Lott
Mrs McKinnon	Julie Wallace
Mackay	Duncan McIntyre
Security Man	Rory McDermot
Miss Montgomery	Sara Branch
Dr Hutchins	Stephen Jack
Todd	John Southworth
Nikita	Ian Flintoff

Directed by Quentin Lawrence

FINGERPRINTS NEVER LIE, so when secret papers are stolen from a briefcase belonging to an atomic research establishment's security officer, Braithwaite, the fingerprints of every member of the staff are taken and compared with those on the briefcase. But there is one set of dabs that cannot be identified: John Drake is called to the scene. The search to identify the fingerprints switches to Scotland Yard and the mystery deepens when the fingerprints turn out to be those of Jock Lawson, a man who has been missing for 20 years. Lawson, Drake learns, was an electrician in the Glasgow shipyards who was on the point of being arrested by the authorities for passing on information about advanced naval radar systems, when he disappeared. No one has heard of him since, and the man was written off as dead. But fingerprints do not lie.

In That's Two Of Us Sorry, *Stuntman Frank Maher threatens to give Drake a headache*

Lawson must be alive. But where, and under what identity? To find out, Drake travels to Scotland to meet Braithwaite. He has never heard of Lawson, and he cannot think of anyone answering the description Drake gives him who is likely to have handled his briefcase. While staying at Braithwaite's house, Drake meets an enchanting girl named Sheila Sutherland, who lives on one of the quiet Scottish islands with her father – author Magnus Sutherland. A chance comment that her father is an expert photographer who has his own darkroom, gives Drake, acting on a hunch, the opportunity to invite himself to the island on the pretext that he would like to take some photographs of his own. Joining Sheila on the ferry, his welcome on the island is cold. They do not like strangers there. Nevertheless, Sheila persuades Donald McKinnon, a young fisherman who hopes to marry her, to give Drake a room at his father's house. Mrs McKinnon makes him welcome and asks Donald to vacate his room for the night. While there, the M9 man finds something strange afoot. The island is crowded with visiting Russian seamen and Drake is quick to investigate their presence. He gets a frosty reception at the local inn until, making the acquaintance of Mr McCloud, the landlord, he is offered a vodka by the Russian seamen. They have been known to trade a tot or two for tobacco and tweed for their womenfolk back home. Attempting to make conversation with a group of the sailors, Drake offers to buy a bottle from one of them, but a man named Euan regards the gesture in an unfriendly manner. When Drake asks if he might photograph the men, Euan and McCloud show real concern: the visit by the Russians is not exactly official, says the landlord. Over supper that evening, Drake meets Donald's father, Angus McKinnon, who explains that the seamen visit the island regularly, although they are only supposed to land there when the weather is bad. McKinnon himself is not an islander by birth, but he has won the affection and respect of all the inhabitants. He has done more for the island than anyone else, his wife tells Drake. Although he shares the guarded attitude of the other islanders towards strangers, the M9 man finds McKinnon friendlier than everyone else. Later, in his room, Drake dusts a bottle handled by several of the villagers for fingerprints. He then takes photographs of it before slipping the bottle into his suitcase. The following morning Drake meets Magnus Sutherland for the first time. Drake's request that he be allowed to use the man's darkroom facilities to develop his photographs, is granted, but Sheila must keep an eye on the newcomer: the equipment is expensive, and Sutherland would not take kindly to it being misused. Sheila shows Drake around her father's estate. She draws his attention to a telescope facing out to sea, explaining that her father uses it to study the stars. Drake's interest is aroused when, peering through the eyeglass, he finds the telescope trained on the Russian trawling fleet. His interest is aroused further when, passing a brick storeroom, he sees Euan leaving the premises. Sheila explains that it is being used by her father as a wine cellar. From Magnus Sutherland he learns that the locals are concerned about the atomic research establishment which the British government have determined will be a boon to the island's economy. Stating that the real future of the Western Islands lies with home rule, Sutherland disagrees. Later, Sheila shows Drake to her father's darkroom. Despite the girl's protestations that she must remain with him, he locks her outside while he develops the film from his camera. Back in his room, he is not surprised when the pictures prove

68

that a set of the dabs taken from the vodka bottle belong to the man he has been looking for: Lawson is somewhere on the island. While taking an evening stroll. Drake discovers Sheila sending light signals with a mirror to someone out at sea. Following the girl to the beach, he sees her greet young Donald McKinnon. A false alarm? Drake's suspicions know no bounds and at midnight, he hides himself away to observe Sutherland's 'wine cellar'. His wait is short. Within minutes, he sees several men carrying packing cases into the building, one of whom locks the door behind him and places the key under a stone slab in the grounds. Leaving his hiding place, Drake picks up the key and is about to enter the storeroom when the man he saw earlier returns. They fight and Drake knocks his adversary unconscious. An inspection of the cellar reveals dozens of crates of vodka, but before the M9 man has the opportunity to investigate further. Sutherland, armed with a shotgun, appears and orders him to leave. The news that Drake has been found snooping travels fast and the following morning, believing the newcomer to be an excise man, the locals turn nasty. Returning to his room at the McKinnon's home, Drake discovers that his belongings have been searched and his camera equipment smashed to pieces. Suspecting this to be the work of Donald McKinnon, Drake reports his disgust at what has happened to the boy's father. Although sympathetic to his guest's charge. Angus tells him that he has been foolish: Drake has abused his hospitality. Nevertheless, he will speak to Donald about his actions. When Drake is adamant that he sees the boy alone. McKinnon tells him that he can be found on the beach. Donald, however, has no wish to talk to the 'snooper'. Seeing Drake approaching him, he casts off his sailing boat and heads out to sea. But Drake leaps into the vessel and before long the men become engaged in a violent brawl, during which they are both swept overboard. Donald is saved by a rope that got entangled around his foot as he fell into the sea. Believing that Drake has drowned, he returns to the island to tell his father the news. However, Drake has been pulled from the sea by a Russian trawler. When Angus McKinnon enters the inn, the prevailing anger of the locals is enough to make him confess that he is the man Drake is searching for. However, as Drake discovers when he takes the man back to the mainland. McKinnon is not a traitor. Met by Braithwaite, it is not long before the scientist remembers that, during a visit to the island a few weeks earlier to see Sutherland, he removed the missing papers from his briefcase to make room for his weekend stuff. Dashing into his home, the scientist finds the documents stowed in a drawer of his desk! McKinnon's fingerprints must have got on the briefcase when Angus helped him to carry his luggage to the ferry. Drake, it appears, has been sent on a wild goose chase. However, the fact remains that McKinnon/Lawson absconded from the law, and it is a sad John Drake who escorts Angus to serve his prison sentence.

THE GALLOPING MAJOR

Teleplay by David Stone

starring

Prime Minister	**William Marshall**
Colonel Nyboto	**Errol John**
Kassawari	**Earl Cameron**
Dr Manudu	**Edric Connor**
Lasalle	**Arnold Diamond**
Suzanne	**Jill Melford**

with

General Powers	**Geoffrey Lumsden**
Mrs Manningham	**Nora Nicholson**
Barman	**Lloyd Reckord**
Personal Asst	**Zakes Mokae**
Adjutant	**Danny Daniels**
Girl	**Heather Emanuel**
NCO	**Ron Blackman**
Attendant	**Jimmy Falana**
Sergeant	**Willie Payne**

Directed by Peter Maxwell

A REQUEST FOR aid in security precautions is sent from Whitehall after the attempted assassination of an African Prime Minister whose country, after one year of independence, is now facing its first general election. Drake adopts the disguise of a British Major, calling himself Major Sullivan and flies out to help shape the destiny of the emergent country. His contact, a barman, recommends that Drake stays at the Laguna Hotel. However, before checking in there, he visits Kassawari, the head of the Prime Minister's security team, who informs him that the Prime Minister has given orders that Drake should be given a free hand – although Kassawari himself feels that importing an agent from London was unnecessary. The security man tells Drake that, since the attempt on his life, the Prime Minister sees danger around every corner. The Prime Minister believes that Dr Manudu, the leader of the opposition party, is preparing to overthrow the government by force – a belief that is not shared by either Kassawari, or General Powers, the British Officer commanding the country's military forces. They are convinced that the forces are loyal. The balance of power is delicate. Dr Manudu has a large following and his policies are popular, even though they mean financial aid from Communist countries. The people are opposed to the more austere policies of the Prime Minister, who wants prosperity, but not at the price of liberty. Introduced to the Prime Minister, the African confirms that it is better that Drake retains his cover: Whitehall seems to have a high regard for Drake's ability to prevent trouble. At the Laguna Hotel, Drake meets its owner, Mrs Manningham, who tells him that it will be a pleasure to have a military man around the place again. She also confirms that Dr Manudu lives in the house opposite. Meeting General Powers, Drake is told that his cover is that of an officer who has been sent out to investigate the possibility of setting up a joint services training area in the bush. The Lasalles are giving a party that evening, perhaps Drake would like to attend. While there, Drake soon has misgivings about Powers' second-in-command. Colonel

Nyboto. He also wonders just where the Belgian financier named Lasalle fits into the picture. When this was a British colony, he is told, Lasalle's mining group was a big money-maker. Since independence, however, all that has gone. Drake is curious as to why the man remains in the country. The behaviour of Lasalle's attractive wife, Suzanne, who so obviously throws herself at him, also puzzles Drake. Introduced by Powers to Dr Manudu, the man seems concerned about Major Sullivan's interest in the forthcoming elections, but Drake allays his suspicions by stating that he is glad that he is just a military man who has no interest in politics. When Drake suggests to Kassawari that he would like to see Colonel Nyboto's regimental training quarters, the security man states that he is doubtful whether the Colonel would like Drake snooping around. Undeterred, Drake does so anyway. But he does not get far. On the outskirts of the training ground he finds himself stopped by one of Nyboto's sergeants, who informs him that he must report to headquarters. Arriving there, Drake sees the adjutant, and is asked to wait until the Colonel has had the chance to speak to him. Nyboto's helicopter flies in and the Colonel ticks Drake off for attempting to visit the camp without his authority. Nevertheless, now that he is there, perhaps he would like to see a demonstration of the Colonel's military strength. It becomes clear that Lasalle and Nyboto are very close to each other and that both men have a good friendship with Dr Manudu. Lasalle, in particular, shares the opposition leader's confidence. However, there is no evidence of any violence until, returning to his hotel, Drake is set upon by an African wielding a knife – the security chief, Kassawari, is murdered just after he has sent the M9 man a message saying that he wishes to see him. The Prime Minister is shattered by this news, and swears to Drake that his killer will be brought to justice. A visit to Dr Manudu takes Drake no nearer to the truth: the man is adamant that he knows nothing about Kassawari's death.

or of any coup to overthrow the Prime Minister, bloodless or otherwise. Events take a dramatic turn, when Drake finds himself arrested and makes a chance discovery that a coup, led by Colonel Nyboto, is about to take place. Escaping from his captors, the M9 man races to inform General Powers of the coup. The General succeeds in foiling the plot, which Nyboto had organised with the help of Dr Manudu and Lasalle. With just a few hours to go before the election takes place, it appears that Drake's task has been fulfilled. By trying to overthrow the government by force, Dr Manudu has defeated himself. Drake now discovers the key to a part of the puzzle that had been worrying him. When he visits Manudu in jail he offers the doctor the chance to be set free – providing Drake is paid handsomely. The African orders him out of his cell. Convinced now of the man's innocence, Drake proposes another scheme, one which the doctor should find interesting. Back at the television station, from which the Prime Minister is due to make his victory broadcast, Drake finds the politician in the company of Lasalle and General Powers. The coup was a sham: a clever way of getting Dr Manudu to frame himself, leaving the door open for the Prime Minister to look after the interests of his friends. But when the Prime Minister attempts to leave his dressing-room, he finds himself a prisoner of his own scheme. Drake forces him to watch an unscheduled transmission in which Dr Manudu explains to the electorate that, earlier that day, he was given news of a plot to overthrow the government led by Colonel Nyboto. However, it is a happy occasion because the coup was forestalled by their Prime Minister, whom he is now delighted to introduce to his followers. Aware that he has been outsmarted, the Prime Minister has no option but to shake hands with the opposition leader. He informs his followers that they must go to the polls and cast their vote for whoever they believe can serve them best!

In order to protect British interests, Drake finds himself adopting the role of The Galloping Major

YESTERDAY'S ENEMIES

Teleplay by Donald Jonson

Starring

Jo Dutton	**Maureen Connell**
Archer	**Howard Marion Crawford**
Attala	**Anton Rogers**
Mrs Curtis	**Joan Hickson**
Brett	**Peter Copeley**
Mrs Archer	**Patricia Driscoll**
Harris	**Aubrey Morris**

with

Hobbs	**Petter Madden**
Bertrand	**Ivor Salter**
Mary Wilson	**April Wilding**
Stewardess	**Lynn Taylor**
Immigration Officer	**George Eugeniou**
Barman	**George Zenios**
Nickolaou	**Nadim Sawalha**
Kemal	**Raul Alkazzi**

Directed by Charles Crichton

HAVING REMINDED her boss, Brett, to lock a classified letter away, Mary Wilson wishes her employer goodnight. As soon as Mary has left, Brett, reading a coded advertisement in his newspaper, makes a copy of the confidential document, tapes it carefully to the inside of the newspaper and leaves his office, taking the news-sheet with him. In a nearby bar, the newspaper is handed over to a contact who leaves the drinking establishment unseen. Arriving at his apartment, the man is sprayed with machine-gun bullets by a stranger, who races off into the night. Drake is called in by Hobbs and is given a briefing which means a trip to Beirut. 'We've got a lead on the opposition network that's operating out there. His name is Brett. He's a British businessman who has to handle a great many classified documents. We've recently discovered that he's been passing it on to the opposition,' Drake is told. Hobbs wants him out there, fast, to find out who Brett's contacts are, how he passes on the information, who runs the receiving centre and, above all, who controls the organisation. Drake's contact in Beirut is Jo Dutton, an attractive young widow who is in charge of the British security there. Arrangements are made for him to be invited to a party at which, disguised as a newspaperman, he will be introduced to Brett. At the party, Drake also meets Brett's secretary, Mary; Mrs Curtis, a playright; a journalist named Archer and his wife Catherine. Jo Dutton is distressed at the suspicions regarding Brett. He is an old friend whom she would have trusted implicitly, but she cooperates in the investigation. This means enlisting the aid of the local Security Chief, Captain Attala. Despite having been told by Hobbs that he will be given full control of the Lebanese network, Drake learns from Jo that she only has six agents at her disposal, all of whom are working on other cases. Nevertheless, she shares a special relationship with Attala and is sure that the man will help. Drake, however, suggests that it would be better if he approaches the Security Chief himself, pretending to be a representative from the Board of Trade.

who knows nothing of Jo Dutton or M9. Told that Brett is being investigated for handing trade secrets over to the foreign competition, Attala agrees to help. He tries to trick Drake into blowing his cover by introducing him to his two assistants, Kemal and Nikolaou. The two throw Drake around the room in an attempt to dupe the M9 man into showing that he has knowledge of unarmed combat. Drake refuses to take the bait. Dressed as office cleaners, Attala's men enter Brett's office and install vision and sound monitors with which Drake, hidden in a cellar immediately below the office, can see and overhear everything that takes place in the room. Brett soon makes his move. Taking receipt of a letter – dictated and mailed by Drake – the traitor heads for the public bar to hand the latest 'document' over to his contact. But Drake and his helpers are waiting. When Brett's contact attempts to drop his package into a post box, the man finds himself arrested and taken to Attala's headquarters for interrogation. But the man's refusal to break leads Attala to become even more suspicious that Drake is not all he appears to be. Believing that Drake works for British Intelligence, the policeman decides to sit on the fence. The evidence Drake has against Brett is conclusive. However, when Drake challenges the man with being a traitor, Brett is taken aback. He claims that he is working for British Intelligence. Under pressure from Drake, he reveals that he was recruited by a journalist named Archer, whom he believes is the head of the British Intelligence network in the area. If Brett is right, Archer is posing as a British agent and recruiting Englishmen who believe that they are working for their own country. This new theory sets Drake off on an entirely fresh trail. Confirmation arrives from London that Archer is a former British agent who was dismissed from the service as unreliable. After eight years, however, he was declassified as a security risk. Drake asks Jo Dutton to get Archer to the Embassy on any pretext. Her attempts to do so, however, are thwarted when Harris, a second-secretary at the Embassy, orders Miss Dutton to attend to her own work and leave her friend the journalist's work for her own leisure hours. Unable to get Archer to the Embassy – and out of Attala's reach – Drake determines to go after the man himself. At

Although Archer is one of Yesterday's Enemies, *Drake calls at his home to investigate reports that Archer is posing as a British agent*

71

Archer's home, he tricks the man into meeting him later, and joins Jo at the Embassy, where she provides Drake with a basement room suitable for the plan he has in mind. Archer makes no attempt to deny the charge that he has set up an espionage network of his own. He maintains, however, that he has only done so to prove his worth to London, and that once he has gathered enough material, his intention is to pass it on to M9. He categorically denies that any of his information has been handed over to the opposition. As a private citizen in a foreign country, he refuses to be bulldozed by Drake into going with him to the British Embassy. When Drake attempts to take him there by force, two of Archer's men overpower the M9 man. The ex-agent now turns on the pressure, threatening to have Drake tortured, but the unexpected arrival of Archer's wife with Mrs Curtis and Harris, saves Drake from further interrogation. By asking Harris and Mrs Curtis whether they would mind giving him a lift back to his hotel, Drake escapes from Archer's clutches. He astonishes the couple when he gets out of the car only a few hundred yards from Archer's home; Drake has 'left something behind' and must return. Although Archer and his henchmen are on guard, Drake makes short work of seeing to the men – only to find himself standing face to face with Attala. Drake's situation has now become awkward. Told by Attala that he will allow Archer to leave the country, the policeman refuses Drake's request to have the man extradited. However, as a gesture of friendship, Attala makes no attempt to hide the fact that Archer will be leaving on Flight 247 to Bagdad; the take-off time is 2.43, and that Archer can be found in seat 3 in the first class cabin. The policeman has also arranged for the flight to be a British one! Escorted by Atalla's men, the unsuspecting Archer boards the plane and takes his seat, unaware that the seat opposite him is occupied by Drake. In the blink of an eye, the ex-agent is rendered unconscious by Drake, who applies his fingers to the pressure points on Archer's neck. He is injected with a sleeping draught to keep him quiet, and whisked away in an ambulance that Drake had waiting. Shaking off the effects of the drug in the basement room provided by Jo Dutton, Archer attempts to make a deal with his abductor. He has a useful and highly-skilled network of agents which London would give their back teeth for; he is willing to trade in this for his freedom. Espionage, however, is a callous, ruthless business, and Drake is having none of it, until Archer plays his trump card. He informs Drake that once his men hear that he has been abducted, his network will go to ground and neither Drake or M9 will hear of them again. His bluff called, Drake has no option but to accede to Archer's request that he relays a message to London for instructions. Back comes the reply, authorising the exchange. The following morning, however, one of Drake's colleagues, Bertrand, arrives with orders signed by Hobbs stating that Drake should hand Archer over to him. Drake does as ordered – unknowingly signing the man's death warrant. The mid-day newspapers carry the report that Archer has been killed in a traffic accident. Told by Drake that her husband died serving his country, a tearful and distraught Mrs Archer threatens to tell what she knows. Drake convinces her that she cannot – must not – say anything. Her husband was a very good agent. In London, disgusted when Hobbs attempts to convince him that Archer's death was necessary and that his wife will be receiving a posthumous award, Drake stalks out of his superior's office in silence.

COLONY THREE

Teleplay by Donald Jonson

Starring

Randall	**Glen Owen**
Donovan	**Niall MacGinnis**
Richardson	**Peter Arne**
Janet	**Catherine Woodville**

with

Student	**George Mikell**
Admiral Hobbs	**Peter Madden**
Lord Denby	**Edward Underdown**
Lady Denby	**Cicely Paget-Bowen**
Fuller	**Peter Jesson**
Soldier	**Laurence Herder**
Agent	**Charles Laszlo**

Directed by Don Chaffey

AWARE OF the fact that hundreds of men and women have defected to one of the Eastern European countries, Department M9 must find out why they were wanted. Only a few are of diplomatic or professional importance. The others are small fry – clerks, teachers, mechanics – people of no conceivable value in the international political sphere. The discovery that a nondescript clerk named Fuller is among the next batch to go, provides Drake with the opportunity to pull Fuller in and have him questioned by Hobbs. But the man knows nothing. He has been contacted to act as an adviser. He is supposed to board a plane, like any other passenger, and someone will meet him at the other end. He has no idea who it will be, or why he is being interrogated; he has done nothing wrong. Accepting this, Hobbs orders Drake to switch identities with Fuller and to go in his place. Simultaneously, in a room marked Sekcja 1, an M9 clerk hands Fuller's file to his boss and the man's photograph is replaced with a picture of Drake. The flight out is by normal passenger plane and Drake finds that Fuller was expected. A courier is waiting for him and he is taken in a blacked-out van to a railway station, then transferred on to a train. There are two other passengers, both of whom have been waiting for some time. Introducing themselves, Drake finds that one is named James Randall; the other Janet Wells. During the journey he learns that Randall, who was working as an electrician when he was notified that he was wanted, has been recruited to work in a combat school; he gained experience with the International Brigade in Spain and with the SAS during the war. Drake tells his companions that he has worked in a Citizens Advice Bureau in England. Janet is a librarian, travelling to join Alan Bayliss, the man she loves, who used to work in the library with her. The rail trip is long and they eventually stop in the middle of nowhere. In the distance, travelling across a field towards them, comes a typical London double-decker bus, its destination sign bearing the legend: Hamden New Town. They still have no idea where they are going, and the bus driver refuses to answer their questions. What they see upon their arrival is a staggering surprise. They can hardly believe their eyes. It seems as though they have been taken back to England. It is a typical English country town, right down to the smallest detail. All the notices are in English. A young policeman in English uniform rides past them on his bicycle. Everyone speaks English. Dropped outside a building denoted as the Civic Centre, they seem to be right back where they started. But this is not England, and they are not dreaming. The reality of the situation is made clear when they are met by a man named Richardson. He takes them to meet Donovan, who he introduces as their Director. It is he who provides them with the explanation:

Installed in Colony Three's *Citizens Advice Bureau, Drake photographs his customers with his specially adapted typewriter*

'This village is one of our best kept secrets.' He regrets that they have had to be brought there in the dark, but they could not risk the possibility of a security leak. 'The agency that recruited you does not even know that we exist.' However, he is sure that they will find life there agreeable, following their normal occupations. The fact that he is expected to work as an electrician, surprises Randall, who had been under the impression that he was going to hold an important post. He is further put out when Donovan explains: 'Hamden, is an induction centre for our intelligence agents. They come here to acclimatise themselves before being sent to work overseas ... we transform our agents into Englishmen. When they arrive, they already speak excellent English, but here they learn to *live* as Englishmen. When they leave they *are* Englishmen, indistinguishable from yourselves.' Stating that he will believe this when he sees it, Randall is amazed when the Director tells him that he already has: until quite recently, he too, was an 'outsider'! It is not long before Janet discovers that Bayliss, the man she had come to join is dead: he had wandered out of the village. There is nothing out there for three hundred miles. In winter, the temperature drops to 30 degrees below zero and he was already dead when they found him. She has been recruited to take his place. All are free to go wherever they please in the village, but no one must attempt to wander outside. Told that none of the residents will ever be allowed to leave the village, Drake assures Richardson that he understands: it is a security measure. However, he would like to learn how they do it. Perhaps there is a

chance of seeing the 'new techniques' mentioned by Donovan? Richardson is only too happy to show the newcomer around the school. Everything is taught from stock-market training to chemistry, explosives and sabotage. Drake's job will be to sit in his CAB office and teach the students English via oral lessons piped through a speaker in their rooms. Perhaps the interrogation room would interest 'Fuller'? It would. So Drake is steered into a room barren of all furniture except for a chair, into which he is strapped by his guide. An arc lamp above Drake's head is switched to full intensity and Richardson crosses to the generator switch. Agents are expected to sit out the interrogation technique for up to eight hours at a time, grins the man. He switches on the current, which races through Drake's body, forcing him to make up answers to his interrogator's questions. The light above his head pierces his eyes, and Richardson's questions explode in his brain as the man increases the voltage. Fortunately for Drake, Donovan arrives at that moment. Explaining that he was simply showing the new man one of the techniques they use to train their agents to withstand torture, Richardson releases Drake from his torment: the M9 man jokingly tells the Director that he would have cracked but for his unexpected arrival. By now, both Randall and Janet are resentful, she because she has been tricked, Randall because he believes that Drake has been singled out as the 'teacher's pet'. Sharing a room with the man becomes increasingly dangerous, particularly when Randall makes a point of needling Drake. His cover is nearly blown by Randall when, finding his room mate's razor (in reality a transmitting device) he angrily casts it aside when he is unable to get it to work. Drake, meanwhile, ensconsed in his CAB office, takes photographs of each of his customers with a camera hidden in his typewriter, which is operated each time he depresses the machine's punctuation key. Randall's unfriendly attitude makes Drake's task more difficult and, for a second time, almost leads to the undercover man being exposed. When Randall's pen runs out of ink, he slips a biro out of Drake's jacket pocket. But this, too, refuses to write. In reality it is one of the M9 man's special gadgets: a cartridge pen, which serves as a container for a micro-transmitter lead which, when attached to his specially-adapted typewriter, allows him to relay coded messages. Fortunately, Drake finds Randall with the object and, accusing him of planting the device in his clothes, adds strength to his threat by telling Randall that if he wishes to stay healthy, he had better learn to keep his nose out of Drake's affairs. Hiding the rest of his pens, Drake readies himself for a party to be held that evening. At the reception, held 'to accustom the students to all the old forms and traditions – all that's good in England', Drake and Randall are introduced to Lord and Lady Denby, the former a foreign office official who is now dubbed 'the Squire' by Donovan. When Randall becomes ill-tempered with Pierce, a student, for attempting to persuade Janet to dance with him, Donovan is forced to intervene. He tells Randall that he must come to terms with his new life, like 'Fuller', for instance. This, of course, annoys Drake's room mate even further. Confronting Drake later, he tells him that he is nothing but a hypocrite who toes the line too easily. That evening, Drake manages to relay a message to Hobbs. His superior is quick to notify Station MR58, telling them to get Drake out at once. However, the following morning brings a dramatic turn of events. Randall has disappeared! Told by Janet that he is attempting to escape, Drake races after his room mate. and eventually catches up with him a few miles from the village. When Randall refuses to return. the men fight and are soon taken back to the village by a helicopter patrolling the area. Brought before a suspicious Donovan. Drake is released but Randall is taken away for interrogation. He tells Richardson everything – including the truth about Drake's special 'pens'. Confronted with this. Drake denies the allegation. stating that the 'pens' are a figment of Randall's wild imagination. However. when Donovan receives a report from Section 1. and a check reveals that the report is genuine. he has no option but to allow Drake to leave. Richardson. however. is still highly suspicious of 'Fuller's' activities and determines that the man will never reach his destination. Before Drake's departure, Janet arrives and. believing they are unobserved. hands him a letter, asking Drake to post it for her. Richardson. accompanying Drake on his rail journey. tells him that he has seen the hand-over. Taking Janet's letter from his fellow passenger. he tears the envelope to pieces. adding the ominous comment that the girl must have realised by now that once someone enters Colony Three. they cease to exist. Richardson tries to kill Drake. but the undercover man is not so easily disposed of. It is Richardson himself who tumbles to his death through the carriage door. In London. having handed over his photographs to Hobbs. he is told that there is nothing his superior can do about the girl – the Department has never heard of her – a saddened Drake recalls Richardson's final words: she no longer exists!

When Colony Three *overlord Richardson follows Drake on board a train, it is a fight to the death*

A MAN TO BE TRUSTED

Teleplay by Raymond Bowers

Starring

Mora	**Harvey Ashby**
Loma Corlander	**Patricia Donahue**
Dorset	**Ralph Michael**
Louise Bancroft	**Eunice Gayson**

with

Stella Dorest	**Wanda Ventham**
Papa Camille	**Christopher Carlos**
Customs Officer	**Alvaro Fontana**
Carlos	**Harry Baird**
Manservant	**Tracy Connell**
The Boscoe Holder Dancers	

Directed by Peter Maxwell

WHEN M9 AGENT Corlander is found dead in his car. John Drake flies to Topeko Bay in the West Indies in the guise of Scotland Yard detective. Superintendent Grant. Corlander's body shows signs of having been tortured and mutilated. as did the body of Bancroft. another agent who had met his death there. Drake's superior is interested to learn why. Drake is met at the airport by Lieutenant Mora. a local Spanish police officer. who is also an M9 agent in charge of the island's security. Drake finds the policeman to be an amusing companion: a man with an audacious air about him that hides his shrewdness. He has most of the information Drake has requested – everything. that is, except for the motives and the identity of the killer. or killers. The island is not a large one and the people of the various nationalities stick together. It is not surprising therefore. that the widows of Bancroft and Corlander are friends. The latter is actually American by birth. and Mrs Bancroft is British, as is the third member of their close circle. Mrs Dorset, whose husband is also an M9 agent. As Corlander's car did not show any evidence of violence. Mora has a theory that the murder took place somewhere other than the place in which the man's body was found. In the house itself. perhaps. after which Mrs Corlander and an accomplice carried her husband's body to the car? Drake rejects this theory. Mora himself proves to be an enigma. Drake is suspicious of the fact that the policeman had to break his cover with the two dead agents. This means that Drake must follow suit in order to talk to Dorset to collaborate statements made by Mora — comments that are flatly refuted by the M9 man. But whether Drake can trust Dorset himself is a matter for further thought. His standard of living. investments and relationship with his wife are all puzzling. Dorset tells him that Bancroft and Corlander were crashing bores: he had never shared a close relationship with the men. He is astounded when Drake tells him that both men were M9 agents. Arriving back at the apartment he is sharing with Mora. Drake disturbs a West Indian man going through his luggage. but Drake tricks him with 'magic'. and the man runs screaming from the building. The mystery deepens further when Mrs Dorset pays him a call and makes it clear that she is willing to sell out her husband who. she says. is engaged in a smuggling racket. Curiously. the widows of Bancroft

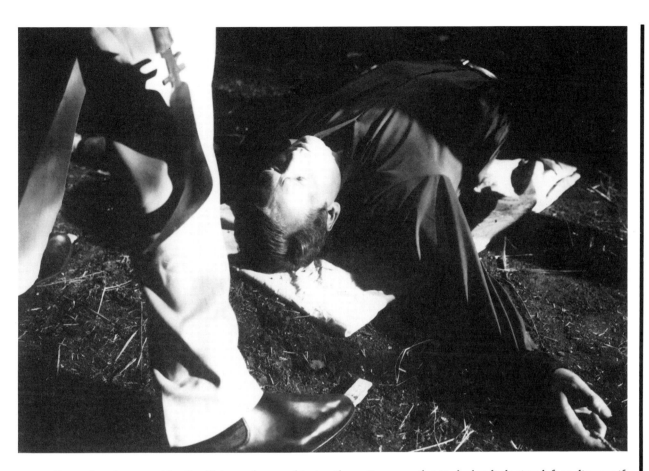

Dragged to the ground by Camille's voodoo-worshipping thugs, it appears that Drake has little time left to discover if Lieutenant Mora is A Man To Be Trusted

and Corlander believed the same about their dead husbands. When Mora returns and Drake tells him about the intruder he frightened away, the policeman theorises that the man may· have been an obeah, a voodoo worshipper. He could have been searching for something that Drake had cast off, believing that such an item would give him power over the owner. It now becomes clear that Mora alone can furnish the two widows with an alibi to prove that they were not connected with their husband's deaths. He was with each of them on the night in question. Drake learns more as Mora explains, disarmingly, that he is also having an affair with Mrs Dorset. The policeman tells him 'I love my wife, amigo. It grieves me that my method of examining the domestic security of our agents requires me so often to deceive her.' When Drake informs Dorest of his wife's activities, the man at first refuses to believe him but, pushing home his advantage, Drake convinces Dorset that he must now break his cover when his wife returns: he must tell her that he works for M9. He must turn himself into a piece of cheese and place himself in the middle of the trap, waiting to be eaten. A telephone call from Mrs Bancroft is instrumental in getting Drake to visit the local museum and to a meeting with the local expert on the voodoo cult, Papa Camille. Drake is told by the man that voodoo is still all-powerful on the island, and that blood sacrifice is still practiced. Papa Camille tells Drake that he can arrange for him to attend a meeting of the sect, but Drake turns the offer down, angering Camille. Later, the M9 man explains to Mora that he is playing a longshot by getting Dorset to

reveal his cover to his wife. But Drake has no option: if the woman is the one they are looking for, she will sell her husband down the river and her contact will have to arrange a rendezvous at which, like Bancroft and Corlander, Dorset will be killed – unless Dorset himself is the killer, of course, in which case Drake himself will be walking into a trap. A few hours later, Dorset telephones with the news that the opposition has made contact: he is to meet them that night in the forest. Aware that he might be putting his head into a noose, Drake is on hand when his M9 colleague arrives at the meeting place. Suddenly, Drake's worst nightmare comes true and he is, literally, strung up in a noose dropped from a tree by Papa Camille's bodyguards. Within seconds, he is dragged to the ground, his shirt is torn open to the waist, and one of Camille's villainous-looking henchmen holds a machete to his neck. Dorset views these proceedings with disgust, but makes no move to help his M9 colleague as the interrogation begins. Fortunately, before the blood-letting ordeal gets going in earnest, Mora and his men arrive. Calmly shooting down Camille's men as he goes, the policeman looks on with amusement as Drake leaps to his feet and struggles to disarm the voodoo man. Camille is accidentally shot during the scuffle, and Mora's men round up the rest of his henchmen. Drake is not surprised, when his audacious ally requests that, on his return to London, Drake tells his superior what a splendid agent they have out there – a man to be trusted, in fact. Drake agrees to do as his colleague asks, and departs for home.

THE BATTLE OF THE CAMERAS

Teleplay by Philip Broadley

Starring

Martine	**Dawn Addams**
Kent	**Niall MacGinnis**
Genicot	**Frederick Bartman**
Hobbs	**Peter Madden**
Alex	**Patrick Newell**

with

Barman	**Jose Berlinka**
Croupier	**Gilbert France**
Senior Executive	**John Serret**
Chief Chemist	**Henry De Bray**
Night Manager	**Hugo De Vernier**

Directed by Don Chaffey

WHEN CONFIDENTIAL documents are stolen from the office of a high-ranking executive of an atomic laboratory, no one connects the theft with the sophisticated, elegant French girl Martine, who is seen in the building. Neither would they have connected her with the shabby, unglamorous waitress who served tea so clumsily in the executive's office – and deftly whisked away the papers from under his very nose. When agent 1056, Alex Boyd, reports to Hobbs of World Travel, he is delighted to be told by his superior that he is off to the South of France to assist Drake, who is already there. Alex, a kind-hearted, lovable, overweight gentleman, is the Department's whipping-boy. Although he is totally incompetent, he is only too eager to join his colleague: 'Perhaps I can teach him a few things, sir?' The latest robbery is the climax to a series of equally audacious thefts on behalf of someone buying and selling technical development secrets. It is the wholesale business; a secrets for sale exchange, and Hobbs believes that it is run by a man called Kent. Drake is already making headway, using a rocket fuel formula known as F-6 as bait. Having kept Martine under surveillance and discovered that she lives at Kent's country mansion, Drake seizes the opportunity to get to know her at the casino tables. Having beaten her at

A none-too friendly beach party develops into danger when femme fatale Martine leads Drake into The Battle Of The Cameras

chemin de fer, he hands her a note addressed to Kent. The note is a picture postcard with a cryptic sign F-6. Kent finds the message challenging. When Drake next meets Martine, a Frenchman named Genicot, is sent to the M9 man's hotel bedroom to search it – quite unaware that Drake, having expected an unannounced caller, has ingeniously hidden cameras which photograph the intruder's every move. With these, and the help of Alex, who has now booked into the hotel, Drake is able to trace the identity of the intruder. He discovers that Genicot runs a gymnasium. Visiting the establishment, the M9 man deliberately goads the Frenchman by telling him that he wishes to take a few lessons in judo – to act as a defence against hotel room pilferers! Delighted at first to oblige, it is Genicot himself who receives a highly effective lesson. He is sent to Kent with further photographs and another tantalising message. Kent orders Genicot to investigate Drake further, but comes up with nothing on the newcomer. After a week during which the secrets broker fails to take the bait Drake has dangled before him, the M9 man increases the pressure by mailing Kent a document that is guaranteed to whet his appetite. Unable to restrain himself any further, Kent finally opens negotiations. But he determines to test Drake out first. His methods are unorthodox; he arranges for Drake to take Martine to a party where the undercover man is attacked by a thug. Drake successfully avoids having his hair parted by his assailant's wicked-looking trident spear, and passes the test with such flying colours that Kent finally comes out into the open and asks Drake to visit him. Drake discovers Kent's reluctance to leave his home. The secrets broker has a badly disfigured face which he keeps hidden behind a mask. He refuses to be seen in public and finds it hard to believe that Martine should be interested in him for himself. The man not only makes him an offer for the formula Drake has dangled before him, but asks the newcomer to work for him. Agreeing to hand over the formula the following morning, for $25,000, Drake leaves, content that the net is now wide open. Nothing it seems, can prevent Kent from falling right into it. Nothing that is, except for a photograph taken with a long-focus lens, of Drake lazing about on the beach and talking to his contact, the bumbling Alex, who has taken the unnecessary risk of contacting Drake in the open. This reveals enough to warn Martine of the danger. Refusing to believe that she has been wrong in trusting Drake, she takes the step of meeting him again and telling him that her employer will have to delay the deal because he has been unable to raise the money in time. When Martine tells him that she has a secret of her own, an apartment that no one has ever seen, and invites Drake to accompany her there, the M9 man plays along, aware that he is walking into an obvious trap. When Martine attempts to drug him, Drake switches their drinks and it is she who passes out. Carrying the woman to her bed, Drake now settles down to await the arrival of whoever has been sent to silence him. It is Genicot, who, finding his quarry the worse for drink, attempts to trick Drake into plunging to his 'accidental' death from the balcony outside Martine's bedroom window. Drake overpowers the Frenchman and forces him into confessing the truth about his link with Kent. The subject of their conversation, meanwhile, has gathered up his documents and prepares to leave. But Drake and the police are waiting for him. Kent is taken into custody, and Drake returns to the still drowsy Martine, who is allowed to dress before she, too, is handed over to the authorities.

NO MARKS FOR SERVILITY

Teleplay by Ralph Smart

Starring

Armstrong	**Mervyn Johns**
Judy	**Francesca Annis**
Gregori	**Howard Marion Crawford**
Helen	**Suzan Farmer**

with

Avraam	**Peter Illing**
Hobbs	**Peter Madden**
Strotti	**John Cazabon**
Lady Fielding	**Elizabeth Ashley**
Sir Charles Fielding	**Frederick Piper**
Joseph	**John G. Heller**

Directed by Don Chaffey

IN ATHENS, Helen Bernares receives a late-night caller to her home, a Mr Avraam. He has arrived at the request of her husband Gregori, who has urgent business to discuss. But when Gregori returns several minutes later, he appears ill at ease to find Avraam waiting for him. Without so much as a glance at his wife, Gregori leads the man into his bedroom. Seconds later, Helen hears the sound of raised voices, in particular Mr Avraam's ordering her husband that he should do as he is told. The guest leaves, and Helen asks her husband whatever was wrong with the man? He stares back in silence. The following morning the newspapers carry reports that Avraam has committed suicide. Helen is concerned that the man's death may be connected with the previous evening's events and asks her husband to explain. His answer surprises her: saying she looks peaky, he declares that they are going to take a holiday. Meanwhile, at M9 headquarters, Drake is informed by Hobbs that Gregori Bernares is an unscrupulous and criminally dangerous man who graces himself with the title 'Financial Adviser' to the Zaibeck government – for 'adviser' should be read 'extortionist'. The man has negotiated several loans from the West, all of which have been misappropriated. While the country's Cabinet live off the fat of the land, the peasant population remains in a state of appalling poverty. The British government has grown tired of Bernares' activities which include bribery, blackmail, extortion and corruption. Several people have taken their own lives, rather than face the disgrace of being exposed as having had dealings with the man. Drake proposes to Hobbs that he would like to have a crack at Bernares and is delighted when his superior tells him that everything has been arranged. He has a very interesting cover for Drake, one which will call for a good deal of discipline. Drake is going back to school – to learn how to become an impeccable manservant! Hobbs, it appears, is dining with Sir Charles and Lady Fielding on Thursday and, after three days of training, Drake will be on hand to show his expertise. Fielding has rented his villa in Rome to the Bernares and Hobbs requests that their butler should be replaced with one of his own – Drake, who has so expertly just served them supper. Arriving at the villa, Gregori and Helen are greeted by their new manservant. Gregori tells Drake not to attempt to throw his weight around with Joseph, his chauffeur, who takes orders only from him. Servile civility is not something that comes naturally to Drake, especially when continuously put in his place by Bernares and he almost breaks his cover when the man mistreats Helen, a girl much younger than her husband. The unsuspecting Gregori has no idea that every preparation has been made for his stay, including the installation of secret television apparatus and microphones which enable Drake to see and hear his every move. Drake is able to observe as Gregori attempts to trap his next victim, Armstrong, a prominent banker and adviser to the British government. Armstrong and his daughter, Judy, are invited to dinner. Gregori offers the banker an enormous bribe in return for his promise to advise the British government to grant a loan that has been requested by the Zaibeck Cabinet. Armstrong indignantly turns the offer down and, in an ugly mood, Bernares plans his next step. Armstrong's daughter is kidnapped and her father is advised to accept Bernares' offer. If he fails to do so, he will never see Judy alive again. It is time for Drake to lend a hand, not only for Armstrong's sake, but to help the ill-treated Helen, who has now unwittingly become involved in the kidnap plan. Drake calls at Armstrong's home to inform the man that he is working undercover and wishes to nail Bernares.

Having shot a hole in Gregori's plans, Drake holds the kidnapper at gunpoint and explains why he expects No Marks For Servility

Confronted with the tape-recorded evidence that Gregori is blackmailing him, Armstrong confesses the truth: his daughter is being held hostage. Promising not to endanger Judy's life, Drake goes to see Sergeant Strotti, Armstrong's friend in the Security Police. But his proposal that they work together to trap Bernares leads to Drake himself being placed under arrest: the policeman wants to help his friend in his own way. Despite being savagely beaten up, Drake manages to escape from Strotti's men and, with events threatening to overtake him, he decides to take matters into his own hands. Telephoning Gregori, the M9 man tricks him into believing that Judy has been rescued. Panicked by the call, the blackmailer flashes a signal to someone in the city. The signal leads Drake, who has been watching from the garden, to the kidnapper's hideout. He enters the seemingly deserted house. Finding a still-warm pot of coffee and an urn of soup simmering away on a stove, the undercover man climbs the staircase with caution, unaware that he is being followed by a man with a gun. In a bedroom upstairs, Drake finds Judy, bound and gagged. Signalling to the girl to remain silent, he is about to remove the gag from her lips when, placed on alert by the sound of a squeaking floorboard from the corridor outside the room, he quickly replaces the gag and hides in a darkened corner of the room. As the intruder enters, Judy, slipping the gag from her lips, fools the gunman into believing that the intruder is hiding above him in the attic. Drake tugs the ladder the man is climbing and the villain tumbles backwards to the floor. A second thug who arrives is treated in a similar matter. Judy is reunited with her father. Arriving back at the villa by taxi, Drake brushes aside Joseph's efforts to restrain him and races into the house to confront Bernares, who, aware that the game is up, is preparing to leave. Gregori leads his servant into the basement, on the pretext that during Drake's absence someone has broken into the cellar. The surveillance equipment which the M9 man had secreted in a wine barrel has disappeared – moved away by Gregori, who, gun in hand, tells Drake that it will make a snug fit for his body. But Drake is prepared for the confrontation. Using a gun he has concealed under his raincoat, Drake shoots the pistol from Bernares' hand. He orders Joseph to refrain from interfering – otherwise, says Drake, his master will join the angels. Alarmed by the sound of the shot, Helen races into the basement to inform her husband that some men have arrived to speak with him. Indicating that Madame is referring to Strotti's security men, whom he telephoned earlier, Drake leads Gregori away. At sunrise the following morning, Judy arrives to ask Helen if she would like to join herself and her father on their trip back to London. Drake gathers up his luggage and departs.

THE UBIQUITOUS MR LOVEGROVE

Teleplay by David Stone

Starring

Elaine	Adrienne Corri
Mr Lovegrove	Eric Barker
Mr Alexander	Francis De Wolff
Mrs Fairbrother	Patsy Rowlands
'Umbrella'	Peter Butterworth

with

Morgan	Edward Underdown
'Briefcase'	Mike Pratt
Man in black	John Cazabon
Doorman	Desmond Llewelyn
Receptionist	Patrick Connor
Fletcher	Peter Gill
Croupier	Terrance Hooper

Directed by Don Chaffey

DRIVING TO London Airport to meet 'Control', Drake (call-sign Ulysees 10), swerves to avoid running down two young boys whose football shoots across the road in front of his car. He crashes into a tree and is knocked unconscious. The time: 12 noon precisely. The next thing Drake knows is that he has a blinding headache, and that one of his superiors, Mr Lovegrove, the Department's treasury man, wishes to see him immediately. Drake finds the man in a sour mood. He wants to know why it is that Drake owes a casino £500? The debt is claimed by a man named Mr Alexander, owner of the club. As Lovegrove points out: 'We don't like people paying undue attention to our agents, and you know the rule about gambling. Gamblers, Drake, are bad security risks.' Denying the charges, Drake is given until the end of the week to come up with a satisfactory explanation, otherwise Lovegrove will have to report the affair to the Minister – and Drake knows what to expect from him. But shocks await Drake when he visits the club. Everyone seems to know him! The doorman is delighted to see him again. Attendants seem to recognise him and an extremely glamorous girl named Elaine Pearson, who works for Mr Alexander, appears to know him *very* well. There is just one snag: to the best of his knowledge, Drake has never seen any of these people before! When Alexander produces the dishonoured cheque, Drake sees that the signature on the IOU is a forgery. Having compared the signature on the cheque with that of one Drake signs in his presence, the club owner accepts Drake's word and apologises: it is an unfortunate coincidence indeed that there should be two John Drakes. The M9 man meets Mrs Fairbrother, a plump amiable widow, who comments that whenever Elaine gambles, she 'gets a look in her eye' and wins. Stating that she knows he will bring her luck, Mrs Fairbrother asks Drake to place a bet for her. Drake does so, his head spinning a little, and he imagines that he can hear Mr Lovegrove's laugh. He gazes at the croupier, and the man's countenance seems to change into that of his superior's. This worries him, but he wins. The next day he discusses the matter with Mr Lovegrove. Saying that he is convinced that there is no other John Drake, he tells Lovegrove that he intends to return to the club, ostensibly as a gambler.

Within seconds of arriving at Mrs Fairbrother's home, Drake succumbs to the nightmarish visions of The Ubiquitous Mr Lovegrove

Drake tells him that his head is still giving him trouble, and Mr Lovegrove orders him to pay the Department's doctor a visit. To Drake's alarm and confusion, the doctor bears an uncanny resemblance to Mr Lovegrove. Haunted by hallucinations, the undercover man finds it difficult to shake off the man's grinning image. Mr Lovegrove's laugh follows him everywhere – every face he sees turns into that of his superior's! Determined to solve the mystery, he revisits the casino and is persuaded by Elaine to drive her home. Mr Alexander is waiting for them and the man puts his cards on the table. He reveals that he has followed Drake's activities for over a year and knows that he is a security agent. Alexander threatens Drake with exposure: if the information in his possession is divulged, say, to the desk of every foreign Embassy in London, Drake's career will be at an end. His price for remaining silent: £10,000. Unless this sum is received within 48 hours . . . What is more, courtesy of the slip of paper Drake handed to him earlier, he now has a valid IOU for that amount, complete with Drake's own signature! Furious at this new development, Mr Lovegrove refuses to honour Drake's debt. To add insult to injury, he assures his junior that should he have to leave the service early, he would, of course, lose all pension rights. Returning to his home more confused than ever, Drake finds he has two unwanted guests waiting for him: 'Umbrella' and 'Briefcase', two heavies sent by Mr Alexander to attempt to force Drake into settling his debt. Disposing of the men in typical secret agent manner, the M9 man returns to the casino intending to ask Mr Alexander to give him more time to pay. Mrs Fairbrother calls him to the roulette table to watch as Elaine plays her next game: she has 'that look' in her eye. Neither are too surprised when the girl wins a hefty sum. However, Drake notices that when the croupier pays Elaine her winnings, he slips a white roulette chip from under his sleeve – a token that is passed on to her playing partner. Something is going on, but what? With his mind plagued by images of Mr Lovegrove's face, Drake finds it difficult to concentrate. When Elaine asks him to drive her home again, he gets closer to the truth. The girl confirms his suspicion that the game is rigged: the table being fixed in Elaine's favour.

She only bets when Alexander tells her to, which is usually when other gamblers, always men, arrive at the club. The numbers she selects are given to her by her employer and are guaranteed to win. The girl, however, never actually profits from her success. She suggests that if Drake bets for her during the next game, they could divide their winnings down the middle and he could pay off his debt. Dropping Elaine at her apartment, Drake agrees to wait for her signal that the next game is due. As he drives away, a policeman on patrol bids him goodnight – a constable who looks amazingly like Mr Lovegrove! Back at the treasury, Drake is shown a photograph of Morgan, the man who had been Elaine's partner during the last game. Drake is told by his superior that Morgan works at the Joint-Planning Naval Department, from which secrets have been stolen. He suggests that the casino could be a link in the spy chain, with the man being paid on the pretext of winning at the tables. Wishing to plug the leak, the men lay a trap to bring Morgan into the open. Still plagued by visions of Lovegrove's face, Drake joins Elaine and Mrs Fairbrother at the roulette table. Selecting the numbers chosen by Elaine, Drake wins handsomely. However, as the croupier slides the white betting chip over, Mrs Fairbrother snatches the token away and exchanges it for one of her own: white being her lucky colour. Refusing the croupier's offer to cash in her chips, she departs with Drake. Finding his exit blocked by 'Mr Lovegrove' look-alikes, Drake is forced to give his superior the slip before racing after the elderly woman. Mrs Fairbrother arrives home at midnight precisely. It comes as no surprise to her when, seconds after she has closed her door, Drake appears at her home. Offering her playing partner a drink, she disappears into the kitchen, allowing her guest the opportunity to take the white gambling chip from her purse. It is then that the croupier arrives and, at gunpoint, orders Drake to hand over the object. Mrs Fairbrother's return from the kitchen allows Drake to dispense with the intruder, but at that moment Alexander races into the room, together with the casino's doorman, who is now exposed as the brains behind the secrets for sale organisation. Drake fires his automatic pistol at the men and is staggered to see them disappear as his bullets enter their bodies! Screaming, the woman races from the room, leaving behind a distraught Drake. Fighting to control his gun hand, which threatens to turn the weapon on its owner, he staggers across the room to finally collapse on a bed occupied by – Mr Lovegrove! Sitting erect, and seeing Mrs Fairbrother approaching the bed with a huge hypodermic syringe, Drake screams out in terror – and finds himself lying on the grass verge where he crashed his car in order to avoid killing the ball-playing children. Cradling his head is Mr Lovegrove – revealed now as the doctor from Drake's *nightmare*!

A DATE WITH DORIS

Teleplay by Philip Broadley

Starring

Juana Romero	**Jane Merrow**
Joaquin Paratore	**Ronald Radd**
Eduardo	**Eric Pohlmann**
Peter Miller	**James Maxwell**

with

Plain clothes Man	**Marne Maitland**
Major Casado	**Richard Bebb**
Chemist	**David Lander**
Van Driver	**David Cargill**
Reception Clerk	**Carlos Douglas**
Bell Boy	**Micky Ventura**
Police Officer	**Alvaro Fontana**
Sergeant	**David Charlesworth**
Jose	**Guido Adorni**
Doorman	**Donald Tandy**
Tavern Keeper	**Charles Hill**
Conchita	**Magda Konopke**
Naval Lieutenant	**Richard Owens**
First Assassin	**Juan Ilinares**
Second Assassin	**Michael Martin**
Soldier	**Roy Vincente**
Sergeant's Man	**Peter Brayham**
Policeman	**Michael Maten**

Directed by Quentin Lawrence

GLAMOUROUS CARIBBEAN ACTRESS, Conchita, is shot by men who break into her home. They leave behind the unconscious body of British agent, Peter Miller, whose cover as a journalist has been blown. John Drake is sent to the island to find Miller and get him to safety. After his arrest for Conchita's murder, Miller has escaped from prison and, though badly wounded, has gone into hiding. Drake poses as journalist John White, ostensibly on the island to interview the veteran Revolutionary Army chief, Joaquin Paratore. Drake books into his hotel and takes the elevator to his room. Within minutes of settling in, he receives a telephone call from a girl named Juana Romero, asking Drake to meet her in the hotel bar in ten minutes. The girl proves to be a surprise. She is young and attractive, speaks near-perfect English – and is dressed in the local uniform of khaki bush shirt and trousers, with low-slung belt and gun holster. She has been sent, she says, to welcome him on behalf of the Ministry of Culture. Drake approves of the choice. She obviously approves of him. However, as much as Drake would like to accept the girl's invitation to dine with her, he pleads a previous appointment and leaves, promising to see her again the following day. His local contact is Eduardo, who gives him the codenumber '3' as the rendezvous for their meeting place. '3', Drake discovers from his code book is the Bamboo Club. Meeting Eduardo there, Drake is told where Miller is hidden, but his contact tells him that the heat is on and nowhere can be considered safe. Nevertheless, Drake must get Miller out that evening. The rescue plan is to get Miller to a submarine that Drake has arranged to have standing by: the code reference is 'Doris'. When everything is ready, Eduardo is to radio her to make an assignation to meet

Drake at a bay at Mira Flores, a deserted corner of the island. Miller is an old friend of Drake's and if he is arrested and talks, matters could get complicated. Drake's first meeting with the local police is in the tavern where Miller has been hiding in the cellar. Arriving there with Eduardo, he finds the place swarming with policemen who, having found blood in the cellar, are interrogating the tavern owner. Drake's attempts to bluff his way out of the place lead to a fight breaking out, but the M9 man and Eduardo escape. Back at his hotel, Drake finds more of the uniformed men searching the premises. Shown a photograph of Miller by a plain clothes policeman, he denies any knowledge of the person they are searching for. However, things become complicated when, returning to his room, he finds Miller waiting for him. The man on the run is in bad shape. Drake bathes his wounds and his friend explains that, having met Conchita at a Ministry of Culture party, their relationship developed from there. He should have pulled out then, but Miller found something out: the girl was Paratore's mistress, so he decided to stick around in the hope of picking up something of interest. But Paratore must have found out and killed the girl. Just when the man's capture seems inevitable, Juana suddenly arrives at Drake's door. She is infuriated. It is her first job for the Ministry and Drake has let her down: he had told her she was pretty and Drake thought she had made a good impression. Consoling the girl, Drake invites her into the room to share a drink to make up for their misunderstanding. Barely have they raised their glasses, when a dozen policemen burst in. Having made an exhaustive but fruitless search, they leave. Juana is about to follow them when a sound from the balcony attracts her attention. Seeing Miller's fingers clutching at the balcony's parapet, Drake and the girl race to hoist him to safety. The M9 man has no option now but to trust Juana with his secret. Miller, however, is alarmed: he is convinced the girl will betray them. But Drake has a hunch about her, and he is prepared to back it. His hunch proves to be justified. Aware that if she reports Miller's

Discovered by Juana, Drake has no option to come clean and ask her to help him keep A Date With Doris

whereabouts, the man will be shot, she agrees to help the men to get out of the hotel. Acting as look-out when Drake and Miller descend to the hotel foyer in the elevator, she conveniently distracts the attention of the doorman and the reception clerk. But their departure is seen by the latter, who sets the police on their tail. Before Drake can make good his escape, the car he is driving becomes ensnared in a traffic hold-up and he is arrested, leaving Juana behind to drive Miller to safety under the very noses of the men searching for him. Soon afterwards, Drake is taken before Paratore, ostensibly for the 'interview' he is seeking. The man apologises for having the journalist arrested and offers to answer the newspaper man's questions. It is not long, however, before the conversation switches to Miller, and Paratore admits that he had been the dead girl's lover. The army chief attempts to bribe Drake into helping him find Miller. Realising that Juana has not yet handed his friend over to the police, Drake convinces Paratore that he will accept the bribe; if only to defray his expenses. Back in Drake's room, Juana contacts Drake by telephone telling him that Miller is in her apartment, but is very ill and must have medical attention or he will die. With time running short, Drake escapes from Paratore's guards by climbing out onto his balcony and edging his way along to the next room. But his troubles are still not over. Stealing into the room, he disturbs the plain clothes policeman who is attempting to snatch forty winks on a couch. He attempts to capture Drake, but by tipping the couch over backwards, the M9 man is able to escape. As he drives away from the hotel, the doorman manages to scribble down the registration number of Drake's car and, informed of what has taken place, Paratore sends out an alert: the Englishman should be arrested on sight. Kissing Juana goodbye, Drake bribes a chemist to supply him with bandages and drugs. He eventually reaches his Mira Flores beach house to await the arrival of 'Doris'. Unknown to them, Drake and Miller were spotted entering the house by a motorcycle policeman and a short time later Paratore and his guards smash down the door. Told that Miller cannot be moved, the Army chief sends for an ambulance, determined to have his shot at interrogating the wounded Englishman. However, as luck would have it, seeing 'Doris' flashing her signal over Paratore's shoulder, Drake's codeword to Miller saves the day. Aware now that rescue is at hand, Miller throws back his blanket to reveal a gun and seconds later Paratore lies dead at his friend's feet. Drake soon dispenses with the rest of the guards and escapes with Miller thrown over his shoulder. It is a relieved M9 man who finds a naval lieutenant waiting for them on the beach.

SUCH MEN ARE DANGEROUS

Teleplay by Ralph Smart

Starring

Major Latour	Lee Montague
Shorty Pratt	Jack McGowran
Mr Sen	Zia Mohyeddin
General	Jack Gwillam
Jack Taylor	John Cairney
Solicitor	Alan Wheatley
Diana	Georgina Ward

with

Hobbs	Peter Madden
Red Johnson	Robert O'Neil
Odzala	Thomas Baptiste
Tweedy Gentleman	Roger Maxwell
Edwin Bowden	Tom Gill
Williams	Ivor Salter
Butler	Eric Chitty
Miss Jackson	Dorinda Stevens
Gateman	Patrick Connor
Harry Hutchinson	David Cargill
Inspector	Henry Kay
Girls	Martine Beswick
	Judy Huxstable
	Ann Colston

Directed by Don Chaffey

A MEETING IN THE countryside with prisoner Edwin Bowden, is instrumental in giving Drake the lead he needs to penetrate a vicious secret society which has the fanatical objective of murdering political leaders. Bowden is due for parole. He has been approached by another prisoner, Williams – who is serving a long sentence for the attempted assassination of minister Odzala – about working for his masters when Bowden is released in a fortnight's time. The job would be well-paid, and Bowden seems to have it made. Why then, asks Drake, did the prisoner report the offer to the prison governor? Bowden, it seems has had enough of being on the wrong side of the law and he wishes to settle down. Offering to help the man accomplish his dream, as long as he in turn helps Drake, the M9 man tells Bowden to report to Williams that he has considered his offer and has decided to accept. What Drake has in mind will mean that Bowden will spend a little more time in jail, but Drake will see that he is moved to another prison for safety. Drake then takes over Bowden's identity and meets the contact arranged for the real prisoner. He soon finds himself passed from one contact to another until he eventually reaches a large mansion in the English countryside. Arriving there, he meets Diana, a beautiful girl who gives him a lift and drops him outside the mansion's front entrance. He is met by a butler who, telling Drake that he is expected, ushers him into a room where he finds himself in the company of other recently-released prisoners. The reason for their presence is soon made clear by a man they are introduced to as the General. Explaining that they have been recruited to serve as members of the organisation he leads, the man tells them that they will be paid well and treated well, but only if they accept the Order's discipline. He continues: 'Our Order is international. It stands for discipline and for the moral authority that derives from discipline. Most people are honest and simple, but they are by nature incapable of deciding their own destiny. They have to be guided, and that must eventually be along the paths our Order lays down, with discipline and moral obedience to those in authority. Meanwhile, the so-called democratic leaders, deceive the people into thinking they are idealists, but in fact, they are decadent and corrupt demagogues. Such men are dangerous. Such men must be removed.' The men find themselves under the direct orders of Major Latour, whose job it is to train them to kill. But before the training begins in earnest, they will be given time to adjust themselves to their new environment, and even be allowed to spend an evening in London. One man, Hutchinson, decides that he is not cut out for such violent work, so Latour reassigns him to 'other duties'. While in London, despite being closely watched the whole time, Drake succeeds in contacting Hobbs and arranges for a miniature transmitting device to be sent to him at the mansion. Drake also arranges for some 'ladies of the night' to be sent to entertain his friends. Meanwhile, Hutchinson's body is found, the victim of a 'road accident' and Taylor, one of the recruits suggests that this is intended as a warning to anyone else foolish enough to speak their mind. One of the ladies sent by Hobbs, is Miss Jackson, an M9 employee, to whom Drake hands a report. From her he learns that the prisoner Williams, started out as a Communist, before changing his allegiance to the British Nazi party and ending up as one of the Order. Now that they have had their fun, Latour expects their full, undivided attention for the remainder of the course. Showing them photographs taken while they were enjoying themselves in the city – pictures which prove that they are being kept under constant surveillance, the Major warns Taylor to keep his nose out of politics: this will be his last warning. It will be their function, they are told, to carry out the judgement of the Order: once the Order has judged a man to be a danger to society, he will be disposed of as silently and as swiftly as is possible. The job is not as difficult as they might suppose. The condemned man will have no idea that he has been judged and sentenced: he will be neither forewarned, or forearmed. From the point of view of the authorities, none of them will have any connection with the condemned man, so the police will have no motive for suspecting them. Warning the group that the Order does not tolerate failure, Latour introduces them to Mr Sen, who has arrived to teach them his particular method of disposing with the enemy – the art of throttling a man to death with his own neck-tie. Thereafter, the recruits are subjected to all sorts of tests to judge their reliability. The transmitter which Drake has asked for, is dropped at a set time in a lane outside the mansion. There is a moment of alarm for Drake when the attractive Diana, who turns out to be the General's wife, and makes no secret of the fact that she has climbed ruthlessly from poverty and intends to remain a top-dog, draws up in her Land Rover as Drake collects the package. However, he manages to dupe the woman into believing that the package was meant for someone else and when Drake refuses her offer of a lift back to the mansion, the woman drives away, leaving Drake with enough time to unwrap the device and hide the 'bug' in the General's study. He is now able to record everything said there. So far, things are going according to plan and the training continues unabated. The recruits are being taught to use explosives and various other weapons

of destruction. Transmitting a message to Hobbs, Drake is told that the FBI are monitoring the department's progress, but they will require at least another 24 hours before they can act. However, if his man gets into real trouble, he has only to give Hobbs the signal, and M9 will close the net within 20 minutes. With the training over, one man appears doubtful that he can proceed as ordered. It is Jack Taylor, who suddenly disappears. But the General knows his whereabouts and Drake is instructed to follow Taylor and kill him. He pretends to do so, but gives Taylor the opportunity to escape. A mistake. Taylor is working for the General: his disappearance was part of the plan to test Drake. Brought before Major Latour, Drake leaps through the window and escapes into the grounds, from where he sends out a signal to Hobbs. Stealing a vehicle, he finds himself pursued across country, and crashes his car into a tree. Recovering consciousness, he finds himself sitting in the General's study with Major Latour and the treacherous Taylor on hand to interrogate him about his activities. Coming clean and exposing his true identity, the M9 man takes great delight in telling the men that the game is up: he has contacted his headquarters and his friends should arrive in two and a half minutes' time.

The game is up. Recovering consciousness in the General's study – with Majour Latour and the treacherous Taylor on hand to interrogate him – Drake discovers why **Such Men Are Dangerous**

However, even Drake is surprised at the next turn of events. Diana enters her husband's study brandishing a shotgun and attempts to kill Drake. But it is the General who dies when the shot meant for Drake fells him to the floor as Drake attempts to wrestle the gun from Diana's hand. Seconds later, the arrival of Drake's M9 colleagues signals the end of the murderous order.

WHATEVER HAPPENED TO GEORGE FOSTER?

Teleplay by David Stone

Starring

Pauline	**Adrienne Corri**
Lord Ammanford	**Bernard Lee**
Certhia	**Jill Medford**
Lady Ammanford	**Joyce Carey**
The Stranger	**Colin Douglas**

with

Nanny	**Patsy Smart**
Sir Joseph Manton	**Richard Caldicot**
Secretary	**Redmond Phillips**
Charlie Hewitt	**Jack Bligh**
Police Sergeant	**Michael Collins**
Miss Jones	**Dorothea Phillips**
Airport Clerk	**Sonia Fox**
Ginger	**Jeremy Ranchev**
Mrs Foster	**Barbara Leake**
Garage Attendant	**Bill Corlett**
Schoolmaster	**Eynon Evans**
Landlord	**Dafydd Havard**
Vicar	**Evan Thomas**
Jones the Boat	**Norman Wynne**
Farmer	**Roderick Jones**
Garage Manager	**Brian Anderson**

Directed by Don Chaffey

DRAKE IS IN Central America, keeping a careful watch on a girl named Certhia Cooper who he believes is involved in a plot to overthrow the lawful government of Santa Marco. His first proof that something is going on comes when he discovers that Certhia has been distributing packets of money to certain people there. He catches up with the woman again at London airport,

A trip to Santa Marco sets Drake on a trail that will lead him to discover **Whatever Happened To George Foster?**

where, having trailed her chauffeur-driven limousine to a building which houses the Society for Cultural Relations with South America, he follows Certhia inside and introduces himself as a member of World Travel, an organisation interested in the country she has just visited. It soon becomes evident, however, that while Drake is interested in the society's activities, someone is also interested in his activities. His apartment is broken into and Drake receives a visit from an unexpected caller – a man wearing an unusual ring on the little finger of his right hand, which is all Drake sees of the intruder as he escapes from his home. Drake's next step is to pay a visit to Fleet Street to see Pauline, a newspaper friend. She remembers Certhia as a girl who had worked her way through the paper's assistant editor, the editor and the managing editor before she left, unable to sink her claws into the editor-in-chief who was away in New York at the time! Pauline remembers the woman as being a predatory, scheming megalomaniac, a career woman of the worst kind who, if Drake is not careful, will use him to achieve her ambitions. As they speak, Certhia telephones, Drake having told her where he could be found. She has a message from someone who wishes to see Drake at six o'clock that evening in his Park Lane penthouse about his ideas for Santa Marco. He learns that his host is Lord Ammanford, a powerful and tremendously wealthy tycoon. As Drake enters the man's study, Ammanford is telling one of his secretaries that he will be delighted to dine with the Prime Minister on Thursday, while asking the other girl to apologise to the Ambassador for not being able to accept his dinner offer because he will be in Washington that evening! Ammanford, the man behind the society, hardly raises an eyebrow when Drake warns him that his money is being channelled into a revolutionary movement. Passing the comment that you cannot trust anyone these days, the tycoon surprises his guest when he reveals that not only does he share a friendship with Drake's superiors, but he also knows his guest's real identity. Introduced to Mrs Ammanford, Drake sees immediately that the two are very much in love with each other. It is not long before he discovers just how far Ammanford's power extends. Without any explanation, he is called to the home of Hobb's immediate superior, Sir Joseph Manton, who tells him that on the orders of the Foreign Office, Drake is to be removed from the case. Like it or not, Drake must take a holiday; his Department has been instructed that they will have to do without him for a month. Understandably, the M9 man does not take too kindly to this. His attempts to continue his investigation alone by catching a plane to Santa Marco are thwarted when he discovers that there are no seats available today, tomorrow or ever; he has overlooked the fact that Lord Ammanford is chairman of the airline. Told by Pauline that no one is prepared to print a story about a man like Ammanford unless he can prove that the man has done something criminal, Drake's plans appear to have died before they have even left the starting post. However, Pauline has been digging into the tycoon's past. She has discovered that before he was given his title, his name was Peter Jones and he came from a village in Wales. On the pretext of researching a book about Ammanford, Drake drives to the man's birthplace and talks to the local residents. Jones, of course, is a very common name, but there are plenty of people who claim they remember the man who became a Lord. They owe a lot to him. Yet, Drake discovers, when they are asked to describe the man, all give different anwers – his eyes were blue or brown, his complexion was dark or fair, his hair was wiry and dark, or soft and blonde. It is difficult for Drake to convince himself that they are describing the same man, unless, of course, there was more than one Peter Jones or, perhaps, as Drake is now beginning to suspect, no Peter Jones at all! A telephone call from Pauline saying that she has found out who the mystery man's parents were, only serves to deepen the puzzle. The real Peter Jones has just died, as Drake sees for himself when he joins the funeral procession and watches as the coffin is lowered into the freshly dug grave! Preparing to leave, a stranger asks Drake if he would mind giving him a lift to the railway station in his car. Drake agrees. A few miles down the road, he has cause to regret his kindness. Forced to stop when a car blocks the road, Drake finds himself beaten around the solar plexus by his fellow passenger – a man wearing an unusual ring. Back in London, Lord Ammanford plays host to the bruised and battered Drake who, Ammanford explains, he thought he would never see again. Drake tells him that he has just returned from the tycoon's birthplace and that a friend, digging in the passport archives has discovered several inaccuracies regarding Ammanford's background. This information fails to dent the tycoon's reserve, but when Drake raises his voice, his host warns him that he obviously has not yet realised how powerful he is; he can break Drake, physically, professionally, mentally and there is nothing that his guest can do to harm him, absolutely nothing at all. From this moment on, Drake not only finds his life endangered, but he comes up against even more drama. Extraordinary moves are made to stop him in whichever direction he turns. With Pauline's help, he discovers that Ammanford married his wife while in Australia in 1930, and that Mrs Ammanford's nanny still lives in the village where she spent her childhood. Armed with this news Drake visits the woman and borrows a photograph of Lady Ammanford's sister's wedding from her on the pretext of requiring it for the book he is researching. When enlarged, the photograph produces a surprising clue: the chauffeur pictured with the wedding party is none other than the man now calling himself Lord Ammanford! Drake must now discover the man's real name. When Drake returns the photograph, the former nanny is unable to tell him anything beyond the fact that the wedding car was hired for the occasion. Drake soon discovers from which establishment and speaks to the garage owner. But he can remember nothing; it was before his time. However, perhaps old Charlie Hewitt can be of help; he was around at that time. A garage mechanic offers to show Drake where Charlie lives, but once again he is led into a trap. The man forces Drake to drive off the road. The following morning, Drake stands before a police sergeant who informs him that the telephone number Drake gave him in London denies all knowledge of anyone of that name. The undercover man is accused of being in possession of stolen property found in the boot of his car. On his way to the cells, Drake once again sees the man with the ring, calmly rubbing his chin as the constable takes Drake away. But he is not in custody for long. Clubbing the constable to the floor, Drake races outside, steals the chief constable's car and drives at speed to Charlie Hewitt's home, where he confirms his theory that Ammanford used to be a chauffeur. His real name was George Foster, and he ran away from the village, leaving behind his wife and children. Mind you says Hewitt, Mrs Foster made him pay: Foster bought her a house in Potts End, where she still lives. As Drake is about

to leave, the man with the ring once again stands before him. But this time it is Drake who gains the upper hand and the stranger is left nursing his bruised jaw amid the shattered remains of Charlie Hewitt's garden railings. A visit to Mrs Foster provides Drake with a chink in Ammanford's armour: the man and his wife have never divorced; she being content to maintain her silence in return for the regular payments her husband deposits in her bank account. Armed with this information, Drake pays the tycoon a final visit. It does not take Drake long to convince George Foster that his evidence is complete.

Attempting to unravel the mystery of Whatever Happened to George Foster? *leads Drake to Wales – and the funeral of a man who died 25 years earlier!*

Drake tells him he has taken the precaution of having typed it out in full and then duplicated. There are 200 copies, all accompanied by photostat copies of birth certificates, passport applications, everything. If Ammanford's team is not out of Santa Marco within the next 20 minutes, a friend of Drake's has been instructed to send the story to every influential editor, politician and public figure that Drake could think of. Beaten, Ammanford accedes to Drake's request. He prepares a statement for the Press saying that he has discovered that his Santa Marco association is being misused and that he is winding it down. This done, Ammanford, joined by his wife, bids his unwelcome guest goodnight, but Drake has not quite finished. Handing the tycoon the file he carried with him, he proposes that Ammanford take good care of it: it is, after all, the only copy!

A ROOM IN THE BASEMENT

· Teleplay by Ralph Smart

Starrring

Susan	**Jane Merrow**
Bernhard	**William Lucas**
Military Attaché	**Michael Gwynn**
British Ambassador	**Mark Dignam**
Dr Huber	**Gerard Heinz**
Keith Turnbull	**John Breslin**
Luke	**Edward Cast**

with

British First Secretary	**John Welsh**
Third Secretary	**Jack May**
Sister Rousseau	**Margo Johns**
Annette	**Kate O'Mara**
Man Receptionist	**John Cater**
Servant	**Jose Berlinka**
Sergeant	**Peter Elliott**

Directed by Don Chaffey

THERE IS nothing more sacrosanct than an Embassy. Any disturbance of diplomatic immunity can result in international complications for all concerned. Nevertheless, this fails to prevent Drake from making an attempt to aid a colleague, Keith Turnbull, who is being held in an East European Embassy in Switzerland. It has been officially denied that Turnbull is there – and, as far as officialdom is concerned, nothing can be done. But when Drake receives a telephone call from Susan Turnbull, appealing to him for help, he disregards his superiors' warnings and hops on the first available plane to Switzerland. The niceties of diplomacy are one thing, but loyalty to one's colleagues means more than this to Drake, especially as Keith and Susan are old friends. Delighted when Drake flies in, Susan offers to help in any way she can. But how on earth can a man be rescued from such a well-guarded building – patrolled not only by its own security guards, but also by the Swiss police? For once, Drake decides that he cannot afford to play the lone wolf. He will need the help of fellow agents. One of these is Bernhard, who is Swiss, and the other is Luke, a Frenchman. Both men think the idea is crazy, but Bernhard tells Drake that Luke is flying in from Paris to join his old friends. Bernhard's chalet becomes their operational headquarters, and his wine cellar is ideal for what Drake has in mind. Installed in a hotel room overlooking the Embassy, it does not take Drake long to lay his plans. But it will not be simple. There is a guard on the door and two on the gate. The Swiss police have four men patrolling outside and a radio vehicle patrols the street. Before they can decide upon a final plan, they will need to acquire the layout of the building and details of the security arrangements. Drake pays the Embassy a formal visit to see if he can find a weak link. Pretending to be a tourist who wishes to apply for a visa, he fills in an application form and is sent to an upper room to see the man who will issue him with a visa. He poses as a Londoner who has a classified job and is eager to sell information. Drake succeeds in duping the man with his story and he soon attracts the attention of the Embassy's military attaché, a Colonel, who falls for the bait Drake dangles before him. Back at his hotel, Drake receives a telephone call from the man with instructions to meet him at a certain rendezvous point in 10 minutes' time. Asked to give Drake a little longer, the caller agrees to allow Drake 20 minutes in which to reach the place, but no more; if the Englishman fails to arrive on time, the other will take it as a sign of bad faith. The extension allows Drake and his friends to put their plans into top gear. When the two men meet, the attaché falls into a trap. Saying that he was worried about being caught, Drake hands the man a tasty tit-bit, and the foreigner allows himself to be driven to the place where Drake says he has hidden the remainder of the documents. A short drive takes them around the corner, up a ramp and into the back of a furniture removal truck parked there by Drake's friends. Taken to Bernhard's wine cellar which, with the help of Susan and Annette, Bernhard's wife, has been decorated to give the impression that the attaché is being held at the British Embassy – and is therefore very much in the same situation as Turnbull, he is threatened that it will be announced that he has defected to the West. Realising how this will affect his wife and family, the abducted man agrees to outline plans of the interior of his own Embassy with details of where Turnbull can be found. Drake tells his friends that as long as they get the prisoner out quickly and no one is caught, sympathy will be on their side and all will be forgiven and forgotten. He scans the Embassy layout, aware that if they are caught it will be political dynamite, with a nice long stretch in prison waiting for them. A private hospital backing onto the Embassy plays a vital part in the rescue operation, and to get inside Bernhard poses as a doctor who has a distinguished English colleague with him. The 'visiting' doctor is Drake, who has a delicate matter to put before the hospital's head, Doctor Huber. He has a patient, an Englishwoman whose unfortunate love affair has ended, leaving her in a state of nervous collapse. She comes from a wealthy family who are away at the moment and Drake considers that she should not be left alone. Assured that the girl's family will show their appreciation in a most practical way, Dr Huber agrees to 'take her in'. In this way Susan enters the hospital as a patient and is placed under the care of Sister Rousseau. This gives Drake and Bernhard the freedom to come and go as they please, on the excuse that they are visiting Susan.

Attempting to discover the secret of A Room In The Basement, *Drake and his companion prepare to break into a foreign Embassy*

During their next visit, Annette arrives as the patient's 'sister-in-law'. The whole rescue party is now in attendance and things move swiftly. By breaking into a room adjacent to Susan's private ward, Drake and Bernhard manage to make their way across to the Embassy where, having edged themselves across the narrow ledge skirting the upper windows of the building, they make their way to the roof. Unfortunately, at that very moment, Sister Rousseau chooses to enter another patient's room where, looking through the window and seeing the intruders on the Embassy roof, she races to a telephone. Attired now in breathing apparatus Drake and Bernhard enter the Embassy through a window. Cutting down guards as they go by firing gas cannisters into their faces, they reach Turnbull's cell and engineer the prisoner's release. Disaster almost strikes when the alarm is raised, but a few further gas cannisters save the day and the three men make good their escape. Having harkened to Sister Rousseau's telephone alert, the hospital is now swarming with Swiss policemen. Nevertheless, Drake and Bernhard manage to reunite Keith Turnbull with his wife. Leaving the couple in Annette's care, the 'doctors' leave the building. Driven by Luke, who is waiting outside, Drake reports to the British Embassy. Confronting a highly-disturbed First Secretary with the news that Turnbull is free, the man tells Drake that he will be reporting his totally irresponsible activities to London: if anything had gone wrong, the embarrassment to the British government would have been unthinkable. It didn't, replies Drake as the Ambassador bursts into the First Secretary's office to congratulate the civil servant on his daring, imaginative and perfectly executed plan! Stammering his apologies to Drake, the Ambassador disregards the credit the First Secretary attempts to bestow on the undercover man – who is more than happy to concede that it is, after all, the 'man behind the desk' who does all the planning, all the thinking, while 'they', the men in the field, simply carry out orders: in fact, Drake would be obliged if the First Secretary took all the credit and his name was not mentioned at all in the report to London. Then, pausing at the door, Drake finds it difficult to resist twisting the knife by reminding the civil servant to give his regards to the Colonel!

Teleplay by James Foster

Starring

Carlos Bisbal	**Eric Pohlmann**
Ramon Torres	**Harold Goldblatt**
General Ventura	**Martin Benson**
Sir Duncan	**Andre Morell**
Van Horn	**Alan Gifford**
Fortunato Santos	**Aubrey Morris**
El Ferro	**Brian Worth**
Maite	**Sonia Fox**

with

Kemp	**Charles Tingwell**
Colonel Montes	**Richard Leech**
Manual	**David Saire**
Detetective	**David Graham**
Immigration Officer	**David Ritch**
Prison Guard	**Clive Cazes**
Policeman in Cafe	**Paul Armstrong**

Directed by Quentin Lawrence

REVOLUTION BEGETS counter-revolution. The victorious forces always face the danger of a new uprising to overthrow them. This is why Ramos Torres' return to his own country has such wide repercussions. Torres, a former Republican leader of the Hispanic country, makes his way back under an assumed name, and his return is looked upon as a signal for a new uprising against the present regime, which is led by General Ventura. But Torres is caught and faces a death sentence which, for political reasons, is something neither Britain nor America wants. John Drake is sent to the country and finds himself working with an American agent, Kemp, in this allied operation. Drake is loath to co-operate with Kemp. The men have worked together before, at which time the American proved unreliable. Nevertheless, informed by Sir Duncan of the British Embassy that he must do so, Drake reluctantly agrees to join forces with Kemp. Life is made somewhat difficult for Drake because a watchdog by the name of Fortunato Santos is assigned by the organiser of the new revolution, El Ferro, to keep tabs on him. Santos is an amiable, inefficient fellow who becomes quite friendly with the man he is supposed to be watching. Over drinks at a cafe, Kemp fills in the background of Torres' arrest. At the end of the Civil War, Torres, a commander in the army is said to have ordered important hostages to be shot at a place called Castelevara. A price was put on his head and he became a national ogre or hero overnight, depending on which side you were on. He has apparently returned home to die in his own land. Their brief is to obtain his release by any means, excluding violence, but Kemp proposes that they snatch Torres and hand him over to the other side. Drake does not agree. If anything goes wrong it would turn into a full scale war. He asks the American to take him to his republican friends. Drake finds himself before El Ferro. However, as Drake arrives at the would-be revolutionary leader's home, one of El Ferro's guards escorts the man who has been following Drake into the room. It is Santos – and Drake is ordered to kill him. He refuses to do so and the man is allowed to go free. Later, Drake meets the lovely Maite, one of El Ferro's followers. She tells him that he is a lucky

Although cinema projectionist, Bisbal, holds the secret to The Affair At Castlelevara, Drake holds the trump card, as revolutionist leader Ferro will soon discover

man: El Ferro could have had him shot. From their conversation, Drake suspects that the plan to release Torres is just empty words. El Ferro and his group wish to see the man dead; in this way he will help their cause by becoming a martyr. The girl refutes his accusations and tells him that the new movement's hopes hinge on the belief that Torres' action at Castelevara was justified because General Ventura himself murdered defenseless women and children. Torres had to execute his swaggering soldiers in retaliation. Told that she has seen a film of Ventura's atrocities, shown to her by a man who now works as a projectionist at a tumbledown little cinema, Drake and the girl pay the man a visit. His name is Carlos Bisbal, a one-time silent film star. At first he is concerned that Maite has revealed the existence of the film, but eventually he agrees to run it, particularly when Drake tells him that he can arrange to get the film shown all over the world. Maite, meanwhile, returns to El Ferro's headquarters. Informed that Bisbal is about to run the film for Drake, El Ferro becomes angry. Kemp, however, sees things differently; if they can buy Torres' release with the film, their problems will be solved. As promised, the celluloid shows Ventura slaying hostages, but Drake is not in a position to use it. As the short movie ends, El Ferro arrives at the cinema with his friends and tells the projectionist to hand the evidence over to him. When he refuses to do so, Bisbal is beaten up and ordered to supply the negative. But Drake interferes. Telling El Ferro that the film was made many years ago and that the negative has been lost, the man almost believes him. However, suspecting Drake of trickery, El Ferro orders him to be searched. With the negative in his pocket, this is the last thing Drake wants, so he turns on his captors and makes good his escape. Finding Bisbal beaten, and the film gone, Maite and Kemp are told by the projectionist that El Ferro has set the police on Drake's tail. Kemp telephones his partner, asking him to meet him at Maite's home. Aware now that he is being hunted, Drake takes the negative to Sir Duncan, but Colonel Montes, the Chief of Police, arrives as he hands over the evidence of Ventura's guilt. Sir Duncan, not wishing to compromise his position in the Embassy, hands both Drake and the film over to the policeman. As they leave, Kemp arrives and asks Sir Duncan to give him the negative. Too late. He is told that both Drake and the evidence are now with the police. Kemp now proves his worth by tricking Colonel Montes into believing that it is already too late: the real roll of film has been posted to England, and the policeman has only the negative. Outfoxed, the policeman has no option but to accede to Drake's request for an audience with General Ventura. Confronted with Drake's news, the man agrees to allow Drake to 'spring' Torres. Watched by a gleeful Kemp and a none-too-happy General, Drake does just that.

HAVE A GLASS OF WINE

Teleplay by David Stone

Starring

Suzanne	**Ann Lynn**
Lamaze	**Warren Mitchell**
Police Chief	**George Benson**
Zelda	**Kathleen Breck**
Jules	**Victor Brookes**

with

Gaston	**Michael Balfour**
Henri	**Larry Taylor**
Duty Officer	**Brian Weske**
Old Lady	**Anita Sharp Bolster**
Madame Lafleur	**Ann Heffernan**
Annette	**Sarah Brackett**
Chateau Guide	**Roger Avon**
Pierre	**Michael Coccoran**

Directed by Peter Maxwell

THE LAUNDERETTE machine contains some very unusual laundry, a brown paper parcel tightly bound with string – a package that Drake has followed for a number of days. Drake observes the package being collected by Zelda, an attractive brunette, and her accomplice. Having photographed the pick-up with his lighter-cum-camera, Drake shows little surprise when a blonde-haired man snatches the latter from his hands, races outside and drives away in his car. The man, an M9 colleague, is soon talking to Drake on his car telephone, confirming that the man in the pictures Drake has taken is Anderson. The girl is a new recruit with no M9 record. Advising his colleague that he will continue his surveillance of the girl's department, just in case she suddenly decides to take a trip abroad, Drake orders his colleague to have his suitcase ready for a quick departure – and in particular, not to forget to pack his fishing rod. Don't worry, comes the reply, this has already been taken care of. Within seconds, a man appears in the street behind Drake's car. Putting the agent's suitcase into the vehicle's boot, and some fishing tackle and a raincoat on the Mini Cooper's rear seat, the man makes a speedy exit. Drake sees Zelda leave her apartment. He trails her to France and books himself into the hotel that the girl is staying in. Other newcomers soon attract his attention. One of these is an attractive French schoolmistress named Suzanne and the other is Lamaze. Having introduced himself to Drake as a wine-merchant, Lamaze insists that the M9 man joins him in sampling the local brew. Deciding to speed up his investigation, Drake confronts Zelda in her room. Although the girl pulls a gun, he soon forces her to admit that the contents of the package she collected – a film – is in her possession. Threatening her with a prison sentence, he explains how he got on her trail. His investigation began at an aircraft and armament establishment at Boscombe Down in the south of England. Secret papers were photographed by someone called Morrison. The film was left under a signpost and collected by Hannard, who posted them to a box number in a London newsagent's shop. The envelope was picked up from there by Machin, who put it into a 24-hour luggage locker. The key was then posted to a man called Anderson, her contact, who collected the film and went to do his washing at the launderette. Confronted with such detailed evidence, Zelda tells him that the film is in her handbag. However, she is not a traitor. She went to meet a man at a party who took some compromising photographs of her. She was then blackmailed into delivering her handbag to a certain wine chateau, where she was supposed to put her bag on a large table while waiting for the guide. The bag would then be exchanged for an identical one. She admits that she is being paid $500, which will be in the other bag. Assuring the girl that if she helps him she will not go to prison, Drake tells Zelda to go ahead as instructed. Lamaze is at the chateau, but Drake pays little attention to him. The girl's handbag is exchanged as planned, by a woman named Annette, who makes off on a bicycle. Grabbing another cycle, Drake chases her through the countryside, eventually arriving at a small farmhouse. Bursting through the door, he stops in amazement when he comes face with face with, not the attractive Annete, but an old lady, who claims that the girl is not on the premises. She is telling the truth. Racing outside, Drake sees his quarry disappearing down a country lane on her bicycle. Another shock awaits him back at his hotel. The door to Zelda's room is wide open and, on entering, he finds the girl dead. She has been shot. Found in the room with the body, Drake is arrested and interrogated by the Chief of Police. He is accused of stealing a bicycle and of stealing Zelda's handbag – what is more, his fingerprints are on a gun found in the dead girl's room. Until the forensic team have proved whether or not this was the murder weapon, Drake will be held in custody in the cells. Later, when the duty officer brings Drake his evening meal, he clubs the policeman to the ground and escapes from the police station. Drake makes his way to Lamaze's home. Appearing to accept Drake's word that he did not kill the girl, the wine-merchant allows his unannounced guest to remain at his home, at least until it is safe enough for Drake to leave. Perhaps Drake would like a meal, asks Lamaze, leaving the room to tell his maid to prepare something for his guest. Minutes later, Annette walks into the room carrying a tray, as do several policemen carrying guns! Drake up-ends the dining table into the wine-merchant's face and escapes from the policemen by hurtling himself through the window into the garden. Surrounded on all sides, Drake finds the window of an outhouse ajar, and climbs into the darkened room .It is Lamaze's wine-cellar, but it offers no

At gunpoint, Suzanne orders Drake to be more cooperative. (Have A Glass Of Wine)

sanctuary. Seconds after he has crept inside, the doors are thrown open by the police and once again he is forced to go on the run. Escaping into the countryside, he is astonished when Suzanne appears before him and offers him a lift in her car. Driven to her cottage in the country, Drake's confession that he is wanted by the police, barely raises the girl's eyebrows. Over supper, he tells her a cock-and-bull story about being a travel agent and visiting the area to examine the possibility of adding it to his holiday brochure.

Suzanne pulls a gun on her guest, and orders him to be more cooperative. Asking her why he should trust her, Drake is told that she works for the French government, but is not prepared to say more. Unconvinced, he attempts to leave, but at a call from Suzanne, two burly thugs enter the room and Drake is forced back in his chair to undergo further questioning. He convinces the girl that, under the threat of blackmail, he was forced to deliver a micro-dot to Lamaze and is astonished when Suzanne tells him that she will give him 20 minutes alone with the wine-merchant; his future depends on his success in convincing Lamaze to join forces with her. Lamaze is surprised when Drake returns to his home, particularly when his guest informs him about Suzanne's offer. It is the wine-merchant's turn to astound Drake by confirming that he himself is an agent for a foreign power; planted in France 20 years earlier, he has been leaking secrets back to his masters. Confirming that Lamaze has but one chance to escape, and that is to return to London with him, Drake and the wine-merchant decide to join forces. But first they must take care of Suzanne's guards who are waiting outside. They determine to achieve this by inviting the men to join them in a glass of wine – drugged, of course. They are joined by Suzanne, whose unexpected arrival concerns the M9 man. Drake realises that he has walked into a trap – the crafty Lamaze has been a cohort of the girl's all along. Drake finds himself back at the police station and is confronted by a relieved Chief of Police – relieved because he now has proof that Drake did not kill the girl. The crime had been committed by the wine-merchant's gardener, who is now under arrest. Hearing this, Drake returns to the wine-merchant's home where, with the aid of his fishing rod – in reality a cleverly-disguised listening device – he overhears Suzanne planning her next move. Drake is waiting for the couple as they arrive at a nearby airport to fly to their next port of call. When Lamaze boards Suzanne's aircraft, he finds Drake at the controls, and his distraught partner is unable to prevent Drake from flying the equally upset wine-merchant back to London.

On the run from the police, Drake seeks refuge in a wine cellar, inviting his pursuers to **Have A Glass Of Wine**

THE MIRROR'S NEW

Teleplay by Philip Broadley

Starring

Bierce	**Donald Houston**
Sir Jeremy	**David Hutcheson**
Penny	**Wanda Ventham**
Nicola	**Nicola Pagett**

with

George Murgia	**Bill Nagy**
Virginia Bierce	**Mary Yeomans**
Esser	**Ernst Walder**
Frances	**Alison Seebohm**
Second Pursuer	**Jerome Willis**
Diana	**Yvonne Marquand**
First Pursuer	**Frank Maher**

Directed by Michael Truman

WHEN EDMUND BIERCE invites a money lender to join him in his apartment in Paris, the 'payment' for the man's services is a bullet through the heart. Bierce turns up the volume on his hi-fi to cover the sound of the shot. Racing outside to unlock the boot of his car, Bierce, on returning to his basement apartment, stumbles down the staircase and knocks his head on a wall. Crawling into the hallway, he slumps into unconsciousness inside his front door. Regaining his senses when a postman delivers the morning mail, the man goes into the bathroom, sponges the dried blood from his head, and returns to the lounge to stare at the dead body lying on the carpet. He must dispose of the dead man quickly, but how? Intending to place the body in the boot of his car, he goes outside but, spotting two strangers watching him, he slams shut the vehicle's boot and returns to his home where, from his observation point at the window, he sees the two men heading towards his apartment. Fearing the worst, he totters backwards into the darkness. A few miles away, M9 man John Drake pays a visit to the British Embassy. Met by Sir Jeremy, the Ambassador, Drake is told that Bierce is missing. The man has worked at the Embassy for five years and goes to Bonn every week to confer with his opposite number. This week was especially important because Bierce was carrying the Dillon Report to hand over to the Chancellor at 9.30 in the morning. It is now after 3 o'clock and Bonn reports that there is still no sign of the man. Should the Dillon Report fall into the wrong hands it would be highly embarrassing. Bierce, Sir Jeremy maintains, is a amiable character, well behaved and happily married for 10 years. Told that the man was carrying the report in an attaché case, Drake proposes that it sounds ominous: in such circumstances foreign agents would normally snatch the case and run away, in which event Bierce would have informed the Ambassador. Could the man have had an accident – or defected and taken the report with him? Drake decides to begin his investigation with Bierce's wife Virginia. She is of little help: she admits that her husband drinks, but denies that he drinks to excess, and is adamant that Edmund is a patriot. Finally, however, she reveals that Bierce is a gambler, and she names George Murgia as one of his gambling friends. Murgia is staggered to hear this. He has never known Bierce to attend one of his all-night gambling

sessions. The mystery deepens when the missing man turns up as though nothing has happened, claiming that he was at home the previous night. Apparently suffering from amnesia, he cannot remember Drake calling there. He is certain that he has to go to Bonn the next day. He tells Drake and his secretary, Frances, that he has somehow lost a day. It is at this point, that Drake notices a small droplet of dried blood on the back of the man's head, but Bierce cannot remember having hit his head. The papers with him are intact, too, but Drake takes the precaution of removing two pages from the Dillon Report, which he then hands to Sir Jeremy for safe-keeping. Believing that there is a possibility that Bierce is lying, Drake determines to discover where the man spent the last 36 hours. He asks Sir Jeremy to allow Bierce to believe that Drake has returned to London. In this way the M9 man keeps a close watch on him. Doing so takes him to some unexpected quarters, and Drake notices the two men who are also shadowing Bierce's every move. Following Bierce when he leaves his office, he sees the man alter his appearance by changing his clothes and his hairstyle. Via a listening bug concealed in a cigarette packet, Drake overhears Bierce telephoning his wife with the excuse that he will not be home until the following day: he is having a late dinner with a colleague. The colleague, Drake discovers, is Penny, an attractive blonde. Having kept an overnight watch on the girl's apartment with Esser, his M9 contact in Paris, Drake sees his quarry leave Penny's apartment block the following morning. Disguised as an encyclopaedia salesman, Drake gains entrance to the woman's flat. Penny is very amorous and immediately makes overtures to her guest. Spotting a photograph of Bierce sitting on the woman's sideboard, Drake comments that there is something familiar about him. He asks Penny if her boyfriend plays poker? Yes, she replies, indicating that the man she knows as Nigel plays often, and never loses.

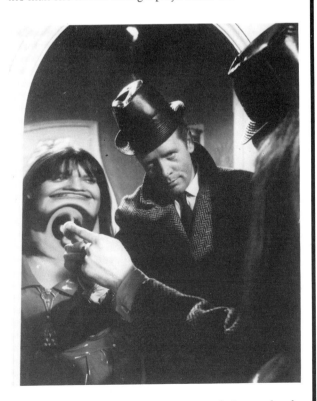

'The Mirror's New', *says actress Nicola Pagett, thereby pointing the finger at a murderer*

Bierce, meanwhile, having returned to his office, is told by Frances that Bonn wishes to speak with him. The Chancellor's news that two pages of the Dillon Report are missing astounds the man. Frances suggests to Bierce that he may have mislaid them while suffering from loss of memory. He has no option but to return to the apartment in which he killed the money lender – leading Drake to his secret hideaway. Frustrated when he is unable to find the missing pages, Bierce climbs into his car and leaves. It takes Drake but a few seconds to gain entrance to the apartment, but a search of the place reveals little beyond the name Dupoirier, which Drake finds scribbled in Bierce's address book. About to leave, Drake is disturbed by the arrival of a pretty young girl named Nicola. Surprised to find Drake in Nigel's apartment, the girl asks the stranger if he is one of her boyfriend's colleagues? Confirming that he is, Drake tells the girl that 'Nigel' has been injured in a fall: he has concussion. Hearing the girl comment that Nigel has replaced the mirror in his lounge, he prods the mirror with his finger: it is plastic. Getting rid of the girl by giving her some money to buy breakfast, Drake visits the premises named in Bierce's address book. A mistake. Arriving there, the thugs he had seen earlier follow him and knock him unconscious. Recovering his senses, he opens his eyes to find himself staring at a photograph held under his nose by one of the thugs. The picture is of the man killed by Bierce. Interrogated by the men, Drake is unable to answer their questions and when the men overplay their inquisition techniques he falls into a stupor. Recovering, he finds the place stripped of both furniture and belongings: the men have gone. Back at his hotel, he receives a visit from Bierce. He has been talking to Penny and wishes to know why Drake followed him: has Drake told Sir Jeremy about his gambling and extra-marital activities? Confirming that he has not, but will be doing so, Drake tricks the man into believing that he has not yet finished his investigation. A second visit to Bierce's secret apartment brings Drake face-to-face with the dead man, Dupoirier, whom he finds hidden behind the mirror Nicola brought to his attention. But the game is up and Bierce enters the apartment before Drake can leave. The man plies Drake with drinks. He turns on the hi-fi and, at gunpoint, orders Drake to sit. Unable to restrain himself, Bierce spills the beans and describes how he enjoyed killing Dupoirier. He now intends to bring about the M9 man's death in the same way. Drake, however, is not so easily trapped. His host turns up the volume to blot out the sound of the gunshot and, as the record reaches a crescendo, Drake disconnects the hi-fi's lead with his foot and springs at his would-be-assassin. Throwing Bierce across the room with a well-aimed kick, Drake leaps after the man. But Bierce escapes – straight into the arms of the men who have pursued him. Two shots ring out simultaneously and the killer slumps down the stairway leading to his apartment, landing in a crumpled heap at Drake's feet.

PARALLEL LINES SOMETIMES MEET

Teleplay by Malcolm Hulke

additional dialogue by Ralph Smart

Starring

Nicola Tarasova	**Moira Redmond**
Dessiles	**Errol John**
Darcy	**Earl Cameron**
Lieutenant Labaste	**Clifton Jones**
James Owen	**Paul Danquah**

with

Victor N'Dias	**Christopher Carlos**
Madame Celeste	**Pearl Prescod**
David Elliot	**Robert Dean**
Vernon Brooks	**Edward Brayshaw**
Mrs Elliot	**Margaret Nolan**
Nero	**Boscoe Holder**
Eirlys Brooks	**Janet Hargreaves**
Guard	**Louis Mahoney**
Anarchist	**Joseph Layode**

Directed by Don Chaffey

WHEN VERNON BROOKS and his wife Eirlys, both employed on atomic weapons research, are hijacked while visiting a quiet English seaport, there is every indication that they have been taken to the West Indies. Posing as John West, a journalist, Drake arrives at Port Au Prince, where, at his hotel, he meets his contact Darcy. Suggesting that the couple Drake is looking for may have defected to the enemy, the M9 man dispels this idea, but agrees with his contact that they have to close every bolt-hole: should the Brooks be found on Tahitian soil, the government will not grant an extradition order. Almost immediately, Drake finds himself involved with another mystery. A body is washed ashore, and a strikingly beautiful young woman who calls herself Madame Courcel, claims that the victim is her husband. Drake, however, contests her claim, putting in a counterbid for the body as being an Englishman named William Hassel. He has very good grounds for disbelieving everything the woman claims. Shown by Darcy where the dead man's body was found, Drake finds himself on a private estate. He is turned away by a guard, but retreats to a secluded spot in the forest and steals back to the house, entering the grounds by swinging over the perimeter fence from a branch of a tree overlooking the estate. But his foot accidentally trips the alarm and he soon finds himself pursued through the grounds by several armed guards. Backtracking, he gives his pursuers the slip, arriving outside the house as a limousine draws up to its entrance. He flicks open the vehicle's rear door and slips into the rear seat. Driven by a chauffeur, the vehicle collects its passenger, a police officer, and Drake slips away unseen by the driver. Back at his hotel, Drake meets Madame Celeste, a coloured woman who appears to know of his interest in the dead man. He listens to her fanciful story of zombies working in the mines operated by Dessiles, the son of Papa Dessiles, a man with great power who recently died. Drake returns to his room. It is here that Elliot, an English artist, introduces himself and invites

Drake to share a pot of tea with himself and his wife. From something Elliot says during their conversation, it becomes clear to Drake that the man was at the English seaport from which the Brooks were kidnapped. Calling at Madame Courcel's room, Drake is told that she will not stand by while he interferes with her claim for her husband's body. The point is rammed home when Drake receives a visit from Lieutenant Labaste, the policeman whom the chauffeur had collected earlier: the island cannot get involved in other people's quarrels, Drake is told. He is then ordered to leave first thing in the morning. However, when the M9 man insists that Labaste must sign a declaration stating that he has ordered him to leave, the man softens his approach and tells Drake that he can go. Later, when Drake receives a telephone call from Darcy, Labaste is monitoring their conversation, but the policeman hears gibberish: Drake has scrambled the call while recording Darcy's news. Played back, the message confirms his suspicion that the dead man was a Russian atomic scientist who disappeared without trace and is suspected by the Russians of having defected. Returning to Madame Courcel's room, Drake forces the woman to admit that she is, in fact, Nicola Tarasova, a Russian agent. They have mutual objectives: Drake to discover what has happened to the Brooks, and Nicola to find out if the dead body is that of the missing scientist. For once, two people who might be expected to be working against each other find that parallel lines sometimes meet. Inevitably, each tries to outwit the other, but their joint operation leads to some interesting discoveries. It now transpires that one of Dessiles' ships is likely to have been used to bring the Brooks to the West Indies, and it is more than probable that the same man had something to do with the death of the Russian. Accepting an invitation to join Dessiles for supper, the mine owner escorts Drake and Nicola around his property and shipping wharf, taking great pride in telling them that he graduated in engineering in England. However, the appearance on the scene of a coloured anarchist named Victor N'Dias, a member of an African organisation which is very anxious to

have nuclear power at its disposal, throws a new light on Dessiles' activities. Returning to his hotel, Drake secretly pockets the key to Elliot's room and, leaving Nicola to make conversation with the English couple, he sneaks upstairs to search their quarters. Discovered in the act of doing so by David Elliot, Drake accuses the artist of having lied when he denied that he was in the vicinity when the Brooks' were kidnapped. Faced with evidence to the contrary, Elliot pulls a gun on Drake, but a powerful blow sends the man sprawling. Drake is joined by Nicola in his bedroom. The girl is showing him a map of the location of Dessiles' mine, when Lieutenant Labaste enters the room. He has learned the truth about Drake's activities from Darcy, who has been arrested. When Drake begs the man to give them 24 hours to complete their enquiries, the policeman agrees. That evening, side by side with his Russian accomplice, Drake gains entrance to the mine. Finding his progress blocked by a newly-erected cement barrier, the M9 man hacks his way through it with a discarded coal-pick. He finds the missing atomic scientists, locked in a cell and protected by a guard. Signalling for them to wait while he engineers their escape route, Drake sets about enlarging the hole he has already hacked through the cement. But one of the prisoners accidentally sets off the escape siren and, escorted by Dessiles, several uniformed guards flood into the pit shaft. Too late: the prisoners have already made their way through the escape hatch provided by Drake. Remaining behind to tackle the guards, Drake is almost buried alive when the roof of the mine collapses, burying Dessiles, and his dreams beneath the tons of falling earth. Their mission complete, Nicola and her 'comrade' climb upwards to freedom.

Finding Drake searching his room, Elliot pulls a gun. A scene from Parallel Lines Sometimes Meet

YOU ARE NOT IN ANY TROUBLE, ARE YOU?

Teleplay by Philip Broadley

Starring

Lena	**Susan Hampshire**
Enzo Bandone	**Andre Van Gyseghem**
Ernesto	**John Cazabon**
Dave	**Bill Edwards**

with

Ellis	**Jeremy Burnham**
Emmerson	**John Welsh**
Receptionist	**Robert Rietty**
Old man	**Andreas Malandrinos**
Barman	**Frank Coda**
Fausto	**Tony Baron**
Left Luggage Clerk	**Harry Tardios**
Boy in Bar	**Ray Barron**
Bell Boy	**Paul Layton**
Masan	**Burt Kwouk**

Directed by Don Chaffey

IN ROOM 600 of a hotel in Rome, Bill Ellis, a British agent who is investigating the death of another agent, Garwood, transmits a message to London: 'I can now state categorically that Garwood's death was not an accident. If you place a message in the personal column of the newspaper *Il Globe*, the message to read "Wolf contact Carl", you will be approached by . . .' His transmission is cut short by the arrival of a man he knows as Dave who, clubbing Ellis to the floor, lifts the unconscious agent's body to his shoulders, walks calmly to the window, and hurtles Ellis to his death on the sidewalk many floors below. At the British Embassy in Rome, Drake – or, for the term of this investigation, Harris – is informed by Embassy official Emmerson, that Ellis' departure has been classed as death by misadventure, due to an excess of alcohol. However, when he points out that the inventory of the dead agent's belongings makes no reference to an electric razor, Drake informs him that Ellis would not have let it out of his sight. Drake smells a rat. The razor, in reality a tape-recorder used by M9 agents in the field to dictate their reports, must have been hidden by Ellis prior to his death: in his hotel bedroom perhaps? Drake secures a room as close as possible to the one occupied by Ellis – room 603. He soon works out that Emmerson would have concealed the device in the room's air conditioner. Drake must retrieve it. But how? His main problem is getting into the room, which is now occupied by an attractive young woman named Lena. On the pretext of returning a glove he has 'found' outside the girl's room, Lena accepts his apology when the glove turns out to be a man's glove; although she is not too concerned, having drunk too much to care, anyway. A little later on, she enters Drake's room to ask for a sleeping pill. Her sleeplessness, she confides, can be attributed to a charming prince whose attentions have ceased abruptly. The pill Drake gives her is a strong one: strong enough for her to collapse on his bed. Picking her up, he takes Lena back to her room and retrieves the razor from the air conditioning unit. Played back, it contains the message about Garwood, and Drake obeys the instructions. Lena,

meanwhile, having recovered from her enforced slumber, shows signs of interest when, sharing a drink with Drake, he explains that he is in Rome to write a book. The reply to the message he has placed in the *Il Globe*, tells him to be at the main entrance of the city's railroad terminus at 10 o'clock the following morning. While purchasing a travel book from a bookstand, a message announced on the platform's public address system informs him that 'Wolf' is waiting to meet him at the car park outside: he is to look for a black Mercedes. The car has no occupant, just a two-way radio over which come the instructions for the amount due and the method of payment, with the questions – who is for disposal and when and where does he want the job to be done? Giving the unseen caller the name of the intended victim as Clive Harris (thereby placing his own head into a noose), he gives the name of his hotel and requests that the man be disposed of as quickly as possible. Confirming that the job will be done upon receipt of the first payment, the voice on the radio breaks transmission. Emmerson is astonished when Drake asks for $10,000 as payment for his own death. He can hardly believe his own ears when Drake adds that this sum is just the deposit: the M9 man will collect the remainder soon. Having commissioned the Murder Incorporated organisation to bump him off, Drake sits back to await developments. When they arrive, they take an unexpected course. Handed his mail by the hotel's receptionist, he tears open an envelope containing a left-luggage ticket, which advises him to take the murder fee to a left-luggage counter, at 3 o'clock that afternoon. Unfortunately, when he arrives at the railway station, Lena races after him, asking him if he is in some sort of trouble: she had knocked on his door earlier and, although she was certain that he was in the room, he did not answer. Telling the girl that he simply wanted to be alone, he arranges to see her later that evening in the American Bar. Having handed over the left-luggage ticket, Drake is given a small package. He tears it open to find a portable transmitter inside with a note saying 'switch on'. He does so, and a voice tells him to sit on a bench by the magazine stand: someone there will relieve him of the briefcase he carries with him. Placing himself next to an elderly man who has his suitcase balanced on his knee, he is soon joined by a beautiful brunette, but it appears that neither person is his contact. Within seconds of taking his seat, the voice on the radio tells him that the man he wants is standing at the news-stand: he will be approached and he is to hand over the briefcase. But as Drake rises to greet the stranger, the other man walks right past him! Drake looks back at his seat, and his briefcase has vanished! (Unseen by Drake, the elderly man seated next to him has 'lifted' the briefcase into a spring-loaded compartment hidden in the base of his suitcase.) Told by the voice that 'they' have the money and that he can keep the radio as a token of their efficiency, Drake returns to his hotel. He dictates a message into his own razor-cum-tape machine: he intends to stick around and give the organisation the opportunity to kill him. In this way, he hopes to net the little fish that will lead him to the big one. Emmerson has been informed, and he is keeping his fingers crossed. So, incidentally, is Drake. However, once again his plan is thwarted by the arrival to his hotel room of Lena, who is proving to be a very persistent young lady. A mysterious individual named Ernesto, who says he has information that will prove of inestimable value to the research material Drake is gathering for his book, tells Drake about Enzo Bandone who, later enquiries reveal, is a very respectable citizen, aged 80, who emigrated to the United States and has since returned to his native Italy.

In this scene from You're Not In Any Trouble, Are You? *Lena obligingly enters Drake's bedroom to ask for a sleeping pill*

While Drake is learning this. Dave. the assassin who killed Ellis. arrives at Drake's hotel and books into room 611. Once there. he dons the disguise of an hotel house boy. When Drake returns to his room. Dave calmly enters. asking if it is convenient to change the towels and draw the curtains. Yes. says Drake. becoming instantly alert when the man calls him to the window to look down at a woman who 'was once the most beautiful girl in Rome'. Once again Lena's unexpected arrival saves the day. Tricking the man into admitting that he does not actually work at the hotel. Drake pounces on the would-be killer as he attempts to leave. But Lena gets in the way and the man escapes. Drake's next step is to visit Bandone. Giving the excuse that Drake wishes to interview him for the book he is writing. Fausto. Bandone's butler. fetches his master. Although he is old and crippled. Bandone soon shows that he still has his wits about him. He asks Drake: 'Why did you arrange to have yourself killed?' 'So I could find you.' answers Drake. He scorns the man's earlier attempt to have him disposed of: will his assassin be using the same feeble technique this time? In answer to Drake's question. a door at the far end of the room slides open and Masan. the crippled man's Oriental assassin marches into the room. Aware that the game is about to begin. Drake asks Bandone who hired him to kill Garwood and Ellis? Delighted to respond. the other replies that he will give Drake the other name. if he in turn tells him who put Drake on his tail. With neither man willing to name

their source. it is stalemate – unless Masan can persuade Drake otherwise. The Oriental is a master of his art – fighting with a type of curved sabre – and what is left of Drake after the encounter will make succulent eating for the crabs. Stating that he is looking forward to the challenge. Bandone orders Masan to 'do it slowly'. At this command. Masan hands Drake his weapon and lunges at the undercover man who almost instantly receives a cut on his forehead from his opponent's blade. He counters Masan's next move with one of his own. Shoved backwards by Drake's angry thrusts. the Oriental lunges at his opponent. sending the undercover man's weapon flying to the floor. Exasperated with Drake's unbowing determination. Bandone sinks his teeth into his cigar as Masan closes in for the kill. Grabbing Masan by the coat sleeve. Drake counters the man's thrust and heaves the Oriental over his shoulder. sending him crashing down on Bandone's hand as. anticipating the outcome of the contest. the crippled man reaches into a drawer of his desk to snatch up a revolver. The shock of defeat proves too great for Bandone's heart and. clutching his chest. he slumps across his desk in a lifeless heap. One final heave and Masan lies unconscious at the foot of the staircase up which he was trying to escape. Having telephoned Emmerson to inform him that the murder cartel has been smashed. Drake returns to his hotel to collect his passport – and the persistent advances of Lena.

THE OUTCAST

Teleplay by Donald Jonson

Starring

Leo Perrins	**Bernard Bresslaw**
Nora Cazalet	**Patricia Haines**
Xavier	**Brian Worth**
Helen Cazalet	**Judy Geeson**

with

Commander Marsden	**Richard Caldicott**
The Stranger	**Stephen Yardley**
Sandra	**Anita West**
'Dead' man	**Frederick Abbott**
Lieutenant Barrington	**Caron Gardner**
Spanish Bus Official	**Paul Armstrong**
Ramon	**Tony Lee**
Flamenco Dancer	**Marina Vasquez**

Directed by Michael Truman

THE MURDER OF Petty Officer Sandra Smith of the WRENS outside the gates of her barracks in Gibraltar, is of sufficient interest to Drake's superiors to bring the M9 agent into the case. Sandra had coded signal documents in her handbag — messages intended only for the eyes of senior command staff, as well as top secret material that her department had no official access to. Told by Commander Marsden that three days after Sandra's death a radio operator named Leo Perrins went absent without official leave, Drake is assigned to find the deserter and, by winning his confidence, trick him into admitting that he killed the girl. Perrins should not be difficult to find: he is 6ft 5in, speaks no Spanish and should stick out like a sore thumb. Having established that the sailor has crossed the border into Spain, Drake eventually finds him in a Spanish fishing village, where he is working in the kitchen of a cafe run by an Englishwoman, Nora Cazalet. Drake does not like anything to do with the set-up — the obvious relationship between Nora Cazalet and a good-looking waiter named Xavier, the fact that Xavier is forcing his attentions on Nora's bored teenage daughter Helen and the jealousy this is causing, and the fact that he has got to win Leo's friendship in the hope of trapping him. However, a job is a job, and Drake soon becomes friendly with the boy, and ends up liking the simple-minded sailor who is at best, conscientious and emotionally immature — an illegitimate, who ran away from home to join the navy. The arrival at Drake's hotel of a mysterious stranger sees the M9 man keeping the newcomer under constant surveillance — a job made easier when Commander Marsden assigns Lieutenant Barrington, one of his security staff to help Drake. A pretty young WRENS officer, she keeps in contact with Drake via a walkie-talkie and has the stranger in her sights when he leaves the hotel. Having planted a miniature viewing device in the man's room — the apartment walls offer no resistance to Drake's cleverly-designed razor-cum-tape recorder-cum-electric drill — the M9 agent is able to observe the stranger lying in wait and ready to shoot Leo as the sailor carries drinks into the man's room. Drake overpowers and disarms the man but the stranger manages to escape by leaping from the balcony outside his window. The attack on Leo's life indicates that he is mixed up in something, but what?

Somehow or other, Drake must trick the sailor into admitting his guilt and, if possible, the name of his contact. It is now that the affair takes a dramatic turn. Told by Helen Cazalet that Leo has been sacked, Drake trails his quarry to the local bus depot where, informed that the bus is delayed, Drake suggests that Leo kills time by sharing a drink with him in the cantina. Later, when Leo offers to pay for his round, he discovers that his wallet has been stolen (Drake has taken it). He is delighted to accept when Drake says that he can share his room: he has a spare cot and he would enjoy the company. By playing on Leo's simple-mindedness, Drake, with Lieutenant Barrington's help, dupes his room mate into believing that he has seen a ghost of the dead girl; that he has seen Drake kill a man, and that Drake is out to double-cross him. Back at the cafe, meanwhile, a furious quarrel breaks out between Nora and Xavier over the man's attentions to Helen. Furious when Xavier makes no attempt to deny her claim, Mrs Cazalet orders him to leave. It is now that Xavier shows his true colours. Finding Drake's spying equipment, together with the photographs of Sandra Smith, he gleefully arranged them in full view of anyone entering Drake's bedroom. The first to arrive is Leo, who catching sight of the objects and aware now that Drake is a spy, is waiting for him when the M9 man returns to the hotel. Confused by what has happened, the simple-minded Leo comes clean: he killed the girl because she was seeing a man named Rodriguez, the man to whom she was passing naval secrets. He had caught them in a compromising position and killed Sandra in a fit of rage. Although he feels sympathy for the boy's story, Drake has no option but to return him to the naval base where Leo is handed over to the authorities.

In The Outcast, *Drake keeps a careful watch on the stranger in the adjoining room*

THE MERCENARIES

Teleplay by Ralph Smart

Starring

Caroline Winter	Patricia Donahue
Prime Minister	John Slater
Sergeant Bates	Percy Herbert
General G'Niore	Peter Arne
Dr Winter	Frederick Peisley
General White	Jack Gwillim
Pierre Deschamps	John Gabriel
Colonel Coote	Derrick DeMarney
Sinclair Jones	Zia Moyheddin

with

Hawkinson	Dervis Ward
Buchanan	Shane Rimmer
Brewster	Patrick Jordan
Cleaner	Paul Danquah
Receptionist	Zorenia Osborne
PM's Secretary	Christopher Carlos
Police Officer	David Lander
Lab Assistant	Heather Emmanuel
Boscoe Holder	Boscoe Holder

Directed by Don Chaffey

THE ACTIVITIES IN Africa of 'Crazy Coote's Commandos', a daredevil volunteer army organised and run by the swaggering Colonel Coote, are the cause of considerable uneasiness to British War Department circles. Department M9 have planted an agent, Johnson, among the mercenaries. Johnson winds up dead, mowed down by the sadistic Sergeant Bates. Drake enters the scene on an assignment to infiltrate Coote's troops and report on their activities. He does so by having General White, a retired military man,' supply him with false army papers and then answering a newspaper advertisement placed by Brewster, the man who vets and enlists Coote's new recruits. In the guise of John Atlee, Drake soon finds himself deep in the African bush and it is not long before he has his first run-in with Sergeant Bates who, in order to test the new recruit's reactions under 'enemy' fire, calmly removes the firing pin from a hand grenade and throws it in Drake's direction. Neatly catching the explosive device, Drake immediately drops to the ground and throws the grenade into the trees, a move greeted with mirth by Bates' men who, aware that their leader is simply testing the newcomer with a dummy grenade, give Drake a round of raucous applause. Reminded by Colonel Coote that his men serve in a private army, and that there is no member of parliament to run to if he finds himself in trouble, the newcomer is dismissed. Recognising Drake as a cut above the rest of his soldiers, Bates informs Drake that they should become friends: he can make a good ally or a bad enemy. They can help each other. Drake helping him sometimes, Bates helping him all the time. Replying that he is nobody's fool, Drake dismisses the Sergeant's request with a smile. The following morning, when Drake is selected in preference to the others to hand out the mail, Buchanan and Deschamps, two of the mercenaries, tease him for having become the Sergeant's new pet. Overhearing this, Bates takes no action; he has other things on his mind. Hawkinson, a private, requests that he be given compassionate leave: his father has died and he wishes to attend his funeral. Flatly refusing the man's request by stating that no one can leave: they could be moving at any time, Bates abruptly dismisses the man. Later that night, when a man named Doctor Winter enters the Colonel's tent, Drake, suspects that something big is being planned, something of significant interest to his masters. Unseen, he steals into Coote's tent and takes photographs of the men with his miniature camera. At reveille the following morning, he learns how ruthless Bates can be when, discovering that Hawkinson has deserted, the Sergeant has Drake drive him after the man. Hawkinson is soon tracked down and Bates attempts to teach him a lesson by lashing him with a bullwhip. But Drake intervenes and gives Bates a lesson in fisticuffs. Leaving the beaten man tied to a tree, Drake drives Hawkinson away in the Sergeant's jeep – Bates' words that he will see them dead ringing in their ears. Sinclair Jones, Drake's contact in Mondow answers the M9 man's request for an introduction to the Prime Minister, by saying it will take some time to organise. The photograph Drake shows him for identification purposes proves to be an easier request: the man pictured with Colonel Coote is Doctor Winter, who runs the country's only hospital. This gives Drake the opportunity to follow up the clues he has by visiting Winter's home and in so doing, meeting the doctor's amorous and neglected wife, Caroline. Over tea, the woman can hardly keep her hands off the newcomer, but her overtures are cut short when Winter arrives. After handing the man several copies of the photograph he took earlier, Drake returns to his car where, via a listening device he has planted next to the doctor's phone, he overhears Winter asking someone called the General to meet him at the hospital. Arriving there, Drake bluffs his way past the girl at the reception desk and enters an elevator, intending to go to the room above. However, while doing so, a military man enters the elevator and asks to be taken to the third floor. Seeing the soldier enter Doctor Winter's surgery, the M9 man returns to the ground floor and asks the receptionist for the name of his fellow passenger. The man was General G'Niore, next in line to rule the independent country should anything happen to the Prime Minister. The Prime Minister has sent a policeman to escort Drake to his residence. Arriving at the mansion, Drake is greeted by the man's private secretary – and a witch doctor, who, dressed in a menacing ensemble of beads and straw, his head covered by a frightening voodoo mask, greets the guest with an incantation. Led into the Prime Minister's bedroom, the M9 man finds his host sitting up in bed removing a thermometer from his lips. Although Westernised and well-educated, the man has one failing. He is a hypochondriac and is one of Doctor Winter's prize patients. Drake learns that he is now awaiting a major operation. The Prime Minister admits that he has called in Coote's mercenaries, to save his people from anarchy – should he die, all the chieftains would make a bid for power. The white mercenaries will maintain the status quo while General G'Niore, who now enters the room, establishes himself. This astounds Drake. Theorising that the General and Doctor Winter are conspiring to get the Prime Minister into the hospital for an operation that will go wrong – leaving him a helpless cripple or, worse still for Britain and America's interests, dead, he takes his leave determined to keep a close eye on future events. Back at his hotel he finds Mrs Winter waiting for him. Aware that the woman wishes to get to know him better, the M9 man informs her that he does not want to upset her husband in case he becomes ill and requires treatment. Mrs Winter states that her husband is far too busy playing around with his hospital and the whims of General G'Niore who, at this very moment is at their home with some idiot Colonel or other. Drake finds an excuse to leave. With the help of Sinclair Jones, who keeps the hospital's receptionist busy while he slips into Doctor Winter's surgery, Drake confirms his suspicions that the men are conspiring together to contrive the Prime Minister's death. Unfortunately, he is seen leaving the building and an alarmed medico alerts General G'Niore of what has taken place. When Drake drives to the Prime Minister's home, the General is waiting to tell him that the patient has already been taken to the hospital; Drake cannot see him until after the operation. Nevertheless, at gunpoint, the General allows Drake to drive him to the hospital where, warned not to interfere, Drake throws his ex-mercenary comrade Buchanan, who is now guarding the hospital's entrance, aside and races inside — to find himself face to face with the sadistic Sergeant Bates. Ordered to dispense with the intruder, the soldier takes great delight in ordering his men to dig Drake's final resting place. But the M9 man outsmarts them. Slipping an incendiary device from beneath his jacket, he turns the tables on the military men and Bates meets his death when a bullet fired at Drake enters the Sergeant's heart. Racing outside, Drake makes a daredevil polevault through a first storey window. Overpowering Bates' men as he goes, he spots the witch doctor in an ante room. Drake hits on a plan. In the operating theatre, drugged by Doctor Winter, the Prime Minister sits up in alarm as the witch doctor enters, scattering aside the men placed on guard. His mask is raised — it is Drake, who under the General's scornful stare, leads the Prime Minister to safety.

Having given The Mercenaries *the slip, Drake finds himself at the mercy of General G'Niore*

STING IN THE TAIL

Teleplay by Philip Broadley

Starring

Alexandros	**Ronald Radd**
Noureddine	**Derren Nesbitt**
James	**John Standing**
Marie Valedon	**Jeanne Roland**
Stephen Miller	**David Collings**
Shah of Assini	**Jeremy Spenser**

with

Police Inspector Roget	**Julian Somers**
Sir Alan	**Andrew Laurence**
Daphne Miller	**Mary Webster**
Bulack	**Ernst Ulman**
Michele	**Juliet Harmer**
Model	**Christine Child**
Messadi	**Neville Becker**
Cafe Owner	**Jose Berlinka**
Airport Clerk	**Zeynep Tarimer**

Directed by Peter Yates

WAKENED BY A telephone call from Police Inspector Roget, Drake telephones Beirut and tells James, a colleague, that the Shah of Assini has been assassinated in his Paris hotel bedroom by Noureddine. Why was Drake not informed that the assassin had left Beirut? Confirming that Noureddine might have slipped out of the country unseen, James answers his colleague's enquiry by stating that Marie Valedon, the assassin's girlfriend is still in Beirut; Noureddine is bound to come back for her. Saying that he will be arriving the next day, Drake rings off. His next step is to collect a watch from Bulack, one of his Department contacts. No ordinary watch this: by lifting its winder, a sharp needle springs from the centre of its dial. A flick of the wrist and the victim is paralysed; pressure on its back, a half-turn of the winder, and the timepiece returns to its normal function. A work of art, says Drake, strapping the watch to his wrist. Step two finds the M9 man calling at the studio of artist Stephen Miller. His wife, Daphne, is delighted when the stranger offers to buy every painting in the room, as well as the artist's easel, palette, brushes, paints — everything in fact, on the proviso that Stephen will draw him a charcoal sketch of the head of a woman whose photograph Drake produces. Arriving in Beirut, Drake poses as a penniless artist. He takes a studio in a house run by Alexandros, a colourful Greek, who takes great pleasure in drink, sleep and women, though not necessarily in that order. Later that evening, James arrives at Drake's room to inform his colleague that Noureddine is not expected to remain in Beirut for more than a few days. The men need at least a fortnight to get the assassin out, so Drake must take a desperate chance and move in at once. The best way of bringing the assassin into the open, he feels, is through Marie Valedon, who works at the local nightclub as a singer. Drake visits the club and gives Marie the charcoal drawing he pretends he has made of her. He suggests that she may like to pose for him, but she is reluctant to agree. However, when Noureddine arrives, he tells the artist that he might be able to arrange the sitting for him — as long as he agrees to make no further approaches of his own. That evening, Drake receives an invitation to visit Noureddine's home, but the undercover man walks into a trap. Two of Noureddine's men, the brothers Messadi are waiting for him. Binding his wrists tightly to a chair, they gag him and beat Drake within an inch of his life. The experience is painful, but suits Drake's plans perfectly. He has made Noureddine jealous, and a jealous man makes mistakes. With Alexandros' help, the M9 man puts his own plan into operation – a plan to make the assassin believe that Marie has run away to Paris with Drake. The infatuated Noureddine is bound to follow. Drake asks James to contact Police Inspector Roget with the news that the assassin will soon be on home ground. That night, Drake joins his quarry at a table in the nightclub. Jesting that he now walks with a slight limp because he 'fell' rather awkwardly earlier that evening, Drake baits the assassin with his durability and the words that Marie would be surprised if she knew the real reason for his injuries. Joined by the girl, Drake rubs salt into the wound by adding that her boyfriend has agreed to allow her to sit for him. Not wanting Marie to know the truth, Noureddine is forced to concede to Drake's request. Followed by the Messadi brothers, Drake and the girl leave. Aware that he is under surveillance, the undercover man boldly crosses the road to the Messadis' car and rips out the vehicle's ignition lead. About to grab Drake, the brothers' attention is drawn to the fact that a policeman stands nearby. Holding aloft the torn-out wiring, Drake climbs into his car and speeds away with Marie beside him – leaving the brothers to explain to the police exactly what was going on. Informed of the incident, a furious Noureddine storms out of his home in pursuit of his girlfriend. Meanwhile, Drake and the girl are sharing an indoor picnic at Alexandros' home. Inside the girl's apartment, James is stowing Marie's clothes for her 'trip' to Paris. Drake tells the girl the truth about her boyfriend – that he is a ruthless, uncaring assassin. Marie is hurt by Drake's deception and begs to be allowed to leave. Insisting that she remains at Alexandros' home until he calls her from Paris to say that Noureddine has arrived, Drake leaves. Marie's boyfriend, meanwhile, having unsuccessfully scoured the city for his sweetheart, enters the girl's apartment expecting the worst. Finding her wardrobe stripped of her clothes, he appears to take the bait. However, the assassin holds a trump card. He finds Marie's teddy bear – a good luck charm which she would never have left behind – and is waiting for Drake when the M9 man arrives at Marie's apartment to collect her luggage. But for the teddy, Noureddine tells him, he would have been on a flight for Paris. Pulling a gun on Drake, the assassin tells him he must die: in a drunken brawl with Alexandros, the man whose body is now being carried into the room by the Messadi boys. But Drake, too, has a trump card. Slipping the wristwatch handed to him by Bulack, to the front of his wrist, he springs at the assassin like a panther, cutting down the Messadi brothers as he does so. Drake destroys the assassin's carefully laid plans in a flurry of flying feet and fists. Grabbing a knife dropped to the floor during the mêlée, Noureddine turns on Drake, but a knife thrown by Alexandros puts paid to the assassin's career. Surveying the destruction in the apartment and the unconscious bodies of the Messadi brothers, the Greek turns to his tenant and states that he needs a Cognac!

A VERY DANGEROUS GAME

Teleplay by Ralph Smart and David Stone

Starring

Lisa Lee	Yvonne Furneaux
Chi Ling	Peter Arne
Suzy	Poulet Tu
Simpson	Anthony Dawson
Khim	Burt Kwouk
Dickinson	Geoffrey Bayldon
Comdr Corbett	Dennis Ramsden

with

George	Charles Carson
British Controller	Mike Pratt
Pauline	Norma West
Questioner	Anthony Chinn
Wardrobe Master	Cyril Chamberlain
Arthur	Christopher Sandford
Watcher	Cecil Cheng
Gunman	Paul Tann
Hostess	Mona Chong
Young Man in Bar	Harry Brookes
Second Hostess	Yu-Ling
Barman	Tommy Yap
Manservant	Donald Chan

Directed by Don Chaffey

IN LONDON, academic Peter Simpson, a man who lectures around the world for the British Cultural Mission, shares a drink with an attractive blonde named Pauline. Their fellow guests have left and Simpson is intent on wooing the girl. Plying her with drinks, he tells her that he is going out to Singapore on a lecture mission. His friends believe that he is wasting his time by accepting such a meagre job, but this time he will show them. The job he has waiting is very big: one that will show his friends, who think they rule the roost, just who are the masters. If Pauline plays her cards right, she can join him out there. The girl plays her cards, but not the hand that the romeo expected. Within seconds, Pauline has thrown Simpson over her shoulder. Landing with a bump on the carpet, he sees the girl about to leave and, determined to continue the game, Simpson races towards her – straight into the arms of two uniformed men, who take the surprised man into custody. Pauline is an M9 agent, and Simpson has unwittingly paved the way for John Drake to take his place and be sent to Singapore to meet his Chinese masters in an attempt to infiltrate the top level opposition Intelligence. But first Drake must visit the Department's 'back-room boys'. Told by George, M9's documents expert, that he must remember that he is attempting a most dangerous game, Drake confirms that he intends to stay alive by all means available to him. One of these 'means' is the undercover man's new 'pipe', a smoking device which has been adapted by Arthur, the Department's armourer. This now has a concealed electronics system – completely insulated, of course. To activate the cell, Drake must turn the stem 180 degrees anti-clockwise. By removing the denture stem the pipe can be used as a blowpipe, firing a miniature radio dart that will transmit a signal that lasts for up to 12 hours. By using the direction-finder attached to Drake's personal radio, he can then locate the dart's approximate distance from his transmitter. Tuned to a wavelength they have chosen for him, there should not be any interference in Singapore. As Arthur points out, there is more – the real box of tricks – but Drake does not have time to look into the satchel the armourer hands to him, telling the man to have it ready for his departure. The Department's wardrobe master has an exact replica of Simpson's herringbone sports jacket, and a lightweight trilby hat completes Drake's wardrobe. His contact in Singapore is an exotic Chinese girl named Lisa Lee, who he meets after making the acquaintance of the man for whom, as Simpson, Drake is supposed to be working – Harold Dickinson. Director of the British Cultural Mission to Malaysia. Feigning intoxication, Drake is told by Dickinson that he has but a short time to sober up; there is a little get-together at the Embassy at seven o'clock that evening. However, before he visits the Embassy, Lisa takes him to meet the Chinese Controller, Chi Ling. Taken to a basement garage, a black hood is placed over the M9 man's head and he is driven to the Controller's headquarters. Stripped of his clothes – but allowed to retain his pipe, Drake is ushered into Chi Ling's domain. Told that 'Simpson' is not armed, the Oriental informs his guest that if he is ordered to kill, he will kill. A bugging device found in the hollowed-out heel of the visitor's shoe, is explained away as being part of the kit he was supplied with before he left England, and Chi Ling accepts his reasons for transferring his allegiance to them. He reveals that his guest has been sent for because 'I have a bold plan. I intend to infiltrate the British Intelligence Service. I need someone who can move freely among the opposition.' The Oriental's words amuse Drake, who now finds himself in the strange position of being required by both sides to infiltrate the other. However, this is not the only double move. Warning his guest that he distrusts Lisa, he orders Drake to keep an eye on her and report every act of disloyalty immediately. In turn, Lisa is told the same about 'Simpson'. His first assignment, Chi Ling tells him, is to find Commander Corbett, who is said to be posing as a British Naval Attaché, but is, in fact, a spy.

Drake is to introduce Corbett to Lisa, and leave the rest up to her. Further, he should not attend the Embassy party but should instead telephone Commander Corbett and invite him to take a drink with him at his hotel. Drake has now no option but to carry out Chi Ling's orders, and thereby places the Commander in a tight spot: there is no way he can warn the man without breaking his cover. Dismissed by Chi Ling, Drake surreptitiously fires his receiver dart into the room's skirting boards as he leaves the man's office. Once again the hood is placed over his head, and it is not long before he finds himself back at his hotel and rings Corbett as ordered. He succeeds, however, in helping the Commander to escape – which, for Lisa, spells death. Dickinson, meanwhile, disgusted that his new employee has failed to attend the Embassy beanfeast, telephones his drunken assistant and tells the man to sleep it off, they can talk about his absence tomorrow. Via the blow dart receiver, Drake learns the whereabouts of Chi Ling's control room, perched high on top of the Singapore New Press building. This is when Arthur's 'box of tricks', which Drake was unable to inspect earlier, comes into play. Unzipping the satchel, the undercover man slips out several attachments: a tube of aluminium, a dart with a sucker-cup attached to its head, a trigger mechanism, a compressed-air capsule and so on. Within minutes the M9 man holds a compressed-air gun in his hands. Sighting its nozzle at the window of Chi Ling's room, Drake releases the trigger and the sucker-tipped dart flies upwards, attaching itself securely to the ornate glass window of Chi Ling's office. Entering the building via a window adjacent to the men's washroom, Drake climbs out onto the narrow ledge that skirts the newspaper block, and begins to climb upwards. A few minutes later, he succeeds in removing his dart and in slicing his way through the window pane, which allows him to reach inside to open the window catch and gain entry. Finding himself confronted with a bank of tape recorders, he plays each one in turn and records fragments of conversation between Chi Ling and his superior. Later, when these are handed to Khim, an M9 man who shares a hidden spy complex with Peter, the local M9 network Controller brings Drake a surprise. Chi Ling, it appears, has incurred the displeasure of his superior by making his own plans to infiltrate the British Intelligence network in Singapore. Because of his acute embarrassment, Chi Ling has ordered Lisa to be killed. With the help of Lola, an M9 agent posing as a nightclub hostess, Drake determines to do everything in his power to discover the identity of the man who is really running the opposition intelligence. An unexpected opportunity to do this arrives when, having tracked down the location of Peter's control room, Chi Ling arrives and accuses Drake of being a British spy. Using this as bait, the M9 man allows himself to be arrested by Ling's men and taken back to the Oriental's headquarters where, accused by Chi Ling of interfering in his business, the opposition Controller informs Drake that he will be tortured until he coughs up the secrets he possesses. But Drake escapes and drives to Dickinson's home with evidence that he is Chi Ling's superior. Confronted with this, the traitor pulls a gun on his English colleague. A mistake. Having traced Drake to Dickinson's home, and believing that his quarry has led him directly to the head of the *British* intelligence group, Chi Ling shoots Dickinson dead. Sadly for the Oriental, he has unknowingly shot his own Controller – a mistake which will rest heavy on Chi Ling's shoulders when his masters find out!

Assigned to A Very Dangerous Game, *Drake is thankful for any help, particularly from Arthur, the Department's armourer.*

THE BLACK BOOK

Teleplay by Philip Broadley

Starring

Simone	Georgina Ward
Sir Noel	Griffith Jones
Blanchard	
General Carteret	Jack Gwillim
Lady Blanchard	Patricia Haines

with

Serge	Mike Pratt
James	Richard Owens
1st Counter Agent	Frederick Abbot
2nd Counter Agent	Ray Roberts
Business Man	Edward Sinclair
Politician	Beresford Williams

Directed by Michael Truman

DRAKE IS flattered when General Carteret, the man who has requested to see him, tells the M9 man that he has followed Drake's 'remarkable' career with unreserved admiration – praise he does not bestow lightly. Nevertheless, Drake feels that it is not really any concern of his when Carteret offers him the opportunity to take a fortnight's vacation in Paris to investigate a case of blackmail: he is not a crime buster. But the General is far too important to displease, and the blackmail victim is the General's brother-in-law, Sir Noel Blanchard, who holds a high ministerial post in Paris. Carteret wants the blackmailer's claws removed and the crook rendered harmless. If a breath of scandal gets out it will kill his sister and do irreparable damage to Carteret's career: Drake's Department has already been told to grant him indefinite leave, and the M9 man must use absolute discretion when investigating the affair. Drake finds Sir Noel reticent about the reasons for his being blackmailed, but far more forthcoming about the methods used. They are different each time. Detailed instructions are given to him which he has to follow faithfully. The initial instructions come over the telephone from a husky-voiced girl with a French accent. He has already made four payments of 20,000 francs. He cannot go to the police: if the secret came out, the result would be politically disastrous. The money has to be packed in bundles of notes, rolled up in a bag and sent to Sir Noel. He has to stay at home until they call, then he has to go to a place they name and from there he is directed by telephone to go to another rendezvous from where he is moved on from place to place until he is given his final instructions. Drake decides to use M9 methods rather than conventional crime detection routines. He gives Sir Noel a miniature transmitter to hide in his jacket pocket so that they can keep in touch while he is keeping his blackmail money assignment. For additional security he also slips a small transistor bug into the wad of bills that Sir Noel will be carrying with him. Once again Drake has come prepared: this time around, he has a cleverly-constructed typewriter/receiver in his luggage. By using its tab-setting key, he will be able to keep track of Sir Noel's progress. Keeping his surveillance activities secret from Blanchard's wife, Drake is able to follow Sir Noel to the spot where he has been told to leave the money. However, the blackmailers are very ingenious. Sir Noel must place the money into the collar of a harness attached to the back of an alsatian dog, which immediately swims off across a river. Drake, is able to follow the animal's progress as he picks up bleeps from the hidden detector transmitter. There are times when he almost loses the trail – then the bleeps ring out clearly as a sleek open-topped sports car swoops past him at speed. The driver is a girl – Simone, and Drake follows her to her apartment. Telling her coolly that he wishes to be cut in on her racket, he passes himself off as a fellow blackmailer who has gone to a tremendous amount of trouble to collect his own evidence on Sir Noel, only to find that she has beaten him to the pay-off. Simone is about to resist when a sound at the door makes her think that her accomplice has arrived. Instead, there are two strangers, gentlemen of sinister appearance, who shove the girl aside and march into the apartment. After a search, during which they question Drake, but are unable to find what they are looking for, they announce in Russian accents that they want 'The Black Book.' Having taken photographs of the men with his lighter-cum-camera. Drake successfully disposes of them. When Serge, the girl's accomplice, arrives, he accepts Simone's explanation that the apartment has been entered by two thugs and Drake, who happened to be passing at the time, raced in to help. Drake now begins to suspect that the whole matter has quite a different aspect than that which he had been led to believe. This is no ordinary blackmailing case: the fact that Serge is also a Russian has clear implications that this is a matter of interest to M9. Keeping tabs on Serge and his accomplice, he is on hand when Simone picks up further packages from Sir Noel. From James, his contact in Paris, Drake learns that the men he photographed are Russian counter-agents who have orders to keep tabs on Serge, a Russian defector and a one-time minor clerk in the Soviet Intelligence network. M9 have nothing on Simone. By shadowing Serge and the girl at every turn, Drake discovers that the two agents have been sent to bring Serge back to Russia. Using this to his own advantage,

Using his cleverly-adapted typewriter/location finder, Drake keeps tabs on Sir Noel as he drives to hand over payment for The Black Book

Drake convinces Simone that her boyfriend is living on borrowed time: his former job gave him access to confidential information which enabled him to compile a Black Book of Westerners who he could blackmail if he defected to the West. But the girl has no idea where the book can be. Serge has stashed it away in a secret place. What is more, she has had enough and is getting out while the going is good: the thought of being arrested and thrown into a French prison frightens her. Drake, however, has his own ideas as to what to do about Serge. He is determined to beat the Russian counter-agents to the punch. While breakfasting with Sir Noel the following morning, he confronts the Englishman with his view that what he had first considered to be a simple case of blackmail, has now become a matter of interest to M9, and no amount of brow-beating by Sir Noel or his brother-in-law General Carteret will detract Drake from his duty. Furthermore, he refuses all attempts by Sir Noel, to persuade him to divulge the names of the counter-agents who are on his trail: if this leads to an enquiry and Blanchard is recalled to London in disgrace, so be it. Back at his hotel, Drake asks James to ring Serge on the hour every hour threatening, in a Russian accent, that unless he produces the Black Book within 12 hours, he will be killed. Drake calls on the Russian at Simone's apartment. He has come to offer Serge the chance to get off the hook: if the Russian will sell the book to him, Drake will ensure that the men following him will be taken care of. The exchange agreed, Serge drives Drake to a derelict house in the country where, hidden behind the wall lies the Russian's little Black Book. However, at the very moment that the blackmailer turns to hand the incriminating evidence to the M9 man, the Russian counter-agents burst into the room. A fight breaks out and, with a flurry of stinging left and right hooks, the undercover man dispenses with the men. Serge, shot by one of the men during the mêlée, collapses to the floor dead. Casually picking up the Black Book, without so much as a second glance at the Russian, Drake departs in silence.

JUDGEMENT DAY

Teleplay by Donald Jonson
Original story by Michael J. Bird

Starring

Jessica	**Alexandra Stewart**
Shimon	**John Woodvine**
Pilot	**Maurice Kaufmann**
Garriga	**Guy Deghy**
Ygal	**David Saire**

with

James	**Peter Halliday**
Airport Official	**Neville Becker**
Hotel Landlord	**Harold Berens**
David	**Ben-Ari**
Carrier	**Mohhammad Moosa Shamsi**
Driver	**Yashar Adem**
Bookseller	**Bakshi Prem**

Directed by Don Chaffey

ATTEMPTS ON THE life of Dr Raphael Garriga lead to Drake being instructed to escort the medical research scientist back from the Middle East to London. It means chartering a plane to the remote spot where Garriga lives. Meanwhile, Drake finds himself having to knuckle under to extortionate airport clearance taxes imposed by the country's airport official, who firmly states that neither Drake or the plane he has chartered can leave until he has done so. Although Drake is not too concerned about this he is taken aback when the official appears to know that he is there to collect Dr Garriga. However, with only 40 minutes left before darkness falls, he dismisses this and is driven to the doctor's home. Asking his driver to wait, he raps on Garriga's door and introduces himself as the man who has been sent to escort the doctor to England. Garriga, however, suspicious since the attempts on his life, pulls a gun on the newcomer and only when its barrel rests firmly on Drake's back does he agree to accompany the newcomer to the airport. But surprises await them when they reach the plane. The aircraft, they are told, has engine trouble and they cannot leave until the following morning. The pilot meanwhile, has booked rooms for them at a nearby hotel. Garriga, is disturbed by this but, as Drake points out, they have no option but to do as instructed. Shown to their room by the hotel's landlord, Garriga again pulls his gun, indicating to Drake that he must hand over the door keys: he is unsure of the other's identity and feels certain that those who attempted to kill him will do so again. His life, he tells Drake, is not only important to the English government, but to the whole world. Drake must protect him, whatever the cost. Convincing Garriga that he must relay a message to London, Drake is allowed to leave and go downstairs. It is here that he meets an attractive young woman who introduces herself as Jessica Shaw. She claims to be an archaeologist just returning from a survey. After three days in the desert, she is looking forward to three things: a hot bath, a strong drink and someone who speaks

English. Looking around the dilapidated hotel, the place does not appear to offer the first two, but at least she has found Drake. When the pilot arrives and appears to know the girl, Drakes leaves them talking while he rejoins his room mate. Throughout the night, Garriga finds it difficult to sleep, tossing and turning in his bunk and, at one stage during his nightmares, even attempting to kill Drake in mistake for someone else. The following morning when they are ready to depart, the M9 man, to his reluctance and annoyance, is forced by the airport offical to take on an extra passenger – Jessica. When the plane has engine trouble over the desert, the pilot makes for an airstrip which was a former RAF staging post, and here they land, miles from anywhere. Concerned that Drake has led him into a trap, Garriga covers his escort with his gun: the exercise is pointless, Drake having removed the automatic's ammunition the evening before. According to the pilot, the aircraft's engine has overheated, but Jessica appears unconcerned, saying that they are bound to send someone after them when they hear that the plane has gone down. However, when Drake proposes to check the aircraft's engine, Jessica reveals her true colours and uses a time bomb to blow up the plane to prevent their escape. Realising that he has been tricked into accepting a bribe to cause what he believed was to be only a delay, the pilot is injured in the explosion when trying to save his aircraft.

an illegal organisation sworn to avenge wartime Nazi atrocities against their loved ones. The man Drake knows as 'Garriga' was, they claim, the chief medical officer in the experimental block at a Nazi concentration camp, and was responsible for hundreds of deaths under appalling circumstances. Realising that there has to be a radio on the truck, Drake convinces the injured pilot to get to it and send out an SOS. Garriga, meanwhile, is taken to a clearing and Shimon begins the war criminal's 'trial'. To the doctor's consternation, his day of judgement is finally at hand. The man at first denies everything, but eventually admits that he did hold the position they accuse him of. He pleads, however, that he had no choice in the matter: he was only working under orders. Drake, too, is acting under orders, and his mean that Garriga must be taken back to London. Although it goes against the grain to save him, he pleads for the man's life: what they are proposing to do is murder and Garriga should be taken back to Germany to be given a fair trial. But Jessica and Shimon are having none of this. Neither is Ygal, whose father was among those slain by the ex-Nazi. In a desperate bid to delay the sentence of death being carried out, Drake acts as the condemned man's defending counsel, pleading eloquently and with skill as the evidence is heard. As the injured pilot crawls to the truck to make radio contact which will bring help, Garriga passes sentence on himself when he acknowledges Shimon's accusation that he experimented on the concentration block inmates with bubonic plague: but only a few prisoners died! It had to be done, says the condemned man, if they were to develop an effective vaccine and save millions of lives. Realising that the man is insane, Drake attempts to persuade his captors that Garriga cannot be held responsible for his actions. At this moment, events take a dramatic turn. Telling Jessica that he must relay their findings to his colleagues, Shimon, having returned to his truck and found the pilot slumped over the radio, races back to the group warning them that the man has radioed for help. Hearing this and unable to restrain himself, Ygal shoots the German dead. For Garriga the judgement has been swift. Not so for Drake and the pilot. When the latter admits that he did not get through, Drake and the man are left standing in the desert while Jessica and her friends speed to safety.

With his Judgement Day *close at hand, Garriga gets his just desserts from undercover man John Drake*

Jessica's colleagues arrive by truck and the pattern of the plan becomes clear. Revealing herself as a former German Jewess, the girl introduces her partners, Shimon and Ygal, who, together with several other men are all members of

ENGLISH LADY TAKES LODGERS

Teleplay by David Stone

Starring

Emma	**Gabriella Licudi**
Pilkington	**Robert Urquhart**
Commander Collinson	**Howard Marion Crawford**
Philippe Granville	**Frederick Bartman**
Colonel Torres	**Gary Hope**

with

Customs Official	**Jerome Willis**
Rosalind Fielding	**Judy Huxtable**
Taxi Driver	**Clive Cazes**
Porter	**Roger Worrod**

Directed by Michael Truman

DRAKE ARRIVES IN Lisbon with precise instructions. Suspecting that there is an agency in the city exchanging stolen secrets and that some very important British ones are being marketed there, the M9 man is told to visit his contact, the local security chief, Pilkington (codename Erasmus). At first the men do not actually meet face to face: having let himself into an empty storage room, Drake lowers himself onto a chair and buries his head in a newspaper. Barely seconds after he has done so, a panel in the wall behind him slides open to reveal a television screen which throbs into life and transmits Pilkington's face into the room: Pilkington is sitting on the opposite side of the wall. Dismissing Drake's theory that his own special talents are required with a shake of his head, Pilkington totally disregards the newcomer's suggestion that 'something is going on': Erasmus, it seems, is fully aware of what is taking place on his own doorstep. Like it or not, Drake is not needed. Further, George Stanway, a Naval Commander who disappeared from Lisbon recently is not, as London suggests, connected with any undercover activities. Pilkington maintains that Stanway is a straightforward smuggler. And, as much as Pilkington deplores his rather unconventional way of earning a living, Stanway is a thoroughly decent fellow, and certainly not the kind of chap to betray his country. Nevertheless, Drake tells him, he must be allowed to make his own assessment. Drake is told that Stanway's partner is a Commander Collinson, a bluff old sea dog, who is also thoroughly reliable. He also learns that Pilkington believes that Stanway simply left his wife Emma, an odious woman. An ex-professional dancer, she made Stanway's life a misery and now takes in paying guests at her villa. Although the majority of the English community have nothing to do with her, Drake determines to take a look at Emma's boarding house. Arriving there, he spins a hardluck yarn of having found himself in trouble in England and having to make a hurried exit, entering Portugal illegally. Emma befriends him and immediately doctors his passport with a succession of forged visa stamps, proving that Drake has travelled from France, via Spain to Portugal, where, courtesy of Emma, he is now given a 60-day visitors' permit! All very clever, all very illegal. At this moment Colonel Torres arrives at the villa. A very important figure in the local police force, he wishes the newcomer a very pleasant stay in his country. However, he is the bearer of 'bad' news for the woman: the man who has been found in a hospital in Naples is not her husband. The news appears to disturb Emma, and Torres' suggestion that she would have felt better if the patient had been Stanway, surprises Drake. Torres asks to see Drake's passport and the newcomer hands it over. However, as Commander Collinson marches into the room, the policeman hands the document back to Drake, saying that everything appears to be in order. It is not long before the M9 man is introduced to another of the villa's regular guests, a Frenchman named Philippe Granville. Keeping tabs on Collinson that evening, Drake follows him into the woods and sees his quarry apparently searching the ground. But Collinson is simply looking for a fox, and Drake narrowly escapes being killed when the hunter fires off a round at the animal. Later, under the cover of darkness, Drake is about to crack open Emma's safe when Philippe disturbs him and orders the Englishman to leave the room. Hearing from Drake that he was simply looking for money, Emma loans him some bank notes – provided he earns them, of course. Drake finds himself recruited into the team's smuggling activities by Philippe. However, when Drake discovers that the first item he is helping to smuggle is a secret bomb fuse, brought into the country disguised as a camera by a girl named Rosalind, he challenges Emma with being involved with espionage work. She admits as much, saying that they are working undercover for British Intelligence! She also reveals that her husband was shot by the opposition, and that his body is buried outside in the grounds. Until his death, she claims, she had no idea that her husband was a British agent but, after Stanway's death, Collinson and Philippe had to tell her the truth about her husband's undercover activities. When told this by Drake, Pilkington has no idea that the group are supposed to be under his control. Drake allays his concern: they do not in fact work for British Intelligence. Emma told him this to get herself off the hook. In reality, Drake believes, they are running the secrets for sale market that he has been sent there to find. Suggesting that he will have one of his informers drop a hint about what is going on to Colonel Torres, Pilkington says that the policeman will arrest Emma and her cohorts and, unaware that he is doing their work for them, will lock them away for a few years. Very neat Drake agrees, but he requests that the Controller allows him enough time to find out what's what and who's fooling who, before Torres puts them out of his reach. Unknown to Drake, Philippe, having followed the M9 man to Pilkington's headquarters, is waiting outside when Drake leaves: barely minutes afterwards the Frenchman has the evidence he needs to cook Drake's goose. It appears now, that the M9 man is going to suffer the same fate as Stanway. 'Duped' into joining Collinson on his next hunting trip, Drake is not surprised to find Philippe waiting for them. As a precaution against being followed, the undercover man has made it his habit to wait for a few minutes whenever he goes to a 'special' appointment. He spotted Philippe leaving Pilkington's place, so Drake is prepared and ready for action when the men strike. Aiming the stem of his pipe in Philippe's direction, the Frenchman is forced to drop the gun he has pulled on Drake, as a jet of acrid gas shoots into his eyes. Unable to shoot Drake for fear of hitting his partner, Collinson can do nothing but watch as the M9 man leaps over a wall and disappears under a lake. They fire several shots into the water as their quarry swims for the shore opposite, then, believing that Drake has been hit and drowned, the men race away. But Drake is far from finished and when Collinson and Philippe arrive back at the villa, a soaked, but very much alive undercover man is waiting for them. The men are soon tricked into confessing that they killed Stanway and cooked up the story that he was working for British Intelligence to keep Emma quiet. However, overhearing their confession, Emma is far from quiet. Attacked by the girl's fists, the Frenchman is only too happy when Colonel Torres arrives to take the traitor away. Realising that Emma has been duped, Drake calmly whisks the girl away from the police and allows her to escape to begin life anew.

An off-duty publicity shot of Danger Man Patrick McGoohan, taken on the set of English Lady Takes Lodgers

LOYALTY ALWAYS PAYS

Teleplay by David Stone

Starring

Beyla	**Johnny Sekka**
Enugu	**Errol John**
Prime Minister	**Earl Cameron**
Major Barrington	**Nigel Stock**
Lucas	**Ray Brooks**
Miss Sefadu	**Dolores Montez**
Colonel M'Bota	**Mark Heath**

with

Mrs Barrington	**Joan Newell**
Susy	**Joan Hooley**
Kanda	**Lloyd Reckord**
Doorman	**Dan Jackson**
Vickers	**Edward Jewesbury**
Chin Lee	**Robert Lee**
Lieut Kankana	**Bari Jonson**
1st Removal Man	**Harry Baird**
2nd Removal Man	**Benny Nightingale**
Barman	**Yemi Ajibade**
3rd Removal Man	**Harcourt Curacao**
Secretary	**George A. Saunders**
Affluent Man	**Joseph Layode**

Directed by Peter Yates

'THIS IS KANDA. There is no doubt that the Minister of Defence has negotiated a secret treaty with the Chinese . . .' This is the last tape-recorded message to be received in Britain from the agent who was killed obtaining the information. John Drake is sent to Africa to discover the truth. In disguise as John Hamilton, of Consolidated Minerals, he is taken to see the Prime Minister. He finds him in a state of anger: if the British government are not prepared to accept his assurances that he is not a political opportunist playing off the East against the West, he is prepared to allow the newcomer to make his own independent enquiry and will offer him all the help he needs. Drake requires only one thing, to be ignored and allowed to go his own way. The Prime Minister agrees. The M9 man's contact is Beyla, who uses his ownership of a cabaret club as his cover. Beyla's assistant is the stunningly attractive, London-educated, African girl, Miss Sefadu. Britain, Drake tells them, is sinking a great deal of money into the country and they have no intention of continuing to do so if the government has sold out to the Chinese. Although the Prime Minister has denied that there is an arms deal, Beyla convinces Drake that their agent Kanda was never wrong: intimating that perhaps the Prime Minister has told Drake a deliberate lie. Miss Sefadu, however, explains this away by saying that there is conflict between the Prime Minister and his Minister of Defence, Enugu. A break between the two men was not unexpected. Enugu is an ambitious man, hopeful of stepping into the Prime Minister's shoes, and it is quite possible that he has signed a secret arms treaty with the Chinese. Drake tells them that if this is the case, his government would want proof: a photographic copy of the treaty. Where would Enugu keep such a document? Proposing that the paper they are looking for is almost certainly kept in the Minister's strong-room, Beyla states that they face an impossible task: the Ministry of Defence is run like a fortress – a fact that Drake discovers for himself when he visits the building. He bluffs his way into the closely-guarded headquarters on the pretext that Consolidated Minerals are interested in mineral deposits in a nearby area, a claim which not only establishes his reasons for being in the country, but enables him to meet an Englishman named Major Barrington, Enugu's head of security. However, before Drake and his friends can get into the strong-room, they must first find a way of getting into the building. Miss Sefadu must find a weak link in the security system, nothing is infallible says Drake. Major Barrington seems to fit the bill, so Drake makes conversation with the man over drinks. The Englishman soon confirms Drake's suspicions: the safe has an excellent alarm system, one protected by the door itself. Once the strong-room door is closed, the alarm is set for the time when the vault will have to be opened again; if the lock is tampered with in any way before that time, the alarm bell sounds. They will need more than brute force on this job. Drake, however, has no intention of forcing the safe open. The Minister has a key and they must get it. This is Beyla's job: he must discover where Enugu keeps it. Meanwhile, Drake sees a way of easing their problem. Barrington, a complex character who, after British Army service, managed to get himself a commission in the Colonial Army, wishes to retire to a little place in the country back in England. The undercover man plays on this when the two next meet. Stoking the man's ego by telling him how impressed he was by Barrington's security arrangements when he visited the Ministry, Drake primes the man for what he has in mind. However, when Drake leaves Beyla's nightclub, he is set upon by a gang of Chinese thugs, who fling him into the back of a removal lorry. It is now that Drake meets Chin Lee, First Secretary at the Chinese Embassy, who tells Drake that he knows his real identity and warns him to leave well alone. But Drake makes good his escape and calls at Major Barrington's home. From this moment on, the Major finds himself unwittingly hooked into helping Drake to lay his hands on the documents he is seeking. Explaining that his colleague in Los Angeles is unable to join him as planned, due to ill-health, Drake dupes Barrington into apparently helping him in a somewhat dubious enterprise by playing on the man's greed. Barrington's action has placed him in Drake's power, forcing him to help the undercover man overcome the Major's own security measures. After this, events move swiftly. When Beyla discovers that Enugu keeps the key to his strong-room locked in a safe at his home, it takes Drake but seconds to make an impression of the key. Well and truly hooked, Barrington has no option but to take Drake into the Minister's private room. Once there, it takes but minutes for Drake to overcome the security lock. He uses the duplicate key to open the inner vault and then photograph the treaty paper. This done, Drake and the Major prepare to leave. However, not everything runs as smoothly as Drake had planned. Enugu, alerted to what has taken place, races into the Ministry and has the men arrested and thrown into a cell. Drake is forced to use his ingenuity – and his miniature spy kit – to extricate himself and Barrington from the building. Banking on the fact that the Prime Minister is completely unaware of what Enugu has been doing behind his back, Drake gets a message to him, and the prisoners are released from the building. However, there still remains the fact that Chin Lee knew that Drake was working for the Prime Minister: someone, either the Prime Minister himself, or his adviser Colonel M'Bota is a traitor! It is the latter, whom the Prime Minister has arrested. Thanking Major Barrington for his part in the affair, the Prime Minister shakes the Major's hand and tells him that his services will not be forgotten for, as Drake observes, 'Loyalty always pays.'

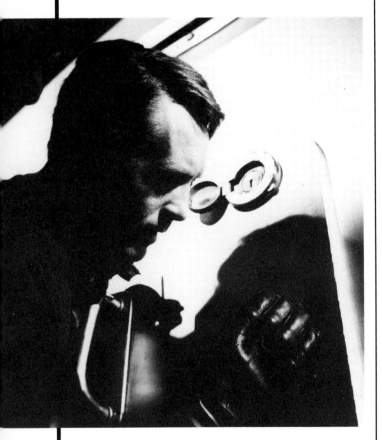

To prove that Loyalty Always Pays, *Drake settles down to tickle the tumblers of Minister Enugu's strong-room safe*

ARE YOU GOING TO BE MORE PERMANENT?

Teleplay by Philip Broadley

Starring

Lesley Arden	**Susan Hampshire**
Kronenberg	**Maxwell Shaw**

with

Joseph Laclos	**Howard Goorney**
Colonel Salmson	**John Miller**
Man in Museum	**George Cormack**
American	**Murray Cash**
Estate Agent	**Denis Shaw**
French Customer	**Cameron Miller**
Jordon	**Desmond Cullum-Jones**
First Agent	**Brian Gilmar**
Second Agent	**Frank Maher**
Vladimir	**Tony Thawnton**
Girl in Taxi	**Lesley Allen**

Directed by Don Chaffey

WHEN JORDAN, THE Controller of M9's cell in Geneva, disappears mysteriously, there is considerable concern in the Department. His predecessor also disappeared in similar circumstances. It is unlikely that two such men would defect, so Drake is called to the 'office', this time a back-street retail shop that bears the legend 'Little Gems, TV and Screen Enterprises', to receive his assignment from Colonel Salmson, one of the many faceless men who head the Department. M9, Drake is told, has three contacts in Geneva. Is one a double agent – someone who has gone over to the other side and betrayed the Department? But first he views a film of the three people he is flying out to investigate. The first face on the screen is Josef Laclos, a waiter. He takes all the reports from East Germany, microfilms them, and hands them over to his Controller at a secret rendezvous. The next man is Wolf Kronenberg, who runs a men's fashion shop and has unique Balkan contacts. His information has always proved to be 100 per cent accurate. Although he is always short of money, he has had an absolutely clear record for over five years. Kronenberg's work follows the same pattern: he hands the microfilm over at a rendezvous. The third contact is Lesley Arden, undoubtedly the prettiest prospect of them all! Half-English, half-French, she is the girlfriend of an Ambassador named Vladimir Synikov who, apparently, says indiscreet things to her. She will pass anything of interest to the Department on to Drake. To make contact, Drake must place an advertisement in the personal column of the local newspaper; it would be indiscreet to call at the girl's apartment, and Drake should only attempt to do this in an extreme emergency. Any one of the three could want to dispose of him. Handed a black book that will tell him everything he needs to know about the contacts, Drake proposes to contact Lesley first. Arriving in Switzerland, ostensibly as the new Controller, Drake is uncomfortably aware that, although the first Controller, Addington may have been unaware of the plot against him, his successor was on the alert. Having placed the

advert in the newspaper's personal column, Drake decides to visit Kronenberg while waiting for Lesley to reply. Having agreed to meet Drake at a seat near the statue in the local park, Drake is immediately suspicious of his contact when Kronenberg insists that Drake gives him an advance payment before he hands over the information. When Drake fails to do so, his suspicions are aroused further when Kronenberg insists on meeting him at a rendezvous point that does not appear in the M9 man's little black book. A visit to the restaurant at which Laclos works sees Drake agreeing to see the contact later, but he has great difficulty in meeting Lesley, who fails to answer the advertisement. Eventually, he decides to break the rules and visits the girl's apartment. While there, he discovers that Lesley is tiring of her latest escort. Vladimir is beginning to bore her. 'But,' she admits, 'I know that I can't walk out on this kind of job.' She confesses that she finds too many men attractive. Quite obviously she finds Drake to her liking because she tells him that she is not worried about the money he has to pay her. That evening, in his hotel room, the undercover man receives an unexpected visit from Kronenberg, who pulls a gun on Drake – it is a joke, the 'gun' being a novelty cigarette lighter. This time Drake agrees to give him $500. His next meeting with Laclos brings Drake disturbing news. Laclos is a shaken man. Someone has tried to kill him, and he realises that his cover is blown. He will now have to pull out of the network. He will leave for Rome the following morning. However, before Drake can pay the man for his services, Laclos is murdered and Drake narrowly escapes with his life when his contact's assailant fires a deadly airgun dart which, had it hit the undercover man's skin and not the collar of his coat, would have rendered Drake unconscious. He now knows the method of disposal, but is as yet unsure as to which of the two remaining contacts is behind the Controller's disappearance. Arriving for a drinks date with Lesley, he shows no surprise when the girl asks him if, during his next contact with London, he could ask the Colonel to arrange for her transfer to a new location. Their drink together has all the beginnings of the perfect romantic evening and, when Lesley suggests that she would like to cook a meal for Drake in her apartment, the M9 man agrees to join her after he has kept his next rendezvous with Kronenberg. He arrives at the designated spot, an empty villa in the country, but the hand-over of his contact's information is forestalled when an estate agent arrives at the villa to show a prospective American buyer around the place and both men are forced to vacate the premises in a hurry. Having already had one attempt made on his life, Drake is alert for any trickery as he arrives for his supper date with Lesley. Unsure of the game that she is playing Vladimir's appearance on the scene is expected rather than embarrassing as far as Drake is concerned. When the girl attempts to drug the M9 man, he is aware that Lesley is responsible for the abduction of the Controller, and Drake is ready when the girl produces a gun. He easily disarms her and learns the truth. She is not a turncoat: she has been working for the opposition all along; a carefully laid plant, who has fooled everyone. Everyone bar Drake it appears, for when Vladimir enters the apartment, it is he who is knocked unconscious and stored into the crate that the girl has made ready to transport the English agent to her masters. As the Ambassador is carted away, Drake allows Lesley to finish her drink before she, too, is taken into custody.

DANGER MAN
(Secret Agent USA)

Season Three

13 monochrome
60 minute episodes

*In the story To Our Best Friend, a reluctant John Drake is
assigned to investigate reports that his friend Bill Vincent
has gone over to the enemy*

TO OUR BEST FRIEND

Teleplay by Ralph Smart

Starring

Bill Vincent	**Donald Houston**
Leslie Vincent	**Ann Bell**
Ivan	**T.P. McKenna**
Colonel	**Jack Allen**
Rutledge	**John Gabriel**
Betrand	**Roderick Lovell**

with

First Secretary	**Charles Lloyd Pack**
Translator	**Robert Rietty**
Natalie	**Gita Denise**
Sayyed	**Julian Sherrier**
Phelps	**Christopher Sandford**
Solomin	**Frederick Farley**
Poltyev	**Cyril Cross**
Watcher	**Simon Brent**
Simpson	**Brian Weske**
Girl in Phone Box	**Rhonda Ryan**

Directed by Patrick McGoohan

THE CODED MESSAGE is short and to the point: M9's agent in Bagdad has 'gone over' – bad news for the Department, and bad news for agent John Drake, who shows great reluctance to fly to the Middle East and investigate the report. The M9 man in Bagdad is Bill Vincent, one of Drake's closest friends. However, as Drake's presence there is unlikely to make Vincent suspicious, he agrees to the assignment. Vincent is delighted to see him, and Drake meets his friend's wife Leslie for the first time. An enchanting Canadian, Leslie insists that her husband's friend stays with them in the lavish apartment she rents from an Arabian princess for a song. Hoping against hope that the trap he is setting for Vincent will prove his friend's innocence, Drake tells Vincent that he has instructions to raid the home of a local politician in the hope of finding documents which will prove that the man is working for the Russians. If the raid goes as planned, it will indicate that Vincent is in the clear. But Drake's hopes are dashed: he is expected. Someone has leaked news of the raid, and it is only because of the precautions he has taken that Drake manages to escape with his life. As Vincent was the only one he told about the raid, this appears to provide conclusive proof of his friend's treachery. Discovering that Drake has tricked him, Vincent, maintaining his innocence and angry that his friend did not take him into his confidence, orders Drake to leave his home. Drake does so and books into a hotel. He tells Leslie that he will return the following morning to give her husband the chance to explain. While at the hotel, Drake spots Phelps, a fellow M9 man, getting into a car. Phelps works for the Colonel, the Department's 'dirty work' organiser – a man who 'tidies up' when all other avenues of persuasion have failed. Worried by the man's presence in the country, Drake tails Phelps to the Colonel's headquarters. He learns from the Colonel that, should Drake fail to clear Vincent's name, the Colonel will arrange for him to meet with an 'accident'. The undercover man warns the Colonel to keep his blood-

hounds off his friend's tail. Later, while keeping tabs on Leslie, he sees the woman leave her home. On the pretext of asking Sayyed, the Vincents' houseboy to take his luggage to his hotel, Drake enters his friend's home. He makes an exhaustive search for hidden bugs, but finds nothing. Returning unexpecedly, Vincent demands to be told what is going on, but Drake can tell him nothing. Told by his friend that Leslie knows that he works for the British Secret Service, Drake suggests that Leslie may be the traitor. The accusation angers Vincent and, once again, Drake is thrown out. Keeping Leslie under surveillance, Drake follows her when she visits the premises of Natalie, a couturière. Having waited for some time for Leslie to reappear, Drake telephones the establishment and learns that she has left. Fortunately, he picks up the woman's trail and sees Leslie leaving a house behind the dress shop. She is followed, several minutes later, by Ivan – a man he discovers later is a Russian agent. Drake tricks Leslie by telephoning her to state that he is leaving; the investigation has been called off. As expected, Leslie races to Ivan's home – and straight into Drake's arms. He is now able to extract the truth: she is a Moscow-trained agent. The girl was given an intensive course in English and provided with a Canadian passport before entering Canada, where Vincent was pointed out to her. She was told that he was an important British agent – marry him. Bill is guilty of confiding to his wife, but he is not a double agent. Leslie has become a victim of divided loyalties: having married Bill, she had fallen in love with him. Confronted with the compact transmitter she used to overhear Drake telling her husband about the raid, the girl is about to tell Drake more when Ivan returns and, at gunpoint, orders Leslie to open the cellar door: his intention is to bury Drake from prying eyes. At that moment, the cigar the undercover man is smoking explodes with a bang, filling the room with acrid smoke. Ivan is knocked unconscious. Drake tells Leslie that as long as she goes straight to the airport and makes no attempt to contact her husband, he will allow her to escape. Told the truth about his wife, a disillusioned Vincent nevertheless thanks Drake for clearing his name and for allowing Leslie to escape. However, this is not the end of the affair. When Leslie calls at a gas station to fill up her vehicle's petrol tank, her husband appears with the intention of telling her that he has forgiven her. Drake, meanwhile, pays the Colonel a final visit. Told that Drake has cleared Vincent's name, the dirty tricks organiser shows his concern. Embarrassed, he confesses to Drake that it is too late, he has ordered his men to dispose of Vincent and he has no way of contacting them to rescind his order! In a desperate attempt to snatch his friend from the jaws of death, Drake and the Colonel speed after the Vincents in the undercover man's car. Too late. Phelps has already planted a gas cylinder device under the passenger seat of the car. The unsuspecting couple have already driven away when Drake and his passenger arrive at the filling station. Several minutes later, the gas begins to take effect. Laughing gaily, Vincent slams his foot hard on the car's accelerator and the vehicle zig-zags crazily across the road. In hot pursuit, Drake catches up with the car and makes a daredevil leap onto the roof of his friend's vehicle. Edging his way to the door, he climbs inside and manages to wrest the steering column from Bill's hands, bringing the vehicle to a stop with a screech of burning rubber. As Leslie is taken away by the authorities, Drake drives his distraught friend back to his apartment.

THE MAN ON THE BEACH

Teleplay by Philip Broadley

Starring

Cleo	**Barbara Steele**
Wykes	**Glyn Houston**
Sir Alan Grose	**David Hutcheson**
Howes	**Peter Hughes**
Lyle	**Clifton Jones**

with

Callaghan	**Fredric Abbot**
Lady Kilrush	**Juliet Harmer**
Mary Ann	**Dolores Mantez**
Rafael	**Gary Hope**
Calypso Singer	**Tommy Eytle**
Cellar Man	**Harry Baird**
Barman	**Paul Danquah**
Millie	**Pearl Prescod**

Directed by Peter Yates

DRAKE IS IN Jamaica to investigate claims that someone in the British espionage network there is a traitor. He receives a telephone call from Callaghan, a colleague. 'Drake, there's a double agent working here, his name . . .' Before Callaghan can give Drake the traitor's name, he winds up dead, floating face downwards in a hotel swimming pool. Since his arrival there, Drake has been aware that Cleo, a beautiful girl has been following him around. They get into conversation at his hotel – a hotel which is, in fact, the headquarters of the British espionage network, its head, Howes, posing as the hotel's manager, and his aide, Wykes, posing as the assistant manager. It is the latter who tells Drake that Howes wishes to see him immediately. Fifteen minutes later, after sharing a drink with Cleo, Drake accepts the hotel manager's summons. Howes is not too pleased with Drake: he has spent a month on the island, drinking in bars and lying on the beach: what the hell is Drake up to? And why has he refused to return to London as ordered? Telling the M9 man that he is insubordinate, Howes reminds Drake who is calling the shots: *he* is Head of Intelligence in the Caribbean, and Drake has been sent there to work under *his* command. Drake will leave the hotel as ordered, or Howes will have his junior placed on a plane under escort! When Drake refuses to explain what he is up to, Howes agrees to allow him just four more days to complete his investigation. Hiring a plane, Drake flies to a small tropical island to meet Sir Alan Grose, an important figure in the echelons of higher espionage: Grose informs him he is staying at the home of Lady Kilrush. Confirming Sir Alan's suspicions that there is a double agent working at the hotel, Drake tells his superior that Howes has ordered him home, leading the other to retort that everyone, including Howes himself is under suspicion until the matter is cleared up. Unknown to the men, their presence on the beach is being observed by a West Indian named Lyle. Drake's hunch is that Cleo can help him, one way or the other. This is why he follows up their first meeting and takes the girl on a picnic. Although the girl plies him with questions as to why he is on the island, it appears that her only interest in Drake is romantic – until a good-looking South American gentleman arrives on the scene, whom the girl introduces as her husband, Rafael! The man hands Drake a wad of money and, as Drake stares down at the gift in amazement, there is a distant click of a camera. Unaware that he has been photographed until he is accused by Howes of the most serious crime an agent can commit – selling out to the other side, Drake demands evidence. Howes has it. A file on the Cuban faction in the West Indies is missing and there is the damaging photograph of Drake receiving money from Rafael Esquerdo, an opposition agent Howes has been keeping tabs on for some time. Denying the charges, Drake asks to talk to Howes alone, and Wykes is told to wait outside. In the privacy of the Controller's office, Drake now informs Howes that he is working directly under the orders of Sir Alan Grose, who, believing that there is a leak at the hotel, prefers to remain out of sight, but has given Drake carte blanche to continue his investigation in any way the M9 man sees fit. To Drake's astonishment, when Howes telephones Lady Kilrush, she flatly denies knowing Sir Alan, and there is no trace of the man! Frustrated by this news, Drake throws his superior aside, tackles Wykes and a guard and escapes. Not knowing what to do next, he meets a young West Indian girl, Mary Ann. Guessing that she probably knows the comings and goings on the island, he tries to bribe some information from the girl, but Lyle arrives and Drake leaves – unaware that the West Indian man immediately reports his presence on the island to Wykes. Finding Lady Kilrush's home, Drake creeps through an open window into her sitting room, but the woman discovers him there. Astounded by Drake's audacity, she maintains that she has never laid eyes on anyone called Sir Alan: Drake has been misinformed. Meanwhile, back at the hotel, Wykes confronts Howes with his observation that, as Drake could have been telling them the truth, the M9 man should be given every opportunity to vindicate his claims: does Wykes have his superior's permission to investigate Drake's story? Acknowledging his aide's concern, Howes agrees. Drake finds Mary Ann alone. The girl is in a more talkative mood: she had seen the man he is looking for – he spent every afternoon with Lady Kilrush on the beach. Faced with the witness, and the blood-stained cravat worn by Sir Alan, Lady Kilrush comes clean: Sir Alan had been mixing business with pleasure, with Lady Kilrush supplying the latter. But where is he now? As Drake discovers, the man is lying dead in shallow water, his body encased in a sheet. However, as Drake climbs from the water, Lyle is waiting for him with an evil-looking machete in his hands. The two men fight and, though Drake is injured by the West Indian, he emerges the victor. Hobbling his way to Mary Ann's cabin, he regains consciousness as Rafael enters, followed by Wykes. Hidden, Drake overhears the M9 man ordering his execution: Wykes will fetch Drake from Lady Kilrush's home and lead him to the beach. Once there, Rafael can shoot the prisoner through the heart! Trailing the traitor, and seeing Wykes turned away by Lady Kilrush, Drake races past her to telephone Howes. But the wires have been cut. Attending to the man's wound, the woman fails to notice Wykes return to her home. Explaining that the wounded man is a spy, the traitor is about to carry Drake away, when Howes and his men arrive. Wykes' attempts to convince his superior that he was about to take Drake into custody are forestalled when Drake produces Sir Alan's tape-recorder – complete with a recording of the traitor telling Rafael to dispense with the undercover man. His life and career intact, Drake collapses to the floor unconscious.

Drake drags himself from his intended resting place to discover the secret of The Man On The Beach

THE MAN WHO WOULDN'T TALK

Teleplay by Donald Jonson and Ralph Smart

Starring

Lydia Greshnova	**Jane Merrow**
Meredith	**Norman Rodway**
Interrogator	**Ralph Michael**
Forbes	**Brian Worth**
Peter	**Simon Brent**

with

Policeman at Garage	**Murray Hayne**
Garage Manager	**Mike Pratt**
Doctor Radev	**Frank Gatliff**
HQ Policeman	**Roy Marsden**
Night Porter	**John Herrington**
2nd Security Man	**David Orchard**
1st Security Man	**Ken Haward**
Girl in Bath	**Angela Lovell**

Directed by Michael Truman

ARRIVING AT Istanbul Airport, Drake nonchalantly takes a seat in the airport's lounge. Using a radio transmitter, he speaks to Forbes, his contact, who is seated some distance away. Told by Forbes that he is being followed, the contact wastes no time in telling Drake that Meredith, M9's regional Controller, hearing that the Eastern Europe network was getting shaky, decided to take matters into his own hands by entering the field: arriving in Bulgaria. Meredith was captured and has been under interrogation for three days. If Meredith talks, the Department will have to shut up shop in the area, and it will take years to re-establish the network: Drake must rescue Meredith, whatever the cost. He must pose as a journalist named Garnet, and book into the Hotel Europa, where he will be contacted by a colleague. Having delivered his message, Forbes leaves, followed by a stranger. Outside, in a darkened alley, Forbes is shot dead. Meredith, meanwhile, is being tortured in an effort to make him talk. His interrogators tell him that, if necessary, they can go on for a week, a month – forever, until he breaks. At his hotel, Drake is greeted by the pretty Lydia Greshnova, whose job, she tells him, is to make him happy: anything he wants, he has only to ask. She is looking after visiting journalists, and insists that she should escort him everywhere. Attractive though' she is, Drake is not happy when Lydia tells him that they have an early start in the morning, and that she will call for him. His contact arrives: it is Peter, a waiter at the hotel. The man does not attempt to hide the fact that he is scared that Meredith may talk. Things are getting hot. The Controller is being held at the Flora Building, a police establishment. Peter has drawn Drake a plan of the building. The interrogation room lies beneath the police office: two guards watch Meredith, one is always stationed at the doorway, the other seated at a desk. The windows are wired. Told that the place is air-conditioned and that the air intake is on the roof, Drake orders Peter to hire a car and wait outside the Flora building at one o'clock in the morning. At first the man refuses, but when Drake tells him that if he is caught he will talk and name names, the waiter agrees to do as asked. Drake's rescue plans are elaborate: by entering an apartment block opposite the police establishment, he reaches the roof unseen and throws two smoke bomb canisters into the Flora building's air conditioning intake. Returning to the ground floor, he enters the police station and easily takes care of the uniformed men positioned at the reception desk by firing gas into their faces from the gas-pistol he has strapped to his wrist. Drake overpowers the interrogator and his assistant in the same way. Tripping the alarm and wearing a gas mask he gets Meredith safely out of the building and into the car Peter has waiting. But something goes wrong with the next part of the plan. Having arranged to meet a man called Demita at a petrol filling station, the contact is not waiting for them. Matters worsen further when Meredith, close to breaking point, sees a police vehicle drive by. He screams in terror. Concerned that his cries will attract unwanted attention, Drake knocks his colleague unconscious. Informed by the garage owner that he has never seen or heard of a man named Demita, Peter suggests that they must leave Meredith behind, but Drake is adamant that the unconscious man returns to the hotel. To keep Meredith quiet, the M9 man injects him with a sleeping drug, thereby quelling any fears that they will be discovered attempting to smuggle Meredith into Drake's room. This is achieved by having Peter distract the attention of the guard placed outside Drake's door while Drake carries his colleague to his room via the fire-escape. All goes well until Meredith wakes up in Drake's bedroom. Terrified by the hotel's pulsating neon sign, and believing that he is still in the interrogation chamber, Meredith kills Peter in a fit of desperation, thinking that he is one of the guards. Drake, meanwhile, pays a second visit to the petrol station. Explaining that he wishes to see Demita, Drake, realises that the garage manager is scared. He allays his

fears telling him that everything is all right: Meredith is safe at his hotel and all he requires from the man – who now confirms that he is Demita – is an escape route. Telling Drake that it will cost him plenty, Demita leaves to contact his friends. He returns shortly afterwards to give Drake the name of his contact. Drake goes back to his hotel and learns from Meredith that he has 'settled his account with the enemy'. Drake becomes increasingly concerned when Lydia arrives at his door bearing a breakfast tray – on which lies a newspaper, complete with Meredith's photograph and news of his escape. Lydia tells Drake that she will collect him after he has eaten. When the M9 man refuses to go with her, pleading that he is not feeling well, Lydia calls in Doctor Radev who, astonished by Drake's temperature reading (the undercover man has 'teased' the thermometer with the flame of his lighter), insists that the patient be taken to hospital. With the secret police searching every one of the hotel's bedrooms, the situation is becoming desperate: the men must leave immediately. But how? The arrival of the ambulance gives Drake an idea. When Lydia returns to the room and finds Drake sprawled out on his bed, she orders a wheelchair to be brought to his room. Unfortunately, she also notices Meredith hiding in the bathroom: the men have no choice but to bind and gag the girl. When the ambulance men arrive, it is Meredith they cart away, dressed in Drake's clothes. Drake leaves the hotel disguised as a waiter. Stealing a van, Drake races off in pursuit of the ambulance, from which Meredith escapes, having knocked out his attendants with Drake's gas pistol. At the petrol filling station, they find Demita waiting for them, their escape route secured. But once again Meredith falls into a state of hysteria and Drake is forced to calm his colleague by administering another dose of the sleeping drug. When the police arrive, alerted by Lydia, the men have escaped to freedom.

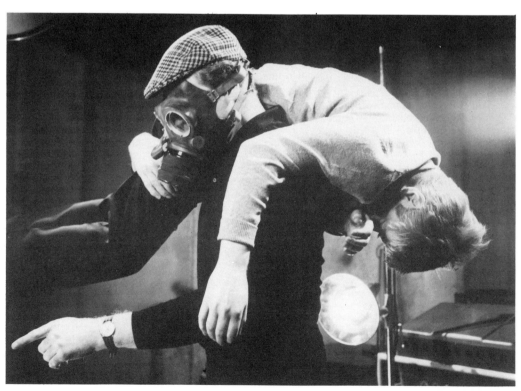

The Man Who Wouldn't Talk *finds Drake donning a gas mask to rescue M9 Controller Meredith*

SAY IT WITH FLOWERS

Teleplay by Jacques Gilles

Starring

Wallace/Hagen	Ian Hendry
Dr Brajanska	John Phillips
Caroline	Jemma Hyde
Krummenacher	Harold Kasket

with

Kasser	Martin Wyldeck
Meyer	William Dexter
Verena	Rachel Herbert
Man in Taxi	Basil Dignam
Buchler	Kevin Stoney
Miss Wallace	Gretchen Franklin
Carl	Frank Maher
Wilhelm	Les White

Directed by Peter Yates

IN A LONDON high-street, a well-dressed man hails a taxi cab. 'Where to, sir?' asks Drake, sitting at the wheel. 'Switzerland', replies his boss, settling himself into his seat. It appears that Hagen, a rather dubious freelance agent who will work for any side providing the money is right, has dropped out of sight: gone over to the opposition, perhaps, in which case things will be highly uncomfortable for Drake's masters. In the guise of an insurance investigator, Drake is to fly to Switzerland and investigate the man's disappearance. Arriving at his hotel in Zurich, a contact tells Drake that Hagen died three months earlier at the Brajanska clinic – a fact that appears to be disproved when Hagen's bank manager confirms to Drake that the man had two accounts: one in the name of Hamilton, the other in the name of Hadleigh, but both have recently been cleared out: the signature on the withdrawal slip is definitely that of his client – unless someone has committed a clever forgery. A visit to the Brajanska clinic is called for, so the M9 man books into the hotel in Heibeck where Hagen was taken ill. The rooming house is run by Krummenacher and his daughter Verena who, when questioned by Drake, confirm that Hagen died of natural causes. However, doubt is cast over their story when Drake learns from the local Chief of Police that six weeks after Hagen's death, his widow arrived in Heibeck to claim her husband's remains, the body was then cremated. When Dr Brajanska confirms the policeman's story, Drake asks Wilhelm, his contact, to transmit a message to London that as all the evidence points to Hagen being dead, he sees little point in continuing his enquiry: Drake will leave for London tomorrow. However, while sharing a cigar with Krummenacher that evening, he is puzzled when the man tells him that another Englishman named Wallace arrived at the hotel on the day that Hagen was taken ill. Drake enquires what happened to the man? Told that Wallace stayed in the hotel for barely two hours and then left after receiving a telephone call from the clinic, never to return, the M9 agent asks London for advice. His inquiry brings swift results: Wallace, it appears, is an industrial scientist who answered an advertisement box number for a job in Switzerland. The advertisement was placed by someone called W. Bernay, but London have been unable to trace

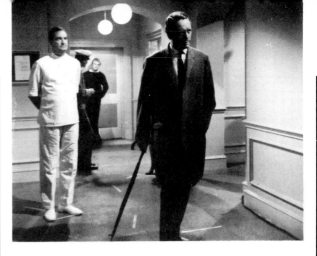

In order to Say It With Flowers, *Drake breaks into the Brajanska Clinic to confront a crooked medical team*

him. Wallace, who has not yet returned, had only one relative, a sister, but she was killed when a fire broke out at her home. It occurs to Drake that if someone has taken over Hagen's money, they could also have taken over his contacts. He tells London that he proposes to continue his enquiry. Furthermore, they must ask Interpol to find out everything they can about Wallace: his appearance, habits, everything – and while they are at it, they should also ask the Americans if they have any information about Dr Brajanska. Drake interviews Buchler, the undertaker who buried the dead man's body. When he shows the funeral director a photograph of Hagen, the mortician denies that this was the man he buried! Informed by Interpol that Wallace is living, quite openly, on the Austrian border, Drake has no difficulty finding him, introducing himself as a lawyer making some inquiries about a man named Hagen. Wallace, a young man wearing thick glasses, does not recall the name at all. He is quite open, too, about his visit to the Brajanska clinic, and says the advertisement he had answered was a bit of a 'sell'. He was sent up to the clinic to see Bernay who was receiving treatment there, but the man told him that he had changed his mind about the job. Seeing no point in returning to England, Wallace went to the Riviera, won a great deal of money on the gambling tables and has been able to retire comfortably to his mountain retreat. But there is something about the man that does not ring true: Drake finds several flaws in his story – particularly when, having been told by London that Wallace was an amateur taxidermist, the man in front of him confirms that he *mounts* stuffed animals. However, Drake has yet to discover a link between Wallace, Hagen and Dr Brajanska. But the latter makes a grave error when, confronted by Wallace, who now says that, thanks to the doctor's incompetence, Drake suspects his real identity. Brajanska issues orders for the undertaker to be killed. Drake rescues the undertaker from certain death when he drags him from his burning home. Buchler throws in his lot with the M9 man. By allowing Brajanska to believe that Buchler is dead, Drake sets out to teach the would-be killers a lesson. Telephoning the clinic, Drake, assumes the identity of Mr Bernay's secretary and convinces the doctor that his employer wishes to return to the clinic. With Wilhelm's help, Drake infiltrates the clinic and confronts the villains with the truth: adept at plastic surgery, Brajanska has been enticing people to the clinic – people with no living relatives – and kills them. He alters the faces of wanted men to assume the dead people's identities. Confronted with the 'dead' undertaker and police officers, Hagen and Brajanska spill the beans and are taken into custody.

SOMEONE IS LIABLE TO GET HURT

Teleplay by Philip Broadley

Starring

Volos	**Maurice Denham**
Dr Sawari	**Zia Mohyeddin**
Magda Kallai	**Geraldine Moffat**
Chand	**Earl Cameron**

with

Manuel	**John G. Heller**
Colonel Maturin	**Jerome Willis**
Holst	**Roy Herrick**
Adam	**George Baisley**

Directed by Michael Truman

SLIPPING OFF his dressing gown and slippers, Drake climbs into his bed, switches the light off and rests his head on his pillow, his eyes closed. But his slumber is short-lived. Within seconds of shutting his eyes, a flashing light beside his bed indicates that a message is being piped through his telephone into the transmitter console by the side of his bed. Wide awake now, he presses a button on the rack of equipment and settles with his back to the pillow as a television monitor screen rises from the footboard at the bottom of his mattress. The screen flickers into life and a female voice gives a running commentary as pictures of men's faces fill the screen. 'This is Dr Sawari, who is trying to take over the government by force. Our agent Davis has discovered that Sawari has been trying to buy arms illegally. Nothing has been heard from Davis for several days and he must be assumed dead. Although Sawari on the surface appears to be loyal to his government, his friend and ally Colonel Maturin, is not so discreet. He has given several interviews to the Press, stating that revolution is the only way to cure the country's problems. Your job, Drake, is to get out there right away, and take over where Davis left off. Find out what Sawari and Maturin are up to, who the gun-runners are, and ensure that there is no illegal arms deal.' Arriving in the Caribbean in the guise of Collins, a journalist seeking an interview with Dr Sawari, Drake reports to the doctor's PRO, Mr Chand, who arranges for Sawari's personal assistant, the mysterious and beautiful Magda Kallai, to take Drake to the doctor. He finds Sawari playing tennis. Drake soon throws off his journalistic pretence, challenging the man with the truth about his plans and offering to help by supplying arms. Sawari refuses to betray himself, but sends Magda to Drake's hotel later to see if he is a genuine arms dealer. The M9 man convinces her that he is. But there is a rival in the field. Who is he, and where can he be found? His questions are answered when a man named Volos arrives at the hotel, using a false name. He warns Drake to keep off; if he does not . . . 'Make no mistake, I will have you killed.' Drake, of course, refuses to heed the advice and, as Volos departs, the M9 man attaches a bugging device to the man's jacket. With this he is able to keep track of his competitor when he drives away – but Volos is too clever for him. The trail runs dry in a forest where Drake discovers his bug, placed ominously on the skull of a skeleton. Back at his hotel, he finds a message telling him to go to the Villa Kiskadee, Rosighol Heights at eight o'clock that evening. He does so and discovers that the villa is owned by Magda. Sawari and Maturin also arrive and Drake settles an arms deal with them. But when he attempts to leave the house, he finds that he is virtually a prisoner. He is to be kept there until the arms arrive. There are, however, compensations. Magda is obviously attracted to Drake but, as he soon discovers, she is lethal. Even though he cannot escape, he is not safe. Volos breaks into the villa and Drake is kidnapped and taken to an old Caribbean fort which has been an impregnable prison for generations. Overhearing Volos tell one of his men to make arrangements to move the arms shipment tomorrow, Drake contemplates escape. But Holst, one of Volos' henchmen follows his every move with a gun. Taken to a cell beneath the battlements, his competitor's statement that escape from the fort is impossible, fails to crack Drake's determination. Stripping the cot in his room, the M9 man hacks off a spring-bracket with the heel of his shoe. Using this, he digs away at a loose concrete flagging stone in the middle of the cell, succeeding, eventually, in prising the stone from the floor. He scoops the earth beneath the floorstone into his blanket and, when Holst next arrives to inspect the prisoner, Drake has magically disappeared! Hearing Volos and Holst depart to search the battlements, Drake emerges from his hiding place beneath the floor of his cell and cautiously makes his way to a room which houses a radio transmitter. Drake manages to relay a message to the authorities telling them to ground all air traffic and to send an airforce helicopter to the fort. When Volos returns, it is he who learns that when people go in for gun-running, someone is liable to get hurt!

Within minutes of being forcibly installed in an old Caribbean fort, Drake will teach Volos that when you deal with John Drake Someone Is Liable To Get Hurt

DANGEROUS SECRET

Teleplay by Ralph Smart and Donald Jonson

Starring

Louise Carron	**Elizabeth Shepherd**
Colin Ashby	**Lyndon Brook**
Fenton	**Derek Francis**
Mather	**John Brooking**

with

Dark Glasses	**Gordon Whiting**
Barbier	**Reginald Barratt**
Barjou	**Michael Anthony**
Jill Preston	**Sheila Steafel**
Barjou's Secretary	**Maureen Davis**
Receptionist	**Nicole Shelby**
Girl	**Jacqueline Hall**
Mark Lester	**Mark Lester**
Alex	**Peter Brace**
Stefan	**Peter Brayham**
Leon	**Derek Baker**
Carl	**Alf Joint**

Directed by Stuart Burge

COLIN ASHBY, a scientist with a British virus research unit, is appalled when, in trying to isolate a virus, he causes a dangerous mutation which, he is quick to realise, could be used in bacteriological warfare. This is why he confides to his colleague, Jill Preston, that he has destroyed his notes. He also refuses to provide Fenton, a representative of a military scientific unit, with details of the virus, when asked to do so by Mather, head of the establishment. Despite being threatened with the Official Secrets Act and with having his passport taken away, Ashby disappears. This security aspect brings Drake into the matter. With an 18 hours start, Asbhy could be anywhere but Drake succeeds in finding a clue that leads himself and Fenton to Barham Yacht Club, and from there to Vieuxville in France. At Vieuxville airport, Drake telephones a French research company headed by a man named Henri Barjou. He attempts to book an appointment with Barjou via his secretary, but he is not expected back until later. Assuming the identity of a newspaper man, Drake succeeds in making contact with Ashby who, he learns, is hoping to work for Barjou, the one man in whom he has confided his secret. Drake tells the scientist that he understands why he has thrown away his career: because he refuses to let 'those bone-headed bureaucrats push him around.' Drake convinces Ashby that he is sympathetic to his cause: he wishes to help the man, he is on Asbhy's side. Drake is somewhat perturbed to discover that the scientist has struck up a friendship with an attractive French woman, Louise Carron, and is even more perturbed when Fenton attempts to force Ashby to return to England by clumsy – and dangerous methods. Drake bugs Ashby's hotel room with a miniature transmitter 'bullet' which, when fired from Drake's umbrella, attaches itself to the window of the scientist's room and magically extends its aerial. Via a receiving bug hidden in the M9 man's typewriter, Drake overhears Barjou telling Ashby that he has mentioned the virus to his director. The scientists is worried by this. He is beginning to suspect, for

the first time, that the job Barjou has promised him has strings attached; but he is still idealistic enough to hope that this is not so. Contacting Drake on his walkie-talkie set, Fenton tells Drake that he can start to pack his clothes: he has read Ashby the riot act and, given time to think it over, Ashby will soon be on his way back to England. Drake retaliates by suggesting that Fenton has picked the wrong man: Ashby will not be frightened into returning home with them: he needs to be persuaded. The next development confirms Drake's statement and worse, indicates that other people are interested in keeping an eye on Ashby's whereabouts. Drake is not the only one to have bugged the scientists's room – a Russian transmitting device is found there! From this moment, wherever Ashby goes, a strange man wearing dark glasses is never far from his side. Drake must find out who the man represents. And who Louise Carron is working for. To enable him to do so, he visits an antique shop run by Barbier, a man he knows to be a dealer in secrets. Drake is surprised to find Louise there. Both, it seems, are after the same thing: a pair of French side-hammer duelling pistols which Barbier proposes that they haggle over, but he will be the out-right winner because he will ask a higher price. Louise, however, is adamant that *she* always gets what she wants!

The beautiful Louise Carron is all that stands between Drake and scientist Ashby's Dangerous Secret

Back at his hotel, Ashby tells Drake that Fenton has been trying to scare him with threats of criminal prosecution. This time he has gone too far and Ashby has already complained to Barjou: his threats carry some weight. True enough. Within minutes, the man in dark glasses approachs Fenton. Introducing himself as an officer of the Sûreté, he orders the Englishman to leave the area immediately. Back at the antique shop, Drake intimating to Barbier that Louise Carron has been told to leave and that he is now the only one in the field, asks Barbier to name his price – for the pistols, of course. As soon as Drake leaves the shop, Barbier runs outside to his car and drives away at speed. Drake has planted a bug in the vehicle and, by turning the shift-key on his typewriter-cum-receiver-cum-direction finder, Drake has no trouble in following the man to a dilapidated farmhouse in the country. Entering the place unobserved, he creeps into an upper room and witnesses the arrival of several men – and Louise Carron. After talking to the men Louise leaves. Drake, meanwhile, having found his way into the farmhouse loft, plays a game of cat-and-mouse with the guards Louise has left behind. Tiring of the game, he returns to his hotel where he is told by the receptionist that Ashby has left with Madame Carron. He is about to race after them when Stefan, one of Louise's men, orders him into his car at gunpoint. Meanwhile, Louise has taken Ashby back to the farmhouse. Accompanied by Alex, Leon and Carl (three members of her team) Louise determines to make the scientist disclose the details of his formula into a tape-recorder. She injects him with a truth drug and within minutes, Ashby is telling her the secret formula. He is still doing so when Drake is shoved into the room by Stefan. Realising that if Ashby and his secrets are to be saved, he must act quickly, Drake overpowers Stefan and races for the attic, snatching up the woman's tape-recorder as he goes. Once again the game of cat-and-mouse ensues, but Drake makes his presence felt in earnest, taking care of each thug in turn. Then, amid the unconscious bodies, he returns the tape-recorder to Louise (minus the tape, of course) and escorts Ashby from the farmhouse. But there is still the matter of the man in dark glasses, who now arrives at the farmhouse astride a powerful motorcycle. Drake jumps into Louise's car to take care of the policeman in true Secret Agent manner. Leaping from his speeding car, he throws a metal rod into the wheel spokes of the oncoming motorcycle, and the rider is thrown to the ground. Removing the unconscious man's helmet and dark shades, Drake stares down at the face of an Oriental.

I CAN ONLY OFFER YOU SHERRY

Teleplay by Ralph Smart

Starring

Jean Smith	**Wendy Craig**
Ma'Suud	**Anthony Newlands**
Nubar	**Bernard Archard**
Seghir	**Henry Gilbert**

with

Police Sergeant	**Tony Jason**
First Watcher	**Ben Ari**
Second Watcher	**Alan Chuntz**
First Thug	**Bob Anderson**
Second Thug	**Eddie Powell**
Military Attaché/ Fortune Teller	**Warren Mitchell**

Directed by George Pollock

WHEN M9 hears that details of oil reserves and potential have fallen into enemy hands, Drake finds himself in the Middle East, assigned to investigate a suspect believed to be behind the leak. The suspect is Jean Smith, an English girl working with the British Embassy. Assuming the identity of journalist John Brown, Drake soon meets Jean and receives a surprise when she turns out to be a quiet, timid but not unattractive girl who, under Drake's influence, thaws somewhat and agrees to dine with him. Later, when he drives her back to her apartment, they find a man waiting for her: an Arab named Ma'Suud. He and the girl are obviously close friends. Having offered to drive Drake back to his hotel, Ma'Suud warns him not to see the girl again. Drake's refusal to agree to this leads to an attempt being made on his life, and to the discovery that Ma'Suud is not all he pretends to be: Miss Smith having told him that she believes Ma'Suud to be a man with a mission, a man with a dedicated social sense, penniless, but anxious to improve conditions in his country. Drake gradually becomes aware that the girl is more than a little in love with the man. Later, when Drake shows her a photograph of a man sitting in his car outside the British Embassy, and two further pictures of the same man taken outside her club and her apartment building, the girl becomes alarmed. Her bemusement increases when Drake tells her that he is a British agent. Informing Jean that she is under surveillance, Drake is about to question her further when Ma'Suud reappears. Once again the Arab plays the host by driving Drake back to his hotel, and once again Drake is warned to leave the girl alone – this time, however, by two of Ma'Suud's heavies, who attack the M9 man. Having dispatched them with a few well-timed punches, Drake is about to return to his hotel when two policemen arrive and take him to the office of the local police chief, Inspector Nubar, an old friend of Drake's. Friendship or not, Nubar demands to be told why Drake has arrived in his country unannounced. He is warned by Nubar that unless he can come up with an explanation about his activities, he will be thrown out of the country. Drake is allowed to leave. Courtesy of a listening device he planted in Ma'Suud's car during their drive, Drake tracks the man to his home where, while retrieving the bug from the man's car, he notices an expensive saloon in the Arab's garage. Drake finds Ma'Suud at the girl's home and produces a photograph he has taken of the vehicle and, more to the point, Ma Suud with a woman – his wife! Furious that Drake has exposed him, the Arab leaves. Apologising to the girl, Drake asks her to tell him what is going on. Saying that she was lonely, Jean explains how she met Ma'Suud and she fell in with his underground political group – at least that's what he told her they were. She now realises that she has been duped into handing over the oil statistics. Just then, a grey-haired figure named Seghir, who Jean has told Drake about, arrives outside her apartment with his men. Concerned by the man's arrival, Drake hurries the girl out of the room and tells her to drive to his hotel. Alone, he faces the newcomers and discovers that Seghir is a member of the secret police. Asking for Drake's passport, the policeman tells him that a flight has been arranged for him: Drake is to leave the country at once. Seghir and his colleagues attempt to force Drake to leave but end up unconscious on the floor. Back in Nubar's office, Drake berates his friend for sending his men to do his dirty work, but Nubar has no idea what Drake is talking about. The men lay a trap. Arriving at Ma'Suud's home carrying a portable transmitter, Drake accuses the Arab of being involved in espionage. Convinced that the game is up, the man turns on Drake with a sword, but the undercover agent is too clever for him. Grabbing a weapon from the wall of the man's lounge, he drives the Arab backwards and knocks him unconscious. However, there still remains the matter of Seghir and his mob. Brought to Nubar's office, Jean offers to make amends no matter how great the danger and listens intently as Drake gives her details of his plan. Dressed as an Arab, the undercover man enters the girl's apartment, and positions hidden cameras at various vantage points. This done, he produces a portable television and settles down with Jean to await the enemy. Convinced that Jean is still on the payroll, Seghir and his men lead her into the apartment block's elevator – and find themselves trapped. Having sabotaged the hoisting machine, Drake is on hand to deliver the villains over to Nubar. The espionage ring broken, Drake accompanies the girl to her room for a drink – sherry, of course, Jean has nothing else!

Drake's refusal to stop seeing Jean Smith leads to an attempt being made on his life (I Can Only Offer You Sherry)

THE HUNTING PARTY

Teleplay by Philip Broadley

Starring

Claudia Jordan	**Moira Lister**
Basil Jordan	**Denholm Elliott**
Max Dell	**Edward Underdown**
Ross	**John Welsh**
Edwards	**Alan White**

with

Coleman	**William Ingram**
Peer	**Oliver Johnston**
Vernon	**John Barcroft**
Gandon	**Michael Godfrey**
Zepos	**Michael Peake**
Annette	**Jean Shaw**
Martine	**Barbara Graley**
House of Lords	
Messenger	**John Dunbar**
French Postman	**Wilfred Grove**

Directed by Pat Jackson

THE HOUSE OF LORDS is an unusual place for Drake to visit in the course of his work as a secret agent, but this is where his enquiries have to begin when confidential information leaks out from very high circles. Only a few people could have possibly had the information which has reached foreign newspapers. One of those people is Lord Gandon, the man who Drake has called to see. Somewhat reluctantly, Gandon agrees to tell him the names of everyone he has met between leaving a cabinet meeting to the time the latest leak has taken place. Out of all the names, there is one that interests Drake more than the others: Basil Jordan whose wife, Claudia, is one of the wealthiest women in the world. The Jordans have a chateau in France, where they are now staying. Faced with the problem of getting into the house, Drake tricks their manservant Ross, into giving up his job and taking a better one in London. Drake applies for the vacant position and is taken on. Claudia's dealing with her husband and staff alike are autocratic. Drake soon realises that she dominates Basil completely. He himself is penniless and only her money holds them together: theirs is not even a love-hate relationship. It is all hate. Masquerading as their manservant is anything but comfortable, but Drake now has the access he needs. He can keep an eye too, on any visitors, and the first of these is an old friend of Basil's, Max Dell. A message from M9 elicits the information that he is a junior minister who is privy to highly confidential information, although he is believed to be totally trustworthy and his reputation is beyond reproach. Drake also receives a message from his M9 contact Ross, that inquiries are being made about him in London, to discover if the references he has given to the Jordans are genuine. This calls for quick action, and Drake takes the bull by the horns by confronting Claudia with the accusation that she is having him investigated. The woman denies this, and the undercover man accepts her denial as being true. Who then, has been making these inquiries? A fortunate chance leads to his learning that it is Basil Jordan. This apart, Drake has a certain sympathy with the unfortunate Basil.

He gets on well with him; they even do some clay-pigeon shooting together, and Drake proves his expertise with a shotgun. That evening, however, Drake makes an interesting discovery when he gets into Basil's den and finds some old newspaper clippings which throw an unexpected sidelight on Basil's interests. There are also some phials of liquid which puzzle Drake. Admonishing Drake for cleaning his private quarters, Basil asks Claudia to sack the manservant, but with several guests due to arrive, she refuses to do so. Keeping tabs on Basil with bugs planted in the house, Drake eventually follows his employer to a forest rendezvous and a meeting with a man Drake recognises as Zepos – a mysterious gentleman who deals in secret information and sells it to the highest bidder. This confirms that Jordan is the man he wants. What is difficult to understand is how Basil gets information out of men like Max Dell. His reason are clear enough: the only chance of freeing himself from Claudia's clutches is to make some money of his own. The transistor bug in Basil's room provides the lead which ties up with the information Drake has culled from the old newspaper clippings. Basil is interested in hypnotism and is getting the information he needs from his guests while they are asleep via a cleverly-devised transmitter set up in their bedrooms. Awakened by the sound of humming, Drake visits Dell's room. The man is fast asleep, but under the influence of drugs administered by Basil over lunch, he is spilling every secret he knows. Unknown to Drake, his presence in Dell's room has been observed by Basil on his television monitor, via a camera hidden in the sleeping man's bedroom. The next morning, on the pretext of needing as many guns as they can get, Jordan invites Drake to join a boar hunt that he has laid on for his guests. Teamed with Basil, Drake tells him that he is aware of what the man is up to. Producing one of the phials he saw earlier, he adds that he knows that Basil is using drugs to obtain secrets. Alarmed by Drake's accusations, Basil calls upon Zepos to get the man. Hidden in the trees, the information buyer attempts to do so, but Drake makes good his escape. Surrounded on all sides by men carrying shotguns, Drake feigns an injury and lures his would-be assassins into a trap. When Claudia arrives on the scene, the undercover man informs her that she will be dining alone that evening – and for some time to come.

TWO BIRDS WITH ONE BULLET

Teleplay by Jesse Lasky Junior and Pat Silver

Starring

Commissioner Winlow	**Geoffrey Keen**
Pilar Lin	**Lelia Goldoni**
Dr Shargis	**Paul Curran**
Singri Rhamin	**John Woodvine**
Aldo Shargis	**Richard O'Sullivan**

with

Jose	**Guido Adorni**
Censor	**Anne Blake**
1st Prison Guard	**Albert Shepherd**
Police Officer	**Malcolm Rogers**
Guard	**Clive Cazes**
2nd Prison Guard	**Reuben Elvy**

Directed by Peter Yates

REVOLUTION IS brewing in the British-ruled Caribbean colony. Drake is sent to the island to protect the would-be new leader, the idealistic Dr Shargis, because the British Government feels that his death would unleash undesirable forces. Alive, Shargis would lose the forthcoming election as quietly as usual, but his death would be quite a different story: the assassination of a popular nationalist candidate would have terrorists pouring in and the British would be held responsible. Shargis would be a martyr and popular sympathy would hand his Party the election. His own people, therefore, want Shargis dead. But who? In the guise of a sympathetic journalist, Drake interviews Dr Shargis and meets his son Aldo; his second-in-command, Singri Rhamin and his glamorous Head of Security, Captain Pilar Lin. Drake needs no introduction to Pilar. She is M9's local agent and it is she who has requested Drake's assistance. She believes that Dr Shargis is to be assassinated by his own Party, but she does not know who has been chosen as the murderer. Shargis runs a training school for what he calls his 'freedom fighters', and any one of the pupils could have been picked for the job. Can Pilar get Drake in there, say, to do a story? Pilar does not know. The place is very hush-hush, but she will see what she can do. Meanwhile, as a result of one of the faked pictures Drake took earlier, (showing a soldier beating a woman and a child) not being passed by Sharis' censor, the M9 man is arrested and taken before Commissioner Winlow. The men are old friends and Winlow believes that Drake is wasting his time: Shargis will lose the election as usual. Whitehall's theory that the man's own people wish to see him dead is ridiculous. Shargis is too popular: he is a man who cares for his people. Warning Drake that if he finds himself in difficulties he will not be able to help him, Winlow cautions his friend to remain alert. Drake is collected from the Commissioner's office in a car driven by Aldo who is chauffering Rhamin to the training school. The M9 man is allowed to join them. Shargis himself leads the trainees and Drake is treated to a demonstration of an exercise designed by the leader; a film show which proves that his men are more than proficient when it comes to protecting him from his enemies. Impressed, Drake volunteers to drive Dr Shargis back to his home. During the drive, the leader confirms that he has complete confidence in the people he has gathered around him. Perhaps so, but that has not prevented someone from trying to kill him. Someone has tampered with the brakes of Aldo's car and the two men barely escape with their lives. Drake is forced to drive the vehicle into the forest in order to halt the car. However. Drake cannot convince the leader that someone wants to kill him. particularly when he insists that the would-be assassin is a member of Shargis' own retinue. Pilar now shows her true colours. She shoots Dr Shargis. making it appear as if Drake is the killer. His arrest follows. The trial will inevitably swing public opinion against the British. Sickened by the discovery that Pilar has tricked him. Drake is forced to wait out his desperate situation in a prison cell. Commissioner Winlow cannot publicly help him and the mob are howling for his head. However Drake has a plan. Winlow smuggles some tools into Drake's cell enabling the M9 man to drill a hole through the wall — a hole into which Jose, a contact. plants some dynamite. The wall is blown apart and Drake escapes to Dr Shargis' home. Climbing through a window, he overhears Rhamin telling Pilar that the tape-recording he has made of Dr Shargis practising his election speech makes it clear that he has nominated Shingri Rhamin as his successor. Watching the girl place the tape into a safe. Drake notes down the combination using his pen-cum-telescope. Creeping into the room when the couple have left. it takes him barely seconds to secure the tape-recording and. by subtle doctoring. to change its content. The outcome is not. perhaps. what his superiors would have liked. but Drake has seen enough to be convinced that the action he is about to take is the right one. Returning to the dead leader's home. he puts the tape back into Pilar's safe and awaits the outcome. When Rhamin ends his election speech by saying that Dr Shagris has left a final message for his people, neither Pilar or her accomplice are prepared for the message that is delivered through the public address system. Aware now that his father's second-in-command was responsible for plotting the doctor's death. Aldo has Rhamin shot. Having convinced the boy that his father was a great man. Drake is given permission to leave; Pilar's fate sealed.

Teleplay by Ralph Smart

Starring

Captain Schulman	**Paul Eddington**
Leanka	**Jeanne Moody**
Leontine	**Guy Deghy**

with

Aurel	**John Cazabon**
Stoian	**Frederic Abbott**
Standfast	**Vincent Harding**
Corbu	**Les White**
Police Sergeant	**Granham Ashley**

Directed by George Pollock

WITHIN MINUTES OF leaving his home. Standfast. Department M9's spymaster in Switzerland, is forced to stop his car in a country lane. There has been a traffic accident and two cars block the road. Believing that the people gathered around the vehicles are attending to the victims of the crash. Standfast gets out of his car to offer assistance. Before he can do so. another car screeches to a stop behind him. A man leaps out of the vehicle and reverses Standfast's car away. A stranger walks towards him and. at gunpoint. the spymaster is forced to watch as the man who has stolen his car races back down the road at speed and crashes the vehicle into a tree, crumpling the car into an untidy heap of scrap metal. In quick succession. Standfast is injected with a drug. his wedding ring is removed and. through drug-glazed eyes. he watches as a man's body is carried from a car. his wedding ring is slipped onto the dead man's finger and the body is squeezed awkwardly into the wrecked remains of his own car. The vehicle is then doused with kerosene and. as Standfast is carried away on a stretcher. the vehicle explodes into a ball of flame. The news of Standfast's death alarms the Department and Drake is sent to Geneva to investigate. Within seconds of arriving at the airport. the undercover man finds himself standing before the local police chief. Captain Schulman, who says that he has a shrewd idea that Standfast was a secret agent. a spymaster who had penetrated the Geneva Embassy and ran a ring of spies. He strongly suspects, too. that Drake is not the legal representative he claims to be. but is also a spy sent to check on Standfast's death: it occurs to Schulman that Drake is working for the British Secret Service. The M9 man denies this, of course. but the policeman informs him that he will remain alert to the newcomer's activities. Nevertheless. he agrees to allow Drake to see the dead man's body – not that this will help for identification purposes. the corpse has been burnt to a crisp. Everything about the body appears to be conclusive: the wedding ring. the height all match Standfast's file. But Drake discovers one clue to prove that the body is not Standfast's: his teeth. Someone. the undercover man is convinced, has gone double. But which member of the team betrayed the spymaster? Returning to his hotel. Drake escapes from two thugs who were lying in wait for him. Emerging the victor, the M9 man once again finds himself before Captain Schulman – accused of attacking his assailants! The policeman has concrete proof of the charge. Shoved into a chair, Drake is confronted with the evidence – a film (taken with hidden cameras) which shows him entering his bedroom and ... If Schulman expects to learn anything from this, he is soon disappointed. Having found the hidden camera when he entered the room, under the cover of darkness, Drake had tampered with the device and the 'evidence' the policeman expected to see shows nothing more incriminating than Stoian and Corbu, the men who attacked him, attempting to beat Drake to a pulp! Having turned the tables on his interrogator, Drake asks Schulman to bring charges against the men! Returning to the privacy of his hotel bedroom, Drake finds what he is looking for: a piece of microdot film containing the names of Standfast's spy network. By contacting each name in turn he elects to play a dangerous game, hoping that by doing so one of the team will reveal himself by trying to kill him. Each agent works for a different Embassy – the rotund Leontine (the first man Drake contacts), as a commercial attaché in one; the rat-like Aurel as a chauffeur in another; the attractive Leanka, who has been having a romantic affair with Standfast, as a secretary at another Embassy. When Drake contacts him by telephone, Leontine tells him he has the wrong number. Nevertheless, the call surprises the fat man and he is soon on his way to a secret rendezvous, set by Drake with a password. When Leontine arrives, the undercover man is waiting hidden in the bushes. Confronted with the evidence that Standfast may still be alive, the fat man is quick to take the bait Drake dangles before him: if the spymaster is alive, Leontine's counter-espionage friends may have him, which will make life at the Embassy very difficult. Next on the hook is Aurel, who is ill – ill with worry that he might be accused of being the man behind Standfast's death. He denies that the spymaster is being held at his Embassy. Leanka also tells Drake that he has the wrong number. But she, too, arrives at the rendezvous and confirms that she expected Standfast to be killed, but was not responsible for leading her lover to his death! However, as Drake soon discovers, she has something to hide. Within minutes of her arrival at the rendezvous point, Drake once again finds himself peering down the barrels of guns held by Stoian and Corbu, who have followed the girl. He escapes and drives away in his car, arriving at Leanka's apartment as the girl is preparing to retire. Under pressure, the girl tells him the truth: she had betrayed Standfast to protect her own life. Unseen by the girl, Drake plants a listening bug next to her telephone and leaves. Barely minutes after he has done so, he tapes a recording of Leanka ringing her colleagues. Repeatedly played, after several hours of dialling telephone digits, the tape coughs up a telephone exchange number ending in the numerals 14. From Aurel, the undercover man learns that this belongs to a safehouse in the country: could this be the place where Standfast is being held? To find out, Drake drives there. Seeing Stoian arrive and enter the building, leaving Corbu outside as lookout, the M9 man knocks out the latter and creeps inside. Hidden behind a desk, Drake sees Stoian and two other men enter a lift shaft concealed by a safe. Unable to crack its code, he telephones Leanka and tricks her into believing that firemen are on their way to the house to crack open the strong-room door. The unsuspecting Leanka telephones her comrades and Drake is waiting in the garden when the thugs emerge from their hiding place, shoving Standfast before them. Hidden in the back of Stoian's car, the M9 man has no difficulty in overpowering the thugs and driving the confused spymaster to safety.

Ill with worry, agent Aurel informs Drake: I'm Afraid You Have The Wrong Number

THE MAN WITH THE FOOT

Teleplay by Raymond Bowers

Starring

Derringham	**Bernard Lee**
Monckton	**Robert Urquhart**
Gomez	**Paul Curran**
Maruja	**Isobel Black**
Soleby	**Hugh McDermott**
Abelardo	**Michael Forest**

with

Reever	**Charles Houston**
Hencke	**Gertan Klauber**

Directed by Jeremy Summers

AN EXTENDED holiday is forced on John Drake when, in going to the aid of his M9 superior, Derringham, his cover is blown and a freelance agent named Soleby discovers Drake's real identity. It looks as though Drake is going to be useless to M9 for some time to come – perhaps forever. The spot he chooses to visit is Banalos, in Spain. It is out of season. The place is almost deserted and Drake is the only guest at the hotel, which is run by the attractive Maruja and her brother Abelardo. Drake is, however, expecting a friend, Gomez, a naturalist who has a scheme with which he thinks Drake can help him. An unexpected visitor also arrives – a clumsy, self-conscious individual named Monckton, the sort of man who, literally and figuratively, puts his foot into everything. He also happens to be a secret agent, as Drake discovers later. Monckton's suspicions are more than aroused when he learns who Drake is and realises that Drake and Gomez are up to something. Moreover, Gomez has with him some strange equipment, including miniature transistor capsules. Monckton is working for Soleby, and that brings his employer onto the scene. Drake, in turn, wonders what game Derringham is playing and a telephone call to his superior brings Derringham there as well. Soleby and Monckton jump to the conclusion that Gomez is somehow mixed up in espionage, quite unaware that he is, in fact, merely there to carry out an experiment to harness the science of tracking animal movements. For this reason, he and Drake go out on a wolf hunt to capture some cubs which, when fitted with Gomez's tracking device capsules, will reveal their movements when they are returned to the freedom of the wild. Shown one of the transistors by Drake, Derringham proposes to his employee that Gomez might be an agent working for the Spanish Intelligence network who, unknown to Drake, have tricked him into working for the other side. Drake tells his superior that if he believes that, he is as wrong as Monckton: the real reason for Gomez's interest is that a certain breed of wolf, usually found only in the Quardrama mountains near Madrid, have suddenly turned up in Banalos and his friend wishes to discover how they got there: the capsules will help him to do this. Soleby and Monckton meanwhile, believe that the capsules are being used for espionage: the devices are small enough to be swallowed, and would enable a spy team to keep track of their man no matter where he travelled. Simultaneously, Drake learns from Derringham that Monckton is the sole remaining member of a network that buy and sell secrets, and Soleby learns from Monckton that he is suspicious of Drake because the man has brought a set of fishing tackle with him – in winter, when there's no fishing to be had! Drake is fishing alright, but not for sprats: he wants to net Soleby. Until he does so, his career is at a standstill. The following day, Derringham keeps watch on Drake as the undercover man smashes a hole through the ice and dangles his fishing hook into the frozen wastes. But Derringham himself is under surveillance by Soleby, who now pulls a gun on Drake's superior. Soleby hands Monckton a gun, and orders him to watch Derringham. He orders Drake not to attempt anything suspicious, on forfeit of his superior's life. But Drake outsmarts his quarry, and hooks the gun from his hand with his fishing rod. Within the blink of an eye, the chase is on, Drake chasing after Soleby while Derringham handles Monckton. After an exhausting chase, Drake's quarry races onto the frozen wastes of the lake and it is here that he is caught by his pursuer and ends up on his back at Drake's feet. Having handed the man over to the authorities, Drake joins his superior for a film show, an epic filmed by Gomez's rifle-camera, which conclusively proves that Monckton's fears are groundless: true to form, he has once again put his foot in it!

In The Man With The Foot, *Drake arouses secret agent Monckton's curiosity when he goes hunting for a four-legged prey*

THE PAPER CHASE

Teleplay by Philip Broadley and Ralph Smart

Starring

Nandina	**Joan Greenwood**
Eddie Gelb	**Kenneth J. Warren**
Tamasio	**Aubrey Morris**
Laprade	**Ferdy Mayne**

with

Gordon Symonds	**Simon Lack**
Joe	**Peter Swanwick**
Frankie	**Peter Stephens**
Sam	**Oliver MacGreevy**
Canesi	**Sandor Eles**
Gloria	**Clair Gordon**
Paula	**Hanja Kochansky**
Constantine	**Steve Plytas**
Waiter	**Guido Adorni**
Customer	**Andreas Malandrinos**
Agent	**Ben Ari**

Directed by Patrick McGoohan

PARKING HIS CAR outside a cafe in Rome, British Embassy official, Gordon Symonds, races through the torrential rain to join Paula, his ladyfriend, in a cafe. Although he is only there for a few minutes, his pockets are rifled and when he returns to his car, his briefcase containing classified secret papers has been stolen. Meeting his friend John Drake, the civil servant explains how he must return the papers by Monday morning. If he cannot do so, the Foreign Office will crucify him. Symonds suspects that the thief was a lottery salesman who he is able to describe. On the surface, it appears that this is petty larceny, not espionage – nevertheless, with 48 hours to go – Drake agrees to help his friend. His enquiries indicate that the lottery salesman was a man named Tamasio. Drake pays a visit to his apartment. The man is immediately on the defensive and escapes into the night. Sometime later, believing Drake to have left, Tamasio creeps back into his home. He finds the Englishman waiting for him. After a heated discussion, Drake forces the man to admit that he has sold the case and its contents to a man named Eddie Gelb, a small-part film actor and inveterate gambler. On the pretext of wishing to join the action, the M9 man makes himself known to Eddie and, during a game of cards, takes him for a large sum, to the fury of Eddie's girlfriend, Gloria. Offering to cancel the debt in exchange for the case he received from Tamasio, the gambler tells Drake it is too late: the case has already been handed to the 'Big Man'. Although he is too scared to give Drake the man's real name, Eddie eventually leads the M9 man to a place run by a woman known as Nandina, who runs it as a hideout for international criminals on the run. The man he wants is a Frenchman, Paul Laprade. Having identified the man, Drake makes use of a transistor bug to overhear Laprade bargaining with a man named Constantine, who says, 'We are interested in the papers. What is your price?' Hearing the Frenchman's

In The Paper Chase, *actor Patrick McGoohan encounters a soon-to-be familiar face – actor Peter Swanwick*

figure Constantine says that he believes the price is more than the papers are worth. Constantine asks for time to consider the offer: he must speak to his superiors before he can accept. Confirming his willingness to wait, Laprade states that he can hand over the papers as soon as a deal is confirmed. Aware now that the Frenchman still has the papers, Drake poses as Troy Davidson, a man on the run. He is given shelter by Nandina, who warns him that there are two rules for the house: no guns, and total respect for the privacy of other guests. Later, however, when she finds Drake searching the Frenchman's room, in the presence of two burly henchmen, her friendly attitude changes and she tells the newcomer that he must be taught a very nasty lesson. Clearing away the furniture, she calmly orders the men to rough Drake up. In the darkened room, however, it is the undercover man who metes out his own brand of justice to the men – only to be knocked out cold when Nandina brings a heavy flower vase crashing down to his head. Afterwards, the woman apologises, and tells Drake that she has a 'good feeling' towards him. Using the tape-recording he made earlier, the M9 man telephones Laprade and, imitating Constantine's voice, fixes a rendezvous where he will be handed the money. Then, by telephoning Symonds, he lays a trap for the Frenchman. Using Tamasio's apartment as the pick-up point, Drake awaits the arrival of Laprade. Symonds, meanwhile, parks his van outside the lottery ticket salesman's apartment block. Arriving on schedule, Laprade, concerned that Constantine is not there to greet him, pulls a gun on Drake and peers through the window. Seeing two men standing in the courtyard below, he believes that he has walked into a trap and threatens to kill Drake should his 'friends' attempt to break into the room. This concerns Drake who, expecting only Symonds, crosses to the stair down to the entrance to Tamasio's apartment block where, sure enough, two men stand on guard. However, before Drake can allay Laprade's fears, a man bursts into the room and shoots the Frenchman dead. Turning the gun in Drake's direction, the man demands that he hands over the papers. He gets them, full in the face, as the undercover man flings the briefcase at the gunman. Then, in the same movement, Drake plunges the room into darkness, retrieves the briefcase and throws himself headlong through the open window, landing with a thump into bales of straw in the alley-way outside. Believing that they now have their quarry cornered, the two thugs move forward. In an instant they are thrown back on their heels as, revving the engine of the machine placed beneath the straw by Symonds, the undercover man zooms past his assailants in a powerful go-cart. A race around the corner, and both Drake and the go-cart are carried off into the night in the back of the truck his friend had waiting.

NOT SO JOLLY ROGER

Teleplay by Tony Williamson

Starring

Marco Janson	**Edwin Richfield**
Corrigan	**Wilfred Lawson**
Linda Janson	**Lisa Daniely**
Susan Wade	**Patsy Ann Noble**

with

Mullins	**Andrew Faulds**
Summers	**Jon Rollason**
Andrews	**Christopher Sandford**
Fisherman	**John Tate**

Directed by Don Chaffey

WISHING HIS Radio Jolly Roger listeners goodnight, disc jockey Andrews, in reality an M9 agent working undercover, leaves his studio and walks outside to transmit a message to his headquarters. Within seconds of warning the Department that the Blue Danube Waltz is being used as a code by the pirate radio station, Andrews is shot by an unseen killer and his body tumbles into the crashing waves below. The following morning, John Drake braves the stormy seas surrounding the old World War II fort in the Thames Estuary which serves as the illegal radio station's base. Joining the station in the guise of 'Johnny' Drake, a replacement disc jockey, Drake meets the radio station's head, Marco Janson, and his wife Linda, before crossing the gantry which leads to the crew's living quarters. The crew's attitude towards him is one of suspicion, particularly the belligerent Mullins, who is the head of administration. Drake soon meets his opposite number, Susie Wade, a pretty but tense girl, who is showing signs of strain and unease. Equally taciturn is the sound engineer Jerry Summers. In contrast to everyone else, the station's cook, Corrigan, shows signs of being over-friendly to the newcomer – and is usually the worse for drink. Drake, however, accepts the man at face value and gives him a bottle of whisky, which leads Corrigan to retort that anytime Drake needs him, he has only to whistle. Once alone, the M9 man produces an item from his arsenal of gadgets: a hairbrush which, when attached to another box of tricks Drake removes from his luggage, forms a cleverly disguised two-way radio transmitter. Dropping this through the port hole of his cabin, Drake makes a tour of his new enviroment. Informed by Susie that rule number one is always to stick to the broadcasting schedule, Drake takes over from her and immediately changes her selection – the Blue Danube Waltz – to a throbbing disco number, a mistake that brings an enraged Marco Janson racing into the studio to berate the new man for his error. His turn at the turn-table over, Drake returns to his cabin and hauls in the 'hairbrush', fitting together several further parts, before lowering it back through the port hole. In between playing records, Drake's investigations lead to him discovering that, as suspected, the fort is being used for something far more sinister than the illegal broadcasting of pop music. A chat with Summers reveals nothing beyond being advised not to snoop around. However, convinced that something is going on, something the station's owner in particular would not wish to see uncovered, Drake plays a dangerous game and climbs to the top of the radio mast where, using one of his transmitting-detector devices, he tunes in to a message being sent by morse code to a submarine somewhere at sea. The following morning, while sharing the breakfast table with Janson and his wife, a chance remark by Corrigan, leads him to check the sound engineer's studio where a number of electric cables disappear into the wall. Pressed about these, Summers tells him that Janson sometimes asks for the generators to be left running during the night; usually during the time when the Blue Danube Waltz is being played! Andrews discovered this before his death and made a note of the transmission times the record was played. Having asked Summers to fetch the notes, Drake forces open the sealed door in Summers' studio and discovers a short-wave directional transmitter. But Mullins arrives with a gun and Drake is taken outside. The men fight on the gantry and Drake is thrown headlong into the ocean. Aware that Susie has seen him throw the newcomer overboard, Mullins forces the girl into Janson's cabin. Concerned that

her employers care nothing for Drake's death, the girl attempts to leave, but is ordered at gunpoint to continue to transmit the coded message. Drake, meanwhile, far from being dead, swims back to the fort, climbs a ladder and makes his way unseen to Summers' cabin. But the sound engineer is dead. Creeping to Janson's cabin window and overhearing Janson berating Mullins for killing Summers, he bursts in through the door, sweeps the men aside and, having disarmed Mullins, forces Janson to show him where the radio telephone is situated. Raising the receiver to his ear, he is about to send a message to the mainland, when Corrigan appears and rams a gun into the side of his neck: the now sober 'drunk' is the head man behind the entire operation! His arms bound behind him, Drake is thrown into the generator room where he finally severs his bonds on the spinning generator wheel. At gunpoint, meanwhile, Susie is forced to spin the final coded record. Having escaped from the generator room, Drake creeps to the studio where, unseen by Mrs Janson, he beckons Susie outside. Drake tells her to get back into the studio and transmit the message: 'It's quiet enough for a drum solo.' The undercover man takes care of Janson while Susie, having aroused Mrs Janson's suspicions, knocks her captor cold. Corrigan, in the meantime, believing that Janson has contacted the submarine, sends for Mullins who, in turn, is flattened by Drake – leaving the M9 man free to take care of Corrigan in his own way.

About to transmit a message to the mainland, Drake discovers that salty old sea-dog Corrigan is a Not So Jolly Roger

DANGER MAN
(Secret Agent USA)

> ## SEASON FOUR
>
> 2 colour
> 60-minute episodes

AUTHOR'S NOTE: These two episodes, made as a proposed fourth series (which was abandoned after only two episodes had been made), were combined and screened as a feature-length television movie in some areas. To facilitate the continuity between the two stories, a short linking passage was filmed. This is included here (in italics) immediately after the first story.

KOROSHI

Teleplay by Norman Hudis

Starring

Ako Nakamura	**Yoko Tani**
Rosemary	**Amanda Barrie**
Sanders	**Ronald Howard**
Tanaka	**Burt Kwouk**
Old Japanese Man	**John Garrie**
Fortune	**Jeremy Longhurst**
Potter	**Christopher Benjamin**
Japanese Granddaughter	**Lilani Young**

Directed by Michael Truman

THE PICTURESQUE neon lights of Tokyo fail to arrest the attention of Japanese girl Ako Nakamura, as she races through the busy streets to escape from her pursuers. Finding refuge in her luxurious apartment, she stares down at the ornate pattern on the medallion she holds in her palm. Checking her balcony window to ensure that she is not being observed, she crosses to the bunch of red carnations placed in a vase on a table. She gently extends a thin telescopic aerial from one of the blossoms, flicks aside a small secret cover on the side of the vase, presses down the lip of the flower container with the tip of her finger, and begins to transmit a message to London: 'K3B calling M9. Priority One. The United Nations' mediator due in New York, will be assassinated within hours of his arrival. This will be the first of a series of killings planned by an organisation centred in Tokyo . . .' Unnoticed by the girl, a second carnation which has now opened its petals as if by magic begins to emit gas into the room. In an instant, Ako collapses to the floor in an untidy heap. Assigned to the case, Drake arrives in Tokyo, ostensibly as Mr Edwards, a radio reporter, and is met by Tanaka, a

chauffeur who has been sent to drive him to the British Embassy. The meeting has been arranged by Potter, the Embassy's cultural attaché, who meets Drake in a record store. Informing the newcomer that Ako Nakamura died of a heart attack, Potter knows nothing else. However, he has got hold of a report from London, obtained he insists with great difficulty, which Drake studies as he is driven through the streets by Tanaka, a man who is suspicious of Drake and offers to be at his *secret* service if ever the newcomer should need a contact! Secrecy, muses Drake, is a somewhat sparse commodity in this Japanese city. At the home of an old Japanese man, Drake takes tea and learns the meaning of the medallion that was found beside Ako's body: it is the emblem of an ancient murder-brotherhood which believed in the poetry of death. Before they were disbanded, they were artists in assassination. It now appears that the brotherhood has been revived. Ako was onto them and she was killed to ensure her silence. A visit to the dead girl's apartment might provide a clue to her killers. Another girl has moved into the flat. She is Rosemary Riley, who tells Drake that she is doing post-graduate research into the Kabuki Theatre, a group that has been around for over 400 years. The girl offers to help Drake by telephoning her friends, but her contacts prove unhelpful and Drake leaves, aware that the girl is trying to stall him. Calling at a florist's shop on the pretext of wishing to purchase 'two dozen red tulips. Japanese style' he is shown by a woman into an ante room at the rear of the premises. Left alone, he transmits a coded message to London saying that he has established the identity of agent K3B, and will affect the infiltration of the murder organisation. Furthermore, London should make no attempt to contact him, through Potter or otherwise. His message complete he thanks the woman for her help and leaves. The following day, while Drake is comparing a photograph of the medallion with several other Japanese artefacts pictured in a book at a museum, Rosemary Riley turns up. Told that he wishes to confirm the existence of the medallion for a programme he is planning, the girl tells him that she knows someone who will be able to help him, an Englishman named Sanders, who is as well informed as anyone about Japan and its customs. They find the man watching a display of the Kabuki Theatre. Told that 'Edwards' is a radio reporter, Sanders enquires whether the newcomer is intending to make a programme about the theatre group, but Drake replies that he is only gathering research material. Goading Sanders as they watch the performance, the M9 man suggests that he has heard that the Kabuki plays are obsessed with violence. Sanders contradicts the opinion, saying that they are simply obsessed with art, and find this in every aspect of life – and death – as the guest will now see for himself, as the players act out the poetry of death. Having studied Sanders' facination with the brutality of the performance – a Kabuki version of 'Hamlet' – Drake realises that the man loves death for its own sake, whether it is acted or not. Afterwards, Drake is shown the man's collection of Kabuki theatre costumes. Sanders is called away to answer the telephone leaving Drake alone in the theatre wardrobe. Drake paces through the storeroom and is instantly alert when he becomes the subject of a bizarre murder attempt: an assassin standing motionless behind him dressed in an eerie Kabuki costume, attempts to cleave his head with a Samurai sword. Drake escapes from the man, who magically disappears from sight by stepping into a lift device that whisks him to the stage above. When Drake reaches the performing area, all he finds is

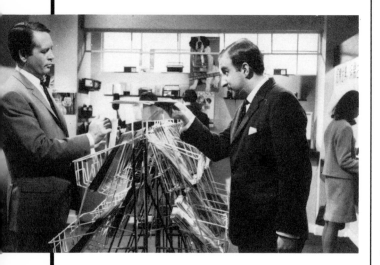

Drake meets M9 agent Potter in a Tokyo record shop. A scene from Koroshi

the would-be assassin's discarded costume! A return visit to the old man brings him a potted Japanese plant – a flower that guides – which is taken by the old man's Number One granddaughter to Rosemary, together with a message card from Drake, thanking the girl for 'the most exciting morning I have *lived* through!' The message disturbs the girl, who now realises that Sanders has been tricking her. Unknown to Rosemary, the flower pot contains a bug with which Drake can plot her progress when she visits Sanders' country home. Fortune, Sanders' colleague discovers the bug that has led Drake to the headquarters and Sanders convinces him that the Englishman is an enemy agent. Rosemary shows surprise, as does Drake, who, stationed in the garden, sees Sanders and the girl, leave and follows them in his car – unaware that one of Sanders' men has planted a bomb under its engine bonnet! Fortunately a warning device on the vehicle's steering column alerts him to the danger and once again, Drake escapes with his life. He is also instrumental in saving Rosemary's life, when Fortune attempts to get rid of her using the method of disposal he designed for Ako. If the dead girl's report was accurate and the United Nations mediator is to be assassinated in New York, time is running out. Discovering that Sanders is going to America, Drake pulls out all the stops. The race

against time reaches a climax in a subterranean temple where the murder-brotherhood is meeting. The means of assassination is being discussed by several black-hooded figures standing before Sanders who is dressed in his high priest's robe of Japanese lilac. Hidden behind a stone pillar, Drake observes as the Kabuki man puts his henchmen through their final training programme, with Fortune elected to strike the first blow. However, when Rosemary is marched into the room, Drake has no option but to make his presence known. Stepping forward, he goads Sanders with the words that in his case, the poetry of death does not rhyme. Telling Sanders that he has no doubt that he will be killed whatever happens next, the M9 man wonders if just one of the man's chivalrous brothers-in-murder could manage this by himself? Fortune is chosen as Drake's killer. Sanders leaves as the two men confront each other. Fortune is proficient, but no match for Drake who, flinging the killer aside, shouts to Rosemary to leave. Turning to face the second assailant, the undercover man disposes of the thug in a similar manner, before running outside to leap into a jeep and driving off after Sanders, who has now reached his private aircraft and is taxiing across the runway. However, seeing Drake's vehicle racing headlong down the runway towards him, Sanders pulls back on the aircraft's control stick. Too late. The plane is unable to respond and the aircraft and its pilot crash into fiery oblivion. However, unnoticed by Drake as he stands amid the ruins of the burning aircraft, Tanaka has crept up behind him. As the man is about to plunge his sword into the undercover man's back, Drake senses the Oriental's presence, and grabs the man's sleeve. Within seconds, the not-so-loyal contact lies unconscious amid the burnt-out remains of his master's aircraft.

...But all is not yet over for Drake. There still remains the secret of who is behind the revived murder-brotherhood? In order to discover this, Drake calls at the office of Commander Yamada, a Tokyo-based Special Branch policeman, who informs him that he has destroyed only the brotherhood's Tokyo cell: Tanaka and the other members of the sect have refused all efforts to get them to talk, and Yamada proposes that it is possible that Rosemary Riley knows nothing of interest – unlike himself, who knows everything that has been going on in Tokyo. He tells Drake that he considers that it may not be entirely a coincidence that Edward Sharp arrives there tomorrow from London. Aware that Sharp, an electronics communications expert, would be of considerable use to Koroshi and company, Drake arranges to have the man paged when he flies into Tokyo airport. Sharp is whisked away by Customs, and it is Drake himself who takes receipt of a package that Sharp was supposed to collect from an airline clerk. Sifting through the luggage in Commander Yamanda's office, the M9 man finds what he was looking for: a wad of banknotes concealed in the lining of Sharp's suitcase; a printed circuit hidden in the man's shaving apparatus; two resistors and a capacitor sewn into the handle of the luggage, and an electrode secreted in the locking-cap's spring attachment, together with a double-diode valve: all vital components of the latest crypton decoder. But who was Sharp going to meet? Someone extremely interested in jigsaw puzzles, offers Yamanda, who has slotted together the pieces of the jigsaw found in the box that Drake collected from the airport clerk – pieces that now point Drake in the direction of ...

Left alone in Sander's Kubuki Theatre wardrobe, Drake finds himself the subject of an eerie murder attempt.
(Koroshi)

SHINDA SHIMA

Teleplay by Norman Hudis

Starring

Miho	**Yoko Tani**
Richards	**Kenneth Griffith**
Controller	**George Coulouris**
Pauline	**Maxine Audley**

with

Commander Yamada	**David Toguri**
Contact Man	**Tommy Yapp**
Edward Sharp	**Edward Ogden**
First Girl Islander	**Mona Chong**
Manager of Two-Tailed Dragon	**Robert Lee**
Second Girl Islander	**Paula Li Shiu**
Passport Official	**Kristopher Kum**
Airline Clerk	**Anna Mai**
Hostess	**Barbara Yu Ling**

Directed by Peter Yates

...the Two-Tailed Dragon nightclub, where, having taken over Sharp's identity, Drake meets Pauline, the electronic expert's contact. An attractive Englishwoman, Pauline tells Drake that she has been swindled: she has bought a jigsaw puzzle, but several pieces are missing. Removing the pieces of Sharp's jigsaw puzzle from his jacket pocket, Drake slots them neatly into the almost completed puzzle which rests on the table before Pauline. The dragon emblem fits precisely into the place denoted by the name of an island: Shinda Shima. Drake must go there. He will be met at a teahouse at 11 o'clock on the morning of his arrival. As expected, he is greeted by Richards, a fellow Englishman who roams the island disguised as a beachcomber. However, when Drake suggests that he would like to go to Shinda Shima, Richards shows his reluctance to escort him there: the island has never had a name before, but a loose translation of the name means 'the murdered island'. It had once been a thriving pearl-diving community, but it was a community which had never felt secure because of a legend that said that the marine gods were jealous of the riches of the sea. One day the heads of three families would die mysteriously: and die they did. Because of this, everyone else moved to the mainland and the island was given its eerie name. Drake can play the enthusiastic geologist if he likes, but he must not get rocks in his head: Richards would not go to the island even if the seas around it were solid pearl! Returning to the teahouse, Drake is escorted to a motor launch by a Japanese contact and then on to Shinda Shima. A secret door hewn from a rockface gives them access to a maze of stone corridors. The contact leads the way to a vast underground complex, which serves as the headquarters of the revived brotherhood. But it is also a neo-Fascist organisation, headed by the Controller, who Drake now meets. Handing over Sharp's crypton decoder, the M9 man asks for the rest of his fee. Informed by the Controller that he knows full well that they need not only the components but his knowledge and skill, Drake learns that his task is to crack UNI, the operations code of the United Nations! He is given a radio room from which to operate and is introduced to a Japanese girl named Miho, who is assigned to work with him. While showing her how to locate the UN operations transmission, after some difficulty he succeeds in obtaining a tele-type message to Potter at the Tokyo Embassy: 'Drake routine report overdue. What is his current assignment? Report his whereabouts immediately. Urgent. M9'! Unaware that he is congratulating the subject of the report, the Controller finds this most impressive, but nevertheless urges the new man to crack the UNI code as quickly as he can. Reminding the Controller that the code is the world's most complicated and flexible code, Drake requests that he be given uninterruped solitude in order to do so. Agreeing to the man's request, the Controller escorts Miho from the room, pausing as he does so to check Drake's movements through a one-way observation window! That night, while Drake is asleep, Miho enters his room and attempts to kill him. Placed on trial by the Controller, it is revealed that she is Ako Nakamura's sister, intent on avenging Ako's death. Believing the girl to be an infiltrator, the Controller orders her death. The method will be a particularly nasty one – an electronic execution, to be carried out by Drake!

When Richards refuses to take Drake to the island of death, Shinda Shima, *the M9 agent is escorted there by a mysterious stranger*

But the undercover man tricks the Controller, and he and Miho make good their escape by swimming to the mainland, where, rising from the waves, they find themselves confronted by Richards, who, at gunpoint, orders them back to his cottage. But Drake is too clever for the man. Having given Richards the slip, Miho leads him to the former islanders who are organised by Drake to agree to invade their former homeland and take it back from those who have forced them away with tales of magic. Richards, meanwhile, crosses to the island and confronts the Controller with the news that the fugitives have given him the slip. Paid handsomely for this information, the man tries to leave, but is killed by an arrow, shot by one of the brotherhood. Meanwhile, back on the mainland, men and women, all of them expert underwater swimmers, meet their enemy on the sea bed. Drake and several islanders return to Shinda Shima to face the Controller for the final reckoning. The result is a spectacular battle that takes place in the vast underground headquarters where dozens of fights take place simultaneously. Cutting down members of the murder-brotherhood as he traverses the maze of corridors, Drake eventually reaches the exterior of the Controller's room. But the villain is ready for him. As the undercover man attempts to force entry, the Controller hooks his finger through the trigger-guard of a machine gun. Bullets ricochet from the walls as Drake smashes his way into the room and lobs a blazing kerosene lamp into the Controller's strong-room. Surprised by the speed of Drake's actions, the Controller attempts to escape, but the undercover man is too clever for him. Within minutes the brotherhood is sent to oblivion, destroying forever the legend of the murdered island.

Shinda Shima destroyed, the islanders prepare to return to their former homeland, led by Miho and Drake

Assistant Directors:
David Tomblin, Gino Marotta, Peter Price, Tony Way,
Doug Hermes

Music Editor:
Alan Killick

Editors:
Lee Doig, John Glen, Gordon Pilkinton, Ann Chegwidden

Casting Director
Rose Tobias-Shaw

32 monochrome 60-minute episodes
Filmed at Metro-Goldwyn-Mayer Studios, Borehamwood
(Episodes 1 to 26)
and
Shepperton Studios
(Episodes 27 to 32)
1964/1965

SEASON THREE

Series Created by:
Ralph Smart

Producer
Sidney Cole

Associate Producer:
Barry Delmaine

Executive Producer:
Ralph Smart

Director of Photography:
Brendan J. Stafford

Art Director:
Lionel Couch

Director of Music:
Edwin Astley

Music Editor:
Alan Killick

Assistant Director:
Doug Hermes (Episodes 33 to 40, 42 to 45)
Peter Price (Episode 41)

Editors:
Lee Doig, John Glen, Bill Lenny

Casting Director:
Rose Tobias-Shaw

13 monochrome 60-minute episodes
Filmed at Shepperton Studios
1965/1966

SEASON FOUR

Series Created by:
Ralph Smart

Producer:
Sidney Cole

Associate Producer:
Barry Delmaine

Art Director:
Albert Witherick

Director of Photography:
Brendan J. Stafford

Story Editor:
George Markstein

Director of Music:
Edwin Astley

Assistant Directors:
Peter Price (Koroshi)
Doug Hermes (Shinda Shima)

Music Editor:
Alan Killick

Editors:
Lee Doig (Koroshi)
John Glen (Shinda Shima)

Casting Director:
Rose Tobias-Shaw

Underwater sequences (for Shinda Shima) photographed
by:
Egil Woxholt

2 colour 60-minute episodes
Filmed at Shepperton Studios
1966

SECRET AGENT

The USA title of the 60-minute *Danger Man* series was known as *Secret Agent*. Complete with new title credits the theme song *Secret Agent Man*, was sung by Johnny Rivers.

THE PRISONER

'I Am Not A Number, I Am A Free Man'

B
Y THE TIME the third series of *Danger Man* went into production in 1965, Patrick McGoohan, in his persona of John Drake, was Britain's most highly paid television star, reputedly earning in excess of £2,000 a week. But the actor was beginning to become tired of the show, and the limitations of the character.

Believing that the series had reached its zenith and was fast running out of steam, McGoohan decided to throw in the towel and hang up the mantle of Drake for good, while the programme was still ahead of its nearest competition. 'It was a wonderful series to do,' he would recount later. 'I had a very enjoyable time. We had some excellent directors and some very good scripts, but then it started, as all series do of that nature, to get stale.' Despite the fact that a further series of *Danger Man* – to be filmed in colour for the first time – had been commissioned, approximately 12 weeks before the current series ended, to everyone's surprise, the star gave notice that he would not be continuing as John Drake. Aware that his contract with ATV still had a number of months to run, and that the company still had an option on his services *after* the agreement expired, McGoohan took stock of his position. Having never lost sight of his idea of the man in isolation standing up against authority and bureaucracy intent on trying to bend his mind into the shape they wanted, he decided to approach Lew Grade, then head of ATV, with his idea for a new series – a concept so special to McGoohan's personal beliefs that, if necessary, the actor was prepared to put both himself and his entire *Danger Man* production unit out of work.

History has it that the actor arrived at Lew Grade's office at 6.30 one Saturday morning. 'I always saw Mr Grade on a Saturday morning between six and six-thirty,' McGoohan has stated. 'He used to get to the office at 6 am and I have always been an early riser, so it was a good time to meet. Any business we had to discuss didn't take long because (that was the wonderful thing about him) you got a decision very quickly.' Told by Grade that he wanted him to do another series, something perhaps of a similar nature, the actor replied that he would rather not do any more. 'I've got this thing with me,' said McGoohan, producing some notes, designs and short plot synopses he had prepared, together with some photographs of Portmeirion, the North Wales *Italiante* village which had so impressed him when he had worked there previously during some 1959 location work for his *Danger Man* series. 'You know I don't like to read such things – tell me about it,' said Grade. The actor chatted away for 15 minutes or so, until Grade replied 'You know, it's so crazy, it might just work. When can you start? How much will it cost? When can you deliver?'

McGoohan, it seems, had the answers. Having 'resigned' as John Drake, the loss of its star meant that the entire *Danger Man* production crew would be looking for new employment. 'I had the whole unit waiting to go onto the new programme,' McGoohan said afterwards. 'Everything was ready. So he gave me the green light. We shook hands – we never had a contract – and I went ahead and did it. He never bothered me, gave me anything I wanted, crazy or not. It was a deal. That's the sort of man Lew Grade is.' (This is slightly untrue. Director of Photography, Brendan Stafford, recalls that ITC officials occasionally came onto the set attempting to cut the budget and interfere with McGoohan's ideas. They were promptly told where to go).

If we are to believe McGoohan's version of events, (and why not?) – in all probability it is as close to the truth as we will ever come (certainly Lew – now Lord Grade, has never cast doubt upon McGoohan's story although, as we will learn, script editor George Markstein would) – then the programme's origins are as remarkable as its content. But a million dollar series, clinched on a handshake?! It is far more likely that Grade, at the time one of the most powerful and astute men in the industry, fully aware that McGoohan was a highly bankable commodity, simply acceded to the actor's request in order to keep a valuable asset on the books.

The finance to produce the new series came from ATV, who were no doubt relying on the programme to sustain the popularity McGoohan had won with his highly successful portrayal of Danger Man John Drake. They were not to be disappointed – although it would take several years before the series recouped its high production outlay. By July 1966, the programme was up and running. It had a budget allocation per story reputed to be in excess of £75,000 – not a lot by today's standards, but then the highest ever assigned to produce a television series. Everyman Films, a subsidiary of ATV formed on 18 August 1960 by McGoohan, David Tomblin and others.

David Tomblin talking to Patrick McGoohan on the set of **Living In Harmony**

under its original name of Keystone Films. was chosen to produce the series. McGoohan elected to become Executive Producer. while Tomblin. a man with whom the actor had shared a long and fruitful relationship. donned the hat of Producer. George Markstein. who had worked in the same capacity on some of the hour-long *Danger Man* stories. was appointed Story Editor for the new programme – and almost immediately laid claim to creating the series' original concept!

Having been attached to British Intelligence in his capacity as the London correspondent for *Overseas Weekly*. a news magazine for the US forces in Europe (as a journalist he had attended over 400 court martial trials. which led to him being engaged as technical co-ordinator on ITC's *Court Martial* series). Markstein had gathered first-hand knowledge of an institution that existed in Inverness. Scotland (Inverlair Lodge. in Glen Spean). During World War II ex-spies who had served their usefulness as agents – together with other people who 'knew too much'. people who had been compromised and had reached a point in their careers when they knew too many secrets to be let loose, but had not actually done anything *wrong* – were sent there on permanent 'holiday' by the State. Although well-treated. the detainees were nevertheless to all intents and purposes. prisoners. Inspired by this knowledge. the writer turned it to his advantage and used it as a basis for his Prisoner concept.

According to Markstein (who was introduced to McGoohan by scriptwriter Lewis Greifer when the then *Danger Man* star was shopping around for a script editor to knock some story synopses McGoohan had written into shape) what happened was this. Close to the end of the *Danger Man* production. McGoohan had approached him to 'come up with an idea that would retain the popularity of *Danger Man*. and keep the production team together.' Exploiting his knowledge of the Inverness real-life situation. Markstein merged fact with fiction and hit upon the idea of combining McGoohan's 'resignation' as John Drake from the spy game. with his concept of a self-contained world where a man with such knowledge could be locked away from prying eyes. Expanding the concept to suit his belief that anyone detained in such a place would be of obvious interest to both sides. the writer proposed the idea to McGoohan. Delighted with the concept, the actor accepted the proposal. However. when Markstein indicated that he intended to pursue the premise that the man locked away was John Drake. McGoohan categorically refused to have the character named and gave him a number – acknowledging to Markstein that if they used the name 'Drake' the character's creator. Ralph Smart. would have to be paid healthy royalties! The first that Markstein knew about the star selling the idea as his own. was when he read about it in a newspaper sometime later. By then the damage was done. Accepting the inevitable. that someone has to take the credit for originating an idea. the writer shrugged things off by stating 'Nobody wants to know about scriptwriters. It is actors who sell a series to the public' – but he never overlooked an opportunity to pursue his claim that McGoohan was taking sole credit for 'his' idea and concept. As to who actually did create the format. I for my part. offer no opinion other than saying that. at the height of his career. I find it doubtful that McGoohan had either the necessity or inclination to 'lift' someone else's idea. However. it is fair to say that, as things turned out. the concept used was not a million miles away from Markstein's original Kafkaesque idea. Of course, there is always another version to be considered. Interviewed by the *Six Of One. Prisoner Society*. director Pat Jackson said 'The germ of the idea was certainly McGoohan's – after hearing from a Home Office official (slightly the worse for drink) that a place such as the Village did exist.' Fuelling the fires of controversy. it is my belief that Markstein provided the canvas (the Village. with its overtones of Orwell's 'Big Brother' and 24-hour surveillance). while McGoohan added the brushstrokes (the numbers. the costumes. and so on).

Despite the actor's protestations to the contrary. I remain convinced that the man numbered '6' was indeed John Drake – a 'fact' confirmed by Frank Maher. the stunt arranger for *The Prisoner* who. when interviewed in 1987 on behalf of the Prisoner Society told Larry Hall and Arabella McIntyre Brown, that one evening after he and McGoohan had played a game of squash. the star gave him a synopsis of the series and confirmed that the man who had been kidnapped and taken to the Village was John Drake.

What is beyond doubt. is that well before the production got under way. Markstein produced a four-page writer's brief. the 'bible' that was necessary to acquaint potential scriptwriters with the vagaries of the plot. action and situations with which the 'man with no name' would eventually be faced – the blueprint which. under McGoohan's control. would develop into the now familiar Prisoner concept. A series that one critic dubbed 'a meaningless muddle of weird. science-fiction orientated twaddle' and another 'an irrelevant load of piffle'!

While McGoohan devoted his attention to the preparatory stages: the design of sets and costumes. the booking of actors who he wished to appear in the programme (his choice of thespians was described by leading casting director Rose Tobias-Shaw as 'off beat') Markstein and Tomblin set about penning the pilot story. Meanwhile. other positions were being filled. In common with other members of the production crew. Brendan J. Stafford had enjoyed a long working relationship with McGoohan during his tenure as *Danger Man*. Having filmed all the original half-hour and hour-long John Drake stories. he was chosen as Director of Photography. (In fact. Stafford was half-way through recording a television series in Hollywood when he got a call from McGoohan asking him to come back to England to photograph *The Prisoner*.) Jack Shampan. another member of the *Danger Man* team was appointed Art Director. and Don Chaffey. a man for whom McGoohan had great respect. was brought in to direct the first story. Chaffey. too. had a story to tell. Having recently completed the Ray Harryhausen fantasy film *Jason and the Argonauts*. Chaffey was about to do another feature in Ireland. when McGoohan. a close friend of Chaffey's family. arrived at the director's home and said he had this idea for a new series and he wanted his friend to direct the first stories. Chaffey refused McGoohan's request and went off to Ireland. In the meantime. however. the actor handed some script synopses to Chaffey's daughter – asking her to show them to her father. Intrigued by what she read. the girl told her father to look at them. insisting that the series was going to make compulsive viewing. and would have people loving to hate him when the series was shown. Chaffey did so. and was hooked. Within days he had called McGoohan and agreed to direct the first episodes.

Approximately one month later. Tomblin and Markstein presented McGoohan with their script for *Arrival* – or. as it was then known. *The Arrival*. Delighted with the result.

particularly as Tomblin had never written a screenplay before, the star directed his story editor to brief his writing team, while he and Tomblin mapped out the location shooting schedule at Portmeirion – the 'perfect' locale McGoohan had had in mind from his very first visit to the place several years previously. (One of the stories that has circulated regarding the selection of Portmeirion as 'The Village' originated from Markstein's lips. Disputing McGoohan's claim that he had stored away the locale as 'somewhere to be used again,' according to Markstein, the location was selected by him, having read about the place in a *Sunday Times* magazine supplement. On the one hand, this can readily be discounted as being inconsistent with the fact that, as Markstein did not actually join the *Danger Man* production team until the second (hour-long) series, his claim was out of sync by quite a few years – McGoohan and his second-unit location crew having visited the locale some seven years earlier in 1959! On the other hand, it could well be that having read the magazine, Markstein *reminded* McGoohan about Portmeirion, the actor claiming that he first thought about the locale when he went there on holiday with his family, some time *after* filming his *Danger Man* stories.

Elsewhere, the runaway success of *Secret Agent* in America, had allowed Lew Grade the opportunity to negotiate both financial and commercial deals with the American buyer, Michael Dann, head of CBS, with the deal to buy *The Prisoner*, being made for a year ahead.

Location filming for the series began in Portmeirion on 6 September 1966, with architect Clough Williams-Ellis, owner and creator of the place, allowing the production team access only on the condition that the hotel's location remained a closely guarded secret. Only members of the public lucky enough to be visiting there were allowed to enjoy the thrill of seeing, at first hand, a film production unit going through its paces.

The initial episodes shot back-to-back were *Arrival* and *Free For All*, a script written by McGoohan, under the pseudonym Paddy Fitz (adapted from his mother's maiden name, Fitzpatrick). With the arrival of Chaffey and the second-unit location team, the serene surroundings of Portmeirion underwent a dramatic change. New notices were erected, strange 'information' kiosks appeared on street corners, canopied mini-mokes (Village buggy taxis) plied their make-believe trade (their presence there was, no doubt, a mystery to the day-trippers who attempted to hire them – only four were used, with usually no more than two appearing on screen at any one time). New arrivals in the shape of local residents, employed as extras (at 50 shillings – £2.50 per day) added colour to the proceedings as they tripped around in their brightly-hued costumes of boaters, frock-coats and top hats which, according to George Markstein, were meant to suggest a holiday camp atmosphere. A penny farthing bicycle (only one was used) tested the nerve of anyone foolish enough to attempt to ride it (in the series, the machine is always *wheeled* around), and a helicopter booked for the series soared low over the golden sands. Within days, Portmeirion had become 'The Village', a far from idyllic haven for its make-believe occupant.

The location shoot lasted for four weeks, during which time the unit worked flat-out to secure enough material for their purpose. As Portmeirion would be closing its doors in October, they worked a seven-day week, 16-hour-a-day schedule. Serendipity allowed them to put several of the location's inanimate objects to specific use: the Stone Boat finding its way into many of the stories; the

Green Dome eventually becoming the permanent residence of Number 2 (the original choice for the Village superior was The Georgian House, ie Portmeirion's Unicorn Cottage); the locale's main hotel being transformed into the Old People's Home, while Portmeirion's Town Hall doubled in the same capacity in the series for the transaction of official Village business, and one building (Battery Cottage) became residence 'Number 6'.

Location material to be used in several other stories was shot during this period. *Checkmate* and *Dance of the Dead* contain scenes filmed at Portmeirion, as does *The Chimes of Big Ben*. Details of the shoot were kept quiet from the media, with McGoohan and Tomblin throwing a veil of secrecy over the location. (Not until *Fall Out*, the final story, was transmitted did the name of Portmeirion appear on the credits).

Rushes – the developed and unedited film shot on the previous day – were viewed at the Coliseum Cinema in nearby Porthmadog, allowing the team to judge their early footage as the cinema's projectionist, Bob Piercy, screened the silent footage every night, including weekends, throughout the four-week period (he would be employed in the same capacity again, when the team paid their second visit to Portmeirion in 1967). As Bob told *Six of One* co-ordinators David Jones and Julie Benson, 'The crew would sit at the front of the stalls, joined sometimes by local extras. Each day's filming was usually about five to eight minutes long. When it had finished, it was sometimes run again. They would sometimes watch it seven or eight times – taking anywhere between 15 minutes and two hours. We used to start at about 10 pm, which sometimes meant that we would not be out until after midnight. Patrick McGoohan would sometimes nip out to the pub. He'd bring little Angelo Muscat up to the projection room and say "Can I leave him here?" and he would sit on a high chair looking out through the projection hole at the film. The highlight for Bob, was when Sir Clough Williams-Ellis arranged a preview of the first episode, *Arrival*. Although the Coliseum only had a six-day licence, and was not officially allowed to show films on a Sunday, they went ahead and did so anyway (without too much concern it appears, the Chief Constable of Caernarvon, being one of the guests). 'It was a great success,' Bob Piercy recalled, confirming that this was the *first* showing of *The Prisoner* anywhere. 'I remember that I had a note inside the film cannister saying something like "Don't scratch this print as it is the only copy." I had to clean the projector first and put Vaseline on all the moving parts. I was quite worried.' Bob remembered that many well-known local characters appeared as extras during the series. 'They picked some good people. One of them, Tecwyn Williams, was employed to recover the balloons when they went astray, and he got wet through running into the sea after them! My son was an extra, doubling for Patrick McGoohan in one scene. They were good wages too!'

The 'balloons' to which Bob Piercy referred were, of course, the now immortal Village guardians, but apparently these came about by chance. An early casualty of the first week's shooting was as an experimental version of Rover, the dreaded Village patrolman, the lighter-than-air membrane bubble-sphere, which served as the community policeman. A prototype machine, designed by art director Jack Shampan to travel over land and water, came under the influence of Murphy's Law and sank to a watery grave. As McGoohan told it, 'We had this thing designed to be the be-all and end-all of mechanical things.

Number 6 is ushered away by the giant menacing bubble

It would go under water, as in submarine, and was supposed to come out of the water onto dry land as in hovercraft. It was supposed to climb up the side of a wall and do all sorts of wonderful things. Valiant efforts were made. We were on location and about to shoot, and there came the day when we needed this thing called Rover, which had a light on top of it – a red blinking eye (the *Arrival* script gives the colour as blue), and issued a horrendous sound. Anyway, we tested it out in the ocean and it didn't come out. It stayed there. So we had to think of something else, and in desperation, Bernard Williams (the series' production manager) and myself were standing there not knowing what to do – we had to have a Rover to shoot on. We were looking up in agony at the heavens, and we saw this white thing, way up in the blue, and he said it must be a meteorological balloon. I said 'Do you think that thing would do? What size is it? Find out . . .' He took off and arrived back with the station wagon full of these balloons in varying sizes, from six inches in diameter up to eight feet in diameter, as well as cylinders of oxygen and helium and various other things. That's how we got what turned out to be the best possible Rover that one could have.' Version one. A second version was put forward by director Don Chaffey who, interviewed for the *Six Into One: The Prisoner File*, (a special Channel 4 documentary, shown in January 1984, immediately after *Fall Out*) expressed the wish to take credit for the Rover balloons. According to Chaffey, the original Rover was

going to be a motor bike, with a sort of igloo stuck over it with a light on the top, which struck the director as not being too effective. 'Rover to me,' he said, 'had to be a sort of abstract thing, it represented bureaucracy, it represented that nameless, faceless lot "out there" who tell you what to do, how to do it and when to do it.' According to Chaffey, what happened was this. At the time he was having arguments in trying to get a telephone installed at his squash court. He had filled out the requisite forms twice, and on both occasions the documents had been mislaid by the Post Office. Finally, in exasperation, he telephoned one of the 'faceless ones' and told him that if he supplied him with his name and address, Chaffey could send the next lot of forms directly to him. When the person on the other end of the telephone told Chaffey that this was not allowed – civil servants had to remain anonymous, the director accused the bureaucrat and his colleagues of being a lot of white balloons. My God, thought Chaffey: 'White balloons!' So he telephoned McGoohan and said: 'Pat, this is it – white balloons! That's what that lot are out there, they're not motor bikes!' Version two. When summing up the 'facts', one must take into account the following: there is certainly *no* meteorological station anywhere near Portmeirion (nor was there at the time the series was being filmed); *no* photographs of the land/sea version of Rover exist, and *no* extras ever saw it! In fact, many people, including noted Prisoner authority and editor of the Prisoner Society magazine, Howard Foy, believe that it never actually existed, or if it did, was rejected at the planning stages. Which version is correct? Who cares. Of such things legends are made. What really counts is that, filled with air, helium and water, the balloons worked amazingly well although, as we will learn, they sometimes had to be motivated by a thin nylon cord attached to a fishing rod, which was tied to McGoohan's heels to make them give chase or, on one occasion at least, were made to earn their supper by camera tricks.

Markstein, meanwhile, having elected to commission scripts from totally different writers than those who had worked on *Danger Man* (he had already received scripts from Anthony Skene, Gerald Kelsey and Vincent Tilsley), approached other scribes to put forward their ideas for storylines. As McGoohan had already promised to write the final story, the script editor commissioned screenplays from writers he believed had the right sort of ideas and attitudes for a series such as *The Prisoner*. Among these were Terence Feely, Michael Cramoy, Roger Woddis and Lewis Greifer. Among the scripts commissioned but not used were ones by Morris Farhi and John Kruse. (History has it that Markstein also approached a number of well-known novelists but none were interested).

In early October, the crew were back at the MGM Studios in Boreham Wood, ready to begin work on the interiors for *Arrival*. At McGoohan's insistence, the set was closed to everyone but the production team. While the location unit had been filming in Portmeirion, permanent sets had been constructed on the sound stages: Number 6's cottage (which, with relatively small changes, also served as his London home); Number 2's Green Dome 'office', with its huge television screen (referred to by Shampan as 'The Living Space') and the Control Room, which, with the addition of ornate arches, also served as the Village Labour Exchange. It was now that McGoohan began to put his stamp of authority on the show. Day after day he would ask to view the previous day's takes, often supervising the editing and, wherever he believed a story could be improved, asking for changes to the script – his habit was to write his alernative ideas on paper which would then be handed over to Markstein for inclusion in that day's filming. To some, his reputation was becoming that of a fearsome ogre, described variously as 'dedicated' and 'difficult'. Flinging his heart and soul into the product, the actor worked long and difficult hours – and expected everyone around him to share his enthusiasm. He replied to the charges by saying 'I know what they're saying and it's true that I have been unpredictable and impatient. You get that way when you're working at high pressure. But I haven't lost a friend in the unit.' Assistant director Gino Marotta said: 'Pat makes strong demands on everyone, and if you try to raise objections all he says is "Get it done!" and you get it done. But I've never known a director like him, because he does his homework so far in advance.' Art director Jack Shampan, concurred: 'He knows what he wants down to the smallest detail. One of the trickiest problems we faced was the control room, with its furniture popping up out of nowhere, and floors that opened. Pat outlined what he had in mind, and left me to work it out. I couldn't see at first how some of the things could be done.' The answer came from a large tank beneath the studio set. It was like a powerhouse, with activators, winches and electrically-controlled hydraulic equipment.

Apart from the prisoner numbered '6', the only other recurring characters were actor Peter Swanwick, who appeared regularly as the Supervisor, and the enigmatic Butler, who tended to Number 2's every whim without so much as a word of complaint – but then he could not complain – the man was mute. But things could have been different. It appears that the draft script for *Arrival* pictured the Butler as being the archetypal Gentleman's Gentleman, a tall, well-spoken, very formal man in obviously good physical shape who would be at home in an E-type Jaguar car. As to why this was changed, who knows? Personally selected by McGoohan after studying 'a vast number of photographs', Angelo Muscat's dimunitive stature became one of the most intriguing characters in the enterprise, leading many viwers to suspect that the black-coated, stocky little servant, who was often hidden beneath a large umbrella was, perhaps, the unidentified, all-powerful 'Number 1'.

After a two-week studio shoot, the pilot story was in the can – although it had still to be edited (both visual and sound) and have the music score added. Hearsay has it that it was McGoohan's original intention that the opener should run to feature length of around 76 minutes (90 minutes when combined with commercials), but the idea was shelved in favour of the standard 52/54 minute transmission time. (See addendum to *Arrival* synopsis). No such mystery surrounds the episode's opening sequence. During an interview, George Markstein had this to say: 'In that episode I set out to define the framework of the whole series – to establish the theme, the mood, the story foundation, and above all, the *characters*. The hub of *Arrival*, was to lay the foundations of the entire concept: to show who the Prisoner was (a man with too many secrets); why they want to put him away (he knows too much); and the place to which he is banished (the Village). The episode is a cry against surveillance, the encroachment of computers, the rubber-stamping of individuals.' His plot device works wonderfully. The opening title sequence (which recurs, in edited form, throughout the remainder of the series – except in *Living In Harmony* and *Fall Out*) is guaranteed to send a shiver down the spine. The Prisoner's fate, when it arrives, has just the right amount of power to make the viewer wish to hang on and await the denouement. However, as Prisoner authority Roger Langley points out in his well-researched *The Making of The Prisoner* souvenir booklet, the opening and closing sequences of the series were originally in different form. As filmed, the original opening titles showed the Prisoner being chased from the beach by a Rover. The guardian finally catches up with him in the Village, bowls him over and sucks the air out of his lungs. In the closing sequence (which was used twice only – see addendum following *Arrival* and *The Chimes of Big Ben* synopses), the penny farthing bicycle motif fades away until the planet earth is viewed in close-up (the large wheel turning into the universe and the small wheel into the earth). The world then explodes with a giant POP, the word emerging from Somalia! Incidentally, the star background was obtained from the makers of *2001 – A Space Odyssey*, which was being filmed at Borehamwood at the same time.

With the pilot story in the can, McGoohan turned his attention to the music. Bearing in mind his admiration for the work of those who had already served their time with him on his *Danger Man* programme, one could have expected the actor to renew his working relationship with composer Edwin Astley, who had scored all the John Drake stories, but it was not to be. At this juncture, Astley was already contracted to provide the theme and incidental music for Roger Moore's *The Saint* television series. as well as composing some incidental music for ITC's *The Champions*. Composer Robert Farnon was the first to be approached to write the title music. but his version of the theme – a zingy. strident Western theme. based on *The Big Country* – did not reflect what McGoohan was looking for. Wilfred Josephs came next. but again McGoohan was not pleased with the result (although a great deal of the music Josephs composed at this time appears throughout the series – notably in *Arrival*). By the year's end the programme was still without a regular title theme. It was at this point that composer Ron Grainer entered the scene. With a track record of popular television themes behind him. *Doctor Who* and *Maigret* to name but two. the musician set to work composing his version of the title music. Although not entirely disatisfied with Grainer's composition. McGoohan nevertheless felt that it was not quite right – it needed 'beefing up'. He explained what he was looking for and the composer went away and revamped his original composition. eventually succeeding in supplying McGoohan with what he wanted. It appears. however. that Grainer was irritated that McGoohan. an actor. had told him. a composer. to change a composition which he believed was right for the series. so when Grainer issued the theme music commercially. he recorded a more 'pop' version of his *original* composition. and not the one heard on the programme! (Incidentally. the majority of the harpsichord music heard in the story *Dance of the Dead*. is composed by Grainer.)

Albert Elms was added to the roster to compose the remaining incidental music. and music editor. Eric Mival. who had recently joined the team to replace Bob Dearberg. was sent along to the Chappell Music Library to. as he put it. 'get to know the library backwards' because. although there would obviously be original music composed for the show. Mival would have to select some previously recorded library music as 'fills'. Mival. whose first story was *Free For All*. was responsible for adding some additional music to the first two stories when they were re-cut. On record as saying that he. for one. understood McGoohan's 'ruffling a few feathers' by telling experienced editors to change this. or alter that. after they believed that they had given their best. Mival said 'Perhaps. as directors are prone to doing. McGoohan

McGoohan flexes his muscles behind the camera

changed his mind and perceived what he saw as a better way of presenting the shot – to give the scene more *impact*. by shortening or lengthening the action.' He added that the first story in particular. went through at least one re-cut of the negative after it had been reprinted. and it is partly because of this that the episode is exciting. (As seen on screen. *Arrival* does have at least one plot flaw. namely that Number 6 claims he saw the woman leave Number 2's residence when in fact – on screen – he sees no such thing. This could be explained by a cut. because the *Arrival* script matches the on-screen action).

After a Christmas break – a nice touch here being that each of the production crew received a Christmas card featuring the Butler with the penny farthing bicycle in a seasonal scene. the crew returned to the studio ready to face new rigours. By this stage. seven stories had been filmed and it was filmsmith Robert A'sher's turn to occupy the director's chair. turning his cameras on McGoohan and company for the story called *It's Your Funeral* – the episode that saw the introduction of the Kosho game. a novel idea dreamed up by McGoohan and developed with input from master stunt arranger Frank Maher. According to Maher. the game was conjured up out of necessity. because McGoohan wanted to use trampolines: 'You're going to *love* what I've got for you in the next episode.' McGoohan told Maher. who went away with Tomblin and came up with the crazy idea. Maher. who had worked with McGoohan throughout the entire hour-long *Danger Man* series. had never been known to bat an eyelid when the actor's fertile imagination came up with yet another complex action sequence that he. as stunt co-ordinator would have to execute. He said of McGoohan: 'He has the nearest approach to a stuntman you'll ever get among straight actors. He is certainly better at action work than any other actor I know. He works just like a good stuntman: everything is perfectly balanced and co-ordinated.' Told what type of fight was required. Maher would work on the fight scenes with the scientific approach of a movie director. Every moment. every punch. every inch of footwork being carefully mapped out on paper. His 'script' would be shown to McGoohan. and each piece of action was then rehearsed. almost in slow motion. until the movements were right. 'Some of them.' Maher said. 'are so dangerous that the slightest mis-timing could cause injury.' The action is then speeded up during rehearsals until it reaches the dizzy rapidity of the final. spectacular shots that reach the screen. with camera angles (also mapped out by Maher) that were as ingenious and imaginative as the fight arrangements themselves.

In March 1967. the second unit team returned to Portmeirion to complete shots for episodes already filmed. Using doubles. pick up shots were obtained as inserts for episodes yet to be made. with some of the footage actually ending up in *Fall Out*. Further location work. including the scenes from *Many Happy Returns*. in which Number 6 arrives at his home from Trafalgar Square. to find Mrs Butterworth driving KAR 120C up to his front door. were filmed in and around London and Borehamwood.

As guardian of the Prisoner's secrets. it could be expected that McGoohan. the only person who knew what was going on. would have kept his crew aware of what he had in mind. It appears that this was not the case. When asked to explain the increasingly bizzare plot. or tell them the identity of the mysterious unseen character. Number 1. he blatantly refused to clarify what he had in mind. Indeed. when asked anything about the production.

he invariably gave half-answers and refused to reveal any of his secrets. After a period of disagreements over the way McGoohan was approaching the series, and frustrated that 'his' original concept was in danger of being buried under a barrage of science-fiction abnormality, Markstein – the man who had elected to play the man seated behind the desk to whom McGoohan repeatedly handed in *his* resignation in the programme's opening title credits and in *Many Happy Returns* – reversed the roles and left the series after 13 episodes. So did most of the production team who had, after all, only been booked to work on the first 13 episodes. To the chagrin of those left behind (among whom numbered several ITC executives who were beginning to show concern that the programme was already way over budget), this allowed McGoohan to flex his muscles and take almost total control of the series by overseeing nearly every aspect of the production. Scenes filmed by well-known directors, including Roy Rossotti and Michael Truman, were thrown out and reshot – usually by McGoohan himself. Unhappy with several of the completed stories, the actor ordered them to be changed, his habit being to edit out the scenes he felt could be improved and replacing them with newly-shot material. Ignoring the protests of his writing team, he began to revise scripts, usually working throughout the night to have the rewrites ready for the following morning. The atmosphere on the studio floor was fraught with tension, and the strain was beginning to tell. Unwilling to relinquish his position, or delegate responsibility to others, McGoohan was beginning to look tired and drawn. Interviewed later, he said 'I worked my way through three nervous breakdowns. First time the doctor ordered three weeks off. Last time he suggested three months. There was only one answer – to keep on working. You can't let up when you're in charge.' (McGoohan, it seemed, was far from prepared to step down off his high horse, but within weeks he was about to climb down from his saddle and hand the reins over to David Tomblin). Meanwhile, however, his commitment to the job knew no bounds. He would work a full day, usually from 7 o'clock in the morning to well into the night, but was always the first to arrive at the studio and be available for the cameras the following morning. Producer David Tomblin said: 'When you're making a television series, you reckon to get through between 15 and 20 set-ups a day. Pat often averaged 33 a day, and in one two-day spell achieved 104!'

Nevertheless, the series was weeks behind schedule and something had to be done. After talks between Everyman Films and ITC, a decision was taken to produce a further four stories and to aim for a season of 17 episodes – an unusual number, but one that would slot neatly into the USA summer schedules. (In his *The Making of The Prisoner* booklet, noted Prisoner authority, Roger Langley, commented that, in a flush of enthusiasm for the series, Lew Grade had originally envisaged 30 episodes, but after almost two years' work, increasingly hostile criticism and the outlay of over £1¼ million, it was decided to call a halt at episode 17. While I defer to Roger's infinitely superior knowledge of the subject, I would suggest that a full season of *26* episodes was far more likely, Roger's assertion seemingly based solely on a press interview that Lew Grade gave at the time. Even shrewd entrepreneurs have been known to be misquoted!

As unlikely as it seems, the next episode to be made, *Do Not Forsake Me Oh My Darling*, would have to be produced without McGoohan taking part – at least, for the majority of the story. Having decided to accept an offer to go to Hollywood to play the role of Jones, the British agent sent to the polar wastes to crack a conspiracy in director John Sturges' version of Alastair McLean's *Ice Station Zebra* (a role not far away from the actor's earlier persona of John Drake), McGoohan, thankful no doubt for any break the filming would allow, decided to hand over his brainchild to David Tomblin. By the time the actor had returned to the studio, his partner had produced the story – a cleverly-woven tale that was scripted by Vincent Tilsley to take into account the absence of Number 6 (although Tilsley's script was heavily rewritten before filming). Feeling infinitely better for his break, McGoohan was soon back in front of the cameras filming his few scenes – with doubles standing in for the actors who, having completed their input prior to McGoohan's return, had left the studio. It was not long, however, before the actor rediscovered his thirst for leadership and he soon slipped back into his old habit of believing that 24-hour days are made for mortals. Within days, he was back at the tiller, steering his ship through the stormy waters that lay ahead.

It was as though he had never been away. Working at a frantic pace, McGoohan once again found himself appearing before the camera during the day and spending each evening consolidating his vision of the next day's shoot – not to mention, one assumes, devoting whatever time he had left to working out the screening order for the programme's imminent debut on television. Barely weeks after his return to the studio, the star and his production team were at each other's throats, the head-to-head spectacle rivalling the fictitious on-screen confrontations between Numbers 2 and 6 – an event that was hardly encouraging to a crew who had seen and heard it all before. Lew Grade, meanwhile, though not overtly worried about the production falling behind schedule (true to his word he had continued to back McGoohan to the hilt) was nevertheless concerned that there would not be a final story ready in time for transmission. 'I knew there *would* be an ending,' he told everyone, 'because Pat *told* me there would.' But the man who refused to be 'pushed, filed, stamped, indexed, briefed, debriefed or numbered' was becoming increasingly intolerant of the charge that he had lost sight of his perspective. With neither the time, finance or inclination to return to Portmeirion for further filming, he threw himself into the

McGoohan rehearses a scene from **The Girl Who Was Death,** *which was made almost entirely on a backlot at MGM studios*

next two stories *Living In Harmony* and *The Girl Who Was Death*. The former broke with tradition by being made almost entirely on a backlot at MGM studios, with location work being restricted to a couple of exterior sequences shot in and around the Borehamwood countryside, the Portmeirion 'Village' footage being courtesy of stock film (as were scenes of the Village used in the episodes *The General*, *The Schizoid Man* and *A Change of Mind*, among others.)

In October 1967, to coincide with the series being premiered on British television, a pre-launch Press conference was arranged, with reporters being invited to question McGoohan about the programme as he sat in the cage used as the Embyro room in *Once Upon a Time* – a story that, though completed many months earlier, had been pulled to serve as the penultimate episode. Dressed in Kosho uniform and a Cossack hat (after a Press screening of *Arrival*, the star would return dressed in *Harmony* western garb), the enigmatic McGoohan, determined to confound and confuse, turned the tables on the media by not only refusing to give straight answers to their questions, but actually asking them questions of his own! A nice anecdote is attached to the *Living In Harmony* episode. Actor Alexis Kanner, contracted to play 'The Kid', received a telegram from McGoohan, who at the time was filming the Alastair McLean story, saying that he was taking quick-draw shooting lessons from Sammy Davis Junior and Steve McQueen. 'So I realised,' Kanner recalled, 'that Patrick was in earnest, and meant this to be shoot-out to end all shoot-outs – the fight wasn't going to be faked by a cut or an edit – and we were really going to have to shoot it out. So I eventually found a gun and practised my own quick draw. Then I wired back the trigger, which was a very dangerous thing to do, because when the trigger is wired off, there is nothing to stop the trigger going off. So the day finally came when we had to film the showdown in *Harmony*, and bets had been placed as to who was the quicker draw, myself or Patrick McGoohan. What actually happened, was that we both drew, but only one shot was heard. So the bets weren't paid out until the next day when the film had been processed and by counting the frames, Patrick had taken 11 frames to draw, while I had taken 7 – a difference of a sixth of a second or something. So after that the healthy competitiveness and respect between us became greater and greater.' (Stunt arranger Frank Maher recalls that when he read McGoohan's cable saying Steve McQueen was teaching him to draw, he had some pencils ready for the star's return, teasing McGoohan by suggesting that the Hollywood actor had been teaching him to draw *pictures*!)

It was during the filming of *The Girl Who Was Death* (in which, incidentally, Kanner made an uncredited appearance) that McGoohan announced that he would be writing the long-awaited finale – but not before he marched into Lew Grade's office and said 'I can't find an ending ... I've become too confused with the project!' Given the fact that the majority of the ITV regions had already transmitted 12 of the episodes, an ending *had* to be found. As McGoohan had always claimed to have had the idea for the finale from the outset, he alone was obliged to deliver the goods. (With the wrap-up story originally due to be screened in January 1968, the final two Prisoner stories were pre-empted, with some ITV regions running the two *Danger Man* colour episodes *Koroshi* and *Shinda Shima* on consecutive weeks, in black and white). Having locked himself away for the weekend, 36 hours

McGoohan attends a Press conference, dressed in Kosho uniform and Cossack hat . . . .

. . . . and returns dressed in Harmony Western Garb

137

later McGoohan presented his crew with the script for *Fall Out*, a tale so wildly ambitious, surreal and pretentious, that neither his allies or the viewing public were prepared for the extraordinary conclusion. Put together at the eleventh hour (the filming and editing were completed with barely days to spare), McGoohan's promise that the story would solve all the mysteries, only served to fuel the

McGoohan directs actor Leo McKern and Alexis Kanner during his extraordinary conclusion story Fall Out

fires of controversy. To the disappointment of many fans – not to mention the actor's colleagues – far from being resolved, the questions that had permeated the programme were forgotten, to be replaced by even more questions. The actor's promise to explain everything was wrapped up in a confusing mixture of ambiguous symbolic imagery which shattered the expectations of just about everyone. *Why* had the one numbered 6 resigned? *Would* he finally throw off the shackles of his captors? *Who* exactly *were* his gaolers? And perhaps most important of all, *who* was Number 1? The episode answered nothing, beyond, perhaps, adding to the mystery. If the doyen of the court was looking for controversy by providing neither a neat resolution or a simple, easy-to-understand answer, he had achieved his aim: the preceding 16 remarkable stories were washed away in a disorderly mixture of pantomimic design that deliberately avoided a tidy conclusion. Viewers who had expected the denouement to answer everything were dumbfounded, with predictable results. During and immediately after *Fall Out* had been transmitted, the ATV duty officer logged well over 150 calls from a confused public.

The following day the mail began to flood in, though strangely enough, the trends of the previous evening were reversed with the majority of the correspondence in favour of the series. The Press were more cautious – their reactions were a mixed bag with some critics asking whether *The Prisoner* was all hokum, while others drew their own conclusion that the programme had been the most vivid of comment on modern civilisation in the history of British television. McGoohan, it seemed was prepared for the outcry. As he told the Press afterwards, 'I *wanted* controversy, arguments and discussion. I was *delighted* with the reaction. It was the intention of the exercise.' Mind you, he was equally liable to claim that the series had reached its perfectly logical and finite conclusion. Answering his critics, he remarked 'I've done a job. I set out to make a specific number of films. I've made them. The series has come to an end. It is just the end of a job, that's all.' Then, with a leprechaunish grin, he invited anyone who failed to appreciate the result of his labours to say, 'Nuts to you, Paddy boy!'

But the job was far from finished, and the actor would experience further hardships before he could slam shut the doors on his creation. As the person responsible for devising the product, there can be little doubt that, despite his claims to the contrary, the man who had strived for perfection in every facet of his career, *must* have been scarred deeply by the initial reaction of both the viewers and critics. Many people regarded the wrap-up story as a betrayal of the established views of the essence of television making: questions are *supposed* to be answered. The good and the bad guys are *supposed* to be defined as such. Programmes are *supposed* to have a beginning, a middle and – in this case in particular – an *end*. They felt let down, hurt and alienated by the actor's total disregard for the established institution of creative television. Many, who seeing the show for the first time had recorded their verdict that the programme was doomed to failure, had long since become hooked on the series and were uniformly unprepared for – to their minds – McGoohan's shocking ending. When the actor came in for a barrage of acidulous Press, many of his former workmates deserted him, only to comment over the years that, with hindsight, they could now understand what McGoohan was about and why he wanted it that way.

Two decades on, it appears that McGoohan's attitude remains resolute. Interviewed for *Six Into One: The Prisoner File* (a 50-minute documentary commissioned by Channel 4 and shown in January 1984, immediately after *Fall Out*), and asked if he had realised that the episode would cause such an outcry, he replied 'Well, I hoped that there would be a bit of an outcry – I *knew* there would be something going on, because it wasn't the conventional ending. People may say "Let's see something original" but basically people like a good solid story that ends up the way it should. This one didn't, of course. There was an outcry – I nearly got lynched and had to go into hiding. They thought they had been cheated, they still had the idea, God love 'em, that it was still John Drake, a secret agent story – *Danger Man* or *The Saint*, or *James Bond*. It had nothing whatsoever to do with any of these. People go to see a James Bond story because they know precisely what they are going to get for their money – a very stylish, bad, bad villain. This had nothing to do with that. This was *not* an action adventure show. It was an allegory. An allegory is a story in which people, places and happenings hide and conceal a message. There is symbolism, therefore there is enormous latitude with what one can do. The main outcry was the evil that had been there throughout, had never been seen. When it turned out to be the evil side of myself, for 12 frames of film in one shot and 18 in another, they were outraged. But what is the greatest evil? If you are going to epitomise evil, what is it? Is it the bomb? The greatest evil that one has to fight constantly, every minute of the day until one dies, is the worser part of oneself. And that is what I did. And I would do the same again.'

But *did* the Prisoner ever *escape*? 'In the final episode,' McGoohan said later in the same programme, 'they all get away, singing "The hip bone's connected to the thigh bone", and he goes back to his house – and the door opens on its own. And he goes in, and the car is there, and you *know* it's going to start all over again. Because we continue to be prisoners. When the door opens on its own – and there is no one behind it – exactly as the doors in the Village open, you *know* that someone's waiting in there, to start it all over again. He has no freedom. Freedom is a myth. There is no *final* conclusion to *The Prisoner*. We were fortunate enough to do something as audacious as that, because people do want the words "The End" put up there. Now, the final two words for *this* should have been "The Beginning"!'

Did McGoohan take the easy way out? Was the ending inconclusive? In retrospect, it is not too difficult to imagine why the actor decided to pull the plug in such an extreme manner. Such a radically innovative series *demanded* an equally radical conclusion. Only much later would the series become accepted as the classic it undoubtedly is – a slice of television history that defies all efforts to catergorise its unique qualities. As Roger Langley sums it up so well: 'The Prisoner can be appreciated for its high standards of creativity, original ideas, direction, acting, scripts, music, camerawork and sets, placing it many years ahead of the time in which it was made. Much of its appeal lies in its unanswered questions. Alternatively, it can be seen as a challenging epic, allegory, parable, fantasy or thriller. It combines Orwell, Kafka and even, when considering Shampan's sketches and set designs, Fritz Lang.'

Another writer, (unnamed) working for the *ATV Newsheet*, the staff newspaper of the (then) ATV network, prepared the following man-in-the-street's guide to *The Prisoner*, in the issue dated February 1968:

The Village	It did not exist in any materialistic form. It symbolised the prison that is man's own mind.
The Numbers, No. 6, etc.	This represents man's lack of freedom – the stifling of individual liberty by authority.
The Balloon – Rover	Symbolises repression and the guardianship of corrupt authority which, when corruption is finally overcome, disintegrates.
The Penny Farthing	Represents the slowness of progress in our modern civilisation.
The Hippy Character (as played by Alexis Kanner)	Symbolises youth in rebellion against the establishment and, as in the closing sequence of the young man trying to thumb a lift first in one direction and then in another on a motorway, youth not knowing, or caring, in which direction it goes.
The Former No. 2 (as played by Leo McKern)	A former trusted member of the establishment who, having broken away, is accused of having bitten the hand that fed him and is being made by authority to pay for his failures.
The Little Butler	He represents the little men of every community, prepared to follow faithfully, like sheep, any established leader.
The 'break-out' sequence, guns, firing – overlaid by the theme 'love, love, love'	This was a protest against the paradoxes which exist in modern civilisation. Man, preaching love, love, love against the holocaust of war. A penetrating comment on the world situation – Vietnam, the Middle East, etc.
No. 1	The unveiling of No.1 as Patrick McGoohan himself is representative of every man's desire to be No. 1 – to be the top dog.
The 'shouting down' of McGoohan by the hooded assembly	The inability of the ordinary man to make his voice heard – to put forward his viewpoint to the world.

Whatever its ultimate aim, *The Prisoner* is a series that demands to be seen over and over again – but not in an attempt to unravel its hidden meaning. In my humble opinion there isn't one – but purely to serve its intended purpose, that of an hour of *entertainment* which has never been equalled for its sheer fortitude in daring to keep the viewer both amused and *alert*. One cannot help being appreciative of its creativity, originality and pure, unabashed excellence!

Before entering into the chronological history behind the making of *The Prisoner*, we should perhaps, look at the picture painted by the *ITC Press Book* for the series, a document that was prepared as the series was still being produced. What follows is reprinted exactly as it appears in the brochure, with only biographical details – not pertinent to the subject matter – being omitted.

THE PRISONER

After John Drake — what?

This was the question asked on all sides when Patrick McGoohan came to an end of the *Danger Man* series — a series acclaimed in almost every corner of the world and one which turned McGoohan into one of the greatest names in television.

It is a question which Patrick McGoohan asked himself. And he himself provided the answer. The answer is **The Prisoner**.

The idea for the series is Patrick McGoohan's own, and it is probably the most original idea ever conceived for a television series. It has so many unique aspects that when the production began, McGoohan insisted that it should be filmed on closed sets, banned to interviewers and other visitors, in a bid to prevent its secrets from leaking out.

The secrets are revealed as the series progresses. Each segment, a complete story in itself, paves the way to intriguing new aspects of the drama. Suspense builds up from the very opening scene in the initial episode.

Patrick McGoohan is not only the star of the series. He is executive producer. He has elected to direct several of the segments. He has written some of the stories and has been closely involved in the scripting of each one that appears on the screen. No actor has ever been more closely identified with a programme.

Who is **The Prisoner**? He has no name. Only a number — Number 6. All references to him in the stories are simply by that number. In the scripts and on the programme billing he is just 'The Prisoner'. Few of the other characters have names either. They, too, are numbers except when story developments demand identification by name — occasions when anonymity is deliberately discarded.

Apart from Number 6, there are no other regular running characters, although some do appear several times. Identification of the characters is probably much simpler for the viewer than when they have names because all wear a numbered disc in their lapels or attached to their clothes.

The Prisoner's background is a mystery. He is a man who has held a highly confidential job of the most secret nature. He has retired, but retirement brings increased vulnerability to men in his position. They still have their secrets — secrets which, in many cases, they have kept even from those who employed them. They are secrets which many, many people, whether friends or enemies, would like to have and, in this new series, are determined to have.

This is why the central character in **The Prisoner** has been abducted. He is among others who have equally vital secrets locked away in their own minds and which only brain-washing can extract . . . and among those who have imparted their secrets and, having done so, can never be allowed freedom again.

He has no idea who abducted him. They could be his own people. They could be enemies. Perhaps both. And he has no idea where he is, except that the compound is a completely self-contained village. It could be anywhere in the world, and there is no way of knowing. He is given a cottage with maid service and every conceivable amenity. But every inch is bugged. His every move is watched constantly on close circuit television. There is a detailed map of the village with all the exits clearly marked — but they are cut off by a deadly ray barrier.

The action is on three levels. The Prisoner is constantly probing to discover the identity of his captors and why they have seized him. He is striving by all means and at risk of death to escape. And he becomes involved with his captors and takes an active part in situations arising in their lives.

Some of the village's residents encourage him to try to escape. Others attempt to dissuade him. He has no way of distinguishing between a possible ally and a potential enemy. He has no idea who are the other prisoners any more than he knows who the captors are. They all speak English, but sometimes a foreign language is heard in distant conversation but ceases upon his approach.

He has no idea if it is the West training him up to top indoctrination resistance, or if it is the East trying to break him. But he does know that he has got to resist every effort to make him talk. The efforts to break him are both physical and mental; but he is a man of integrity, determination and willpower, with an inflexibility of purpose that cannot be defeated.

Suspense is the keynote of the series. The action is electrifying but, more than anything, these are stories of a man's personal courage and convictions. The emotional impact is intensely moving. 'It tears at your heart,' one member of the unit declared after seeing a rough-cut of the first episode.

The Prisoner is *not* John Drake. Patrick McGoohan is emphatic on that point. But there is one thing in common with the *Danger Man* hero, and this is in keeping with Patrick McGoohan's well-known refusal to introduce anything of a nature which cannot be viewed by family audiences. There is no sadism. There is no flamboyant sex.

The Prisoner will not become emotionally involved with girls, but this does not mean that there is any lack of feminine appeal. On the contrary, the series introduces some of the most excitingly glamorous and talented of Britain's actresses; and women do, in fact, play a much more vital part in the stories than they did in *Danger Man*.

But Number 6 can trust no-one, not even those he believes to be friends and particularly the girls who display their femine appeal . . .

McGoohan refuses to reveal, except for an undertaking to do so at a later date, where *The Prisoner* was filmed while on location. A large amount of the action takes place out of doors in and around the mysterious village, and the programmes have been filmed in one of the most fascinating and colourful villages in the world — a village which is unique in that it is privately owned and has no permanent residents.

Interior scenes have been filmed at the Metro-Goldwyn-Mayer Studios in England, where some of the most imaginative and ingenious sets ever devised for a television series have been created by set designer Jack Shampan. Nothing like them has ever before been seen on the screen, and it is part of McGoohan's puckish sense of mystery that they will convey to the viewer no indication of the time in which the stories are set. They could be taking place today or tomorrow.

The hour-long stories have been filmed in colour, but whether in black-and-white or colour, they introduce a new element into the making of television films, with their unusual settings, intriguing costumes and fresh, vital ideas.

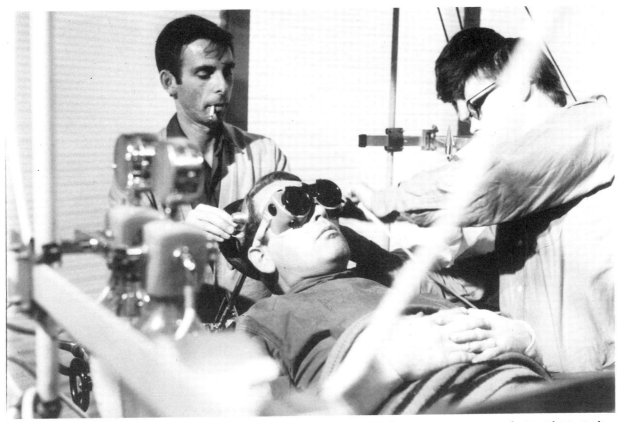

Studio technicians prepare Number 6 for the reversal process in Do Not Forsake Me Oh My Darling

THE VILLAGE

It is known simply as The Village. It has no name. Its occupants have no idea where it is, and they no longer have names themselves: they have become numbers. But they have one thing in common. All are prisoners of one sort or another, and all have been associated with highly confidential jobs of the most secret nature for one country or another. Some have been brainwashed and have accepted their new life. Others are still fighting for survival as individuals.

The Prisoner is one of the fighters, and this is the role Patrick McGoohan plays in his new series of one-hour episodes in colour, **The Prisoner**.

The village to which he finds himself abducted is fascinating. It's colourful, unusual to a high degree, and entirely self-contained. Geographically beautiful, it is built on a hilly peninsula, isolated by a range of mountains, dense forests and the sea. It could be anywhere in the world. Its buildings suggest that it might be in Italy, but everything about it refutes this. It could be a village built especially for the grim purpose for which it exists, but it could be one that has been taken over completely for this purpose.

Viewers might well imagine that it is a vast film set built especially for the series. But it is not. The village really does exist, and all the location scenes for *The Prisoner* were filmed there. Its very existence, known personally to McGoohan for some years, was partly responsible for inspiring the idea for the series, devised by Patrick McGoohan himself.

But what it is, and even which country it is in, is a secret which Pat McGoohan is hoping to keep during the initial airing of the episodes, at any rate, not only because secrecy will add provocative interest to the programme but because further scenes might have to be filmed there and the presence of the public would hinder production.

Fact and fiction have been skilfully blended. The village, and what it stands for, is an integral part of the story construction, and The Prisoner's efforts to discover its secrets are thwarted at every turn.

He has a map, but there are no place names. The map is detailed. There is 'The Sea' — but what sea? There is 'The Beach'. There are 'The Mountains'.

The Village has two kinds of inmates — those who have been taken there and those who run it. But it is almost impossible to tell who is who. Surveillance is constant. Television cameras record every move and activity, both indoors and outside. Every type of modern electronic watching device is used to keep tabs on everyone.

Standing in a clearing by itself is the Castle, which is used as a hospital. It is also, in actual fact, a conditioning centre using the latest methods to break down the prisoners. But the prisoners, except when being brain-washed, are well catered for. There are entertainment facilities of all kinds, from chess, dancing, gambling and film shows to a Palace of Fun and amateur theatricals.

There are shops, a Citizens Advice Bureau, cafes, an hotel, a village square; the village has its own Council, its own water supply, electricity, telephone exchange and, ominously, its own graveyard. It even has its own newspaper and local TV and radio service.

There is no single industry, but the people are kept busy doing all kinds of work, with a factory manufacturing local requisites. There is a Labour Exchange which assigns people varied tasks, drafts them to wherever they are needed, and organises the inhabitants. And there is a Town Hall which is the municipal office and headquarters of the chairman. No-one can get away from The Village, which has flying strip facilities for helicopters but no railway station. A local taxi service is run for the benefit of the inhabitants, and consists of mini-mokes driven by girls.

Life is self-contained and, for those who have accepted what they feel is the inevitable, it is leisurely and even enjoyable. But for those who have accepted there is no longer self-respect and no freedom. The Prisoner is one man who is determined not to be broken. Over it all hangs a menacing shadow . . . a threat that provides **The Prisoner** series with spine-tingling suspense and seat-riveting excitement. And the Village itself is part of its unusual appeal.

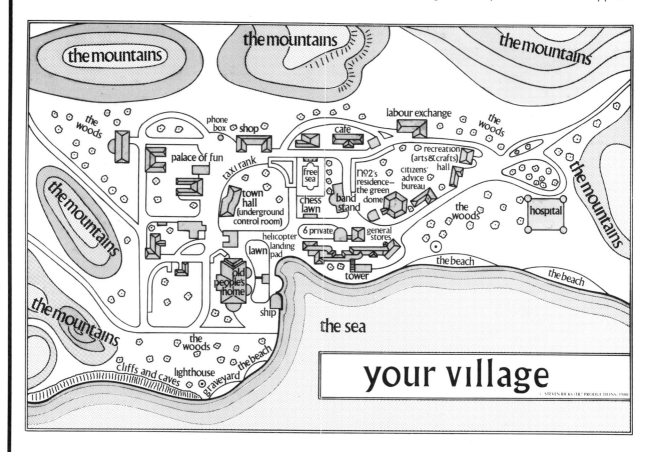

PAT MCGOOHAN IS A PRISONER OF HIS OWN SECRETS

The Irish in Patrick McGoohan surges to the surface when asked about his new television series **The Prisoner**. A leprechaunish smile creeps over his face as he admits that he is the only person in the world who knows the answer to all the questions that are going to be fired at him when the programme is shown.

The Prisoner is Pat McGoohan's first series since his phenomenally successful *Danger Man* (*Secret Agent*). He has conceived the idea himself. And originality is the keynote of the most off-beat stories ever filmed for television.

Who is The Prisoner and what is his name? 'Wait and see,' is McGoohan's enigmatic retort to this initial question, and all he will say about this is that the character is not John Drake of *Danger Man* and that he is a man who has retired from a highly confidential job. And this makes him vulnerable: there are many who want to learn his secrets.

McGoohan reveals that The Prisoner (he is simply known as that or as 'Number Six') has been abducted from his home and taken, unconscious, to a mysterious village.

Where is The Village? Again no answer; viewers will have to wait, and follow the series, to find out.

Who has captured him and why? 'The Prisoner,' McGoohan explains, 'has no idea. This is one of the main points of the series — something he himself is trying to find out. But the reasons are fairly clear: he has secrets they want to get out of him. What isn't so clear, though, is if this is just a method of training him to top indoctrination resistance . . . to see how far he can go without breaking.'

The man behind the organisation is known simply as 'Number One'. Who is he and will he ever be seen?

McGoohan grins impishly. 'The scriptwriters, directors and every single member of the unit have been plying me with these questions,' he comments, 'and I am hoping that viewers will be sufficiently intrigued to follow the series until they find out!'

The Prisoner's direct contact is 'Number Two'. But 'Number Two' is never the same man twice running. This position in the organisation changes regularly, with the Prisoner himself put forward as a candidate in one segment. By why? Just watch the series to find out! It's a hot seat for anyone to occupy.

The Village emblem is an old-fashioned Penny Farthing bicycle with a colourful, modernistic canopy. Once again, this is something Patrick McGoohan has dreamed up, but when asked if there is anything symbolic about it, he just smiles mysteriously. It has no personal associations with his private life and he admits: 'I've never been on one, and it's going to take a lot to get me on one!'

Who is the strange dwarf who wanders in and out of the stories, oddly garbed and frequently with an umbrella over his head? Could he be 'Number One'? A lot of the members of the unit believe he might be, and viewers will undoubtedly wonder as well.

Here again, McGoohan is giving nothing away. There is a good reason for the dwarf's presence, just as there is a good reason for the presence of other unusual characters and for the odd things that happen. Beyond that, McGoohan refuses to be drawn.

What is the Rover? What is the significance of the salute everyone gives? Again . . . wait and see!

Within a short time of **The Prisoner** becoming established on the air, a new slogan is likely to catch on among the viewers. It is, 'Be seeing you.' Why? 'Just watch, and you'll find out!' McGoohan exclaims.

Throughout the production of *Danger Man*, it was widely publicised that Patrick McGoohan would have nothing to do with the opposite sex in a romantic manner. McGoohan still feels that sex, as such, has no place in a popular television series intended for family viewing. There are, however, plenty of girls in **The Prisoner**, but what they will be doing is McGoohan's secret.

Actresses Mary Morris and Norma West pictured with McGoohan during a break from filming Dance Of The Dead

The series will have viewers asking one question after another, and McGoohan will assure you that he knows all the answers. They are locked in his own head and interviewing him presents problems: he is a prisoner of his own secrets.

He will not even reveal where the location scenes for the programme have been filmed. 'It's a real village,' he says, 'and it's one of the most unusual villages in the world.' He is not, he avers, simply trying to puzzle viewers. Each story is complete in itself, and the unaswered questions are part of the developing theme: 'Questions the Prisoner himself is asking, and once he finds the answers he will be well on his way towards solving the mysteries that are baffling him.'

Inevitably, he is repeatedly asked if **The Prisoner** has anything in common with *The Fugitive*? His answer to that is emphatic. It has not. It has nothing in common with any other television series ever filmed. It's new . . . unusual . . . and challengingly intriguing!

PATRICK MCGOOHAN

Three of the most important men attending a production conference on a film are the executive producer, the director and the star.

In the case of **The Prisoner** series, one man sometimes represents all three. Patrick McGoohan is not only starring but is executive producer, and is personally directing several of the episodes.

It is a challengingly formidable undertaking for one man, even if only on the grounds of physical stamina. Few actors would accept such a challenge, but Patrick McGoohan does so with an air of undisguised enjoyment and restless energy.

'If things go wrong,' he exclaims, 'I am the only one to shoulder the blame!'

The idea for **The Prisoner** is his own, and in playing the title role he is taking over a brand new character to follow the long-running and phenomenally successful John Drake of *Danger Man (Secret Agent)* and certainly in stories which bear no resemblance to any series previously filmed for television.

McGoohan has never disputed the fact that he entered television because he wanted to prove that a film series could attain the quality of the best in feature film production and the theatre, with a distinctive flavour of its own. He also wanted to prove that action-filled adventure could be presented without sadism and sex.

The success of *Danger Man*, even though it kept him away from the theatre and film projects he had in mind, was so great that, the moment the series came to an end, he began work on the preparation of *The Prisoner*.

Now he continues his television career in his most provocative role yet.

THE PRISONER

17 colour
52–minute episodes

ARRIVAL

Written by George Markstein and David Tomblin

Guest stars

The Woman	**Virginia Maskell**
Number 2	**Guy Doleman**
Cobb	**Paul Eddington**
The New Number 2	**George Baker**

with

The Butler	**Angelo Muscat**
Taxi Driver	**Barbara Yu Ling**
Maid	**Stephanie Randall**
Doctor	**Jack Allen**
Welfare Worker	**Fabia Drake**
Shopkeeper	**Denis Shaw**
Gardener/Electrician	**Oliver MacGreevy**

and

Ex-Admiral	**Frederick Piper**
Waitress	**Patsy Smart**
Labour Exchange Manager	**Christopher Benjamin**
Supervisor	**Peter Swanick**
Hospital Attendant	**David Garfield**
1st Croquet player	**Peter Brace**
2nd Croquet player	**Keith Peacock**

Directed by Don Chaffey

AS THE mid-morning sunlight gives way to slow-moving storm clouds and thunder shatters the heavens, from a distant horizon, an open-topped, yellow and green Lotus 7 sports car appears, racing at speed down a deserted airport runway. Its driver, clad entirely in black, his face set in determination, steers the machine into the busy London streets, proceeding at speed across the city's Westminster Bridge, and weaving its way past the Houses of Parliament. Making a right turn, the vehicle descends into a dimly-lit underground car park, its driver pausing only to snatch a ticket from the building's automatic ticket dispenser before impatiently driving the car at speed beneath the ascending checkout barrier. Grinding to a halt before two closed doors marked 'Way Out', the man climbs from his seat and strides purposefully along an empty corridor towards a second set of doors, his footsteps punctuated by the pulsating musical accompaniment. Throwing the barriers aside, he enters an ante-room furnished to serve as an office. Seated impassively before him is his bespectacled superior, his squat body framed against a large wall map of the world. Pacing angrily before the man (his words lost in repeated thunder claps) the intruder slaps down a white envelope from his inside suit pocket. Then, bringing his fist forcefully down onto the desk, upsetting a cup and saucer in the process, the man turns on his heel and storms back to his car; back into the sunlight and *clean* morning air.

Simultaneously, we see a sterile room, empty save for lengthy rows of metal filing cabinets, above which glides a mechanical arm. Plucking a computer-identity card adorned with the man's photograph from a file, the machine methodically types a row of X's across the man's picture, before depositing the card into a drawer marked 'Resigned'. Driving home, the man mysteriously finds

himself behind the hearse he passed earlier. Watched by its driver, who is dressed in mortician's garb, the man overtakes and enters a nearby residential street. Bringing the Lotus to a stop outside a genteel Victorian house, the driver springs from the vehicle and enters his home. Unseen by the man, the hearse draws silently to the pavement behind him. Inside the house, the man selects a suitcase and begins to pack. (He is identified now, by the on-screen title *The Prisoner*.) Outside, the driver of the hearse climbs the three concrete steps leading to the tenant's front door. Stowing travel brochures on top of his clothes, the man snaps shut his luggage, then, as clouds of billowing gas begin to seep into the room through a keyhole, he pauses, a quizzical look on his face. Blurred visions of spinning sky-scrapers float across his face as, finally overcome by the gas, the man falls backwards onto his studio couch. Waking, he sits up dazed. His surroundings seem familiar – and yet? Climbing to his feet, he crosses to the window, draws back the venetian curtain and stares in disbelief at . . . The London view he knows so well has disappeared. His eyes stare out at a village he has never seen before. Onto the screen comes just one word: 'Arrival'.

His eyes stare out at a village he has never seen before

The place is so architecturally puzzling and difficult to identify that, confused, he looks again at his room, before he realises that it is an exact replica of his London home. Uncertainly he paces to the veranda outside to take stock of his surroundings. He now stands outside a small cottage. London's landmark, Big Ben, has been replaced by a lofty bell tower, perched high on a rocky tor. Believing he sees a figure staring down at him, the man races upwards. The 'person' is just a statue and, glancing downwards, the man sees no sign of activity. Just then the bells begin to chime and in the distance he sees the figure of a woman erecting a colourful sun canopy over a cafe table. Racing to the spot, the girl informs him that the establishment will open shortly. Demanding to know where he is, the girl makes small talk. 'Where is this?' (The Village?) 'Where's the police station?' (There isn't one). 'Can I use your phone?' (She doesn't have one, but there is a phone box around the corner.) He locates the device, an odd-looking telephone booth marked 'For information lift and press,' it carries a white circle containing a canopied penny farthing bicycle motif. The stranger lifts the cordless telephone receiver. (A chance to learn his whereabouts?) It is not to be. After some verbal banter about exchanges and numbers, a female voice cuts the line dead when the man is unable to give her his number. Resuming his walk, he passes quaint little buildings of elaborate design, before arriving at a roadside board displaying a map denoted 'Free Information'. Selecting a category from the dozen or so listed, he presses one of its many buttons, and the machine clicks into life. Within seconds, he is picked up by an Oriental girl driving a Village taxi (a motorised buggy, topped with a colourful canopy). She, too, refuses to answer his questions and, telling the newcomer that the taxi is for local use only, refuses to take him to the nearest town as requested, dropping him instead outside a charming little village shop sign-posted 'General Stores'. The charge for the journey is two units. Realising the man does not have the fare the girl says that he can pay next time. Entering the shop, which has a large penny farthing emblem in its window and stocks only one brand of goods – Village Food, each can bearing the penny farthing motif (a symbol he is now growing used to, having seen it worn in badge-form by every Village inhabitant he has encountered, each of whom appears to have their own individual number printed over the bicycle's large wheel). The stranger finds the shopkeeper, a rotund man wearing an apron and straw boater, talking to a female customer. As he enters, they are speaking in some foreign language but, catching sight of the newcomer, they revert to English. 'Be seeing you.' the shopkeeper calls as the woman leaves. Requesting a map of the area, the stranger is asked if he requires colour or black and white? Handed the latter, its cover titled 'Map of your Village.' the man becomes further disillusioned. The chart provides no additional information to the one he had seen earlier at the Free Information directory: useless detail, with vague names. The colour version, containing slightly more detail, proves just as vague: an 'Old People's Home', the sea, the beach, and again 'the mountains', which appear to dominate the region on all four sides of the map. Learning that there is no demand for a map of the larger area, the newcomer leaves in disgust, the shopkeeper's 'Be seeing you,' and forefinger-and-thumb-together salute ringing in his ears.

Walking back to the cottage in which he awoke, the man hears a message being transmitted on the public address system; a woman's voice wishing everyone 'Good morning all. It's another beautiful day.' Approaching 'his' home, and seeing a maid shaking her dust cloth from 'his' verandah, he breaks into a run, arriving at the cottage to find a newly-erected sign pointing to his front door. It reads '6 Private'. The door opens automatically, he enters and it closes behind him with a gentle hum. The girl is winding her way down the steps outside the cottage. Looking around the room, he spots a stick-like doll resting on his writing bureau. It holds a message card. 'Welcome to your home from home.' At that moment a telephone, its subscriber exchange and number dial bearing the solitary numeral '6', purrs into life. It is an invitation to join someone for breakfast. 'Number 2, the Green Dome' – an opportunity, perhaps, to learn more about his strange surroundings?

Climbing the building's ornamental rock-garden steps, where a gardener is tending some plants, the visitor approaches its large white door and tugs at the bell push. Once again the door opens of its own volition, beckoning the man into a richly-furnished room where, as the door swings shut behind him, he is led across the room to another set of doors, steel ones this time, by a mute dwarf Butler wearing a tailcoat. Stepping inside the dimly-lit chamber, the man takes stock of the room. The chamber is huge. Rising vertically from the centre of the floor is a large black orb, before which rests a console of switches, colourful glowing lights and buttons. Seconds later, as the black sphere revolves, he notices that its rear side is hollow. Inside it sits a middle-aged man, dressed in a dark blazer, roll neck jumper, flannels and plimsoles. In his hands rests a furled-up umbrella, and drapped around his neck is a long woollen scarf. Pinned to his blazer, he wears a penny farthing badge, boasting a red numeral '2'. Approaching his host, the visitor notices that one entire wall of the chamber consists of a giant television screen, with soft psychedelic patterns floating across its surface. 'Do sit down.' invites the host, the absence of a second seat being remedied by the man extending his umbrella to press a control button on the console before him. A circular floor aperture opens and a small chair and table rise at the visitor's feet. The dwarf Butler enters pushing a breakfast trolley. To the visitor's bemusement, his request for China tea with lemon, plus bacon and two eggs, is served instantly. (Did they already have knowledge of his preferences?) The giant metal doors open and close as the Butler leaves, and the question-and-answer session begins in earnest. 'I suppose you're wondering what you are doing here?' (It has crossed the visitor's mind.) 'It's a question of your resignation.' (Go on.) 'The information in your head is priceless. I don't think you realise what a valuable property you've become.' (The visitor paces the floor, refusing the offer of another seat.) 'A man like you is worth a great deal on the open market.' (The pacing stops.) 'Who brought me here?' demands the visitor. (I know how you feel, believe me, they have taken quite a liberty.) 'Who are they?' Whoever they are, they are apparently curious about what lies behind the man's resignation. He had a brilliant career. His record is impeccable and they want to know why he suddenly left? The bout continues until, realising that the session has turned into an interrogation, the visitor, making to leave, announces 'I don't know who you are or who you work for and I don't care. I'm leaving.' Reaching the top of the ramp, the doors slam in his face. Stepping out of the globe. Number '2' leans towards his control panel, on the top of which sit a row of coloured telephones – green, yellow, red, all cordless – and reaches for a black-covered book. As this is opened, the wall screen begins to flash pictures of moments from the visitor's life – large reproductions of those in the album. Snatching the book the visitor begins to flick through its pages ('Oh, feel free.' snorts his host.) The large screen now shows the man in his London home, getting ready to meet a colleague named Chambers. ('A nice guy, Chambers – and so talkative.' comments his host.) Slamming the book shut, the visitor ponders his position, realising now that every facet of his former life is accessible to his enemy: his former life has been monitored and filmed. Reopening the book brings further images from his past career, revealing that not a single moment of his life has been overlooked, entered and filed. 'The time of my birth is missing.' observes the man. 'Well there you are!' exclaims the other, feigning surprise. 'Now let's bring it all up to date. 4.31 am, 19th of March, 1928. 'I've nothing to say. Is that clear? Absolutely nothing!' replies the visitor, throwing the book to the floor. His interrogator whines on that it is just a matter of time before he does tell them what they wish to know and, who knows, if he co-operates, he might even be given a position of authority. It is finally out in the open. The man has been captured by an unknown power who are after the priceless information stored in his head. He will be kept in this place until he divulges his secrets. His response is immediate. Pacing angrily before his host, he tells him that he refuses to make any deals. He has resigned! And he will not be pushed, filed, stamped, indexed, briefed, debriefed or numbered! His life is his own. 'Is it?' asks Number 2. 'Yes, you won't hold *me*' retorts his guest. '*Won't we*,' the other replies confidently. To prove that they will, he leads the man from the room. The time has arrived to show the newcomer exactly what he is up against.

With the dwarf Butler at its controls, a Village helicopter takes off with the two men as passengers, for an aerial tour. From aloft, the Village can be seen as a self-contained area. With pride, Number 2 shows the newcomer the community. 'Quite a beautiful place, really, isn't it? Almost like a world of its own.' (I shall miss it when I'm gone) quips the other. Number 2 pinpoints the Council Building, the restaurant, commentating that they even have their own newspaper. (You must send me a copy.) And their own graveyard. A social club – members only, of course, but Number 2 will see what he can do . . . If the new man has any problems, he should visit their Citizens Advice Bureau. 'They do a marvellous job. Everybody's very nice. You might even meet people you know!' The helicopter lands and the newcomer is shown a group of senior citizens, several of whom are climbing the rigging of a stationary stone boat moored by the

'They're our senior citizens. Of course, they have every comfort'

beach. Then it's off in a taxi to the Village square. A band is playing, and the now familiar female voice reports over the public address system that strawberry ice cream is on sale, and there is a possibility of intermittent showers later. Everyone appears to be enjoying themselves, all save the newcomer who, frowning, is urged forward by Number 2 to approach the Town Hall's balcony, on which

he stands, a megaphone is his hands ready to address the Villagers. Bidding the newcomer a beautiful day, an elderly couple salute the man as they pass. 'They didn't settle in for ages. Now they wouldn't leave for the world,' says Number 2. Suddenly Number 2 repeats the word 'wait'. All save the new man stop dead in their tracks. He continues to walk forward, until he sees a small white circular ball spinning on top of a jet of water in the fountain nearby. In the wink of an eye, it has increased its girth a hundred fold and has soared upwards to nestle between two ornamental stone pillars overlooking the square. Setting eyes on the apparition from his position by the Village pool, a man wearing sun-glasses lets out a scream, and races between the immobile villagers. Ignoring the warning by Number 2 to 'Stop – Come back,' the man races away. A mistake. Watched by the newcomer, the vibrating white sphere glides down from its perch and propels itself after the running man, homing in on its victim to suck the life from his lungs. The thing departs as quickly as it came and the Village returns to normal. Watching the amoeba-like thing bounce away, the newcomer asks 'What was that?' '*That* would be telling,' replies Number 2, through his megaphone.

The next initiation takes place at the Labour Exchange. Passing two rows of villagers waiting outside, one formed by men, the other by women, Number 2 and his guest venture inside. Greeted by an official, who eyes the new man with disapproval, Number 2 is told to go straight through. Placards adorn the walls: 'A still tongue makes a happy life'; 'Questions are a burden to others, answers a prison for oneself'. Eyeing these with amusement, the man follows Number 2 into a huge hall, adorned with ornate arches. Everything is ready, and the new man is given an aptitude test. Placed before a display panel showing a square hole, the man's attempts to frustrate Number 2 by selecting a round peg, fail to materialise: the hole magically shrinking to accommodate the round peg like a glove. Like it or not, he has passed. The questionnaire is next, the man being asked to fill in details of his race, religion, hobbies, reading matter, food preferences, what he was, what he wishes to be, any

'Any family illnesses? Any politics?'

148

family illnesses – any politics . . .? The last phrase spurs the newcomer into action. Smashing a contraption consisting of wheels, cogs and spokes which sits upon the Exchange Manager's desk, he storms out of the building – leaving Number 2 to console his colleague with the words, 'Never mind, you can get all you need from this.' Handing the man the black book we saw earlier, he adds 'I think we have a challenge.'

Back at 'his' cottage, the man finds a lovely blonde girl working there, sent by the Labour Exchange. 'That's another mistake *they* have made. Get out!' Alarmed by the man's demeanour, the girl leaves. Immediately she does so, a central wall panel in the lounge rises with a hum, revealing a part of the accommodation which has hitherto remained hidden: a bedroom, a bathroom, and a kitchen stocked with tins of Village Food, each bearing the ubiquitous penny farthing motif. Examining everything as he paces the room, he confirms that it is an exact replica of his London home – with two additions. Music is being piped into the room from a loudspeaker, and a lamp containing floating globules of oil immersed in liquid, rests upon his furniture. Opening 'his' writing bureau, he produces a day-by-day memo/diary – with neatly written pre-printed daily entries. Things to do: TODAY 'Don't forget to send thank you note for flowers at earliest.' TODAY'S Memoranda: 'Arrived today. Made very welcome.' Another drawer contains a bound volume of the 'Map of your Village,' but again this offers no further clues to the ones he has seen earlier. Finally, when his aimless pacing before the speaker turns to annoyance, he angrily crosses to the device and throws it to the floor. Disintegrating, it nevertheless continues to pour out its music, despite being kicked and trampled on by the man. As he does this, a voice from the speaker announces: 'Attention Electrics Department, please go to Number 6 where adjustment is needed.' At that moment, the maid returns on the pretext of having forgotten something. Demanding to know how to stop the music, the man is told that they cannot. It's automatic. 'Who controls it?' (She doesn't know – she *really* doesn't know.) 'Have you never tried to find out?' Relenting a little, he questions her further, but she does not have, or refuses to give, the answers he is seeking. (We have a saying here, a still tongue makes for a happy life.) The man moves on. People must have tried to get away from the Village 'How many have succeeded?' (Don't ask.) 'Has *anyone* ever escaped?' (Some have tried, but have been brought back – not always alive.) At that point the girl breaks down and begins to cry. Eventually confessing that she was ordered to gain his confidence, in exchange for her freedom, the man mocks her by saying 'You believe that. With all that knowledge in your head, you really believe that they would let you go?' (They might – if he gave her some sort of information.) Her words find no sympathy. 'Your services will *not* be required tomorrow!' he exclaims. Tearfully, the girl leaves.

Every move and word of this scene has been watched and monitored on a closed circuit television by Number 2 and his Supervisor, a bald-headed, bespectacled official, who stand side-by-side in the enormous control room – an impressive place, laid out with ultra-modern machinery. Banks of monitors are punching out ticker-tape messages. An enormous rotating shaft with an observer seated at each end manning surveillance cameras, spins backwards and forwards before a huge map of the world and a star chart. The Village nerve-centre. An all-knowing, endlessly-watching operations room which controls everything outside. Staring impassively at the monitor screen, the Supervisor confesses that the girl was most convincing. He was sure that she would pull it off. 'He's no ordinary man,' observes Number 2. 'This one has got to be handled very differently.' Pointing out that that could be dangerous, the Supervisor takes solace when his colleague reminds him, 'You know how important this is.' Back in 'his' cottage, the new man receives a visit from an electrician carrying a replacement speaker unit – the tenant is neither chided for breaking the original, or asked if he wants a replacement! After several minutes of small talk, the occupier decides to take a stroll. 'Be seeing you,' he smirks. 'And you,' returns the repair man. Reaching the gardens the man acknowledges a passing cyclist and bumps into a gardener – an exact double of the man he left repairing his speaker unit! Startled by the likeness, the newcomer makes for the nearby woods, passing rows of stone statues during his progress. Suddenly he is forced to drop behind a bush when he sees one of the huge white balloons, patroling a nearby road. Changing direction, the man reverses back towards the column statues, whose heads turn to follow his progress, their 'eyes' emitting flashes of light. Back in the control room, the Supervisor is watching the man's every move. Sensing that he is under surveillance, the newcomer breaks into a run, but his progress is blocked by the return of the bouncing white sphere which, uttering a fearsome roar, pursues the man. Back in the control room, the Supervisor speaks into a red telephone: 'Attention Post 14 – Yellow Alert. Now leaving Northern perimeter, Number 6 – Repeat, Number 6.' Hearing the approaching wail of sirens, the pursued man keeps going. Observing the man's progress on his monitor screen, the Supervisor adds: 'Now approaching, contact imminent.' A motorised buggy takes to the beach and pursues the running man who, zig-zagging, races along the sands to evade his pursuers. He falls, then quickly regains his feet to engage the man leaping from the vehicle. They fight and the buggy's passenger is knocked to the ground. Leaping onto the back of the speeding machine, the would-be escaper tosses its driver overboard and drives away at speed. 'Number 6, heading for Outer Zone, in our vehicle. Orange Alert,' warns the Supervisor. As if by magic, an obstruction now appears before the racing buggy – the quivering white balloon. Approaching at speed, the man leaps from the vehicle and attacks the glutinous thing with his fists, but his adversary engulfs him. Immobilising the man, the Village guardian bounces away, then sits on guard beside the prostrate figure as a second mini-vehicle, summoned by the Supervisor, arrives and carts the unconscious man away.

Wearing pyjamas, the prisoner awakes in a hospital bed. An old woman sits before him, knitting as she rocks back and forth in her chair. Asking how he feels after his nasty experience, his immediate response is to ask where he is. 'You're in the hospital, son,' she retorts, feigning sympathy. As the woman leaves to fetch the doctor, he recognises the face of a patient in an adjacent bed. He slips from his bed and crosses to the figure. The man is Cobb, an old colleague. The figure stirs as the man questions him. 'Cobb. What are you doing here?' he asks. 'And you?' says the other, recognising his vistor. His story matches that of his friend. 'How long have you been here?' (Days? Weeks? Months? Cobb cannot be certain.) 'Who brought you here?' (The patient remembers nothing beyond returning to his hotel room in Germany, climbing into bed, and waking up in the Village.) Any further conversation between the two is cut short by the arrival of the doctor who, handing the new patient a dressing gown, leads him on a tour of the hospital. Perusing the corridor outside his ward, the newcomer stares through an observation window in a door. In a passage flooded with red light, he sees two rows of people, each attired in dressing gowns, each apparently doing nothing. 'Group therapy,' explains the doctor. 'Counteracts obsessional guilt complexes producing neurosis.' As they walk away, an infantile man with electrodes taped to his shaven head is being led to a room, his expression blank. Accompanying the doctor to a medical room, the patient is invited to sit in an examination chair. At its base are a pair of slippers, his

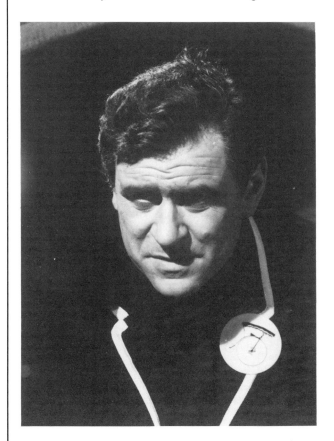

'. . . Just listen to the old ticker'

size! The patient is examined and a machine produces a perforated card pronouncing the man absolutely fit. In the control room sits Number 2, engaged in conversation on a red telephone. 'He's having a medical. Mmm, no, course I don't mind. One has to make sure of these things.' Telling his patient that he is free to leave the following morning, whereupon he will be issued with new clothes (his own have been burned), the trip back to his ward allows the patient to catch sight of the infantile man again. Looking into the man's room, he sees the figure watching a small white ball dancing gaily on a water fountain, a demented look upon his face as he sings in time with the bubbling water jets. An alarm bell sounds, and the doctor's assistant races forward to announce that Cobb, the amnesia case, has jumped to his death from a window. Back in his ward, staring at his deceased colleague's bed, the newcomer ponders what the future holds for him.

The following morning, wearing his newly-acquired clothes, the patient is discharged and escorted from the hospital by a male nurse. The man now looks very different. He is wearing a dark blazer with white piping lapel trims, fawn-coloured slacks, and thick black plimsoles with white rubber soles. A straw boater adorns his head and he is carrying an umbrella. Most notable of all is the fact that he now wears a badge pinned to his

jacket's left lapel, a badge identical to the ones worn by every Village inhabitant, save for one small diference, the man's badge is numbered '6'. Handing the man a folder containing his employment, identity, health, welfare and credit card, the medico returns to the hospital. As he does so, the new Number 6, casts his hat, umbrella and badge into the back of the taxi waiting to take him 'home'. Glancing back at the hospital as he is driven away, to the female driver's consternation, the man abruptly jerks back the vehicle's handbrake and runs up the steps leading to the Green Dome. As before, the door marked '2' opens of its own volition and the mechanical steel doors are thrown back by the mute drawf. Marching down the

'I have taken his place. I am the new Number 2'

interior ramp towards the figure seated in the oval shaped chair, he is astonished to see a new face. 'Get him,' he shouts to the seated figure. 'I have taken his place. I am the new Number 2!' (Get Number 1.) 'As far as you are concerned I'm in charge! What can I do for you?' (Cobb!) 'What we do here has to be done. It's the law of survival. It's either them or us.' (Imprison people. Steal their minds. Destroy them!) 'Depends on whose side you're on, doesn't it?' (I'm on our side.) 'Then we'll have to find out where your sympathies lie,' retorts the new Number 2, leaning forward to pick up a black book. (You know where they lie.) Reading from the book, the man in the chair recites the intruder's record: the subject shows great enthusiasm for his work. He is utterly loyal. Pausing he comments 'Is this a man who suddenly walks out?' (I didn't walk out – I *resigned*!) 'People change, exactly, as do loyalties.' (Not mine!) Telling the intruder that his words are all very commendable, but he is interested only in the facts, and the only chance the man has of getting out is to give him the facts. 'If you don't give them, I'll take them. It's up to you.' The new Number 2 dismisses the intruder with a flippant 'Good day – Number 6.' Number what? Quizzes the man. 'Six,' replies his tormentor. 'For official purposes everyone has a number. Yours is Number Six!' 'I am not a number. I am a person,' the intruder throws back defiantly. 'Six of one, half-a-dozen of the other!' exclaims Number 2, as the so-called Number 6, exits through the steel doors. Staring at the man, Number 2 dictates an addition to the man's file. 'Report on Number 6. Normal classification. On arrival subject showed shock symptoms, followed by accepted behaviour pattern. Since then has been unco-operative and distinctly aggressive. Attempted to escape. Subject proving exceptionally difficult, but in view of his importance, no extreme measure to be used yet.'

At 'home' again, the man denoted Number 6 paces his room. Hearing the sound of a band approaching his cottage, he steps out onto the balcony. A procession of villagers, some carrying umbrellas, are marching up the hill towards him. At the rear is a flower covered coffin, towed in a trailer by a buggy. Some way behind walks the solitary figure of a woman, her face a mask of sorrow. Leaving the balcony, the man follows the procession to where the woman stands alone. She is looking at a section of the beach where gravestones mark a small cemetry, towards which pallbearers are carrying the coffin. His intuition tells him that the casket contains his ex-colleague Cobb. The man crosses to the woman, who wears a badge numbered '9'. Seeing the tears clouding her eyes, he tells her that he was a friend of the dead man, and offers to help. Expressing some doubt as to whether she can trust him, she says that she knew Cobb but a short time. Told by the man the cause of his death, she flinches, turning her head away. A bell chimes and she warns him to leave. Grabbing the woman's arm and explaining that they must talk further, the woman agrees to meet him at the concert centre at 12 o'clock.

Shortly after the appointed hour, the woman joins him before the grandstand on which a band is playing. This time she is more forthcoming. Pretending to read a book, she explains that Cobb had been planning to escape from the Village. They had an escape route planned but 'they' came sooner than Cobb had expected them to. In order to use Cobb's method of escape, he will need to fly a helicopter (one is due at two o'clock) and will need an electropass which, synchronised with the alarm system, will allow them to reach the machine. (She can supply this. She knew the last pilot.) Agreeing to meet again by the stone boat at two o'clock, they leave – the man watching her climb the steps to the Green Dome.

Inside his home, Number 2 is dictating a further report on the new Number 6, up to and including his attendance at the concert just a few minutes earlier. Looking up, he offers the woman sitting opposite him a congratulatory 'Thank you, my dear. More tea?' Then, adding that she has done well and should not worry too much about Cobb, it was not her fault, he hands Number 9 a black-fronted folder containing details of her new assignment. Turning back its cover, the photograph of Number 6 stares back from the page!

Later that day, Number 6 is playing chess with Number 66, an ex-Admiral, but his mind is not on the game for. As a helicopter approaches and lands nearby, his attention is distracted further by the arrival of Number 9. His partner cries 'Checkmate!' Refusing the offer of a second game in favour of a stroll, the ancient mariner recommends the boat. 'She's great in any weather. Sailed her myself many a time. Have a good trip.' Leaving the seadog humming the melody of 'The Drunken Sailor', Number 6 joins the woman inside the mock stone boat. Handing over the electropass (a kind of wristwatch, with rather more dials than usual), the woman is taken aback when he intimates that it was sent by her 'boss' Number 2. Confirming that she has been assigned to him, and was previously assigned to Cobb, Number 9 denies that she has betrayed either of them. 'We were trying to get out, before it was too late. Soon it will be too late for you.' Declining his offer to join him, she leaves, instructing the man to go right away. Watching her depart, the man begins his long walk to the helicopter pad. Passing merrymakers swimming in the pool, and the mute dwarf Butler, he arrives unseen to where the flying machine waits unmanned, guarded only by the hovering white sphere. Flicking on the electro device, its hands being to rotate, punctuating a flashing light on its dial. Hesitantly, he approaches the helicopter. The device works and the guardian withdraws. Climbing into the pilot's seat, he slips the device into his pocket, starts the machine and roars skywards. Back in the control room, Number 2 observes the man's departure with a smile. He nods, and one of his staff coaxes back a lever. Inside the helicopter, Number 6 loses control of the machine: the control stick freezing in his hands as, of its own accord, the helicopter banks sharply and heads back to base. Resigned to his fate, the pilot removes his hands from the controls.

Below on the lawn, Number 9 looks concerned when, having told the chess-playing seadog that she does not play his game, he advises 'You should. We're all pawns m'dear.' Within minutes, the helicopter makes a gentle landing at the very point from where only moments before, escape looked assured. Watching the touch-down with glee, Number 2 turns to his companion (Cobb, now very much alive and dressed in a businessman's suit, ready to meet his new masters in London), and tells him 'I think I'll let him keep the watch, just to remind him that escape

Hesitantly, he climbs into the helicopter

151

is not possible.' Then, assuring his companion that the woman will be well taken care of, he bids Cobb au revoir. 'They'll be delighted with you,' he calls after the retreating figure. 'Give them our compliments.' Promising to tell his new masters that there are no loopholes, Cobb gives the familiar hand salute and bids his colleagues 'auf wiedersehen.'

Ushered away by the giant menacing bubble, Number 6 walks, defeated, across the lawn, the bouncing glutinous bodyguard following close behind him. As he walks to his fate, the mute Butler, his umbrella raised above him, watches the *prisoner's* return!

The prisoner's face zooms from a panoramic aerial view of the Village. Filling the screen, bars snap closed across the face with a deafening thud. The man is now THE PRISONER.

AUTHOR'S NOTE: Originally filmed as *The Arrival,* this story features the only full version of the title sequence and theme music.

To achieve the effect of the Rover *closing in* to smother its victim, the production staff sometimes used a fishing rod with a thin line tied to Rover's 'neck'. On other occasions, the film was shot in reverse, with people walking *backwards* to give the impression that the balloons were passing them when the film was played projected *forwards*. In an alternative version of *Arrival* (a pre-broadcast print, shipped to America for the early 1970s syndicated run of *The Prisoner*) Rover had a mechanised 'heartbeat' and its progress was accompanied by 'heavy breathing'.

As mentioned earlier, the alternative version (which probably still exists, but has yet to be found — although an *audio-taped* recording of the episode does exist, courtesy of USA Prisoner enthusiast Christopher Campbell, who had the presence of mind to make a reel-to-reel recording of the story when it was transmitted by WHDH Channel 5, in Boston, Massachusetts on 10 May 1974) also contains the POP closing credits.

FREE FOR ALL

Written by Paddy Fitz (Patrick McGoohan)

Guest star

Number 2	**Eric Portman**

with

Number Fifty Eight	**Rachel Herbert**
Labour Exchange Manager	**George Benson**
The Butler	**Angelo Muscat**
Reporter	**Harold Berens**
Man in Cave	**John Cazabon**

and

Photographer	**Dene Cooper**
Supervisor	**Kenneth Benda**
Waitress	**Holly Doone**
1st Mechanic	**Peter Brace**
2nd Mechanic	**Alf Joint**

Directed by Patrick McGoohan

'WHERE AM I?' (In the Village.) 'What do you want?' (Information.) 'Whose side are you on?' (That would be telling. We want information, information . . . *information.*) 'You won't get it!' (By hook or by crook, we will.) 'Who are you?' (The new Number 2.) 'Who is Number 1?' (*You* are Number 6.) 'I am not a *number* I am a free man!' (Laughter).

The telephone marked 6 purrs into life: an early morning call from Number 2. 'Good morning, good morning. Any complaints?' (I'd like to mind my own business!) 'Fancy a chat?' (The mountain can come to Mohammed!) Almost immediately, Number 2, sporting a light-coloured blazer and his long woollen scarf piped with white trims, walks into the man's cottage. 'Mohammed?' (Everest, I presume?) 'I've never had a head for heights.' (How's Number 1?) 'Past the summit.' (Play it according to Hoyle?) 'Oh, all cards on the table. They rely on that.' (Whose move?) 'Your turn next. Confide and we concede. Breakfast?' As the words leave the elder man's lips, Number 58, dressed as a maid, walks into the cottage, carrying a breakfast tray. Introduced to the reluctant host, she is addressed by Number 2 in a foreign language, then leaves. Informing Number 6 that the woman used to work in records and has a great variety of information, the elder adds that she has a wonderful gift, a photographic memory. She has done well during her stay and should not be with them for long. Over breakfast — international cuisine — Number 2 turns the conversation to the forthcoming election campaign beginning that day. 'Are you going to run?' quizzes Number 2. (Like blazes — the first chance I get.) 'I meant run for office,' retorts the elder. (Whose?) 'Mine, for instance.' (You have a delicate sense of humour.) 'Naturally,' replies Number 2. 'Humour is the very essence of a democratic society.' Their conversation is interrupted by a fanfare of trumpets broadcast over the host's loudspeaker unit. Then, hearing campaign music being played outside, they rise; the one known as 6 follows his guest to the door. Stepping out onto the veranda, the elder man returns the salute from the crowd gathered in the street below the cottage, many of whom carry colourful

Numbers 2 and 6 relax during a break in the filming

umbrellas. A placard bearing the man's photograph and the words 'Vote – No 2' is being held aloft. Passing comment that it appears as if his guest has a unanimous majority, Number 6 is told by Number 2 that that is why he is worried – 'It's bad for morale. The good people don't seem to appreciate the value of *free* elections.' Told that he, Number 6, is the sort of candidate they need, the younger man asks what the outcome would be if he chose to run against Number 2 – 'What *physically* happens, if *I* win?' 'Then you're the boss!' answers the elder, inviting Number 6 to step back into the cottage. 'If you win,' suggests Number 2, 'Number 1 will no longer be a mystery to you. I'll introduce you properly, and we'll see how you feel after accessing the maddening crowd.' Leading Number 6 outside, they climb into a taxi and are driven to the Village square. Entering the Town Hall, they emerge onto a balcony and Number 2 calls for silence. Informing the congregation that the lack of opposition in the matter of the pre-election is not good for the community and reflects an acceptance of things as they are, he adds that they are, however, fortunate in having among them a recent recruit whose outlook is particularly militant and individualistic; he hopes that the man will not deny his duty to the community by refusing to take up the challenge. Turning to his guest, he introduces Number 6 to the congregation. The younger man's opening announcement that he is *not* a number, but a person, is greeted with great amusement. 'In some place, at some time,' he continues unabashed, 'all of you, held positions of a secret nature, and had knowledge that was invaluable to an enemy. Like me, you are here to have that knowledge protected or extracted.' 'That's the stuff to give them,' smiles Number 2. 'Unlike me,' the younger man continues, 'many of you have accepted the situation

of your imprisonment and will die here like rotting cabbages.' 'Keeping going. They love it,' goads Number 2. 'The rest of you have gone over to the side of our keepers. Which is which? How many of each? Who's standing beside you now?' continues Number 6, informing the onlookers that he intends to discover who are the prisoners, and who are the warders. 'I shall be running for office in this . . . *election*?' he ends, purposefully. Asking the crowd to applaud a 'citizen of character', Number 2 barely raises an eyebrow as 'Vote for 6' placards appear throughout the crowd, as if by magic. 'Be seeing you,' grins Number 2, as the candidate finds himself hustled by his newly-won supporters into his election vehicle, a Village taxi, decked out with placards bearing his image.

Leaving his cottage at sunrise, Number 6 is angry to find Number 58 waiting for him in a taxi. Ringing Number 2, he is informed that the girl has been selected as his aide, because she, too, is new. She will be at his disposal for the election period – and for anything he might desire, within reason, of course. Number 6 is expected to attend the dissolution of the outgoing council in 30 minutes' time in the Town Hall chambers. The girl can speak no English and cannot, therefore, understand him when he requests to be driven to the establishment, so he determines to walk. Leaving the girl behind, he crosses the Village green and arrives at the 'Free Information' board. Seconds later, he is joined by Number 58 who, witnessing him selecting a number from the board's control panel, joins him and presses the button marked 6. Babbling in some foreign language, the girl heads back to her vehicle, beckoning her unwilling passenger to join her. As he does so, two Village reporters race after the taxi and bombard the man with questions. Introducing himself as Number 113, and his photographic colleague as Number 113B, one of them states that they work for the Village newspaper, the *Tally Ho*. The reporter asks how the candidate will handle his campaign? 'No comment,' comes the reply. Further questions bring the same response, but undeterred, the journalist makes up his own answers for each question asked: 'Intends to fight for freedom at all costs. Will tighten up on Village security etc.' Arriving at their destination, the newspaper team move away, thanking the candidate for his answers as they go. Paged by an announcement over the public address system, Number 6 is about to enter the building when a voice causes him to turn. Standing a few feet away, is a young man selling newspapers – a man looking remarkably similar to the newspaper photographer now racing away to develop his pictures! Crossing to a printing device signposted 'The Tally Ho', the candidate is astonished to be handed a hot-off-the-press edition of the newspaper carrying the headline 'Number 6 Speaks His Mind' – barely seconds after he gave the reporter *no* story! Puzzling over the headline, it takes a split second before the man becomes aware that a Village guardian is approaching his position. Ushering the candidate towards the Town Hall entrance, the bouncing monster departs once the man is safely inside.

Directed by Number 2's voice, the candidate enters a vast subterranean chamber, akin in size to a circular aircraft hanger. Before him sits Number 2, surrounded by 12 candidates, each of whom wears a top hat. All stare blankly before them. Asked by the elder man if he wishes to question the council, the candidate nods. The dais on which he stands begins to rotate and the interrogation begins. 'Who do you represent? Who elected you? To what place and public do you owe your allegiance? Whose side are you on?' he asks. No reply is forthcoming and the dais ceases to revolve. 'Any further questions?' mocks Number 2. The candidate retaliates. 'This *farce*. This 20th-century bastille that pretends to be a pocket democracy . . . Why don't you put us all into solitary confinement until you get what you're after and have done with it!' Furious, Number 2 bangs his gavel, calling the man to order. 'Brainwashed imbeciles,' continues the candidate, ignoring the man's fury. Then, staring at the rows of blank faces, 'Can you laugh? Can you cry? Can you think?' Holding aloft the *Tally Ho* headline purporting to contain his words, he berates the silent onlookers, ignoring the elder man's attempts to silence him. With the push of a button, the dais occupied by Number 6 begins to rotate again. Gaining in momentum, faster and faster it whirls as Number 2 orders that the man undergoes the 'test'. Deposited with a thud into a strangely-lit corridor, the man struggles against dizziness to rise to his feet. Traversing the corridor by clutching straps suspended from the ceiling, the fear-stricken man stumbles into a room, to be greeted by the manager of the Village Labour Exchange. Purporting to be a friend, the bespectacled man offers the new arrival tea – unsweetened, he declares, acknowledging that he is aware of the man's preferences: the records show that the man gave up sugar four years and three months earlier on medical advice, which shows that he is afraid – afraid of death. 'I'm afraid of nothing!' exclaims the guest. 'You're afraid of yourself,' comes the reply. 'You're aware of that? Good. Honesty attracts confidence, and confidences are the core of our business.' In the Green Dome, Number 2 receives a telephone call from Number 1. Apologising that his experiment got out of hand and, yes, he is aware of how valuable Number 6 is to them, he offers to be more careful in the future. Then, telephoning Number 6's

companion, he informs him that the Prisoner must be taken to the first stage only, the tissue must not be damaged. Looking sideways at his guest, the interrogator presses a button on the control panel before him. The chair occupied by Number 6 is now electrofied and its occupant is forced to grip its arm rests for support. On a screen behind him appears a silhouette of the man's head, with two triangular lines running from the shadow's eye-line. Questioned as to why he wishes to run for electoral office, Number 6 stares impassively ahead. The question is repeated. The man's eyelids flicker and a circular black spot appears on the screen, moving along the top line towards the silhouette's face. The man is lying. Informed that everything he thinks there is treated in the strictest confidence, a black square moves inwards on the bottom line. The man being interrogated understands: he is acknowledging the truth. Asked again why he is running for office, both objects move, leading the interrogator to postulate that he believes that had the man won and took over the Village, he would be able to control an organised breakout – correct? The black square moves forward. That was a mistake, wasn't it, asks the interrogator. The circular spot urges forward. Told to think only of his responsibility, both objects reverse. A challenge. Fighting to regain control of his thoughts, the man in the chair makes an all-out attempt to defeat the device. Within seconds, both objects being to move forward and converge. As they enter the head on the screen, Number 6 slumps into unconsciousness. Having witnessed these events on the control room monitor screen, Number 2 orders Central Area to stand by. Staring at his helpless prisoner, the interrogator remarks, 'Good. Simply splendid.' Seconds later, the prisoners awakes and rises cautiously from his chair. Looking around him, he acknowledges his gratitude for the tea. He shakes hands with his interrogator, thanks the man for voting for him and with a cheery 'Be seeing you' leaves the chamber, a changed man. Outside the establishment, he acknowledges the cheers of the villagers and willingly gives answers to a reporter from the *Tally Ho* newspaper.

Back in the residence marked '6 – Private', in the company of Number 58, the man watches his televised election speech with pride. He advises the girl to learn her lesson quickly; if she obeys the rules, *they* will take good care of her. Gradually, however, he begins to struggle for clarity of thought and runs away from the girl, driving off in a buggy parked outside. Weaving his way through throngs of villagers, he slams the vehicle to a halt and races away towards the beach – pursued on all sides by Number 58, people carrying 'Vote 6' placards, an helicopter and the mute Butler. Jumping into a small powerboat, he guns its motor and heads out to sea at speed. Staving off attempts by two engineers who try to impede his progress, the man regains control and races away at full throttle – ignoring the warnings from Number 2 in his helicopter to stop being foolish and to turn back before it is too late. Alerted by the control room Supervisor, a guardian rises from its anchor point on the ocean floor. The white sphere looms before him and he is forced to leap overboard as the pulsating mass heads directly for the boat. Too late. The swimmer's attempts to forge ahead are doomed. Exhausted, he is soon overtaken and the guardian engulfs him in its glutinous mass, suffocating the man into submission. Carried to the shore, the man recites his election speech in delirium as an ambulance arrives to carry him away. Its mission over, the guardian returns to its undersea lair.

Staving off attempts to impede him, Number 6 throttles away at speed

Disturbed by dreams of the election, Number 6 regains consciousness back in his room, as a pulsating lamp above his bed flashes into his eyes. He is conditioned by messages flashed to his brain: perched on the stone boat he addresses the Villagers with words put into his mouth by Number 2: give *them* information and the community will be a better place to live. *He* can fulfil their dreams. Whatever they require *he* can supply it: winter, spring, summer or fall, all can be theirs. Apply to *him*, and it will be easier and better. Number 2 makes an alternative campaign speech. Beware, be careful. There are those among them with a fresh face and an enthusiasm that cannot be denied. *Their* promises ring richly in their ears. Number 6 has explained his record. He has adapted admirably, but he has no experience whatsoever of the manipulation of a community such as theirs. Beware. Ask yourselves if he has got the administrational ability to implement his priorities? Can you trust *him*? The prisoner's slogan '6 for 2, and 2 for nothing, 6 for free for all, for free for *all*. Vote, vote for 6.' Watching his opponent whipping the crowd into a frenzy, Number 2 opens a debate about spare time, stating that *he* cannot afford such a luxury. Telling *his* supporters that *everyone* is entitled to spare time, Number 6 proposes that should *he* win the contest, he will make spare time for 'less work and more play.' Hearing this, the people roar, 6, 6, 6!

Evening finds the junior candidate in a bar. The beverage on offer is supposed to be non-alcoholic, but Number 6 puts on a good display of being intoxicated. Screaming for drink, he is led outside by Number 58, who he accuses of spying on him. Driven by her to a secluded spot in the woods, she indicates that real alcohol can be found in a cave, kisses him and departs. Entering, he finds a still – and an intoxicated Number 2 sprawled out on a makeshift cot. The man confesses the need to keep his nerves steady: he is worried about the forthcoming election and what will happen to Number 6 during it. Handed drinks by a brewer and confirming that they are not under surveillance in the therapy zone, the older man sits up. Told by Number 6 that he does not approve of the Village, Number 2 exclaims: 'To hell with the Village!' Then, leading the other into an ante-room, he shows his guest a large blackboard on which is written a complicated equation. The brewer, he is told, was once a brilliant scientist. He now brews his brew, plays with his chalk

and, once a week, they come down to photograph what he has written, then clean it away so that the man can begin over again. 'Clever', says Number 6, keeling over at the man's feet. 'Quicker than usual,' remarks the brewer entering the room, to which a now sober Number 2 replies that he warned the man not to make it too strong – 'we must not damage the tissue.' Telling his superior not to worry, the brewer explains that Number 6 has been given just enough to take him through the election: he will remember nothing.

The beverage is non-alcoholic, but Number 6 puts on a great display of being intoxicated

'6 for 2, 6 for 2' chant the villagers outside the election hall. Inside, the votes for Number 6 overflow the ballot box. Conceding defeat, removing his opponent's rosette and replacing it with that of his own – one bearing the number 2 – the older candidate leads the victor outside. Acknowledging the bemused and silent faces of the crowd, the men are driven by Number 58 to the Green Dome. Beckoning the victor into his new home, the defeated candidate makes to leave, pausing for a moment to tell the new man 'Anything you need to know, press a button. You're the boss.' As the door glides shut behind him, the new Number 2 and his aide enter the building's vast circular chamber. A press of a button by Number 58 and the recently-vacated oval-shaped chair rises from the floor. A telephone purrs. It is the Labour Exchange Manager, asking if there is anything he can do for them. 'Be seeing you,' gloats Number 2. 'And you,' comes the reply. In a moment of mad exhilaration, Number 2 follows the woman's lead and experiments by pushing buttons. Chairs rise from the floor and retreat to their nests. The monitor screen flashes into life. Further equipment appears from all corners of the room until, at the touch of a button, a piercing blue and white light

'Anything you want to know, press a button'

begins to pulsate in front of the man's eyes. He stiffens, unsure of his surroundings. Led by Number 58 he is placed before the psychedelic patterns flitting across the monitor screen. Turning the man around, his eyes remain glazed as the woman tears off his rosette and slaps him forcibly across the face. The hypnotic trance broken, the man reels backwards, landing awkwardly in the oval-shaped seat. It revolves, bringing him back to the woman's icy stare. Terrified, he regains his feet and races to the bank of telephones – his babbling words being piped around the Village cause barely a second of interest. Two security men rise from beneath the floor and attempt to pin his arms by his side. He escapes to an ante-room, but the men follow him and rain vicious blows to his body. Within minutes his bruised and battered body is carried back into the room to face the new Number 2 – the girl he left behind just a few minutes previously. Speaking in perfect English, the woman tells him that this is only the beginning: they have ways and means of getting the information they require, but have no wish to harm him permanently. Is he ready to talk? Silence is her answer as, falling backwards on a stretcher provided for him, the prisoner is returned to his residence.

At the controls of his helicopter, the out-going Number 2 telephones his replacement. 'Just on my way. Everything go according to plan?' 'Don't worry, all was satisfactory in the end. Give my regards to the homeland,' replies Number 2. Leaving the Village behind, the helicopter rises skywards.

AUTHOR'S NOTE: The violent, some say sadistic, fight between Number 6 and the two 'guardians' which takes place in the Rover cave was deleted when the episode was first broadcast in the UK. This was later restored, and appears intact in the *Channel 5* video cassettes. Stuntmen Alf Joint and Peter Brace played the 'guardians', with the former being responsible for choreography.

Although not credited in the story, the Supervisor was played by Peter Swanwick, who is seen courtesy of some stock footage from 'Arrival'.

This was the only view of the Cat and Mouse nightspot.

CHECKMATE

Written by Gerald Kelsey

Guest stars

Rook	Ronald Radd
1st Psychiatrist	Patricia Jessel
Number Two	Peter Wyngarde
Queen	Rosalie Crutchley
Man with the stick	George Coulouris

with

The Butler	Angelo Muscat
2nd Psychiatrist	Bee Duffell
Supervisor	Basil Dignam
Painter	Danvers Walker
Shopkeeper	Denis Shaw

and

Ass. Supervisor	Victor Platt
Nurse	Shivaun O'Casey
Skipper	Geoffrey Reed
Sailor	Terence Donovan
1st Tower Guard	Joe Dunne
2nd Tower Guard	Romo Gorrara

Directed by Don Chaffey

A BEAUTIFUL SUNNY morning in the Village. Its inhabitants go about their business as usual until, emitting a fearful roar, a guardian bounces into view. Moving aside to allow the gelatinous thing to pass, the Villagers freeze in their tracks – all save one, an elderly gentleman who hobbles along on his walking stick without so much as a glance at the malign beast. Watched by Number 6, whose curiosity is aroused by the man's apparant unconcern, the man disappears through an archway leading to the gardens. The guardian continues its progress ,and the Prisoner races after the man as the community returns to their normal activities. Catching up with his quarry in a courtyard, the floor of which has been designed to represent a giant chessboard, the man with the stick invites Number 6 to take part in the unusual game. Joined by the Queen, a woman dressed to represent a chesspiece who invites the Prisoner to be her pawn, it becomes clear that this is no ordinary game of chess. Only the man with the stick and his opponent actually play while others, dressed in colourful costumes which represent chessmen, 'move' across the board as indicated by the two players. Taking up his position as the Queen's pawn, Number 6 begins to question the woman as to the man's identity. He is the champion, she replies as the man climbs into his high chair to commence play. 'Who *was* he?' he urges. The woman has heard that the man is an ex-Count, whose ancestors are supposed to have played chess using their retainers: rumour has it that they were beheaded as they were wiped off the board. 'Charming,' quips Number 6. 'Oh, don't worry,' says the Queen 'that's not allowed here.' The game continues, as do the pawn's questions. 'Who is Number 1?' (It doesn't do to ask questions.) 'Why were you brought here?' Keeping her eyes on the play, the girl repliies. 'That was a good move, wasn't it?' 'I know a better one.' says he. (Oh?) 'Away from this place.' (Oh, that's impossible.) 'For chessmen – not

156

for *me*,' he retorts. (They told me there wasn't a hope.) '*I don't believe what they tell me. Are you surprised?*' he continues, missing his cue to move as the man with the stick orders the Queen's pawn to another square. 'Maybe I could help,' offers the woman. 'How? ... How? ... HOW?' he shouts, as the address speakers surrounding the chessboard bark out the player's request for the Queen's pawn to move to Queen's 4. Urged on by other 'chessmen', he finally moves as ordered and a Bishop from the opposing side tells him not to worry, he is quite safe, protected by the Queen. The game proceeds, observed from the Control Room by Number 2 and the Supervisor, who have the Queen and her pawn under surveillance. Passing comment that Number 6 looks placid, the Supervisor is reminded by his colleague that the man is just a pawn – one false move and he will be wiped out. 'Not while the Queen is protecting him,' the Supervisor replies. 'The Queen!' exclaims Number 2. 'She'll take no risks to help him.' Reminding his colleague that he knows where he will be if he needs him, Number 2 leaves. The chess game continues until, confused by the bombardment of moves indicated by the players, the Rook, standing in the next square to Number 6, walks off the board in disgust. Entering an unoccupied square, he yells 'Check!' Informing Number 2 that the White Queen's Rook has moved without orders, the Supervisor is told to bring him in for treatment. In seconds, the 'chesspiece' has been carried away to the hospital and the game proceeds with a substitute chesspiece. Asking the Queen why the man has been removed, Number 6 is told 'for using his initiatve' – the forbidden cult of the individual. Four moves later and the game is over, won convincingly by the man with the stick. Congratulating the winner on his performance, Number 6 joins the man for a stroll. Inquiring why the man uses people for his game, the elderly man replies that, according to psychiatrists, it satisfies his desire for power. As they walk, Number 6 turns the conversation to the possibility of escape. Admitting that he has given it some thought, the other says that he has now learned to distinguish between the blacks and the whites – indicating that the attitudes of the villagers gives away the difference between the prisoners and the warders. Everybody has an attempt, but they all fail, the Prisoner is told. Leaving the man behind, Number 6 walks off alone, but is soon overtaken by the Queen, who wishes to know how he plans to escape. If he will tell her his plan, she will be willing to help: she likes Number 6, and if it is a good plan she would be willing to join him. Unsure as to whether he can trust the woman, he tells her as much and returns to his residence.

At sunrise the following morning, as Number 6 is taking a stroll, he is greeted by Number 2, who wishes to know if the Prisoner enjoyed the chess game? 'Don't tell me you care?' comes the reply. (But of course, *we* want you to be happy.) 'Fine. Just give me a one-way ticket home!' barks Number 6. 'Won't you ever give up?' asks the superior, indicating that they have ways of making him see sense – ways that are carried out under the strictest medical supervision, of course. 'I can guess what,' the Prisoner retorts, pointing to the hospital, 'from the state of the man you took yesterday.' 'The Rook? Oh he'll come to no harm, he's been put on a rehabilitation course.' 'You make it sound very attractive – what do you want me to do, envy him?' replies the other. The outburst is greeted with a smile and Number 2 offers to drive the man to see the patient. At the hospital they see the Rook being wheeled into a room. It contains three coloured water coolers, and Number 2 explains that the patient has been dehydrated: when he awakes he will be suffering from an insatiable thirst. As they watch, a woman psychiatrist enters the room, administers an injection into the sleeping man's arm and leaves as the patient stirs. Joined by the woman, the men watch as the Rook rises from his chair and attempts to quench his thirst from the first of the water dispensers. A voice piped over the room's public address system tells him to wait, but his thirst is too great. Ignoring the command he picks up a cup and turns on the dispenser. The container is empty. In desperation, he sidles along to the second dispenser. Again the voice orders him to desist. Failing to heed the advice, he receives an electric shock and falls to the floor, his body racked with pain. Viewing this in disgust, Number 6 turns to his host. 'Don't tell me,' he growls, 'it hurts *you* more than it hurts him.' The superior sighs. 'In a society, one must learn to conform.' Regaining his feet, the Rook staggers around the room pleading for an end to the ordeal. Do as you are told and you will be given water, he is scolded. He is directed by the voice to the dispenser coloured blue. Approaching the container with caution, after further coaxing the Rook turns on its tap. It yields water and the patient drinks, refilling his cup several times over. According to the psychiatrist, the man is now cured. 'You must be proud of yourself,' snaps a disgusted Number 6 to the man at his side, leading Number 2 to quip that they are proud of the patient: in future, the man will be fully cooperative, a statement which leads the doctor to observe that she, for one, is glad, the patient had proved troublesome. Marching to the door, Number 6 warns them that their troubles are only just beginning, a comment that spurs the woman to ask her superior if he, Number 6, is there for treatment. His negative response bringing forth the comment that it is a shame, the man is an interesting case – one whose breaking point she would love to discover. 'You could make that your life's

'Psychiatrists say it satisfies my desire for power'

ambition,' throws back Number 6, departing with a grin.

Later that day, as he is wandering through the Village, filling out chess moves in the *Tally Ho* newspaper chess competition, Number 6 comes across the Rook sitting alone on the steps of a fountain. Seeing the man staring at him, the Rook races away, but he is overtaken and questioned by the stranger. He learns that the man was brought to the Village after a new electronic defence system he had invented was stolen. Believing that the man can be trusted, despite the treatment he has received, Number 6 tells him they will meet again. In the Green Dome, Number 2, informed by the Supervisor that his prize subject is getting friendly with the Rook, orders his colleague to give him vision. Within seconds his monitor screen glows into life, showing the two men sitting together on a veranda, deep in conversation. Unable to decipher their words, Number 2 asks the control room to connect the audio link. However, having noticed the head of a statue nearby turning in their direction and aware that their conversation is being monitored, Number 6 is ready for them. When the audio link buzzes into life, the two men are discussing nothing more suspicious than chess moves. Reassured by the doctor that the Rook is cured and content that anything Number 6 learns from the man will only serve to teach him that there is no point in rebellion, Number 2 orders the surveillance to be closed down. Free from observation, the men continue their talk of escape. Informing the Rook that they must determine who they can trust, the Prisoner and his new ally circulate through the Village to discover a nucleus of prisoners who could be reliable allies. A gardener ignores them, but others show more promise.

'I'd like a word with you.' (Then you'll have to wait.)

Observing the men talking to several villagers, Number 2 orders the audio link to be reconnected; it is not working, having been sabotaged by the Rook. Concerned that the men may be planning something, he has Number 6 taken to hospital for psychiatric examination. Interrogated by a woman doctor, the question-and-answer session produces nothing significant. But a second test, conducted by the doctor who attended the Rook's ordeal shows that Number 6 shows positive signs of an abnormality: a total disregard for his personal safety, and a negative reaction to pain – something no prisoner could fake, unless he possessed superhuman willpower. Elsewhere, the Queen is brought before Number 2. Hypnotised, she is ready to undergo a new experiment, one which if it works, will prove invaluable to the superior: a development of studies carried out on dolphins which, when performed on humans could prove highly effective for Number 2's purpose. Delighted by what is planned, the superior watches with interest as the psychiatrist implants in the patient's brain the belief that she is in love with Number 6: she will do anything for him, even betray him to save him from his own folly. She is given a necklace which she is told is a gift from her sweetheart – a locket that contains a detection transmitter which will relay all her emotions to Control. She will now dote on Number 6, follow him like a lap dog. When her true love is out of sight she will sigh, when she sees him her pulses will quicken and if she thinks she is about to lose him – if he attempts to escape – she will be frantic and her emotions will send an alarm to the control room, the device is foolproof. Released from hospital, the Queen follows Number 6 everywhere, observed by the doctor and the control room Supervisor on their monitor screen. Each time the woman catches sight of the Prisoner, her pulse-rate quickens and the detector in the locket keeps the onlookers informed of their whereabouts. Meanwhile, handed a report of the tests carried out on Number 6 by her medical colleague, the doctor's suspicions are confirmed. She suggests to Number 2 that she be allowed to perform an operation on the man in order to lock out the aggressive tendencies in his brain. Telling her that the man is too valuable to take such a risk, her superior refuses her request. Meanwhile, the man they are discussing steals a buggy and drives away from the Village. The Queen follows suit, racing after her *beau*, honking her buggy's horn as she tears after him. Informed of this event, Number 2 orders the control room to take no action: he wishes the device to be given a proper test. The couple should be kept under observation, but no further action is to be taken unless it reaches a Yellow Alert situation. Giving the woman the slip, Number 6 picks up the Rook and drives into the woods. Concerned that the girl has lost her quarry, the doctor urges the Controller to try to locate her on the monitors, but camera 34 is not working, the Rook has ripped out its innards. Together with Number 6, he steals a cordless telephone and an electronic device from the tool kit belonging to the repair man sent to repair the broken camera. Driving away, the men are spotted by the girl, her pulse-rate quickening as she spies Number 6. Leaving the Rook to drive away with the stolen equipment, the Prisoner joins the girl in her buggy. When the woman confesses her love for him, he tells her she is crazy; they hardly know each other. The woman begins to sob; he is waterproof and a slight drizzle will not wash away his doubts. 'But I want you near me,' she sobs. 'Everybody's near in this place – far too near,' he replies, climbing out of the vehicle. Try as he may, he cannot shake his lap dog. That evening she appears at his cottage, singing merrily as she prepares to brew him a hot cup of chocolate. Their conversation continues as before: she vowing her love, he distrusting her words. Eventually, as curfew beckons and the girl refuses to tell him who sent her, he orders her to leave. She begins to sob and he softens. Asking if she can see him again, he replies dryly 'Oh, I'm here all the time.'

'I'm waterproof. A slight drizzle won't wash away my doubts'

Number 6 sees the Rook safely out to sea

The sun beats down on the shoreline as the Rook approaches the beach. Greeted by Number 2. who asks if the man feels well. the man confirms that he is and enters a beach tent. Not long afterwards he is joined by Number 6 who. told by his partner that they require further transistors for the device he is preparing. offers to collect them. Leaving the beach. he stumbles across the Queen sitting alone. When asked if he still loves her. he smiles. saying that he never did. 'How can you say that.' she teases. 'If you don't love me. then why give me this locket?' Suggesting that she has mistaken him for someone else and has picked the wrong man. her reply throws him. 'If I've got the wrong man. then why have I got the right photograph?' Curious. he takes the locket from her hand. Opened. it reveals his photograph in one half and a miniature transistor device in the other. Telling the woman that he is not very happy with the photograph and will have it replaced with a better one. he takes the trinket to the Rook. The man confirms his suspicions: the device is a reactive transmitter – the girl has become his automatic watchdog. However. providence has provided them with exactly what the Rook is looking for to complete his electronic device. It will be ready that night: tomorrow they will be free. Called to the control room. the doctor is told that her gadget has gone dead. Monitoring the girl as she crosses the beach and noting that she no longer has the necklace around her neck. the psychiatrist asks the Controller to locate Number 6. He does so and they think no more about the device. believing that it slipped from the girl's neck while she was swimming. Moments later. Number 6 and the Rook begin to circulate through the Village. advising their allies that the escape attempt is planned for that night: each being given the codeword 'Rook to Queen's Pawn 6.'

As darkness falls. Number 6 transmits a mayday signal on the device put together by the Rook. The weak signal is picked up by the *Polotska*. a ship somewhere out at sea. Receiving the message that 'Trans-Ocean flight D-for Delta 250 Zero. is on fire and losing height.' the ship asks the mayday caller to give his position. Unaware of the Village coordinates. Number 6 transmits a garbled reply. Crumpling paper into the transmitter's mouthpiece to convince the *Polotska* that static is responsible for breaking up the signal. he breaks off in mid-sentence.

Picked up by the control room. the mayday call is ignored on the advice of Number 2. Number 6 joins his colleague on the beach and. before seeing his partner safely out to sea. fixes a bleeper device onto the Rook's makeshift raft. Hearing the distress signal. the men in the control room. suspicious that the signal is coming from close to the shore. telephone to the radio tower in the mountains to give them a cross-reference. Number 6. meanwhile. having arrived at the stone boat. which harbours prisoners waiting to escape. is aware that they will need to knock out the radio tower's searchlight and sets out to head an attack on the observation post. The guards are quickly overpowered and the lamp is doused. Number 2. meanwhile. angry that his hour for meditation has been interrupted. becomes interested when his control room staff telephone him with an emergency alert. Too late. By the time the man is ready to leave his home. Number 6 and his friends are waiting at his door – not wishing to leave without thanking the man for having had them as his 'guests'. Bound by the men. Number 2 retains his reserve: he is disappointed that Number 6 in particular could not devise a more original escape attempt. Crossing to the Green Dome's master control panel. the subject of his indignation is about to switch off the Village surveillance cameras when the Rook's distress signal ceases its transmission. Suspicious that it has stopped too soon. Number 6 races to the beach alone. Finding his colleague's empty raft and spying a boat a few hundred yards from the shore. he uses the makeshift structure to reach the *Polotska*. Helped aboard by its captain. the would-be escapee stops dead in his tracks when he comes face to face with a grinning Number 2! No longer bound. the man's face stares at him from a television monitor in the captain's cabin. Taunting Number 6. the Village superior smiles with satisfaction as he confirms that the ship belongs to the Village – and besides. the weather report was unfavourable. Number 6 would not have stood a chance of escaping in such a frail craft. As the control room camera pans to the man standing at Number 2's side. the Prisoner learns what went wrong with the plan. Believing Number 6 to be a *warder*. and suspicious when he was not given the psychiatric treatment that the Rook was subjected to. his ally had convinced the others that their leader was a traitor: the Prisoner's air of authority

159

convincing the Rook that Number 6 was one of *them*. 'You only have yourself to blame,' gloats the triumphant Number 2, stating that the others will be back tomorrow – on the chessboard, as pawns! Spotting a single yellow chesspiece, a Queen's pawn, standing solitary on the control unit before Number 2, the Prisoner snatches up an ashtray from the bulkhead beside him and throws it through the television screen. Watched by an unconcerned Number 2, the Prisoner turns on his heel and fights off the attempts of the captain and his crew to detain him. One by one the men are thrown overboard. Bored with this entertainment, Number 2 reaches out with his umbrella and selects a button on the display panel before him. Called to alert, a guardian rises from the depths, bursts to the surface in an eddy of bubbles and bounces its way towards the ship. On board, the Prisoner attempts to steer the vessel away from the beast, but the *Polotska's* controls have a mind of their own and refuse to respond. Growing in size, the guardian draws alongside. Watched with caution by the helpless Number 6, the shimmering spectre bounces to the vessel's stern to push the *Polotska* back to the Village. In the control room, the mute Butler, his face a mask of complacency, places a yellow-coloured pawn back onto its rightful position on his superior's chessboard!

AUTHOR'S NOTE: Originally made under the working title *The Queen's Pawn*.

This story contains the first (and only) interior view of the Watchtower.

The shots of the *Polotska* at sea and the mock-up of its deck were re-used in the gun-runner boat scenes of *Many Happy Returns*.

DANCE OF THE DEAD

Written by Anthony Skene

Guest stars

Number 2	Mary Morris
Doctor	Duncan Macrae
Girl Bo-Peep	Norma West

with

The Butler	Angelo Muscat
Town Crier	Aubrey Morris
Psychiatrist	Bee Duffell
Day Supervisor	Camilla Hasse
Dutton	Alan White
Night Supervisor	Michael Nightingale

and

Night Maid	Patsy Smart
Maid	Denise Buckley
Postman	George Merritt
Flowerman	John Frawley
Lady in Corridor	Luck Griffiths
2nd Doctor	William Lyon Brown

Directed by Don Chaffey

NIGHT. Observed by a doctor and his colleague from the control room, three men in white medical coats enter the Prisoner's residence. Straps are attached to the sleeping figure's wrists and a device with wires running from it is secured to the Prisoner's forehead. 'Shouldn't you be doing this in the hospital?' asks the man standing at the doctor's side. 'I know what I'm doing,' replies the doctor. 'What about Number 2? Has it been agreed?' queries the other. 'I'll take responsibility. If we wait for orders, we'll never get results,' snaps the doctor. Responding to a nod from the man strapping the devices to the sleeping man's body, the doctor crosses to a control unit and turns on a machine. 'I hope you *do* know what you're doing,' says the other, a look of concern crossing his

'They always do that. Don't worry, he'll be alright in a moment'

brow. Throwing back his arms for support, Number 6 suddenly sits up erect. 'Don't worry,' says the doctor, seeing the look of concern on his colleague's face. 'They always do that. He'll be alright in a moment.' Telling his associate that he is aware about the instructions for Number 6, if any damage is done ... Silencing the man with a move of his finger, the doctor tells him that the man in the bed will talk before that happens. Viewed on the monitor screen, Number 6 blinks his eyes, shakes his head, then with a hint of a grin, looks around him. 'It's going to work. I knew it would!' exclaims the doctor, crossing to a third man, a zombie-like figure sitting upright in a chair, his left hand raised as if talking to someone on the telephone – but his hand is empty! Placing an L-shaped telephone in the man's right hand, the doctor puts the drugged figure's finger on its dialling button. The phone by the Prisoner's bed purrs. Placing the receiver to his ear, Number 6 listens as the man tells him that *they* want to break them down on everything they know; you, me, Arthur, the Colonel, everybody. Apparently it is a suspected security leak: all the files he has seen, the projects he knows about. Just headings, not details. The phone is scrambled and the man has a recorder: Number 6 may as well tell him now. Drawing a waist-high console towards him, the doctor switches on a tape machine. Pausing for an instant, Number 6 stammers 'You ... you must ... not ... ask me about that ...' The doctor advises the man in the chair to tell Number 6 that *he* is not asking the questions, it is the committee who require answers. Trembling now, Number 6 grasps the telephone tightly and stammers 'Who ... is that? Who ... is THAT?' Alarmed by the Prisoner's condition, Number 2's associate attempts to switch off the machine, but the doctor probes further, telling the drugged man to answer that it is Dutton. The man does so. Number 6 trembles and falls backwards in a helpless heap. 'Stop. Stop!' cries the associate. 'You'll damage the brain, then we'll all be ...' 'Stop!' cries Number 2, as she enters the control room. 'Get that man to hospital.' Crossing to greet her, the doctor hastily interjects 'Number 6 was about to talk ...' 'Don't you believe it,' she snaps. 'He'd have died first. You can't force it out of this man, he's not like the others.' '*I* would have made him talk – every man has his breaking point,' says the doctor staring at the monitor screen. 'I don't want him broken. He must be won over. It may seem a long process to your practical mind,' Number 2 tells him, 'but this man has a future with us.' As they talk, the zombie-like man is led away behind them. 'There are *other* ways,' Number 2 concludes.

As sunlight filters through his cottage window, Number 6 rises to the ubiquitous piped music and the Village Voice greeting everyone with a cheery good morning. Donning his dressing gown, he crosses to the window, peers outside and turns as his television monitor flickers into life. 'How did I sleep?' he asks Number 2, pictured in the Green Dome. 'Sound as a bell,' she replies. 'Have a nice day. Feel *free*.' Observed by the woman, the Prisoner crosses to his bathroom, sliding the door closed behind him. His ablutions complete, the man begins shaving. Number 2 speaks to someone on the telephone. 'Yes. Splendid,' she says, turning her chair to view Number 6 on her monitor screen. 'Oh he'll be no trouble. It's just a matter of time. Tomorrow night ... we're preparing for it now. Yes. *I* wish you could come, too.' Transported in a trailer pulled by a Village buggy, a young woman attired in an old-fashioned dress enters the Prisoner's residence carrying a breakfast tray. 'Don't tell me that time-travel

has been invented as well?' quips Number 6, catching sight of her dress. 'A woman is always impatient to wear a new dress,' the girl replies, pirouetting to display her finery. 'How do you like it?' 'Different from the others,' he replies, passing comment that maids come and go. 'I'll get along,' says the girl, passing the man on her way out. 'I'm sure you get along with everybody,' he returns. 'I've a good mind to report you,' the girl throws back. 'I'm new here,' quips Number 6, following the maid to the door, where a postman stands holding a special delivery for the resident. It is a card inviting him to attend the Village Carnival and Dance. Asked to sign with his number, the occupant replies by slamming the door in the postman's face. The Village is alive with people carrying their colourful parasols. A brass band marches through the streets and a bell-ringer rides past the Prisoner's cottage in a colourful buggy. While stroking a black cat, Number 6 views the festivities from a balcony overlooking the Village square. He is joined by Number 2, who informs him that the forthcoming festival is one of the Village traditions: each year they hold a fancy-dress party and a ball in the evening. This year, they are promised a cabaret. Will Number 6 be present? Has he a choice? Of course, she says, he can do as he wants. 'As long as it is what *you* want,' he sneers. 'As long as it's what the *majority* wants.'

'We're democratic – in some ways' (Scene different to *tx* version)

We're democratic – in *some* ways,' replies the woman, joining Number 6 as he walks to a table on the cafe veranda. 'No game is worth playing if you can't win,' she continues, keeping apace with the man. 'That's not very English I know ...' 'Are you – *English*?' he smiles. Advised that he is too independent, and should find himself a nice young lady, Number 6 spots a girl sitting alone towards the rear of the cafe. He teases, 'What about her?' Turning to the girl, Number 2 states that she is quite unsuitable. 'I'm independent, don't forget,' says the other, ignoring her advice by crossing over to the attractive blonde wearing a white cap. Seeing his approach, the girl makes to leave. 'Don't go,' he says, as the girl rises from her seat. 'I must,' she replies – indicating that Number 2 wants her to go. Pausing for a second to consider if, perhaps, he is entering a game with rules set by Number 2 (is he playing *her* game or his own? He tells the girl that she can leave if she likes and when she fails to do so, he plies her with questions. 'How long have you been here?' 'Questions are a burden to others. Answers a prison to oneself,' she replies, showing signs of being nervous. He tries again. 'What did you do, to have yourself brought here?' 'Questions are a burden . . .' she begins. Losing his temper, he finishes the quote. Upset by his outbursts the girl races away up some steps. He tries to follow her, but a guardian blocks his progress, and the girl vanishes into the Town Hall courtyard. Attempting to follow her, an electronic barrier halts him in his tracks as his body receives a mild electric shock. 'Are you alright?' asks a gardener. 'You tried to go in. By mistake? It's fussy about who it lets in – this is the Town Hall.'

In the control room, the girl he chased after is explaining to her colleague that it was not her fault that Number 6 tried to follow her. As she watches the man leave on her monitor screen her colleague replies, 'Funny though. You being his observer. Remember, keep a sharp watch.' Outside his residence, Number 6 finds the black cat he had befriended earlier. Carrying the animal inside, he is surprised to find the maid dusting his room. 'Where did you find it?' she asks. 'It found me,' he replies, stroking the animal's ebony fur. Telling him that it is against the rules to have pets, and moving towards the cat to pick up the animal, the girl is shocked by his comment that *he* is not subject to *their* rules – besides, she may get scratched! In full-flow now, he bombards the girl with questions: where does *it* come from? How did it get here? The milk? The ice cream? The potatoes and the aspirins? Staggered by his onslaught, the girl leaves, his questions unanswered. 'At night? When everyone's asleep?' he throws after her, adding that he has never seen a night. Prowling his room, he picks up a cushion and places it over the television monitor screen, short-circuiting the device. A man is placing flowers in a window-box outside his room. He jovially answers the Prisoner's comment that he does not want any by stating that everyone has flowers during carnival time. With a Village salute and a cheery 'Be seeing you,' the man leaves. Later, an elderly maid brings Number 6 a nightcap. 'Drink it while it's hot,' he is told. Sniffing the drink suspiciously, he lays the cup to one side and enters his living room. Observed by the girl he had raced after earlier, he smiles when the lights go out.

'What is it?' (It's good for you.)

Number 2, meanwhile, is telling the doctor that his earlier attempts to condition Number 6 will not be reported: she will put it down to enthusiasm. Thanking the woman, the man asks her for a directive about Dutton – the man is being difficult. At 10.32, curfew time, Number 6 paces the floor, ignoring the fact that his cottage is in darkness. He crosses to his door: it refuses to open. Retreating to his bedroom and finding the cat stretched out on his bed, he returns to his living room and seats himself in a chair. In seconds, the light above his head begins to pulsate. His eyelids flicker as the soothing voice of Number 2 attempts to send him to sleep. 'Sleep, sleep. Sleep softly until tomorrow,' purrs the voice. The attempt to hypnotise him fails. Throwing back his curtains he races from the cottage – the door is open now – and steals off into the night. Seeing this, his observer telephones Number 2, who tells the girl not to worry, the man's actions will test their efficiency. On her control room wall screen, the woman watches the man's progress along the beach. Released from the depths, a guardian rises from the sea and shadows Number 6 as he races along the shoreline until, exhausted, he falls to his knees. Hovering a few feet away, at the flick of a switch the guardian is returned to its nest by a delighted Number 2 who, turning to the cat at her side, tells the animal that the man will eventually go back to his room. 'It's the only place he can ever go.' At dawn, waking on the beach, the Prisoner spots a body lying in shallow water. Turning it over he removes the dead man's wallet and a small leather pouch. The former contains some photographs, the latter a small transistor radio. He tests the receiver. It works.

A town crier proclaims that the carnival is decreed for that night. He informs the villagers that there will be music, dancing and happiness – by order, sending them into a frenzy of anticipation – a sight greeted with apathy by Number 6 who, walking into his cottage is informed by his maid that his bed has not been slept in. Replying that he thought he would save her the trouble, he shows little interest when the girl tells him that they have given her a new dress – something special. He asks about the cat. 'Gone,' the girl replies, adding that she played no part in its leaving. Passing the comment that everyone appears to be having a good time, the girl tells him to wait until evening. 'Do you mean we're allowed out after hours?' he mocks. Anyone would think they were locked in the way he talks, says the girl, informing Number 6 that his costume has arrived. It's not of the man's choice. 'Other people choose,' says the maid. 'It's a game.' Opening the box, the man produces his own evening suit, specially delivered for the occasion. 'What does that mean?' asks the girl, expecting to see fancy-dress. 'That I'm *still – myself*,' he suggests. 'Lucky you,' says the maid, leaving. Number 2 watches as the Prisoner attempts to tune in the radio he found earlier, and warns the doctor not to be so eager with his attempts to crush the Prisoner's reserve. His techniques are efficient, but not always beneficial and Number 6 will be of great value yet. 'He can't do as he likes,' says the doctor. 'He's an individual and *they* are always trying. Don't worry, his observer will ring me the moment he puts a bomb in your lovely hospital. Incidentally, how's Dutton?' Informing Number 2 that the man has given him lots of information, but he is reluctant to go any further, the medico confesses that he will have to use more extreme measures if he is to win in the end – as he always does. Commenting that Dutton is a small fish, the woman nevertheless agrees to allow her colleague to continue his work on the patient: it will of course, give him the opportunity to experiment. 'After all,' she adds, '*he* (meaning Dutton) is expendable.' In the meantime, Number 6 has climbed to the Bell Tower and managed to get the radio working. He has just picked up an English-speaking station when Number 2 approaches, followed by his observer. Asking Number 6 if it works, he contemptuously retunes the device, and an announcer invites listeners to take part in a shorthand typing exercise. 'Hardly useful,' grins Number 2, switching the radio off. Telling the man that she is sad and believed he was about to ... 'Give in?' fires back Number 6, anticipating her words. '... why not? Everything you ever wanted is here,' she suggests. 'Everything's elsewhere,' he replies. Told that they will only stand for so long, he adds, 'Yes, I know. I've been to the hospital and seen.' 'You've seen only a fraction,' threatens Number 2, as, glancing at the other woman, the man states that he knows where her loyalties lie. The superior explains that the girl is one of their best observers. 'We have one each?' queries Number 6. 'Only our more fractious children,' states the superior, inviting the man to return to the Village. When he fails to answer, she departs alone, taking the transistor radio with her. 'I have my duty,' says the girl, as Number 6 moves towards her. 'To whom?' he asks. 'To everyone,' comes the reply. 'It's the rules. *Of* the people, *by* the people, *for* the people.' 'It takes on a new meaning,' he counters. 'You're a wicked man,' states the girl. 'Wicked?' 'You have no values,' she says. '*Different* values,' he replies. 'You want to be helped!' she exclaims. 'Destroyed.' 'You want to spoil things,' she snaps. He retaliates, stating that he won't be a goldfish in a bowl. 'I must go. I will see you later?' questions the girl, softly. 'Can you avoid it?' Indicating that his radio is alright, he questions her as to what she would do if she had found it? She would report it. Ask for instructions. 'From Number 1?' (Yes) 'Who ...?' (No) '...Tell me.' (That's all I know – all there is to know.) 'In the place where you work?' 'Don't keep asking me questions,' says the girl, leaving the man standing alone. Slipping out the wallet he took from the dead man, the Prisoner takes out a photograph of a father and child. Descending to the Village, on the pretext of joining a crew renovating the Stone Boat, he steals a lifebuoy and a length of cord. Racing down to a cave on the beach in which he had earlier placed the dead man's body, he removes his Village identity card and some paper from his pocket and begins to write a note: 'To whoever may find this ...' In the control room, his observer, scanning the Village for her ward, but unable to locate his whereabouts, telephones her superior to confess that she has lost contact with Number 6. 'Don't worry,' says an unconcerned Number 2, 'he'll turn up. It's only a matter of time, he's very undisciplined.' Turning to her colleague, the observer asks if she should watch Number 34 instead? 'No, he's dead,' reports the other. 'Dead! When?' exclaims the girl. 'That's none of our business,' snaps her colleague. 'I got to know him quite well,' sighs the girl. 'He didn't get to know *you*, did he?' comes the reply. Back in the cave, his message complete, Number 6 seals the wallet containing his own documents into a plastic envelope, puts them into the dead man's inside jacket pocket and drags the body out of the cave and into the sea. The lifebuoy strapped around the man's lifeless body carries the figure away on the outgoing tide. Turning back to the cave, the Prisoner sees a man observing him. It is Dutton, the man to whom the doctor handed the telephone in the opening sequence. 'You. You of all people. I'd never have believed it,' says the man, as the Prisoner approaches him. 'Roland ... Walter ... Dutton,' stammers Number 6. 'Who was he?' asks the other, indicating the body floating away on the tide. 'His body was washed up on the shore,' answers Number 6. 'How long have you been here?' 'You don't know?' asks Dutton. 'Would I ask?' The other, his face and body showing signs of interrogation, staggers to support himself by the rockface. 'It's difficult to say ... a couple of months? And you?' 'Quite recently,' Number 6 replies. 'How's London?' Dutton wishes to know. 'About the same.' 'Yes. Places don't change – only people,' sighs Dutton. '*Some* people,' suggests Number 6, helping the man into the cave. Safely inside, Dutton confesses that he has told them everything he knows, the irony being that they still do not believe that he told them the truth – that he never had access to the vital information. Telling Number 6 that they will take him back to the hospital and by the time they learn that he was telling them the truth it will be too late, he adds that he has been released for 72 hours, so that he can reconsider in the peaceful atmosphere of the Village. 'There's still hope,' the Prisoner tells him. 'No my friend, not for me,' Dutton replies. 'Such noble thoughts are long dead. Soon, Roland Walter Dutton will cease to exist.'

Later that evening, dressed in his tuxedo and looking out to sea, the Prisoner is joined on the beach by Number 2. 'You're waiting for someone, Mr Tuxedo?' she calls. 'Or expecting someone?' Turning, and catching sight of her costume, a skimpy pantomime outfit depicting the creation of author J.M. Barrie, he retorts 'Mr Peter Pan?' 'So it seems,' says the woman. 'With his *shadow*!' he mocks. 'You're being hostile again,' says the imp-like figure. 'What were you looking at?' 'A light?' (A star?) 'A boat?' (An insect?) 'A plane.' (A flying fish!) Bridging the gap between them, he quips 'Somebody who belongs to *my* world.' 'This is your world. *I* am your world,' says Peter Pan. 'If you insist on living a dream, you may be taken for mad.' 'I like my dream,' he replies. 'Then you *are* mad! Now go on up to the Town Hall.' 'May I?' he taunts. 'You *may* enter tonight – it's carnival.'

As deadly as the male

Entering the great hall, they find the place bedecked with rows of white masks, those in attendance dressed in a variety of colourful fancy dress costumes. 'What, no dancing?' shouts Number 2, to the rows of villagers who stand agape at the sight of Number 6 who, dressed in his tuxedo, is completely out of step with the spirit of the event. 'Tonight's for dancing!' exclaims Peter Pan. Then, with a glance in the Prisoner's direction, 'amongst other things.' As the man wearing the tuxedo strolls through the crowd, Number 2 signals to the orchestra to begin. Handed a glass of wine by his host, the Prisoner confesses that he rarely partakes. 'Then you'll enjoy it all the more,' she says. 'Self-denial is a great sweetner. It's undoctored, for the carnival.' She raises her glass. 'Your administration is effective, but you have no opposition,' he says, looking at his glass. 'An irritation we've dispensed with. Even at best, free democracy is remarkably inefficient,' she returns. After some small talk about the vintage of the wine, he asks why he has not been given a costume. 'Perhaps because you don't exist,' Number 2 replies, commenting how lovely his observer looks as she arrives dressed in her costume. 'Little Bo Peep,' says the girl proudly. 'Who always knows where to find her sheep,' Number 6 replies. While Number 2 offers the doctor, (dressed as Napoleon) a glass of wine, Bo Peep leads Mr Tuxedo to the dance floor; he stands with his arms crossed, while she sways before him. 'How many of these have you been to?' he asks, adding that this is his first – and last. 'Don't be silly,' Bo Peep replies, attempting to cajole him to dance. 'Who's saying that,' he replies, 'you or the computer?' 'Me!' she exclaims, stopping dead in her tracks. 'Oh, don't behave like a human being, it might confuse people.' 'Only you are confused,' says the girl, picking up the rythmn, 'but not for long. They have treatments for people like you.' Apologising for bumping into the doctor and Number 2, the couple continue to dance, he walking in time to the music, she attempting to persuade her partner to join in. The questions continue. '*She* must get instructions. Who do they come from?' asks Number 6, indicating Number 2. 'Is he here tonight . . . the man behind the big door?' 'There's no need to know,' says Bo-Peep, 'this place has been going for a long time.' 'Since the war? *Before* the war? *Which* war?' 'A *long* time,' replies the girl, storming off the dance floor. Brushing aside two doormen attending the hall's entrance, Number 6 dons a white hospital coat from a clothes stand in the corridor then, placing the pair of spectacles he finds in the coat's pocket onto the bridge of his nose he patrols the corridor until he finds an unlocked door. Mistaking him for a doctor, a woman wearing a similar white smock enquires if he has seen Number 2. 'I'll *be* seeing her,' he mocks, taking the urgent termination order from the woman's hand. 'Much obliged,' she says, reminding him that the matter is urgent. 'Right away,' states Number 6, giving the impression that he is on his way. Alone in the corridor, however, he opens the missive. In white lettering on a black background it contains just three words: 'Roland Walter Dutton'! Musing over his colleague's fate, the Prisoner enters a darkened room. The lights switch on automatically as he does so, and two doors, which swing open of their own volition, beckon the man into a second darkened room. As before, the lights come on and he finds himself standing in a huge room. Crossing to a third door, he tries to open it. It is locked, but entrance is secured when he notices a key hanging from a hook by the side of the door. Passing through, he finds himself in a vast ante-chamber, containing two rows of metal cabinets – a repository

where, sliding open one of the drawers, he discovers the body of the dead sailor that he had cast out to sea! 'You make the most of your opportunities,' calls Number 2, entering with the cat at her heels. 'You don't blame us for doing the same.' Meowing its affection, the cat crosses to the man. 'Ah, she's taken to you,' grins Peter Pan. 'I'm jealous. Oh she's mine. She works here too. She's *very* efficient – almost ruthless.' 'Never trust a woman,' grins Number 6 weakly, 'even the four-legged variety.' 'You can trust everyone,' mocks Number 2, sliding the mortuary cabinet closed, 'and will – in time. Let's go back. The cabaret's beginning.' Indicating the body in the closed cabinet, Number 6 asks 'In his pocket . . . ' 'The wallet?' retorts Peter Pan, anticipating his question. 'It's still there – "amended" slightly. We'll amend him slightly. It's you who's died – in an accident at sea.' 'So the outside world . . . ' says the Prisoner, removing his coat and handing her the keys to the room. ' . . . Which you only dream about,' reminds Number 2. ' . . . I'll be dead,' he concedes. 'A small confirmation of a known fact,' concludes Peter Pan. 'Don't blame me. It's a question of waste not, want not.' Leaving the mortuary, they rejoin the festivities in the dance hall. But the dancing has ended. All those in attendance are now gathered around a large circular platform placed in the centre of the dance area. 'I thought there was a cabaret?' asks the Prisoner, as Number 2 struts to her throne, a large chair positioned at the end of the room. 'There is. You are *it*!' says Peter Pan. Addressing the gathering, she brings the court to order. 'In the matter of the People versuses this person,' she begins, 'the court is now in session.' 'What is my crime?' asks Number 6. Telling the accused that they will come to that, Number 2 explains that their legal system is unusual. 'No jury?' mocks the Prisoner. 'Three judges decide here,' continues Peter Pan, ignoring the man. 'As in the French Revolution,' suggests the Prisoner. 'They got through the dead wood, didn't they,' retorts Number 2 unamused, adding that she has been appointed by the court to act as his defence and Bo-Peep will prosecute. The judges have been chosen: Marie Antoinette, Nero and Napoleon, take their seats on the circular platform. 'Proceed,' orders Peter Pan. The Town Crier opens the proceedings. 'You are charged with having on your person and using for unlawful purposes and against the interests of the community, an object the possession and use of which breaks our Rules. A radio set.' 'Don't you ask how I plead?' enquires the accused. Ignoring the man, the Town Crier orders the prosecution to proceed. Confirming that she saw the device twice, once in his room and again on the bell tower, Bo Peep gives way to the maid, who steps forward to say that she saw the device while dusting the man's residence. The accused was listening to the radio; as it is improper to listen, she has no idea as to the programme. 'Quite right,' confirms the Town Crier, turning to Number 2. 'Did you listen Madam?' 'How can my Defender be a prosecution witness?' asks the accused. 'No, my lords, but it did work,' says Peter Pan, ignoring her charge yet again. 'It is the duty of all of us to care for each other . . . ' continues Bo-Peep, ' . . . and to see that the Rules are obeyed. Without this discipline we should exist in a state of anarchy.' 'Hear, hear,' mocks the Prisoner. 'You do yourself no good,' pipes up Napoleon. Stating that the accused had no radio of his own but, by acquiring one he made a positive effort against the community, indicating a malicious breaking of the Rules, the prosecution turns to the Prisoner. It is the duty of the court to pass the severest possible sentence. Number 6 joins Peter Pan in applauding the girl's words.

As the judges have no wish to question the Prosecution, the Defence can open its case. Number 2 takes the stand and tells everyone that the accused is a human being, with the weaknesses and failings of his kind. The fact that he had the radio and has broken rule after rule cannot be denied, but she pleads with their Lordships for clemency. The accused is new and guilty only of folly. No more. They must treat folly with kindness, knowing that soon his wild spirit will quieten and the foolishness will fall away to reveal a model citizen. 'That day you will never see,' challenges the accused. 'The Prisoner will be silent . . . this is a serious matter,' says the Town Crier. 'Very serious,' mocks Number 6. Stating that both officers have presented their pleas with creditable simplicity, Nero suggests that they now consider their findings. 'I wish to call a witness,' says the accused. 'Witness?' quizzes Napoleon, a look of concern crossing his face. Looking at Bo-Peep, Number 2 states that they are the sole witnesses

'He was listening to a programme'

to the man's guilt. 'What manner of witness?' asks Marie Antoinette, indicating to the others that the accused has rights. 'A *character* witness,' states Number 6. 'I want the court to call Roland Walter Dutton!' A look of consternation crosses the judges faces. 'No names are used here,' states Nero. 'He's a man I think I knew. A man who is scheduled to die, and therefore better fitted than I to say the things that need to be said,' pleads the accused. Rising from her seat Peter Pan brings forth Dutton, dressed now in a jester's suit. The man shows signs of having become an imbecile: his head droops forward onto his chest, his eyes stare unseeing. 'Your *character* witness,' mocks Peter Pan, returning to her throne. The judges begin their deliberations. They find the accused guilty of a breach of the Rules, which his folly and inexperience cannot excuse. In accordance with the Rules, sentence is passed and Nero hands the mute Butler a proclamation. 'No. Stop it!' exclaims Bo-Peep, rising from her chair. 'It's the Rules my dear,' says Peter Pan, as Nero places a black cap on his head. The sentence is death! The accused has been sentenced in the name of the people. The people carry it out in the name of Justice. With a final stare at his friend Dutton, the Prisoner marches warily through the crowd.

As he reaches the Town Hall's entrance, they surge forward after him, like a hungry pack of wolves howling for blood. Racing down the corridor, he runs through the doors he passed through earlier and enters the mortuary room, lights to each chamber coming on as he rushes through them. Entering the ante-room, he prises up a trapdoor in the floor and disappears into the blackness beyond, the howls of the villagers ringing in his ears. Traversing the underground vault, he ascends a staircase and slips back unseen, into the corridor through a concealed door. A second set of doors slide open to admit him into a lavishly-furnished room where, hidden behind a ticker-tape machine, its keyboard criss-crossing numerals onto a piece of blank paper beneath its platen, he attempts to switch off its staccato chattering by tearing out its electric wiring. Through a mirror set into a wall, he sees his pursuers still searching for him. 'It's a one-way mirror,' says Number 2, entering the room with Bo-Peep. 'They can't see you. They've never seen in here, and they never will. They lack initiative.' Turning to Bo-Peep, she tells the girl to deal with them. Nodding her approval, the girl leaves. 'Why are they trying to kill me?' asks Number 6, softly. 'They don't know you're already dead . . . locked up in a long box . . . in that little room,' replies Number 2, witnessing the crowd outside being dispersed by Bo-Peep. 'She's no longer your observer. Observers of life should never get involved.' 'You'll never win,' maintains the Prisoner. 'Then how very uncomfortable for you, old chap,' laughs Number 2, as the tele-printer behind Number 6 magically begins to chatter back into life. In unison with Peter Pan's cruel and mirthless laugh, the bars slam shut across the Prisoner's image.

AUTHOR'S NOTE: The part of Number 2 (played by Mary Morris) was originally written for a man, actor Trevor Howard, but due to ill-health the actor had to be replaced.

THE CHIMES OF BIG BEN

Written by Vincent Tilsley

Guest stars

Number 2	Leo McKern
Nadia	Nadia Gray
The General	Finlay Currie
Fotheringay	Richard Wattis

with

The Butler	Angelo Muscat
Colonel J	Kevin Stoney
Number 2 Asst	Christopher Benjamin
Karel	David Arlen
Supervisor	Peter Swanwick

and

Number 38	Hilda Barry
First Judge	Jack Le-White
Second Judge	John Maxim
Third Judge	Lucy Griffiths

Directed by Don Chaffey

THE VILLAGE is stirred into a new day by a fanfare of music piped over its personal address system: the Village voice, wishing everyone 'Good morning, good morning, and what a lovely day it is. Rise and shine. Rise and shine.' Inside the cottage signposted '6 – Private', its resident endeavours to sleep on. The strident announcement continues: a weather forecast, stating that the fine spell will continue for at least a month, and the local council – democratically elected by the villagers – has decided to organise a great new competition. 'Can you paint? Can you draw? Can you mould clay? If you can, then *your* day is just six weeks today!' The recumbent figure stirs, his eyelids flickering open to stare at the radio speaker in his room, struggling against this intrusion of his dreams. The voice gives way to music, a raucous brass band march. Resigned now, the figure turns back his sheets, slips into his slippers and dressing gown, and walks to his bathroom. Watching these proceedings from from his over-sized oval-shaped chair, sits a bearded, slightly balding, rotund figure dressed in the ubiquitous flannels and blazer, a badge denoting a red Number 2 pinned to its left lapel. 'He can make even the act of putting on his dressing gown appear as a gesture of defiance,' observes the man. Then, reacting to his duty officer's claim that there are methods they have not yet used, he rises from his seat, stating.'I want *him* with a whole heart, body and soul.' Crossing to his kitchen, the man being observed withdraws a food carton and two eggs from his refrigerator. 'He'll crack,' observes the man standing next to Number 2, watching the man select a saucepan from a shelf. 'Perhaps,' replies his superior, raising his morning cup of tea from his breakfast tray. 'One tiny piece at a time?! I don't want a man in *fragments!* Setting his breakfast aside, Number 6 crosses to the loudspeaker unit, clutches the device to his chest (it has no exterior wiring) and transports it to the refrigerator, placing it untidily on top of a chicken breast and a sliced roll of pastrami! 'Fascinating,' declares Number 2, sipping from his cup. 'He doesn't even *bend* a little,' observes his

colleague dryly. 'That's why he'll break,' states the older man. 'It only needs one small thing. If he will answer one simple question, the rest will follow. WHY DID HE RESIGN?'

Attired in his Village uniform, Number 6 takes an early morning stroll. Observing this, Number 2 frowns as he is forced to respond to a flashing light on the red telephone sitting behind him on the console unit. It is a message from the Controller. The helicopter Number 2 is expecting has been sighted. Stating that he has no wish to make radio contact, Number 2 requests that he be informed when the machine lands: he wishes to meet it personally. Watching the helicopter's approach, Number 6, is sitting at a table on the terrace, playing a game of chess with an elderly gentleman wearing a military cap. He allows his attention to be distracted from the game, leaving his opponent to regain his attention by stating 'Your move, young man.' Turning half-heartedly back to the game, Number 6 makes a random move. 'Mmm,' says his opponent, perplexed by the man's foolishness. 'Know what I'll do.' 'Resign?' teases the younger man. 'No,' his opponent grumbles, picking up a chess piece and stating that he will make a new set for the Arts and Crafts exhibition. 'Are you entering? No! You're a fool Number 6, that's my opinion. You'll be here for as long as you live.' 'However long that is,' retorts his companion. 'Might as well try to settle down. No point in being uncooperative,' replies the military man. 'Was there ever a time when *you* were not cooperative?' queries his playing companion. 'No point in fighting battles you can't win.' 'Perhaps you came here of your own free will?' throws back the man denoted as 6. 'Wish I'd had you in my regiment for a few months,' states the chess player. 'Which regiment was that? Which Army?' counters his opponent. The helicopter lands nearby and the elderly man is rescued from further interrogation by the arrival of Number 2 and his dwarf Butler. Bidding the ex-soldier good morning, Number 2 appears non-plussed when the man nods expression of disapproval at Number 6, and departs in disgust at his playing companion's attitude. 'The General seems a little sour,' comments Number 2, selecting a chair opposite Number 6. 'Mate in 7 moves,' sneers the man, removing his hand from a chesspiece. 'How many more do you know?' inquires the newcomer. 'A few more,' comes the reply. '*We* must play sometime,' smiles Number 2. 'Certainly we must – by post!' retorts the other, rising from his seat and moving towards the helicopter. 'I must add humour to your file,' chuckles Number 2 behind him. 'They tend to leave out things like that. Very important.' An unconscious woman is being carried from the machine on a stretcher. Covered by a red blanket, she is young and attractive. 'What *crime* did she commit?' demands Number 6. 'Nervous tension,' calls back the elder. 'She's come here to recuperate.' 'How much are you charging her?' A hearty chuckle. The man's new file really must be brought up to date.

Having adjourned to Number 2's quarters, the mute Butler wheels in tea on a trolley as his master dictates an addendum to his visitor's file. Joining his guest, he enquires how many sugar lumps he takes. One lump or two? 'It's in the file,' snaps back Number 6 (Yes, but it would save time if the man answered.) 'Why? Are you running out of time?' quips his guest. Number 2 checks the man's file. (He does not take sugar – frightened of putting on weight perhaps?) 'No. Nor of being *reduced.*' (You really are a model.) 'But I don't run on clockwork.' (You will, my dear chap. You will!) 'Do you think so?' (Do you still think that you can escape, Number 6?) 'I'm going to do better than that!' (Oh?) 'I'm going to escape and come back . . .' (Come *back*!?) ' . . . Escape, come back, wipe this place off the face of the Earth, obliterate it, and you with it!' Seething now, Number 2 hastily dictates a sub-section six update on his guest's 'Persecution complex, amounting to mania – paranoid delusions of grandeur.' To add insult to injury, his guest calmly pours himself tea and, with great deliberation drops three sugar lumps into his cup. Apparently beaten, Number 2 sinks back in his chair. Then, renewing his resolve he adds, 'Don't worry, Number 6, you'll be cured. *I'll* see to it. No more nightmares. If you have so much as a bad dream, you will come *whimpering* to tell it to me. *Whimpering!* Watch, just watch!'

Viewing the giant monitor screen, the two men see the ambulance men leaving the cottage denoted '8 – Private'. 'Your new neighbour, the new Number 8,' the host tells his guest. 'What happened to the old one?' asks the listener. (Oh, he vacated the premises.) 'He escaped?' (A chuckle) 'There was no funeral?' (That's not always possible – you need a body.) 'Oh look, she's getting up,' begins Number 2. 'It's quite like old times, isn't it, Number 6? Do you remember *your* first day?' In her room – an exact replica of the one she lived in before she was kidnapped – the girl stirs. Taking her first faltering steps, she stares at her surroundings, then crosses to look out of the window. The view is a shock to her senses. Guffawing aloud, Number 2 reaches for his telephone and requests to be connected to Number 8. Their conversation is short, culminating with Number 2 inviting the girl to lunch. Distraught when the line goes dead, the woman trembles in fear. Sickened by his host's behaviour, Number 6 makes to leave. 'I trust you'll be neighbourly?' queries Number 2. 'I'll do a deal with you Number 6. You tell me one thing and I'll release you. *Why did you RESIGN?*' Unmoved by the man's false promise, the visitor turns his back and raps loudly on the giant metal doors before him. Number 2's plea that he should take part in community life, falling on deaf ears. 'At the age of fifteen, was top of the class in woodwork.' Number 2 reads from the man's file. 'Now that's the sort of thing I mean. Join in.' 'I'll make you a handle for this door,' quips back his guest, pacing determinedly through the now open doors. 'You'll be back,' echoes his host. 'Whimpering!'

Outside, further news of the Arts and Crafts competition is being broadcast by the Village voice. There are to be five categories to be judged, the winner to receive 2,000 work units. Outside his residence, Number 6 meets the new girl. She hails him, seeking directions to the Green Dome. 'Across the square, across the street, up the steps, you can't miss it,' he replies. 'I know it sounds crazy,' she stammers, 'but I don't know where I am.' 'In the Village,' he replies, as two villagers pass by, proferring the Village hand salute, which he returns. The woman is puzzled by the greeting and the stream of Village taxis plying their trade. At her request, Number 6 accompanies her to her destination, explaining as they walk that the taxi service is only local. 'Who are these people?' she asks. 'Why are they here?' 'Why are *you*?' he answers. At the door marked '2', the girl asks 'Who is Number 2?' 'Who is Number 1?' says he, as the door opens of its own volition. He makes to leave. Puzzled, she calls 'I've done nothing wrong. I've committed no crimes. All I did was resign.' 'No use telling me,' replies Number 6, with a hint of suspicion.

They meet again as the girl returns from her luncheon date. As curfew is approaching, the man offers her a nightcap: genuine non-alcoholic whisky, or would she prefer genuine non-alcoholic vodka, 24 and 16 work units respectively. 'Thank you, Mister . . .?' he replies, pouring her drink. '*I* am Number 6. You are *Number 8*.' Inspecting his quarters, the woman informs him that she is Estonian. Commenting that she speaks good English, she explains that it was her job. 'From which you *resigned*?' he queries, a hint of suspicion in his voice. Remarking that Number 2 was a charming man and she would expect his assistant to be the same, he retaliates with: 'And what about *you* – Number 8?' 'I'm no Number 8, or number anything else,' she protests, adding that her name is Nadia Rakovski, and she has been interrogated enough for one day. Putting down her glass, she bids her host goodnight. 'Be seeing you,' he calls after the retreating figure.

'Taxis . . . local service only'

The following morning, the new girl joins the merry-makers on the beach. She selects a spot on the sand, immediately below the veranda on which her neighbour is sitting. Sipping coffee, she ignores the man's stare. 'May I join you?' asks Number 2, approaching the man's table. Indicating a vacant seat with a nod of his head, Number 6 peers over his shoulder at the girl. His reverie is broken when the man denoted '2' asks if he and the girl are now good neighbours? Imparting the comment that there are some people who leave this place and some who do *not* leave, Number 2 continues '*You* are obviously staying.' He awaits the man's reply. (Has it ever occured to Number 2 that he is just as much a prisoner as Number 6?) 'Ah, my dear chap, of course. I know too much. We're *both* lifers. *I* am definately an optimist, that's why it doesn't matter *who* Number 1 is.'

The woman rises and heads for the sea. 'It doesn't matter which *side* runs the Village,' continues the elder. (It's run by *one* side or the other?) 'Oh, certainly. But both sides are becoming identical.' Removing her sunglasses and bathing robe, the girl enters the water. 'What in fact has been created, is an *international* community, a perfect blueprint for world order. When the sides facing each other suddenly realise that they are looking into a mirror,

167

they will see that *this* is the pattern for the future.' (The whole earth, as the Village?) 'That is my hope. What's yours?' (I'd like to be the first man on the moon.) Taking the joke agreeably, and thanking Number 6 for a delightful chat, Number 2 leaves his junior staring quizzically at the woman who has now entered the sea, and is pulling away from the shore using powerful swimming strokes. Back in the Green Dome, Number 2 opens the woman's file. Reading the entry 'International Swimmer; at the age of 17 was Olympic bronze medallist' with a mixture of interest and alarm, he telephones the control room Supervisor to ascertain what visual range he has out at sea. Two miles visual, comes the reply, radar after that. He joins his colleague in the control room, where Number 8's progress is being monitored on the wall screen. Aware that the woman is almost out of range, with a shrug of his shoulders the leader presses a button and orders 'Orange Alert'. Within the wink of an eye, a guardian is released from the bed of the ocean floor. Bursting to the surface with a high-pitched howl, the lighter-than-air monster rolls across the water after the girl. Watched knowingly by Number 6 from the beach, with a terrifying roar, the guardian overtakes the swimmer and engulfs her in its glutinous mass. Stretching its balloon-like fabric over her face, it sucks the air from her lungs and the swimmer is lost in a swirling eddy. Dividing into three (a 'parent' and its 'children') the grotesque creatures floats her body back to the shoreline where, watched by a quizzical Number 6, the limp body is carried away on a stretcher.

Told by Number 2 to meet him at the hospital, Number 6 is ushered into an observation room, and is treated to another demonstration of the interrogation methods of the Village. Looking through a one-sided observation window, he sees the woman sitting alone, being questioned by the Supervisor from the control room. 'What was the purpose of your swim? Were you attempting suicide?' drones the voice from a speaker placed in the room. 'Did you think you could escape?' Stating that he does not want to be hard on the girl – she is not that important, Number 2 asks the prisoner if he noticed any suicidal tendencies in the woman?' 'What are you doing to her?' demands Number 6. 'Oh, there's an alternating current in the floor, four seconds on, four seconds off.' replies the other. 'It takes just three seconds to get to the door. If she times it correctly, she can leave whenever she likes.' The woman's salvation is a glass of water on the table before her. By sprinkling a few drops upon the floor she can discover when the current is harmless and make her escape. Watched by the all-seeing mechanical eye positioned in the room, her every move is being monitored. 'I believe she's going to do it,' says Number 2, as the girl sprinkles further water droplets onto the floor's surface, counting the seconds that elapse between its evaporation. Suddenly, the girl makes her dash for freedom, but her bid comes to nothing. With the Supervisor's voice droning in her ears, she falters as she reaches the door, standing a split-second away from extinction. Falling helplessly to her knees she cries 'Kill me . . . kill me . . .' 'No!' screams Number 2. 'Switch off. Switch off!' Staring at the hapless figure, a distraught Number 2 turns to his fellow-observer. 'Well, well. We'll just have to try something else.' Outside in the corridor, he beseeches Number 6 to help; the lesson was very distasteful. 'Let her go!' demands the prisoner. (Looks like a suicidal tendency, doesn't it – but one must be sure.) 'Let her GO!' (Is that an order, Number 6?) 'All right,' says

Number 6. 'You wanted a deal. I'll make a deal with you.' He crosses to peer into a therapy room. 'Let her go and I'll collaborate.' (You'll what?) 'That's what you wanted.' (So obvious a weakness – in *you*?) 'Why not?' (For which you'll collaborate?) 'Don't get too excited. I'll tell you nothing. I'll join in, try to settle down, even carve something for the exhibition.' (If I turn her over to you, *you'll* do some woodwork for me. Is that your *deal*?) 'The best you'll get.' Amused by the man's arrogance, Number 2 dictates a further update on the prisoner's 'self-importance and egomania.' Turning to face the man, Number 6 asks 'Well?' 'All right! She's all yours,' concedes Number 2. 'Be seeing you,' smiles the other, leaving.

Preparing breakfast the following morning, Number 6, attired now in a zip-up anorak-type wind-cheater, with the ubiquitous white piping lapels, grins as Number 8 arrives and offers to complete his chore – a scene that is being observed by Number 2 and his aide from the control room. Commenting that things could not be going better, Number 2 decides to pay them a call. Meeting the couple as they leave the prisoner's residence, he bids them a joyful good morning, then asks if they are settling down. A nod from Number 6 brings the reply 'No swimming, I hope?' 'Off to the woods,' states the prisoner. 'Naughty, naughty,' chides Number 2. Explaining that he has decided to do a series of abstracts, and is off to the woods to carve something with tools he has made himself, the prisoner leads the girl away.

Their progress through the trees is followed by the turning heads of the statues. Safe in the knowledge that they can see, but cannot hear, the man gives them a Village salute and tells the girl that they can talk freely; or does she still believe that it is a trap? Reaching the spot where he has buried his tools, he asks 'Were you sent here because you discovered the whereabouts of the Village?' Alarmed by his knowledge, the girls begs him not to tell them. Digging further by suggesting that she does know its location, the girl maintains that there is no escape. Not even by sea, he suggests, indicating that if he knew where he was sailing *from* he could calculate where he was sailing *to*. 'Sail?' queries the girl. 'By boat,' he replies, commencing to chop down a tree with his home-made stone-headed axe – unaware that a delighted Number 2 sits watching them from his chair in the Green Dome. Before long the tree has been felled and hewn into the skeleton of a dug-out canoe. Intrigued. Number 2 leaves his residence and joins the woodcutter in the forest. 'I say, I say. What is it?' he asks. 'It doesn't make sense without the whole group. There'll be three pieces.' replies the wood carver. Reminding Number 6 that entries must by in by two weeks from the following day and that, technically, an axe and stone chisels are outside the pale of the law, the senior man asks the woodsman if he can give him a lift back to the Village. Declining the offer. Number 6 states that he wishes to continue his work while there is still daylight. 'Be seeing you.' says the departing Number 2. 'And you,' mocks Number 6 dryly. 'But not for long.'

'Were you sent here because you know the whereabouts of the Village?'

Curfew time. Sleep time.' says the Village voice. 'Allow us to lull you with . . .' A soft lullabye is transmitted through the speaker unit as Nadia calls on her neighbour. Signalling the man to speak softly, she takes him outside and sits close beside him at a table on his veranda. 'The language of love.' comments Number 2, seeing but unable to hear the man's words as he gently strokes the woman's hair. Walking arm in arm with her neighbour, Nadia finally concedes that she does know the Village coordinates. The government she worked for gave her access to a secret file on the place. Its location: Lithuania. The prisoner plans his escape route: from the Baltic, that means making for West Germany, then Denmark. 300 miles at least. Not so, says Nadia, offering her own plan. If he will take her along, they can travel to Danzig, in Poland. He tells the girl that although he cannot answer for the British authorities, he will give her his personal guarantee, for whatever that is worth, of her safety. Number 6 listens intently as she continues her story. They are only thirty miles away from the Polish border. Beyond

that is a small village and her contact who will help them. Explaining that her greatest need is to hear the sounds of Big Bill – 'Big Ben', he corrects – as the curfew bell chimes, Nadia bids her comrade sleep well 'Goodnight, Big Ben.' 'Big *Bill*.' quips Number 6.

The day of the Arts and Crafts exhibition arrives with a fanfare from a brass band. A banner outside the exhibitors' hall proclaims the admission times. Together with other excited entrants. Numbers 6 and 8 arrive, to be greeted by an enthusiastic Number 2, shadowed as ever, by the mute dwarf Butler. Informing Number 6 that the Awards Committee are intrigued. though somewhat mystified by his exhibit, its creator promises to explain things. The room they enter contains paintings and sculptures, all of an obvious subject: Number 2. 'Remarkably high standard. Don't you agree?' boasts the leader proudly. 'Highly original.' throws back Number 6. Revolving merrily on a circular rostrum towards the back of the hall, sits the 'pride' of the exhibition, the younger man's abstract: a montage of three pieces, the dug-out canoe, a cross-member, and a long pole running through its centre. Introducing Number 6 as their 'very own Epstein'. Number 2 takes credit for superior deductive powers when, asked by several visitors what the montage means. Number 6 replies 'It means what it is.' 'Brilliant.' echoes Number 2. 'It means what is *is*. Brilliant!' Then, realising, perhaps that he has spoken out of turn he quickly adds, 'Oh no! You mustn't let *me* influence you. *You* are the Awards Committee.' What puzzles a lady judge, however, is the fact that Number 6 has titled his work 'Escape'. Standing before his masterpiece, the creator, points out various portions of his work, stating that depending on how it is viewed, the structure represents freedom or a barrier. Popping his head through a circular hole in its rear, he proposes that the barrier is down, the door is open, you are free to go. *free* to escape, to escape . . . to this, the symbols of human aspirations, knowledge, freedom – escape. Moved by the man's words, the first judge removes his boater. 'But why the crosspiece?' he ventures. 'Why not!' fires back Number 6. 'Good. Splendid!' exclaims the lady judge. 'I was really quite worried for a moment.' The only thing she *really* does not understand, is the omission of any representation of Number 2! The subject of her consternation is at that moment waiting on the stage to hand out the prizes. Having presented the 'Over 60s' special award to Number 38. for her magnificent tapestry bearing his image. Number 2 announces the outright winner in all categories. The Awards Committee have selected Number 6. Stepping forward to receive his prize, the man proudly accepts his reward, but soberly airs his view that another is more worthy than he – Number 38, whose long life and work in the Village is a glowing example to them all. Offering his 2.000 work units in exchange for her tapestry, he proudly boasts that he will be honoured to hang it in his own home. To applause from the gathering, he joins Number 38 and leads the procession outside.

Night finds Nadia acting as a lookout while Number 6 carries his exhibit from the Arts centre. On the beach, they unroll a tarpaulin, which is in turn secured to the skeleton framework of the dug-out structure. The crosspiece and centre pole are added and the tapestry bought by Number 6 becomes a sail. Huddled together beneath the woven image of Number 2, the couple sail away under cover of darkness.

Their absence and location is soon pin-pointed by the control room's all-seeing eye. Requesting his superior's presence, the Supervisor picks out the vessel on his radar screen. 'There, almost out of range,' the bespectacled man tells Number 2. Advising his colleague to contact Post 5 as a precaution, the elder man turns to a map of the area behind him. Summoned into action by the Supervisor's orange alert command, a ghostly guardian rises from the depths and bounces off in pursuit of its quarry. Barely two miles from a welcoming shoreline, the would-be escapers fail to notice the white orb speeding towards them. Not so a man on the shore who, seeing their approach through his binoculars and aware that the guardian is almost upon them, raises his rifle and fires at the beast. Alerted now to the approaching danger, Number 6 orders Nadia to swim for it. As the rifleman's bullets bounce off the guardian's skin, the couple reach the beach unscathed. Scrambling to safety, they turn as, outwitted, with a terrifying roar, the guardian bounces away. 'Nadia,' calls her contact, conversing with her in a foreign language. Number 6 requests pencil and paper, wishing to write a coded message for the man to transmit to London. Asking what route they will be taking, the man tells him by sea to Gadansk, then Danzig; by air to Copenhagen and by air again to London. Asking the man for his watch, his own having been damaged by seawater, Number 6 straps the timepiece to his wrist and joins Nadia in a large wooden crate labelled 'London, via Danzig, Cophenhagen.' Aboard a lorry, the crate is transported to the docks and then by boat to its destination. During the long journey, the couple converse: Nadia asking if Big Ben has a wife, he telling her to hold out as she feels nauseous.

Fortheringay, a bespectacled civil servant answers his telephone. Confirming that he has seen a copy of the deciphered message, he adds that he cannot wait to see them. Simultaneously, the crate is being transported by plane. Consulting his watch, Number 6 tells his companion that there is less than an hour-and-a-half to go, adding that if his message has been properly received, they will land in a London office well-known to him. Jostled and bumped about, the packing case is unloaded, its occupants hearing a voice proclaiming 'Stone the crows, this one's a weight.' Back in Fotheringay's office, three

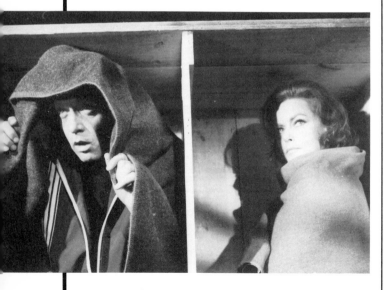

Safe in Fotheringay's office, Number 6 and Nadia step out of their transit crate

smartly dressed men arrive, followed by other men carrying the packing case. 'Good evening, Colonel,' the civil servant greets the group's leader. Announcing that everything has gone according to schedule, the Colonel bids his men open the crate. Peering out at the face before him, Number 6 extends his hand to the man. To peals from Big Ben, Nadia is introduced. 'Is it . . .?' she queries. Pausing to listen to the chimes, her travelling companion confirms that it is. Politely asking the girl if she would wait in the next room, the Colonel turns to the newcomer. 'The return of the prodigal son.' 'I don't see any fatted calf,' returns his subordinate, stretching his legs. 'Did you expect one?' asks the other. 'No,' replies Number 6, as the Colonel slams the door behind him to a close. 'Who's *she*?' asks the man. Answering that the girl is named Nadia Rokovsky, the junior becomes annoyed when his superior fires back 'and what was her name before she left Peckham Rye to join the Bolshoi Ballet?' Aware now that nothing has changed, the junior man attempts to explain the details of his capture, Nadia's nationality, the Village, Number 2, and how the girl had known the location of the Village, thereby enabling him to escape. Telling the subordinate that *he* is there to answer questions, the Colonel nevertheless becomes interested when the man continues to mention the Village. 'What *Village*?' he asks. 'The *VILLAGE*,' snorts the newcomer, pacing the room. 'It's a place where people turn up. People who have resigned from a certain sort of job, have defected, or have been extracted, the specialised knowledge in their heads being of great value to one side or the other — are you sure you haven't got a village *here*?' (Where's the Village?) 'Lithuania, in the Baltic, thirty miles off the Polish border.' (How did you find out?) 'Nadia told me. I risked my life and hers to come back here, home, because I thought it was *different*! It is, isn't it? It's DIFFERENT!' Apologising, the Colonel asks the man if he would like a drink. 'Scotch?' '24 work units.' 'What?' asks the superior. 'That's how much it costs in the Village.' 'The Village!' scoffs the Colonel. 'Surely you know about it?' asks his junior. All the man knows is that his guest resigned from a post of the highest possible secrecy. Refused to give his reasons for doing so, then promptly vanished. 'I was kidnapped!' 'Oh really. How dramatic.' Taking a harder line, the senior man intimates that his guest is a traitor, sent from behind the Iron Curtain to carry on the good work. 'No!' exclaims the other. 'No! Neit! Neit! What sort of imbeciles do you think we are?' Handed his drink, the subordinate asks the man what he wants him to do? 'Quite a lot of things,' the Colonel replies. 'But let's start at square one, shall we? First. Why did you resign?' 'It was a matter of conscience!' the man shoots back, as the chimes of Big Ben strike outside the window. 'Oh listen. Sonny Boy. Do you think you're safe in London?' Chime one. 'If they thought it worth kidnapping you, it's worth killing you.' Chime two. 'I doubt if you'll be alive 24 hours after leaving this building.' Chime three. 'Unless you get protection. Do you want it?' Chime Four. 'For the girl as well?' answers the man. The chimes continue. 'If you come across with the goodies, yes.' 'Political asylum *guaranteed* for the girl?' Big Ben continues to chime. 'Well, that depends.' 'It depends on *nothing*! It's guaranteed!' 'All right. As long as you stick to your side of the bargain.' The man being interrogated peers at his watch. 'Question one,' says the other. 'Why did you resign?' The man starts pacing the room. 'I resigned . . . because . . . for a very long time . . .' He pauses in mid-sentence, stops pacing the floor and crosses to the window. 'Just a minute.' he says, mystified. 'Eight o'clock?' (Big Ben has just chimed eight.) 'That's right.' says the Colonel. 'The night is young – and there are many questions. First, why did you resign?' A quizzical look furrows the other man's brow. 'Big Ben has just struck 8. *My* watch says *8*?' 'So?' comes the reply. 'I was given this watch by a man in Poland. I particularly wanted it to check the time, to make sure that the trip *tallied* with a journey to London.' 'Which it presumably did?' says the elder, as the other removes his watch. 'Of course.' replies the man

'. . . Just a minute. Eight o'clock?'

being interrogated, moving towards the man before him. 'Would you like to explain to me how a man in Poland came to have a watch showing English time when there is one hour's time DIFFERENCE!?' he shouts, realisation dawning. 'Maybe he was slow.' stammers the Colonel, his jacket lapel crumpled in the man's fists. 'I bet he was.' growls the other, regaining his composure. Searching the office, tugging out electric cables as he goes, the man pulls the plug on the interrogator's designs. Throwing back the doors of a cupboard, he exposes the reel-to-reel tape recorder which the man has used to assimilate the sounds of London. Resigned to his fate, Number 6 leaves the defeated Villager behind and paces determindly down the corridor outside. Pushing open a set of white painted doors, he enters – the Village.

As Number 6 surveys the familiar surroundings, on the steps of the exhibition hall Number 2 thanks Fotheringay for his help: the latter being told to return to London quickly, before any embarrassing questions are asked. Joined by Nadia, Number 2 glances across to where

Number 6 is pacing up and down. Turning to face them, with a Village salute and a 'Be seeing you,' the prisoner turns on his heels and walks back to his cottage.

In the control room, Number 2 dictates a further update on the man's file. 'You were right about him.' states Nadia, dressed now as a civilian, her expensive fur coat draped around her shoulders. 'I told you.' replies Number 2. 'Don't worry.' she calls back, climbing a staircase. 'It was a good idea and you did your best. I'll stress it in my report.'

AUTHOR'S NOTE: Two versions of this story are in existence. The one that played on television and the much-vaunted 'Alternative' version, located by *Six Of One* American co-ordinator Bruce Clark in a film vault in Toronto, Canada – a version that is believed to have been produced for Press screenings before *The Prisoner* was aired (although it did play on the show's first American outing). The alternative version (released on video in the USA, but not available in Great Britain contained several notable differences. The opening credits contained several scenes showing Number 6 attempting to escape from a Rover, and the closing credits saw the wheels of the penny farthing bicycle start turning, before changing into an image of the earth and the universe (see page 134). Other notable differences include a scene in which, having payed her first visit to the Green Dome, Nadia returns to her cottage after her 'long lunch' with Number 2 to find Number 6 outside his residence standing beside a tall wooden contraption, which is pointed skywards. Armed with a notebook and pencil, he is recording navigational observations and explains to the girl that his 'Triquetrum', is a device for plotting the location of the Village by studying the movements of the stars.

The alternative version also includes the Wilfred Josephs theme, and further incidental music by the composer – vestiges of which can be heard in *Arrival* (as Number 6 walks towards the helicopter and again after the helicopter lands and a Rover herds Number 6 back to the Village.

As transmitted, this episode has very little in the way of actual Portmeirion footage: the Village and its beach exteriors being filmed on a backlot at MGM Studios.

THE SCHIZOID MAN

Written by Terence Feely

Guest stars

Alison	**Jane Merrow**
Number 2	**Anton Rodgers**

with

The Butler	**Angelo Muscat**
Supervisor	**Earl Cameron**
Number 36	**Gay Cameron**
Doctor	**David Nettheim**
Nurse	**Pat Green**
1st Guardian	**Gerry Crampton**
2nd Guardian	**Dinny Powell**

Directed by Pat Jackson

NUMBER 6 is selecting cards from a pack placed on the table before him. Unlike a normal playing deck, the face of each card bears a geometric pattern. He is testing his guest Alison, who, displaying a close telepathic understanding with the Prisoner, is able to identify each card he selects – although she sits several feet away from her host. She thanks Number 6 for allowing her to practice her mind-reading act on him: no one else believed in her ability. 'They had no imagination.' he says, picking up a card marked with a broad red cross. 'You should concentrate, otherwise you won't be let into the Village festival.' Saying that she still has a month to prepare, Alison continues to identify each card he selects. An amateur photographer, she asks if she can take another picture of him with her Polaroid camera. Crossing over to her host, she accidentally knocks a soda-syphon onto his left hand, bruising the Prisoner's fingernail. 'Don't worry,' he says, as the girl asks if she can still take the picture, 'it will mend itself.' The girl has identified 17 cards out of the 25 he selected at random, a remarkable feat. 'It could mean that we're simpatico.' the girls suggests. 'It might,' he replies, adding up some numbers he has written in a note book, 'but there's more to it than that. Out of the last 4 runs you've got 73 out of 100.' The girls shows him the photograph she's taken. 'Like it?' Seeing his image slightly off-centre, he returns it with a smile. 'As you say. You need a little more practice.' Asking if they could try another, she requests that he adopts a certain pose. 'Put you hand to your face.' He does so, covering his profile. 'Yes, but not over your face ... just to your mouth.' Number 6 teasingly places his finger to his lips. 'Yes, yes that's marvellous,' says Alison, releasing the camera's shutter. 'I'll keep this one for myself.' Would he like to try another run of the cards? 'No,' he replies, adding that it is late and she might reduce her average and get discouraged. 'Don't forget the cards,' he reminds her, as the girl takes her leave. Can they play again tomorrow? Telling the girl that they might, he bids her a cheery 'Be seeing you' and Alison departs. Elsewhere, the steel doors of the Control Room slide to a close behind the new Number 2. Descending the steps to the chamber's main observation area, he orders an operator to switch him to Number 6. Joined by a doctor, he stares into the darkness of the Prisoner's bedroom. 'Closer,' he commands. 'Infra-red.' Covered by a duvet, Number 6 is asleep. 'His breathing is shallow. His sleep is light,' the doctor observes. 'Let's deepen it for him shall we? ... Pulsator ... visual ... oral.' orders Number 2. The patient sleeps on, oblivious to the pulsating lamp that slowly descends to a few feet above his head, or to the arrival of two white-coated medics. Injecting a serum into the Prisoner's arm, the men lift him from his bed, collect his wristwatch and calender from the living room, and carry the sleeping figure away. While he is still deep in slumber, a probe device is inserted into the skin above the patient's left wrist, and a further injection is administered into his right arm. Some time later, sitting up in his bed the patient receives two uninvited guests – the medics, who treat him to a series of therapy shocks with a long metal probe; the men insist that he should use his *left* hand to ward off the device. On Wednesday, 10 February, year unknown, a man bearing a remarkable likeness to Number 6 awakens in the patient's bed. Save for his black hair and moustache, he is the mirror image of the Prisoner. Stirring, he rubs the sleep from his eyes then, feeling the unfamiliar growth above his top lip, he surveys his changed surroundings. Peering at his reflection in a mirror, he staggers around the room, taking everything in at a glance. His wardrobe contains his own blazer, with one small but noticeable difference, his identification badge is now numbered '12'. Snatching the jacket from its hanger, he stares at the numerals in confused curiosity. A red telephone sitting on a table nearby purrs into life; it is Number 2. 'Good morning, Number 12. I hope you slept well after your flight. I'll expect you for breakfast in 15 minutes.' Leaving the residence denoted '12 – Private', he is greeted by one of the villagers, an Indian. 'Good morning Number 12,' the Asian man says, acknowledging the man's salute. A nurse pushing a patient in a wheelchair greets him in a similar manner. 'Why do you call me Number 12?' asks the man. 'Well, that's what you were called when I last saw you,' the woman replies continuing her journey. As the door to the Green Dome swings open to greet him, the mute Butler leads him into Number 2's quarters. 'My dear chap, delighted to see you,' greets the new Number 2. 'You're looking fine, you really are ... I don't mind telling you, we had to pull every string in order to get you seconded back to us.' Breakfast is à la carte, or table d'hote. The guest lifts the lids of the dishes served on a table trolly in turn. Selecting three pancakes, he walks to the table and uncovers a hooded plate to reveal sliced lemon. 'Did you think I'd forgotten we used to call you Flapjack Charlie?' grins Number 2. 'Even in those days it was obvious that you were going to make a top field man. Here am I, stuck in Admin ... you always did enjoy your food. Even before a job from the Black File.' 'Sorry I didn't shave ... couldn't find a razor,' says the man denoted '12'. 'My dear chap, I'm so sorry ...' begins the host. 'Must have been mislaid ... strange apartment,' apologises the guest. '... And after all that flying,' says Number 2. 'You must feel a bit disorientated.' 'What's it all about?' questions the guest. 'Our prize prisoner. The one we call Number 6.' replies the superior. 'Toughest case I've ever handled. I could crack him, of course. But I can't use the normal techniques. He's too valuable. Mustn't damage him permanently say our Masters. That's why I need you.' 'Why do you need *me*?' quips the man, a thought lodged somewhere in his brain telling him not to play the other's game. 'You bring two great gifts to bear. Firstly your ability as an agent ...' 'Oh yes,' mocks the guest. 'Secondly?' '... You have a unique physical advantage.' concludes the other. 'Physical *advantage* of growing a *moustache* overNIGHT!' fires back the one numbered '12'. Amused by the man's words, Number 2 proceeds to give his guest details of his plan. 'No not quite. You took longer that time in Bucharest.' 'Bucharest?' 'You remember how Susan hated you without it? She told me she wouldn't kiss you till you grew it again.' 'Good for Susan,' snaps the guest. 'You know, you really do bear a remarkable resemblance . . . remarkable . . . Your job Number 12, is to impersonate him. To take his sense of reality away. Once he begins to doubt his own identity, he'll crack. What do you think of the idea?' Maintaining his reserve, the one denoted '12' replies 'I think it has fascinating possibilities, but you'll have an awful job convincing me that I am not *your* Number 6.' 'Excellent,' smiles Number 2, maintaining that the other is ever the professional. 'You've started living the part already eh. Oh, that reminds me . . .' He delves into his blazer pocket and places a badge numbered 6 on the man's left lapel. '. . . you're now officially Number 6.' Removing the button and returning the man's stare, the guest replies 'I shan't need *this* to remind me that I am *your* Number 6.' Unbowed, the superior throws the other a leather-bound file. 'You'll find all *his* background details in here.

'You want to watch that Number 12. Number 6 is right-handed'

Study it.' The guest catches the file with his left hand, leading the other to comment. 'You should watch that Number 12. Number 6 is right-handed.' A puzzled look crosses the guest's face as Number 2 tells him that they will only have to make a few small changes; the moustache, the hair. 'Oh don't worry. I'll get a couple of my girls to work you over a little . . . but they're very pretty.' The girls go to work, shaving off the moustache, dyeing and changing the man's hairstyle. Surveying the finished product, a delighted Number 2 remarks. 'You'd hardly know yourself, would you Number 12?'

Taken by Number 2 to his own residence, Number 6 (it *is* Number 6, *isn't* it?) points out that things have been changed; a magazine, an ornamental bust, they're not *his*. Showing disinterest, the superior tells him that the idea is that when *he* comes back, in a few short minutes, the new man will be in residence. Once the project has started, even Number 2 will not be able to tell the two men apart, in which event the imposter will need a password to identify himself: this will be Gemini. Aware that Number 6 is expected, Number 2 proposes that it would be better if the men met each other alone. Wishing 'his' man good luck, Number 2 leaves the cottage.

(Author's note: From this point onwards, life for Number 6 (and the author!) becomes somewhat confusing. With two identical Prisoners, the real and the fake, I have simplified matters by referring to the Prisoner as 'the Prisoner', and his double (The Schizoid Man) as 'White'.

As the resident is about to enter 'his' bedroom, the door behind him swings open and in walks a man identical to himself save for the fact that the newcomer's blazer is white, and trimmed with black piping. Catching sight of himself, the new arrival immediately begins to bait the other as to his true identity. 'What the devil . . . oh, very good, very good indeed. One of Number 2's little ideas I suppose. Where'd they get you? A people's copying service? . . . or are you one of those *double* agents we hear so much about these days?' 'Seeing that you've gone to so much trouble,' says the Prisoner, 'the least I can do is offer you a drink.' 'Scotch!' snaps back White. 'I take it I'm supposed to go all fuzzy round the edges and run off into the distance screaming; Who am I?' 'Probably,' replies the Prisoner flatly, asking the newcomer if he would like ice. But the Prisoner can not find his drinks cabinet, and White pours his own drink from a bottle placed on the *opposite* side of the room to where the resident normally keeps his drinks supply. 'Thank you,' mocks White, dropping two cubes of ice into his glass from *his* ice bucket. 'I think it spoils it myself.' '*I* always keep it in that thermos bucket over there . . .' continues the newcomer. 'Do you know I never realised I had a freckle on the right side of my nose . . . when they come to film my life story, you've got the part. Cigar?' he asks, indicating a tabacco box inlaid with ivory. Selecting a panatella with his left hand, the Prisoner places it between his lips. Reminding his twin that he will have to learn to smoke it right-handed, White offers him his lighter. Ignoring the offer and striking a match with his left hand, the Prisoner coughs as he inhales the smoke. 'And how to smoke *my* brand, without having a heart attack,' sneers the other, informing his double that there are some black Russian cigarettes in a box on the table. 'I never touch them myself . . .' 'It's not going to work you know!' exclaims the Prisoner. 'It certainly isn't . . . why don't you run away and play somewhere else.' 'I have a very strong sense of identity,' mocks the Prisoner. '*You* have?' laughs White. 'Oh yes, of course. I'm sorry, I was forgetting – you're supposed to be *me*. *You* are the goodie Number 6, and *I* am the baddie who is supposed to be proving you wrong. Is that it?' 'That's right. Except there's no *supposed* about it,' confirms the Prisoner. 'Tell you what, why don't we settle this like gentlemen?' suggests White. 'You're claiming to be a gentleman too . . .' comes the reply. 'Very good, very good indeed . . . that line is worthy of me. We're both claiming to be Number 6. Are we not?' says White. '*I* am Number 6, *you* are doing the claiming,' snaps the Prisoner. 'Well let's prove which one is correct,' White challenges. 'How?' 'Oh there are many ways . . . pistol shooting for instance. What is Number 6's average?' '90 per cent' says the Prisoner. 'Correct,' snaps White. 'Shall we go?'

In the recreation room, the two men test their shooting abilities on the firing range with electronic guns, with White commenting to the other that he does not wish to take an unfair advantage. 'Check into position . . . One,

'It's uncanny. Number 12 has caught the man's whole style'

two, three ... Electronic gun you see, no bullets ... can't kill anyone with them ... Number 2 takes no chances ... 3-second intervals, alright?' 'Whatever you say,' smirks the Prisoner. Noting that his opponent is gripping his pistol in his *left*(?) hand, White reminds the other that Number 6 is a right-handed shot. Bewildered, the Prisoner reverses his hold. Each man fires five shots – several of the Prisoner's going astray. Watching the contest from the Control Room, a delighted Number 2 comments that the way that Number 12 has caught the man's whole style is uncanny. 'In Haiti, we'd say that he has stolen his soul,' says his coloured Supervisor. The contest has proved nothing except, as White puts it, that the other should have put in more shooting practice before taking on the job of imposter. 'How's your fencing?' he asks. 'You should know, you've studied my file,' the Prisoner retorts. 'Turning the tables. Very neat. These foils have all a length,' mocks White, teasing his opponent with quotes from Shakespeare. Handing the Prisoner an épée, White engages his double in a fencing match. The Prisoner is beaten. Leaving the recreation hall, they go outside where, although he continues to claim to be Number 6, the Prisoner when challenged to a boxing match is unable to decide whether he is an orthodox or southpaw. He soon finds himself on the wrong end of his opponent's fist. A roar announces the approach of a Rover. 'Oh dear,' says White, staring at the man he has knocked to the ground, 'it looks as though we're in trouble with the headmaster.' The Rover hustles them forwards. 'It must be confusing for it – not knowing which one of us to bite,' he continues, leading his twin towards the Green Dome.

But a surprise awaits White. Entering Number 2's front door, he is hauled away and taken to be interrogated by Number 2. The Prisoner, meanwhile is greeted personally by the superior – a recognition that raises a smile – and is taken to the interrogation room as a guest. Under guard, White is placed before Number 2's latest thought-probing device. The man is invited to spill the beans, the machine vibrating with a hum as Number 2 asks his first question.

'Who are you?' 'Switch that idiot thing off. I'm getting cramp,' returns the Prisoner's twin. 'Who are you?' repeats Number 2. 'You know who I am. I am Number 6,' says White. 'Where did you come from?' demands Number 2. 'You know that too.' 'How did you get here?' '*You* know that better than I do. *I* was unconscious at the time, if you remember,' states White. 'What was your purpose in coming here?' 'I had *none*! I'll go away again if you like.' 'How did your people know that Number 6 was here?' 'What people?' 'How did they know enough about *him* to produce *you*?' 'I do not understand.' Number 2 signals to his colleague to increase the machine's strength. 'What were you doing in the recreation room?' 'Teaching that synthetic twin of mine how to shoot and fence,' says White. At a further signal from Number 2, an oval-shaped dot appears on White's forehead. 'For the last time. What do your people want with Number 6?' shouts the superior. '*I* am Number 6. I am Number *6* ... Number 6! 6! 6! 6! ...' The light grows in intensity and the man being interrogated collapses to the floor. 'Ugh,' says the Prisoner. 'Your boy is dedicated to his work.' 'I told you he was a tough nut Number 12,' replies Number 2. 'Er – 6, 6' reminds the Prisoner, turning to face the Superior. 'Yes, you're quite right, of course. Careless of me. He might have heard,' smiles Number 2, as the one dressed in the white blazer is dragged before him. 'Do you still insist that you're Number 6?' he asks the Prisoner's twin. White remains silent. 'Your mind can lie, but your body can't. You'll see,' confirms Number 2, signalling for the guards to take the man into custody. The superior proposes to test the man's fingerprints against those of Number 6's. 'Yes, I know my own fingerprints,' quips the Prisoner. 'Let's start with the thumb nail shall we,' says Number 2, as the records as flashed onto a screen. 'That's mine,' says the Prisoner, as the print appears. Turning to the man constrained by the guards, Number 2 asks if he knows his fingerprints? 'Yes,' says White, looking at the screen, 'that's mine.' 'So that if I say that on the contrary, it belongs to Number 6, one of us is lying?' says Number 2. 'Not at all,' returns White. 'As I am Number 6, we'd both be telling the truth.' 'Let's find out, shall we?' says Number 2. 'There, that's my thumbprint ... now it's your turn.' The man being guarded is taken to the console and his thumbprint is flashed onto the screen. Viewed side by

'Simple. Foolproof'

side with the first print, they do not match. 'Simple, foolproof,' boasts Number 2 to the Prisoner. 'Too simple, too foolproof,' states White. 'Oh?' says Number 2. 'Very ingenious and scientific. The trouble with science is that it can be *perverted*' The Prisoner is inclined to agree. 'You agree?' says an astonished Number 2. Stating that he is inclined to believe in *human* instinct and agrees with his twin that he would rather be convinced by a human being than by a piece of machinery, the Prisoner rests his case. 'You have something in mind?' asks Number 2. Proposing a test that will conclusively prove which man is which, the Prisoner begs leave to telephone Number 24 – Alison, the girl with whom he did the card test. 'Yes,' answers the girl when the Prisoner phones her. 'I'm at Number 2's residence. Could you come over right away.' The girl was about to wash her hair, but as it's important, she's on her way. 'What do you hope to achieve?' asks Number 2. 'To prove that I am Number 6, and he is a fake,' states the Prisoner. 'That's what you wanted isn't it? That's what all this is about?' 'Yes,' confirms the superior. 'Good heavens, it can't be ...' says Alison, appearing in the chamber, amazed to find two identical men waiting for her. 'Mother nature has been up to her tricks again,' quips the Prisoner. 'It's weird ... Who is ... Which one ...?' 'I am the original. He is the economy pack,' confirms her card-playing friend. 'It's impossible,' says Alison. 'On the contrary ...' quips the Prisoner. 'But I still don't understand which of you ...' 'That is what you are here to settle ... Number 2 says it's not possible.' 'I see,' says the girl. 'That's why you wanted me to bring the cards.' 'That's right,' confirms the Prisoner. 'I don't follow,' says a bemused Number 2. 'Number 6 and I have a mental link ...' Alison confirms. 'So let's see which one of us has a mental link with her,' says the Prisoner. The girl agrees to the test. Selecting a card, the Prisoner concentrates on the picture on its face. The girl fails to identify it. He tries a second card, with the same result. Another, and another, but the girl is still unable to come up with the right answers. White goes next – and scores 5 out of 5! The Prisoner has lost! Forced to concede that the man in the white blazer is the real Number 6, Alison produces the photograph she took of him earlier. 'Isn't it awful, I took it last night, he's all arms and legs. Actually, there was a much simpler way to identify Number 6. He has mole on his left wrist.' 'Of course,' sneers White, slipping back his cuff. The Prisoner does the same – his wrist is spotless! 'Well if we've finished for the day, and you don't mind, I'll see the young lady home,' says White, leading Alison from the room. Number 2 is furious. 'What in heavens name made you do a stupid thing like that?' he asks the man left behind. 'Surely you must realise Number 6 and that girl have got a genuine rapport. Someone's going to have to pay dearly for this!' He signals to Number 118, the medic who took Number 6 from his bed earlier. 'Number 118, why was there no mole on Number 12's left wrist?' The man remains silent. 'I said why was there no mole? Don't you realise that you've jeopardised the whole operation ... report to me first thing in the morning. First thing!'

Back in his room, the Prisoner contemplates his position, summoning his willpower to fight against the steadily-mounting evidence that he is someone else – a man simply masquerading as the man he believed himself to be. Watching the man writhe in nightmares, Number 2 tells Number 12 that it will not be long before he cracks. Rising from his bed, the Prisoner notices his bruised fingernail. The congealed blood has moved downwards,

indicating several month's growth. Musing this over in his mind, he removes Alison's photograph from his pocket. The mark on his nail is clearly displayed. So too is the date on the calender behind him. A magnifying glass allows comparison of the fingernail then and now: the bruise is just beginning to form, the date on the calendar reads 10 February. Memories from the past begin to flood into his mind. Crossing to the mirror he recalls being drugged and placed into a bed, while someone operated on his left wrist – a wrist that no longer bears a mole! He recalls being given therapy treatment to change his right-handedness; the days spent indoors growing the beard that was trimmed to a moustache; a tape-machine ploughing the knowledge into his brain that he was Number 12: the flapjacks, the cigars ... Picking up a box of cigarettes timidly with his left hand, he drops the container into his right palm. He selects a cigarette and shreds it. It appears to be normal. The cigar box comes next. Breaking open a panatella, he discovers the plastic filament which made the cigars unpalatable to the smoker. Crossing to the settee, he selects a second cigarette from the box on the table, left-handed. Is that right? Pausing, he peers beneath the table lamp, inspecting it for hidden microphones, but finds nothing. Raising it gently, he places it before the fire grate and reaches towards the cottage's gas appliance. Gripping the supply pipe, he cautiously reaches for the table lamp with his other hand. Upon contact, the appliance short-circuits, throwing the Prisoner to the floor. Gripping a table for support, he regains his feet, knocking a trinket box from the table as he does so. He catches it – an automatic response – with his *right* hand! He is now cured, ready to take on anyone – including Number 2!

It is night time and Number 2 is being treated to a massage by the mute Butler. 'Let's see how Number 6 is getting on, shall we,' he says, rising to switch on the monitor screen. Number 6 is not at home. Guards are alerted to the find the Prisoner. They do so as he traverses a street. He gives them the password, 'Gemini', which is wrong and a fight ensues. The men beaten, the Prisoner escapes from a Rover by pretending to race off in a buggy In the Control Room, the Supervisor informs a distraught Number 2 that Number 6 cannot be found. 'Send out a general alarm. Orange Alert,' orders the superior. The Prisoner, meanwhile, has crept back to his residence to confront his twin. Hearing the man enter, White is waiting for him in the bedroom with a nerve gas gun: 5-yard range, one squirt will paralyse, two squirts will kill. 'Couldn't sleep,' says the Prisoner to the man lying on his bed. 'Came here to ... Who am I?' 'You know who you are, you're Number 12,' says White, believing his twin to be disorientated. 'Yes, I'm Number 12 ...' the Prisoner begins. '...but sometimes in my dreams I'm ... I'm somebody else.' 'Who?' mocks White, covering the other with his gas gun. 'I don't know ... Sometimes in my dreams, I resign my job.' 'Why did you resign your job – in your dream?' asks White. 'Sometimes I'm here in my dreams, and then I come back,' sobs the Prisoner, feigning exhaustion. 'I want to know ... Who am I? Why am I here?' Believing that his twin has reached the end of his tether, White offers to ring Number 2. He might be able to help. A mistake. His defences are down and the Prisoner makes full use of the opportunity. Leaping onto his double, he throws White to the floor. A no-holds-barred fight ensues, which culminates in White's defeat. 'The password,' threatens the Prisoner. 'I don't know what you're talking about,' denies the other. 'What is it?'

'Nerve gas. One squirt you're paralysed. Two squirts, you're dead'

says the victor, his fist raised in a threatening manner. 'What password?' 'What is IT!' exclaims the Prisoner. 'Schizoid . . . Schizoid Man . . .' 'Schizoid man . . . what's your name?' 'Curtis,' gasps White. Catching Number 6 off-guard, White makes a run for it. His second mistake. Racing outside, he is swallowed up by a Rover. Back in his residence, the Prisoner telephones Number 2. 'Password,' asks the superior, taking no chances. 'Curtis . . . Schizoid Man,' says Number 6, hastily correcting his mistake. 'Number 6 is dead. Rover got him.' 'WHAT!' exclaims Number 2. 'He's dead,' replies the Prisoner, savouring the taste of victory. 'Rover got him.' Furious at this news, Number 2 issues orders for Rover to be deactivated immediately, pending further instructions. Donning White's blazer, Curtis, the Prisoner visits the superior in the Green Dome. Still trying to discover why Rover killed the Prisoner, Number 2 tells the man he believes to be Curtis that he is to return immediately to report his failure. 'My failure,' mocks Number 6. 'You wanted him broken. I've broken him. I wasn't to know he'd go beserk.' 'Nor was I,' Number 2 confirms. 'You studied him. You should have known. It was your idea.' 'That's a strange thing to say,' retorts the superior. 'You know it wasn't.' 'Well, you certainly didn't resist . . .' 'Bearing in mind its origin, no I didn't! Nor did you.' 'Recriminations aren't going to help. It's a disgrace to us both, when do I leave?' He is due to depart in an hour's time, but *they* want to talk to Alison before he goes; they believe that she may have some insight into the Prisoner's motivations. Watching the man leave, a thought enters Number 2's head, but dismissing the idea he returns to his desk. At Alison's home, the girl states that she has nothing significant to report. 'I don't believe in such things myself,' Number 6 tells the girl, 'but you were supposed to be able to read each other's minds.' 'It doesn't work like that,' says the girl, sensing something different about the man. 'Oh. How does it work?' quips Number 6. 'In spasms . . . little things. Sudden coincidences which aren't really coincidences,' Alison replies, picking up a cigarette. 'Oh,' says he, turning to offer her a light. The girl stares at him. 'It's a bad habit of mine, playing with lighters,' he mocks. 'I'll probably start a fire one day. Well if you've got nothing to tell me, I'll be on my way. Be seeing you.' He leaves to prepare for his journey home. Dressed in civilian clothes for the first time in many months, he takes Curtis' wallet out of his jacket. It contains a photograph of a pretty blonde girl – the dead man's wife, and is signed 'From your loving wife, Susan.' Joined by Number 2, the men climb aboard a Village taxi. During the short trip to the helicopter pad, the superior questions him about a proposition he put to Curtis when he arrived: has he thought about it further? 'Sorry, haven't had the time,' the Prisoner replies. 'But you must have some views . . .' probes Number 2. 'I'm afraid not.' '. . . Look old chap, we've been through many scrapes before, but we've never fallen out over them. The General's not going to behead you.' 'We won't know – until I've reported to the General, will we?' comes the terse reply. 'Report to the General . . . that's a new one.' 'I don't mean report to him personally . . . for Pete's sake you know what I mean,' throws back Number 6, aware that he's on dangerous ground. 'You are edgy,' replies Number 2. 'I've never known you quite so strung up.' 'You mean I'm not as I was,' replies Number 6. 'Yes . . . I remember Susan saying only a month ago, that you're genuinely quite unflappable. You have changed,' returns Number 2, a hint of suspicion in his voice. 'We *all* change. The job, it changes us.' 'Yes,' says Number 2 as they arrive outside the recreation hall where a helicopter waits to take 'Curtis' away from the Village. 'It's just a quick flip in the helicopter to the landing strip and the jet picks you up there. Excuse me . . .' Alison is waiting for them. 'I'm ashamed of what I did to Number 6 yesterday,' she tells the man. 'Why are you telling *me*?' he asks. 'Everyone has to tell someone.' 'It was your job,' he smiles. 'It was a betrayal,' she replies. 'Isn't everything we do *here* a *betrayal*,' he retorts. 'It's not often one gets a second chance,' quips Alison. 'There are *no* second chances,' he points out. 'There are sometimes. For the *lucky* ones. If *I* had a second chance, I want you to know that I wouldn't do it again.' She knows. But he realises that his secret is safe with her. 'Bon voyage,' bids Number 2, as Number 6 turns to board the helicopter. 'Thank you,' grins the Prisoner. 'Oh, one last thing,' says the superior. 'Yes?' 'You forgot the security regulations. Must be obeyed. The blindfold old chap.' 'Oh yes, of course,' sighs Number 6 with relief. 'You won't forget to give Susan my regards, will you?' asks Number 2, as the departing man boards the machine and slips the blindfold to his eyes. 'I won't. *Goodbye*' The helicopter blades begin to rotate and the machine climbs skywards, taking its passenger to freedom. High over the Village it soars until, unseen by the man in the blindfold, it lands back at its departure point outside the recreation hall. Unaware of what is going on, Number 6 is man-handled back to face a grinning Number 2. His blindfold is stripped away and a triumphant superior reminds him 'Susan died a year ago!' The man is still a PRISONER!

So that's how it's done. Patrick McGoohan faces up to himself – stunt double, Frank Maher

AUTHOR'S NOTE: This is the only story to refer to Rover by name.

The extensive split screen shots showing Number 6 and Curtis (The Schizoid Man) on screen together, was achieved by use of McGoohan's regular stunt double, Frank Maher.

IT'S YOUR FUNERAL

Written by Michael Cramoy

Guest Stars

New Number 2	Derren Nesbitt
Watchmaker's Daughter	Annette Andre
Number 100	Mark Eden

with

Retiring Number 2	Andre Van Gyseghem
Watchmaker	Martin Miller
Computer Attendant	Wanda Ventham
The Butler	Angelo Muscat
Number 2's Assistant	Mark Burns

and

Supervisor	Peter Swanwick
Artist	Charles Lloyd Pack
Number 36	Grace Arnold
Stall Holder	Arthur White
M.C. Councillor	Michael Bilton
Kosho Opponent	Gerry Cramptom

Directed by Robert Asher

WATCHED BY Number 2 and the Supervisor, a beautiful young girl enters the residence denoted '6 – Private'. Its occupant, apparently asleep, lies in his bed. But as the girl stretches out her hand to wake him, she finds herself flung onto the bed, the man's hand tightly clasping her wrist. 'What are you doing here?' he growls. 'I was just going to wake you up,' stammers the girl. 'You have. Who are you?' he yells, releasing the girl. 'I'm a number, just like you. Does it matter which?' she replies. 'How did you get in?' 'The door was open,' comes the answer. 'It always is, isn't it . . . to *them*!' the Prisoner snaps back, as he tightens the belt on the dressing gown he has donned. 'I'm not one of *them*,' the girl replies forcefully, rising from the bed. 'No? What do you want?' 'Help,' she throws back. 'Go to the Town Hall, the Citizens Council promises help and advice to everyone,' he retorts. '*Their* citizens council,' sobs the girl. 'As far as I'm concerned what's theirs is *yours*,' shouts Number 6, approaching the intruder. 'I am *not* one of *them*!' she fires back, her eyes beginning to well with tears. 'No. No one is,' he replies, suspicious that the girl may be a plant. 'Go back. Tell them that I was *not* interested . . . that I wouldn't even listen . . .' Then, acknowledging the fact that everyone in the Village is always under surveillance, he adds 'What's the point. They know already.' He peers around the room at the unseen surveillance cameras. 'I won't go for it, whatever *it* is . . . so you may as well stop trying,' he shouts, opening the door to see the intruder out. '*We* never stop, Number 6,' says Number 2, observing the man's outburst on the control room wall screen. With a glance at his wristwatch, he adds 'Now we'll see how accurately they've timed it.' Back in the Prisoner's cottage, the girl suddenly collapses to the flooor. 'She was given the drug yesterday,' Number 2 tells his Supervisor. 'One of the new super-strength moprobomates that we've developed. *She* doesn't know anything about it, of course.' 'Yesterday?' questions the Supervisor. 'Well the drug remains dormant until triggered by the nervous system.

and then it releases itself, to the desired quantities, to produce instant tranquility, or temporary oblivion,' the Superior replies. 'But why?' queries the bespectacled man. 'Well in anticipation of Number 6 throwing her out . . . which he was about to do.' 'And *will*, when she revives,' replies the Supervisor. 'Oh no no,' a grinning Number 2 replies. 'You see she has now become a lady in distress. He's going to be all good deeds and sympathy.' Then, noticing that the door to Number 6's residence is still ajar, he tells his assistant that he can't recall his procedure agenda authorising this. Told by the Supervisor that it was an after-thought — to make certain that once the girl had made up her mind to go and see Number 6, she'd have access, Number 2 points out the obvious. 'Doesn't she know how to knock on a door, then?' 'He doesn't always answer,' defends the Supervisor, realising his mistake. 'It seemed like a good idea . . .' 'It *wasn't*,' snaps Number 2, 'because now he is going to assume that we sent her. Now we don't want that — do we?' 'No!' the assistant admits. 'This plan,' continues the superior, 'is too important for little slapdash improvisations, you know. No matter how good the idea may seem at the moment.' 'Yes Number 2,' says the Supervisor as the other draws his attention to the fact that the girl in Number 6's room is coming round. 'Look at that,' giggles Number 2 pointing to his wristwatch, 'exactly the time the chemists anticipated.' Apologising for making a fool of herself, having accepted a glass of water from Number 6, the girl pleads

exhaustion. 'No,' says the tenant, lifting the girl's eyelid. 'Drugs! Your pupils are contracted.' 'I don't take drugs,' she answers in alarm. 'Forced feeding then,' he suggests. 'Why should they?' she queries. 'You tell me,' he says, acknowledging that he is prepared to listen — as long as what she tells him does not become too obviously phoney. Convinced that she is wasting her time, the girl makes to leave. 'I'll find help somewhere else.' 'They told you to find it here, didn't they?' 'Believe what you like . . .' says the girl. 'I . . . it doesn't matter any more.' Then, pausing to gather her thoughts, she turns and acknowledges that it does matter. 'This concerns the welfare of everyone in the Village.' 'And welfare is our biggest consumer item. Yes,' quips Number 6. 'Joke about this if you can — assassination!' she exclaims. 'Are you trying to organise, or prevent one?' he throws back, uninterested. 'Prevent!' she acknowledges. 'They would have to take reprisals, everybody would suffer.' 'Alright,' he concedes. 'What can *I* do for you?' She replies by saying that she needs his help to prevent the assassination attempt. '*They've* heard. They are aware and *they* don't need anyone's help!' '*They* don't believe me,' cries the girl. 'No comment,' he says. 'So much caution, in a man like *you* it seems so wrong.' 'Many times bitten, forever shy. But *they* are not shy. *They* love to listen,' says the Prisoner. Informing him that he does not understand: her name, her number is on a list, she replies to his quipped 'Honours or Deportment' with just one word: 'Jamming'.

'Jamming?' he says. 'Oh. domestic science.' Informing him that he will learn all about jamming soon enough and that it is one of the most important ways of fighting back. his comment that he is prepared to learn all about it at that very moment leads the girl to remind him that he was formerly convinced that she was lying. 'I'm sorry I ever bothered you.' she says. walking towards the door. 'Call in anytime you like.' he calls after her. Disappointed that his first attempt has failed. Number 2. told by an unseen caller (whom we learn later is an elderly Number 2) that he must find a way of making Number 6 take an interest in the girl, the young Number 2 promises to do so. 'Yes. I realise that Sir. but what put us behind was the girl's hesitancy. As you know she took a long time making up her mind to see him. I had hoped to catch up. but Number 6 flatly refused to have anything to do with her . . . and that's caused another delay. Well, perhaps if we could replace him with someone more tractable, less suspicious . . . Yes. I realise that sir, the reason why we selected Number 6 . . . A matter of credibility, without which the plan might backfire. Indeed I will sir. As you say. I must find a way to make him interested.' Turning to the Supervisor. he calls for the day's Activities Prognosis on Number 6. 'As quickly as possible!' Within minutes the Control Room is a hive of activity. The Computer Attendant orders her colleagues to maintain a top priority interest on the Prisoner, and an audio-taped record is kept of the man's every move: 6.30 am subject exercises daily with a walk around the Village; daily the subject climbs to the bell tower – reason unknown . . . subject eccentric: certainly watching. waiting, constantly aggressive . . . it is possible the subject likes the view. 7.30 am physical workout using subject's home made apparatus . . . 8.15 am, the subject cooling off by skiing on the lake. 9 o'clock. coffee at cafe and buys some newspapers. 9.20 am, subject will proceed on foot to Old People's Home where he plays a game of chess with an elderly man – the game ending with an 11-move checkmate win, by subject . . . He then humours other eccentric resident. by sitting for portrait – or perhaps subject has an ulterior motive for doing so? As the Prisoner sits with the portrait painter, the computer attendant seals the report on his activities into an envelope addressed: 'Official. For the attention of the acting Number 2. Day's activities prognosis. No: 6.'

In the control room, the young Number 2 is holding a conversation with Number 100. one of his assistants. who. dressed as a villager. spies on the community. 'Then you're satisfied with your progress to date on Plan Division Q?' asks the young Number 2. 'My division will be operational exactly on time . . . you can quote me in your report.' confirms the other. 'Mmm mmm. well I shall. You're still confident of your cover? There's no sign of penetration?' 'No. They still think of me as just another prisoner. We're kindred spirits, comrades.' says Number 100. referring to the Prisoner. 'There'll be no trouble from him.' Number 6. meanwhile. converses with the man painting his portrait. 'You moved.' says the artist. 'Sorry . . .' 'What they do. these jammers.' continues the other. 'is talk. They talk about the plots they've been hatching.' 'Plots?' queries the poser. 'Well escapes mostly. But plans and developments for all kinds of mischief. They do it to confuse the observers. Still – please!' 'So sorry.' says the Prisoner. resuming his pose. 'The plots they talk about are always make-believe. Non-existent. But control can't know that until they've checked them out. Used to run themselves ragged investigating the schemes of jammers.' 'Used to?' 'They don't bother much anymore. Now they keep a list of all known jammers. Anything control picks up from these. they just let it ride.' the artist replies picking up the completed canvas. 'What do you think?' he adds. showing the subject his 'portrait' – a wild abstract of confusing daubs of paint. 'A perfect likeness.' confirms Number 6. Marching into the control room with the envelope she sealed earlier, the computer attendant stands before the young Number 2, who asks her to detail the prognosis' reliability. 'I'm afraid we don't know that.' replies the woman. 'Why not. asks the superior. 'Twice we programmed our machines for percental appraisals of their own efficiencies. Each time they've refused to give back the requested information.' 'Refused? How?' challenges the young Number 2. 'Simply by not returning the data to us.' the attendant replies. Sipping his tea. an astonished Number 2 suggests that they'll be wanting their own trade union next. 'Well go ahead and read it to me.' Reading from the report. the woman looks at her wristwatch and begins 'It is now 10.19 exactly. According to the prognosis, the subject is now taking his daily stroll through the village. At approximately 10.20. he will go to the kiosk . . .' The young Number 2 stretches out on his lounger, anticipating a boring display of the assistant's thoroughness. He turns to the monitor screen where, as confirmed by the report. Number 6 is handing over his credits for a copy of the *Tally Ho* news-sheet. '. . . there he will buy a copy of the newspaper. a bar of soap, and a bag of sweets . . .' 'Oh no no . . . he *never* eats candy.' cries the superior. 'According to the prognosis he . . .' the girl begins. 'It doesn't matter about the prognosis. it's wrong – it doesn't work!' insists the young Number 2. Explaining that it will only take a moment to find out and told by the superior to continue. the girl and Number 2 turn their attention to the monitor screen. They watch as an old lady standing next to Number 6 pleads with the kiosk attendant. 'But I must have them.' she sobs. 'For the last time . . . your week's credit allowance is all used up.' states the attendant. 'Come back tomorrow.' 'But I can't go through an entire day without my sweets.' pleads the woman. her eyes welling with tears. 'Sorry.' says the trader. ignoring her and devoting his attention to Number 6. 'Yes sir?' 'Er. a bag of candy for the lady.' says Number 6. The onlookers watch these proceedings with rapt attention. 'My apologies. How did you know?' asks the young Number 2. 'An efficient prognosis progamming must include a quantum permutation of the cause and effect of all supplementary elements.' replies the computer attendant. 'In other words the computer calculated the old woman's behaviour would change the behaviour pattern of Number 6.' states the superior. Sighing. and aware that her position has been vindicated. the woman continues to record what Number 6 will be doing for the rest of the day. Hearing that the Prisoner will arrive at the gymnasium between 11.40 and 11.50 for his semi-weekly Kosho practice, the young Number 2 stops the woman in mid-sentence. He has heard enough. He's found what he was looking for. The girl is dismissed and the superior turns to Number 100. 'You know what I have in mind.' his colleague is told.

In the gymnasium. Number 6. dressed in a red cossack-style coat with his left wrist covered by a guantlet-type glove. his right encased in a white cotton mitten. and his head protected by a white helmet. stands challengingly before his similarly-attired opponent – although his opponent's helmet is black. Each man is balanced precariously on a trampoline. The trampolines are separated by a six-foot divide and erected over a huge water tank, the objective being to knock your opponent into the water below. Bowing to each other as the competition begins, the opponent leaps into the air, clears the divide and lands at the other's feet. But Number 6 is no longer there. He has sprung to the safety of the ledge behind him, his hands firmly grasping the handrail to prevent him falling backwards onto the spring mat. In the wink of an eye, the men have swapped places. Time and again they leap from the ledge, to escape each other's grasp. Landing together on the Prisoner's side of the trampoline, the opponent gains the advantage, pressing the Prisoner's body precariously close to the edge of the divide. A kick sends the man reeling backwards, but he quickly regains his feet and springs back into the attack.

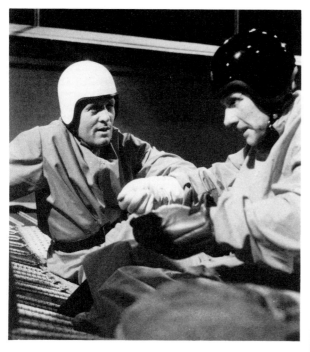

Patrick McGoohan and stuntman Gerry Crampton discuss the Kosho fight

Unseen by either man, the one numbered 100 has entered the gymnasium and found his way into the men's locker room. Locating the Prisoner's locker, he exchanges the man's wristwatch for an identical one and departs, unobserved. The Kosho battle rages on, each man somersaulting to escape the other's clutches. Again and again they leap into the air until, anticipating his opponent's next move, Number 6 leaps to the handrail a split second before the other and with a tug of the man's collar, sends him headlong into the water below. Triumphant, the Prisoner springs to the trampoline and then to the floor of the gymnasium, executing a perfect headlong flip as he does so. Bowing twice to his water-logged opponent, he retreats to the locker room to dress. Discovering that his wristwatch is broken, he takes the timepiece into the watchmaker's shop. 'It's stopped,' says Number 6, handing the device to the wizened old shopkeeper. Inspecting the wristwatch, the man asks him to wait and retreats into the rear of his shop. The Prisoner finds an odd-looking device the watchmaker had been working on when he entered, and lifts it from the man's workdesk. As a plunger is pressed on its uppermost side, an equally strange looking device left on the worktop clicks into motion, its tubular finger turning clockwise. Having made a small adjustment to the customer's timepiece, the watchmaker returns and hands the watch back to its owner, stating that it is working again. Clipping the Prisoner's credit card, the old man tells him that the device he has been playing with is simply a toy. As the customer exits, Number 100 appears from his hiding place at the rear of the shop. 'Well?' he enquires. Acknowledging that he has done the man's bidding, the watchmaker says that he cannot understand why the other asked him to expose their methods. 'All will be explained to you in time.' replies the spy. 'No, now! What can we gain by letting *them* know what we're up to? The enemy?' demands the watchmaker. 'We add to *their* confusion. That's what we stand to gain.' replies the other. 'You see, they don't believe anything we say. Or do. Or intend to do. That's why we are able to carry out our plan,' he ends, handing the device which the customer had been playing with back to the watchmaker. In the street outside, Number 6 bumps into the girl who passed out in his cottage. 'How did you find out?' she asks, acknowledging that she saw him enter the shop. 'Beg pardon?' says he, confused. 'I never mentioned the watchmaker to you. What did you want with him?' Indicating that his wristwatch had stopped and that he had taken it to the shop to be repaired, the man grins when the girl tells him that she is the shopkeeper's daughter. 'Ah, that explains why you're so concerned, doesn't it,' he mocks, his senses alert to a trap. 'And you?' she asks. 'The same total disinterest?' 'Not quite the same, no.' he confirms. 'What happened?' What's made you so interested?' she queries. 'Because I don't believe that a device to detonate explosives by radio is a toy – and neither does your father.' he replies. Number 2's assistant, meanwhile, watching this scene with his superior in the control room, acknowledges that Number 2's plan could work. 'It *is* working,' grins the young Number 2. 'But I'll take the bows later on.' 'Whatever you like to call it. Plan Division Q is still murder,' states the other. Sneering, the young Number 2 retaliates: 'You have *your* specific duties, stick to them and leave the rest to one double zero. 'You think Number 6 has fallen for it?' asks the other. 'No, no not yet.' replies the young Number 2 shaking his head. 'But he will . . . he *will*.' 'And after it's all over you'll be showered with official congratulations.' 'Yes,' nods the superior, 'well after he's been here to warn me that an assassination is being plotted . . . and that *I* am the intended victim!'

Sitting with the girl at a table in the café outside the Old People's Home, Number 6 asks the girl what she knows. Precious little appears to be the answer: she is aware that her father and another man – one she has never seen – intend to assassinate Number 2, but she has no knowledge as to when they intend to do it, nor how, nor where. In an attempt to make the girl's father see reason, they visit the watchmaker. But the old man flatly refuses to abandon his plan, even when told by Number 6 that the whole Village will suffer because of his foolishness. 'Maybe it's what they need to wake them up. To shake them out of their lethargy. To make them angry enough to fight.' he states. 'Assuming they survive the punishment,' an irate Number 6 points out. 'What's the use? You'll never understand,' replies the confused an angry watchmaker, retiring to his work room, as an equally frustrated Number 6 storms out of the shop. In the control room, a delighted Number 2 congratulates the one numbered 100 on a job well done. 'Since he cannot reason with the watchmaker,' confirms Number 100, 'he must now come here to warn you.' At that very second, that is exactly what the Prisoner is doing. Watched by the men on the monitor screen, Number 6 is tracked by the surveillance cameras to the Green Dome, from which Number 100 is leaving as the Prisoner enters. 'Ah, Number 6, my dear fellow, do come in,' greets the young Number 2 as the Prisoner enters. 'Shall I order you coffee, or would you prefer some tea?' 'You can forego the amenities,' quips the newcomer, 'this is not a social call.' 'To what then do I owe the pleasure of your company?' asks the superior. 'I'm here to deliver a warning.' 'A warning? What about?' asks the young Number 2. 'A plot to kill you.' 'To what?' asks the other, feigning surprise. 'To kill you ... assassinate you,' grunts Number 2. 'Mmm.' 'To ass-ass-in-ate YOU!!' 'I don't believe it,' mocks the superior. 'They should have told you. There are some unhappy people here,' confirms Number 6. 'Yes ...' replies the young Number 2, '... well I have seen the list of malcontents ... it might interest you to know that *you* happen to be top of the bill.' 'I'll do my best to live up to it,' quips the Prisoner, confessing that the only reason he is warning the man is to prevent the mass reprisal that would surely take place after the killing. A smug and confident Number 2 pooh-poos the man's words, informing him that he knows all about the jammers and the watchmaker. 'Yes well we expected something like this ... that they'd try to get through to us through a dupe. Hmm, so they chose *you* to lead us into believing their fantasy eh? Tell me, how did they sell you the idea Number 6? Did they show you the gun?' 'Oh they're not going to shoot you,' grins the Prisoner, 'they're going to *blow you up!*' 'Did they tell you how they were going to go about it. When? Where?' asks the young Number 2. 'Would you find out for me, because, well, a laugh would do me an awful lot of good!' Riled by the man's over-confidence, Number 6 marches from the room, turning while doing so to tell the other that he may find out himself, quite suddenly, in which case, he certainly will not be laughing. Alone, a delighted Number 2 is informed that both cameras and audio-tape have captured the conversation.

'Oh don't tell me. It's the little watchmaker that concerns you'

Meeting the watchmaker's daughter, Number 6 explains that he has no choice but to continue his attempts to defuse the situation. Number 2 believes him to be a communications medium and did not believe him. As they talk, the Village voice announces that the Citizens Council have officially proclaimed Thursday, the day after tomorrow, as Appreciation Day, a day when the Village community pays due honour to those brave and noble people who govern them so wisely. Everyone will be delighted to hear that the proceedings will be opened with an address by Number 2 himself, and concluded by the unveiling of the new appreciation monument. There will be speeches, thrills and excitement. 'Maybe *more* excitement than planned,' quips Number 6 to his partner. That night, in her father's shop, the girl and Number 6 find Number 2's Great Seal of Office, which he always wears at ceremonies. The pendant contains a slab of explosive which can be detonated by radio.

The following morning, Number 6 enters the control room with the intention of informing Number 2 about his discovery. The oval-shaped chair rises from the floor to greet him, but as it turns to face the newcomer, a new man is sitting in the seat – a man Number 6 has never seen before! 'Number 6 isn't it?' asks the figure. 'I've been expecting you.' 'I want to see Number 2,' informs the newcomer. '*I* am Number 2,' says the other with a grin. 'You've come to tell me that there's a plot against my life, haven't you?' Confused by this turn of events, the Prisoner begins to pace the room. 'You know my colleague is very concerned about these imminent death by violence projects that you've been reporting during my absence,' confirms the new Number 2, a man with silvery hair. 'Plots?' replies the Prisoner, coming to a halt in front of the stranger. 'I've reported one only.' 'Not so,' snaps the elderly Number 2, 'my every efficient colleague – or should I say my heir presumptive, has been collecting evidence, that every interim Number 2 who has served here while I've been on leave, has been cautioned by you, about some improbable conspiracy to murder him.' Number 6 stares at the man. 'Really,' he replies with obvious distrust. 'You obviously don't believe me. Well the psychiatrist warned me that that might be the case. Shall I show you proof?' With a wave of his hand, Number 6 bids him do so. Leaning forward in his chair to press a button on the control console before him with the tip of his rolled parasol, the superior leans back in his seat as the television monitor glows into life – to show Number 6 warning a succession of Number 2's – all bar the first (the young Number 2 seen earlier) people the Prisoner has never laid eyes on – that their lives are under threat of assassination. 'More?' asks the confident voice behind him. 'Why bother,' replies Number 6. 'So you're convinced?' asks the other switching off the device. 'I'm convinced that those excerpts are fakes!' retorts the other, aware that his earlier warning to the young Number 2 had been monitored and that the sequence which has just been paraded before him is a compilation of events which occured earlier, spliced together with additional material. 'You think they've been *doctored*. For what purpose? Why should we want to convince you that you're not well?' returns the man in the chair. 'Perhaps it is *you they* want to convince,' offers Number 6. 'Me? Tomorrow I hand over to my successor – I retire!' states the other. 'Perhaps they are trying to save a pension,' the Prisoner throws back, as he departs from the room, leaving the elderly Number 2 to consider his words.

Joining the girl, Number 6 shows little surprise when she

(You're going on with it?) 'I haven't much choice'

points out that Number 100, sitting at a table opposite them is her father's fellow conspirator. Hearing the Prisoner tell the girl that he has seen the man earlier, leaving the Green Dome – no doubt after plotting the assassination attempt with 'another', the retiring Number 2, strokes his chin, considering the truth of the man's words. Joined by his assistant, he orders the man to have the tapes made by the incoming Number 2 to be brought to him; he wishes to review them. 'At once,' says the junior. 'Subject?' 'Subject – warning of assassination plot. Persons Number 6 and my successor,' replies the elderly Number 2. The assistant falters, considering the request. 'Well get on with it,' urges the superior. 'It would be a waste of time. There is no recording of that description,' confirms the assistant. 'How strange,' states the elderly Number 2. 'You must have been misinformed,' tries the junior. 'Strange that although you have no duty functions with the Bureau of Visual Records, you can think instantly, and with total assurance, that the records I require are non-existent. Please explain,' orders the superior. 'Number ... Number 2. I'm not able to,' stammers the assistant. The fact that his junior will not explain is proof enough for the departing Number 2: the Prisoner has told him the truth, his successor means to kill him! His successor, meanwhile, telephones Number 1. 'Absolutely sir, just as it's been planned, it's going like clockwork ... oh thank you sir ... No no, there's no danger of that, Number 6 is no problem ... we have fully convinced him ... and you do have my word.' Sitting outside the Old People's Home, the girl pleads with the Prisoner to prevent the assassination, for her father's sake. 'For everybody's sake,' he reminds her.

The outgoing Number 2 receives a visitor – Number 6. Worried now, he informs the guest that he now realises that he was telling him the truth. 'I'm to be assassinated.' 'For assassinated substitute *executed*!' the Prisoner returns. 'Since it's arranged by my own people you mean?' stammers the elderly Number 2. 'You don't *mind*?' yells Number 6. 'Of course I mind. It's just that I thought it would never happen to me.' 'It never does,' mocks the Prisoner, 'to anybody. But it can be prevented.' Informing

the visitor that prevention is only a postponement, the superior tells his guest some home truths. 'You've never understood us Number 6. We *never* fail. Anyway, why should you care what happens to me?' 'I don't,' replies Number 6. 'But innocent people will be blamed.' 'Yes, I know,' confirms the elder sympathetically, apologising that he is unable to do anything. 'The ceremony can take place *without* the seal,' offers Number 6. 'The seal *is* the ceremony,' replies the superior. 'It's hollowed out! It's packed with explosives ...' the other begins. 'And before I hand it over to my successor.' '... it will be detonated by radio,' says Number 6, confirming the elder's suspicions. 'I can think of better ways to die,' concedes Number 2. 'And better *causes* to die for !' snaps Number 6, leaving the man shivering in his chair. Elsewhere, the incoming Number 2 updates his report to Number 1: Plan Division Q is running according to schedule. It is set to succeed. It is working beautifully, *dead* on schedule in fact. (A joke?) 'No sir, no no, just the way you ordered it ... the people are already gathering, it will be very, er, very spectacular. Nothing can go wrong now, I'll stake my future on it.'

The holiday Thursday arrives. Exuberant, the villagers acknowledge the Master of Ceremonies with joyous applause. The retiring and the incoming Number 2s stand side-by-side on the Town Hall balcony, the former frowning as the Master of Ceremonies mouths words of joy, the latter contacting Number 100 via a transmitter secreted in the stem of his eye glasses. 'Can you hear me? Come in please ...' 'I can hear you,' confirms his confederate. 'Is everything alright?' 'Everything is alright. Stop worrying ... repeat, stop worrying,' replies Number 100, as Number 6 joins the crowd. Everyone appears happy, all save the watchmaker's daughter who, joining the Prisoner, admits that she is worried: her father did not come home last night. 'The shop?' asks Number 6. 'He's not there, he must be here somewhere,' she confirms. 'Not necessarily ...' he replies, confirming that the transmitter her father had made has a very wide range. 'He could be anywhere.' Scanning the crowd and catching sight of the watchmaker in the bell tower, he pushes his way through the crowd and races upwards, followed by the girl. Simultaneously, the mute Butler carries the Seal of Office to the Master of Ceremonies. Lifting the medallion from its red, velvet tray, the speaker places it snugly around the neck of the outgoing Number 2. His successor stands to one side, his carefully-laid plan only seconds away from fruition. Arriving at the bell tower at the very second the watchmaker lifts the radio-controlled detonator to his chest, Number 6 wrestles with the man for control of the device. Below them, the outgoing Number 2 makes his farewell speech, aware that at any moment his retirement will end too early. The young Number 2, meanwhile, worried that the explosion is overdue, signals to his confederate to find out what is wrong. Having snatched the radio detonator from the watchmaker's hands, Number 6 hastily descends the clock tower. 'Farewell my friends,' says the departing Number 2, anticipating that his words will send him to heaven. But the explosion he expects fails to occur. At that very moment, Numbers 6 and 100 are fighting each other to regain possession of the detonator trigger, which has been knocked from the Prisoner's hand by his opponent. As the men fight, a confused but nonetheless relieved ex-Number 2 is only too glad when the Master of Ceremonies lifts the seal of office from his shoulders and crosses the balcony to place the medallion around the neck of his successor. A look of terror and bemusement fills his eyes as, via the transmitter in his glasses, he hears Number 6 ordering his defeated opponent to confess his involvement in the affair. At the foot of the bell tower, the one numbered 100 throws the Prisoner backwards, but the struggle soon ends when Number 100 is punched into submission. Back on the balcony, the achievement sculpture is unveiled and the new Number 2 looks on with anger as Number 6 hands over the detonator trigger to the out-going Number 2. 'Take it,' he says. 'What for?' begs the other. 'It's your passport. No one will question its authority. The helicopter's waiting.' 'But they'll get me eventually,' stammers the elder. 'Fly now, pay later,' jousts the Prisoner. 'They'll find me, wherever I am,' confirms the other. 'As long as it's not here. Take it and go,' Number 6 advises, returning the new Number 2's icy stare. Watched helplessly by his successor, the retired Number 2 leaves. As the villain of the piece attempts to raise the medallion over his head, Number 6 springs forwards to pin his arms to his sides. 'And so the great day is nearly over ...' mocks the Prisoner. '... Came off rather well I thought. Better than planned. And now you can look forward to your own retirement and I'm sure they'll arrange something equally suitable for you, when the day comes.' Seething, the new Number 2 is unable to do anything as, patting the man on the shoulder, the Prisoner quips 'Be seeing you ... Won't I?' and strides from the balcony.

'Went off rather well I thought. Better than planned'

A Change of Mind

Written by Roger Parkes

Guest stars

Number 86	Angela Browne
Number 2	John Sharpe

with

The Butler	Angelo Muscat
Doctor	George Pravda
Number 42	Kathleen Breck
Supervisor	Peter Swanwick
Lobo Man	Thomas Heathcote
Committee Chairman	Bartlett Mullins

and

Number 93	Michael Miller
1st Member of Social Group	Joseph Cuby
2nd Member of Social Group	Michael Chow
Number 48	June Ellis
1st Woodland Man	John Hamblin
2nd Woodland Man	Michael Billington

Directed by: Joseph Serf (alias Patrick McGoohan)

WORKING OUT ON his home made high-bar gymnasium apparatus in the woods, Number 6 finishes his exercise with a rope swing and a few well-placed blows to his punch-bag. He instantly becomes aware that his fitness routine is being monitored by two thugs. 'Training for the big break?' asks the first man, entering the clearing. 'Why not use the Village gymnasium?' probes the second, joining his accomplice. 'Perhaps I prefer privacy,' quips the athlete, his senses alert for trouble. His reply provokes a fight. Using his home-made equipment to good advantage, the Prisoner

Number 6 lays out the opposition

soundly thrashes the men. Racing away, the taller of the two thugs swears to have Number 6 brought before the committee. Later that day, while waiting in the council chamber ante-room for their cases to be heard, Number 6 joins other miscreants and listens as a tape recording piped in from the chamber below informs those gathered that: The council chamber has considered Number 93's case, but already there are signs of disharmony in his behaviour: he appears to be a reasonable man, but there is plenty of evidence showing his unwillingness to work for the community. There are several cases waiting to be dealt with: Number 6 is seriously in need of help, and they want to do something for Number 42, who appears to be in a permanent state of depression; she is always in tears. It is Number 93's clear duty to prove that he is once again a suitable member of society. The only way he can achieve this and regain the respect of his fellows is to publicly acknowledge his shortcomings. He must go to the rostrum and confess. They will tell him what to say. In the space of a second, Number 93 enters through the door leading to the chamber below. He mounts the rostrum at the rear of the ante-room and, repeating verbatim what a voice on the public-address system tells him, the man tells the gathering that he is in turn: inadequate, disharmonious, and truly grateful, believe me . . . believe me . . . The authoritative voice over the public-address system, continues to echo the word until, sobbing now, Number 93 leaves the rostrum and marches from the chamber to the hearty applause of those gathered in the room. 'Number 6 enter,' pipes the voice. Entering the council chamber, a vast circular auditorium containing a semi-circle of tables behind which sit the committee members, the Prisoner descends the elongated ramp to the arena below. As the mute Butler wheels away a control console which records the court's proceedings, Number 6 sidles through the opening. To applause from his companions, the Committee Chairman, a bespectacled man, dressed in a striped vest and top hat, opens the proceedings. 'I take it you have completed the written questionnaire of confession?' he asks. 'Of course,' mocks the Prisoner, tearing the document he carries into shreds. 'Naturally!' 'Please do not be hostile to the committee. We are here to help you,' says a bodyless voice, as the accused sits scornfully in the chair provided for him, scattering the torn pieces of the questionaire to the floor. 'I take it you've checked my file . . . regarding hostility?' he quips with an air of indifference. 'Your files are no concern of ours,' drones the voice. 'Any information about *you* is with Number 2.' 'Really,' replies the accused, twiddling his thumbs as the chair he occupies begins to rise and rotate. 'It is the duty of this committee to deal with complaints,' says the chairman. 'Complaints!' snaps Number 6, rotating rapidly in his chair. 'Well done, I have several.' The voice from the console drones on. 'You realise a serious charge has been levelled at you, particularly regarding your attitude towards your fellow citizens . . . we deplore your spirit of disharmony.' 'That's a *common* complaint around here, isn't it,' grins Number 6, as the chairman counsels him to be discreet. 'You do appreciate that everything you say is being recorded . . .' challenges the voice. '. . . and may be used as evidence against me . . .' mocks the Prisoner. 'This is a strictly impartial committee . . .' says the voice, interrupted by the chairman who informs Number 6 that he has not been called before them to defend himself. '. . . All we ask,' continues the voice, 'is for your complete confession.' Advising the accused to cooperate, the bespectacled man informs the others that

it is time they all had a tea break: the accused man's group and medical records will be considered in full at the resumed hearing of the committee. Applauding Number 6, the committee leaves the chamber and the accused man does likewise. As the doors leading to the chamber slide shut behind them, the Butler reappears to push away a section of the circular tables to allow the Prisoner to exit. Passing through the ante-room above, Number 6 pauses for a moment at the confessional rostrum where, hearing a re-run of Number 93's confession, he salutes his fellow miscreants and marches from the room, applauding as he goes. While returning to his cottage, the Villagers show their hostility by avoiding him and refusing to acknowledge his salute. The *Tally Ho* newspaper magically carries the hot-off-the-press headline: 'The Committee Hearing Continues; Number 93 confesses disharmony and Number 6 awaits further investigation'! Entering his cottage, the ostracised man crumples up the newspaper and flings it into the hearth. Number 2 waits for him. 'There is a saying, the slowest mule is nearest to the whip,' greets the elder. Countering with one of his

A jovial, but devious Number 2

own – he who digs a pit will one day lie in it, the Prisoner presumes that his guest is above investigation? '*Nobody* is above investigation,' retorts the other, adding that failure to cooperate makes one an outcast. 'What? No more taxis. No more credit?' quips Number 6. 'Believe me, it could be only a beginning,' suggests Number 2, placing a biscuit to his lips. 'You should know,' the Prisoner replies, preparing to brew himself a drink. 'I hope that you do not think that *I* am a member of the committee?' questions the superior. 'Oh no, of course no – never.' 'I assure you,' smiles

Number 2, 'no matter what significance you may hold for me, to the Village and its committee, you are merely a citizen Number 6, who has to be tolerated – and if necessary shaped to fit.' 'Public Enemy Number 6,' mocks the Prisoner. 'If you insist. But public enemies cannot be tolerated *indefinitely*. Be careful. Do not defy this committee. If the hearings go against you, *I* am powerless to help,' sneers Number 2. The other is about to reply, when a beautiful blonde girl enters the cottage. Greeted by the Superior as Number 86, it appears that she has had valuable experience of the committee. 'As a member?' asks the Prisoner. 'I suffered the shame of being posted. Disharmonious,' the girl replies. 'How terrible for you,' grins Number 6. 'The hearings were fair and just. *I* was at fault,' she replies turning to Number 2. 'Oh but this is irrelevant. With your permission sir, Number 6 has a busy schedule. First the social group, then the medical.' 'Of course,' replies the elder, placing another biscuit into his mouth. 'Do carry on.' 'No time for tea?' quips the Prisoner playfully. 'No. Only your future,' confirms Number 2. Stating that the man's attitude towards the committee is both frivolous and dangerous, the girl informs him that the hearings are televised. That is why his behaviour is so important. 'You stand before the entire community. The social group is your one hope. Fortunately I, too, have been attached to the Group.' 'Most fortunate, yes,' quips Number 6, pouring the girl a cup of tea. 'Oh please, you must try to cooperate . . .' He confirms that he will. '. . . Join in with the Group's spirit.' 'Naturally.' 'Only they can help you with the committee.' 'Naturally.' Frustrated now, the girl looks at her wristwatch. Indicating that they are already overdue, she ignores the man's offer of tea, and bundles him through the door. Watching this with his Supervisor on his monitor screen, Number 2 remarks 'Females! If that woman makes one mistake we could lose Number 6. D'you hear that. Lose him!'

Determined to show her pupil community life, Number 86 leads the Prisoner into the Village to where, gathered in a group, a bunch of citizens are discussing ways of curing Number 42 of her depression. Stating that there can be no mitigation, they all have a social obligation to stand together, the senior member of the group shouts down a second member who, though not contesting the validity of her claim nevertheless feels that . . . 'No exceptions,' says the senior. 'All right, so you say you're a poet. You were composing when you failed to hear Number 10's greeting.' 'Neglect of a social principle,' cries another. 'Poetry has social value,' pipes up the Prisoner. 'He's trying to divide us,' claims the senior member. 'His intentions are obvious,' says Number 86. 'To stop us from helping this unfortunate girl.' 'You're trying to undermine my rehabilitation, disrupt my social progress . . .' claims the girl. 'Strange talk for a poet,' says Number 6. 'Rebel. Disharmonious. Rebel' cry the group. 'Reactionary!' Scornful of the group's attempts to reinstate Number 42 into society, the Prisoner breaks up the debate, elbows his way past the group and heads for the woods – ignoring Number 86 as he goes. But he does not get far. Three white-coated medical men wait for him, and he is driven to the hospital for his medical. 'First rate, Number 6,' says a doctor unstrapping a blood pressure sleeve from the patient's arm. 'Life here suits you.' 'Finished?' throws back Number 6, rolling his sleeve to his wrist. 'Just your patelia reflexes,' replies the medical man, tapping the Prisoner's knees in turn. 'Excellent. Fit for any contingency.' 'Anything specific in mind?' asks the patient donning his blazer. 'How suspicious you are of us all,' grins the doctor,

bidding the patient a cheery 'Be seeing you'. Outside in the corridor, the Prisoner's attention is drawn to a door marked 'Aversion Therapy.' Peering through its observation glass, he sees a drugged man strapped to a chair. Before him sits a television screen on which are projected images of a Rover which appears to be bouncing towards him, an image that is intercut with shots of Number 2's face and the word 'unmutual'. Time and again the word flashes onto the screen as the fraught man attempts to break his bonds. Concerned by what he sees, Number 6 attempts to enter the room. The door is locked. Behind him in the corridor, another patient calls for him to be calm. 'Are you his keeper?' the Prisoner challenges, crossing to the man's side. 'So excited all of you. Rushing and shouting,' the patient replies, his glassy stare showing that he is not quite at peace with his surroundings. 'Have *you* been in there?' 'Not in *there*,' replies the patient, staring at the therapy room door. 'That's odd.' 'Not odd, please . . .' stammers the deranged man, stroking a scar on his forehead. '. . . *different* maybe.' 'Different?' The patient gives a weak smile. 'I'm one of the lucky ones . . . the happy ones . . . I was . . .' 'Yes?' 'I was unmutual,' replies the 'cured' man.

In a darkened council chamber, the Chairman submits his report to an apparently unconcerned Number 6. Submitted by the social group, the report leaves the Chairman no choice but to classify the accused as unmutual! He is warned that if any further complaint is lodged against him, it will be necessary to propose him for the treatment known as Instant Social Conversion. As the sentence is passed, the chair upon which the Prisoner sits grinds to a halt, the chamber is flooded with light and Number 6 finds himself staring into the face of the Butler. The committee have vanished! Number 6 and the po-faced servant are alone. Rising from his seat, the Prisoner storms out of the room. Outside he passes a poster bearing the legend 'Your Community Needs You', its image of Number 2 mocking his progress. The streets outside are void of life, not a citizen to be seen. The *Tally Ho* newspaper headline carries a report of the committee's declaration, and the Village Voice rings out over the public address system: 'Your attention please, here is an important announcement. Number 6 has been declared Unmutual until further notice. Any unsocial incident involving Number 6 should be reported immediately to the appeals sub committee. Thank you for your attention.' Arriving at the cottage denoted '6 – Private', he lifts the telephone receiver. The line is dead. Within seconds of his arrival, a group of female villagers arrive at his door, led by Number 42. They represent the appeals sub committee and wish to help him. He refuses their help and they leave, a spokeswoman advising her colleagues that their offer is premature. Monitoring all this from the control room, Number 2 grins and tells his Supervisor that they will shortly be able to see how the loner withstands real loneliness – although he hopes, for the Prisoner's sake, that it will not take too long for the man to reach his senses. They continue to monitor the subject's progress as he walks alone through the woods, his eyes staring skywards as a flock of geese fly overhead, taking an avenue of escape that is beyond his reach.

The following morning finds Number 6 ordering coffee at a table in the cafe. His request is ignored. The other customers rise as one from their seats and walk to the sidewalk, their presence there forcing him to return to his cottage. Inside he is greeted by the female sub committee who tell him it is no longer a game. Number 42 informs him that they are socially conscious citizens and are provoked by the loathsome presence of an unmutual. 'They are sheep!' he throws back, leading the spokeswoman to declare that if he insists on rejecting their offer of help, so be it, there remains but one course open to them. The door to the cottage swings open and the women leave, at which point his telephone purrs into life. It is Number 2. 'I warned you. The community will not tolerate you indefinitely,' confirms the superior. 'You need a scapegoat ... Citizens unite to denounce this menace in our presence,' challenges Number 6. 'A scapegoat. Is that what you think it is? Allow me to reassure you that after conversion, you won't care what it is ... you just won't *care*,' states the elder. 'Oh yes,' jests Number 6. 'The ordeal of social conversion.' 'You'll soon have lasting peace of mind and adjustment to the social system here,' explains Number 2. 'Drugs?' 'Would *drugs* be lasting?' asks the other, suggesting that the only available treatment for one such as Number 6 is the isolation of the Prisoner's aggressive, frontal lobes of the brain! The line goes dead. The tenant's in-house speaker-system carries a message to all staff psychologists and psychiatrists, stating that those wishing to study the conversion of Number 6 on the hospital's closed-circuit television should report immediately to the hospital common room! Retreating outside, the Prisoner finds himself confronted by hoards of angry citizens. Led by the social sub committee's spokeswoman and Number 42, they begin to attack him with their umbrellas. Thrown to the ground, Number 6 finds himself man-handled into the hospital's theatre. Through a dazed stupor, he sees an injection administered into his arm by a doctor, and feels himself being wheeled into an operating theatre on a stretcher. Secured to a table, he struggles as an ultrasonic device is lowered over his head, and muff-like attachments are placed over his ears. Outside in the common room, the Chairman and his committee take their seats in front of the closed-circuit television, its cameras focused on Number 86 who, dressed in an operating smock, is describing the step-by-step conversion process. They are using standard equipment. The unit suspended over the patient's head contains a quartz crystal, which is activated by a variable electro-magnetic field, governed by two high-voltage condensers. The crystal emits ultrasonic sound waves, which are then bounced off a parabolic reflector. The focal point of the reflector can be seen by the use of light waves. Number 86 demonstrates the molecular turbulence by burning a hole in a block of white-coloured material. Throughout the demonstration, unable to move a limb, the Prisoner blinks his eyes, alarmed by what may lie ahead. As the girl continues to describe the operating procedure, the committee members shuffle in their seats, craning their heads forward to obtain a better view. The prime concern, states Number 86, is to locate the link point of the frontal lobes. To achieve this, the machine will be changed to a low voltage rating and the surgeons will feel the focal point. A circular white dot appears on the patient's forehead, a few centimeters above his right eyebrow. Controlling the light, the girl moves the beam four centimeters to the right, then point two-three-zero centimeters down and the position is held, the ultrasonic beam focussed now on the exact link point they require.

'The crystal is activated by a variable electro-magnetic field'

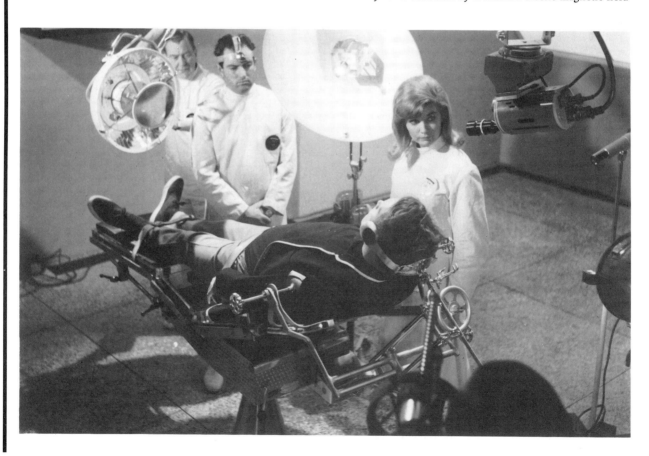

Moving close to the patient's head, the girl applies a lanolin barrier to the spot she has selected: this will minimise external cell breakdown and subsequent scar tissue. The patient is then injected with a relaxant to preclude muscular reaction. The patient is now ready, the voltage being stepped up until the ultrasonic bombardment causes permanent dislocation. The machine purrs into a higher frequency, and the patient's lips contract into a grotesque grin.

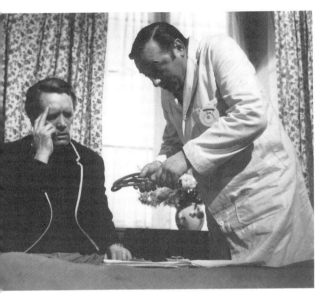

'If I were you I'd keep it on for a couple of days'

Number 6 wakes up in a hospital bed. 'You went to sleep Number 6. Just at the most interesting point you went to sleep,' a doctor relates. Warned against any physical exertion, the patient grins as he discovers the plaster above his right eyebrow – a dressing he is advised to keep in place for a couple of days – to remind himself to take things easy. From the far side of the hospital ward, Number 86 promises the doctor that she will take good care of him. Together they leave, he stopping for a moment to catch up on the progress of the patient being subjected to the aversion treatment, she beckoning him outside. A group of villagers race forward to greet them, delighted that the 'loner' is cured. Throughout their drive back to his cottage, citizens line the streets, each acknowledging their joy at his return to the community. Indoors they are greeted by Number 2, who welcomes the lamb back to the fold and suggests that the girl makes Number 6 a soothing cup of tea – a celebration drink. Saying that he will see them later, he leaves as Number 86 leads her charge to a couch: he looks tired after his ordeal and she wishes him to relax. With lowered eyelids, the Prisoner spots the girl slip a pill into his tea cup. Handed this, he avoids sipping its contents by pretending to need a blanket. 'Cold,' he suggests, in a childlike whimper. 'Cold?' says the girl. 'Rug . . . bedroom . . . rug.' 'Rug?' 'Rug! Wardrobe.' Disturbed by his request, Number 86 crosses into the bedroom. Alone, he pours the contents of his cup into a nearby flower vase. Returning with a blanket, she covers the man and removes the empty cup from his hand. Believing that the drug has taken effect, she strokes his brow. 'Rest well,' she remarks heading for the door. 'Be seeing you,' he quips to the retreating figure. The door has barely closed behind her, when Number 2 snaps his fingers in front of the sleeping man's eyes. 'It's time for our talk Number 6,' says the elder. 'Our talk?' the Prisoner replies, his eyes flickering open. 'Oh yes, now that all your aggressive anxieties have been expunged – let us say forever, I know that you'll feel free to speak.' 'Feel free to speak,' repeats the other. 'Yes, particularly about that little incident which has been causing you such absurd distress,' coaxes Number 2. Through half-closed eyes, his lips drawn back in a grimace of drug-induced stupor, the Prisoner mutters some unintelligible comments. The elder continues. 'The trivia . . . the trivia of your *res-ig-nation* . . .' The Prisoner stirs. '. . . Yes . . . you resigned. But why? . . . why prematurely . . . Why-did-you-resign?' 'It's difficult,' stammers Number 6, indicating that he needs time to think. 'Oh time, that was it was it?' urges Number 2. 'No, it wasn't *time*,' says the other. 'You couldn't stand your job . . . you needed time to think.' 'No! No!' 'I'm asking you, not telling you,' hisses Number 2, anxious to calm the one being interrogated. 'Please don't be angry,' smiles the other weakly. 'I'm not angry my dear friend. That is just the way things seem to be to you . . .' whispers the superior. '. . . Because your new world is so quiet by contrast . . .' 'Is it?' '. . . for you agitation is a thing of the past. Lay back and rest, lay back and rest,' smiles Number 2, rising and heading for the door. 'We can have our little chat later on . . . when you've had time to collect your thoughts.' Alone now, the Prisoner rises from his couch and walks into the bathroom. Standing in front of a mirror, he peels off the plaster, gently rubs the scar with his fingertips and replaces the dressing. Joined in the Control Room by Number 2, the girl denoted Number 86 watches the Prisoner's actions with interest. 'Strange. Very strange,' she comments. 'What is?' asks the superior. 'Already he suspects.' 'The scar at any rate is genuine. He'll learn nothing from that,' observes Number 2. 'No, but he suspects already. I gave him 8 grains of Mytol,' confirms the girl, explaining that the drug should preclude all such reactions. 'He's still very confused,' the elder points out, observing Number 6 slam down his fist on the kitchen divider. 'He's shocked, as I anticipated,' says Number 86. 'Well he's seen what he *thought* was the operation. He should be convinced . . .' Commenting that there is really no reason for Number 6 to suspect that the operation never really took place, the girl is astounded when Number 2 orders her to go back to the man's cottage and repeat the dose. 'Now? But 16 grains of Mytol is quite impossible!' Drawing her attention to the man being observed, who is now racing around his kitchen pounding the units with his fist, Number 2 points out that the patient is already beginning to show aggression and suspicion; they cannot afford a relapse. 'Yes, but this drug . . .' 'The man is as strong as a bull. You simply *must* step up the injection!' exclaims the other.

To the accompaniment of the Prisoner's nervous finger-tapping, a tattoo played out on a table top, the girl brews Number 6 a cup of tea – drugged of course. 'You still have some impatience, impulsiveness,' she says placing the drink before him. 'Do you like my dress?' 'More feminine than slacks,' he replies. 'One thing though,' he adds rising to carry the cup and saucer to the kitchen sink. 'I cannot stand girls who don't know how to make a decent cup of tea.' Emptying the teapot, he then demonstrates the correct procedure: warm the pot, one scoop of tea for himself, one for his guest, one for the pot – and an extra one for luck. Add boiling water, allow the pot to stand for a moment and . . . He turns back to the girl, asking her to pour the milk. While she is doing so, he collects a second cup and saucer, instantly aware that the girl has dropped a pill into his own – a cup he exchanges for hers while the girl's back is turned. 'All charming and domestic,' Number 2 tells the Supervisor and his mute servant, suggesting to the latter that he, too, would enjoy some tea. 'Excellent my dear,' he continues as the couple being observed lift their tea cups to their lips. 'Just leave him . . . leave him to *me*.' By now, the girl has fallen victim to her own drug. Observing this on his television monitor screen, an angry Number 2 leaps to his feet. 'Stupid woman!' he cries, crossing to the console to relay a message to the girl that she is to report to him immediately. 'Stupid woman,' he repeats to the Supervisor, 'she'll ruin everything!' 'Be seeing you,' calls Number 6 as the girl leaves his cottage. Aware that Number 6 is about to take his daily stroll, the elder's attitude mellows. 'Why not. Let him go out, feel free. He'll sift it out if he has doubts. A little outside contact will soon reassure him.' Outside, the Prisoner meets the man with the scarred forehead who he spoke to earlier – the unmutual who was 'saved' by social conversion. Asked by Number 6 if he feels different, the man breaks into laughter. 'You should know,' he says, indicating the sticking-plaster on the Prisoner's forehead. 'I should?' queries a bemused Number 6. 'Who better? See you soon,' grins the imbecile, laughing as he walks away.

At his woodland gym, Number 6 wrestles with his changed personality. The exercise apparatus looks familiar but he appears to lack the know-how to put them to their intended use. The sound of a twig snapping underfoot heralds the return of the thugs he met earlier. 'Back here again,' says the first man. 'But not so sure of himself now,' quips the other. 'Not so much punch in him this time,' grins the first man. 'We have some unfinished business,' confirms his companion, baiting the man. The taller of the two calls Number 6 a social convert, while the other sends the Prisoner reeling backwards by swinging his home-made punchbag into his face. Suddenly, both thugs begin to throw punches to the Prisoner's jaw. 'Remember?' grins the tall one, sending his fist into the bemused man's face. The jolt to his senses does the trick. Springing upwards to the high-bar, Number 6 reverts to his acrobatic self. Casting the men aside in a flurry of flying feet and well-timed punches the contest is over within minutes and the thugs are nursing their bruised egos.

Returning to the Village, the Prisoner meets Number 86. Still drugged, she is picking flowers to take to Number 2. 'Having a funeral?' quips Number 6. 'I have to report . . .' grins the girl. 'On plant life?' '. . . To Number 2. I want to make him happy.' 'The ecstasy of illusion,' mocks the Prisoner. 'I'm higher . . .' she begins. 'Are you?' he teases. '. . . Higher than Number 2.' 'Are you?' She insists that she has to report. 'Go on then, report,' he says. In the Control Room, her superior orders the Supervisor to put out a general call for the girl. Hearing the order.over the Village loudspeaker system, Number 6 hits on an idea. With the girl under the influence of drugs meant for him, he hypnotises her into accepting that he is her superior. At his command, she then makes a full report on his social conversion. Told by the girl that the ultrasonic device was just a prop, and that the tranquilisers he was given were fakes and the illusion is being maintained by keeping the patient heavily tranquilised, he gives the girl her final instructions. 'Listen carefully, this is what I want you to do. When the Village clock strikes four . . .'

Number 2 receives a welcome guest. It is Number 6 who, confessing that he feels much happier, wishes to have a little chat. 'Why yes,' grins Number 2. 'Clearer in your mind now?' 'Oh much clearer, and happier. I want you to know that . . . such peace of mind,' teases Number 6. 'Well of course, only to be expected,' confirms the other. 'And I resisted, to think that I resisted for so long . . .' 'Understandable. A man of your training, but now you er . . .' invites Number 2. 'Yes, everything's clear cut now. Quite simple,' says Number 6, telling the other what he wishes to hear. 'Quite so. No more problems eh . . . and now at last we can have our little chat.' 'Yes I hope so. But . . .' 'But?' challenges the elder. Number 6 asks if he can tell everyone how grateful he is for his treatment; such a confession might inspire others to speak out also. Pleased with himself and seeing victory within his reach, Number 2 issues a radio announcement that, following his successful conversion, Number 6 has expressed his touching desire to address the community in person. All those that are not otherwise occupied, should report immediately to the Village square. Turning to his guest, he tells Number 6 a proverb. 'He who ploughs a straight furrow needs owe for nothing.'

The Villagers arrive in droves, all applauding loudly as Number 6 begins his speech from the Town Hall balcony. 'Citizens,' begins the 'cured' man, 'you're cheering me, but that is a mistake. It is Number 2 you should applaud.' The superior can hardly restrain his excitement. 'Until he brought about my social conversion . . .' continues Number 6, '. . . and believe me, it was *him* and not your committee, until then I was a rebel – an unmutual.

senselessly resisting this, our fine community.' An ecstatic Number 2 leads the applause. 'To borrow one of Number 2's sayings,' the speaker continues, 'the butcher with the sharpest knife has the warmest heart.' A murmur of discontent runs through the crowd. Smiling in the elder's direction, Number 6 carries on. 'Some of *you* have resisted in the past – have withheld *knowledge* that was important to Number 2. Now, thanks to social conversion, I want to tell you all something, and I trust that my example will inspire you all to tell ... to tell ...' Stopping in mid-sentence as the Village clock strikes four, the speaker glances at Number 2 and smiles as Number 86 steps forward to declare that Number 2 is unmutual. 'Social conversion for Number 2,' she yells, as Number 6 takes up her cause. 'Number 86 has a confession that Number 2 is unmutual – an unmutual who desires to deceive you all!' he shouts. The elder can hardly believe his ears, as, led by Number 86, the crowd takes up the chant and the 'convert' standing beside him accuses him of being a tool of those who wish to possess their minds. A look of failure crossing his face, the elder races from the balcony, the Prisoner's words that the community should reject the superior's false world echoing in his ears as, attempting to fight his way through the angry villagers, he finds himself jostled and pushed. Chanting for his blood, the crowd race after the fleeing figure, leaving behind the Butler who, following alone, raises his black and white striped parasol aloft to block out the sun's rays.

'There's something I have to show you. Very important –
Number 2's orders'

A. B. AND C

Written by Anthony Skene

Guest stars

Engadine	Katherine Kath
Number 14	Sheila Allen
Number 2	Colin Gordon
'A'	Peter Bowles

with

The Butler	Angelo Muscat
Blonde Lady	Georgina Cookson
'B'	Annette Carel
Flower Girl	Lucille Soong

and

Maid at Party	Bettine Le Beau
Thug	Terry Yorke
Thug	Peter Brayham
Henchman	Bill Cummings

Directed by Pat Jackson

HIS HANDS clasped tightly behind his back, Number 2 paces backwards and forwards across the vast expanse of his Green Dome control room. Without warning, the large red cordless telephone dominating his control console purrs into life, its high-pitched hum bringing a look of concern to the elder's face. Crossing to the instrument, he tentatively lifts the receiver to his ear. 'Number 2 here. Yes sir. I am doing my best. He's very difficult. I know it's important sir ...' Sighing, he swallows, determined that the unseen caller should be made aware of the difficulties. 'He's no ordinary person sir, but if I had a free hand ...' Pausing in mid-sentence, he listens to the other's opinion. '... I know sir yes. I'm not indispensable.' Lowering the receiver, his head drops in abject despair. Pouring himself a glass of milk, he ponders the caller's words. Then, with resolve, he lifts a second telephone and asks to be connected with Number 14. 'Number 14? The experiment must come forward!' he snaps. A woman's voice is heard to reply that that is not possible, she will require at least a week's preparation. 'I haven't got a week!' barks Number 2, as the voice informs him that she has not even finished testing it on animals, let alone people. 'Then now's your chance,' snaps Number 2 impatiently. 'When?' asks the voice. 'Tonight!'

As darkness falls over the Village, lightning accompanied by rolls of thunder and a deluge of rain heralds the arrival of two men in oilskins to a laboratory corridor. A third figure wrapped in a black plastic shroud, lies unconscious on the stretcher-trolley which the men wheel into the building. As the metal door they entered through glides to a close behind them, a woman dressed in a white surgical smock orders them to stop. 'Don't bring that wet in here, take your macs and boots off,' she yells. Having done so, the men wheel the man on the trolley down a ramp and into a chamber – a laboratory occupied by Numbers 2 and 14, the woman who called to them. Having unwrapped the body, the two men lift the intended victim onto an examination couch. The patient is Number 6. Their work done, the men leave. Number 2 reminds Number 14 that, for her own sake, her brainchild had better work; if the

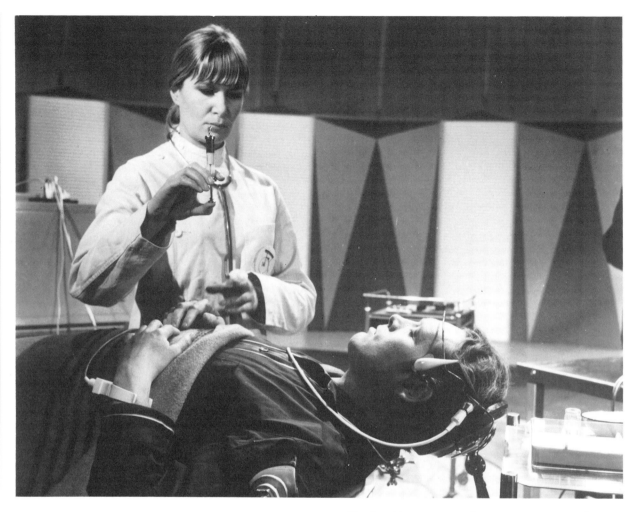

Number 14 prepares to administer injection number one

patient is damaged she will be held responsible. He looks on as the girl, an attractive blonde, attaches plastic bracelets to the patient's wrists and electrodes to his head. 'You know I haven't had the time to prove the drug.' she throws back. 'Just get it *right*, or I'll see that it's proved on you.' threatens Number 2, as the girl attaches wires leading from the electrodes on the patient's head to a monitor machine, which immediately begins to display the drugged man's brain patterns. 'What's all that about?' questions Number 2 staring at the monitor screen. 'Energy from his brain.' answers Number 14. 'Thoughts, like sound waves converted into electrical impulses and finally . . .' crossing to a tuning console, she tweaks a control. '. . . into pictures.' 'Extraordinary.' comments Number 2 as the patient's sub-conscious thoughts are converted into pictures and a television screen displays images of the one known as Number 6 handing in his resignation. 'How very single-minded.' comments Number 2, witnessing the event for the first time as the dreamer conjures up the sequence time and again. 'He's not conventional.' says Number 14. 'I sometimes think he's not human.' states the other. 'It's an anguish pattern.' sighs the girl, crossing to select an hypodermic syringe from a plastic container containing three injection cartridges marked 1, 2 and 3 respectively. Each is filled with a pinky-brown liquid. 'So this is your wonder drug.' the elder remarks. 'Yes.' she confirms, dabbing the tip of the syringe she has selected

with a wad of cotton wool. 'Three doses . . . and that's the absolute limit.' 'Why?' the superior demands. 'Three is dangerous enough. Four would kill him.' Crossing to Number 6, she swabs the patient's right wrist and prepares to administer the injection. Subconsiously, Number 6 raises his eyelids, but with a gentle stroke of her hand she closes his lids. Injected with the drug, the patient slips further into drowsiness. 'His mind is now yours.' the girl instructs. 'What do you want from it?' 'Why he resigned.' replies Number 2. 'I believe he was going to sell out. I want to know what he had to sell and to whom he was going to sell it. We've researched and computed his whole life and it boils down to three people . . . A, B, and C.' Crossing to three red-coloured box files perched on top of a filing cabinet, each of which bears the label 'a', 'b', or 'c', he taps each one in turn, as he informs his junior that the patient must meet each one of them. This way they will learn what *would* have happened had they not got to him first. 'Where do you want them to meet?' asks Number 14. 'Paris.' replies the superior. 'They all had one thing in common. They all attended Madame Engadine's celebrated parties. Here's some film of the most recent.' He hands the girl a film cassette. Placing the film spool into its slot on the master console, Number 14 presses a button. Almost instantly the television monitor displays film of the garden of a luxurious French chateau. People in evening dress enter and exit from the house. 'Ah,

190

nothing like a good party.' smiles the girl. 'I'm sure he'll welcome the change of environment.' Frowning at this remark and anxious for the experiment to proceed. Number 2 orders the junior to begin. 'Go on, feed it into him.' As bidden, Number 14 crosses to the console and trails a long electric lead feeding from the film cassette holder to the recumbent figure on the operating couch. Contacts are snapped tightly around the patient's wrists and a jack-plug attached to the lead is slotted into a device on the Prisoner's head. As she turns to rejoin her superior, Number 6 utters a single cry. Swinging back in alarm, the woman checks his heartbeat with a stethoscope. 'Is he all right?' calls a concerned Number 2. 'So far,' she answers, staring at the patient, as she turns a knob on the console a half-circle. The moment of truth has arrived.

Mentally transported to Paris, Number 6, now dressed in a tuxedo and black bow-tie, meets his hostess Engadine, a middle-aged, vivacious lady. 'You look tired darling,' greets the woman. 'Things are bad?' 'No, not now,' replies Number 6, explaining that he has started his holiday. 'The *English* holiday,' she jokes. 'Big boots and fishing sticks.' 'Not quite like that. Somewhere different. Somewhere quiet, where I can think,' he replies. Engadine laughs. 'There is no quiet anywhere.' She apologises that she has to mingle. However, before doing so, she cannot resist reminding her guest that he 'belongs' to her. 'Be horrible to other women,' she teases as, blowing him a kiss, she departs to rejoin her guests. 'Of course, yes,' smiles Number 6. 'I think it's time we introduced "A",' Number 2 decides, opening the box file labelled 'a', which contains a photograph of a suave-looking man with a moustache. Beneath a clip lies another can of film which, handed to Number 14, is attached to its relevant slot on her equipment. 'His face looks vaguely familiar,' she comments as the man's face fills the monitor screen. 'What's his real name?' 'I'm surprised you don't remember him. He made world news a few years ago,' confirms Number 2. With the flick of a switch, they watch as the man denoted 'A' sidles over to Number 6. 'I'm surprised,' greets Number 6. 'Not unpleasantly I trust,' says the newcomer, handing his fellow guest a glass of champagne. 'I knew you came to these parties . . .' begins Number 6. 'And wondered why we'd never met?' answers 'A', suggesting that Engadine has tactfully kept them apart. 'Until tonight,' grins Number 6. 'Perhaps tonight is

'I hope you're happy with your new life'

special,' suggests 'A'. 'I feel it is special too,' smiles the other. 'To us,' returns 'A', raising his glass. 'As we are, or as we were?' quips Number 6. 'Oh I remember him,' recalls Number 14 watching the scene. 'He defected about 6 years ago.' 'It's been a long time,' the defector confirms, continuing his conversation with Number 6. 'Not long enough!' quips the other. 'We used to be friends.' 'Once,' comes the short reply, 'but that's in the past.' 'Then let's think of the future,' tries 'A'. 'We're still the same people.' 'Working for different sides,' snaps Number 6, acknowledging a greeting from a fellow guest with a nod. 'Sides don't matter, only success.' 'In that case, we should still have a great deal in common,' counters the other. 'We do the same jobs.' 'For different reasons,' reminds Number 6. 'I see you still overrate absolute truth,' condemns 'A'. 'Whatever way you look at it, we both want to conquer the world. I hope you're happy with your new life?' 'New life?' enquires the other, leaning forward to catch the other man's words. 'Well news of old friends travels quickly.' 'In a few hours.' 'To you and to me, news is like air. We breathe it deeply, draw it from far and wide.' 'If it's interesting,' smiles Number 6. 'What are you going to do with your freedom?' quizzes the other. 'Go fishing,' replies Number 6. 'Perhaps you're fishing now? What's your price?' 'What am I selling?' grins Number 6. 'I'm anxious to find out,' whispers 'A', broaching the subject of a deal being struck. 'Madame's wine is always excellent,' mocks the other ignoring the remark. 'If you haven't got a price, you must have a reason,' prompts the other. He receives no reply. Tiring of the game, Number 6 moves away. 'They're not always the same thing. Excuse me.' 'He's going!' exclaims a deflated Number 2 from his laboratory observation point. 'And we haven't found out if he . . . He must not *go*!' 'He's only doing what he *would* have done. I can only create the situation,' explains Number 14 watching the screen as Number 6 is handed his topcoat by a footman. 'Get him *back!*' demands Number 2. 'It's his *dream*,' the girl replies helplessly. 'It must take its course.' Back at the party, it comes as no surprise to Number 6 that, as the footman swings back the door to allow him to leave, 'A' is waiting for him, also dressed in his topcoat. 'You never could take a hint,' he tells his determined ex-colleague. 'I don't want a hint. I want *you*,' mocks "A".' With a snap of his fingers, the defector signals for his colleague, the previously benign footman, who grabs the Prisoner's arms and Number 6 is led away. 'I'm saving myself money,' quips the kidnapper as Number 6 is shoved into the back seat of his car, between 'A' and his henchman. Driven away at speed, the vehicle soars down the Champs-Elysées, cutting its way through the traffic like a knife. 'Paris hasn't changed much, has it . . .' comments Number 6. 'Where are they going?' asks a concerned and puzzled Number 2. 'I don't know,' replies Number 14, 'but it's what would have happened. That's what you wanted.' After a long journey, the vehicle arrives at a deserted country chateau and the hostage is ushered out of the car at gunpoint. 'Well you're in my country now,' grins 'A'. Feigning levity and saying that he enjoys travel. Number 6 plants a solid right hook to the kidnapper's jaw. A fist fight ensues, Number 6 emerging victorious. Squaring his bow-tie, the hostage departs the scene with a cheerful 'Be seeing you'.

The outcome is a disappointment for Number 2; the Prisoner's actions indicating that he would never have sold out to subject 'A'. Anxious to continue, he demands that the patient be given a second dose, but Number 14 says the risk is too great to give him a second injection immediately: at least 24 hours must elapse. 'Why?' demands the impatient elder. 'It's a very dangerous drug,' reminds Number 14. 'He must have time to re-adjust.' Looking nervously at the large red telephone sitting ominously on his control console, the superior sighs in anticipation of what the future may hold.

It is morning. Sitting on the foot of his bed, a still dazed Number 6 stands up, stretches his spine and dons his bathrobe. The front door magically opens of its own accord and his attention is drawn to two women talking on the terrace outside his residence. One, a pretty Oriental, is handing the other a bouquet of carnations she has selected from her flower cart. Accepting the flowers, the purchaser turns and gives the onlooker a brief glance. Recognition is hazy until, focusing his eyes on the woman's badge numbered '14', Number 6 instinctively glances at his right wrist. It bears a small but distinct puncture mark, the skin around it showing signs of bruising. Somewhere, in the back of his confused mind, the girl's face seems familiar . . .

Later that day, dressed now in his Village uniform of blazer and flannels, the Prisoner seats himself at a canopied table outside the Old People's Home. The table is already occupied – by Number 14, who is reading the latest edition of the *Tally Ho* newspaper. 'My handbook on social etiquette doesn't deal with this,' he confides, seating himself opposite the girl. 'How does one talk to someone that one has met in a dream?' Folding her newspaper, the girl gives him a quizzical stare. 'Look er, Number . . .?' The man is not wearing a badge. 'Six,' he offers, eyebrows raised. 'Six. I'm usually a social animal, but not now. Another time?' She attempts to continue reading the newspaper. 'Last week, Number 14 was an old lady in a wheelchair,' he continues. 'You're new here, and you're one of *them*!' 'Your nonsense bores me,' she returns, folding her newspaper a second time and preparing to leave. 'Oh, my mistake!' he throws back as the girl gathers up the bunch of carnations she purchased earlier. 'Don't worry, we all make mistakes . . . sometimes we have to,' replies the girl leaving the table. Seated in his oval chair inside the Green Dome, Number 2 receives a visitor – Number 6, escorted into the chamber by the mute manservant. 'Come in my dear fellow,' calls the superior from behind his control console. 'Come in and sit down.' 'I'm not tired. I slept well,' throws back the newcomer, descending the ramp with his arms clasped tightly behind his back. (Good. We don't seem to have seen a lot of each other) 'I haven't seen very much of *you*,' quips Number 6, staring quizzically at the bespectacled man. (I don't spend *all* my time spying) 'Don't you. Your predecessors *did*,' replies the other. A grin, and a statement that *he* has other things to do, Number 2 raises the subject of the Prisoner's resignation. 'Now all this nonsense about why you resigned. If people can't chuck up a job, things have come to a pretty mess. Do sit down.' 'I'm still not tired,' confirms Number 6. 'In that case, perhaps you'd pour me out some milk . . . *I* didn't have a very good night.' The newcomer does as requested handing Number 2 his glass of milk in such a way that he cannot fail to catch sight of the puncture mark on the Prisoner's wrist. The superior attempts to ignore the injection scar by extolling the virtues of milk. 'Milk is the perfect food. It creates good temper . . . would you like some?' 'My temper's fine,' snaps the other. 'Anyone who had nothing to hide would ask where I got it,' he plies, raising his wrist before the elder. 'Where did you get it Number 6?' 'In my sleep.' 'Oh you must have been

restless. Perhaps you need a check up.' 'I have a favourite doctor,' mocks the Prisoner. 'Really.' 'Number 14,' grins the other. Having delivered his trump card, Number 6 turns and walks out of the chamber. Lowering his glass, Number 2 raises his body from his seat and begins to pace the room, deep in thought. Behind him, sitting ominously on the control console, the large red telephone bleeps into life. Walking hesitantly to the instrument, the bespectacled man answers the summons. 'Sir,' he sighs. 'Yes sir, within two days. You have my word.' He swallows deeply. 'Yes sir, I realise my future's at stake. Two days. I guarantee.'

Night, and an elderly maid brings Number 6 his evening drink. Laying it on the unit by the side of the Prisoner's bed, she bids Number 6 goodnight and leaves. Dressed in pyjamas and dressing gown, the Prisoner sits on the edge of his bed, raises the cup to his lips and drinks deeply. One mouthful achieves the desired effect and he stumbles to the carpet in an unconscious heap, the cup and saucer clattering to the floor beside him. Within seconds he is back on the operating couch and the hypodermic numbered '2' returns him to his dream and Engadine's party in Paris. Seated on a balcony overlooking the garden, he is approached by the hostess. 'Where have you been darling?' she asks, enquiring what has happened to her other handsome guest, the 'old friend' he was talking to. 'Oh he's gone,' he replies. 'Just like that,' she asks with a wave of her hand. 'Yes.' 'How very rude, without saying goodbye. Anyway, I never did like that man . . . it doesn't matter.' Called away by a footman to greet new arrivals, she says that she will see him later and re-enters her home. Observing this in the company of Number 14, Number 2 snaps shut another file. 'Time for "B",' he suggests handing the girl another film cassette, which she snaps into place on her machine. The face that materialises on the television monitor is that of an attractive dark-haired woman. 'She even looks like a spy,' comments Number 14. 'A very good one. From a long line of spies,' confirms the elder as he joins Number 14 before the monitor screen where the subject being observed is seated at a table. 'He's full of the party spirit, isn't he,' quips Number 2, staring at the man sitting alone. 'Where *is* she?' 'I don't know,' replies his assistant. 'She should be there,' insists the elder with concern. 'I think he's resisting,' states Number 14 crossing to the patient who, covered by a red blanket, is lying immediately below the monitor screen. 'It may take longer for the drug to work this time,' she comments checking the patient's pulse. As her superior joins her, the man on the screen rises from his chair. 'I imagine she's coming,' grins Number 2, catching sight of a girl's head flitting through the folliage which blocks her face from sight. It is only a maid going about her business. 'No, no that's certainly not "B",' corrects Number 2. 'I expect she's there somewhere,' comments the woman beside him, holding the patient's wrist tightly in her hands. 'I very much hope so,' says the superior with a shrug of his shoulders. They watch as the maid reaches the man on the balcony and Engadine walks out to meet her. 'Ah Lucette, I was looking for you. What have you been up to?' 'Nothing madame,' replies the maid. 'I was helping Louis to collect the glasses.' Spotting the envelope the girl carries in her hand, Engadine asks what it is. 'A note madame. A lady she gave it to me.' Believing it to be meant for her, the hostess reaches out her hand. 'No madame, it's for the man.' 'Thank you Lucette,' says her mistress, handing the note to her guest with the comment that it is in a woman's handwriting. 'I am jealous. What does she want?' asks Engadine as Number 6 slices open the envelope. 'I dare not tell you,' he quips, happy to play the game as he shoves the note under the hostess' nose. 'Oh,' she says reading the letter. 'to meet her in the arbour? My guest, at my party, in the arbour?' 'She's an old friend,' replies Number 6. 'There's no name,' the woman points out. 'Old friends don't need names,' he says, as feigning indignation and joking that for her the party is over, ended because her escort has been 'stolen' by another woman. Engadine rejoins her guests, pausing momentarily to tell her guest to enjoy himself. Walking into the garden, Number 6 enters a maze of neatly-trimmed bushes. The letter writer is nowhere to be seen until, led by the familiar pop of a champagne cork being drawn from a magnum, he finds 'B' seated at a solitary white table in a clearing. 'I'd recognise that signal anywhere,' he calls, crossing to the beautiful woman as she fills a second glass with champagne. 'Let's get distressed together,' she responds. 'There you are,' boasts Number 14 as she and Number 2 watch the man approach the mysterious newcomer. 'You are still the most intriguing spy I have ever met,' grins Number 6. 'It's taken a lot of thought and experience,' confirms 'B'. 'The last I remember you were hiking across the mountains to Switzerland,' he teases, pointing his finger. 'I got sore feet,' grins the girl. 'You should have stayed,' he says, joining the woman and accepting the glass she offers. 'I have no friends there.' 'Your enemy is a very bad loser. He was here earlier. Does he know you're back?' 'His chums are all over the place,' she confides, glancing over her shoulder. 'He and I had a little ride together. I left him in a most unforgiving mood. He may return.' Apparently unconcerned, 'B' remarks that being killed is an occupational hazard. 'Like a sitting duck,' he suggests. 'Don't worry. Tonight's a party,' she smiles dismissing his challenge. Taking her by the hand, he leads her from the table. 'You used to be a very good dancer,' he acknowledges, placing his arm around her waist. 'I still am.' 'Are you?' They begin to glide around the clearing, picking up the tempo of the music that filters through the trees from the chateau. 'Where are you going for your holiday?' she asks. He laughs. 'So you've heard. I don't know yet.' 'A long one?' she queries, gliding away from his arms. 'Oh a very long one.' 'Why?' 'I need time to think,' he says. She glides back into his arms. 'I can't bear to think. I can't bear to be alone. That's why I like parties. I drown myself in chatter.' 'Tonight,' he says, 'there is no need for that. Just dance.'

'He's far too relaxed,' complains an impatient Number 2, staring at the patient as the man on the operating couch grunts. 'He may be there, but he's not here,' confirms Number 14 peering at her scanning machine. 'With this kind of resistance he'll burn up the drug in no time,' she predicts, telling her superior that they have not got long. 'Then you'd better do something about it,' demands Number 2. Pondering the elder's words, Number 14 paces the floor. 'The only way to manipulate his dreams is to get into them,' she states, toying with her stethoscope. The superior is intrigued. 'Is that possible?' 'I was wondering . . .' she begins. 'What?' '. . . If we can put words into her mouth?' 'How?' The assistant patrols the floor. 'We've fed him the pictures. Why can't we feed him with sound.' 'But the voice? Would he hear yours or hers?' questions the elder. 'That's the danger. If he hears *my* voice and recognises it, the shock would wake him, he'd see everything and we'll have failed.' 'We *must* make the most of this chance, or we'll never know if it was "B"',' insists Number 2. His assistant throws up her arms in exasperation. 'It's the worst time to try anything. Look at the state he's in,' she urges, pointing at the patient. 'Where's your scientific enthusiasm?' challenges the superior. Resigned to the fact that she has but one course left open to her, the assistant crosses to her console, connects a microphone handset to the machine and pauses, awaiting instructions. 'What shall I say?,' she asks the bespectacled man. 'Anything, try it. Go on!' Above them on the screen the couple are still dancing. 'Shall we have some more?' says Number 14, attempting to put words into the mouth of the man's dancing partner. 'Shall we have some more?' repeats the woman in the man's arms. 'More?' says he. 'Champagne,' whispers Number 14. 'Champagne,' echoes 'B'. Aware now that the audio link works, Number 2 urges his assistant to get to the point. 'You said we haven't long.' 'I wonder if they will kill me?' says 'B', repeating Number 14's words. 'I thought you didn't care,' replies her partner pausing in mid step. 'I do.' 'I'll help you. You know that,' confirms Number 6 as the woman returns to her seat at the table. 'They are here to kill me,' replies 'B' nervously. 'They want me to make a deal with you. They want to know why you resigned.' Her words, manipulated by the girl in the laboratory, appear to shock Number 6. 'Go on!' urges Number 2. 'If you'd just talk about it they'd let me off the hook,' says Number 14. 'If you'd just talk about it they'd let me off the hook,' repeats 'B'. 'Are you shocked?' 'I'm surprised,' hisses Number 6. 'I can't believe it's you.' 'I'm in such a mess. I need something to swap. Will you meet them? They're here now,' says 'B' nervously, her voice reaching a higher register. 'Are *you* asking this?' 'Don't hate me. We all make mistakes. Sometimes we have to,' pleads 'B', inserting the final nail into her coffin. The man has heard this before. 'Have you the feeling that you're being manipulated?' he asks calmly. 'Manipulated?' 'Who are you?' yells Number 6, lunging at the woman, his anger a shock to her senses. 'They're here . . .' she stammers. He turns to see a man dressed in an evening suit observing them from the trees. She implores him to tell them. 'If you don't, they'll kill me!' she exclaims. 'You're not who you pretend to be. Excuse me,' yells Number 6 striding away. The one watching them is joined by a second man. His exit blocked, the Prisoner engages them in a fight, attacking the tuxedo-attired thugs with venom. No match for his expertise, the men soon wind up at his feet. Staring at the woman at the table, Number 6 sees a third assailant holding the barrel of a gun at the girl's right temple. 'Tell him! He'll kill me!' she screams. 'I don't believe in you,' the Prisoner confirms. 'He'll kill me!' pleads 'B'. 'How long

Number 6 dispenses with one of A's thugs

has your husband been dead?' the man calls back. 'B' shakes her head, unable to comprehend the man's question. From his observation point, a concerned Number 2 hurriedly gives his assistant the reply. 'Four years,' states Number 14. 'Four years,' 'B' replies. 'How old is your son now?' This startles Number 2, who, leafing through the woman's file, is unable to come up with the right answer. Number 6 tries again. 'What is your son's name? That's an easier question.' The woman at the table pleads with him to help. 'Son? Husband yes. There's no son . . .' says a panicked Number 2. 'Help me please,' screams 'B'. 'Thought you couldn't answer,' mocks Number 6, turning on his heel and walking from the clearing. 'Come back, don't leave me, come back. I can explain everything. Please,' screams 'B' to the man's back. In the laboratory, a mortified Number 2 raises his arm to cast aside the woman's file but, seeing the large red telephone sitting on top of his console, he resignedly shrugs his shoulders.

Morning in the Village, and Number 6 slips from beneath the duvet on his bed. Easing himself to the edge of the divan, he blinks, a thought nagging his brain. Slipping up the sleeve of his pyjamas, he finds another puncture mark alongside the first one on his wrist. He ponders this, his mind recalling earlier events and the conversation he had with Number 14. Dressing swiftly, he races over the woman's residence, arriving there as the girl leaves. Hidden behind some foliage, he follows her from a safe distance and watches her enter a steel door set into the side of a rock face. Racing after her, he attempts to prise open the barrier but it refuses to open. Undeterred, he climbs up the rock face to search for another entry point. Meanwhile, in the laboratory below, Number 14 goes about her business unaware that the subject of her careful preparations, having discovered an air vent, is climbing down the laboratory's air duct. By the time that Number 14 has completed her task, Number 6 has edged his way down the chimney to floor level and is at that very moment watching the girl leave the operation room through a mesh-covered grill. As Number 14 vacates the corridor, the Prisoner kicks out the mesh and gently lowers himself into the deserted passageway, replacing the air vent cover behind him. The doors to the laboratory slide open to greet him and he enters the chamber where, hours before, he was the unwilling victim of Number 2's latest endeavour to break him – although, at this stage of course, Number 6 cannot know this. However, he soon realises what has been going on: the pictures of Engadine's party flashed onto the monitor screen giving him a clue to the doubts which have been nagging his brain. Finding the box files marked 'a', 'b', and 'c', he throws back their covers, noting the faces of boxes 'a' and 'b' – file 'c' containing nothing but papers. Carefully replacing them, he switches off the television monitor and prepares to leave. It is now that he sees the last remaining hypodermic, numbered '3'. He holds it to his wrist and makes the obvious deduction. Spotting a carafe of drinking water nearby, he removes the handkerchief from his breast pocket and siphons off two-thirds of the hypodermic's pinky-brown contents into the handkerchief's white absorbent cotton. Making up the deficiency by siphoning in an equivalent volume of the drinking water, he carefully replaces the syringe into its plastic container, returns the water carafe to its former position and swiftly departs from the chamber.

In the Green Dome, the mute Butler serves Number 2 his early-morning jug of milk. Dressed in pyjamas and silk dressing gown, his bespectacled superior is far from being his usual confident self. Worry lines etch his forehead and he is nursing a headache. 'I couldn't sleep,' he confides to the silent figure, the strain of the last few days obviously beginning to tell. Rising from his chair, he thumps down a button on the control console and crosses to gaze at the exterior scene of his giant television screen. 'What's that Number 6 doing?' he says aloud. 'He's always walking. Irritating man. Don't you ever get tired?' he shouts as the figure on the screen turns to the surveillance camera, performs a mock salute and bids the observer 'Be seeing you.' 'No! I'll be seeing *you*!', returns the man in the dressing gown. That evening, Number 6 exits from his bathroom to find the usual hot night-cap waiting for him in its cup and saucer. Forewarned this time, he calmly pours the contents of the cup into his kitchen sink. Selecting a clean glass from the sink unit's top, he turns on the tap, fills the glass to its brim and gulps down a mouthful. Nevertheless, the previous night's events are repeated. Crossing to his bedroom, he staggers, the glass slips from his grasp and he topples to the floor.

He is once again recumbent on the operating couch. Having administered the contents of her syringe marked '3', Number 14 raises the patient's wrist, confirms that his pulse-rate is normal and turns to Number 2 who is pacing the floor behind her. Confirming that they can go ahead, she flicks on her machine and the experiment enters its third stage. But something is wrong. The monitor screen lights up as usual, but the picture is distorted. 'What? . . . What's gone wrong?' demands a concerned Number 2 as the picture on the screen waves drunkenly before them. 'The strain's too much for him. I'm going to stop it,' yells the girl, racing to the patient's side. 'No!' shouts her superior, grabbing her arm. 'It's our last chance. It's now or never.' 'It's on your own head,' reminds Number 14. 'I'll worry about *them* later,' groans Number 2 staring at the on-screen events. Dressed immaculately in an evening suit, Number 6 walks behind a lovely brunette. 'Haven't they killed you yet?' he quips behind the girl's back. The girl turns, he fails to recognise her. 'Sorry, must have been thinking of someone else,' he apologises, rejoining the other guests. Spotting him out of the corner of her eye, Engadine walks towards him. 'It's so wild darling. It will end in tears,' she warns. 'All the best parties do,' he returns. 'Oh you're so . . .' Engadine's reply is lost in laughter as she rejoins her guests. '. . . Not terrible,' Number 6 calls back. 'It's dreamy. This is a DREAMY PARTY!' The guests turn. The man appears to have had one glass too many. Raising his fingertips to his temples, Number 6 cups his head in his hands. Staggering, he sways across the room towards an ornate mirror suspended on a wall. He stares. His reflection appears lopsided. He attempts to ease the glass back into its perpendicular position. The strain of doing so wrinkles his brow as, back in the laboratory, a concerned Number 14 tells her superior that they have to hurry. 'Get me 'C's picture.' Her colleague reaches behind him, snatching up the papers from the file denoted 'c'. 'There isn't one,' he confesses, picking up the typewritten pages. 'This is all we have on him.' He reads from the file. 'Known to be French. Known to have attended Engadine's parties, probably disguised. Known to have been in contact with Number 6.' The girl looks perplexed. 'How do you expect me to bring them together if there's no picture?' she asks. 'It's a process of elimination!' snaps the superior. '"C" is the only one left. He'll find him.' 'Well he'll have to hurry,' confirms Number 14. Miraculously, the picture behind them returns to normal. 'Champagne,' says Engadine to Number 6. 'We all need champagne.' She attracts the attention of a pretty blonde woman, wearing a low-cut evening gown. 'Watch him for me will you darling. He's the last man in the world.' 'I like sane men. Are you in business?' asks the girl approaching the man. 'I was.' 'You're too young to retire.' 'Age is relative,' he replies. 'Meaning you're *free*?' 'Possibly,' he ponders. '*I* know of something and the pay is very good.' 'I'm free!' he grins. Removing her left earring, she hands it to him with a smile. 'Number 6. I'm sure it's your lucky number.' Taking the earring to the roulette table, he lays the glittering bauble squarely on the square numbered 6. Closing the betting, the croupier spins the wheel. Giving the gambler a knowing smile, the blonde girl walks away. 'Six, noir!' announces the croupier, lifting the trinket and placing an overlarge key in its place. Tapping the key in time with the party music, Number 6 walks across the room. Unannounced, a hand stretches out before him – a hand holding an identical key. 'It can't be,' gasps an astonished Number 2. *She* can't be 'C'.' The hand belongs to Engadine. 'It takes you a long time to sell yourself darling,' smiles the hostess. 'It took a lot of thought,' the Prisoner replies. 'Come on,' grins the woman, waving the key before her and beckoning her guest to follow. 'She's fooled us for years. But not any longer!' hisses Number 2. 'We're bringing her to the Village?' asks Number 14, as the elder races to position himself before the monitor screen. 'Yes!' he snaps, staring at the woman on the screen.

Leaving the partygoers behind, Engadine escorts the man into the ground of her home. 'You are sure? No change of mind?' she probes. 'No change of mind,' he confirms. 'And no doubts?' 'Not any more.' 'It's a one-way journey. You have the fare?' 'Yes' he sighs, drawing a sheaf of papers from his pocket, 'these papers from London.' 'If you want to go back you can. Back to the party. Back to your life. But once through this door, you can never return,' the woman confirms. In reply, he proffers his key. She does the same and both are inserted into the heavy wooden door before them. 'This is what I've been waiting for,' whispers

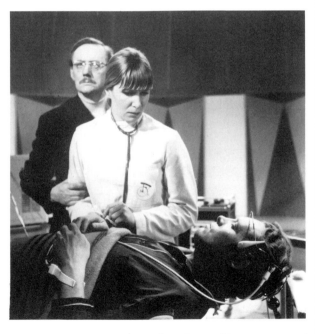

'No. It's our last chance. It's now or never'

Number 2, his face pressed to the wall screen, his index finger pointing towards Number 14, who is holding the patient's wrist as the figure on the operating couch stirs restlessly, his eyelids flickering as a concerned Number 14 strokes his perspiring brow. Suddenly, the picture starts to rotate, spinning faster and faster until, with a final grunt, the patient's head flops to one side and the television screen goes blank. 'It's gone dead. What's happened?' shouts an exasperated Number 2. 'He's collapsed!' exclaims the assistant. The patient is fed oxygen. 'That's it,' states Number 14 staring at the helpless Number 6. 'We've pushed him as far as we dare!' 'No! I must have the dream back, screams her superior over her shoulder. 'You know who 'C' is,' says Number 14, anxious to stop the experiment. 'Yes! But I still don't know what he was selling.' The girl turns. 'And if it kills him?' she warns. 'I shall have to take that risk, replies the superior biting his lip. 'I'll try a heart stimulent,' sighs Number 14, resigned to the fact that she must follow orders. The injection is given, and the tuxedo-suited man and Engadine reappear on the screen, she at the wheel of his open-topped sports car, motoring at speed down the Champs-Elysees. 'Where are you taking me?' asks the passenger. 'To the summit, to hand over your papers,' the driver replies, her hair flowing in the wind. 'Not to *you*?' 'Even *I* work for someone,' she confides with a grin. 'Someone else . . .?' hisses Number 2, unable to believe what he hears. 'Who?' asks the passenger. 'I've never seen him,' Engadine confesses. '*No one* has ever seen him.' 'I thought you'd boiled it down to three,' comments Number 14. 'I *had*,' confirms the superior, staring at the television screen, a smile of anticipation widening his lips. 'I didn't know about this one. It's great!' 'You'll have to call him "D"', concludes Number 14 her eyes twinkling at this unexpected departure from the script. The car draws up at a large country estate akin to a mediaeval castle, minus its moat. 'We're here,' says the driver, switching off the engine. 'Are we?' grins the passenger unable to believe his eyes. 'Oh yes he likes impressive offices,' smiles Engadine, nodding her head and wishing her passenger good luck. 'Aren't you coming?' he asks. 'I must go back. I can't leave the party for long, people will talk.' Number 6 climbs out of the car. 'How will I know him?' he turns to ask. '*He* will know you.' Crossing the courtyard as Engadine reverses away, the man approaches the huge wooden doors that bar his way. Unlocked, they glide open at the touch of his fingertips. Passing through, he receives a surprise. The doors lead not into a room but a dimly-lit cul-de-sac; the exterior of the building being but a facade. A voice greets him from the darkness. 'I am *glad* that you could come.' 'Where are you?' yells Number 6. 'It doesn't matter.' 'I want to see you!' the visitor affirms, staring around him. 'I've been dying to see you.' 'It won't make any *difference*.' 'People who *hide* are *afraid*!' exclaims the intruder, casting a glance over his shoulder, his own voice resounding from the darkness. In the distance, he hears the sound of a bell, not too dissimilar from that of the Village tower bell. As he makes his way forward, another figure appears at the end of the passage. In the laboratory, Number 2 leans forward in anticipation. Stopping within a few feet of his host – a man shrouded in black, his face concealed behind a black face mask – Number 6 acknowledges that he did not know that the other existed. 'It is often the case with really important people. Anonymity is always the best disguise,' mocks the stranger. 'You are afraid,' asserts Number 6, reaching into his pocket for the papers from London. 'This is very important to me.' he turns the papers over in his hand. 'It is only a commodity,' suggests the masked man. 'No! It's my future,' says the other. 'You belong to me now. You were told, there is no return.' Leaning forward, transfixed by the events unfolding before him, Number 2 stares avidly at the screen. 'Not until I know who *you* are. I've never liked *secrets*,' says the man with the papers defiantly. 'Nor have I!' exclaims Number 2, racing up the steps towards the television screen. 'I want to see him!' 'No one will ever see me,' the shrouded figure insists. '*I* will. I want to know who I'm selling out to. We must *all* know,' challenges Number 6. '*All*? Aren't you alone?' questions the faceless one. 'No . . . but *you* are,' confirms the other, replacing the papers in his inside jacket pocket. 'Violence will do you no good,' warns the hooded man, as the intruder steps forward. 'It relieves the feelings,' grins the antagonist, raising his hands to strip off the other's mask. It's wearer grabs the assailant's wrists. 'Does it matter?' he asks staring into the other man's face. 'It does to *them*. We mustn't disappoint them . . . the people who are *watching*.' The masked man's grip is broken and the hood is ripped from his face, the assailant turning the figure around so that only the back of his head is seen by the onlookers. Number 2 gasps as the man in the street studies the exposed face. 'I *knew* of course. Now show *them*!' shouts Number 6. Grabbing the man's shoulder, the assailant spins the unmasked man around to face the observers. Number 2 gasps, his head slumped back in amazement. Number 14 throws up her hands to stifle a scream. The revealed face is that of Number 2: the superior is staring at himself! 'You see,' shouts Number 6, as the limp Number 2 hobbles down the laboratory steps, his shoulders slumped, his knees sapped of strength. Behind him the man on the screen approaches the foreground. The heavy wooden doors swing closed in his face. Undeterred, he eases them open to bring into focus – the Village! He knew all the time. He was playing with you.' Number 14 confirms to her dejected superior. The man on the screen, dressed now in his Village blazer, has passed through the doors and entered the Village, turning as he does so to give the shrunken Number 2 a knowing smile. 'Your drug failed,' croaks a weary Number 2, his shoulders bowed in an admission of defeat. But the girl is not prepared to accept his accusation. 'No! *He* succeeded,' she chides. But Number 6 has not yet ended the game. As they watch, he is climbing the rock face and, carrying the papers from London, he enters the corridor outside the laboratory. Viewing the screen, the observers watch in amazement as the doors behind them slide open and Number 6 enters the laboratory.

But this cannot be taking place: Number 2 and 14 are now viewing *themselves* standing over a sleeping Number 6, who, on the television screen at least, has now entered the room – but he is not behind them! Are they going mad? As one they turn to look at the metal doors behind them: they are still closed. Returning their eyes to the screen, they stare in bemusement as Number 6 enters the laboratory to confirm to the man on the screen – the *other* Number 2 – that he owes him an apology. 'I forgot to give you this,' says Number 6, handing the superior the white envelope he carries with him. 'A bargain is a bargain.' 'Open it you fool open it!' exclaims Number 2 to his image. 'I must see what's in it!' The man on the screen does so, removing some papers from the envelope. They are travel brochures! 'He *was* going on holiday,' confirms Number 14. 'I wasn't selling out,' says Number 6 from the screen. 'That wasn't the reason I resigned.' Totally

dejected, an ashen-faced Number 2 stares at the screen as the man in the piped blazer reclines on the operation couch, his body twinned with that of the patient sleeping peacefully behind the onlookers. His 'dream' completed, the screen fades to black. One second later, the man reappears to act out his original resignation scene and the beaten Number 2 lowers his head in defeated silence as Number 14 removes the electrodes from the sleeping patient's head.

Preparing to leave, Number 2's attention is drawn to the ominous red telephone, its bleeping a portent of the horror in store. He rests his weary body against the control console behind him, his brain unable to blot out his failure – a failure that will cost him dear.

AUTHOR'S NOTE:

Originally known as *Play in Three Acts*, before final editing the episode became *1, 2 and 3* and finally *A, B and C*.

Actor Colin Gordon's first appearance as Number 2. He would reprise the part in *The General*.

THE GENERAL

Written by Joshua Adam

Guest stars

Number 2	**Colin Gordon**
Number 12	**John Castle**
Professor	**Peter Howell**

with

The Butler	**Angelo Muscat**
The Announcer	**Al Mancini**
Professor's Wife	**Betty McDowall**
Supervisor	**Peter Swanwick**
Doctor	**Conrad Phillips**
Man in Buggy	**Michael Miller**

and

Waiter	**Keith Pyott**
Man at Cafe and First	**Ian Fleming**
Top Hat	
Mechanic	**Norman Mitchell**
Projection Operator	**Peter Bourne**
1st Corridor Guard	**George Leech**
2nd Corridor Guard	**Jackie Cooper**

Directed by Peter Graham Scott

SEATED AT A table of the cafe, Number 6 watches a helicopter soar high over the Village. A young man is staring at him from a neighbouring table. Their eyes meet and the second man turns away as a proclamation is piped over the Village public address system. 'Attention. This is an announcement from the General's department. Will all students taking the Three Part History Course, please return to their dwellings immediately. The Professor will be lecturing in approximately 30 minutes. I will repeat that. This is an . . .'. The message is repeated, and the inmates sitting on either side of the Prisoner cease their conversations, rise as one and depart. Although he has no intention of leaving, Number 6's request for a second cup of coffee is refused by the elderly waiter who arrives with a tray to clear away the vacated tea and coffee cups. 'Sorry sir, we're closed. You did hear the announcement sir, about the Professor?' 'I'm not one of his students,' the Prisoner states. Sweeping the speaker's cup and saucer from the table, the waiter, adamant that the cafe will remain closed, asks the customer to settle his account. 'One coffee sir. Two credit units if you please.' The other hands him his credit card. 'You're never too old to learn sir,' reflects the waiter, handing the customer back his duly clipped credit slip. 'Who told you that? The Professor?' queries Number 6. 'No sir, the General.' 'The General?' probes the customer. 'Best of luck with your exams sir,' returns the old man, lifting his tray and leaving the solitary figure behind. The announcement drones on. Rising from his seat, Number 6 crosses to view a poster attached to the wall of an archway. It bears a photograph of a man he has never seen before and the message: 'Our Aim. One hundred per cent entry, one hundred per cent pass. Speed Learn, a 3-year course in 3 minutes. It can be done. Trust me.' Pondering its meaning, the Prisoner's thoughts are disturbed by a voice behind him. It is the young man who was staring at him a few minutes earlier.

'You don't believe it. A university degree in 3 minutes,' says the newcomer. 'It's improbable,' Number 6 replies. 'But not impossible?' 'Nothing's impossible in this place,' returns the other. 'You should enrol Number 6. You'll find the Professor most interesting.' 'Really?' 'He has an extraordinary range of knowledge,' adds the other. 'The only subject I'm interested in is getting away from this place,' comments Number 6. 'Exactly,' says the newcomer forcibly, gaining the other's attention. 'Who are you?' the man smiles. 'A cog in the machine.' 'And the General?' asks the Prisoner. Their conversation is interrupted by the helicopter flying low overhead and the sound of a siren as a buggy towing a trailer swoops down a nearby lane. People are racing across the broad expanse of the beach onto which the buggy now races at speed. 'Who are they after?' asks Number 6 turning back to the newcomer. 'The Professor I think,' says the other. 'Why?' 'You know Professors. Absent minded. Best of luck with your exams,' returns the other, making his exit. From the Control Room, the Supervisor sends out an Orange Alert. 'All units. All Posts. Orange Alert,' comes the message as, pursued by several villagers, a figure races across the beach. Following at a distance, the Prisoner treads on something buried in the sand and his attention is attracted by a voice coming from the sand beneath his feet. Kneeling, he uncovers a portable tape-recorder. Turning up its volume control, he listens to its urgent message: 'Ladies and gentlemen, fellow villagers, students . . . This is the Professor speaking, this is the Professor speaking. I have an urgent message for you . . .' Hearing the sound of approaching sirens, he climbs to his feet, walks several paces then, switching off the machine, he drops the tape machine in a short tuft of grass. A buggy races up to him, its shrill-sounding siren settling to a hum as he surreptitiously buries the tape-recorder with his foot. Leaping from the buggy, two men approach him. 'Are you a student?' asks the bearded one. 'Who isn't. Are you prefects?' jokes Number 6. 'What are you doing here?' the man wishes to know. 'Playing truant?' quips the one being questioned. In the distance, the crowd who have been pursuing the man across the beach finally overtake him and pounce on their quarry – the Professor. Stumbling to the sand he is manhandled back to the Village. The bearded thug meanwhile offers to give Number 6 a lift in his buggy. 'Where to?' 'Home. Hundred per cent entry. Hundred per cent pass,' boasts the man. 'You know what the General said.' 'Who's the General?,' the Prisoner interjects. 'C'mon,' says the other walking to his buggy. 'You don't want to start the term with a black mark.' 'Alright . . .' concedes Number 6, climbing into the vehicle, ' . . . let's go.'

Dropped at his cottage, the Prisoner enters to find his television set switched on. From it emits a torrent of propaganda proclaiming the significance of their friend the Professor's discovery. ' . . . a significance far beyond the confines of this community,' says the announcer on the screen. 'To quote the Professor's own words, Speed Learn is nothing less than a revolution in educational techniques . . .' Entering his kitchen, the announcer's words resounding in his ears, Number 6 helps himself to a glass of tomato juice from his refrigerator, before returning to his lounge and easing himself into a chair in front of the television set. ' . . . And now,' continues the announcer, 'someone who needs no introduction . . .' A short pause, and an attractive middle-aged woman appears on the screen. It is the Professor's wife who brings her husband's apologies for detaining the viewers for a few moments. As they know, the huge success of his course has placed an added strain upon her husband, who, even as she speaks, is completing his notes for the second lecture and should be with them shortly. Meanwhile, poor substitute though she is, she will bring them up to date on their programme. 'The extra Curricular Seminar for Post Graduate and Advanced students will be held next week . . .' At that moment, the announcer sitting next to her receives a telephone call. Offering his apology to the woman, he lifts the receiver then, having been given a message, he turns back to the Professor's wife and informs her that her husband is now ready to complete the lecture. 'We now take you over to the Professor in his study. Best of luck with the exams . . .' concludes the man on the screen. Panning to another room, the cameras turn their lenses onto the subject of the broadcast. Seated behind his desk, the Professor makes an apology for the delay and tells the viewers that he would like to say a brief word about his teaching method. Sipping his tomato juice, Number 6 settles back in his chair, his attention devoted to the Professor's words. 'Speed Learn . . .' begins the elderly man, '. . . is quite simply the most important, the most far-reaching, most beneficient development in mass education since the beginning of time. A marriage of science and mass communication which results in the abolition of years of tedious and wasteful schooling. A 3-year course indelibly impressed on the mind in 3 minutes. Impossible? That's what I said until I was introduced to the General. And then I realised that not only was it possible but that Education was ready for a giant leap forward from the dark Ages into the twentieth and twenty-first centuries. Ladies and Gentlemen, I have been a teacher for 30 years. Speed Learn has made me as obsolete as the Dodo. And we are going to prove it . . .!' A fanfare of trumpets reintroduces the television announcer who tells viewers that the subject of tonight's lecture is Europe since Napoleon. A hard, complicated 6 months study. 'Ladies and gentlemen, sit back and relax. Watch the screen. We are going to cover it in 15 seconds flat!' The television picture changes to black and white, and the Professor's face is projected onto the screen, the camera focussing on the man's intense stare, zooms in on the subject's left eye and enters the cornea, which appears to change to an intense blue dot, the centre of which burns with a piercing white orb. Accompanied by weird electronic music, the image expands and contracts, the blue-coloured spot pulsating in time with the accompaniment. Even the Prisoner cannot avert his gaze from the uncanny effect. His eyes focussed intently on the television screen, the glass he holds slips from his hand, its contents spilling onto the carpet. Fifteen seconds later, a fanfare of trumpets brings the Speed Learn course to an end. Blinking his eyes in bemusement, Number 6 shakes his head and kneels to mop up the tomato juice from the carpet. '. . . 15 seconds flat,' proclaims the televison announcer, advising those students who want supplementary information to address their queries to 'The General, Speed Learn, the Town Hall.'

'Mopping up operations Number 6?' says a voice behind him, as the Prisoner places his empty glass on a table beside him. The speaker is Number 2, who, entering with a man carrying a Geiger counter, shows little concern when the man crosses to the occupant and scans the Prisoner's body with the device. 'Have you lost something?' quips the tenant. 'Not me, the Professor,' returns the superior with a grin. 'Oh.' 'I believe you took a stroll on the beach?' 'What beach?' queries Number 6

sarcastically, as he mounts the steps leading to his kitchen. 'Poor old Professor,' says the Number 2 ignoring the man's insolence, and following the tenant up the steps, 'losing his recorder with all his notes in it. *You* didn't see it of course?' 'Would it be something about that big?' enquires Number 6, indicating a size with his hands. 'The Professor is rather worried about it,' snaps Number 2, dismissing the tenant's attempts to goad him. 'Why doesn't your man look in the wardrobe,' proposes the Prisoner as the man with the Geiger counter runs his locating device around the walls of the cottage. At a nod from the superior the man does so, sliding back the doors of the unit to reveal nothing but the tenant's clothing. 'Very amusing,' growls

Number 2. 'Tell me. Are you as keen as ever to leave us . . .?' 'Any more questions?' replies Number 6, tiring of the intrusion. '. . . I was thinking that a compromise could be arranged – in exchange for the recorder,' tries the superior, his face a mask of determination. 'I wonder who has it?' mocks the Prisoner with a grin. The superior and the man with the locating device turn to leave. 'Enjoy the lecture?' asks Number 2, turning back to his inhospitable host. 'What lecture?' asks the tenant. 'It's a great experiment

Number 6. You can learn a lot,' sneers the superior. 'History is not my subject.' 'Isn't it? When was the treaty of Adrianople?' Without thinking. Number 6 gives the correct answer. 'September 1829.' What happened in 1830?' asks Number 2. 'Greek independence was assured and guaranteed.' 'By whom?' barks the superior. 'Russia. France and Britain.' 'Who was Bismark's ally against the Danish Prince Christian of Glucksburg?' Suddenly. Number 6 finds himself giving all the right answers to the questions fired at him by Number 2 – questions that yesterday, *before* the Speed Learn telecast. he would have been hard-pressed. if not totally unable to answer! 'Very good,' grins the superior. '10 out of 10. Don't

'Tell me. Are you as keen as ever to leave us?'

underestimate yourself Number 6 . . .' he grins as he turns to leave '. . . and don't underestimate *me*!' Satisfied that he gained the upper hand. the superior leaves. Shocked and bewildered by his knowledgeable performance. Number 6 races over to his telephone. 'Can I help you?' asks the operator. 'When was the Treaty of Adrianople? What happened in 1830 . . .?' asks the bemused caller. laying down the receiver as the voice rattles off the replies that he himself had barely seconds earlier recited to

Number 2. 'Curfew time . . . 15 minutes.' calls a voice from the loudspeaker across the room. 'Curfew time 15 minutes.' Pacing backwards and forwards, deep in thought. Number 6 halts in mid-step. Staring at his front door. he departs in haste into the blackness beyond. Back on the beach. he searches in vain for the Professor's tape machine. Hearing the sound of a twig being snapped underfoot behind him. he rises and with a sudden movement. pulls the man he met earlier from behind a bush. 'Anything I can do for you?' he growls. his hands clasped firmly on the man's collar. 'You want to get out of this don't you?' asks the other. 'So?' whispers the Prisoner through clenched teeth. The other is about to reach into his jacket pocket. but Number 6 grabs his wrist. Easing the missing tape recorder from his pocket. the intruder raises it to his assailant's face. 'Here's your passport. Number 2 offered you a deal didn't he? Don't you trust him?' asks the man. handing the tape machine to the Prisoner. 'People don't trust Number 2 . . . I don't trust you and I don't trust your tame Professor.' hisses Number 6. 'Who do you trust Number 6?' asks the man we now learn is Number 12. 'I trust *me*!' 'Join the club,' grins Number 12. turning to leave. He stops a few feet away. 'Oh. what was the Treaty of Adrianople?' 'September 1829,' snaps Number 6 without thinking. 'Wrong,' says Number 12. 'I said *what*, not when. You need some special coaching.' Satisfield with the outcome. the man leaves the bemused Number 6 staring at the tape recorder which. flicked into motion by its holder's finger. sounds out the warning: 'This is the Professor speaking. I have an urgent message for you. You are being tricked. Speed Learn is an abomination. It is slavery. If you wish to be free. there is only one way. Destroy the General. Learn this and learn it well. The General must be DESTROYED.'

It is morning. In the Green Dome. the mute manservant wheels in Number 2's breakfast trolley and finds his superior talking to Number 1 on the telephone. Handing Number 2 a glass of milk. the Butler wheels away the trolley as the bespectacled man assures his superior that everything is going well. 'I assure you there is no problem sir. We're getting a 100 per cent co-operation from everyone. I'm anticipating a truly exciting result . . . who sir? Oh the Professor . . . just a mild aberration. I assure you. A couple of days rest and adjustment and he'll be doing everything we need . . . yes yes I will keep in touch sir. closest touch . . . thank you sir.' Laying down the receiver. he mutters under his breath. 'Probably the most important human experiment we've ever had to conduct and it's treated like a military exercise.' At that moment. Number 12 enters the chamber through the sliding steel doors. 'Anything on the Professor yet?' asks Number 2. 'He is responding sir. The doctor will be in to see you personally.' 'Get over there and tell them to hurry things up,' snaps the superior. The man makes to leave. 'No,' calls Number 2 changing his mind. 'No I'll do it myself.' he calls. sipping milk from his glass. 'Yes sir,' replies Number 12. turning back to face the superior. 'Frankly sir. I think we're going the wrong way about it with him.' He begins to descend the ramp. his hands clasped firmly behind his back. his tongue flicking over his dry lips. Number 2 stares at the newcomer. 'You mean about the Professor?' 'We indulge his idiocies far too much. He's a crank and should be treated as such.' Number 2 can scarcely believe the man's nerve. 'You think so.' he purrs. 'I know he's the corner stone of Speed Learn sir but . . .' the younger man begins. 'Yes?' quips the superior inclining his head. '. . . I can't help feeling he's a trouble maker.

And he attracts trouble-makers.' 'How long have you been with us Number 12?' asks the bespectacled man, his tone placing the other on guard. 'Me sir? Quite a long time sir,' the junior confirms. 'But obviously not long enough!' snaps Number 2, indicating that juniors should be seen and not heard. 'Yes sir. Sorry sir,' whispers the other lowering his eyes. 'Number 12,' calls the superior as the junior turns to leave. 'Your opinions about the Professor should be carefully guarded.' Duly reprimanded, Number 12 makes a hasty retreat.

Entering the master Control Room at a brisk pace, Number 2 calls upon the Supervisor to put up Section 32, sound and vision. At the assistant's command, the Village cameras focus on the Professor's study, where the subject being viewed is busily typing at his desk. A doctor and a nurse enter without warning and, despite the typist's protestations, the Professor is lifted bodily from his chair and taken away for some mild therapy treatment after which, he is told, he will be able to work twice as fast. The doctor, however, remains in the study and removes the sheet of paper from the man's typewriter. Together with further papers taken off the Professor's desk, these are placed into a machine and are instantly converted into a long strip of negative film. 'Track the Professor?' asks the Supervisor. 'No, the Seminar,' orders Number 2. The scene on the monitor screen changes to an exterior view of the grounds outside the Old People's Home. Numerous villagers are seated in rows, each busily sketching away on their drawing boards. In the foreground sits Number 6, his pencil putting the finishing touches to a sketch he has drawn of a woman's head. 'It's Number 6!' exclaims the supervisor in astonishment. 'Really. How very odd,' states Number 2 peering at the monitor screen, as the subject of his attention raises his hand to attract the attention of a middle-aged woman. It is the Professor's wife. 'Can I help you?' she asks, crossing towards to the Prisoner's chair. 'I don't know. Can you?' he asks. 'Finding things a bit strange?' she says, reclining her head. 'That is the trouble. I can't find anything at all,' quips the man in the piped blazer. 'Well what exactly are you looking for?' 'What are we *all* looking for?' he challenges. 'Well, let's see,' replies the woman turning to a solitary figure sitting alone on the veranda tearing pages from a book. 'What do you think he's doing?' 'Tearing up a book!' exclaims Number 6 twisting his pencil in his fingers. 'He's creating a fresh concept,' says the woman. 'Construction arises out of the ashes of destruction.' She turns, indicating a woman standing on her head. 'She's developing a new perspective.' 'Really!' grins the Prisoner, indicating a man dozing nearby. 'And him?' 'He's asleep. One learns only when the mind wants to. Not at set times.' 'Is that what your husband believes?' he probes. 'It's self-evident, surely? What's your subject?' 'What's *yours*?' he retaliates. 'Mine? Modern art.' 'Really,' he replies, tearing the sketch he has been working on from his pad and handing it to the woman with a flourish. 'What do you think of this?' He has pictured her in a military uniform. The woman is not pleased. 'Not altogether flattering. So art's your subject too?' Informing her that he has a preference for military history, *Generals* and that kind of thing, the woman replies that he is wasting his time. 'What a pity,' he says, telling her that he understood that her husband was quite an authority on the subject. 'He may be,' snaps the woman, tearing the sketch in half, 'But I'm not!' 'Creation out of destruction?' he taunts. Giving him an icy stare, the woman rejoins the seminar. Rising from his chair, he flings his torn sketch onto his chair and strolls into the garden.

'Number 6 out of vision,' calls a Control Room operator. 'Scan,' orders Number 2. By now, the Prisoner has made his way to the Professor's house and gained entrance to the man's unlit study. Switching on the lights, he finds the room filled with sculptures of people's heads, each sitting on top of a pedestal, each covered with a white sheet. Venturing to the window, he peers out onto the veranda and observes nothing except two of the artists innocently going about their seminar lesson. Unseen by the man, the Professor's wife has entered the room and is standing behind him. 'This is a private room,' she calls, attracting the attention of the man at the window. 'Interesting view,' he throws back. 'Who are you? A spy?' 'How long have you been in this place?' he asks, staring around the room. Stating that she does not have to answer his questions, the woman asks him to leave. Pacing the floor, he points out that the house is most elegant. 'Books, paintings and a very beautiful garden.' 'The Professor and I have certain privileges,' she retaliates, snatching from him a book he has picked up from the desk. 'As prisoners? Or as warders?' Pointing out that they came here voluntarily, have everything they need and are perfectly happy, the woman loses her temper when, uncovering one of the sculptures, he intimates that as her husband is the teacher, she must be the artist. 'For the last time,' she demands, 'I'm asking you to leave.' 'Subjects from life?' he queries, uncovering further clay busts and ignoring her request. '*Rough* exercises,' she snaps. 'Very good,' he acknowledges, snatching the sheet from each sculpture in turn. 'You really have a considerable talent.' 'What are you looking for?' 'I would have thought that with all these privileges we might find at least one study of er . . .' He stops in front of another bust. Ripping off its cover, he stares at a bust of – himself. '. . . the General!' His lips widen to a grin. Turning swiftly, he tears away the cover of the next bust to reveal . . . 'It's really not a bad likeness, is it?' confirms Number 2, as he arrives in the room and stares at the bust of himself. 'Are you playing truant?' 'Doing a little homework,' quips Number 6. 'I didn't ask him here. I found him . . .' begins the woman nervously. 'You don't have to explain, my dear. Number 6 and I are old friends,' the superior interjects allaying the woman's fears. 'I can recommend him as a thoroughly zealous student . . . with a tendency to overdo it.' 'How's the Professor? Cooperating?' asks Number 6, selecting a heavy walking stick from the umbrella stand before him, and noticing for the first time a white-coated doctor and nurse in the adjoining room. 'I've given him some sedation,' confirms the Doctor, through the open door. 'Has *he* been overdoing it too?' quips Number 6, rejoining the Number 2 and the woman. 'Probably a bit excited,' the superior tells the Professor's wife. 'You know your husband my dear. This Speed Learn. He's as enthusiastic as a child.' 'And now he's sleeping like a babe,' the Prisoner whispers. 'He's not to be disturbed,' confirms the doctor. 'I wouldn't dream of it,' mocks Number 6, who, followed by the woman, slips past the doctor into the adjacent room where the Professor, supposedly ill, lies in his bed. 'Get out,' cries the woman as Number 6 raises his walking stick over the sleeping man's head. 'Stop him!' she calls to the doctor. Too late. With a determined stroke, the Prisoner brings his club crashing down on the head of the figure before him. The woman screams. The 'face' of the recumbent figure shatters as an eggshell. It is only a carefully-modelled clay bust. 'You should take better care of him Ma'am . . . he gone to pieces,' quips Number 6, handing the woman a fragment of her husband's 'head'.

'You are an odd fellow . . .' sighs Number 2 as the Prisoner struts past him. '. . . You have the wrong end of the stick.' 'I haven't.' grins Number 6. throwing the weapon of destruction into the doctor's arms, 'the doctor has.' 'Just a minute . . .' snaps Number 2, pacing after the man. '. . . the offer I made to you about the Professor's notes. It's cancelled!' 'Is it?' mocks Number 6. 'He's changed his mind. He doesn't need them now.' confirms the sarcastic superior. 'That's extraordinary, neither do I.' teases the Prisoner. Taking the tape recorder from his pocket, he throws it to Number 2. 'Best of luck with your exams. Why don't you open the blinds and let in some daylight . . . You've got nothing to hide – have you.' he mocks. spinning on his heel and leaving the room. 'I'd better warn control.' says the doctor joining Number 2. 'Don't warn *anyone*.' the superior snaps back. 'But he'll . . .' *You* do your job, *I'll* do mine.' growls Number 2 then, crossing to the Professor's wife he remarks that the man has made quite a mess of her masterpiece. 'What does he want?' she asks. as the superior takes the fragment of clay from her hand. 'What some of us want, ultimately . . . to escape.' replies Number 2. 'He persists about the General.' she says. 'I shouldn't worry too much about him my dear. I have an obsession about him myself.' confirms Number 2 staring intently at the clay bust of the man who has left.

The streets of the Village are thronged with people in festive mood. their costumes appropriate to their attendance at the Mardi Gras. Radio and television reporters weave their way through the jostling crowd seeking interviews from the excited villagers as they fall over themselves to proclaim the joys of Speed Learn. Watched by a solemn Number 12, the television announcer walks over to Number 6 and plies him with questions about historical events. Without realising that he is doing so, the Prisoner rattles out the correct answers. 'Well done. Coming along nicely Number 6.' congratulates the television man. 'Yes.' replies Number 6. Viewing this, a saddened Number 12 walks away from the festivities. as does the Prisoner. He returns to his cottage to find the place in darkness and flicks on the lights. Seconds after he has done so, the room is plunged into darkness again and his telephone purrs into life. 'Please stay where you are Number 6. Do not move. The fault on the electrical circuit will be attended to forthwith. Electrics and Adminis-tration are on their way. You will find a candle for such an emergency in the upper kitchen cabinet second right . . .' Within a mili-second, a mechanic arrives, followed by Number 12. who. claiming to be from administration. shines his torch into the room and asks what has gone wrong. 'This sir.' calls the mechanic gazing beneath a lampshade. 'A deliberate short circuit across the contacts.' 'Sabotage. That's punishable.' says Number 12 entering the room. Having informed the administrator that they will require a replacement. the mechanic goes outside to his buggy to contact control and asks them to switch on the temporary reserve. Left alone in the dark interior, its resident asks the other if the power failure is his doing. 'Some. Listen carefully.' whispers Number 12. 'We have about 15 seconds. The Professor's real lecture . . . the one you heard on the tape recorder . . . Would you like it to go out?' 'I might.' returns the Prisoner cautiously.. The other hands him a pen-like device. 'Take it. In the ink cylinder. Micro. Be careful.' 'How?' asks Number 6. 'With these.' bids the other. handing him two circular white plastic chips. 'Passes.' 'When?' asks the Prisoner. twisting the chips in his fingers. 'Tomorrow.' 'Where?' Suddenly the room is bathed in brightness as the lights are switched

'I'll fix it. I'll fix it Number 6 . . .'

back on and the mechanic returns. 'I'll fix it.' states Number 12 resuming his authoritative tone. 'I'll fix it Number 6. so that you become aware that deliberate destruction of official property is a most serious offence. I must recommend the full penalty.' 'Which is?' enquires the Prisoner. stroking the pen he has been handed with his index finger. 'It could be imprisonment. It could be a fine.' snaps Number 12 as the mechanic leaves the cottage. 'I'll take the fine.' quips the man being being chastised. 'Yes. I thought you might. Report to my office in Administration tomorrow morning.' barks Number 12. aware now that the surveillance cameras are now recording their every word and movement. 'Yes . . . sir.' says Number 6.

The doctor lifts the Professor's eyelid. Sedated, the Speed Learn teacher lies in his bed. a nurse and his wife looking on. 'How is he, doctor?' asks the latter. 'Fine. Beautiful response.' replies the doctor. 'Will he be able to complete the lecture?' 'Able . . . and willing.' the doctor confirms. entering the patient's pulse rate on a medical chart.

A buggy races through the Village and two men dressed in black, each wearing a top hat. enter the Council Room. 'Your business please?' asks a voice from a red-coloured monitor box installed immediately inside the steel entrance door. 'Board member. Lecture approval session. Education.' answers the first man. staring at the device through his dark sunglasses. 'Proceed to pass . . . pass.' confirms the voice. Delving deep into his pocket, the man produces a special pass chip. identical to the ones given to the Prisoner by Number 12. When placed into a slot on the machine. an elongated finger emerges from the monitor, snatches the chip and the man and his colleague are allowed to enter the Council Chamber ante room where, waiting to greet them, is a similarly attired Number 2. 'You have them?' seeks the superior. Handing the briefcase he is carrying to Number 2, the newcomer confirms that he has and they have been processed. 'Excellent.' grins Number 2 handing another man a sheaf of papers. 'Summon the Board.' Taking receipt of the second man's briefcase. the superior removes its contents and lays them on the unit before him. Carefully sliding an inner sleeve from what appears to be a cigar case. he gently eases a long metal rod from the inner container. 'Micro reduction report satisfactory?' he queries, holding the object before his eyes. 'Oh first class sir,' confirms the first top-hatted man. 'Good,' grins Number 2 placing his fingertip on a button positioned on the unit's top. 'Number 2 calling the General's office. The lectures have arrived. Full security alert.' 'Everything all right sir?' enquires the first top-hatted man, clutching the top of the unit. 'I don't know about the General, but I think I can say in advance that the experiment is going to be a 100 per cent . . .' returns Number 2, removing a second object, a glass circuit tube from the sleeve, '. . . success.' In the corridor outside, several other top-hatted board members arrive and follow the routine set by top hat one earlier, each acknowledging their business before being allowed to pass into the ante-room. Among them is Number 6, his identity masked by the long black dress coat, his eyes unseen behind his dark glasses. Inside, Number 2 carries the lecture devices past two uniformed guards. 'Number 2, for Sublimator,'. he snaps, entering a room denoted 'Projection Room.' Having handed the objects to the projection operator, the superior answers the junior's question whether the material has been cleared by the board. He tells the operator to prepare to transmit; clearance to do so will be forthcoming. Racing hurriedly down a corridor and placing a white-coloured chip into a second monitor box, the superior proceeds as directed, to the board room – unknowingly passing Number 6 who stands in the corridor, his face hidden behind a copy of the *Tally Ho* newspaper. '90 seconds to session time,' announces a voice over the corridor's loud speaker. Having watched Number 2 depart, the Prisoner places the paper he had been reading into his briefcase, and throws the document case in the direction of the control console on the wall. An electronic force field flips it back at him and he is forced to resort to following the departed Number 2's routine of placing his white pass chip into the monitor's mouth. After a few seconds of indecision, the monitor allows him to pass into a long corridor. As he cautiously walks along the corridor in the board room proper, Number 12 is addressing the education ministers. In return for their confidence in the General, he proposes to give them a breakdown of the entire operation – in confidence of course. Rising to his feet as the gathering applauds him, Number 12 opens his account. 'Speed Learn is the outcome of the general's prolific knowledge. Its basis is the students confidence in the tried and trusted Professor, and the Professor's confidence in Science . . .' Outside in the corridor, Number 6 weaves towards his objective, but finds the corridor patrolled by two guards. Snapping his fingers, he attracts one of the uniformed men's attention and within a second the man lies unconscious at his feet, his senses reeling from the knockout punch to his chin. Dragging the man into a room, Number 6 treats the second guard to the same fate. Then, having stretched the man out alongside his companion, he cautiously walks down the corridor and enters the projection room. It is five minutes to projection time when Number 6 dispenses with the projectionist and reports that the projection room is clear. He ignores the trickle of blood that runs down his wrist from a wound he received when the projectionist stabbed him during their fight. In the Board Room, Number 12 is ending his report as Number 6 removes the thin metal rod from the Sublimitor transmitter and replaces it with an identical one secreted in the pen handed to him by the man who is addressing the assembly. '. . . Thus the miniaturised course can be projected through the Sublimator at a speed

thousands of times faster than the eye can record,' continues Number 12. 'It is imposed directly onto the cortex of the brain and is, with occasional boosts, virtually indelible. Tonight's lecture for instance . . .' His words are cut short by an interruption from Number 2, who says to the board that so much is theory, now for the practice. At the push of a button from Number 12, a wall screen in front of the assembly flickers into life and the men are given a visual rundown of the various departments that will be involved in the lesson. 'Final clearance please,' says a voice over the public address system. 'Sound studio. General's studio, Lecture studio . . . Cameras? Projection . . .?' However, when the surveillance camera zooms in on the man in the projection room, Number 2 spots the trickle of blood running down the man's hand and, recognising Number 6, a confused Number 2 has the projectionist replaced – unkindly – by having Number 6 clubbed on the head. The transmission begins as scheduled, and once again the Speed Learn process is broadcast throughout the Village, ending with the television announcer wishing its unknowing participants 'sweet dreams'.

'Projection! Will you clear please'

Seated in the centre of the circular row of boardroom tables, his head slumped onto his chest, Number 6 is being interrogated by Number 12. 'Who were they Number 6? Who let you in? What are their names? There's an organisation, isn't there? Dissidents. Who is the head man?' 'Santa Claus,' the Prisoner fires back. 'Who's the head of the organisation? You'd be wise to tell us,' replies Number 12. '*He* won't tell you anything. He's a trained conspirator . . . a very hard man!' pipes up Number 2 from his chair directly in front of the man being interrogated. 'This reactionary drivel that you were on the point of sending out to our conscientious students,' he continues, picking up a report from the table, 'The freedom to learn. The liberty to make mistakes . . . old fashioned slogans. You are an odd fellow Number 6. Full of surprises.' As he speaks, he receives a telephone call. It is the Professor's wife, wishing to know if the lecture was a success. Indeed it was. Number 2 is delighted. Can she see her husband? 'Of course. As soon as he has completed the first phase of the next instalment. He's performing so well, it seems a pity to disturb him now,' confirms the superior. 'How long? Oh who can tell?' But not too long my dear . . . he needs you.' 'You'll let me know?' asks the woman. 'Naturally,' replies Number 2, replacing the receiver. 'Lovely woman,' he confirms to Numbers 6 and 12. 'Warm. Sympathetic . . . she'd talk him into anything, to keep him alive.' 'The Professor?' whispers Number 6. 'Indeed. Such is the course of true love.' grins back Number 2. 'Do you need him?' 'They're both necessary. The one for the other. Even essential,' states the superior. springing to his feet. 'Now! To the matter in hand. I'm sure that a man of your calibre will appreciate that rebels must be kept under the closest possible surveillance with a view to their extinction if the rebellion is absolute.' 'The professor?' 'No, no, not the Professor. He's no problem. He has an adoring wife and an even more attentive doctor. No no, he's a lovely fellow. People love him. They'll take anything from him. It is the image you see, that is important. The kindly image.' confirms Number 2, raising a telephone to his ear and placing a call to the General's office. Staring at Number 12, the superior tells him that though they will not get an answer from Number 6, the General will know – he can answer anything . . . given the basic facts. A knowing glance passes between numbers 6 and 12, each considering their respective fates. 'Yes,' says Number 2, into the receiver's mouthpiece. 'Yes, it all went splendidly. Delighted, absolutely delighted. Er, just a slight problem for you. Mind if we come round? Thank you, right away.' Donning his top hat, he confirms that the General awaits them: they will soon know what's what? Escorted by Numbers 2, 12 and two guards, the Prisoner finds himself frogmarched without ceremony, through a maze of corridors to the General's office. Inside, the Professor sits unmoved at his desk, his fingers caressing the keys of his typewriter. 'Plato, Aristotle, Voltaire, Rousseau . . . and the rest, they're all here.' states Number 2, indicating the well-stocked book shelves immediately behind the typist. 'All available to the General. There is no question, no question from advanced mathematics to molecular structure, from philosophy to crop-spraying that the General cannot answer.' Behind him, the Professor rises from his chair and inserts the paper he has been working on into the jaws of a machine. In an instant this is converted to a strip of celluloid microfilm, which slides from beneath the roller of a complex printing module. 'This is how it works,' whispers Number 2, 'allow me to introduce you to the General.' A curtain behind the Professor slides back to reveal a long ante-room: the General, a huge computer with flashing lights and revolving tape spools, spanning the wall to wall division at the top of an approach ramp. 'All the Professor's own work.' boasts Number 2, joining the machine's creator. 'He gave birth to it and loves it with a passionate love . . . but probably hates it even more.' At a nod from Number 2, the Professor carries the strip of microfilm up the ramp and hands it to a blonde female assistant who is attending the machine. Number 2 meanwhile, continues his description. 'That mass of circuits, my dear fellow, is as revolutionary as nuclear fission. No more wastage in schools. No more tedious learning by rote . . . A brilliantly devised course, delivered by a leading teacher, subliminally learned and checked and corrected by an infallible authority . . . and what have we got?' 'A row of *cabbages*.' mocks Number 6, moving forward to seek a better view of the General. 'Indeed,' nods Number 2, '*knowledgeable* cabbages.' 'What sort of knowledge?' 'For the time being past history will have to do. But shortly we shall be making our own,' boasts the superior. 'Napoleon could have used it.' mocks Number 6. Ignoring the remark, Number 2 calls to the Professor and asks him to take down a problem for the General, an illustration of its infallibility. Inserting a fresh piece of paper into his typewriter, the teacher awaits the superior's

command. 'Point one: a traitor in the Village,' begins Number 2. 'Point two: Security pass discs were issued to Number 6. Point three: Access to these is through . . .' He crosses over to stare at Number 12. '. . . through where?' 'Administration sir.' falters the accused. 'Exactly!' exclaims Number 2, turning back to the typist. 'Put that down. Also that Number 12 is an official in Administration. *Now* ask the General . . .!' '. . . A question that can't be answered,' interjects Number 6. 'What's that?' retorts the superior. 'There is a question that the General *cannot* answer.' the Prisoner insists. 'Impossible!' exclaims Number 2. 'Allow me to ask it.' 'No!' 'Are you afraid.' challenges the other. A pause. Then the superior gives his consent. 'Excuse me Professor,' says Number 6, crossing to the desk. Replacing the paper the teacher was working on with a blank sheet, the Prisoner types out four letters. Leaning forward in an attempt to read what the other has typed. Number 2's attempt to do so is thwarted as, with a flourish, Number 6 slides the paper from beneath the machine's platen. Then, asking the Professor's permission to proceed, he inserts the paper into the micro-processing printer. Handed the duly received microfilm, Number 2 gives it to the Professor and tells him to place it into the computer. Having done so, the teacher turns several knobs and adjusts the computer's memory circuits. To the consternation of both the Professor and Number 2, the machine goes into overload: the needle on its safety dial hovering dangerously close to the red danger level. Smoke issues from the General's ventilation grids and the Professor himself is soon enshrouded in dense smoke as the computer short circuits and blows a fuse. 'Switch it off . . .!' screams Number 2. '. . . Switch it off!' Racing up the ramp to detach the Professor from the machine, Number 2 falters in his tracks as Number 12 overtakes him and drags the Professor free from the General's hold: both men screaming as, electrocuted, they fall helplessly back down the ramp. Having successfully beaten off his two guards, Number 6 calmly joins Number 2 on the ramp as the latter, removing the burn-out strip of microfilm from the molten wreckage that was once the General, turns to ask. 'What was your question?' 'It's insoluble . . . for man or machine.' returns the Prisoner. 'What was it?' demands Number 2, his face a mask of defeat. 'W.H.Y. Question mark.' 'Why?' sighs the superior. 'Why.' gloats Number 6 'Why?' returns the other, through trembling lips. 'Why?' shrugs the Prisoner, staring at the blackened and scorched remains of the microfilm the superior holds in his hands.

AUTHOR'S NOTE:

The second episode to feature Colin Gordon as the milk drinking (but hard-as-nails) Number 2.

Joshua Adam is the pen-name of Lewis Greifer.

This episode contains the first view of the metal corridors which lie beneath the Village.

The basic interior set that was used as Number 2's Green Dome 'office', also doubled as the Council Chamber, the Control Room, the Labour Exchange and the laboratory in *A. B. and C.*

HAMMER INTO ANVIL

Written by Roger Woddis

Guest star

Number 2	**Patrick Cargill**

with

Band Master	**Victor Maddern**
Number 14	**Basil Hoskins**
Psychiatric Director	**Norman Scace**
New Supervisor	**Derek Aylward**

and

The Butler	**Angelo Muscat**
Number 73	**Hilary Dwyer**
Control Room Operator	**Arthur Gross**
Supervisor	**Peter Swanwick**
Shop Assistant	**Victor Woolf**
Laboratory Technician	**Michael Segal**
Shop Kiosk Girl	**Margo Andrew**
Female Code Expert	**Susan Sheers**
1st Guardian	**Jackie Cooper**
2nd Guardian	**Fred Haggerty**
3rd Guardian	**Eddie Powell**
4th Guardian	**George Leach**

Directed by Pat Jackson

W HY DID you slash your wrists, 73?' The attractive girl in the hospital bed attempts to hide her bandaged wrists beneath the sheets that cover her shapely figure. 'Aren't you happy here?' The girl rocks her head from side to side. 'You're not being very cooperative my dear.' 'There's nothing I can tell you,' she replies, choking back a tear. 'Come now,' the voice continues, 'you must know where your husband is.' 'He's still over there,' sighs the girl. 'Where?' 'Oh somewhere there. He had some work to finish.' 'Was he devoted to you?' He *is* devoted to me,' challenges the patient, her face showing signs of nervousness as the interrogator walks into view. It is the new Number 2. 'Oh, so you don't mind about him and the woman Maryka?' 'That's a lie!' exclaims the girl, shuffling her body beneath the sheets. 'Stop protecting your husband's memory, 73. He went to her hotel several times ... then there was the villa, of course ...' the patient clenches her teeth, her eyes welling forth tears as the man unzips an inner pocket of his blazer. Removing a photograph, he sighs. ' ... Let me show you just how loyal your dear husband is to you ...' he sneers looking at the photograph. ' ... They look quite at home – together. Would you like to know the date, place ... look.' He lays the picture on the bed, the evidence a challenge to the girl's resolve as she refuses to look at the photograph. 'I've wasted enough time,' insists Number 2, thumping down the girl's file in threatening manner. He turns to approach the patient's bed. Walking through the grounds of the hospital and hearing the girl's hysterical screams coming through an open window, Number 6 races into the building and bursts into the girl's room at the very second that the screaming patient breaks free of her captors and throws herself through the window. Ignoring Number 2 and his companions, the Prisoner crosses to the window and gazes down at the girl's broken body several stories below, her red dressing gown resembling a dried spot of blood on blotting paper. 'You shouldn't have interfered Number 6. You'll pay for this,' threatens Number 2. 'No ... *you* will,' returns the Prisoner earnestly.

Back in his cottage, Number 6 receives a telephone call. It is Number 2, who wants him at the Green Dome immediately. 'We've got nothing to talk about,' replies the Prisoner, slamming down his receiver. But like it or not, Number 6 will obey the superior's instructions. Taking his daily stroll through the Village, his activity is terminated by force when three thugs appear before him to force home Number 2's request. Although he gives a good account of himself, the odds prove too strong and the Prisoner is carried, struggling, to a buggy. Seconds later he is dumped before Number 2. 'You defied my instructions to come here. We have things to discuss.'

'You defied my instructions to come here'
(Scene unseen in tx version)

greets the elder. 'About the girl you murdered?' 'Oh never mind about the girl,' dismisses Number 2. 'I want to talk about you.' 'You're wasting your time. Many have tried.' 'Amateurs!' the other fires back. 'You're a professional ... a professional sadist.' With a flick of his wrist, Number 2 unsheathes a rapier from his umbrella. Approaching to within an inch of the Prisoner's chair, he places its blade directly over the bridge of the seated man's nose. 'Light blue ... fearless ... or are you? Each man has his breaking point you know. And you are no exception.' The tip of the rapier is lifted to the Prisoner's forehead. 'Ah you react ... are you afraid of *me*? What is going on up there?' mocks the sadist. 'Disgust ...' Strengthening his resolve, the superior stands erect and slaps Number 6 heavily across the face. 'You think you're strong. Mmm, we'll see. Du musst Amboss oder Hammer sein.' 'You must be *anvil* or *hammer*,' quips the Prisoner. 'I see you know your Goethe,' acknowledges Number 2. 'And you see me as the *anvil*?' 'Precisely,' confirms the superior. 'I am going to hammer you!' The red telephone sitting on top of the control console bleeps into life. A call from Number 1. 'Number 2. Yes sir. Yes sir, everything is under control. No sir, no problems. Assistance? No no sir, I can manage. Yes sir, of course. Be seeing you.' 'You were saying? ... Something about a hammer,' taunts Number 6, aware that the other does not have things entirely his own way. 'Get out!' exclaims Number 2. 'Thank you very much.' returns the other. climbing to his feet. 'I'll break *you* Number 6.' Pausing to look back. the one about to leave hisses a knowing affirmative. Alone. Number 2 picks up the telephone. 'Get me the Supervisor ... Supervisor? Number 2. Alert all posts. Special surveillance on Number 6. Report any unusual activity to me personally.'

Meanwhile. the subject of his report calls at the General Store. 'Good morning sir.' greets the shop assistant. '*Tally Ho*. That will be two units sir.' Pocketing his clipped credit slip. Number 6 turns his attention to a rack of classical record albums on display by the counter. 'These new records. I like to hear L'Arlesienne.' 'Ah yes sir. The Davier recording. Beautiful. There's no one to touch him on Bizet. It takes a Frenchman ...' 'I'd like to hear them *all*.' The assistant can hardly believe his ears. 'I beg your pardon sir?' 'How many copies have you got?' asks the customer. 'Six'. 'May I have them?' 'If you insist sir. but they're all the same.' 'I doubt it.' grins Number 6. 'Yes sir.' replies the assistant. reaching behind him to gather up the required albums. 'Thank you. thank you very much.' grins the customer carrying the records to a listening booth. Selecting the first album. he places it onto the record deck provided. listens to several bars of music while viewing his wristwatch then. returning the record to its dust sleeve does exactly the same to the second record. The third album is given a longer hearing. and the listener makes notes on his *Tally Ho* newspaper. Apparently satisfied. the customer collects up the albums and returns them to the bemused shop assistant. 'Well sir?' asks the man. 'I'm afraid not. Not a very satisfactory recording.' replies Number 6. 'Really sir.' replies the assistant. 'I thought it was first class.' 'It's a matter of taste.' observes the customer. 'nevertheless. thank you very much. Be seeing you.' 'Be seeing you sir.' calls the assistant as the customer leaves. While replacing each of the records back into its sleeve. he notices that the customer has left behind his newspaper. The assistant peers at the words the man had written. Seeing that Number 6 has circled the word 'Security' on the bye-line of a feature and denoted the word with a question mark. the assistant urgently telephones Number 2. The Prisoner. meanwhile. having hidden himself behind a stone pillar outside the store. is on hand to witness the shop assistant leave his premises and race with the newspaper to the Green Dome. His plan is working.

Having played the L'Arlesienne recordings. Number 2 is as confused as the shop assistant. 'I don't understand. They sound identical.' 'Yes sir.' confirms the man from the stores. 'And you say that he was timing them?' 'Yes sir.' replies the one in the apron. 'There was one in particular.' 'I don't suppose you know which one?' enquires Number 2. comparing the album sleeves. 'I. er. have no idea sir. He kept looking at his watch and then he wrote something down on a piece of paper.' 'Did he now.' muses the superior. laying the records down on a table. 'The sleeves are all the same. There's no variation in tempo. What was Number 6 listening for? What makes one of these records different?' 'I've no idea sir.' replies the shop assistant. Then. producing the copy of the *Tally Ho* newspaper the customer had left behind. he adds. 'Oh and that's not all sir. He left his *Tally Ho* behind.' 'And?' sneers a confused Number 2. 'Well look at the front page sir.' The superior does so. glancing at the circled word. 'All right. you can go.' he says. dismissing the shop assistant. 'Yes sir.' 'And take these with you.' calls Number 2 indicating the record

albums. The assistant moves to gather the items together. 'Ah. leave the paper ...' orders Number 2. sliding the *Tally Ho* from the top of the pile as the shop assistant clutches the albums to his chest and departs from the chamber. Pacing the floor. his eyes scanning the by-line with its additional scrawl. the superior muses over what the Prisoner is up to. He crosses to the control console behind him and. with the flick of a switch his quarry is brought into view as he crosses the floor of his cottage and sits at his writing bureau. After scribbling a few words on a writing pad. he tears off the sheet. folds it carefully in two and places the note into his inside jacket pocket. Scanning the top sheet of the writing pad. he tears this off also before. folding it neatly. he strolls out of the cottage.

Number 2 watches with interest as the Prisoner scribbles a few words on his note pad

Within seconds. Number 14 (an agent of Number 2) enters the vacated residence. tears the top sheet off the writing pad and takes it to his superior at the Green Dome – unaware that Number 6 has been observing his every movement. Having inspected the notepaper by hand. Number 2 places the sheet into a projection enlarger. dismisses Number 14 and stares at the blown-up impressions left on the paper by the writer's pen. 'To XQ4. Ref your query via Bizet record. Number 2's instability confirmed. Detailed report follows. D6.' he reads. unable to believe his eyes. 'Number 6 ... a plant?' Meanwhile. in the residence denoted '6-Private'. the Prisoner glances at his wristwatch. lays down the book he has been reading while lounging on his bed. rises and slides a white folder from beneath the mattress. Surveilled by Number 2. he leaves his cottage under the cover of darkness. 'Come on.' says Number 2. handing

Number 14 a walkie-talkie, 'we'll follow him.' Together they set out on foot after the Prisoner, who has now crossed through the Village and is heading for the beach. Having followed their quarry for a short distance, the pursuers separate, Number 2 remaining behind in the darkness while his companion continues to follow the Prisoner alone. The men keep in contact via their communication devices. 'Where is he now?' demands Number 2. 'He's going down towards the beach sir,' replies the pursuer, keeping Number 6 in sight as he tiptoes down the steps leading to the broad expanse of sand. 'Keep on his tail. I'll follow you down,' comes the reply. 'Which way is he heading?' Confirming that Number 6 is going around the sea wall towards the swimming pool, Number 14 is told to keep after him, but to be careful. Then, after a short space of time, 'What's he doing?' 'He's going towards the Stone Boat,' replies Number 14. 'Keep out of sight and go on reporting,' comes the order. Seeing Number 6 reach his permanently-moored objective, the pursuer picks up his commentary. 'He's going aboard ... He's going into the cabin. Now he's come out ... he's heading back.' 'Let him go. I'll join you at the Stone Boat,' comes the reply. Having made his way up from the beach, Number 6 pauses for a moment to stare back at the sands. Then with a knowing grin, he returns to his cottage.

Numbers 2 and 14 enter the Stone Boat. 'You're sure he didn't have it with him when he left?' asks the superior. 'Yes quite sure sir,' confirms his companion, crouching to enter the vessel's cabin. Bending over a bunk, Number 2 easily finds what they are looking for – the white folder left there by their quarry. Carrying the folder back to the Green Dome, the superior once again dismisses the underling. 'But I thought ...' 'Don't!' snaps Number 2. 'Just obey orders.' 'Yes sir,' returns the junior leaving the chamber. Alone now, the superior tears open his prize. It contains nothing but sheets of blank paper. A look of puzzlement crosses his face as he shuffles through the white sheets, his eyes searching for any hidden writing. Selecting a telephone from his console, he asks for the laboratory and orders a technician to join him. 'I want these tested immediately,' growls Number 2 as the laboratory technician enters the chamber. 'For what sir?' asks the newcomer taking receipt of the papers. 'Anything ... words, figures, whatever is written on them!' exclaims the superior. The man stares at the papers again. 'There seems ...' he begins. 'Don't argue with me!' snaps Number 2. 'I'm telling you there is ... a message of some kind. Try everything. X-rays, infra-red ... what are you staring at?' 'Nothing sir,' replies the confused technician. 'Then get on with it!' barks Number 2. With a stare of disbelief, the laboratory man leaves. Having had the papers tested, he turns to his assistant for confirmation. 'Well?' 'This one's negative too,' replies his junior, handing his companion a blank sheet of paper. 'Of course. I didn't expect anything else,' confirms the senior technician. 'Shall we put them through again?' asks the other. 'What's the point. We've tried everything,' confirms the senior. 'He isn't going to like this,' he tells his companion with a shrug of his shoulders. Waiting anxiously back in the Green Dome, a concerned Number 2 is astounded when the technician reports that the papers are blank. 'I'm sorry sir, but there's nothing.' 'Nothing! Nothing at all?' quizzes the frustrated Number 2. The other confirms that the papers are blank. 'They CAN'T be!' exclaims the superior, snatching the papers from the lab man's hands. 'Why should he hide blank sheets of paper in the Stone Boat?'

He ponders for a moment before, looking curiously at the other he adds, 'Or are you hiding something?' 'What do you mean sir?' 'I mean was there a message here and you're not telling me?' growls the superior, turning to face the man. 'Why should I do that sir?' pleads the accused. 'Perhaps you're in with him!' shouts Number 2. 'In with whom?' 'Six ... Number 6!' returns an aggressive Number 2. The technician looks back in confusion. 'Oh, you don't know what I'm talking about. Get out!' concludes Number 2, ordering the man from the room. Relieved that the torment is over, the technician races back to his laboratory.

'Increased Vigilance Call From New Number 2' reads the headline of the *Tally Ho* paper which lies with its companions on the newspaper vendor's kiosk. 'Good morning,' greets the Prisoner to the pretty young girl behind the counter. 'Good morning sir, can I help you?' 'Yes. I'd like to place a private advert in the personal column of the next issue please.' 'Certainly sir. What is it?' asks the girl, sliding her advertising pad and pencil across the counter. 'I have it written down,' smiles Number 6, reaching into his inside pocket and handing the girl a slip of paper. 'There you are.' The girl reads the first three words aloud, struggling to get the pronunciation correct. 'Hay mas mal. ...' she falters. 'Hay mas aml en el aldea que se suena,' corrects Number 6, confirming the message. 'Nine words. That will be three units please sir.' 'Good.' 'Spanish isn't it?' asks the girl while clipping the customer's credit card. 'That's right. Cervantes – Don Quixote,' he confirms. 'Oh yes,' replies the girl acknowledging her ignorance. 'Sort of personal joke between myself and a certain friend.' 'I see,' she replies. 'That word Aldea. Doesn't it mean village?' 'Yes!' he confirms with a grin. Pocketing his clipped credit card, he walks over to a telephone kiosk. 'Hospital ... Yeah ... Hospital? Psychiatrics, Head of the Department.' 'Director of Psychiatrics,' replies a voice. 'Ah yes Doctor, what's the verdict on our friend?' 'Friend. Friend, who is this?' quizzes the doctor. 'Your report ... on *Number 2*,' urges the caller. 'Number 2? What are you talking about? Who ... who is this speaking?' asks the somewhat bemused doctor. 'I understand. You'd rather not talk on the telephone. You're probably very wise. Never mind. I'll be seeing you later on ...' grins Number 6 replacing the receiver.

'... I understand. You'd rather not talk on the telephone. You're probably very wise. Never mind. I'll be seeing you later on ...' repeats the words from the tape machine which Number 2 now switches off, its ominous message sending a shiver down the spine of the doctor who now stands before his superior. 'Perhaps you'd explain,' says Number 2. 'I can't. I'm as much in the dark as you are,' pleads the psychiatrist. 'Are you?' mocks the superior, placing his hands on the tape machine. 'You don't know who it was who telephoned you?' 'No,' confirms the other. 'It was Number 6, and the oscilloscope will prove it,' warns Number 2, inserting the jack-plugged end of a cable that leads from the tape machine into an oscilloscope monitor. 'Voices are like fingerprints,' explains Number 2, tweaking a control on the monitor. 'No two are the same. Even if the voice is disguised, the pattern doesn't change. I'll now show you the voice pattern of your caller ...' He reverses the tape recording and the doctor is treated to a visual display of the caller's voice pattern. Replaying the word 'you', after comparison with the voice of Number 6, the superior confirms that they match. 'It was Number 6 who telephoned you. Do you still plead innocent?' 'I tell you I haven't the faintest idea...' 'You aren't preparing a report on my ... my mental health?' quizzes Number 2. 'Of course not,' grins the psychiatrist. 'And Number 6 *didn't* see you later ...?' 'No!' '... Then why did he ring you?' barks the superior forcibly. The doctor goes on the defensive. 'I told you. I don't know!' 'You're a psychiatrist aren't you ...' affirms Number 2, crossing to the doctor. '... Would you say that Number 6 was mad?' 'Not according to our records.' 'Then he had a *reason* for telephoning you, didn't he. What was IT?' growls the superior. 'Why don't you ask him?' 'Would you like to sit in this chair?' Number 2 snaps back, angry at the other man's sarcasm. 'I was merely suggesting ...' 'DON'T TELL ME WHAT TO DO!!' bawls the superior. 'You can go.' 'Thank you,' sighs the doctor, turning to exit through the metal doors.

Approaching the bandstand, Number 6 pauses to whisper a few words into the bandmaster's ear, then continues his stroll, glancing momentarily at the green-coloured dome of Number 2's residence.

'A request you say?' 'Yes sir. That's all,' confirms the musician, relating that Number 6 asked him to play the Farandole from the L'Arlesienne Suite. 'What *else*?' asks the suspicious superior. 'I don't understand sir,' replies the bandmaster shaking his head. 'What else did he *say*?' urges Number 2. 'Nothing sir.' 'Nothing,' repeats the superior, linking his hands behind his back and pacing before the musician. 'Number 6 just asked you to play a tune ... and then walked away.' 'Did he sir? I didn't notice,' replies the man being questioned. 'Does that make sense to you?' 'No sir.' 'No, it doesn't does it,' confirms Number 2. 'I'll ask you once again ... Did Number 6 say anything else ... about *me* for example?' 'About you sir?' 'Well, did he?' 'No sir,' says the other, his eyebrows raised. 'Perhaps you've forgotten. Try and remember!' 'He didn't sir,' confirms the bandmaster after a moment of thought. 'You're lying aren't you?!' screams Number 2, turning to face the man. Closing the gap between them, the superior glares into the musician's face. 'There's something going on!' 'I don't know what you mean sir,' stammers the bandleader. *'I don't know what you mean sir.* I'm as much in the dark as you are ...' mocks Number 2. '... You're all lying! It's a plot! Going behind my back. Who do they think they're dealing with? Pygmies! Oh get out, get OUT!'

In the Village graveyard, Number 6 stares at a bouquet of daffodils which someone has placed on the deceased Number 73's tombstone. He leans forwards to peer at the headstone of the adjacent grave, one denoted by the numerals 113. Returning to the Village, he acknowledges a salute from a passing inmate as he drops the note he is carrying into a post box. In the Control Room, having completed his daily broadcast, the Supervisor, turns back the pages of his request folder and finds a message he has overlooked. He reads out its contents over the air: 'And here is a personal message for Number 6. It is from 113 ...' Number 2 hears the broadcast as he is making a telephone call. Telling the caller that he will contact them later, Number 2 rests the receiver in its cradle and devotes his attention to the message being broadcast. '... and it reads, warmest greetings on your birthday ... May the sun shine on you today and every day. And that concludes the personal messages. We continue with music ...' Snatching up a file from a shelf below his control console, Number 2 flicks through its pages. Confirming his suspicions, he repeats the procedure with a second file. Slamming the folder closed he beckons Number 14 to follow him, and stalks angrily from the chamber, carrying his sporting stick. Observing the two men leaving the

Green Dome, Number 6 continues his stroll with a wry smile.

Entering the Control Room with his lap dog at his heels Number 2 finds the Supervisor surrounded by assistants, each sitting at their observation posts. From his position on the ramp by the entrance doors, Number 2 calls 'What's going on here?' 'Going on, Number 2?' quizzes the Supervisor. 'That personal message for Number 6 ...' 'What about it?' questions the bespectacled man, as everyone in the room turns to watch their superior. '... Do you all think I'm stupid?' barks Number 2. 'I ... I don't understand sir,' replies the Supervisor. 'Don't you? Birthday greetings for Number 6 from 113.' 'That's right,' nods the Supervisor, confirming that the superior had heard the message correctly. 'It's NOT right! It's all wrong and you know it!' screams Number 2, losing his patience. He beckons for the Supervisor to come closer. The bespectacled man does so. 'It is not Number 6's birthday today ...' 'Oh,' whispers the Supervisor, confused as to what is taking place. '... Yes "oh". And Number 113 doesn't exist!' snaps Number 2. 'Doesn't exist?' questions the man being admonished. 'An old woman ... she died a month ago ...' confirms Number 2. 'Well?' 'I swear Number 2, I ...' 'You're innocent ... you know nothing,' mocks the elder, taking the words out of the Supervisor's mouth. 'Nothing at all,' confirms the bespectacled man. 'And that message ... May the sun shine on you today and every day ... *You* don't know what it means?' 'It ... means ... what it says,' stammers the Supervisor. 'It isn't a coded message for Number 6?' accuses the superior. 'I've no idea,' pleads the other. 'You're finished,' screams Number 2. 'Finished?' whispers the Supervisor. 'I'm relieving you from your post as Supervisor.' Not wishing to tempt the elder's wrath further, the dismissed man slouches his way up the staircase. Pointing to another operator with his finger, Number 2 orders the junior to take over. 'Yes,' says the new Supervisor as the previous one joins Number 2 on the ramp. 'And steer clear of Number 6. Or you'll lose more than your job. Understand?' yells the red-faced elder. 'Yes Number 2,' says the newly-elected man. 'And that goes for all of you,' screams Number 2, as the deposed Supervisor is led away by Number 14. 'I'll BREAK THIS CONSPIRACY!' comes the departing shot as the metal doors slide to a close.

Inside his residence, Number 2 studies the personal message dictated by Number 6 for the *Tally Ho* newspaper. 'You say Number 6 put this personal ad in?' he asks, turning to Number 14. 'Yes sir. I checked as soon as I saw it.' Lowering himself into his oval-shaped chair, the superior reads the message aloud. 'Hay mas mal en el aldea que se suena ... there is more harm in the Village than is dreamt of.' 'Something ought to be done about Number 6,' proposes the other. 'I can take care of him,' confirms Number 2. 'It's got to be done *soon*,' insists Number 14. 'Every day he's a bigger threat to you personally. Let *me* deal with him. He's undermining your authority. Give me the word.' Number 2 appears untroubled by the warning. 'He doesn't hide it. He's out to poison the whole Village,' says Number 14. 'He's a plant,' proposes Number 2. 'If anything happened to him, our masters would know who was responsible.' 'Leave it to me. They'll never connect you with it,' coaxes the lap dog. 'An accident. It's the *only* way.' Rising to his feet, Number 2 begins to pace the room. After several minutes, he turns back to his assistant and, with a sharp nod of his head, leads him from the chamber into the entrance hall of his home. 'What do you want?' he enquires, stopping

A Kosho contest to settle a dispute

in his tracks as Number 6 enters through the front door. 'I don't want anything. *You* sent for me.' grins the newcomer. 'I did?' 'Yes. You telephoned. You said you wanted to see me urgently.' quips the other with a smile. 'I didn't phone you.' contradicts Number 2. 'It was *your* voice . . . *he* said he was Number 2. Someone in this village is impersonating you.' says the Prisoner. 'I have some calls to make. I shan't need you.' the superior informs Number 14. 'Right sir.' acknowledges the lap dog. as Number 2 leaves the two men alone. 'You're a troublemaker Number 6. Do you know what I'd like . . . really like? To dust you down. I'd really enjoy that.' 'Well nothing's stopping you – Kosho?' grins the other. 'I challenge you.' '*I* accept!' Within the space of a second. the two men stand facing each other on the gymnasium trampoline mats positioned over the giant water tank. The contest begins, but Number 14 is prevented from using any foul moves when other Kosho opponents enter the gym and remain to watch the match. The contest over. Number 6 strips off his Kosho attire and heads for the General Store. Spotting several pigeons dancing on the roof of the premises, a wry grin crosses his face. Entering the establishment. he declares that he wishes to purchase a small notebook. 'Very good sir.' says the assistant. reaching behind him and placing a selection of writing pads on the counter. 'Will that be all sir?' 'No.' the customer replies selecting a small notepad. 'I'd like one of these.' He crosses to a selection of cuckoo clocks which are on display at a nearby stand. 'Ah yes sir . . . yes sir. very good value. Special import. What about this type sir?' smiles the shop assistant. proffering an ornate timepiece. 'No. I'll take this one.' says Number 6. indicating the clock in front of him. which is sitting on top of a wooden box. the hinged lid of which the customer has been playing with. 'As you please sir. Now sir. that will be 42 units in all sir.'

'And a what?' asks Number 2. while receiving a telephone report from the shop assistant. 'A cuckoo clock sir. And that's not all. I think he was looking for a special one sir. He didn't want the one I picked . . . he seemed to be searching for a specific box.' 'All right. Thank you.' replies Number 2. laying down the telephone. Puzzled by the Prisoner's antics. he considers what his quarry may be up to.

The specific box now sits on a table outside the purchaser's cottage. Lifting up the box. Number 6 places it on the gravel at his feet. Raising its hinged lid. he props it open with a thin rod which he removes from his pocket. takes a bite from the half-eaten sandwich that lies on a plate on the table top and throws the remainder of the bread into the back of the box. Picking up the cuckoo clock. he totes it carefully through the Village. mounts the steps leading to Number 2's residence and, peering around him. nestles the timepiece snuggly against the foot of the building's entrance door. Having watched these events with growing concern on the Control Room monitor screen. Number 2 takes the bait. He calls out in alarm: 'What's he up to with that clock . . .? It's a bomb, that's it . . . it must be a bomb!' His trap laid. Number 6 descends the Green Dome's steps and returns to his residence. He has barely left the street when a Village buggy screeches to a halt below the Green Dome. Two men in helmets race up to the door and the 'bomb' is safely stowed away in a container of sand. Simultaneously. Number 6 has returned to his residence. collected his home-made pigeon trap (which now contains a bird. tempted into the snare during his absence) and carried the box and its prisoner into the woods. Meanwhile. in a sand-bagged dug-out. a thoroughly frustrated Number 2 joins an equally bemused Bomb Disposal mechanic to stare at the skeleton remains of the cuckoo clock which now adorn a table top before them – the technician's raised eyebrows clearly indicate his thoughts: is it Number 2, or the timepiece who is going cuckoo! 'Supervisor. Number 6 is now approaching Restricted Area,' calls out a camera operator. 'Let's have him on the screen,' orders the newly-promoted Supervisor. Seeing Number 6 approach the forbidden area, the senior operator telephones Number 2 and reports that the Prisoner is in the mangrove walk. 'He could be making for the shores, or the hills.' 'Don't lose him. I'm coming over,' orders the superior, as, deep in the woods, Number 6 lays the box he is carrying on the ground. Removing the notebook he bought earlier, from his pocket and pausing to consider the next part of his plan, he carefully writes several numbers onto the blank sheet. This done, he folds the paper several times, attaches it to the pigeon's leg and releases the bird into the blue. 'Track that bird,' orders the new Supervisor. 'Tracking sir,' replies an operator. 'Beam.' 'Beam on sir. Yellow . . . tracking . . . Orange . . . ,' confirms the operator, as a pencil-like aerial rod eases its way through the hinged-top of a flag pole sitting on top of the Control Room roof. '. . . It's out of sight!' 'Get a fix. Radar,' orders the senior. 'We've got a fix sir,' confirms the man at the radar screen. 'Prepare to fire . . .' 'What do you think you're doing?' exclaims Number 2, racing into the control chamber. 'But sir,' calls out the new Supervisor, indicating the monitor screen, 'that pigeon. Number 6 is sending a message!' Mumbling to himself, Number 2 orders the bird to be brought down. 'I want that message. Beam. Minimum strength.' 'Minimum strength,' repeats the other. 'Fire!' orders Number 2. Seconds later the lifeless bird is carried into the chamber and the note attached to its leg is handed to Number 2. Unfolding it and seeing the set of numbers, the elder gives orders for it to be deciphered right away. 'Yes sir,' calls out the female code expert, reciting the numbers to her assistant. '20, 60, 40, 47, 67, 81, 91, 80.' The decoding machine clatters out its reply and Number 2 is handed the result. 'Vital message tomorrow 06.00 hours by visual signal . . .' he reads. '. . . Visual signal . . .?'

The time on the Prisoner's wristwatch, which lies side by side with a looking glass on the waiting man's table, reads 5.36 am. Leaving his cottage while the rest of the Village sleeps – all that is except Number 2 and his Control Room operators, who have the Prisoner under constant surveillance – Number 6 makes his way down to the beach and heads off across the sand. 'Stand by observers . . .' orders Number 2, following the man's progress as Number 6 kneels on the sand and begins to flash a message with the hand mirror. 'Get that Morse down . . . get it down! Get in closer . . . get in as close as you can,' orders Number 2. 'Who can he be signalling to?' queries the new Supervisor. 'We'll find out. Radar . . . anything?' asks Number 2, shoving the assistant aside and crossing to join the radar operator. 'No sir . . . not at sea,' says the man. 'There must be!' 'No sir. There's no ship sir,' confirms the radar man. Number 2 lowers his eyes. 'There must be an aircraft, helicopter . . . something?' he yells, running to each operator in turn. 'There's nothing sir.' 'Under the sea . . .' tries Number 2. '. . . a submarine? We'll try the sonar.' He races to the sonar operator. 'No sir,' he replies, 'there's nothing coming through.' Number 2 looks concerned. 'But he must be signalling to *someone*. Morse, did you get it?' 'Yes sir,' replies the operator staring intently at his monitor screen. At last, Number 2 grins. 'What's it say?' The operator looks silently over his shoulder. 'Well!?' exclaims the superior, demanding an answer. 'Pat a cake, pat a cake baker's man. Bake me a cake as fast as you can,' stammers the Morse operator.

Number 2 is aghast. 'it must be a special code,' he mumbles to himself, crossing to the control console which is now pumping out its ticker-tape decoded result. '*Pat a cake, pat a cake* . . .' reads Number 2. 'But this is what you put in!' 'And that's what came out sir,' confirms the female operator. 'It must be a new code,' insists the elder. 'And the computer's not programmed for it!' The girl looks startled. Number 6, meanwhile, joins Number 14 at his cafe table. 'Morning . . . did you sleep well? I didn't. I had a terrible night . . .' he whispers to the man eating his breakfast. '. . . Insomnia, couldn't sleep, so restless . . . and there's no point in lying in bed when you're awake . . . is there?' Number 14 gulps down a mouthful of food. 'What are you talking about?' he asks. Ignoring him, Number 6 drones on '. . . So I got up, went out, had a long walk on the beach . . . marvellous at that time of day, invigorating, the air, it's brisk and clear . . .' 'You must be out of your mind,' suggests the diner. '. . . the rain on your face, the wind in your cheeks . . . don't look now, the waiter's watching . . .' Then, raising his voice he ends '. . . Yes, it's the only way. I'm so glad you agree with me.' The trap sprung, he leaves the bemused man staring after him. 'Get me Number 2. Quickly,' says the waiter, lifting his telephone receiver.

'You expect me to believe that?' growls Number 2, to the man standing in front of him – an ashen-faced and concerned Number 14. 'But that's what happened. He came over and . . .' 'And asked if you'd slept well!' mocks the superior from his chair. 'Yes sir.' Number 2 laughs. 'The waiter said you were whispering.' '*I* wasn't, but he was,' pleads Number 14. 'What about?' challenges the superior. 'Well, he said . . .' 'Yes!' 'Well he talked a lot of rubbish. Then he said the waiter was watching us . . .' 'Why?' scowls the superior, rising to his feet. 'Why did Number 6 say that?' 'I don't know sir.' '*Don't* you. You're *working* with Number 6!' exclaims Number 2, his face a mask of suspicion. 'Me sir?' 'And I thought you were the one man I could trust,' the superior throws back, his voice sobbing with despair. 'But you can. I'm loyal.' 'Traitor!' screams Number 2, slapping the man heavily across the cheek. 'Traitor! Traitor!' he sobs, his shoulders hunched, his eyes welling with tears. Unable to believe what is taking place, Number 14 strides from the chamber, leaving the broken man behind. But Number 2 is not quite finished with him. As the mute Butler accompanies Number 14 to the door, an hysterical Number 2 races up behind them. 'You've lost, you and your friends!' he screams. 'I'll break the lot of you . . . You too,' he yells, staring down at his black-coated manservant as Number 14 walks through the door in disgust. 'You're in this plot, aren't you?' The small man stares back blankly, unable to comprehend what is going on. 'Oh yes!' exclaims Number 2, raising his arm as if to strike the defenceless figure. 'Get out! Get out of this house!' Lowering his head, the Butler calmly walks to the double doors through which the superior has passed, pulls them closed and returns to his duties.

Leaning back in his chair, Number 6 is listening to a record when Number 14 races into his cottage. 'Turn that thing off,' orders the intruder. 'I beg your pardon?' grins Number 6. 'Turn it off I said,' insists Number 14. 'I'm listening. Music makes for a quiet mind,' quips the tenant as the intruder bends over him to flick off the record player. 'I'd rather you didn't,' grins the listener, grabbing the man's arm and throwing him effortlessly onto the carpet. Rising from his chair, Number 6 asks what's on the other man's mind. 'You put the poison in,' hisses Number

14, scrambling to his feet. 'Did I?' grins the tenant. 'With Number 2 . . .' continues the intruder. '. . . I'm finished!' 'Sorry to hear that,' mocks Number 6. 'I'll kill you!' yells the other, leaping at the Prisoner, his fist raised. 'Will you?' grins Number 6, stepping backwards to ward off the blow. The men enter into a vicious fight. Bedsheets are torn and scattered to the floor. Crockery from the tenant's kitchen is smashed to the floor as the kitchen divider gives way under the strain of the men's weight as they battle their way around the cottage. The fight is long and arduous until, with a final lunge from his opponent, Number 14 is sent crashing through the Prisoner's front door. Meanwhile in the Green Dome, the Butler is preparing to leave. Having packed his suitcase, he gathers up his raincoat and marches to the door – leaving behind a babbling superior, his bloodless hands clasped tightly to the large wheel of the penny farthing bicycle; his tormented face a mask of self-pity.

Number 2 stands alone, his face a mask of torment

'What are you doing here?' sighs Number 2 as the Prisoner strides into the chamber. 'I've come to keep you company. I hear all your friends have deserted you,' mocks the newcomer. 'You can't trust anyone anymore . . . Pity. It's odd isn't it . . .' he peers around the huge chamber. '. . . all this power at your disposal, and yet, you're alone. You do feel alone don't you?' 'What do you want?' sobs Number 2. 'To talk and to listen.' 'I have *nothing* to say.' 'That's not like the old Number 2,' grins Number 6, descending the ramp and approaching the trembling figure. 'Where is the strong man. The hammer. You have to be *hammer* or *anvil*, remember?' 'I know . . . who . . . you are,' stammers Number 2, crossing to face the newcomer. 'I'm Number 6.' 'No! *D6*.' 'D6?' grins the Prisoner breaking into laughter. 'Yes . . . sent here by our masters to *spy* on me,' babbles Number 2. 'Sorry, I'm not quite with you,' replies Number 6, striding away from the elder. 'Oh yes, oh yes, you can stop acting now, you know.

I was onto you from the beginning. *I* knew what you were doing!' 'Tell me,' mocks Number 6 while pacing the floor, the superior trailing him like a lap dog. The roles are reversed now. 'All those messages you sent, and all the people you recruited. I knew you were a plant. *You* didn't fool ME!' 'Maybe you fooled yourself,' quips the other, raising an eyebrow. 'What does that mean?' 'Let us suppose for arguments sake, that what you say is true . . . that I was planted here.' 'By X04,' yells the elder. 'X04?'

'I know who you are!' (I'm Number 6.)

'Mmm,' returns Number 2, nodding his head in confirmation. He has his quarry on the run now. 'Oh very well then, by X04 . . . to check on Village security. To check on you . . .' 'You were!' '. . . What would have been your first duty as a loyal citizen? Not to interfere . . .' confirms the Prisoner. Number 2 bites his lip. '. . . But you did . . . *interfere* . . . You have admitted it yourself.' The elder's bottom lip begins to twitch. 'There is a name for that . . . sabotage!' Realisation dawning. Number 2 begins to sob. 'No.' Pressing home his advantage, the other takes on the role of interrogator. 'Who are you working for Number 2?' 'For us. For US!' pleads the distraught superior. 'That is not the way it is going to sound to X04.' 'I swear to you . . .' 'You could be working for the enemy. Or you could be a blunderer who's lost his head. Either way you've failed. And *they* do not like failures here,' insists Number 6, his words cutting deep into the other man's pride. Head bowed, his words racked with sobs, the defeated man sighs. 'You've . . . destroyed me.' 'You've destroyed yourself,' retorts the interrogator, shaking his head. 'A character flaw . . . you're afraid of your masters. A weak link in the chain of command . . . waiting to be broken.' 'Don't tell them. Don't report me,' pleads Number 2 through tear-stained eyes. 'I don't intend to. You are going to report yourself,' confirms Number 6, handing the broken man the instrument of his resignation – the ominous over-size red telephone – the superior's direct line to Number 1. Clutching the cordless receiver to his chest, the luckless man settles himself into his soon-to-be vacated oval chair. A drawn out sigh, then, regaining his composure, under the watchful eyes of Number 6, the out-going Number 2 reports to his superior. 'I have to report a breakdown in control. Number 2 needs to be replaced . . .' His battle won, Number 6 paces slowly from the chamber. '. . . Yes, this is Number 2 reporting . . .' confirms the man behind him, as he falls back sobbing into his chair. Glancing back, the Prisoner leaves and the bars slam closed.

MANY HAPPY RETURNS

Written by Anthony Skene

Guest stars

The Colonel	**Donald Sinden**
Thorpe	**Patrick Cargill**
Mrs Butterworth	**Georgina Cookson**

with

Group Captain	**Brian Worth**
Commander	**Richard Caldicott**
Gunther	**Dennis Chinnery**
Ernst	**Jon Laurimore**
Gypsy Girl	**Nike Arrighi**
Maid	**Grace Arnold**
Gypsy Man	**Larry Taylor**

Directed by Joseph Serf (Alias Patrick McGoohan)

IT IS MORNING. Sunbeams flow through the windows of the cottage denoted '6 - Private', their golden rays casting shadows across the resident's bedroom. Looking at his wristwatch, the Prisoner flings back his bedsheets, dons his dressing gown and crosses to the kitchen. Checking that his coffee percolator has water, he flicks on the switch and enters the bathroom with the intention of taking a shower. But the faucet is not working. Neither are the bath or wash-basin taps . . . nor the radio speaker in his lounge, which, for the first time since he became a resident of the cottage, sits on its shelf as silent as the grave. Strolling outside, he paces the veranda and views the Village. The square and the swimming pool are void of life. As far as he can tell, the Prisoner is alone – except for a solitary figure, a black cat, whose yellow eyes gaze in his direction. Discovering that his telephone is dead, he gets dressed and ventures outside. The Village is deserted. Empty coffee cups sit on top of the vacated cafe tables; the Village Store is closed, the cottages devoid of tenants. The Stone Boat carries no passengers, its blue, yellow and red banners blowing merrily in the wind. Save for the screeching of seagulls flying overhead, there are no voices. It seems as though the Village has died, very suddenly. Climbing to the bell tower, he scans the deserted horizon. He rings the bell, but the panoramic view remains unchanged. Back at ground level, he spots a deserted buggy. Its engine starts easily. Removing its ignition key, he strolls to the Green Dome. Unlike previous occasions, the entrance door remains closed. He raps on the barrier without success. Easing open the door, he passes into the lavishly-furnished hallway, expecting the Butler to appear. When no one arrives, he approaches the steel doors that lead to Number 2's seat of power. The barriers remain closed and he is forced to prise them apart by hand. The circular chamber and the superior's seat are deserted, an air of eerie silence hanging over the vast dome-shaped Control Room. Returning to the sunlight, he fires the buggy's engine and drives deep into the woods. The mountains rise before him. No Rover blocks his way, no Orange Alert is forthcoming. For the first time since being abducted, he sees the real promise of escape. With no one to stop him he hacks down some trees and builds a raft. Breaking into the General Store, he gathers together some supplies: food, a radio speaker, a camera and so on.

Leaving an IOU for 964 units scrawled in chalk across the shop assistant's counter, he races outside to take several photographs of the strangely silent community. Back at the raft, he is about to depart when he is startled by the sound of breaking crockery. A look of alarm flicks across his face. Has he been discovered? Are *they* playing another cruel game – allowing him to believe that he was alone and holding back on interference until that last glorious second when, believing that escape was finally in his grasp, *they* strike. A barely-discernible smile crosses his lips as he turns and sees the black cat sitting on top of a cafe table, a smashed dinner plate resting at its feet. Hopping aboard his make-shift vessel, he poles himself out to sea.

Far out on the ocean, he removes the film cartridge from his camera, seals it into a plastic bag and stows it safely away. Dismantling the radio speaker, he removes a darning needle from a needlecase. When rubbed against the speaker's magnetic coil and attached to a home-made sextant, this serves as a compass. Torn into squares and folded, a copy of the *Tally Ho* newspaper becomes a seaman's log. On his seventh day at sea, he eats and shaves. On day 18, he adjusts the vessel's sail and collapses from exhaustion, waking as darkness descends and the distant throb of an engine pounds in his ears. Through heavy eyes, he perceives a movement on the raft beside him. A seaman is passing his boxes of possessions to his companion aboard a fishing trawler. Rescue at last, he believes, as his body is heaved forward. It is not to be. With a grunt, the stranger heaves the Prisoner's body into the murky cold ocean and clambers back onto the trawler. Munching on a slice of chewing tobacco, the seaman casts the raft off and walks to his bridge to fire the trawler's engine. He is unaware that the man he pushed overboard has swum to the trawler and is now descending below deck. Observing the seaman's companion carrying a tray of food and drink to the man at the wheel, the stowaway enters a cabin, prises open a crate and discovers a cache of guns. Hearing the sound of a radio playing in another cabin, he enters sliding the door shut behind him. It is the vessel's galley. He places a frying pan on the stove, fills it

Entering a cabin, the stowaway discovers a cache of arms

with rag and douses the dish with alcohol. Stretching out to pick up a box of matches, he strikes one and ignites the alcohol-drenched rags. Adding further strips of cloth to the inferno, he waits until the dish is well alight, then, smothering the flames with a dampened table cloth, he departs from the smoke-filled galley. Alarmed by the whisps of smoke from below, the seaman who dumped the Prisoner into the water races below where, hidden in a cabin, the Number 6 takes revenge for his untimely swim. In swift succession, the stowaway deals with the second man and both sailors find themselves trussed up with rope and pushed into a cabin. Slipping a length of chain through the cabin's door, the victor ascends to the bridge, grabs the controls and steers a new course.

Sometime later, the captives recover and struggle to loosen their bonds. Above them on the bridge, Number 6 sees a light flashing far out at sea, and sets a new course, heading for the beacon at full throttle. Free now, the men below decks attack the chained door. Unable to get through, they remove several items from a cupboard and smash their way through into the adjoining cabin. Unaware of what is taking place below him, the Prisoner races at full speed towards the shoreline which is now in view. Attacked unawares by the gun-runners, he gives as good as he gets. However, when one of the men runs below to return with a gun, he has no option but to dive overboard and swim for the shore.

Waking on a beach, the Prisoner surveys his surroundings. The rock-strewn sand stretches out before him, a chalky-white cliff face towers above his head. Confirming that he still has the waterproof bag containing the film cartridge in his trouser pocket, he sets forth to explore his new environment. He weaves his way carefully over the rocks and climbs to the plateau above. Pausing to get his breath, he looks down at a lighthouse on the beach and traverses the grassy cliff top until, wonder of wonders, he meets a man walking his dog. 'Where is this?' he asks. The man passes the unkempt stranger in silence, urging his dog forward, and continues his stroll. Following them, the Prisoner stops in his tracks as the man joins a woman and her male companion sitting around a campfire. The people are gypsies. The woman gets to her feet and approaches the stranger, inviting him in a foreign tongue, to join them. Finding herself ignored, she returns to the campfire, pours the newcomer a cup of bubbling-hot liquid and offers it to the man, indicating to the stranger to drink. 'Where is this place?' he tries. 'Ah . . .' says the woman in Romany tongue. 'A road. Where is there a road?' asks the stranger, sipping his drink. Unable to understand her reply, he sets off down the hill in the direction in which she points. Descending a grassy knoll, he is forced to take refuge in the trees as, to his astonishment, he sees an English policeman directing traffic along a country lane. Racing back up the hill, he rejoins the road at a spot a few yards further on. But again his escape route is blocked; this time by two uniformed policemen who stand by their patrol car stopping and searching the oncoming traffic. Noting that one of the stopped vehicles is an open backed removal van, he races back into the woods and crouches hidden in the trees some distance further up the road. As the removal van motors past him, he leaps from the trees. Racing after the vehicle, he hops over the van's tailboard and lands in the back of the van with a bump. Climbing to his feet, he snuggles down on a platform directly above the unsuspecting driver's head where, covered by a hessian sack, he drifts off to sleep. Hearing the sound of a siren,

he awakens with a start and tumbles from the back of the removal van – to find himself standing precariously in the middle of a busy London street! A red bus drives by. A London taxi plies its trade a few feet behind him. He is home! Staring at the familiar London landmarks he can hardly believe his eyes. He has done the impossible. He has beaten them. He has escaped. He is a FREE man!

Making his way to the most familiar landmark of all, the white-painted front door of the elegant Georgian house that had once served as his residence, he tentatively raps its door knocker. The door is opened by an elderly maid. 'Yes?' she queries, staring at the unshaven, scruffily-dressed stranger. 'Who owns this house?' 'I beg your pardon!' 'I'm sorry. What I meant was I'd like to see your master.' 'My *mistress* is not at home,' snaps the maid. 'Do you mind if I wait . . .?' She slams the door in the man's face. Left alone on the doorstep, the man descends the steps and begins to walk away. At that moment, a familiar sound causes him to stop. Peering back up the street, he sees an attractive woman stepping out of a sporty customised yellow and green Lotus 7 sports car – the very machine which he had built with his own hands! Racing after the woman as she enters the house he asks 'What's the number of that car?' About to close the door, the woman thinks better of it and joins him on the steps, her eyes taking in his dishevelled appearance with a smirk. 'Terribly interesting,' she retorts. '*KAR 120C*. What's the engine number?' 'Do tell me,' mocks the woman. '461034 TZ,' he states. 'Marvellous!' she exclaims, nodding her head as the stranger continues his mysterious approach. 'I know every nut and bolt and cog. I built it with my own hands!' he confirms. 'Then you're just the man I want to see. I'm having a good deal of overheating in traffic. Perhaps you'd care to advise me,' smiles the woman. Entering her home, she invites the stranger inside. Easing his way past the woman, he enters the familiar surroundings, his eyes lovingly surveying his one-time home. 'This way,' she calls from her lounge. He joins her. 'Make yourself at home and I'll organise some tea . . . You would like some tea?' 'Very much.' 'I am Mrs Butterworth,' she establishes, removing her stylish motoring cap. 'And you are?' 'An exile.' 'A nameless exile?' 'Smith . . . Peter Smith,' says the guest looking around the lounge. 'Enchanting. Be comfortable and I'll be back in a moment . . .' smiles Mrs Butterworth, leaving to arrange for tea. '. . . and then you can enlighten me on the intricacies of KAR 120C.' Left alone in the room, the man lovingly runs his fingers over the oh-so-familiar objects. Crossing to the window, he eases back the curtains and stares out at the London skyline, recalling perhaps that the last time he did so, he ended up in a place . . . but no, all that is now behind him. Lifting the telephone and hearing the familiar post office dialling tone, he lays the receiver back onto its cradle as the woman reappears. 'Refreshments on the way. Now, tell me more.' 'What's the date?' he asks. 'Saturday, March 18,' the woman confirms, selecting a cigarette from a silver cigarette box. 'Tomorrow's my birthday,' he says, pacing the floor. 'You are an odd fellow.' 'Yes . . . you er . . . you must think I'm crazy.' 'Who isn't these days.' Mrs Butterworth replies, placing the cigarette between her lips and igniting a match. 'Do you know, this er, this was my house,' he states. 'Really. In better days. Before I went away.' 'You must miss it,' she says igniting her cigarette and placing the dead match into an ashtray. 'The lease had 6 months to run,' he recalls. 'Then it's been renewed. I have it for 10 years, fully furnished.' 'Oh yes,' says he, pushing his hands into his trouser pockets as he crosses the room to join the woman. 'Is the inventory in order?' 'I'll bet . . .' he snaps. '. . . The only thing that's missing is a body.' 'Don't tell me that you've been prying into my private affairs,' she grins. 'Forgive me. I'm very sorry,' he pleads. 'Er, would you do me a very great favour?' 'Are you growing a beard?' she asks. 'No.' 'Pity,' she replies, crossing to stand by the fire hearth. 'I've always had rather a soft spot for bearded men. But I could never get dear Arthur to grow one.' 'Arthur?' 'My late husband. Navy you know. Unhappily, now deceased.' Hearing a knock on the lounge door, Mrs Butterworth calls for the person to come in. The maid enters carrying a tray bearing refreshments. 'Oh thank you Martha,' says her mistress, removing a flower vase from a table to accommodate the tray. 'Is this the gentleman you said called earlier?' 'It is madam,' confirms the maid, staring at the stranger with disdain. 'Her description of you was hardly flattering Mr Smith. You must learn to delve beneath the surface Martha, who knows what treasures we may find. Alright.' Thanking her employer, the maid leaves. 'Come and sit down Mr Smith,' smiles Mrs Butterworth indicating the cushion on the settee beside her. The man does so. 'Sandwich?' asks the hostess, proffering a plate. 'You're very kind,' he says munching on the triangular slice of bread and accepting the paper napkin the woman hands to him. 'It's a pleasure,' she smiles, as the guest gobbles down each morsel in turn, followed in rapid succession by a three-tiered variety of pastries. 'That was the best fruit cake I've ever tasted,' he says dabbing his lips with the napkin. 'I'm a very good cook. It's one of my hobbies.' 'Mrs Butterworth,' says the guest rising to his feet. 'I asked if you would do me a very great favour?' 'Certainly.' 'Behind that desk . . .' he begins, indicating a piece of furniture on the far side of the room. '. . . there was an area of dry rot. It was made good about 12 months ago. The bathroom door is sliding, it opens to the left. The sink is on the right as you go in. The hot and cold taps on the shower were put in the wrong way round . . .' The hostess giggles. 'I had them changed. Don't be so silly, you haven't got to prove anything. I believe you.' 'Sorry. I'm not used to that,' he confirms. 'What can I do for you?' she asks. 'I would like to see, the lease of the house and the log-book

'That was the best fruit cake I've ever tasted'

of the car.' 'How mysterious . . .' says the tenant, rising from the settee to reach into a bureau drawer. Finding the log-book, she hands it to him. He points out that the document is new. 'Yours is the first name on it. There's no indication of the previous owner.' 'The estate agents arranged it all,' she explains rifling through the bureau to find the house lease document. 'They said the car was for sale. It was reasonable. And I've always had a taste for a little speed,' she smiles, handing her guest the lease to the property. 'The estate agents were Stumbell and Croydon?' he queries, reading the name at the top of the document. 'Most reputable. And a charming man dealt with me – Mr Croydon himself. Did you ever meet him?' 'No,' he confirms. 'That wasn't the firm that I did business with.' 'How odd?' she says, aware that his reply contained a hint of suspicion. 'Yes indeed Mrs Butterworth . . . You've been extremely kind in allowing me to intrude on your privacy in this way . . . I have to make two important calls. One in the country, one in town. So if you will please excuse me, I'll say goodbye.' He opens the door preparing to leave, but the woman calls out to him to stay. 'Mr Smith, you mustn't . . .' 'I'm sorry, I have to.' '. . . You mustn't go like that . . . Some of Arthur's things. You're very welcome. I've kept them all you see. Stupid but, even though there isn't a man about the place, I like to feel that there is. Do you understand what I mean?' she says, crossing to the lounge door. 'Yes I . . .' 'I just know that you're in some kind of trouble. Have you got any money?' 'No . . .' 'There you are you see. How are you going to get about?' Easing his way past her, the guest informs her that it is perfectly all right. He can manage. 'Thank you. Thank you very much indeed . . . you've been terribly kind.' 'Don't be silly . . .' says Mrs Butterworth chasing after him and grabbing his arm '. . . and independent and proud.' She manoeuvres the guest towards the staircase. 'Now go on up. You'll find everything you want in the bathroom. And I'll lay some of Arthur's clothes out for you . . .'

After a shave and a change of clothes, the man is sitting behind the wheel of his beloved Lotus. '. . . on condition that you stop that nasty overheating,' continues Mrs Butterworth, leaning over the man at the wheel. 'It's a deal,' he replies. 'Bon voyage,' she calls, turning back to her home. 'Mrs Butterworth, you've been tremendously k . . .' 'No speeches,' she says, raising her hand. 'Off you go . . .' Then, pausing for a moment as the driver revs the vehicle's engine, '. . . Don't forget to come back.' 'I'll be back,' he calls, his reply lost in the throb of the powerful engine. 'I might even bake you a birthday cake,' she promises as the Lotus pulls away from the pavement. It is though he has never been away. His hair blowing in the wind, he guns the car's engine and accelerates through the busy London streets. Making a right turn, he once again drives into the underground garage, throws back the double doors of the establishment's secret ante-room and enters his superior's office. The room has not changed. The large map of the world still hangs behind the solid wooden desk behind which sits a man in a chair. Nor has its occupant, the bespectacled man to whom he handed in his resignation many months before altered. Unaware of the newcomer's arrival, the bald-headed superior sips from his tea cup and places it back on its saucer. Picking up a pen, he lowers his head over several sheets of writing paper lying on the blotting pad before him. 'Anyone at home?' asks the intruder, leaning over the desk to attract the man's attention. Raising his head, the superior answers the newcomer's request with a silent, but knowing smile.

In his lavishly-furnished home, the Colonel is inspecting the photographs the newcomer has taken of the Village. 'Pretty spot . . .' he comments, looking at each picture in turn. '. . . Mixture of architectures. Italianate . . . Difficult. Certainly has a Mediterranean flavour. What do you think Thorpe?' he calls to a department executive standing beside a table in the adjacent room. Meanwhile, the man once known as Number 6, is patrolling the carpet between them with his hands clasped firmly behind his back. 'I think I wouldn't mind a fortnight's leave there. Prison for life eh?' replies Thorpe, placing duplicates of the photographs back onto a table. 'It's a far cry from Sing Sing.' 'I'm sorry to interrupt on an afternoon's golf Colonel . . .' interjects the newcomer, crossing to where the Colonel sits astride a balustrade '. . . but this is not a

'Anyone at home?'

joking matter.' 'My dear fellow,' says the military man, getting to his feet, his eyes glued to the pictures he holds. 'You really mustn't blame Thorpe. After all, you yourself on occasion could be, a little sceptical. That's why you were such a good man. Why we were so sorry to lose you.' 'The evidence is there,' says the newcomer. 'A set of photographs from ground level, of a holiday resort,' mocks the man known as Thorpe, as he adds a splash of soda water to his drink. 'And a schoolboy navigational log on the back of what *you* call the Village newspaper.' 'I'm sorry. It was the best I could do in the circumstances. You'd hardly expect the Village store to issue sextants would you!' exclaims the guest, raising his voice. 'Indeed, indeed . . .' the Colonel pipes up '. . . if the place is as you say it was. The *Tally Ho* . . .' he adds, peering at the newspaper. 'A daily issue,' informs the newcomer. '. . . Morning or evening?' 'Daily, at noon,' says the guest. 'What are facts behind Town Hall?' says the Colonel, reading out the paper's headline. 'Town Hall?' 'That's right,' confirms the newcomer. 'Town Council?' asks Thorpe. 'Correct.' 'Were you a member?' 'I could have been . . . It's democratically elected once a year.' 'Democratically,' queries the Colonel. 'That is what they claim,' answers the newcomer from across the room, his reply raising a smirk on Thorpe's face. 'And they're all *numbers*. No names. No names at all?' he challenges, tapping his fingers on the side of his whisky glass. 'Just

numbers,' the man continues. 'I see,' says the military man, as the guest informs them that each inhabitant was a number in a village which is a complete unit of its own society. A place to put people who cannot be left in ordinary society. 'People who know too much or too little. A place with many means of breaking a man!' he ends, his voice showing signs of anger because their minds are closed to the evidence. 'Intriguing,' mocks Thorpe, raising his glass to his mouth in total disinterest. 'They have their own cinema, their own newspaper . . . their own television station,' growls the newcomer pacing the room. 'A credit card system and if you're a good boy and cough up the secrets, you are gracefully retired into the Old People's Home!' He turns to face the men. 'But er . . . no escape?' asks the Colonel. 'They also have a very impressive graveyard,' confirms the man. 'Which you avoided,' states Thorpe. 'The Village was deserted,' confirms the other. Why don't they believe him? 'Perhaps they were on the democratic annual outing,' quips Thorpe, casting doubt upon the man's version of events. Snatching up several photographs from the table, the man shoves them under the Colonel's nose, leafing through them as he confirms the evidence – evidence which the men appear to dismiss out of hand. 'The Town Hall . . . Number 2's residence . . . *My* house . . . the Old People's Home . . .!' 'My dear fellow, you really mustn't get excited,' calms the Colonel. 'You must forgive us. You see we have a problem . . . Tell him of our problem Thorpe.' 'You resign. You disappear. You return. You spin a yarn that Hans Christian Anderson would reject for a fairy tale,' condemns the Colonel. 'And we must be sure . . .' '. . . People defect. An unhappy thought, but a fact of life. They defect, from one side to the other . . .' '*I* also have a problem,' growls the guest. '*I'm* not sure which side runs this Village.' 'A mutual problem,' confirms the military man. 'One which *I'm* going to solve . . .' states the guest. 'Quite,' replies the Colonel. '. . . If not here, then elsewhere,' threatens the other. 'Thorpe,' calls the military man. 'Sir?' 'Check.' 'Yes sir,' says the other rising

'You must forgive us. You see, we have a problem'

from his chair. 'Check every detail contained in our ... ex-colleague's report,' snaps the Colonel.

'Of course I helped him. I'd help anyone in trouble, wouldn't you?' says Mrs Butterworth, seating herself next to Thorpe's assistant, who silently writes her reply into his notebook. Having shuffled the ashes of the gypsies' campfire with his boot, a policeman mounts his bicycle and departs from the scene. 'Never mind,' says Thorpe, addressing an unseen caller on the telephone. 'Keep checking and report when you have anything. All corroborated, apart from the boat,' he tells the Colonel who sits at his desk, the remains of his breakfast lying on a tray before him. 'The beach?' 'Gypsies,' confirms Thorpe. 'Romanys,' says the man once known as Number 6. 'What about the road-block?' confirming that the police patrol had nothing to do with their guest and they were looking for an escaped convict, the Colonel asks the guest if he can tell them anything more about the boat. 'No name?' 'Would *you* advertise if you were gun-running?' asks the man, emptying his coffee cup. 'No I would not. I most certainly would not. Would you Thorpe?' grins the Colonel to his junior. 'No,' answers the assistant, picking up his cup and saucer and crossing to a table where several other men have their heads bent low, studying the newcomer's *Tally Ho* log. 'Are you satisfied?' asks the log-owner. 'Let us say that the dice are heavily loaded in your favour,' the Colonel agrees. 'Right,' says the guest. 'Let's get to work.' He joins the men at the table. 'Commander, how's it going?' The elderly man dressed in naval officer's uniform gives his verdict. 'On the basis of your log, and allowing for the variance of your primitive device and the laggard speed of your craft, I estimate that you would have averaged some three and a half knots.' Agreeing that this was the case, the guest inclines his head as the naval man asks if he had fair winds. 'Mostly,' says the man. 'You'll appreciate that there is no allowance for tide.' 'No there couldn't have been. I had no charts nor any means of assessing them.' 'Precisely,' affirms the Commander. 'You slept for how long?' 'Four hours out of each twenty four.' 'Remarkable,' says the naval man. 'So, in 25 days at sea, you proceeded at an average of three and a half knots for 24 hours out of each 24, on a north easterly course, which would have put us at ...' He looks at the map spread before him on the table. '... four hours sleep, 24 under fair sail. Maximum travel on a true course ... 1,750 miles,' interjects an RAF Group Captain. 'Where was the lighthouse?' asks the man attempting to prove his story. 'Here,' says Thorpe, indicating a spot on a map pinned to a board and easel. '250 miles to the inch ...' states the Group Captain, calibrating the mileage on a slide rule. His calculations complete, he draws a circle on the map with a compass. After further discussion, the RAF man pinpoints an area on the chart. If the Village exists, it lies somewhere on the coast of Morocco, South West of Portugal and Spain: an island perhaps. With over 1,750 square miles to search, its quite an undertaking. Nevertheless the ex-prisoner has got to discover the truth, and the authorities agree to give him every assistance — even if it means scouring every inch of the world. Early next morning, a milk float arrives at an aerodrome in the country. Inside a mission control room, the Group Captain confirms that clearance has been given for refuelling at Gibraltar. 'Good,' says the man once known as Number 6. 'Then we'll sweep as far as we can today, and again tomorrow.' 'And tomorrow and tomorrow ... you're a stubborn fellow Number 6,' grins the Colonel. 'James, you call me that once again, and you're liable for a bout in the

hospital,' threatens the ex-prisoner, dressed now in RAF flying gear. 'I won't be a minute,' calls the Group Captain from inside the changing room. 'Good luck,' smiles the Colonel shaking his ex-colleagues' hand, paying little attention to the milkman walking into the building behind him. 'Thanks,' says the other striding over to the reconnaissance plane. Watched by the Colonel and Thorpe, the man climbs into the jet and the pilot taxies down the runway. 'Interesting fellow,' says Thorpe. 'He's an old, old friend ... who *never* gives up,' says the Colonel as the jet soars over their heads.

'Turn. Sweep back 15 degrees south-west,' the man in the cockpit directs the pilot, as he plots their course on a chart resting on his knee. 'Sweep nine degrees south-west. That could be it,' he urges, leaning forward in his seat as an island sweeps into view below them. 'Get closer. There it is ... we've found it! That's it!,' he confirms as the Village is found nestled on the coast. Lowering his sun visor, the co-pilot prepares for a low level fly past. But the pilot has other ideas. Sliding back his visor and releasing his breathing mask, the man at the controls edges his hand towards the aircraft's yellow ejection lever. 'Be seeing you,' grins the milkman turning to stare at the man behind him. A tug of the lever and the co-pilot is ejected high into the clouds, his parachute opening atuomatically. Down, down he falls, watched by a solitary figure – the grinning black cat, who sits immobile on the wall of the cafe. Landing with a thump on the golden sand, the man releases his harness and climbs to his feet. Watched by the cat, he paces through the familiar streets and returns to his cottage. Pausing on the veranda, he scans the still-deserted Village, his face betraying his thoughts. This round is theirs. But there will be others. Turning, he walks into his residence. As he steps into the lounge, the shower which he had turned on before he had left gushes forth a fountain of water. The lights come on. The coffee percolator begins to bubble away and the black cat creeps into the room – followed by Mrs Butterworth, carrying the Prisoner's birthday cake! 'Many happy returns,' she grins, as crossing to the window. Number 6 peers outside to see a procession of villagers parading the square!

Author's Note: The first episode to break the tradition of showing the identity of the current Number 2 during the opening credit sequence — necessary, of course, to achieve the 'twist in the tail' finalé (although the voice used for Number 2 is that of a male — actor Robert Rietty).

Courtesy of stock footage from *Arrival*, Script Editor George Markstein 'returns' as the man behind the desk.

Number 6's birthday is given as 19th March — McGoohan's own birthdate.

Slides are being projected onto a screen which stands mounted on an easel before the doors of an office. The majority are of landscapes: a scenic Scottish loch, the Eiffel Tower in Paris, a rugged, wind-swept coastline. Viewing the screen sit two men, a silver-haired civil servant (and head of the British Secret Service) named Sir Charles, and a man whose head is barely visible over the rear of a high-backed chair. A third man is operating the slide projector. 'Cipher, coding, optics – still known as computers, experts in every field . . . and yet we're still left 36 dreary and badly photographed colour shots,' complains the man in the high-backed chair. 'Yet I'm convinced they contain the clue we want,' says Sir Charles. 'Have you tried superimposing?' 'Yes we have sir,' replies the other. 'But as you'll appreciate, the permutations on 36 runs into millions.' 'Well, coming to them relatively fresh, one of us may get a sudden flash,' proposes the slide operator. 'That you say is Loch Ness?' asks Sir Charles, peering at the screen. 'Yes sir. We've pinpointed the position exactly,' confirms the other, shuffling in his chair. 'Not an inspired photographer, however brilliant a scientist,' quips the silver-haired man. 'Extraordinary order of filming isn't it . . . Loch Ness, the Yorkshire Moors, Dartmouth, the Eiffel Tower, Beachy Head . . . What's Number 6?' A man's photograph is flashed onto the screen. 'Hopelessly over-exposed . . .' comments Sir Charles '. . . I wonder if there's a reason?' 'Well there are nine on the roll very over-exposed, and as many under, the rest are correctly exposed,' confirms the man in the high-backed chair. We see his face now, and learn his codename: another civil servant called 'V'. 'I hate to mention this Sir Charles, but er . . . it is possible that there is no clue to be found in these shots.' 'How do you work that out?' asks the silver-haired man. 'Breaking a code or a cipher is a finite problem, but as I said, with these we don't know that there is a problem, and if there is, on what level of reasoning it is set.' 'We just haven't thought of it,' proposes Sir Charles, 'and I don't accept that it is impossible to do so. Do we know where Seltzman is?' He turns to look back at the blurred image of the man on the screen . . . .

DO NOT FORSAKE ME, OH MY DARLING

Written by Vincent Tilsley

Guest stars

Janet	Zena Walker
Number 2	Clifford Evans
The Colonel	Nigel Stock

with

The Butler	Angelo Muscat
Seltzman	Hugo Schuster
Sir Charles	John Wentworth
Villiers	James Bree
Minister	Kynaston Reeves
Danvers	Lloyd Lamble

and

Camera Shop Manager	Lockwood West
Potter	Frederic Abbott
Cafe Waiter	Gertan Klauber
Old Guest	Henry Longhurst
1st Young Man	Danvers Walker
Young Guest	John Nolan

Directed by Pat Jackson

A helicopter hovers over the Village and lands softly on the lawn beside the swimming pool. Pictured on Number 2's monitor screen, Number 6 walks from his kitchen and enters his lounge carrying a coffee cup and a slice of toast. Biting into the bread, he crosses the room to peer out of his window then turns to stalk the room like a caged cat. 'Relax, relax old boy . . .' murmurs Number 2 '. . . it won't be long now.' Having raced through the streets and deposited its passenger outside the Green Dome, a Village taxi drives away at speed. Inside the building, Number 2 rises from his oval-shaped chair to greet the man flown in by the helicopter. 'Ah, Colonel. Had a good trip?' he asks, shaking the newcomer's hand. 'Yes thank you,' says the guest, descending the ramp, his eyes taking in the bizarre surroundings. Asking the newcomer if he's had breakfast, Number 2 leads the middle-aged man to his control console. 'I'd appreciate knowing my duties as soon as possible,' says the Colonel. 'You've no idea why you're here?' grins the superior. 'All I know is I was sent here by the highest authority,' returns the other, anxious to proceed. 'You were indeed. You should be very proud.' 'I'm gratified certainly . . . and now, if you'd be kind enough to explain what I'm supposed to do?' Draining the last drop of coffee from his cup, then dismissing the mute Butler with a nod of his head, the superior motions for the newcomer to look at the monitor screen, on which is pictured Number 6 still pacing his room. 'What sort of opinion do you form? . . . of that fellow,' asks Number 2. The Colonel watches the man's actions with interest. 'Anybody who spends his time doing that, must be rather stupid,' he comments. 'You couldn't be more wrong, because *he's* our most interesting citizen from every point of view,' says Number 2. 'Particularly yours.' 'Why's that?' 'You'll find out,' grins the superior, crossing to join his guest. 'Tell me, have you heard of Professor Seltzman . . . Professor Jacob

Seltzman?' 'I don't seem to recall the name ... should I?' asks the Colonel. 'No. in your line of business I suppose not.' confirms Number 2. 'Doctor Seltzman is a great neurologist who became fascinated with the study of thought transference.' 'I've actually seen it done. in India.' says the newcomer. '... Where Seltzman studied for many years. As you know the advanced Yogi is capable of living in a state of suspended animation for months. his mind and body disassociate ...' says Number 2. '... Now what Seltzman did. was to take this dicipline several stages further. and with scientific aid. he was able to transmit the psyche of one person into *another*.' 'The mind of one man into another. Impossible. I don't believe it!' exclaims the Colonel. 'Where is this Seltzman?' 'Nobody knows.' sighs Number 2. 'The only man who may because he. had the last contact with him. hmm. is our friend.' he concludes. leaving the other to stare at the man pictured on the monitor screen. 'Are you asking me to believe that it's possible for me to become you and you to become me?' asks the Colonel. turning back to the superior. 'Not exactly. but near enough.' confirms Number 2. 'I don't believe it!' challenges the guest. 'Colonel. if I told you that ten years ago that you could've flown a rocket around the moon would you have believed that?' 'No. I suppose not ... but *why* all this interest in Seltzman?' 'Colonel.' replies Number 2. enjoying the game. 'You must be aware that all major powers have in their prisons one or two of each other's spies ...' 'Yes.' '... From time to time diplomatic swaps take place ... imagine the power we could have if the spies we returned had the mind of *our* choosing. We could break the security of any nation. Let me show you one or two other things that will interest you.' Leading the Colonel out of the chamber. Number 2 shows him in to an examination

room. 'Now we call this our amnesia room. d'you like the title? With it we can erase the memory back to any point in time we choose ...' instructs Number 2. crossing to where a man lies strapped to an operating couch. his head connected by wires to a machine. on which is projected the silhouette of a soldier. 'This man you see. was extremely cooperative. he told us all we needed to know in three days ... with hardly any persuasion ... so now we can wipe out all unhappy memories of the Village. and put him back into circulation to gather more information.' A doctor arrives to check the patient's pulse. Elsewhere. four uniformed guards push their way into the Prisoner's cottage. 'And this ...' continues Number 2. leading the Colonel to a row of banked electrical machinery. '... is a Seltzman machine ...' A struggling Number 6 is dragged from his cottage by the four guards and thrown. without ceremony. into the back of a canopied buggy trailer. '... Let me give you a dummy run.' continues Number 2. handing the Colonel a pair of tinted goggles. Indicating to a technician to switch on the machine. the superior gives a running commentary as the bank of machinery buzzes into life and the room is bathed in a piercing blue light. 'A device with which Seltzman finally succeeded in switching the minds of two people ...' informs Number 2. Watching in astonishment. the Colonel can scarcely believe his eyes as the room itself appears to pulsate and a pink vapourish cloud begins to form over two empty operating couches sitting at the rear of the room.

Back before his monitor screen. Number 2 stares at the image of a drugged Number 6 who lies on one of the operating couches. His eyes are covered by opaque goggles and wires are attached to the side of his head. 'Sleep well my friend. and forget us ... tomorrow you will wake up a new man.' whispers the superior wryly.

'This man you see was extremely cooperative'

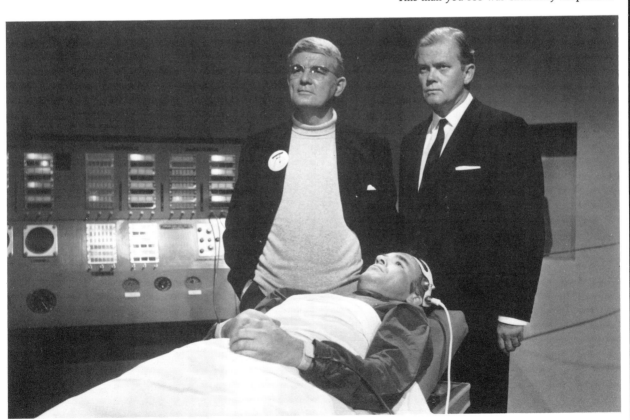

'Hmm,' growls the figure in the bed (we do not see his face). Humming, he stares at his wristwatch, throws back the bedsheets, slips on his dressing gown and walks to the window to peer through the venetian blind. A familiar London street is seen. 'Yes, not a bad day,' he says. 'Let's see ...' He spots a framed photograph of a pretty young girl. '... oh yes, Janet's birthday present ...' He lifts the picture. '... Hope she likes it ... can always change it if she doesn't.' Replacing the photograph in its position next to the telephone, he crosses over to his day-to-day jotter sitting on top of the writing bureau. 'What's on for today? Let's see ... car service, dentist's appointment, no no, we'll have to cancel that because Sir Charles' lunches go on forever, but who can blame him ... he's the boss.' (Although we have yet to see his face, the voice we hear is definitely that of the Prisoner.) Passing into his entrance hall, he catches sight of his reflection in the mirror there – and stops dead in his tracks. He has the face and body of the Colonel! Back in his control room, with the mute Butler in attendance, Number 2 concentrates hard on the image of the drugged Number 6 pictured on his monitor screen. '... *Seltzman machine ... a device with which Seltzman finally succeeded in switching the mind, switching the mind ...*' drones a voice in the Prisoner's brain. '*Relax ...*' begins Number 2, as scenes from the drugged man's past flicker through the patient's mind: 'I am not a number, I am a person ...' The soothing voice urges him not to be aggressive. '*You mustn't resist ... Take it easy, take it easy ... it will all be won in the end ... The thing to do now is keep calm ... Keep your head...*' 'I will not be pushed, filed, stamped, indexed, briefed, debriefed, or numbered,' warns the image on the monitor screen. '... *Just bear in mind your ultimate objective ... We want information*' drones the voice. '... Information!' exclaims Number 2. '*Seltzman ... Seltzman ...*' the voice tears at his brain '... *Proceed as our friend would have done ... relax ... good ... now go boy ... go ... This is the time ... Now ... Move or leave it ... move move move ... Seltzman...!* Will the voice never end?

It does, abruptly, as the doorbell behind the Prisoner confirms that he has a caller.

AUTHOR'S NOTE: Once again, life for the Prisoner becomes more complicated than usual. Like it or not, he now occupies the Colonel's body. In order to make the plot more lucid, from this point onwards, the actions and dialogue of Number 6, will be attributed to the Colonel's given name – Oscar.

With a final glance at his reflection, Oscar opens the door. His caller is Janet, the girl in the photograph. 'His car,' says the girl, nodding in the direction of the pavement. 'Is he back? ... is he with you?' Confused, Oscar gulps. 'Yes,' he confirms as the girl walks past him. 'Darling, darling,' she calls, entering the house and climbing the stairs. The man holds his head. What can he do? How should he act? 'His' mind is in another man's body. 'Where is he?' asks the girl behind him. 'Janet ... however fantastic what I'm going to tell you may sound, you must believe me ...' 'Who are you? How do you know my name?' asks the confused girl. 'What are you doing here any ... How did you get hold of his car? Why ... why did you tell me he was here? Who are you?' 'A friend,' he returns weakly. 'Well then, where is he? Why did he leave without a word to *me*?' 'Leave! But he saw you, he told me he saw you last night.' 'Last night? I didn't

see him last night.' 'But he had dinner with you, after your fitting.' 'What fitting?' asks Janet, perplexed by the man's words. 'Your dress, for the party, your birthday party, he even told me the colour, yellow silk.' 'Yellow silk? The only y ...' she stares back at the other in amazement. '... that was a year ago. Yes, I took him to the final fitting ... I haven't seen him since.' 'A year!' exclaims Oscar. 'A year ... what's happened?' 'You couldn't have seen him ... even if you had, he couldn't have made *that* mistake,' confirms Janet, following the man into the sitting room. 'No, but *I* could have ...' he falters. '... I *must* have got it wrong.' 'Yes you must have ... What are you doing here? How did you get in anyway?' 'Miss Portland, you must be aware of the sort of work he did?' 'Obviously, working for my father,' she confirms. 'So it won't come as a surprise to you to learn that ...' He falters, biting his lip '... it may not be possible for him to get in touch with you for a year, or even longer.' Lowering her eyes, she replies 'Thanks, that's a big help.' Sighing, she turns to leave. 'Miss Portland,' he calls 'I may have a message for you soon.' 'When?' 'I'll bring it to your birthday party,' he says, as Janet leaves. Catching sight of his reflection in the hall mirror, Oscar angrily smashes the looking glass into fragments with his fist.

Having returned to her home and entered her father's study, Janet finds Sir Charles talking to two men. 'Father, I must have a word with you,' she calls, ignoring the guard posted by the door. He points out that it is not a very convenient time and that he sincerely hopes that she is not about to make a practice of bursting into his room unannounced. Told by his daughter that her business is both important and personal, Sir Charles asks the men to give them a few minutes alone. 'Now my dear?' he asks sitting at his desk. 'You know where he is ... all this time you've known and you've let me go through this hell. You sent him on a mission, he can't get in touch with me.' 'I presume we're talking about your fiancé,' says Sir Charles. 'His house, his car, he's lent them to a friend,' she says. 'A friend? Tell me about him ... what sort of a man is he?' asks her father. 'He's perfectly ordinary ... Is he able to get in touch with me?' 'I honestly don't know.' 'Do you mean you haven't sent him on a mission?' 'No,' shrugs her father. 'And you must realise I'm telling you more than I should. I shouldn't even tell you that.' 'You mean even you don't know where he is?' asks Janet. 'I have no idea,' her father replies shaking his head. 'But you must know someone who does.' 'There again I can't help you.' 'It's awful. I don't know whether you're telling me the truth or not,' she accuses, turning her head away in disgust. When her father remains passive in his seat, Janet leaves. At that moment, outside 'his' residence, Oscar leaps into the yellow and green customised Lotus 7 which stands parked at the curb. Revving its engine, he sets out at speed and weaves the machine through the busy London traffic, following the route indelibly etched in his mind – a mind which now occupies the body of another. The drive to the underground car park is accomplished in minutes, as is the purposeful march along its dimly-lit corridor. The metal 'exit' doors offer no resistance, nor does the man sitting beneath the map of the world – a new face this time, a younger man climbing his way up the ladder of seniority – who offers little beyond a token 'Who are you? What are you doing here?' The young man finds himself being grabbed by the collar and hoisted from his chair by the intruder who demands that he gets him Sir Charles Portland at once! Supported by his jacket lapels, the executive knocks over his tea cup as his fingers snake out across his desk to press an alarm button.

Their roles are now reversed, with the man back in his seat and Oscar standing erect before the desk. His determination unchanged, despite the two burly guards who stand but a few feet away, the intruder's daring knows no limits. 'You're still as pompous as ever Danvers,' Oscar grins to the man behind the desk. 'Where did you get my name?' demands the seated man. 'Jonathan Peregrine Danvers. Born in Bootle. Took elocution lessons . . . came to London in 1948 as a junior clerk. Was moved to this department some three years later, mainly at the request of the typing pool . . . Am I going to see Sir Charles? Well . . . or would you prefer me to go on . . . I'm sure these 'gentlemen' would be most intrigued to hear of your little jaunt to Paris in March 1958 . . . Let me see now, what was her name . . .' Danvers is saved from further embarrassment by the arrival in the room of another man. Walking calmly to Oscar's side, he demands the intruder's name. 'Code or real?' taunts the intruder. 'Code.' 'In France, Duval. In Germany, Schmit. You would know me best as ZM 73, and your code number is PR12. Do you want more . . . Seltzman,' grins Oscar. 'Alright, thank you,' says PR12, dismissing the two heavies who stand at the door. 'Danvers, I must ask you to leave.' 'Yes sir,' says the man behind the desk, rising to follow his companions out of the room. 'What do you know about Seltzman?' asks the superior when the men are alone. 'He invented the device that makes it possible to put one man's mind into another man's head,' states the intruder. The one denoted PR12, is aghast, particularly when the other slips a photograph of Number 6 from his pocket. Aware now that the intruder knows something, the superior escorts him into an elevator. Several stories above their departure point, the two men step into a corridor. Having shown his pass to the guard at an office door PR12 and his companion are allowed to enter. Ushered into Sir Charles' study, Oscar marches to the man's desk. 'Sir Charles, at last . . . I am ZM73.' 'You claim to be ZM73,' challenges the silver-haired man. 'And I can prove it!' 'Do so,' bids Sir Charles. 'I could pitch this on a very personal level Sir Charles . . .' 'Oh don't spare my feelings,' grins the other 'speak as freely as you wish.' 'Very well,' says Oscar. 'I will confine myself to simple domestic details, of no interest to anyone accept the family . . . Details incidentally which couldn't possibly be known to anyone except ourselves, would you accept that . . .?' 'Yes, I suppose so,' says Sir Charles. The newcomer proceeds with his claim: Sir Charles is a rosarian and it was while he was pruning his baccara, the one down by the little goldfish pool, that ZM73 asked for the hand of his daughter. He remembers that Sir Charles dropped his secateurs — he had never understood why, because it could not have been all that much of a surprise. The next day Sir Charles had taken him to lunch at his club. They had their favourite dish, jugged hare. But still Sir Charles refutes his story. 'I don't dispute the accuracy of your statement, it's correct in every detail. The trouble is, you see, there's nothing you can tell me which may not have been told to you by the person you claim to be under sedation or hypnosis,' says Sir Charles. 'It could have all been recorded and you could have learned it parrot fashion.' 'Ask me the minutest details of anything you know that we did together,' urges Oscar. The same problem applies, the other confirms. 'I could never convince you then,' states Oscar. 'Only sufficiently to intrigue me . . . to make sure that you are watched and followed every inch of wherever you go,' confirms the

silver-haired man. 'It's a waste of somebody's time,' growls Oscar. 'He'll be paid for it.' 'Thank you, thank you very much,' says Oscar, making his way back to the elevator alone, the words of his alter-ego urging him onward. 'Where is he? . . . where is he? . . . where is he? . . . Did he perfect the reversion process? If he didn't . . . it's a pity.' Driving back to his home, he overtakes a long black saloon – a hearse. Are they after him again? A false alarm. The hearse has followed a different route . . . perhaps so, but why is he now passing the ominous vehicle again as he brakes the Lotus to a stop outside his home – and what dark business in the street does the gaunt-faced undertaker have, the one standing by the parked hearse just a few feet down the road? Entering the house, the words of his alter-ego begin anew. 'Before I know it, I'll be inside for forgery . . . Talking of forgery, is my handwriting still the same? Let's see, lets try it . . .' he checks the Prisoner's handwriting against his own. They are the same. The alter-ego laughs '. . . That's rather interesting isn't it . . . that's something . . . Well let's be grateful for small mercies . . . Now, money. Unless the rats have been at it . . .' He opens a safe, secreted behind his television set. '. . . good . . . still intact . . . fresh as ever. Splendid.' Oscar counts the wad of bank notes he has removed from the safe. '. . . That should be adequate.' Placing the bank notes into his wallet, Oscar picks up the framed photograph of Janet. An idea.

'Are you sure he's being followed,' Sir Charles asks PR12, as the superior enters his boss' study. 'We've attached a homing device to his car, our man will be there by now,'

Entering the Portlands' mansion, Oscar finds the party in full swing

confirms the junior. It is dark when a tuxedo-suited Oscar enters the Portlands' mansion. A party is in full swing and a waiter hands him a glass of champagne. Of course, it is Janet's birthday. Draining his glass, he elbows his way through the guests and escorts Janet to the dance floor. 'I didn't invite you,' she says, as they glide around the floor. 'Our friend lent me his card, a year out of date . . .' 'You've seen him?' 'Not exactly,' he grins. 'Look. Do you work for my father. Did he send you here?' 'No, but I've no doubt that he knows that I'm here . . . When I arrived they were playing a waltz, the first I danced with my love . . .' The girl stares at him in astonishment. '. . . my dear beloved in Kitzbühel.' This cannot be happening. 'How do you know all this? Where is he? Please,' pleads Janet. 'I have a message from him . . . before he went, he left something with you for safe keeping in case of trouble. A slip of paper.' 'Yes, yes I have it,' she says, unable to comprehend how 'he' can know so much about 'him'. 'Do you want to see him again? Will you get it . . . I'll be in the arbour,' he urges, ending their dance and retreating through the French windows. 'May I?' asks a young man, inviting the girl to dance. *Was she just trying to get rid of me? Will she come? Will she have the receipt?* whispers his alter-ego as Oscar waits in the garden. But Janet does arrive and she has the receipt. 'I'm sorry I was so long . . . here it is,' she apologises handing Oscar a scrap of paper. 'What was the message?' 'Simply this . . .' he replies, raising his hand to caress her cheek. Following this with a peck to each cheek and one to her nose, he embraces the girl and they share a long passionate kiss. Pulling away, she steps backwards, her thoughts unable to grasp what has happened. 'Who else could have given you *that* message?' he asks over his shoulder. 'Nobody . . . but . . .?' 'Couldn't you say, nobody but you . . . I need your faith.' Janet turns. 'Nobody but . . . *you*,' she concedes. She knows now. As difficult as it is for her to understand, she knows.

Bright and early the next morning, Oscar makes his way to a high street camera shop to collect an order 'he' left there 12 months earlier; a roll of film which he had left to be developed into transparencies. Handed the receipt, the camera shop owner confirms that the order had been collected by a Mr Carmichael – a clerical error. However, discovering his mistake the man had returned them, so no harm has been done. 'How very good of Mr Carmichael,' says Oscar. 'It's very kind of you to take it that way sir. Alas, no business can be entirely free from the occasional clerical error. Is there anything else sir?' 'Yes.' 'What is that sir?' 'Can I get a photograph taken?' asks Oscar. 'A photograph?' 'Yes. A passport photograph.' 'I'm afraid our photographer's away on holiday at the moment sir,' replies the shop owner. 'Hmm, he would be.' However, the other is happy to oblige – as long as the customer does not require a flattering study, but one that will be satisfactory for the passport authorities. 'Thank you,' says Oscar. 'It's a pleasure sir. This way . . .' grins the camera shop owner leading the customer into a back room.

'He has collected the transparencies sir,' confirms PR12, reporting to Sir Charles. 'Condones my conviction . . . somewhere they contain a clue and our own bright boys have missed it,' states the superior. Followed back to his home by Potter, one of Sir Charles' men, Oscar parks his Lotus at the curb and enters his home. 'XB4,' reports Potter, from his car parked outside the house. 'He's gone inside . . . and now the living room curtains are being drawn.' The lookout is ordered to stay at his post and follow his quarry when he leaves. Having erected a projection screen in his living room, Oscar moves to his desk, pulls a writing pad towards him and writes two rows of figures on the blank page. One above the other they read: SELT and ZMAN. This done, he counts on his fingers and writes the number five above the letter E. A further finger count and the number 20 is placed above the letter T. Muttering aloud he whispers, 'Miss out the one M . . .' then, counting aloud on his fingers, '. . . A, b,c,d,e,f,g,h,i,j,k,l,m – 13, and N must be 14 . . .' The letters M and N on the paper before him are numbered 13

and 14 respectively. Shuffling the numbered slides into a certain order, he begins to lay each one by its equivalent number on the writing pad. This done, he sets aside the unwanted slides and places the remainder into the projector, superimposing one on top of the other. By using a special set of dark lenses which are snapped into place over his reading glasses, he reads off the words that are now magically brought into view on the screen, KANDERSFELD, AUSTRIA. Shutting off the projector, he locates the town in an Atlas, destroys his notes and stows the projector away. 'Hello sir,' reports Potter from his car, 'the curtains are now being opened . . . he's coming out of the house and getting into the Lotus.' 'Follow him,' orders Sir Charles.

'Our route is definitely Dover,' reports Potter, following the Lotus as its speeds down the A20 to the ferry port. Using the electronic bug planted on Oscar's car, the pursuer follows his quarry aboard. A short time later, Oscar steers the Lotus into the forecourt of an Austrian cafe. 'Welcome to the village sir,' greets a waiter. 'What would you like to order?' 'I took some photographs, look . . . here's one,' says the customer, handing the waiter one of his colour slides. 'Is he still here?' 'Yes, Herr Hallen sir,' confirms the other. 'Where is he now?' 'In the barber's shop I suppose,' grins the waiter, pointing to a building across the street. Entering the establishment, Oscar is greeted by a grey-haired old man wearing a barber's smock. The man greets him in a foreign tongue. 'Good afternoon, Herr Hallen. The waiter at the cafe told me I could get a shave here.' 'That is correct sir,' confirms the barber, lapsing into foreign dialect again as he motions for the customer to sit in a chair by a sink. 'Please sit down mein herr.' 'Your English is very good,' says Oscar lowering himself into the seat. 'Yes,' replies the other, explaining that he learned his trade in London, but returned to the village in which he was born. 'Herr Hallen, I may as well come to the point,' says Oscar, resisting the man's attempts to drape a smock around his shoulders. 'I don't want a shave, I want your help, desperately . . .' 'In what way sir?' asks the other. 'We have met before. But you couldn't possibly remember me because the first time we met I looked like this.' He hands the other a photograph of himself. (The Prisoner). 'It is not possible!' exclaims the man. 'You see, Professor Seltzman, your invention works . . . only too well.' 'I am simply a village barber,' tries the other. 'Don't play tricks on an old man, I beg of you.' 'Believe me, Herr Professor, you're the last person in the world I would choose but somebody's played a wretched trick on me. Do you recognise that face?' 'Of course, he was a friend . . . But anyone who has that photograph could claim to be him.' 'For what reason?' asks the customer. 'Perhaps you will tell me,' says the other returning the photograph. 'I understand,' says Oscar, rising to his feet. 'Incognito, until I can prove that I *am* that man. When everything I tell you can be countered by you. By saying that I have extracted the information by fair means or foul.' 'Yes, that is so,' says the barber. 'Herr Professor, would you admit that, as with fingerprints no, two handwritings could be the same?' 'I would.' 'Then the only way that I can prove to you that I am that man, depends on whether or not you kept that letter I sent you over a year ago from London when you were staying in Scotland.' 'If you really are who you say you are, you would not have expected me to keep it. Would you?' challenges the other. 'No . . .' sighs Oscar. 'It's a hopeless situation.' 'If I had kept it I would have been very stupid, silly.' 'You've made your point, I accept it,' sighs the customer accepting his fate. 'But you overlook one thing ...' grins the other '... Sentimental people *are* sometimes stupid, very stupid. Wait please,' he smiles, disappearing from the room. Potter, meanwhile, guided by the blips from the hidden bug, is approaching the village at speed. The barber soon returns, carrying with him a letter. Having written the man's Scottish address on his note pad, Oscar tears off the page and hands it to the Professor for comparison. The handwriting matches the envelope the customer mailed to his friend 12 months earlier. 'My poor young friend ... but *who?*' 'I don't know,' replies the other. 'The motive is clear. You will lead them to me, that is what they hope. Do you think your people have done this to you?' 'No, I'm sure ...' Oscar says. 'Then it must be your enemies.' 'My enemies presumably having my other half.' 'Precisely. If you are taken by the side that hasn't you must learn to accept yourself as you are.' As they speak, Potter enters the village and parks his car at the cafe across the street. 'As both sides want my reversal process it will be a close race,' says the Professor. 'Then the reversal process *does* exist?' 'In theory, but put into practice, it could be dangerous. Very,' warns the elderly man, leading Oscar to the window. Drawing back the curtain and seeing Potter heading across the street towards them, the Professor asks his friend if his face is familiar. 'Potter,' confirms Oscar. 'We must not be taken by *him*.' 'Then hide behind this door,' urges his friend, leading the other into a room at the rear of the shop. Closing the door behind him, Oscar stares down into the darkened cellar below. 'Come in, come in,' calls the Professor, as Potter stalks into the shop. 'Don't move please, Professor,' warns the thug, ignoring the man in the chair. Having searched the shop thoroughly, he notices the door at the rear of the premises. Sliding his gun from its holster, Potter rams open the door. Grabbing the thug's arm, Oscar pulls him into the cellar and the men fight on the staircase. Downwards they tumble, picking up where they left off on the cellar floor. Snatching up a chair, Potter brings it crashing down onto his opponent's head, but still Oscar fights back, the fury and strength of his punches sending the other reeling backwards. The fight is hard-fought and culminates with both men lying unconscious – overcome by the clouds of acrid gas emitting from a strange gun held by a third man, who, having descended the staircase unseen, grins as the men fall backwards into oblivion.

'Ah, Herr Professor,' greets Number 2, as Oscar and the scientist are ushered into the dome shaped chamber. 'Welcome to *our* humble village. Had a good trip? At least let me offer you some breakfast,' grins the superior, turning to the po-faced Butler. 'You have kidnapped me for one reason ... my answer is no!' challenges the Professor. 'You are livery this morning Professor,' laughs Number 2. 'Surely neither of us wants to prolong this interview,' says the scientist. 'Life has not brought you sweet resignation,' quips Number 2. 'Nor has it for many other scientists. Rutherford, for example. How he must regret having split the atom.' 'Yes ...' mocks Number 2, '... almost as bad as splitting two human beings. Unlike all the king's men, only you can put them together again.' 'Don't rely on it,' warns the Professor. 'Why make this stand now. You must have known what you were doing when you invented the wretched process,' states the superior. 'Only people like you have made it wretched.'

The fury of Oscar's punches send Potter reeling

'Can you really leave this poor man with his mind wrongly housed,' challenges Number 2, indicating Oscar. 'Surely you owe him some slight responsibility.' Pausing for a moment to glance sideways at his friend and then at the monitor screen on which is pictured Number 6 – his head strapped to a concoction of wires, his eyes unseen behind the black-tinted goggles – the Professor gathers his thoughts. 'I will do it . . . on certain conditions,' he concedes. 'I'm sure they will be reasonable,' grins Number 2, putting on his glasses. 'For once *I* am dictating,' snaps the scientist. 'Heil . . .', mocks the superior, raising his arm in a Nazi salute. 'I will do it . . . but alone, under this condition only,' states the Professor. 'I accept,' nods Number 2. 'Very well. I shall need time to prepare myself. In 12 hours . . .' stipulates the scientist, departing from the chamber with his friend. Alone, the superior's lips draw back into an insidious grin. Twelve hours later, the experiment gets under way, watched from his Control Room by Number 2 and a group of white-coated observers. 'All cameras turn . . . make a note of everything he does,' orders the superior, as the Professor enters the laboratory to begin the reversal process. Viewed on the monitor screen, the scientist flicks on the bank of machinery. Then, placing an electrode device over his head, he sits down in a chair positioned between Oscar and his alter-ego, who are strapped to the operating couches within arms-reach of the scientist. At the flick of a switch, a milky-pink cloud begins to form over the head of Number 6, while a blue haze shimmers above Oscar's head. The power is increased and a flickering array of electrical disturbance channels its way across the divide between the recumbent men; the man in the chair forming a three-way link between them. But the power is too great. With trembling hands, the Professor slumps forward, his teeth biting his lips, his face a mask of torment. 'Emergency . . . examination room, immediate treatment,' screams Number 2. *'Emergency, emergency,'* echoes a voice over the public address system. Within seconds, two male orderlies race into the laboratory and place the Professor's unconscious body onto a stretcher. *'Emergency, emergency,'* screams the voice from the public address system as an ambulance races away from the building. 'He must not die . . . I need him,' orders Number 2, to the group of medical people attending the scientist's body. 'Thank you Colonel,' he says to Oscar 'Your help has been invaluable.' 'I trust I've been of service,' comments the other. 'Yes. You'll be suitably rewarded . . . the helicopter is waiting for you.' Slipping on his jacket, the Colonel leaves. 'You assured me that he was in good health,' whispers the Professor, raising himself from the couch. 'You must contact Number 1, and tell him that I did my duty . . .' With a final gasp of breath, the patient slumps backwards onto the stretcher. 'The *Colonel* . . .?' hisses Number 2, concerned by the dead man's words ' . . . the man who is just flying out of here . . .?' He stares to the ceiling as the helicopter passes over head. ' . . . Is not who you thought it was,' confirms Number 6, sitting erect on the couch. 'I don't believe it . . . I *watched.* I saw *everything,'* whispers a resigned Number 2. Stripping off his goggles, and tearing the wires from his person, Number 6 delivers the coup de grace. 'The good doctor's mind now inhabits a body perhaps not to his liking . . . the Colonel's . . . Dr Seltzman had progressed more than any of us had anticipated. He *can* and *did change three minds at the* same time.' The ashen-faced superior stares back at him in total amazement. 'He's now free to continue his experiments in peace,' concludes

Number 6, as the helicopter soars high over the Village. With the Colonel dead in the Professor's body, Number 2 has lost both the game and his post!

'The man flying out of here is not the man you thought it was'

AUTHOR'S NOTE: A different pre-credit scene and slightly different title sequence appear in this story.

The letter to Professor Seltzman is addressed in McGoohan's own hand and the address on the envelope 'Portmeirion Road' was an in-joke. All McGoohan's scenes were done in a one day shoot.

Originally filmed under the working title *Face Unknown.*

A lone rider gallops across the prairie, his mount given free rein to increase its speed. At his desk in a nearby town sits a Marshal, pen in hand, filling in a report. As if by magic, the Prisoner appears before him, his dark-piped blazer replaced by a thigh-length buckskin range coat, his legs protected by western-style riding breetches, a low-slung Colt 45 strapped to his right hip. Staring at the Marshal from beneath the brim of his stetson, the intruder flicks out his hand and a badge lands squarely on the lawman's desk – but not, as could be expected, one bearing the numeral '6', but a star-shaped Sheriff's badge of office. Returning the newcomer's stare, the lawman pays scant attention as the intruder unbuckles his gun belt and slams it forcefully down on the desk to join the Sheriff's star. Heaving his saddle to his shoulder, the Prisoner leaves and sets out on foot across the hills. Descending a slope, he finds his way blocked by a cowboy toting a gun. Ignoring the man, he attempts to move past him but finds himself looking up the barrell of the man's revolver. The saddle, thrown with lighting speed, hits the cowboy square on the jaw, sending him reeling backwards down a grassy knoll. In a flash the Prisoner is upon him and the two men fight. Knocked to the ground, the Prisoner crawls to his knees – to find himself facing five other men. His refusal to concede brings punches raining down on his head and he is forced to his knees in an onslaught of flailing fists . . .

Having handed in his tin star, he sets out on foot

LIVING IN HARMONY

Written by David Tomblin

(from an original story by David Tomblin and Ian L. Rakoff)

Guest stars

The Kid	Alexis Kanner
The Judge	David Bauer
Cathy	Valerie French

with

Town Elder	Gordon Tanner
Bystander	Gordon Sterne
Will	Michael Balfour
Mexican Sam	Larry Taylor
Town Dignitary	Monti De Lyle

and

Horse Dealer	Douglas Jones
1st Gunman	Bill Nick
2nd Gunman	Les Crawford
3rd Gunman	Frank Maher
1st Horseman	Max Faulkner
2nd Horseman	Bill Cummings
3rd Horseman	Eddie Eddon

Directed by David Tomblin

POUNDED INTO unconsciousness, the man's body is strapped to a horse which gallops away to a nearby town. His saddle thongs are sliced and the helpless man is dumped onto a dusty street. Their work done, the horsemen ride away. Climbing groggily to his feet, he dusts himself down and stares around the town. Its streets are deserted save for one man, a Mexican who sits with his back to a watering-trough. 'Welcome to Harmony, stranger,' calls the man, as the newcomer hoists his saddle onto his shoulder. 'Harmony. Never heard of it,' states the Prisoner. 'Not many people have senor, it's sorta exclusive,' grins the other. 'So am I,' quips the stranger. 'Where is this town?' 'You'll find out senor, it's not wise to ask too many questions.' The stranger makes to leave. 'Hey hombre,' calls the Mexican, inclining his head in the direction of the cantina behind him, 'you look like a man who could use a drink . . . why not try the saloon.'

Carrying his saddle, the newcomer enters the saloon. As he does so, the place becomes silent; the pianist removes his fingers from the keys; the drinkers and card players look at him in astonishment. Ignoring their stares, he crosses over to the bar, dumps his saddle at his feet and is joined by a pretty girl. 'Regulars get the first one on the house,' she says as the bartender slides a glass of whisky down the bar. 'I'm not regular,' he quips staring at the glass. 'I'm Cathy.' 'Nice name,' he returns reaching for the drink. A shot rings out and the glass disintegrates. 'Come and join me Sheriff,' shouts a voice. 'Whisky,' he calls, ignoring the voice. The bartender fills a new glass. Downing it in one gulp, the Prisoner turns, his eyes trained on a grey-haired man – the town Judge – who sits at a table playing solitaire. Crossing to the card-player, he pauses for an instant to stare at the young man who stands at the Judge's side – the baby-faced gunslinger who shot the whisky glass from his fingers. Without warning, he sends the youngster reeling with a powerful right hand to the jaw, then pulls up a chair and joins the card-player. 'You know me,' he says. 'You shouldn'ta done that. A man needs all the friends he can find,' warns the Judge. 'I don't know you,' states the Prisoner. 'I know you. I know all about you. That's why you're here,' insists the card player. 'Where?' asks the newcomer. 'Here,' says the other gulping back his drink. 'Cathy, bring us more whisky.' At that moment, the young man the Prisoner punched recovers consciousness. The gunslinger staggers to his feet, grabs his top hat, dusts it and, given a barely perceptible nod from the Judge, leaves the saloon. 'He's good. Sensitive, but one of the best . . . but he's mean,' the card player relates. 'You've got plenty of those,' mocks the stranger. 'I could use some more . . . like yourself for instance.' 'I'm not for hire.' 'You've turned in your badge.' 'And my gun,' the Prisoner confirms. 'What were your reasons?' '*My* reasons,' replies the other with a grin. 'You've already taken a job. Who with?' 'With whom?' mocks the other. 'Look,' grins the Judge, '*I'm* offering you

a job. Harmony's a good town . . .' The saloon doors swing back and three newcomers swagger up to the bar and order drinks. ' . . . Runs smooth and peaceful. Now let's be friendly,' says the card player. 'Red two on black three,' quips the Prisoner, laying a red deuce on the card player's hand. Drawing another card from the pack, a black ace, the Judge grins. 'Think it over.' 'I already have . . . ' says the other, easing back his chair. 'And?' ' . . . I'm moving on,' grins the Prisoner, climbing to his feet and crossing to the bar where he left his saddle. Picking it up, he starts to leave. He stops, thoughtfully. Drops the saddle and walks back to the men at the bar. Removing a gambling chip from his pocket, he holds it under the nose of one of the men and flings it to the bar. Then, hoisting the saddle onto his shoulder he leaves.

'How much?' he asks, indicating a horse tethered to a post outside the stable. 'Sold,' replies the stable keeper from his rocking chair. 'The bay?' tries the Prisoner, looking at a second horse. 'How much?' '$5,000.' 'The rest?' 'They're expensive,' mocks the other. 'How's business?' quips the Prisoner, making to leave. Before him stands the town elder. 'Well stranger, fancy living in Harmony?' 'Not

'Harmony's a good town . . runs smooth and peaceful'

my kind of town.' retorts the other, walking next to the man. 'It's a good town.' says the elder, picking up the stranger's step. 'Enjoy it.' grins the other. 'Why, What's wrong with out town mister?' 'Maybe I don't like the way it's run.' replies the other. 'Oh if you just do as the Judge says, he'll look after you.' '*I* look after myself.' 'It's a good town.' the elder insists. 'Keep it!' the Prisoner exclaims, as Mexican Sam (the man who welcomed him to Harmony) grabs his saddle and heaves it to the ground. 'So you don't like our town huh. You insult us.' roars the Mexican, turning to address the group of townsfolk who have appeared on the scene. 'Are we going to let him do this?' he growls. 'He's insulted our town.' yells a resident. As the stranger picks up a length of timber to stave off their attack, a man with a gun appears on the scene. Firing the weapon in the air, he points the Colt at the stranger's chest. 'All right folks. We'll take care of him . . . now git.' At gun-point, the Prisoner is taken to the Sheriff's office. Inside he finds the Judge, sitting calmly at his desk. 'Change your mind yet?' he grins, as the crowd gathered outside scream for the stranger's head. 'Charge?' asks the Prisoner. 'Protective custody.' grins the Judge. 'Lock him up and bring Johnson out here . . . We mustn't disappoint the crowd.' Two men step forward and drag the Prisoner to a cell. As the bars slam shut in his face, another man is pulled from the adjoining cell and thrown screaming into the street. 'There he is.' yells Mexican Sam, as the crowd surges forward. Dragged beneath a tree in the town square, a noose is thrown over the man's head. His hands are tied behind his back and the lariat is thrown upwards, its trailing end looped over a sturdy branch. 'Stop it . . . stop it!' screams Cathy, arriving on the scene and racing to the intended victim's side. 'You can't hang my brother, he's done nothing wrong . . . you promised . . . ' she screams, as the blood-crazy crowd surges forwards to get a better view of the hanging. ' . . . Let go of me, let go!' the girl screams as two cowboys drag her away, her words lost in the roar of the crowd. Screaming, she faints as a blood-thirsty cowboy whips the horse from under her brother. Watching this from his cell window, the Prisoner lowers his eyes. Behind him, the young gunslinger he had earlier knocked cold, calmly quenches his thirst from a bottle.

Drunk now, and finding it difficult to maintain his equilibrium, the top-hatted youngster plays a game of now-you-see-me-now-you-don't with the Prisoner, goading the man by leaping into sight with his revolver raised in threatening manner and then back again to snatch his Colt from its holster with lightning speed. Observing the young man's antics with total disregard, the Prisoner calmly rolls himself a cigarette and sits unmoved on his bunk. After a few minutes, Cathy arrives carrying a bottle. 'I've brought you a drink Kid.' she smiles, placing the bottle on the desk next to the youngster's feet. Lowering his boots from the desk, the Kid, who is mute, walks behind her. 'You know I've always liked you Kid.' smiles the girl, as the baby-faced gunslinger grabs her and kisses her passionately on the lips, his hands clutching at her dress. 'Hey, how about pouring me one?' grins Cathy, pulling free of his hold. As the youngster searches the desk for glasses, Cathy slips the keys to the cells from a hook on the wall and hides them inside her dress. The glasses found, the mute pours her a drink and attempts to kiss her again. 'Not now Kid, I've got to get back to the saloon.' she teases. 'I'll drop by later.' Before he can offer any resistance, she quickly walks out of the door. Stunned by this new development, the Kid begins to sob, while

outside in the alley, Cathy places the keys she has stolen onto the window ledge of the Prisoner's cell. Intoxicated, the Kid curls up in a chair and drifts off to sleep. Donning his stetson, the Prisoner gently unlocks the door of his cell and slips out into the darkness. Having saddled a horse at the stable, he is about to depart when Cathy arrives carrying a canteen of water. Advised by the girl that there is only one way out, due north, the fugitive rides off into the night.

Returning to the jailhouse and finding the Prisoner gone, the Judge throws the Kid from his chair. Dazed from his drinking bout, the mute goes for his gun, but his employer slaps his face several times. Galloping away from the town, the Prisoner is lassoed by two lookouts. The lariat is tied to the pommel of a rider's horse and the Prisoner is dragged back to the town. 'Let justice be done.' grins the Judge, banging his glass on a table as the fugitive is thrown at his feet. Anticipating some fun and games, several cowboys line up their chairs in front of the Judge who, banging his gavel hard on a table, calls for order. 'Order! The court is now in session.' grins the Judge. 'What's the charge?' sneers the Prisoner. 'Against *you*, none.' smiles the Judge. 'You were only held in protective custody. You're free to go.' Turning, the Prisoner joins Cathy at the bar and pours himself a whisky. 'The people of Harmony against Catherine Johnson.' calls the Judge. 'The accused step forward.' The words burn into the Prisoner's brain. Turning to face the court, he pours himself another drink as the girl at his shoulder steps forward to face the Judge. 'You are accused of aiding a criminal to escape. How do you plead?' 'But Judge, you just said that he wasn't a criminal, he was just being held in protective custody.' a bystander pipes up. '*She* didn't know that!' snaps the Judge, quelling the outburst. 'How do you plead?' Cathy says nothing. Sometime later, the jury returns. 'Have you reached a verdict?' barks the Judge. 'We have your honour.' confirms a town dignitary. 'Do you find the defendant guilty or not guilty?' 'Guilty!' comes the reply. 'I will pass sentence later. Take her away.' Cathy is taken off to the jail and all, save the bartender, the Prisoner and the Judge leave the saloon. 'When you work for me, I'll let her go.' grins the latter, joining the Prisoner. 'You're a bad judge.' whispers the other. 'We'll see, we'll see.' grins the arbitrator, edging his way past the one he wishes to employ. Turning back to the barman, the Prisoner calls for another drink.

Placed on the far end of the bar counter, a top hat and a Colt 45 are swept along the bar to rest at the Prisoner's right wrist. It is the Kid. Peering at the newcomer from beneath his stetson, the Prisoner sighs, draws himself to his full height and turns to face the gunslinger. As if by magic, a gun appears in the Kid's hand. A shot rings out, and the Prisoner flinches as the bullet grazes his cheek. Another shot, and a trickle of blood appears on the man's left hand. 'Hold it!' cries the Judge, re-entering the saloon. 'I've been looking for you Kid . . . decided to give you your old job back. Go take care of the jail.' This pacifies the gunslinger, who, sliding his gun back into its holster, reaches across to the bar to pick up his top hat. 'You'll need two of these to take care of the woman.' taunts the Prisoner, sliding back the Kid's gun. A look of anger crosses the Kid's face. Snatching up the Colt, he aims it at the man standing at the bar. 'There's always another time Kid.' warns the Judge, grabbing the gunman's wrist. Placing his topper squarely on his head, the youngster leaves the saloon. 'The Kid's real fond of Cathy. But he does tend to get *over*-affectionate.' the grey-haired man admits. 'If anything happens, it will be paid for,' threatens the Prisoner, elbowing his way past the man. 'Nothing could happen . . . if *you* were Sheriff,' grins the Judge.

Watching the girl pacing the floor of her cell, the Kid licks his lips in anticipation of the pleasure in store. Entering the jail and seeing the gunslinger ogling Cathy's every move, the Prisoner snorts in disgust when the Judge shoves a sheriff's badge under his nose. 'Let her go!' he exclaims, snatching the star from the other man's hand. 'Let her out Kid,' orders the Judge, walking into the cell block. The youngster stares back in silence. 'I said let her out!' warns his employer. Gritting his teeth, the Kid rises from his chair and unlocks the door to Cathy's cell, his intense stare never leaving the face of his master. 'Don't give me any problems,' snarls the Judge as the girl joins the newly-elected Sheriff. 'I'm sorry,' she says. 'It's alright,' he confirms as the girl leaves the office. 'She's safe now. Safe for as long as you work for me . . . ' the Judge tells the Prisoner. ' . . . But enough of that. We don't want to start off on the wrong foot. You're gonna like this job, it's most rewarding . . . ' he says, leaving the Prisoner to bandage his hand. ' . . . No Sheriff, you won't regret joining my outfit.' 'No, but *you* may,' goads the other. 'You're just sore at the moment. Here, put this on, you'll feel better,' says the Judge, offering the other a gunbelt he has fetched from his desk. 'Nothing but the best.' 'I agreed to wear the badge. But not the guns,' states the Sheriff, knotting the bandage he has taped round his wrist. 'It's a start. But you'll find this a rough town without a gun,' warns the other, placing the gunbelt back on his desk. Later, while out on his rounds, the Sheriff is confronted by a cowboy. 'Mornin' Sheriff . . . I'm Zeke. I don't carry no gun either, but then *I* don't need one.' The Sheriff attempts to push his way past the man, but Zeke blocks his way. A mistake. Within seconds the cowboy lies flat on his back, his head resting on a pile of logs. Two others arrive, but Zeke calls them off. 'He's mine!' he screams, picking up a short piece of timber with the intention of clubbing the other into the dust. A long fight ensues and Zeke is decisively thrashed. The others join in and the Sheriff is attacked from all sides. In the saloon, the Judge rejoins his card school. 'The boys are just teaching him it's not safe to walk around without guns,' he grins, puffing on his cheroot. Outnumbered, the Prisoner gives a good account of himself as one after the other, Zeke and his companions rain blows to his jaw. Watched by the townsfolk, the men fight their way across the street until, tired and exhausted, the Sheriff is clubbed to the ground. Down but not out, he drags himself to within reaching distance of his remaining assailant (the others litter the street) crawls to his feet, and throws one final punishing knockout blow to the other man's jaw. Grabbing his groggy opponent by the shirt, he throws him sideways into the horse trough and then into the dirt. Back in his office, Cathy enters to help him bathe his wounds. 'Are you hurt?' 'Nothing a bit of water won't take care of,' he says splashing water to his face. 'I'm sorry, I'm blushing . . . I didn't think I could blush anymore,' she sighs. 'It's alright.' 'Get out or they'll kill you,' she pleads. 'The last time I got out, they dragged me back and er . . . I can't refuse that kind of hospitality. Can I?' 'You saw what they did to my brother.' 'That's one of the reasons I'm staying . . . ' 'He was a stubborn man too,' Cathy interjects. 'I'll be in the saloon tonight . . . Regulars get the first one . . . ' 'On the house,' he finishes as the girl leaves.

Things in the saloon are rowdy. A cheroot between his lips, the Kid stands at the bar, his eyes glued on Cathy,

Watched by the townsfolk, the Sheriff throws a final punishing blow to his opponent's jaw

who is enjoying a drink. At a table in the corner, two old-timers engage in an arm-wrestling contest, the man who spoke up in defence of Cathy emerging the winner. The loser, a small man, leads the victor to the bar. 'Come on bartender, let's have some whisky . . . Drink up, they're on me,' he calls throwing his arm around Cathy's shoulder. 'C'mon Cathy, you're going to have one on me,' he slurs. 'Okay Will, but don't let your wife catch you,' she teases. Witnessing this, the Kid removes the cheroot from his lips and purposefully rams the cigar into the drunken man's neck. Staggering away in pain, Will turns on his attacker. Seeing the Kid standing silently by the bar, the lethal Colt strapped to his hip, the small man stops in his tracks. Inclining his head to one side, the Kid stares back in silence. As one, everyone in the room races for cover, all save Cathy, who, approaching the youngster cautions him to wait. But he shoves her aside. Drawing his gun, Will makes no attempt to shoot, the Kid doing likewise. Backing towards the bar in a mock expression of defeat, the youngster draws with frightening speed and shoots the man through the heart. Looking silently at the crowd, the gunslinger turns to leave. At that moment, the Sheriff enters the saloon. 'Will drew first Sheriff,' confirms a bystander, as the Kid leaves the saloon. 'You're the Sheriff, it's up to you,' calls a voice from the crowd. 'It's time you did something . . . Get some guns on.' 'You're wearing the star, you know Sheriff, c'mon,' challenges another as, watched by the Judge, the lawman leaves. Later that evening, the man who spoke the loudest, pays the Sheriff a visit. 'Some of us have been talking Sheriff . . . ' 'Yeah,' replies the lawman. ' . . .

You're the only man who stood up to the Judge. So we're with you.' 'Yeah?' 'We'll help you clean up this town.' confirms the visitor. 'You're-going-to-help-*me*-clean-up-the-town.' quizzes the lawman. 'We can't do it by ourselves.' the other concedes. 'and Sheriff, neither can you.' 'Get yourself some coffee.' smiles the lawman.

'Whisky.' calls the bystander, a few minutes later as he enters the saloon. 'That one's on me.' calls the Judge over the man's shoulder. 'Come over Jim.' he bids from his table. The Sheriff's new ally joins him. 'Jim, you disappoint me . . . your choice of friends. Jim, *old* friends are the best friends. What were you talking to the Sheriff about?' The newcomer remains silent. 'Well if you won't tell me, I'm sure you'll tell the boys.' warns the Judge, signalling for his men to join them. They do so and beat the man to death! Returning from his rounds, the Sheriff finds Jim's body propped up in his chair. He snatches up his gunbelt. Checking that the Colt is loaded, he rotates its chamber and slips it snugly into its holster. He will make them pay – but not with a gun. Flinging the gunbelt aside, he stalks from the jail-house and enters the saloon. 'And *still* he doesn't wear guns.' observes the town elder from his seat next to the Judge. 'We're leaving tonight.' the Sheriff whispers to Cathy. 'But I told you, the pass is guarded. You'll never make it with me.' she states. 'Be on the edge of town . . . after the saloon closes.' he says, dismissing her warning. 'I'll be there.' she promises. 'The Kid wouldn't be too happy if he saw them with their heads together like that.' says the Judge to the man sitting next to him. 'I think someone should tell him.'

Under the cloak of darkness, the Sheriff rides into the hills where, having crept up behind a lookout, he slugs the man guarding the pass. Spotting the relief lookout sitting beside a camp-fire, he throws a lasso over the limb of a tree and swings into the campside, his feet connecting squarely on the chin of the second man who, knocked unconscious, is trussed up in his sleeping blanket. Back in the town, meanwhile, Cathy finds her way blocked by the Kid. 'Get out of my way.' she yells as the baby-faced gunslinger stares silently into her face. 'You're crazy. Now get out of my way!' she exclaims as the Kid tries to kiss her. Biting his lip, she breaks free of his hold and tries to escape from the saloon. But there is nowhere to run. Grabbing her firmly by the throat, the crazed assassin throttles her to death! Having waited for Cathy to join him, the Sheriff creeps back into the town. Seeing the Kid leaving the saloon, he races inside and finds Cathy's body. At dawn, he buries her in the town's graveyard, his solitary figure silhouetted in the early-morning sunlight, taking on the spectre of vengeance. It is war now, and they will be made to pay. Entering the jailhouse, he strips off his jacket, washes his hands and buckles the gunbelt to his hip. Tightening the holster's drawstring firmly to his calf, he slides open the Colt's chamber, spins the gun's chamber with his palm, flicks on the safety guard and replaces the revolver back in its holster. Placing his badge on the desk, he purposefully steps through the door, his jaw set, his eyes cold. The Kid stands before him, his hands held tightly at his side, shadowing the pearl-handled Colt strapped to his thigh. They stare at each other in silence until, drawing together, they fire simultaneously. Rotating the gun, the Kid slides his Colt back into its holster – and keels over dead! Walking past the dead figure, the Prisoner enters the saloon, grabs a bottle and a glass from the bar, and squats at a table. 'You *beat* him! And he was the fastest I've ever seen.' grins the Judge, entering with his henchmen. 'The fastest you will

Patrick McGoohan rehearses a scene

ever see. I just quit!' barks the Prisoner downing his whisky. 'You aren't quittin' while I've got Cathy. Just get it clear, *you* work for *me*, guns an' all.' threatens the other. 'You haven't got Cathy any longer . . . she's dead.' 'But he was only supposed to . . . ' '*Rough* her up a little bit!' snarls the Prisoner, leaping to his feet. 'Wait' calls the Judge, as the ex-Sheriff turns to leave. 'You work for me whether you like it or not! *Nobody* walks out on me . . . I'm not lettin' you join some other outfit . . . I'll *kill* you first.' Looking around him, the Prisoner weighs up the opposition: before him stand two of the Judge's gunslingers. Another peers down from the balcony. 'You've got five seconds to make up your mind.' warns the Judge, carefully edging his way out of the firing line. 'One . . . two . . . three . . . four . . .' Staring at the man on the balcony, the Prisoner draws, fires and leaps for cover behind the bar. The shot finds its target. The gunslinger above him tumbles down the stairs. Another falls backwards over a table, his face etched in agony as the Prisoner's lead pierces his heart. As the gunman's bullet strikes him in the chest, the third gunslinger is thrown backwards through the saloon window. Now for the Judge. But the Prisoner is too late. Drawing a gun from beneath his jacket, the Judge fires twice, the bullets entering the Prisoner's head. Clutching his ears, he falls backwards to the floor . . .

Still holding his head, the Prisoner wakes up on the sawdust-covered floor of the saloon. His western attire has magically vanished and he is dressed once again in his familiar Village blazer. Scrambling to his feet, he tears off the strange ear-muffs which cover his ears. Staring around the saloon and seeing the Judge, he leaps at his enemy, grabbing the man by the throat – but the figure is nothing but a lifesize cardboard cut-out. Confused, he races outside to snatch up the two-dimensional cut-out of the Kid. A cardboard horse waits in the street to carry him away. Is he going mad? Terrified, he races back into the saloon and out again, pausing to slump over a hitching-post hewn from a tree. A *wooden* hitching post! Wood! He runs his hands along its length. It is real! Hearing the sound of a brass band playing in the distance, he races towards the direction of the sound. Running down a tree-covered country lane, he finds himself staring down at – the Village! A visit to the Green Dome and the nightmare becomes clearer. Cathy is there, or at least a girl wearing the ubiquitous Village clothing and a badge numbered '22'. Aware of what has happened, he retreats from the control room, leaving the girl behind – together with the Judge and the Kid, who are now exposed as numbers 2 and 8 respectively. 'Interesting that he could separate fact from fantasy so quickly,' states Number 8. 'I told you he was different. I *knew* it wouldn't work!' exclaims Number 2. 'Fill him with hallucinatory drugs! Put him in a dangerous environment! Talk to him through microphones.' 'It's always worked, and it *would* have worked *this* time, if you hadn't . . . ' Number 8 begins. 'But it DIDN'T did it?' interjects an angry Number 2. 'Give

him love, take it away. Isolate him. Make him kill, then face him with death . . . He'll crack. Break him, even in his mind, and the rest will be easy. I should never have listened to you!' 'It would have worked, if *you* had kept your head and not created the crisis too soon,' challenges Number 8. 'How could I control it? Tell me that. You said yourself we would get involved and do what we would in a real situation.' Throwing back his head, Number 8 laughs. 'Well then, don't blame my method just your own damned lack of self-control.' 'It's alright for *you*. I have to answer for this failure,' says Number 2. Standing by the penny farthing bicycle, 'Cathy' begins to sob. 'It seems as though I'm not the only one who got involved,' says Number 2, as the girl numbered '22' races out of the chamber. Sighing, with a shrug of his shoulders, Number 8 concedes defeat.

Elsewhere, the girl enters the dummy saloon of the town called 'Harmony'. Walking to the staircase, she positions herself at exactly the spot where 'Cathy' lay when the 'Sheriff' found her. Having followed her, Number 8 now stares at the woman through the gap beneath the stairs. 'What are you doing here Number 8,' asks the one numbered '22'. Receiving no reply, she descends the staircase. 'The *game's* over Number 8,' she calls to the man in the shadows. For her perhaps, but the other has played his role too well. Edging into the light,

The Sheriff faces the townsfolk. (Scene does not appear in tx version)

he paces slowly towards the girl – his face a distorted mask of terror. Number 8 is the Kid again, reliving the role he played so well. In a flash, his hands are at the girl's throat, his nerve-shattering scream ringing in the ears of Number 6, who, strolling through the town, races into the saloon. Seeing the crazed youngster throttling the girl, he punches the maniac to the floor. Too late. Kneeling at the girl's side her dying words cut through his soul. 'I wish it had been real,' she gasps. Having driven to the town in a buggy, Number 2 dashes into the saloon as the Prisoner lays the girl's head gently to the floor. Turning to greet the newcomer in silence, Number 6, climbs to his feet as the superior looks first at the girl and then to the Kid, whose glassy-eyed stare convinces the superior that his colleague is insane. 'Keep away from me Judge, keep away . . .' screams the Kid, climbing the staircase. 'I'm getting no more . . . not going to hit me . . . no more,' he screams racing along the balcony. 'No mo...re . . . ' he yells, throwing himself to his death at the superior's feet. Leaving Number 2 staring at the girl's body, the Prisoner walks out in the darkness.

AUTHOR'S NOTE: The standard title sequence, with its newly-shot western style resignation sequence, was without the usual *The Prisoner* title theme. However, much against McGoohan's wishes, several UK television companies superimposed the words 'The Prisoner' over the title credits when the story was transmitted.

This was the only story that was NOT aired in the United States when the series premiered on American television. Five sequences hit censorship problems and were either edited or deleted altogether: Johnson's hanging, the no-holds-barred fight with Zeke, the Prisoner being dragged back to Harmony and both sequences in which 'The Kid' strangles Cathy.

This episode marks the only credited appearances of stuntmen Frank Maher and Les Crawford as the 3rd and 2nd gunmen respectively.

THE GIRL WHO WAS DEATH

Written by Terence Feely

(from an idea by David Tomblin)

Guest stars

Schnipps	Kenneth Griffith
Sonia	Justice Lord

with

Potter	Christopher Benjamin
Killer Kaminski	Michael Brennan
Boxing M.C.	Harold Berens
Barmaid	Sheena Marsh

and

Scots Napoleon	Max Faulkner
Welsh Napoleon	John Rees
Yorkshire Napoleon	Joe Gladwin
Bowler	John Drake
Little Girl	Gaynor Steward
1st Little Boy	Graham Steward
2nd Little Boy	Stephen Howe

(Alexis Kanner . . . uncredited appearance as Young Man with Camera)

Directed by David Tomblin

LIKE ALL GOOD fairy stories, our tale begins with a book whose colourful pages are turned back to reveal a picturesque English scene – a cricket match being played on a village green. Spectators sit around the perimeter and applaud as the man at the wicket swings back his bat and scores a four. The score-keeper, a man named Potter, registers the hit on his scoreboard, then taking a pair of binoculars from his sports bag, he fastens his sights on a pair of shapely legs. They belong to a pretty young blonde who sits away from the crowd in a deckchair. From the tips of her shoes to the parasol she holds aloft, she is dressed entirely in virginal white. Shifting his attention to the batsman, Potter smiles as the whiskered man gives him a wink. Awaiting the next ball, the batsman steadies himself as the lady in white eases herself from her chair and walks to the edge of the green. To raucous applause, the batsman receives the ball with a whack, and sends it skittering away to the deep clusters of grass which determine the boundary. A six! Ecstatic, Potter registers the score on his board as a fielder races after the ball. Unseen by either players or spectators, the leather-bound cricket ball is exchanged for an identical one. Snatching this up, the fielder runs back onto the green and pitches the ball back to the bowler who, catching it neatly in his hand, takes several determined paces past the umpire to ready himself for his next delivery. The spectators are agog; Potter watches in anticipation, the girl in white grins. Steadying himself, the bowler surges forward, his arm aloft, his face a mask of grinning teeth. The ball leaves his hand, the batsman whacks it – and in a busy London street, the Prisoner reads the stop press newspaper headline: 'Col. Hawke – English. Murdered at cricket match . . . one short of his century!' Placing the newspaper under his arm, the Prisoner walks several paces down the street, stopping at an outdoor stand where a shoe-shine boy is plying his trade. It is Potter, the ex-scorekeeper and ex-Secret Agent (retribution for failure travels swiftly it appears). 'Busy Potter?' quips the newcomer. 'It's our form of Siberia,' grunts the shoe-shine man, confirming that he is serving his punishment for allowing the batsman to be killed. 'What was the Colonel up to?' asks the other. 'Doctor Schnipps. Crazy scientist. For the last 26 years he's been building a super rocket . . . to destroy London.' 'Where?' 'Well that's just what the Colonel was about to find out,' returns the other, scouring the newcomer's brogues with a wire brush. A transmitter device in his shoe box indicates that someone wishes to talk with him. 'Excuse me,' says Potter, placing a receiver to his ear. 'Where do I start?' asks the other. 'You're to go to the Magnum record shop. Booth 7. The chief will speak to you there.' 'Chin up Potter,' quips the Prisoner. 'It was so damned unsporting,' pleads the shoeshine, 'It certainly wasn't cricket,' confirms the other, handing his ex-colleague a bank note. 'Keep the change.' Leaving, the Prisoner fails to see the girl in white watching his progress from inside a shop window. The Prisoner enters the record shop, asks the assistant for a record and enters booth numbered 7. Placing the disc on the turntable provided, he listens to the voice of his chief. 'Mission. Find and destroy Professor Schnipps' rocket. There is very little *I* can give you I'm afraid, the opposition have been one step ahead of us all along.' 'Thank you very much,' quips the listener. 'What was that?' asks the record. 'Nothing.' 'Standard disguise. Take over where the Colonel left off . . . ' orders the voice.

The Prisoner does so. Wearing a false moustache and side-whiskers, he stands at the wicket dressed as a batsman. The girl in white sits as before, her parasol raised over her head. Marking his crease, the Prisoner accepts the ball and scores a run. The bowler tries again: the batsman lifting the ball aloft and sending it soaring to the boundary, where, as before, the ball is exchanged for an identical one. Repeating his actions, the fielder races after the sixer, grabs it in his hand and throws it back to the bowler. A toothy grin, and the bowler retreats to his bowling crease. The Prisoner's score rests at 99: the girl in white stands by a tree. Lowering his bat to protect the middle stump, the batsman prepares to accept the next ball. His arm aloft, his face set in a toothy grin, the bowler races forward. Leaving his hand, the ball soars through the air towards the batsman, who, *catching* it in his gloved hand, throws it high in the air, where it explodes above the trees. Racing after the bomb, the batsman finds nothing but a lace handkerchief draped over a bush. It carries a message scrawled in lipstick: 'Let's meet again – at your local pub!' Having parked his sports car on the forecourt, the Prisoner enters the pub and orders his usual from Doris, a barmaid. He removes his white raincoat, hangs it on a coat stand and returns to the bar. Sitting on a stool, he sips from his beer glass – a drink with a difference. When drained of its nutty-brown liquid, the glass contains a message written on its base: 'You . . . have . . . just . . . been . . . poisoned!' 'Same again sir?' asks Doris. 'No thank you,' he replies, 'one of those is quite enough. Brandy.' The girl hands him his drink. ' . . . Whisky, Vodka, Drambuie, Tia Maria, Cointreau, Grand Marnier . . . ' he orders, gulping down each drink in turn. 'SIR!,' cries Doris, 'You'll make yourself sick.' Counting each empty glass before him, with a wry smile, he staggers from the bar and stumbles to the washroom – holding back the door to allow the girl in white to ease past him, her arrival heralded by an 18-inch long white cigarette

holder. Having emptied the contents of his stomach, he splashes cold water onto his face and reaches for the towel dispenser. This, too, carries a message: 'Upset Tummy? Try Benny's Turkish Baths around the corner!' Wearing his phoney moustache and sideburns, the Prisoner sweats it out in a steam box. The girl in white is there too. Dressed in the briefest of mini skirts, the perspiration trickling down her shapely legs, she carries a broom handle as she creeps from her steam-box and slides the pole through the handles of the cabinet in which the Prisoner sits humming merrily away. Unseen through the billowing clouds of steam, she places a perspex globe over the man's head. Catching sight of the retreating figure's shapely ankles, he kicks out in anger, splitting the broom handle in two and engineering his release. Dressed now in a Sherlock Holmes ensemble of dog-tooth cape and deer-stalker hat, he is about to chase after the girl, pausing at the door first. Crossing swiftly back to the steam box vacated by the girl, he again finds a message inviting him to follow her to Barney's Boxing Booth, front row. The message ends in a PS: 'Who would be a goldfish.' The fairground is in full swing as he enters the large marquée and squats in a chair at the ringside. The master of ceremonies issues a challenge: 'Ladies and gentlemen. It is my pleasure to introduce to you, for the first time in this country, at 207 pounds, the Polish giant, Killer Karminski . . . ' Stepping into the boxing ring, a huge brute of a man bows to the crowd. ' . . . And now Ladies and Gentlemen, another hand I want for a gallant and courageous opponent who has undertaken to go three rounds with the Killer . . . A man of mystery . . . in the front row . . . Mr X.' He points at the Prisoner. The spectators go wild, and two men step forward to divest the Prisoner of his Edwardian motoring cloak. Climbing into the ring, he removes his coat and sits on the stool in his corner. 'Good luck young man,' says an old lady behind him, dressed in a black funeral dress, a black shawl pulled tightly around her shoulders (we have seen her before – clad entirely in white). A second enters the ring and straps a pair of gloves over the Prisoner's hands. The referee calls the opponents together in the centre of the ring. 'Now I want a good clean fight,' he orders. 'No kicking, butting or gouging – except in moderation . . . and when I say break, break. Don't forget eh. May the best man win. Go back to your corners . . . ' Before he can do so, the Prisoner is stripped of his dark sunglasses! 'Seconds out. Round 1,' calls the master of ceremonies. As the boxers close on each other, the girl in white takes her seat in the crowd. A sharp jab to the stomach throws the Prisoner, followed by a second punch. About to throw a blow at his opponent's head, the Killer blocks his arm. 'Take it easy sorr, will you . . . me face is me fortune . . . You might knock it back in shape,' grunts the Killer in a sharp Irish brogue. Coming between them the referee intervenes, splitting the two men apart as the Prisoner's glove is about to clip his opponents's nose. A right to the jaw and the Prisoner reels backwards to the ropes. He rallies, closing on his opponent in a bear hug. The girl in white grins, the Killer grunts. 'Let's go to the Tunnel of Love,' he gasps, dancing with his opponent around the canvas. 'The what?' growls the Prisoner, planting a solid right hand into the man's solar plexus. 'The tunnel of love . . . ' gasps the Killer, returning the blow. 'Who . . . gave . . . you . . . the . . . message?' asks the other, peppering the Killer's face with forceful left hooks. 'The lady . . . ' grunts his opponent, giving as good as he gets. 'Who was she?' seeks the Prisoner, landing a punch in the man's midriff. 'I don't know.' 'Who . . . *was* she?' challenges his opponent. 'Didn't I tell you,' utters the Killer, closing in for the kill. 'I don't *know*!' His glove, lands squarely on the other's waistline, bringing a gasp from the Prisoner. 'In the tunnel of LOVE!' exclaims the Killer, following up his advantage by swinging a vicious right cross to his opponent's jaw. Beaten now, the Prisoner collapses to the canvas and smiling, the girl in white leaves the marqueé.

Wearing his Sherlock Holmes attire, his false moustache and side-whiskers back in place, the Prisoner sails through the fairground's Tunnel of Love. Hideous white masks adorn the rock walls and the vessel floats past the immobile figure of the girl in white, her arm raised erect as she stands motionless, disguised as Aphrodite. As the unsuspecting passenger floats past her she calls to him. 'Hello . . . No don't turn around. I have you covered. The tunnel of love is very fitting, because I'm beginning to love you . . . in my way.' All my life I've been looking for a worthy opponent. *You* have passed my first little test brilliantly. You will be hearing from me again. Auf Wiedersehen.' She laughs. He turns quickly. The girl is nowhere in sight, but a tiny white box has been placed in the rear seat of the boat. Hearing the girl's hysterical scream, he flings it into the water behind him. It explodes, the force of the blast drowning her hideous laughter.

Beckoned on by the girl, he sees her board a roller-coaster and disappear from view. Climbing into a roller-cart, he finds himself alone, high on the fun-machine: the girl now stands watching him from the ground. She blows him a kiss from the merry-go-round, but by the time he boards the ride the girl has disappeared again. Catching sight of her racing through the crowd, he follows, seeing her board a caterpillar ride. He polevaults a fence and jumps into the seat beside her, but when the canvas hood is raised at the end of the ride, he is sitting with a stranger, the girl in white mocking him from the pay booth. A slap from the woman beside him and he is off and running again, following his beautiful but deadly quarry as she hails him again from the seat of her roller-coaster carriage. Leaping aboard, he begins to climb, hand-over-hand, towards her, his cloak flowing in the wind as several seats in front of him, the girl stands precariously aloft swinging her arms in pantomimic defiance. Faster and faster speeds the ride, climbing high up the tracks and plummeting down at speed to the water-splash. Wilder and wilder become the girl's antics until, having dropped into the carriage behind her, the Prisoner is about to grab her when she turns. She is a stranger – as is the young man with a camera who magically appears from behind her and threatens the pursuer. 'Here, what's your game Sherlock Holmes . . . I'll spread your nose all over your face . . . I'll bust you up and down this fairground . . . you'll never pick up your teeth with a broken arm. I'll tear off your leg and I'll beat you over the head . . . ' shrieks the man, placing a protective arm around the girl's shoulder. Staring downwards, the Prisoner sees the girl in white beckoning him from the ground.

Back on the ground, he spots her again standing before

'Hello. No, don't turn around, I have you covered'

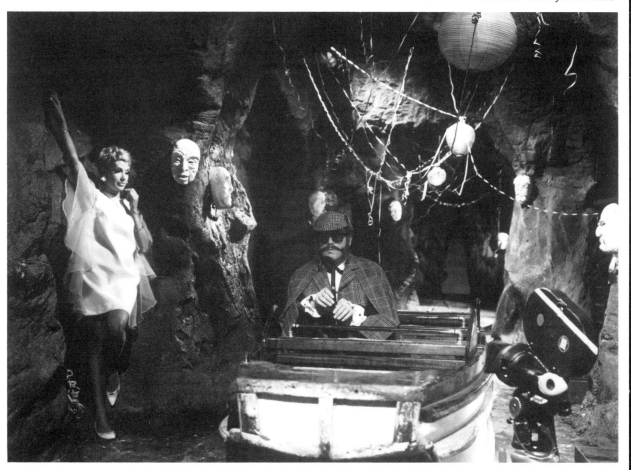

a carousel, her face hidden beneath a billowing web of white lace. But is it his quarry or another dupe? The reappearance of the young man with the camera suggests the latter, so the Prisoner makes a hasty retreat. A mistake. As the pursuer makes his exit, she pulls back her veil - it is *she*. The youth with the camera plants a kiss to her lips and the girl races away to her gleaming white sports car – pursued by the Prisoner who, failing to impede her progress, strips off his disguise, climbs into his speedster and roars off in pursuit. Within minutes he is behind her as they race along a motorway. Supremely confident, the girl raises her hand in salute, beckoning him on – but to what? Entering a country lane, the cars speed on, he endeavouring to overtake, she raising a telephone to her lips. 'I love you madly. I love the way your hair curls on the back of your neck. You'll make a *beautiful* corpse!' she confirms, her words being piped into the pursuer's car. 'I'm going to do you the honour of letting you die *superbly* . . .' Gritting his teeth, the pursuer changes gear, his foot going down hard on the accelerator. Looking over her shoulder, she stretches out her hand, her finger pointing at his vehicle. As her hand sways back and forth, so does his car. She draws a circle in the air, his car appears to follow suit, doing a 360 degree turn, although its wheels never actually leave the ground. What magic is this? '. . . But not yet darling. There's more fun to come . . .' she purrs, as her car streaks around a bend in the road. In an attempt to follow, for a second he loses control of his car. Reversing, he continues his pursuit, losing the girl in a maze of roundabouts and country lanes.

Having located her parked car on the outskirts of a deserted village, he climbs out of his vehicle and peers up and down the street. A shopsign denoted 'Candlestick Maker'. Another a baker, a third a butcher. 'I'm glad you came,' echoes her voice 'This is to be our love tryst. You may not see my face, but you may know my name . . . *my* name is Death!' She laughs as he wanders through the streets endeavouring to locate the building from which the voice emanates. 'I'm sorry my father could not be here to greet you, but he's busy with his rocket. Besides, he did not wish to play gooseberry. *You* are a born survivor. *I* am a born killer. *We* were made for each other . . .' Above him, pinned to a wall, he spots a loudspeaker. '. . . But I fear this is where it must end. Your reflexes cannot save you now. It will come swiftly, suddenly . . . when your luck runs out . . .' He finds himself standing in front of the door of the building. '. . . With my love . . .' He crouches, his shoulder ready to crash down the door. 'Come, come inside my darling . . .' He bursts through the flimsy door, landing inside on the dilapidated floor of the room. Crouching, he crawls to peer through the vents of a door that leads into an adjoining room. Flinging the door back on its hinges, he dives to the floor as a machine gun erected on a bracket rotates and spits its bullets into the rotted timbers of the wall behind him. Crawling on his hands and knees, he makes his way towards the weapon, placing his hands over its infra-red trigger control to halt its chattering progress. '. . . Is your heart pounding,' continues her voice. '. . . Your hand shaking? That's *love* my darling! My father was a great man, but the war ended before he was recognised . . .' Listening to her words, he begins to disconnect the machine gun from its moorings. '. . . But when London lies in ruins he will be a God . . .' The machine gun is free now. Ramming it firmly into his hip, he turns its barrel towards the walls, raking his way through them with a clip full of bullets and leaps through the opening he has made. Spotting a figure standing in the darkness, he sends a spray of bullets into its chest. It is a dummy assembled from sacks and a balloon. Angry, he races forwards, the floor giving way under his feet. He falls, but the gun saves him, its barrel jammed tight across the gaping jaws of a pit. 'Nice of you to drop in . . .' quips the voice. '. . . I can see you're having a swinging time, but that's not quite what I had in mind . . .' He stares into the pit below his feet. The heels of his shoes are barely fractions of an inch away from a bed of iron spikes, their tips filed into jagged points, inviting him to be skewered. '. . . Perhaps this will help . . .?' At her cue, the spikes begin to rise, threatening to pierce the soles of his feet. '. . . You'll soon get the point . . .' mocks the voice. '. . . Incidentally, they're electrified . . .' He attempts to haul himself upwards, but succeeds only in bringing a discarded wardrobe drawer crashing to the floor. It is release enough. The drawer falls neatly over the spikes, forming the base of an elevator which, much to the girl's disappointment, raises him out of the pit. '. . . Ingenious. Nobody has ever thought of that before. You really are the most entertaining love I've ever had . . .' Recocking the machine gun, he rakes bullets into the walls of the room. '. . . That was ill-mannered *and* dangerous. I might not have been able to inform you that the rest of this floor is mined . . . Very small, but very sensitive. And quite deadly . . .' she warns as he lays down the weapon. Snatching up a brick, he flings it several feet away and the floor disintegrates in a puff of smoke! '. . . Oh, I almost forgot, they will all explode anyway in 90 seconds . . .' Using the drawer beneath his feet as a platform, he pulls himself onto a pipe above his head. '. . . That's the hot line,' informs the voice, as the scalding hot pipe sears at his hands. '. . . Or had you noticed . . .?' Blocking out the pain, hand-over-hand he approaches the door and leaps across to an adjoining pipe. Gathering momentum, he swings backwards and forwards and leaps into the adjacent room. The floor behind him explodes into sheets of smoke. '. . . You've been through the butcher's and the baker's, now you're in the candle-stick makers . . .' drones the voice as the man drops to his feet. '. . . only he never made candles like these. These are *my* invention . . .' Rising from the rubble, he traverses the room. It is decked out with thousands of candles. 'They have a cyanide derivative mixed with wax. As the candle burns, it gives off a cyanide gas. Every candle in this room is breathing poison into the air . . .' He attempts to escape, but two steel doors crash down from the ceiling blocking his path. He races to the door, the windows; these too are blocked. '. . . I do so believe in double glazing, don't you? Keeps out the noise . . . of course it does keep out the air too . . . Oh a last word of advice. If the candles are blown out, they explode . . .' Choking now, the man is about to blow out the candle in front of his face. Hearing the girl's warning, he stops in mid-breath. Picking up a candle-snuffer he raises it above him to the chandelier and fluffs out its wick. The result is devastating – the device being blown apart. '. . . And that's just one of the little ones. I warned you your luck would run out. I've got to go now. I'm glad it's to be this way. I *hate* quick farewells, don't you?' mocks the girl. But he is not outsmarted so easily. Gathering together as many of the candles as he can, he places them en masse next to the steel exit doors. Witnessing this the voice tells him that she has noticed that mice get irrational in just the same way when they are about to die. 'In this village in the past, when a great man was dying . . .' she continues. '. . . they sounded the death knell. I think that was a charming idea . . .' By now, the Prisoner has collected a pair of bellows from the corner of the room. Standing behind a counter. he sends a jet of air from the device and ... an explosion ensues. allowing him to race through the wrecked door and out into the street. He immediately comes under fire as the girl in white. attired now in a snow-white version of a World War I battledress. a spiked soldier's helmet adorning her head. eases back the trigger of a Gatling-gun. Racing into a blacksmith's shop. the Prisoner slams the doors closed behind him. 'Alright darling. you win ... ' greets her voice from a speaker positioned on the wall over his head. ' ... I've *just* realised something. I don't want to kill you anymore. You are the *best*. If I kill you. what will be left for *me*? Life would be a bore ... Why don't you join us. my father and me. We'd have a wonderful time together. You would be a constant challenge to me ... ' He. too. has realised something: no matter what she says. he is now fully aware that she does intend to kill him – he is aware. too. that his enemy is a girl. although he doesn't know her by her given name (Sonia). but only by the name she has given herself : 'Death'. He realises. too. that he has a chance of escape. Behind him in the blacksmith's shop stands a bulldozer – if only ... ? 'Come and join me in the bell tower.' she

suggests. 'What do you say darling? Don't let silly pride stand in your way ... ' He doesn't. Having fired up the bulldozer's engine. he leaps behind its controls and releases the throttle. In an instant. the massive wooden doors of the building are smashed aside and the Prisoner is free – free to elevate the bulldozer's steel shovel to act as a shield against the bullets. the mortar bombs. and World War I hand-grenades that his enemy unleashes as he steers the machine towards the bell tower. 'Wheee. wheee. Wheee!' she grins. as the bulldozer grinds to a halt. its gears ripped apart by the onslaught. Staring upwards. he sees with alarm that the girl has the sights of a huge bazooka trained at his chest. 'Bye bye lover ... ' she grins. releasing the weapon's trigger mechanism. In a heartbeat. the bulldozer is blown apart. its tattered burning remnants littering the street. As the tower bell chimes its death knell. the girl calmly powders her nose. Placing a white leather helmet to her golden locks. she descends from the bell tower to savour her opponent's defeat. Behind her. the Prisoner rises from a manhole and follows her from a safe distance.

Seeing the girl climb into a helicopter. he races after the machine and firmly grabs the aircraft's landing gear. As the machine soars skywards. he crawls up into the

'Don't let silly pride stand in your way'

helicopter's skeleton tailpiece and holds on for dear life. Unaware of her stowaway's presence, Sonia lands the machine in a field where, as the engine cuts out and its rotor blades grind to a halt, the Prisoner runs away from the machine and seeks refuge in some bushes. Pursuing her, he follows the girl over a hill, before losing sight of her in the rocks. Climbing to the top of the hill, he sees a lighthouse out at sea. But how can he reach it? The drop below would test the nerve of even the most ambitious climber – 100 feet of sheer rock face. A nearby cave appears to offer a solution. Entering its darkness, he urges his way forward along a passage, which empties into a large room hewn from the rock. In front of him stands an impressive bank of machinery; to the left of the cavern stands a row of bunk beds. The walls are adorned with pictures and reproductions, each representing a Napoleonic scene. Hearing a sound behind him, he seeks refuge behind a rock as a man dressed in a scarlet Napoleonic uniform descends a ladder leading from the area above. 'From glen to glen, and down the mountain side . . . The summer's gone and all the roses dying . . . ' sings the newcomer, crossing to a record player and placing its needle on a record. ' . . . 'Tis you 'tis you must bide and I must go,' pipes the Prisoner, knocking the stranger unconscious with a blow to the head. Removing the unconscious man's uniform, he puts the scarlet tunic over his own coat. Above him, in a room decked out with machinery, stands a row of half-a-dozen men, each wearing the scarlet finery of Napoleonic times. Parading before them walks 'Napoleon'. It is Professor Schnipps, the scientist intent on blowing up London. Inspecting his troops and noticing that each man has their hand concealed beneath his tunic in true Napoleonic fashion, he races down the row hitting each man in turn, removing their hands at a blow. Regaining his dignity, he walks over to his daughter Sonia, who is now dressed as Marie Antoinette. 'Everybody's doing it now you see . . . You're quite sure you killed him?' he asks. 'Father, Who taught me?' she sighs. 'You're a girl after my own heart. If only your dear mother could see you now . . . Good old Josephine,' he sobs, wiping a tear-stained eye. 'Tell me again about her last cavalry charge,' asks Sonia. 'Not now child, we have work to do,' he says, turning back to his troops. 'Gentlemen,' he begins, addressing the fairy tale soldiers. 'In one hour's time, London will be entirely in ruins . . . ' Meanwhile the Prisoner has broken into the armoury and dealt swiftly with its guard, dumping the man's body down a safety-hatch. Gathering up each rifle in turn, he flicks back their firing pins and begins to prise open the bullets he has ejected onto a table. Above him,

The intruder punches the armoury guard

234

'Napoleon' continues to relay his plan of battle. ' ... And then of course, as I was saying, there will be no more Trafalgar Square, it will be Napoleon Square ... and of course, Nelson's Column will go to become Napoleon's Column ... and er ... and then my little girl here will be taking over Bond Street ... ' 'Oh,' cries a delighted Sonia. ' ... and you merry lads can have ... Chelsea Barracks ... ' One of the troops mutters something under his breath. ' ... Ungrateful swine!' yells the Professor ' ... and then we'll be taking over the entire regions ... Is the Scottish Marshal here?' 'Present,' nods one of the men. 'You keen on soccer?' growls Schnipps. 'Oh aye sir, I am, I am ... ' 'Like Wembley Stadium?' 'Oh aye, aye I would,' gushes the Marshal as the leader pushes his finger into the man's chest. 'It's yours ... Welsh Marshal?' 'Here sir ... What a great day for the Nationalists sir.' 'Thank you Marshal Jones,' grins the Professor. 'Irish?' 'He's gone down stairs to the armoury sir,' says the Scot. 'He'll not be long.' Schnipps grits his teeth. 'Blast O'Rorke ... what on earth does he do down there?' O'Rorke, of course, is unconscious, courtesy of the man now replacing the 'doctored' rifles back into the weapons rack. This done, the Prisoner begins to ease the fuses out of several hand-grenades. However, as he is tipping the black explosive powder into the tubular *handles* of the grenades, one of

'The countdown has now been started ... ' confirms 'Napoleon' Schnipps, switching on his control machine and arming the red trigger button. Sonia, however, glancing behind her and aware that her father has overlooked something (he is, after all, a 'nutty' professor), taps him on the shoulder and draws his attention to the fact that the rocket's guidance system *wasn't* really armed! 'Mmm,' sighs her exasperated father, attempting to regain his dignity. Turning back to his troops, he picks up where he left off. ' ... As I was saying, the countdown has already started. In a few minutes we transfer to the speedboat and control the final phase of the operation from the sea. O'Rorke will ... where is Marshal O'Rorke? Find him at once. All of you!' As one, the men trip over each other as they bump into one another and attempt to go their different ways, each of them stumbling down the staircase in total mass confusion. Staring at them Schnipps cannot help but mumble 'Oh ... it's Waterloo all over again.' 'Oh,' smiles Sonia, stroking his brow. Finally regaining some semblance of order, the men descend the stairs where, believing the man at the table to be one of their companions, one of them asks if he has seen O'Rorke. 'No,' returns the Prisoner. 'But he must have come through here,' says the Scottish Marshal, who demands to know what O'Rorke is up to. 'I don't *KNOW*!'

'This one won't backfire darling'

the Professor's soldiers descends the staircase behind him. Identifying the intruder by his trousers (the Prisoner has donned only O'Rorke's tunic and tri-corn hat) the newcomer creeps up behind the stranger – and receives a blow to the head for his pains. He, too, joins O'Rorke in the safety hatch.

grins the Prisoner, swinging the grenades he is holding over his shoulder and laying two of the troops out unconscious. Turning, he easily slips through the arms of the other men as, panicking, they stumble over themselves in their attempts to grab him. Knocking them out, he flees through the door and descends the outside of the lighthouse via a metal ladder. Above him, running around in circles of confusion, the men each grab a rifle from the weapons rack. Seeing the intruder racing along the pier towards the motor launch, the Scot orders the men to fire. As one they do so – and fall backwards into the armoury as the 'doctored' rifles explode in their faces! Having climbed back up to the armoury, the Prisoner eases his way upwards to the room above – to find himself staring down the barrel of a gun held by Sonia. 'This one won't backfire, darling,' she warns.

'Mountaineering rope,' confirms Sonia, tying her enemy to a chair. 'It would hold an elephant.' 'I must remember that the next time I go climbing with one,' quips the Prisoner. 'Oh I'm afraid there won't be a next time for you darling. I'm going to give you the most original death in history ... You're going for a rocket ride,' grins the girl. 'Oh the rocket. That reminds me ... Where is it?' asks the bound man. 'It is here,' grins 'Napoleon' Schnipps, with a wave of his hand. ' ... all around you.' 'All around us?' quizzes the Prisoner. 'The light ... house itself is the rocket!' confirms Schnipps, Sonia and the Prisoner as one. 'You've guessed,' mocks the Professor. 'I say, you're not the Duke of Wellington are you? Ah, well I guess you're surprised to meet me. Don't you think it's clever? Aren't I an extraordinary man?' 'Crazy,' grins the bound man. 'This is the nose cone we're in now,' confirms Sonia, indicating the lighthouse walls with her hand. 'So you see, when the rocket reaches London, you'll be the first to know. Won't that be exciting?' she grins, staring at the man tied to the chair. 'I'll just go to pieces,' he jokes. A red warning light flashes on the control panel. 'It's time to go aboard the boat,' grins 'Napoleon', confirming that the flight pattern is set and all that remains is for them to fire the 'lighthouse' when they get out to sea. 'Bon voyage darling ... ' waves Sonia, as she follows her father down the staircase. ' ... Think of me when you hit town.'

'Warning' says the red sign below the flashing danger signal that rests before the man bound to the chair. 'When red light is flashing, it is strictly forbidden to enter upper chamber.' The clock on the control panel reads .2 minutes to countdown as the Prisoner struggles to unfree his hands. Far below him Sonia and her father fall over each other to cram documents into their briefcase. 01.78 registers the countdown clock as the man above them struggles against his bonds. 'Please hurry. It's less that 2 minutes to blast off,' urges Sonia. 'I must have my papers ... these are the history,' insists the Professor, shoving further sheets of paper into his brief-case. 01.55 ... 01.41 ticks the countdown. Pausing for a second, the Prisoner eases the back of his chair upwards. It springs free with a pop (like everything else connected to Schnipps' plan, his attempts to defeat our hero are doomed to failure). Easing his bound wrists over the back of the chair's backrest, the Prisoner stands and the bonds fall free of his wrists. Stripping off his Napoleonic tunic, he crosses to the control console, manipulating its dials, levers and buttons until sparks begin to emit from the machine and a dense cloud of smoke pours from its innards. Grabbing up the coil of the mountaineering rope which Sonia laid aside, he hurriedly climbs the ladder to the lamp-house room. Far below him lies the sea. Tying one end of the rope to the inspection gantry's guard rail, he casts the rope over the side and carefully eases himself over the railing, before descending hand-over-hand to the rocks far below. Their packing complete, Sonia and her father race from the documents room and prepare to descend to their boat. Pausing with his foot on the top rung of the metal ladder,

'Napoleon' races back inside. 'What is it?' asks his daughter. 'I forgot to turn the gas off ... ' 'Oh father!' she says. Peering below and seeing the man they left above them leaping into the motor launch, Sonia calls on her father to stop him. Racing together back into the armoury, she grabs a hand-grenade while he picks up two rifles. 'Not those ... ' cries Sonia, handing her father a grenade, ' ... these!' Armed with a grenade apiece, they race back to the door, prime the devices and fling them into the boat – and stare in amazement as the Prisoner throttles the motor launch out to sea. Bemused when the hand-grenades fail to explode, Schnipps and his daughter stare at each other in astonishment as their lives and hopes are blown away when the booby-trapped grenade *handles* they hold explode in a sheet of flame. Out at sea, the man on the boat stares back as the lighthouse disintegrates into a million pieces.

'And that is how I saved London from the mad scientist,' a seated Number 6 tells three children, who squat before him in a nursery, their eyes trained on the cover of *The Village Story Book* which he now lays aside. 'Go on tell us more ... just one, one,' scream the children. 'No, no more for tonight, it's way past your bedtime,' grins Number 6, rising from his chair to gather up a little girl sitting on a rocking horse. 'Come on now to bed ... there's a good girl,' he soothes, placing the girl onto her cot. 'You will come tomorrow, please, please,' sobs the infant. 'Yes yes, we'll see ... ' 'Oh promise you will come,' cry the others, hopping into their bunks. ' ... We'll see,' smiles the storyteller. 'Come tomorrow, yes tomorrow,' chant all three, snuggling beneath their sheets. 'You will come?' 'Sshhh ... sleep ... I'll come tomorrow,' whispers Number 6 ' ... I don't think I have any other important appointments,' he grins, staring at the Village surveillance camera, on which Number 2 (Schnipps) is avidly watching his every move. Switching off the monitor screen, the superior turns in his chair with a shrug. 'He might drop his guard with children ... he might give something away ... ' he sighs, to the girl dressed in black (Sonia) standing behind him with her arm resting on the saddle of the penny farthing bicycle. 'Well it was worth a try Number 2,' she confirms, realising now that their plan has gone wrong. 'He told them *nothing*! He told them a blessed fairytale ... ' sighs the disillusioned superior. 'That one wouldn't drop his guard with his own grandmother,' he roars, pointing to the monitor screen with his umbrella. 'Goodnight children ... *Everywhere*,' mocks the image of Number 6 from the screen which has magically switched itself back on – to show a picture of the little girl's toy doll ... a grinning red-faced clown!

AUTHOR'S NOTE: Reappearance of actor Christopher Benjamin as 'Potter', John Drake's contact man in the *Danger Man/Secret Agent* story *Koroshi/Shinda Shima*.

The countdown mechanism that triggers the rocket, was actually a stock shot originally filmed for the Gerry Anderson *Thunderbirds* series. The same shot reappears in *Fall Out*.

ONCE UPON A TIME

Written by Patrick McGoohan

Guest star

Number 2 Leo McKern

with

The Butler **Angelo Muscat**
The Supervisor **Peter Swanwick**
Umbrella Man **John Cazabon**
Number 86 **John Maxim**

Directed by Patrick McGoohan

DESCENDING THE ramp of Number 2's Green Dome residence, the mute Butler parks the breakfast trolley he is wheeling by the side of the superior's control console, reaches out his gloved hand and depresses three buttons from its vast array. In a fraction of a second, a curtain covering the monitor screen behind him slides open, a table magically appears from the depths and Number 2's oval-shaped chair rises from the floor; the shell of the seat now contains a spherical white ball – a Rover. The manservant places cutlery on the table before the pulsating balloon and puts a tray containing toast and coffee on the console's counter top. The silent Butler then picks up and shakes a small dinner bell. In the space of a breath, a second black leather chair rises from the depths, followed by Number 2, his head bowed, his hands clasped firmly behind his back. Crossing to the breakfast tray, he removes a silver cover from one of the plates and tastes the food. 'Wait!' he calls to the retreating servant. 'Remove it!' The Butler stand immobile. 'I told you to REMOVE IT!' screams Number 2, crossing to the other man's side. The manservant begins to clear away the breakfast tray. 'And *you* can remove that *thing* too ...' snarls the superior to someone (Number 1?) on the telephone. ' ... I'm not an *inmate*! You can say what you like. *You* brought me back here. I told you the last time, you were using the wrong approach. I do it *my* way, or you find somebody else ...' Spotting the Butler about to carry the breakfast tray from the chamber, he holds the telephone receiver behind his back as he asks the little man to leave the coffee. 'The coffee. LEAVE IT.' he screams replacing the receiver to his ear. 'How many times do I have to *ask*?' he inquires as the chair containing the Rover descends back into the floor and the manservant leaves. Pouring himself coffee, he turns to view the monitor screen on which Number 6 is pictured prowling his cottage while eating breakfast. 'A likely lad ...' says Number 2, standing directly in front of the screen. ' ... Why do you care? Take it easy, relax ... why do you care ...?' he yells pointing his finger at the figure on the screen. Crossing back to his control panel he picks up a telephone and asks to be connected with the Prisoner. 'Why do you care?' he asks when the connection is made. 'I know your voice.' returns Number 6. 'I've been here before ... Why-do-you-care?' 'You'll never know.' replies the other, laying the telephone receiver back on its cradle rest and walking out of the cottage. He pauses on the doorstep to clap his hands twice, and the door obeys his command and swings to a close behind him. '*Wait and see*.' whispers a determined Number 2. Outside in the Village, Number 6 bumps into a man strolling by the

swimming pool. 'How?' asks the Prisoner raising his hand in mock greeting. 'Don't do that.' says the man with the umbrella. 'What?' 'Enquire.' whispers the other. 'What's your number?' asks Number 6. 'What?' enquires the man. 'Your number. What is it?' urges the Prisoner. 'Be careful.' warns the man staring around him. '1,2,3,4,5,6,7,8 ... ?' 'Quiet.' urges the one being questioned. '9,10,11,12,13,14,15,16?' screams the Prisoner, his raised voice echoing around the deserted square. In the Green Dome, Number 2 is scanning the pages of the Prisoner's 'Progress Report', as scenes from Number 6's past life are flashed at speed across the monitor screen. '*Going to escape and come back ...*' says the voice from the screen. '*... wipe this place off the face of the earth, obliterate it and you with it ...*' The screen changes ' *... This is what they did to you, is this how they started to break you before you gave them what they were after ...*' continues the voice. ' *... I've resigned. I will not be pushed, filed, stamped, indexed, briefed, debriefed or numbered ...*' This continues for quite some time until, tired of the game, Number 2 grabs a telephone as the man on the screen ends with ' *... I want to call a witness – a character witness.*' 'Degree *absolute*.' snarls Number 2 to his unseen superior 'I require approval ... If you think he's that important ... there's certainly no other alternative! You *must* risk either one of us. I am a good man ... I *was* a good man ... but if you get *him*, he will be BETTER! ... and there's no other way. I repeat, no *other WAY*! Degree absolute, tonight please ...' he orders, as the man on the screen behind him repeats his challenge that he will not be pushed, filed, stamped, indexed, briefed, debriefed or numbered.' 'A week! That's not long enough ...' barks Number 2, ' ... you don't want me to damage him ...' Apparently he is given no choice ' ... Very well then ... Tonight!'

That evening, he marches into the main Control Room. 'Degree absolute ... you're under orders.' he snaps to the Supervisor. 'What period?' requests the bespectacled man as the superior races down the staircase to join him. 'One week!' 'Emergency?' asks the Supervisor. 'Well it has to be hasn't it.' sneers Number 2. 'Mind if I check?' asks the other. 'You check NOTHING!' growls Number 2 patrolling the floor. 'Recall all subsidiary personnel.' 'First shift, early release. Time sheets as normal. Double night time ... double night time.' the Supervisor barks to his staff. As one the majority of the controllers in the chamber leave their posts and exit from the room. Sitting down in front of a control viewing console, Number 2 pulls back on its control stick and the sleeping figure of Number 6 appears on the screen. 'Blow up Channel 3 ...' orders the superior. 'Channel Three.' snaps the Supervisor. 'Check profundity.' calls Number 2. '1,2,3,4,5, 6, ... first waveband clear.' confirms the bespectacled assistant. 'Repeat and increase.' comes the demand. '1,2,3,4,5,6 ... still clear.' confirms the Supervisor. 'Third waveband ... slow ... and hold on 5.' states Number 2. '1,2,3,4,5 ... 5,5,5,5,5 ...' calls the assistant through clenched teeth. On screen, the Prisoner tosses to and fro in his bed. 'Diminish ... !' the superior calls. '5,5,5,5,5 ... 5.' the bespectacled man replies, his words softening with each number called. '5 ... 5 ... 5 ...' Number 6 calms down, his head nestling snuggly into his pillow. 'Safe enough.' nods Number 2, walking briskly from the room. 'I'll take over.' 'It's a risk ... I'd hate to see you go.' says the Supervisor, aware of the risk the superior is running. 'It's all yours. For one week.' throws back Number 2. 'Get moving. Degree *Absolute*. OPERATE!'

The lampshade above the Prisoner's bed begins to descend from the ceiling until it completely covers the sleeping man's face. As the lamp begins to oscillate and increase in intensity, Number 2, who is now standing by the side of the man's bed, leans over the sleeping figure and begins to recite a nursery rhyme. 'Humpty Dumpty sat on a wall. Humpty Dumpty had a great fall. All the king's horses and all the king's men, couldn't put Humpty together again ... ' Stepping backwards, he enters the Prisoner's lounge, his voice increasing in intensity. ' ... Jack and Jill went up the hill, to fetch a pail of WATER. Jack fell down and broke his crown and JILL came tumbling after ... ' Seated now in the sleeping man's lounge, he settles back and begins to sing. 'Oh the grand old Duke of York, he had 10,000 men. He marched them up to the top of the hill, and he marched them down again ... ' The figure in the bed sleeps on, the light above his head increasing in its intensity, pulsating in time with the superior's reversal to the lines of *Humpty Dumpty*, his childish babbering sinking deep into the Prisoner's brain – but to what purpose? It is morning, and Number 2 throws back the curtains and squints out into the sunshine. Throwing his blazer over his shoulder, he changes his mind and lays the jacket onto a chair then crosses to the sleeping man's bed. Lifting the lampshade from his head, he shoves it aside then whispers an invitation into the sleeping man's ear. 'Want to go walkies,' he grins as Number 6 leaps from his bed and turns to face the intruder. 'Wash and dress quickly, and I'll show you some nice things,' he quips, handing the man his dressing gown. With a childlike grin, Number 6 retreats to his bathroom – the promise of goodies in store ringing in his ears. A few minutes later, his hand clutching an ice cream cone, his body slumped in a wheelchair, the Prisoner is wheeled into the Green Dome by the mute Butler. Licking his ice cream, he looks on blankly as the manservant disappears into the floor and Number 2 beckons him to join him at the control console. They, too, descend into the floor where, led by Number 2, the lap dog follows his minder through several corridors until they reach a steel door set into the rock. The barrier slides open and Number 2 steps into the darkness. Beckoned inside, the Prisoner finds himself surrounded by a rocking horse, a child's swing, an infant's play pen, a blackboard and other toys; items one would associate with a well-stocked children's play room – all save an ominous huge metal cage which contains a replica of his own cottage kitchen. (From this moment on, Number 6 will be put through days of savage and relentless interrogation, his regressed mind to be taken back through his early childhood, as Number 2 leads him through the seven ages of man. Only one can return – the victor; the loser to remain a prisoner of life – or death.) 'This is it,' confirms Number 2. 'For better or for worse ... who knows? One week ... one teeny weeny week my boy. Neither of us can leave. Till death do us part ... And I brought it upon myself ... Who knows?' he says, setting the time lock on the massive steel door and drawing a heavy curtain over the exit. 'Come ahead son, let's see what you're made of ... find out what's in that noddle of yours ... ' He marches past the Butler, who now stands in the children's playpen shaking a baby's rattle. 'All the world's a stage and the men and women merely players. They have their exits and their entrances, and one man in his time plays many parts ... ' Donning a pair of white plastic spectacles, the lenses of which are narrow slits, he turns around to push a portable control, tape-recorder console towards the playpen occupied by the Butler. ' ...

'Till death do us part. And I brought it upon myself'

His acts being seven ages ... ' A piercing white light spotlights Number 6 who stands by the playpen with a childlike grin, staring intently at the antics of the silent manservant. Turning to the blackboard, the superior wipes it clean with a damp cloth. ' ... William Shakespeare, he summed it all up ... so they say. At first the infant, mewling and puking in the nurse's arms ... Be still!' he calls, distracted by the Butler, who, also adorned in the weird-looking spectacles, flings the rattle at the onlooker and climbs out of the playpen. ' ... Even as a child there is something in your brain that is a puzzlement. I intend to discover it ... ' He turns to write on the blackboard. 'A ... find missing link ... and when I have found it, I will refine it, tune it, and you will play our game ... ' he threatens, pointing at Number 6, who, shaking the rattle, stares intently at the piercing blue light beaming down on his head. 'B ... put it together ... and if I fail ... then ... ' He writes the word 'BANG' on the blackboard. Laying down his chalk, he walks past the Butler whose short legs are now dangling several inches from the floor as he sits on the swing. Taking the rattle from the Prisoner's hand he looks down at the kneeling man. 'I am your father ... do I ever say anything that makes you want to hate me?' Number 6 climbs to his feet, joining the superior as they walk around the floor. 'We're going for a walk aren't we ... ?' suggests Number 2, taking the other by the arm. ' ... Into the park isn't it? I always speak well of your mother don't I?' The two men climb onto a seesaw, the Prisoner falling flat onto the seat of his pants when, in his childlike innocence, he takes his seat before the superior can do likewise. Up and down they rock, the Butler swinging in time with their momentum. 'See-saw Marjorie Daw ... ' coaxes Number 2 ' ... Jacky shall have a new master ... ' 'See-saw,' picks up Number 6. (Margery Daw.) 'Jacky ... ' (Shall have) ' ... a new master.' (A new *Master*.) 'Master.' (Jacky.) 'Master.' (Jacky.) 'Master.'

(Jacky.) Faster and faster they go. 'Master,' says Number 6. 'Mother!' 'Master.' (Father.) With the word 'father' Number 6 stops the see-saw abruptly and steps off. Thrown to the floor, a distraught Number 2 picks himself up and grins as the other says 'Brother.' 'Friends,' nods the elder. 'Brother . . . brother . . .' queries Number 6 timidly. 'Friends,' confirms Number 2. 'Friends . . . push!' grins the other, walking to the swing. 'Friends,' confirms Number 2, from over his shoulder. 'Friends push . . . push,' smiles Number 6, placing his hands on the Butler's shoulders and easing him forwards. 'School!' growls the superior. 'School?' 'School,' says the other, as the manservant vacates the swing and walks over to the console. He presses a button and the tape-recorder begins to revolve. ' . . . Creeping like snails, unwillingly to school . . . to school, school . . . school . . . school,' states Number 2, pushing the Prisoner who now sits on the swing. The Butler, meanwhile, has crossed to a cupboard and placed a straw boater on his head. Taking out a headmaster's cape, mortar-board and cane, he hands the attire to Number 2 and places the boater on the head of the man on the swing. Dressed now in his robes and square hat, the superior coughs out an order. 'Report to my study in the morning break,' he yells to the man on the swing.

To the sound of organ music (played by Number 2) the Prisoner stands at a mock-up door denoted 'Headmaster'. Escorted inside by the Butler, the manservant stands to attention behind the superior's back, while the 'pupil' waits to be chastised. 'Take off your hat in my presence,' barks Number 2, looking over his shoulder. 'Sorry sir,' says the pupil, removing his boater. 'You were talking in class . . .' accuses the headmaster. 'No sir.' 'You refuse to admit it.' 'I wasn't sir,' begs the pupil. 'Do you know who was?' 'Yes sir.' 'Who was it . . . ?' questions the man sitting at the organ. The pupil remains silent. 'This is the ninth day since the incident,' challenges the headmaster. 'You have been in my study every morning at this time and still you refuse to cooperate. TODAY IS YOUR LAST CHANCE! It wasn't *you*?' 'No sir.' 'You know who it was?' 'Yes sir.' 'Who was it . . . ?' Again no reply. ' . . . This is cowardice!' 'That's honour sir,' challenges the pupil. 'We don't talk about such things,' states the headmaster. 'You should teach it sir.' (You're a fool) 'Yes sir, not a rat.' (Rat?) 'Rat.' Lifting his fingers from the keyboard in front of him, Number 2 swings round to face his accuser. 'I'm a rat?' he barks. 'No sir, I'm a fool . . .' smirks the pupil, 'not a rat.' The superior gulps. 'Society,' he begins. 'Yes sir?' ' . . . Society is a place where people exist together . . .' (Yes sir) ' . . . That is civilisation . . .' (Yes sir) ' . . . The lone wolf belongs in the wilderness . . .' (Yes sir) ' . . . and you must not grow up to be a lone *wolf*!' (No sir) 'You must *conform*!' (Yes sir) 'It is my sworn duty to see that you *do* conform!' (Yes sir) 'You will take SIX . . .' grins Number 2. (Six?) ' . . . of the best.' 'I'm not guilty sir,' replies the pupil. 'TEN!' snaps the superior. (12!) 'What?' hisses the headmaster. 'Twelve sir . . . so that I can remember!' 'Huh,' shrugs Number 2. At a nod from the superior, the Butler passes through the door. Swishing the cane in the air, the servant closes the door behind him as Number 6 bends over the organ stool to receive his 12 whacks.

'And so we come to another graduation day. A joyous moment for any boy . . . but especially for our prize pupil . . .' states Number 2, getting to his feet from his throne-like chair positioned on the top of a stage. Peering down at the duly chastised pupil, he continues his graduation speech. ' . . . As we launch him into the rapids of adulthood, we look back on the ups and downs of his childhood and view with some satisfaction, the fine specimen you see before you now. Have you anything to say?' 'Nothing,' replies the Prisoner. 'Nothing? Nothing at all?' 'Thank you for everything,' replies Number 6, peering down at the diploma he has been given. 'Congratulations my boy, you will do very well. *We* are proud of you. Proud that you have learned to manage your rebellious spirit. Proud that your obedience is absolute. Why did you resign?' (What's that sir?) 'Oh come along boy . . . why did you resign?' (From what sir?) 'Now my boy, you know perfectly well what I'm talking about . . .' grins Number 2, descending the steps to face the pupil. ' . . . Why did you resign?' (I can't tell that sir.) 'Was it Secret . . . ?' (Secret sir?) ' . . . and Confidential?' (No sir.) 'Top Secret?' (No sir.) 'Top Secret!' (State Secret.) 'Yes!' urges Number 2. (State Secret sir.) 'Top. State. Confidential . . . !' screams Number 2, grabbing the lapels of the pupil's jacket ' . . . Why? Why? Why did you resign?' 'No . . . No-ooo!!!' screams Number 6, throwing the interrogator around in circles. 'Alright boy . . . alright boy . . .' calms Number 2 ' . . . Leave school boy . . . just tell me, no more school . . . Tell me why DID YOU RESIGN?' Grunting, the Prisoner grits his teeth, draws back his fist and, with a vicious right hand, sends the other reeling to the floor. Leaping on top of the man, he grabs at his throat. As the two men wrestle and tug at each other's clothes, the Butler walks past them, places the bamboo cane into the cupboard, and returns to the men carrying a billy club. 'State . . .

'State . . . Confidential . . . Secret' Ugh!

Confidential . . . Secret!' screams the Prisoner as the club descends onto his head, knocking him sideways to the floor. Walking to a lamp, the silent servant pushes it across the floor and returns to help Number 2 gather up the unconscious man. Placed on a table top, Number 6 lies helpless as the superior lowers the perspex hood of the lamp level with the unconscious man's head. 'I'm beginning to like him,' puffs Number 2, his breathing pattern taking on the rhythm of the pulsating lamp.

'A.B.C.D.E. say them' orders Number 2. to the man sitting on a rocking horse. '1.2.3.4.5 ... ' begins the Prisoner. (Six!) 'Five.' (Six!) 'Five.' (Six!) 'Five.' (Six!) 'Five.' repeats Number 6. Six-five they continue until. breaking the pattern. Number 2 tries another tack. 'Six of One!' 'Five.' counters the Prisoner. (Six of One.) 'Five.' (Six of One!) 'Five ... ' On and on they go. neither man prepared to concede ground. 'Six of One. half-a-dozen of the other ... ' snaps Number 2. 'Pop goes the weasel ... pop, goes the weasel.' counters Number 6. (Pop.) 'Pop.' (Pop.) 'Pop.' (Pop.) 'Pop. pop. pop ... ' each throws back in turn. 'Pop protect.' yells Number 2. 'Protect?' quizzes the other. (Protect Pop.) 'Pop.' (Protect pop. pop protect.) 'Pop.' (Protect other people.) 'Protect.' repeats Number 6. staring into the blue light over his head. (People's own protection.) 'Protect other pop.' grins Number 6. as the superior circles around the rocking horse. (Protect other people.) 'Pop.' (Why?) 'Pop.' (Why?) 'Pop.' (Why. why. why. why. why?) 'Pop pop pop-pop.' grins the man on the horse. (Why pop?) ' ... goes the weasel.' sings Number 6. (WHY? WHY? WHY? WHY? WHY?) 'Half a pound of tuppenny rice. half a pound of treacle. That's the way the money goes. pop goes the weasel ... ' (Why? Why? Why?) 'Half a pound of pop ... ' grins the Prisoner. (Why pop?) 'Pop.' (Why pop?) 'Pop.' (Why pop?) 'Pop pop ... ' 'Why?' asks Number 2. ' ... POP!' grins the other.

Magically. the two men continue their verbal sparring in boxing gear. with Number 2 as the teacher and the Prisoner as the trainee. 'Pop.' says Number 2. protecting his chin from his opponent's swing. 'Too much swing boy ... swings are for kids boy ... not too much swing ... keep 'em down ... keep 'em short ... again. again. again ... Good boy ... he puffs. warding off the Prisoner's blows as he backs across the room to stand with his back at the blackboard. 'Hit me ... Hit me!' he challenges. dropping his guard. 'Like this?' lunges his opponent. swinging his gloves wildly at the superior's head. 'Too much swing boy ... swings are for kids boy ... ' confirms Number 2. throwing back a right. 'Don't move that right and leave the left asleep boy – Hit me! ... Hook. hook. hook. hook ... good that's it boy ... it's the left boy. keep the left or I'll kill you boy ... I'll KILL you boy ...!' Their remaining words are lost in mumbles as the two close in on one another. Number 6 throwing wild jabs. the superior warding off each blow with a supremely timed counter-punch. 'Take it easy boy ... you're the champ boy ... take it easy ... ' grunts Number 2 as the men stand face to face. the perspiration trickling down their faces. 'I made you ... you're the champ boy. champ. champ ... eh?' Number 6 is sitting exhausted in the children's playpen. being fanned with a white towel by the Butler. 'Pop ... pop ... pop ... ' he murmurs as the piercing blue light burns into his eyes. 'That's it boy.' calms Number 2. The other stares blankly into the tutor's face. 'Son ... tell me boy. why did you resign boy? Tell me son ... you're the *champ* boy ... the champ ... ' The superior's words burn into the exhausted pupil's brain. 'Tell me boy ... tell me something. *why-did-you-resign-boy* ... ?' Clenching his gloved fist. the Prisoner holds it squarely under the other man's nose. A lightning upper-cut. and Number 2's head is jolted back!

It is épées now. A fencing lesson. 'That's my boy ... that's my boy, touché ... light and easy young man ... no muscle ... finesse ... good. nice and easy ... good! ... But you ran ... mustn't run young man. don't hit and run ... don't treat it as a game young man ... You're the champ ... Kill! Kill! Kill ... !' Countering his opponent's

thrust. the Prisoner sends Number 2's duelling weapon soaring to the back of the room. Removing his head guard. the superior stares at his opponent. daring Number 6 to end the game. ' ... Now kill!' pants the superior as the other plants the top of his epee sharply to Number 2's throat. easing him backwards to the mock-up door. 'Afraid to prove you're a man ... ' gasps Number 2 ' ... Your resignation was cowardice wasn't it?' Circling his opponent's head with the epee's tip. the Prisoner thrusts his arm forward. 'Ah!' yells Number 2. as the weapon flicks past his ear and rattles into the door. the force of the lunge removing its safety cap. Drawing back his arm. the one being challenged places its razor-sharp point to the tip of the superior's nose. 'Kill!' grins Number 2. 'Kill boy ... you can do it boy. you're the one-man band ... ' The words penetrate the Prisoner's brain. Tearing off his face guard. he gives his opponent a bemused stare. ' ... but you won't step over the threshold because you're scared ... go on *kill*.' defies Number 2. Emitting a fearful scream. Number 6 rams his épée into the superior's shoulder. 'You missed boy ... ' mocks Number 2 ' ... You still can't do it.' 'Sorry ... sorry.' pleads Number 6. 'Sorry ... ' growls

'You have no respect for tradition'

do you mean?) The Butler crosses behind them to pick up the coffee perculator. 'I mean I can work.' (Tell me what hours.) 'I don't care.' 'Why?' asks Number 2, as the mute manservant places the coffee pot next to the Prisoner's right wrist. 'Well, it's the way I'm made,' replies Number 6 quietly. 'Oh excellent,' confirms Number 2, placing his hand on the other's shoulder. 'Are you ready? C'mon, c'mon . . . ' 'Ready for *what*?' asks the other nervously. '*You* are to meet our Managing Director!' exclaims Number 2. 'Right away?' cries Number 6, leaping to his feet and crossing the room to hop into a children's motorised toy car. Snuggling into its seat, he motors his way across the chamber, bringing the vehicle to a halt beside the mock-up door. As ever, the mute manservant appears and swings it open for him, bringing Number 2 into view, who now sits behind a bright yellow desk, reporting to someone on the telephone. 'It is approved and passed into the minutes,' he orders, slamming down the receiver as the man in the toy vehicle appears before him. 'Yes sir?' barks the superior, staring at the newcomer. 'I'd like a job,' replies Number 6. 'You have it!' 'Thank you,' grins the Prisoner turning to leave. 'Wait a minute . . . !' calls the other. ' . . . Close the door . . . come here . . . come, come, come . . . ' he whispers, as the successful applicant approaches him with caution. 'Just . . . hmm . . . just one slight matter . . . ' 'Yes?' 'We've been watching *you*.' 'Have you?' 'Yes . . . you're . . . you're just right,' confesses Number 2. (Right for here?) 'Yes, of course, my dear boy . . . you don't expect a man of your talents would be wasted in licking stamps do you?' (Never.) 'Never. No *you're* with us.' (To death do us part.) 'Exactly.' 'This is a cover?' asks the Prisoner. (Exactly.) 'For . . . ?' (Ssh . . . Secret.) ' . . . Good.' (This *is* a cover.) 'Secret?' (Secret work.) '*Top* Secret. Confidential job . . . thank you . . . ' smiles Number 6.

Back at the controls of the motorised car, Number 6 zig-zags around the nursery. Dressed in a policeman's uniform and giving an occasional blast of the whistle in his mouth, the Butler directs the motorist around the room, their madcap antics accompanied by the tape-recorded sounds of London traffic. Round and round drives the childlike Number 6 until, braking his car in front of the tiny policeman, he stares in bewilderment as the constable

the wounded man. ' . . . You're sorry for *everybody* . . . is that why you resigned?'

Day lengthens into night, night into day . . . and day after day the ruthless penetrating questioning continues, each man pitting his wits against the other, the macabre charade continuing unbroken against the ludicrous backdrop of the children's nursery and the huge metal cage in which the two men now sit, attended by the silent onlooker, the Butler, who serves them breakfast. Washed and refreshed after their last encounter, Number 2 begins the interrogation anew. 'I like it here,' he says, sitting at the breakfast table and toasting Number 6 with a glass of claret. 'Always use it for interviews. Nice and quiet . . . yes, well, I must say I am considerably impressed. Of course, naturally I shall have to discuss with my directors, but you seem admirably suited. Just to bring matters up to date . . . why exactly do you want this *job*?' 'It's a job,' whispers Number 6. (No other reasons at all?) 'No.' (You have no respect for tradition?) 'Pardon?' (No respect for tradition for an old established firm of bankers?) 'I was very good at mathematics.' (So were we all, otherwise we wouldn't be in it, would we?) 'I don't mean that.' (What

Number 6 stares in bewilderment as the 'constable' halts his progress

241

dangles a pair of handcuffs before his face. Number 2, dressed now in the scarlet robes of a judge, a shoulder-length white wig perched on top of his head, sits before the spinning wheel of a wooden children's toy, harkening to the defendant's plea. 'I am very good, I'm no angel . . .' pleads Number 6, his head bowed in abject apology ' . . . but I'm very good at mathematics.' 'Two and two?' snaps his lordship. 'Four!' 'Congratulations,' grins Number 2. 'Ask the manager.' (Manager?) 'The bank manager. He knows I'm good at figures,' says the defendant. (How many DEAD?) 'What?' (You were driving at *great* speed.) 'Yes, but nobody was hurt.' (In a restricted zone.) 'I had to.' (Had to?) 'Yes . . . I had a reason.' (Good, good. Tell me the reason.) 'I was on a mission . . . matter of life or death.' (Life or death eh?) 'Yes.' (Whose life or death?) 'I'm not allowed to say.' (Why?) 'It was secret business.' (Confidential . . .) 'State Confidential.' (. . . of the *highest* order . . .) 'Yes.' grins Number 6, warming to the game. (. . . International . . . *State Secret* business) 'Yes, yes indeed.' (Tell me.) 'Can't!' (*Can't?*) 'Such . . . such . . . b . . . b . . . business is above the law!' 'Above the law,' throws back the judge, challenging now, he means to get to the bottom of this. 'Above the law, yes . . . ' (Tell me.) 'Never!' (You're GUILTY . . .) 'Yes?' (. . . of speeding on a public highway, no excuses!) 'Ask the manager,' pleads Number 6 as the Butler flicks the uppermost wheel of the toy sitting on the desk before his lordship. 'Alternating even numbers,' grins the Number 2. 'What?' 'Test.' 'Test?' queries the defendant. 'Test, alternating even numbers. Go . . . ' 'Two' says the Prisoner. (Two.) 'Four.' (Two Four.) 'Four.' (Six!) 'Four, four . . . ' repeats Number 6, lifting up his hand to block out the light. (Six!) 'Two . . . two . . . ' stammers the defendant banging his fist on a table ' . . . four FIVE!' (Six!) 'FIVE!' screams the Prisoner. (Two, four, *six*!) '*Five* . . . that's me.' seethes Number 6. 'Two, four, SIX, that's you . . . Six, you are *six* . . . alternating *even* numbers, go . . . 2.4.6.8.' 'Guilty,' whispers the Prisoner, lowering his head. 'Unrestricted murder on the public highways . . . Thinks he knows it all . . . too fast. Why did you risk the murder of innocent human beings by exceeding the speed limit?' 'I'm good at figures,' mocks the defendant. 'Don't you like it?' 'I'll work any hours of the day,' confirms the Prisoner. 'Fine 20 units.' 'I appeal.' 'What?' blusters Number 2. 'I appeal.' (Not allowed.) 'I can't pay.' (20 units!) '*I can't* pay.' (Nothing?) 'Units are not for me.' '*You* are a *member* . . . of the Village!' bawls Number 2. 'No!' denies the defendant. '*You* are a *unit* . . .' 'No-oo!' ' . . . of *society*.' 'No-ooo!' screams the defendant. '*Contempt!*' 'No.' '*Contempt* of Court.' 'I accept . . . ' nods the condemned. ' . . . I accept the ruling. Thank you.' 'Six days in jail.' sentences the Judge, leaving his chair to cross and hug the defendant. 'I was rebelling, my lord,' sobs the Prisoner. 'Six days,' says the other, grabbing the distraught man's arm. 'I was rebelling against the figures, my lord.' 'Six days. Take him away.' With the manservant's aid, Number 2 drags Number 6 down a table top, sweeping all before them as the condemned man is thrown into the cage. 'I shall appeal against unfair treatment,' swears Number 6 as he is forced into a chair and the metal door is slammed shut in his face. 'You've had the same treatment as everybody else,' growls Number 2. 'That's why I'm going to appeal.' yells the Prisoner grabbing the metal bars. 'Let me out. This is unfair treatment! Why, why, why did I resign? Am I a sick man . . . ?' mumbles Number 6 as the superior storms across the room to the Butler.

Wakened by the manservant, Number 2 struggles off the table top on which he has been sleeping. Although still tired, he quickly regains his composure, buttons up his blazer and mounts the steps leading up to the cage. Steadying himself by holding on to the bars, he paces backwards and forwards before the man locked inside, stopping to stare into the Prisoner's face. 'Why did you resign?' he grunts. 'For peace,' grins the handcuffed man. (For peace?) 'Let me out,' shouts the Prisoner pacing the cell floor. (You resigned, for peace?) 'Yes. Let me out.' (You're a fool.) 'For peace of mind.' (What?) 'For PEACE OF MIND!' barks the man in the cage. (Why?) 'Too many people know too much.' (Never!) '*I* know too much.' (Tell me) 'I know too much about *you*.' (Don't.) 'I *do*.' (Don't.) 'I *know* you,' growls the prisoner, pacing the floor of his cell like a caged tiger. (Who am I?) '*You* are an enemy.' (I'm on *your* side.) 'Yeah.' (Why did you resign?) 'You've been told.' (Tell me again.) 'I know *you*.' (You're smart.) 'In my *mind* . . . ' (Yes?) ' . . . in my mind, *you're* smart!' growls Number 6, pointing an accusing finger at the other's face. (WHY DID YOU RESIGN?!) 'There . . . you see,' sobs Number 6. (Why did you resign?) ' . . . Know who you are?' mocks the Prisoner. (What?) 'A fool!' (What?) 'Yes . . . (No, don't.) ' . . . Yes, you're an idiot.' (I'll kill you.) 'I'll die,' whispers the caged man, staring defiantly into the other man's face. 'You're dead,' mocks Number 2. Grabbing the bars, Number 6 rattles them in anger. 'Let me out,' he pleads. 'Dead!' exclaims the other. Racing to the kitchen cabinet behind him, the Prisoner grabs a carving knife from a drawer, and hands it to the superior through the bars. '*Kill* me,' dares Number 6. 'Open it,' orders the superior. 'Open it!' mocks the man in the cage as the silent figure of the Butler places the key into the locked door. 'Open the door,' repeats Number 2 with a sigh. Raising the knife to his shoulder, the tip of the blade a threat to the Prisoner's life, Number 2 enters the cage and holds the tip of the carving knife to the other man's neck. 'Kill.' mocks Number 6, falling backwards to the floor. 'Kill me lying down.' 'Get up you fool.' 'You can't?' challenges the Prisoner. 'In the was *you've* killed.' 'Yes.' 'You killed for fun!' 'For *peace*,' swears Number 6. 'DO AS I SAY!' orders the man with the knife. 'I did as I was told.' mocks the man on the floor.

Sometime later, dressed in pilot's flying helmets, Numbers 2 and 6 are sitting on a wooden beam high above the floor, their legs dangling above the head of the Butler who sits at the controls of a dry-ice machine which is pumping dense clouds of silky-white smoke into the nursery. 'Twelve seconds to zero.' Number 2 warns his co-pilot. 'Stand by to release. All set?' 'Set,' confirms Number 6. 'Eleven,' says Number 2, commencing the countdown. (Eleven.) 'Ten.' (Ten.) 'Nine.' (Nine.) 'Eight.' (Eight.) 'Seven.' (Seven.) 'Six.' (Five.) '*Six*' (Five.) 'Six!' (Five!) 'Six!' (Five.) 'Six!' (Five!) 'SIX . . .! Fire . . . ' screams Number 2, as the sound effects controlled by the manservant simulate the sounds of exploding bombs. 'Three.' (Three.) 'Two.' (Two.) 'One.' (One.) 'Zero go . . . zero go . . . zero, zero, go, go, go. . . . overshot you fool, wake up . . . ' yells Number 2. ' . . . Coming in again on the re-run, let 'em go as soon as the turn's completed . . . stand by . . . ' (Stand by.) 'Approaching . . . let go . . . Now!' 'Bombs gone,' confirms Number 6, pressing the make-believe bomb release button. 'Good boy . . . bull's-eye . . . We're hit . . . bail out, bail out . . . ' yells Number 2, leaping from the beam. After a slight pause, his co-pilot follows him. Back inside the cage, the Prisoner is being questioned by Number 2, who has now adopted the role of a German officer. (German dialogue, accompanied by the sounds of

'Bail out. Bail out. Bail out!'

German troops saluting their Führer.) 'I do not wish to kill,' confirms Number 6 in a German accent. Marching in time with the music being piped into the cell by the tape-player, the superior continues his cross-interrogation in German. 'The aircraft was hit. I had to bail out, over your territory,' pleads Number 6, with a shrug of his shoulders. 'It's not my fault . . . I cannot help bailing out!' The two men continue their conversation in German. 'My arrival is a fact, but I have to tell you nothing,' mocks the Prisoner. The superior replies in German. 'Zero go . . . ' shrugs Number 6. 'How dare you . . . ' snaps Number 2. ' . . . Go, go, go, go-oo,' laughs the Prisoner. 'Zero, zero go!' 'I'm a friend,' confides Number 2. 'Yes.' 'Why did you resign? I'm a friend . . . I'm a friend.' 'Eight,' replies Number 6. (Why did you resign?) 'Eight.' (Why?) 'Six.' (Six?) 'Yes . . . Four.' (No.) 'Two!' grins the Prisoner, leading the superior out of the cage. (No!) 'One.' (NO!) 'Zero . . . go.' (No!) 'I'm hungry.' 'What would you like?' asks Number 2. 'Supper.'

In a reversal of their roles, Number 2 now lies on a table, as Number 6 hovers over him like a hawk. 'You chose this method because you knew the only way to beat me, was to gain my respect,' coaxes the Prisoner. 'That is correct,' nods Number 2. 'And then I would confide?' 'I hoped that you would come to trust me,' nods the other, dancing his fingers over his ample tummy. 'This is a recognised method?' probes the interrogator. 'Used in psychoanalysis . . . the patient must come to trust his doctor totally.' 'Sometimes,' mocks Number 6, bending over the reclining man's head, 'they change places.' 'It is essential in extreme cases,' giggles Number 2. 'Also a risk.' 'A grave risk,' laughs the other. 'If the doctor has his own problems.' 'I have,' confirms the superior with a grin. 'That is why the system is known as "degree absolute"?' coaxes the Prisoner. 'It's one or the other of us,' giggles the superior. 'Why don't you resign?' The man lying on the table laughs. 'Very good,' giggles Number 2, raising himself aloft. 'You're very good at it.' Easing himself to the floor, Number 2 crosses over to where the Butler is playing the organ. 'Play something cheerful,' he requests. 'I'd like to know more,' says the Prisoner. 'You'll have every opportunity before we're through,' confirms Number 2, gazing around the room. 'Join me,' he calls, racing into the cage. Number 6 enters the cell. 'There you

are,' grins the superior handing the Prisoner a glass of whisky. 'Straight?' 'One-hundred per cent proof,' confirms the elder, recorking the bottle. 'No additions?' 'My word of honour,' grins Number 2. 'Cheers,' toasts the Prisoner raising the glass to his lips. 'Mind if I er, look around our home from home?' 'Not at all,' chortles the elder. Offering to show his guest around, the superior leads him back into the nursery area. 'This delightful residence is known as the Embryo Room. In it you can re-live from the cradle to the grave. Seven ages of man, William Shakespeare.' 'Last seen all, that ends this strange eventful history, of this second childishness and near oblivion,' quotes Number 2. 'Sans eyes . . . ' whispers the superior. 'Yes.' ' . . . Sans teeth . . . ' 'Yes.' ' . . . Sans taste . . . ' 'Yes.' ' . . . Sans everything.' 'Correct,' confirms Number 6, placing his hand on the other man's shoulder. 'No there's no way out until our time is up . . . If we can solve our mutual problems, that will be soon . . . You can take my word for it,' confirms the weary elder. 'Naturally I would,' grins the Prisoner. 'Let me show you the DOOR!' invites the other. Racing across the room, he tugs on the curtain pull and the deep blue curtains slide apart to reveal the massive steel door. 'We are protected from intrusion in a most efficient way. No one can interrupt our, shall I say, deliberations? Totally encased in solid finest steel,' confirms Number 2, rapping his fist on the door. 'Behold the clock!' he yells, indicating its red dial, its triangular white minute hand denoting that only five minutes are left before the time-lock releases the door's locking mechanism. 'FIVE MINUTES!' he exclaims, resetting the dial to open at a new phase of their relationship. 'That is, if we are still here?' 'Are we likely to move?' quips the other. 'It's possible!' yells Number 2, racing back into the cage to refill his empty whisky glass. 'Somewhere nice?' mocks Number 6, following the superior to the bars of the cell, but remaining poised at the door. 'Built in bars?' he whispers, sliding the cell door almost to a close. 'Also self-contained,' grins the superior, walking around the interior. 'Kitchen, bathroom, air conditioning. Food supplies for six months. You could go anywhere in it . . . It even has a waste disposal unit.' 'It *moves*?' quizzes Number 6. 'It's detachable,' confirms the elder. 'What's behind it?' grins Number 6, sliding the cell door closed with a clunk. 'Steel . . . steel,' nods Number 2, as he leaps at the door. Too late. The one outside has turned the key in its lock and handed it to the Butler, who, bowing to the victor, carries it away. 'Ah . . . ha,ha,ha,' laughs the one locked in the cage. 'He thinks you're the boss now,' yells Number 2 in the direction of the silent manservant. 'I am,' gloats the Prisoner. 'I'm Number 2. I'm the *boss*! Open this door!' yells the one in the cell. 'Number 1 is the boss,' says the one standing outside. 'No!' 'Three minutes,' goads Number 6. 'You're scared.' 'No.' 'You can't take it.' 'FOOL!' exclaims Number 2, thumping his fist on the bars. 'Yes, a fool . . . but not a rat,' quips the other. '*You're* scared,' challenges the one in the cage. 'Want me to come in?' 'Keep out!' warns the elder. 'Let you out?' mocks Number 6. 'Stay away,' calls the one inside. 'Wanna come out?' grins the Prisoner. 'KEEP OUT!' screams Number 2. 'You're mine,' threatens Number 6, descending the steps to urge the Butler to open the cage. As beckoned, the mute manservant approaches the cage. 'STOP HIM . . . !' screams the elder, as his once loyal companion inserts the key into the lock. 'Two minutes,' confirms the Prisoner. 'STOP HIM.' pleads the hysterical Number 2. '*Two minutes . . . thank you,' grins Number 6 sliding open the door to the cage. 'You're free!' he snaps, indicating that the superior can leave. 'No, I'm Number 2 . . . ' stammers the elder. 'You are number nothing,' sneers the Prisoner. 'I am Number 2!' 'One minute, thirty-five seconds,' warns Number 6. 'Why did you resign?' tries Number 2. 'I didn't accept, why did *you* accept,' snaps the Prisoner. 'You resigned!' confirms Number 2. 'I *rejected*!' 'You *accepted* before you resigned.' 'I *rejected*!' 'Who?' throws back Number 2. 'You.' 'Why me?' pleads the elder. 'You're big!' 'Not tall.' 'Not tall . . . ' confirms Number 6, ' . . . big . . . Humpty Dumpty. All the king's horses. All the king's men!' snaps the Prisoner. 'That's right,' confirms the elder. 'Couldn't put *Humpty* together again,' confirms Number 6. 'Wh..what . . . ' stammers Number 2, staring at the clock. 'One minute to go.' He sighs. Clutching his heart, he elbows his way past his tormentor and races down the steps, stumbling while so doing and rolling past the mute figure of the Butler who sits unconcerned playing the organ. '59 seconds . . . 58 seconds,' counts the Prisoner. Climbing to his knees, the superior rests his hand on the organ's top. 'I'm big,' he boasts. '57,' counts Number 6. '*You're* tall,' concedes the elder to the one standing over him. '56 . . . ' grins Number 6 continuing the count. Crawling his way backwards, the superior cowers at the Prisoner's feet. (55) 'Be glad.' (54) 'God.' (53) 'Not for *me*,' pleads the elder, clutching at the playpen. '52, 51,' yells the Prisoner, snatching away the superior's hand. '50, 49, 48 . . . ' 'Why?' (47) 'WHY?' (46) 'Why RESIGN?' screams Number 2, his fingers clutching at the rocking horse. (45) 'Tell me.' pleads the elder. (44) 'WHY DID YOU . . . ?' (43)

'39' (I'll tell.) '38'

'I don't know.' (42) 'Yes?' (41) 'Any minute now,' whispers Number 2. '40!' yells Number 6. 'I'll tell . . . ' screams the superior crawling to his knees. (39) ' . . . I'll tell!' (38!) ' . . . Got no time . . . ' (37!) ' . . . No time . . . ' sobs Number 2 stumbling into the spotlight. '36!' shouts Number 6. ' . . .

No time . . . ' '35,' whispers the Prisoner staring at the clock as the second hand creeps towards zero hour. 'Still time . . . ' grunts the exhausted Number 2. ' . . . not too late.' 'For *me*?' mocks Number 6. 'For *mee-ee* . . . ' screams the man on his knees patting his chest. 'You snivel and grovel!' 'I *ask*.' 'You crawl.' 'Yes . . . look,' confirms Number 2, crawling towards the other man's feet. 'To ask?' 'Yes, to ask.' 'Why?' Smiles Number 6. Head raised, the elder grunts. Then, leaping to his feet with his arms outstretched, he grabs his tormentor by the throat. 'Ask on,' grins the Prisoner. 'Ask YOURSELF!' he yells, throwing the trembling man aside. Racing back into the cage, the superior begs why. 'Why? . . . Why?' '15,' snaps the Prisoner. 'Please,' sobs Number 2. 'Don't say please,' mocks Number 6. 'I say it.' 'Don't!' 'Please . . . I plead!' exclaims the terrified man, placing his hands together in a gesture of prayer. 'Nine!' 'Too late,' concedes the other. 'Eight.' 'Seven!' barks Number 2, picking up the count. 'Six!' 'Six!' echoes Number 2. 'Die Six, Die!' yells the other. 'Five' wheezes Number 2. 'Die!' The superior gasps for breath. 'Die!' growls the Prisoner. 'Four,' gasps Number 2. 'Die!' '*Threeee*,' wheezes the other. His breathing is heavy now. 'Die!' The defeated superior raises a glass to his lips. '*Two-ooo*' he gurgles. '*DIE!*' snorts Number 6. The clock stops ticking. Number 2 collapses to the floor. Crouching, the Prisoner places his fingers to the man's neck. The superior has paid the price of defeat. His glazed eyes stare unseeing at the ceiling, no breath emits from his lips. Drawing his hand back gently across the defeated man's face, the victor climbs to his feet. With a final glance at the body lying on the floor of the cage, he retreats from the cell, slides the door to a close and locks it with the key. As the mute Butler ascends the steps to take one final look at his former master, the steel door slides open and the Supervisor marches into the room. 'Congratulations . . . we shall need the body for evidence,' he says, joining the men by the cage. In a fit of pique, Number 6 flings his glass to the floor. 'What do you desire?' asks the newcomer. 'Number 1.' 'I'll take you,' confirms the Supervisor. Crossing over to the time lock, he depresses a switch and a huge metal shield descends from the ceiling to cover Number 2's well-protected tomb. To the tune of the nursery rhyme 'Baa-Baa Black Sheep' the three men depart from the room — a room that is now as silent as a grave.

AUTHOR'S NOTE: Originally conceived as the final (13th) story of the first series, this episode was put on the shelf to be shown as the penultimate story - leading directly into *Fall Out*. (The episodes should always be viewed together!)

A time span of over 12 months separated the production of this story and the final denouement, by which time Leo McKern was beardless. As the actor had an aversion to false whiskers, the production personnel came up with an ingenious solution — the bizarre machine which brought the 'dead' Number 2 back to life and, in so doing, gave him a shave and a new haircut!

Although credited, actor John Maxim as 'Number 86' does not actually appear in the story - his scenes being trimmed prior to transmission.

Almost all of the answers Number 6 gives to Number 2 are based on McGoohan's own life.

Filmed under the working title *Degree Absolute*.

THIS IS IT . . . for better or for worse . . . who knows. One week . . . one teeny-weeny week my boyboy . . . Neither of us can leave, till death do us part . . . and I've brought it on myself . . . who knows,' says Number 2, setting the time lock of the massive steel door and drawing a heavy curtain over the exit door. 'Come ahead son . . . let's see what you're made of . . . find out what's in that noddle of yours . . . ' Turning, he writes on a blackboard. 'A . . . find missing link, and when I have found it, I will refine it, tune it and you will play our game . . . ' 'No sir,' says the Prisoner, staring into the superior's face. 'Top Secret . . . ?' 'State Secret,' snaps Number 6. 'Yes,' sighs the other. 'State Secret sir . . . ' 'Top. State. Confidential . . . !' screams Number 2, grabbing the lapels of the pupil's jacket. ' . . . Why? Why? Why did you resign?' 'No . . . No-ooo!!!' screams Number 6, throwing the interrogator round in circles. Grunting, he grits his teeth, draws back his fist and with a vicious right hand sends the other reeling to the floor.

'Don't move that right and leave the left asleep boy – Hit me!' exclaims Number 2 throwing a short right cross to the Prisoner's jaw.

'Kill! Kill! Kill!' screams Number 2. Countering his opponent's thrust, the Prisoner sends Number 2's duelling weapon soaring to the back of the room. Removing his head guard, the superior stares at his opponent, daring Number 6 to end the game. ' . . . Now kill!' Circling Number 2's head with the epee's tip, the Prisoner thrusts his arm forward. 'Ah!' yells Number 2, as the weapon flicks past his ear and rattles into the door, the force of the lunge removing its safety cap. Drawing back his arm, the one being challenged places the razor sharp point to the tip of the superior's nose. 'Kill!' grins Number 2. 'Kill boy . . . you can do it boy, you're the one-man band . . . but you can't step over the threshold because you're scared . . . go on kill.' defies Number 2. Emitting a fearful scream, Number 6 rams the epee into the superior's shoulder.

'WHY DID YOU RESIGN?' snorts Number 2 to the man in the cage. 'Know who you are?' mocks the Prisoner. (What?) 'A fool.' (What?) 'Yes . . . ' (No don't) ' . . . yes, you're an idiot.' (I'll kill you.) 'I'll die,' whispers the caged man, staring defiantly into the other man's face. 'You're dead,' mocks Number 2.

'Twelve seconds to zero.' Number 2 warns his co-pilot. 'Stand by to release. All set?' 'Set,' confirms Number 6. 'Eleven,' says Number 2. (Eleven.) 'Ten.' (Ten.) 'Nine.' (Nine.) 'Eight.' (Eight.) 'Seven.' (Seven.) 'Six.' (Five.) 'Six.' 'Stand by,' replies Number 6. 'Approaching . . . let go . . . Now!' 'Bombs gone,' confirms Number 6, pressing the make-believe bomb release button. 'Good boy . . . bull's-eye!' confirms Number 2.

'Built in bars?' whispers Number 6, sliding the cell door almost to a close. 'Also self-contained,' grins the superior, walking around the interior. 'Kitchen, bathroom, air conditioning. Food supplies for six months. You could go anywhere in it . . . It even has a waste disposal unit.' 'It moves?' quizzes Number 6. 'It's detachable,' confirms the elder. 'What's behind it?' grins Number 6, sliding the cell door closed with a clunk. 'Steel . . . steel,' nods Number 2, as he leaps at the door.

'Die Six Die!' yells the Prisoner. 'Five,' wheezes Number 2. 'Die!' 'Four,' gasps Number 2. 'Die!' 'Three-ee,' wheezes the superior. 'Die!' The defeated Number 2 raises a glass to his lips. 'Two-ooo,' he gurgles. 'DIE!' 'One,' gasps the drinker, removing the glass from his lips. 'DIE!' snorts Number 6. The clock stops ticking. Number 2 collapses to the floor. With a final glance at the body lying on the floor

of the cage, Number 6 retreats from the cell, slides the door to a close and locks it with the key. The steel entrance door slides open and the Supervisor marches into the room. 'Congratulations . . . we shall need the body for evidence.' In a fit of pique, Number 6 flings his glass to the floor. 'What do you desire?' asks the newcomer. 'Number 1.' 'I'll take you,' confirms the Supervisor. Crossing over to the time lock, he depresses a switch and a huge metal shield descends from the ceiling to cover Number 2's well protected tomb. His duty done, the Supervisor follows Number 6 and the Butler out of the Embryo Room . . . .

FALL OUT

Written by **Patrick McGoohan**
with guest star **Leo McKern**

The President   **Kenneth Griffith**

Alexis Kanner

The Butler   **Angelo Muscat**
The Supervisor   **Peter Swanwick**
The Delegate   **Michael Miller**

Directed by Patrick McGoohan

ESCORTED BY THE Supervisor, Number 6 and the mute manservant walk down a long corridor to the blackness beyond – a darkness which contains a circular elevator platform. When mounted, this takes them deep into the bowels of the earth. But to what? What new nightmares await the Prisoner in this underground world far beneath the Village? What further torment lies ahead for the man who dared to take on the opposition – and win! After a long descent, the elevator grinds to a halt. Its steel-encased doors slide open to reveal a solitary motionless figure beckoning them onward – a figure bearing a clay mask modelled in the likeness of . . . himself! 'We . . . thought you would feel . . . happier as yourself,' greets a disembodied voice. Stepping over to his likeness, the Prisoner blinks as a fanfare of trumpets pipe out the opening bars of a pop song. (All You Need Is Love).

'All you need is love'

245

Moving forwards the trio pass through a gauntlet of colourful juke boxes and approach a huge wooden door set into the rock, its rusted hinges beckoning ... what? The Butler inserts his key and the huge door swings open to reveal a vast subterranean cavern. 'Well Come' invites a sign on the back of the door as the Butler and Supervisor stand aside to allow Number 6 to enter. The chamber is immense. Stalactites hang from the ceiling. Banks of computers and other machinery stand on metal gantries, attended by men in white robes, their faces hidden from view beneath white hoods. A squad of troops march proudly in unison across the cavern floor, their white helmets, gloves and boots matching the white rifle harness they carry strapped to their shoulders. Along one wall of the room sits an assembly of robed figures – delegates representing the defectors, reactionists, rationalists and every shade of opinion and activity in the village. In the centre of the room is a throne standing on a majestic blue-carpeted dais, its place of honour guarded by four of the uniformed troops. Walking past Number 6, the Supervisor and Butler pace proudly across the floor, the former accepting a white robe and mask from a hooded attendant. (The black and white mask matching those of the delegates.) 'All you need is love ... all you need is love ... ' sing the juke boxes as, to an ovation from the assembly, the Supervisor pulls the robe over his head and dons his face mask ready to take his place with his fellow representatives. The music ceases abruptly and Number 6 is greeted by a bewigged man dressed in the scarlet robes of a judge. 'Welcome,' bids the President, as the Prisoner walks slowly towards the pulpit on which the man stands. Behind him, the Supervisor sits in the seat designated 'Identification.' As he does so, the assembly breaks into applause. 'This session is called in a matter of democratic crisis ...' opens the President, banging down his gavel to bring the assembly to order. ' ... and we are here gathered to resolve the question of revolt.' Applause from the delegates. 'We desire that these proceedings be conducted in a civilised manner, but remind ourselves that humanity is not humanised without force and that errant children ... ' he points in the direction of the Prisoner ' ... must sometimes be brought to book with a smack on their *backsides.*' Gleefully smacking his hands together, he silences further applause with a bank of his gavel. 'We draw your attention to the regrettable bullet ... The community is at stake ... and we have the means to protect it. The assembly is now in security ... ' he ends, looking down at the white-robed figure of the Supervisor standing before him. 'Number 6 is presented to you,' announces the mask-covered face. 'I understand he survived the ultimate test,' says the President. 'Indeed,' confirms the Supervisor. 'Then he must no longer be referred to as Number 6 ... or a number of any kind. He has gloriously vindicated the right of the individual to be individual ... and this assembly rises to you ... Sir,' grins the President. As one, the delegates rise to their feet and give the newcomer a hearty ovation. Raising his hand for silence and staring directly at the Prisoner, the President continues. 'Sir. We crave your indulgence for a short while ... the er, transfer of ultimate power requires some tedious ceremony and perhaps you would care to observe the preliminaries from the chair of honour.' Directed to the throne, the Prisoner mounts the steps to a fanfare of trumpets, and seats himself comfortably in the chair. A wry smile crossing his lips as the President continues. 'Sir. We thank you and promise to be as brief as possible.' A machine attendant pushes a button and amid clouds of

steam, the huge self-contained metal 'tomb' containing the body of the dead Number 2 descends from the ceiling, coming to rest with a gentle thud behind four uniformed guards. The metal shield slides to one side and two green-coated medical men wheel a stretcher-trolley into position in front of the cage. Turning to look at a tubelike silver metal container – its foremost side denoted by a large red number '1' – the President barks out the command 'Resusitate.' In an instant, the huge television monitor screen in front of him flickers into life and displays the lifeless body of the deposed Number 2. A second machine operator slides a lever to the right, and the final minutes of the encounter between the man sitting in the chair of honour and the dead superior is played in reverse: the 'dead' Number 2 leaping back to his feet and placing the whisky glass to his lips! 'A revolution ... ' grins the President ' ... Get him out. Key!' Appearing from nowhere, the Butler unlocks the cage door. Then, crossing to mount the dais steps, he bows to the man seated in the throne and positions himself at the man's shoulder. The body of Number 2 is carried out of his tomb by the medical men, placed on the stretcher and wheeled into an area occupied by more green-coated figures. Carried to a

An individual at last

breaking into the words of a well-known song: 'The collar bone's connected to the neck bone and the neck bone's connected to the head bone. Now hear the word of the Lord ... ' 'Number 48!' exclaims the President, banging his gavel. Shaking their black and white faces in disgust, the assembly rises to its feet. 'Dem bones 'dem bones gonna walk around. Dem bones 'dem bones gonna walk around ... ' continues the one strapped to the piston arm. 'Number 48!' screams the President, attempting to regain order. ' ... Them bones, them bones them dry bones.

'Dem bones, dem bones, dem dry bones'

seat, a flashing white light encased in a metal hood is lowered over the reclining figure's head and its visor is lowered over the man's face. Canvas straps are snapped into place around his wrists and ankles and a resusitator device is placed against the dead man's ample belly. As the visor is lifted from the seated figure's face, a circular rubber face pad extending from an elongated metal arm slides forwards to encase the bearded face and the apparatus purrs into motion with a throbbing electrical hum.

'Revolt, can take many forms ... ' announces the President. ' ... and here we have three specific instances ... ' On the far side of the chamber, a piston-like pole rises from a circular pit. ' ... Number 48!' confirms the President. From the smoke-filled pit emerges a young man dressed in black, a top hat perched rakishly on his head. He is strapped to the pole by a wide metal belt, unable to move anything but his head. The newcomer stares at the assembly. 'Thanks for the trip dad,' sings the youngster tunefully. 'Be grateful for the opportunity of pleading your case before the assembly,' cautions the figure in the scarlet robe. 'Oh baby ... what a crazy scene ... ' laughs the youngster, rocking his head from side to side and

them bones them bones them dry bones ... ' sings the grinning Number 48 as, in total confusion, the delegates dance around in their seats, keeping time with the young man's words. 'NUMBER 48!' screams the bewigged man. ' ... Now hear dat word of the Lord,' continues the vocalist, ignoring all attempts to shut him up. Suddenly, a flashing green light attracts the President's attention. Looking over his shoulder towards the large camera eye positioned on the wall beside the tubular metal container and seeing its inner lens pulsating with an intense white light, the President calls for order. 'Order, order ... release him, release him.' Accompanied by another uniformed guard, a sentry walks swiftly over to the young man and releases the wide metal strap that ties him to the pole. 'Youth ... with its enthusiasm ... ' begins the President, as the released man climbs, cat-like, out of the pit. ' ... which rebels against any accepted norm because it must and we sympathise ... It may wear flowers in its hair, bells on its toes, but ... ' The young man takes several faltering steps forward – approaching the area where the Prisoner sits in his chair of honour. ' ... when the common good is threatened, when the function of society is endangered, such revolts must cease ... ' states the President. Passing the group of medical men working on the dead Number 2, the young man moves forward. ' ... The are non-productive and *must* be *abolished*!' concludes the bewigged President. Standing motionless before the man seated on the throne, the young man raises the small golden cow bell that hangs around his neck and rings it defiantly. 'Number 48,' sighs the man dressed in scarlet. 'Hmm,' says the youngster. 'Hear the word ... of the Lord.' Without warning, he begins to race around the chamber singing the words of his song. The medics leap out of his way as he jumps down from a rock and sends his pursuers flying like skittles as he leaps aboard the stretcher trolley and propels himself towards them like a torpedo. Escaping from their clutches, he races up a gantry, grabbing a microphone from a controller as the delegates race across the floor and attempt to ensnare him. The chamber is in uproar. Total confusion reigns as he races around the room, pushing a button here, pulling a lever there, running, running from the uniformed men who chase after him. Falling to the floor, he rolls over in a heap and finds himself surrounded by soldiers, their rifles directed to his head. 'Young man,' snaps the man sitting in the chair of honour. 'Give it to me again,' calls Number 48. 'Don't knock yourself out ... ' says the Prisoner. 'Give me a rest,' pleads the youngster. ' ... Young ... man,' the Prisoner concludes. 'I'm born all over,' quips the top-hatted youth, springing to his feet amid the circle of gun-toting troops. 'Sir, we thank you for your intervention, but fear that such familiarity is not in keeping with procedure,' grins the President. ' ... we must maintain the status quo ... Now, Number... ' A siren screams and the man dressed in scarlet turns back to the flashing green light which emits from the tube-shaped cylinder denoted by the large letter '1'. 'Yes, of course,' confirms the President as the pulsating green light flashes out its warning. 'Naturally, it would expedite matters. Very well ... to your places.' As one, the troops guarding Number 48 break formation and return to their posts, leaving the youngster standing motionless in the centre of the chamber. 'Sir, it would appear that temporarily, we may use the new form of address in order to bring these proceedings to an early and satisfactory conclusion,' announces the President, turning to the assembly to invite them to cast their vote. 'Those in favour?' As one the delegates applaud. 'Carried. We are obliged ... sir,' he concludes, staring at the Prisoner. 'Don't mention it, Dad,' returns the one seated in the chair of honour.

This appears to please the young man, who, his face breaking into a grin, turns to face the President. 'Young ... man,' says the one in the scarlet robe. 'You got the message?' quips the youngster. 'I just got it,' confirms the President. (What gives?) 'You've never been with it ... I mean us,' corrects the one wearing the wig. (I'm gone, gone away.) 'But you were then you went and gone.' (Got da word.) 'Oh yes, yes,' nods the President. (The bright light, Dad. Got the sign.) 'The sign?' (The light.) 'The light?' (The Message.) 'Then you went and gone,' grins the President. 'Why?' smiles Number 48. 'Give it to me, baby,' laughs the man in the scarlet robe. 'That's it,' urges the young man. 'Give me the rest!' 'Give. All you want is give. That's it,' nods Number 48. 'That's it,' mocks the President. 'And take,' confirms the other. 'That's it.' (Take is all you want.) 'That's it.' (Take.) 'That's it!' 'And take,' grins the young man. 'Take, take, take ... ' yells the President. 'Take ... take,' growls Number 48, spreading his arms to lead the assembly into a chant. '*Take, take, take, take, take* ... ' shout the delegates, thumping their fists to their desks as the young man sinks to his knees arms outstretched. 'Take, take, take,' mouths the President, turning to the large television lens, his words lost in the babble of voices. The man sitting in the chair

of honour and the Butler remain silent, watching stoically from the dais. 'TAKE!' yells the President, crashing down his gavel to bring the assembly to order. Still kneeling, the young man rings his bell. 'Now you're high,' barks the man wearing the wig. 'I'm *low*,' smirks the other. 'Give it to me baby! Confess!' exclaims the President. 'Oh Dad, I'm your baby, Dad. You owe your baby something, Daddy.' 'Confess now you're hep,' hisses the man in the red robe. 'Hip dad,' mocks Number 48. '*Hip!*' 'Confess!' 'Ah hip bone ... ' grins the one on the floor. 'Confess!' ' ... and de thigh bone ... ' 'Confess!' ' ... Shin bone, knee bone ... ' 'Confess!' ' ... Back bone, all yours, Dad ... ' 'Confess!' 'Knee bone ... ' yells the young man, stretching out his arms as a record of 'Dem Bones' blasts out from a juke box. Within seconds, the entire assembly including the President picks up the words of the song and begins to sing and sway in time with the music – the instigator. Number 48, turning his head to give a mock salute to the silent figure seated behind him on the dais. Dancing to his feet, the young man begins to snap his fingers and join in with the chant. The delegates sway more and more wildly, their white-gloved hands clapping in silent beat with the music. Grinning, Number 48 slides to a kneeling position, then, crossing his legs beneath him into a yoga position, he sits back, content to let the court make a mockery of itself. 'Hip Hip,' yells the President, as the music ceases abruptly. 'Hurrah,' yell the delegates throwing their hands in the air as they thump back into their seats in unison. ' ... And hear de word of the Lord,' sighs the man on the floor. 'Guilty!' roars the President, bringing his gavel crashing down before him. 'Read the charge.' Climbing to his feet, the delegate representing the anarchist division of the assembly addresses the court. 'The prisoner has been charged with the most serious breach of social etiquette ... ' The young man rings his bell. ' ... total defiance of the elementary laws which sustain our community ... questioning the decisions of those voted to govern us ... unhealthy aspects of speech and dress not in accordance with general practice, and the refusal to observe, wear or respond, to his NUMBER ... !' Grinning, Number 48 turns to the delegate and rings his bell mockingly. 'Sir, you approve the proceedings?' the President asks the man sitting on the throne. 'I *note* them,' comes the wry reply. 'Sir, I take it you have no comment at this stage.' 'Not at this stage,' replies the Prisoner after a pause. 'Then the accused will be held in a place of sentence until after your inauguration. Remove him,' orders the President. Carried away by two guards, the young man is strapped back onto the pole from whence he came. 'Hear the word of the Lord, Dem bones dem bones, dem dry bones ... ' sings Number 48 as a button is pressed and the condemned man sinks back into the smoke-filled pit. 'A most regrettable demonstration,' the President comments, turning to look at the Prisoner. 'My apologies, sir.' 'Oh don't mention it,' grins the man in the chair. 'I think you'll find our next revolutionary a different kettle of fish altogether,' grins the bewigged man as, looking at the television monitor screen, he begins to laugh.

'Next,' grins the President as the circular rubber pad extending from the elongated arm is removed from Number 2's face, which has now been shorn of its beard, although he still retains his neatly-trimmed moustache. Seeing this, the President and the delegates break into laughter. Miraculously the 'dead' man stirs. His eyes flicker open and stare blankly at the ceiling. The medical team remove the straps from the patient's wrists and feet and, rising to his feet, the 'reborn' Number 2 takes a few faltering steps forward, his fingers stroking his now naked chin. Pausing before the assembly he raises his hand. The laughter ceases abruptly. 'I FEEL A NEW MAN ... !' he exclaims. With a hearty chuckle, he turns to look at the man sitting in the chair of honour. 'My dear chap!' he exclaims, mounting the dais steps to shake the Prisoner's hand. 'How've you been keeping? The throne at last eh ... I knew it. It had to be ... And you my little friend ... ' he greets the silent Butler ' ... Ever faithful.' Descending the steps, he beckons for the manservant to follow him. 'Come on ... come on come on ... ' Staring at the Prisoner, the Butler does not budge. ' ... New allegiances,' says Number 2, shrugging his shoulders. 'Such is the price of fame ... and failure. Dear me, how sad.' Spreading his arms, he begins to address the large assembly. 'My Lords, Ladies and Gentlemen ... a most extraordinary thing happened to me on my way ... here.' Breaking into laughter, the delegates give him a rousing ovation. Mounting the President's pulpit, the superior calls for silence by raising his hand. 'It has been my lot, in the past, to wield a not inconsiderable power. Nay, I have had the ear of statesmen, kings and princes of many lands. Governments have been swayed, policies defined and revolutions nipped in the bud at a word from me in the right place and at the propitious time ... ' A pause, a wry grin and he turns to address himself directly to the President. ' ... not surprising therefore, that this *community* should find a use for me. Not altogether by accident, that one day I should be *abducted* and wake up here amongst you ... ' He returns his attention to the assembly. ' ... What is deplorable, is that *I* resisted for so *short* a time ... a fine tribute to your methods.' To a man, the delegates applaud his words. Again he motions for silence. 'I wish to thank you for recognition of my talents, which placed me in a position of power second only – to ONE ... ' Descending from the pulpit, he continues his address from the floor. 'This authority, gave me the right to make decisions. My last decision concerned this gentleman here ... ' Holding out his arm, he points to the man sitting in the chair of honour. ' ... which could be resolved only in the death of either one or the other of us. He emerged victorious ... I ... apparently ... ' Pausing, he turns to state at the man who 'killed' him. Confused, his attention is drawn to the monitor screen on which is being played out the final excruciating seconds of his final defeat. '*Die Six Die!*' says the figure on the screen. '*Four* ... ' he hears himself mutter. '*Die!*' screams the figure of the screen. '*Two-ooo*' his image gurgles. Bemused, the superior stares at the assembly. ' ... *Died?*' says the revived Number 2. '*Die!*' echoes the voice from the screen. In graphic detail, his 'death' continues to unfold before him. '*Die!*' screams the image of Number 6. '*One-oone,*' wheezes his voice. '*DIE!*' 'Was it the drink?' yells Number 2, turning to the President, who stares back in silence. 'You couldn't even let me rest in peace.' sneers the superior, having watched the man on the screen sink into oblivion. 'How was it DONE?' 'There have to be some security secrets that are kept from a ... late Number 2,' confirms the man on the pulpit. 'Did you ever meet him,' asks the Prisoner. 'What's that?' asks the dejected Number 2. 'Did you ever *meet* Number 1?' 'Face to face?' 'Yes,' urges the one once denoted as '6'. 'Meet *HIM* ... ' laughs the other, walking across the chamber to stand mockingly in front of the tubular metal container denoted '1'. ' ... Meet him.' The metal eye set into the column emits a green light into the superior's face, daring the deposed

man to continue. 'Shall I ... give him a stare?' whispers Number 2 in a show of boldness. 'You transgress!' yells the President. 'I *shall* give him a stare ... ' mocks the man standing in the pulsating green light. Defiantly, he turns to stare at the metal-lidded lens. 'Look me in the eye ... ' he sneers. The eye flickers open, its intense white cornea defying the deposed leader's challenge. His face a mask of determination. Number 2 walks purposefully towards the mechanical eye. ' ... Whoever you are ... *whatever* you are ... ' 'You'll die!' screams the man in the scarlet robe. 'Then ... I'll die ... with my own mind ... ' returns Number 2, tearing the '2' badge off his blazer lapel. ' ... You'll hypnotise me no longer.' he challenges. In reply, a dense cloud of gas emits from the hooded-eye and envelopes the superior's head. Gritting his teeth, in a mock gesture of submission, Number 2 lunges forwards – and spits directly into the cortex of the mechanical eye. In an instant clouds of acrid dense smoke pour out of the container. Triumphant, Number 2 holds his arms aloft in victory – arms that are grabbed by two uniformed guards who drag the deposed leader before the President's pulpit. 'Sir?' calls the bewigged man. 'Hold him.' snaps the Prisoner. 'In the place of sentence?' 'Until my inaugur-ation.' commands the seated man. 'Secure him!' orders the President and Number 2 is dragged away to be strapped to a second piston-pole and suffers the same fate as Number 48 – but not before he holds up a challenging finger in a gesture of warning and guffaws an ominous 'Be seeing

'Be seeing you'

you' as he descends into the darkness of the pit. 'We have just witnessed two forms of revolt ... ' sighs the President. ' ... The first, uncoordinated *youth*, rebelling against nothing it can define. The second, an established, successful, secure member of the establishment, turning upon, and biting the hand that feeds him. Well these attitudes are dangerous, they contribute nothing to our culture and are to be stamped *out* ... !' Applause from the assembly, which stops abruptly as the flasing green light emits from the container, denoted with a large red letter '1'. As if by magic, two civilians appear on the monitor screen and are seen removing a 'For Sale' sign from the railings outside the Prisoner's London home. ' ... At the other end of the scale ... ' continues the President. ' ...

we are honoured to have with us. a revolutionary of different calibre . . . ' On screen. the one once known as Number 6 is pictured driving up to his front door in KAR 120C. ' . . . He has revolted. Resisted. Fought. Held fast. Maintained. Destroyed resistance. Overcome coercion. The right to be Person. Someone or Individual . . . ' A man dressed in maintenance overalls is seen cleaning the yellow and green Lotus. ' . . . We applaud his private war. and we concede that despite materialistic efforts he has survived intact and secure . . . All that remains is. recognition of a *man* – a man of steel . . . A man magnificently equipped to lead us . . . That is . . . lead us or *go*. In this connection. we have a prize . . . ' Below him. one of the robed figures wheels an ornate coffee table on castors into the chamber. On its top sits a golden chest. ' . . . You will see that your home is being made ready. Above and beyond this. we have the means for you to desert us and go *anywhere* . . . ' informs the President. Having parked the table before the dais. the hooded delegate delves into the chest and holds up an object. ' . . . The key to your house.' states the man dressed in the scarlet robe. as the robed figure holds up several other items in turn. 'Travellers' cheques . . . a million. Passport . . . valid for anywhere. And er, petty cash . . . You are free to go!' confirms the man in the pulpit. 'Free to go?' echoes the Prisoner. 'Anywhere.' grins the President. 'Why?' 'You have been such an example to us . . . ' 'Why?' asks the man sitting in the chair of honour. ' . . . You have convinced us of our mistakes . . . ' *'Why?'* ' . . . You are pure. *You* know the way. Show *us* . . . ' 'Why?' enquires the seated man. ' . . . Your revolt is good and honest. You are the only individual. We *need* you.' 'I see.' quips the man on the dais. ' . . . You do.' confirms the President. *'You see all.' 'I'm* an individual?' urges the one being addressed. 'You are on your own.' 'I fail to see.' mocks the other. Leaning forwards. the bewigged President spreads his arms. 'All about you is . . . *yours*. We *concede*. We offer. We *plead* . . . ' states the speaker. leaving his pulpit and pacing the floor ' . . . for *you* to lead *us*.' 'Or go.' 'Go if you wish.' 'Well, I . . . I . . . don't know.' says the seated man. inclining his head in a gesture of thought. 'Take the stand. Address us.' pleads the President. 'Should I?' enquires the Prisoner. 'You *must*. You *are* the greatest. Make a statement . . . a *true* statement which could only be yours . . . but for us. Remember us. don't forget us . . . ' says the other. ' . . . Keep *us* in mind. Sir, we are all yours.' Having given some thought to the President's words, the man sat on the throne rises to his feet. To a flourish of music. he purposefully descends the dais steps and picks up his passport from the table. The delegates applaud. Acknowledging their ovation. he slips his possessions into the pockets of his jacket and, picking up the stringed purse containing the petty cash. walks proudly to the pulpit vacated by the President. Placing the coins into his trouser pocket and silencing the assembly with a bang of his gavel. he begins his address. 'I . . . ' 'Aye. aye. aye. aye, aye . . . ' echo the delegates. He brings down his gavel a second time. 'I feel . . . ' His words are lost in shouts from the delegates. He tries again. 'I . . . ' 'Aye. aye. aye. aye . . . ' *'I* feel . . . ' 'Aye. aye. aye. aye. aye. aye,' stamp the delegates. drowning out his words. His attempts to get across his message continues for several minutes until. losing his temper. he is about to scream for silence. when. with a solitary raised finger. the President motions the assembly to silence. 'Sir, on behalf of us all.' states the man dressed in scarlet. 'We thank you. And now I take it that you are prepared to meet . . . er.

Number 1. Follow me if you would be so kind. sir.' Following the bewigged figure across the floor of the chamber. the Prisoner walks over to stand beside one of the pits. Bowing as the President leaves. he steps onto a platform and descends into the darkness below. The doors before him slide open and. passing the rows of uniformed guards who stand at attention on either side of a long passage. he walks down the brightly-lit corridor to find the youth and the deposed Number 2 encased in two plastic tubes denoted Orbit 48 and Orbit 2 respectively. The young man is still humming the garbled words of his song. the other continuing his raucous laughter. To the right of the figures stands a third tube labelled 'Orbit'. Empty. it opens at the push of a button from a robed controller. A claxon sounds and turning. the intruder sees the Butler striding down the corridor towards him. Passing silently before the uniformed guards. bowing to his new master. the manservant invites the Prisoner to ascend a spiral staircase. Having climbed cautiously upwards. he finds his way blocked by a huge metal door. At the push of a button. it slides back to reveal a circular antechamber protected by glass. Globes of varying sizes sit on top of a circular glass table. Rotating slowly. each represents the planet earth. Before him stands a robed figure. watching the ubiquitous television monitor screen on which events from the onlooker's past life are being projected. *'I will not be pushed. filed. stamped. indexed. briefed. debriefed or numbered. . . . I will not be push . . .* ' drones the image behind him. as. accepting the clear glass orb. the white-robed figure hands to him. the hooded figure suddenly lifts up its arms and rears like a spectre before him. For the first time. the intruder notices the circled numeral painted over the robed man's heart – an ominous black number '1'! Dropping the glass orb to the floor. he reaches out his hand to tear away the black and white mask that covers the spectre's face. (At last. Number 1!) Snatched away. the mask reveals the grinning countenance of a grinning ape. This. too. is torn aside to reveal . . . the hideous distorted face of himself!! To the accompaniment of the spectre's hysterical laughter. the intruder chases his duplicate around the room. Round and round they race until. emitting a terrifying scream. the duplicate races up a ladder and escapes through a safety hatch into the chamber above. Its grotesque face is shut off from sight when its pursuer pulls down the safety hatch cover and swings the locking device shut. Above them. sitting on the Prisoner's vacated throne. the President twitches his fingers nervously across his lips as. staring at the metallic container marked '1'. he sees the mechanical eye snap shut with a clunk. Grabbing up a fire-extinguisher from the wall. the Prisoner quietly descends the spiral staircase. to find the mute manservant standing silently on its lower rung. Although unable to speak. the servant motions with his eyes that danger lies ahead. Leaping down from the staircase. his master springs into action. blasting the hooded figures in the room with the fire-extinguisher. Having cut down several of the opposition. he flings the fire-extinguisher to the Butler and turns on the guards with his fists. To the accompaniment of Number 2's raucous laughter. the man and the Butler cut down the opposition like nine-pins. Several minutes later. the door to the ante-room slides back to expose a hooded figure inviting the uniformed guards into the room. They enter and find themselves mowed down by the Butler who. wielding the fire-extinguisher like a tommy-gun. soon puts a stop to their antics. Stripping off his robe as he races back up the spiral staircase. the Prisoner flicks on the controls of the television monitor. Seeing the President and the assembly patrolling the floor of the cavern, he depresses a red button on the panel in front of him – a red fuel injection button. The room is not a room at all, but a rocket! For a second, nothing happens, until, noting that the man dressed in scarlet is staring directly at the rocket labelled '1', the Prisoner jams his finger onto the button a second time. He then rotates a disc marked 'Maximum Hold'. 'Contact ... Control ...' screams the President's voice over the public address system above the Prisoner's head. ' ... Confirm contact. Priority ...' Spotting the rocket's countdown button, the man at the control console flicks it downwards. ' ... Contact Priority ... contact.' screams the President, as he races to the gantry and attempts to reach the control room by radio. ' ... Emergency, contact ... Contact ... Control, emergency.' he screams into a microphone as he races before the rows of computers and machinery. 'All personnel take cover ...' Disguised under a mask and robe, the Prisoner rises from a pit. He tears off his hood and opens fire on the troops with a machine gun. An all-out battle ensues on the floor of the chamber during which, released by the Prisoner earlier, Numbers 2 and 48 join in, mowing down the uniformed guards with glee. 'All You Need Is Love' throbs the juke box as the Prisoner and his comrades embark on their orgy of destruction. Within minutes the President, delegates and the uniformed guards are forced to race from the cavern. Above them in the Village, the sirens scream and the President's voice calls out 'Evacuate, evacuate, evacuate ...' Pouring out of their cottages in droves, the inhabitants race wildly through the streets of the Village. Helicopters take off and soar high over the community. Below ground, the Prisoner and his companions leap into the self-contained cage that had until recently served as Number 2's tomb. With the Butler at its controls, the unit slowly departs from the cavern, the wheels of its trailer picking up speed as the 'home from home' enters a long, dark corridor.

Zero minus two minutes registers the dial of the countdown clock as the Butler eases the trailer down towards the daylight ahead. 'Evacuate, evacuate ...' screams the voice of the Village public address system as the Villagers race for their lives across the golden sands of the beach. The noise of sirens from buggies driven at speed combine with the drone of the helicopter engines as, within minutes of the alarm being raised, the Village is evacuated. 'Five, four, three, two, one' ticks the countdown clock as the Butler rams his foot on the accelerator and smashes down the iron gates that protect the tunnel's mouth. In the intense white heat of its exhaust flame, the rocket rises high over the Village, its seering white tail-flames lighting up the dome of the residence once occupied by Number 2. A Rover rises from the bubbling ocean, gurgling its way to the surface. Dying, it sinks back into the bubbling mud that was once the cavern floor. High above the once-thriving community, a helicopter soars across the sky, leaving the panoramic view of the Village far behind.

Out on the road, the free men throw sections of the kitchen out onto the highway. Some distance behind them, a bowler-hatted civil servant switches on his car radio, the words of 'Dem Bones' blaring out from its speaker. Drawing alongside the unusual trailer the escapee and his companions pick up the rhythm through the car's open window and dance a jig in the cage. Seeing their frivolous antics, the man at the wheel of the car rams his foot hard on the accelerator and speeds away from the madmen. A roadside sign informs him that London is but 27 miles away.

Braking to a stop at the roadside, the trailer deposits the man once known as Number 48 onto a grass verge. Waving goodbye to his friends, the top-hatted figure sets out on foot to hitch-hike his way home. Entering the busy London streets, the somewhat odd-looking transport pulls over to the curb, waved down by a policeman on a motorcycle. Barely a hundred yards down the street, loom the Houses of Parliament, the tower of Big Ben beckoning

Home at last. The man and his Butler allow a hearse to pass before he climbs into the seat of his beloved Lotus and drives off to face – what?

the citizens home. Its passengers alight and the former Number 2 walks proudly in the direction of the seat of power. Hopping down from the vehicle the Butler joins his new master at the roadside in front of the bemused constable. Alone with his thoughts, the ex-Number 2 stares up at Big Ben, then trots across the road and turns to give his companions a wave. Turning to see the Butler standing some distance away, the man once known as Number 6 smiles wryly. Turning to look over his shoulder at the strangely-garbed manservant, the policeman approaches him. The scene which ensues (seen through the Butler's eyes) is nothing if not ludicrous. Engaging the policeman in conversation, the ex-Number 6 breaks into a pantomimic description of how he and his oddly-dressed little friend came to be walking the streets of London in such unusual circumstances. Before the bemused law officer can catch his breath, the ex-Prisoner walks calmly to the small man, clasps him by the hand and together they race away from the scene to hop on board a number 59 double-decker bus.

In the closing minutes of the story, the young man in the top-hat is seen hitch-hiking his way down a dual carriageway. (The actor's name, Alexis Kanner, is flashed onto the screen.) Placing his thumbs into his belt, he races across the highway and lifts his thumb high to hitch-hike in the opposite direction.

In a London street, the man and his Butler reach the man's former home. Pausing for a moment to allow a long black hearse to drive past, the man climbs into the seat of his beloved yellow and green Lotus which sits parked at the curb. He guns its engine. It throbs into life. Turning, the Butler mounts the steps of the house (the name Angelo Muscat appears on the screen) and passes through the door which has opened of its own volition. Behind him, the man at the wheel of the Lotus guns its engine and joins the busy London traffic. (A single word appears on the screen 'Prisoner'.)

Dressed now in a smart pin-stripe business suit, a black bowler perched on his head, a white carnation in the lapel of his jacket, the one once known as Number 2 stares up at the Houses of Parliament. (The name Leo McKern appears on the screen.) Smiling as thunderclaps heave across the sky, swinging his umbrella and briefcase, he marches purposefully past a policeman who stands beneath an archway, and enters the building's forecourt.

Having left the London streets far behind, the custom built Lotus races at speed down a deserted highway. Its driver, clad entirely in black, his face set in determination, places his foot on the accelerator and motors on at speed.

AUTHOR'S NOTE: After a reprise of scenes from *Once Upon A Time*, a special credit sequence with a different version of the theme music, revealed (for the very first time) that the Village location was set 'In the grounds of Portmeirion, Penrhyndeudraeth, North Wales, by courtesy of Mr Clough William Ellis.'

KAR 120C, seen in this story, was a 'lookalike' — the one used in the standard opening sequence having been sold and exported overseas.

PRODUCTION CREDITS

(Episodes 1 to 12 inclusive, and Episode 16)

Produced by:
David Tomblin

Executive Producer:
Patrick McGoohan

Script Editor:
George Markstein

Production Manager:
Bernard Williams

Director of Photography:
Brendan J. Stafford B.S.C.

Art Director:
Jack Shampan

Editors:
Lee Doig, Geoffrey Foot, John S. Smith, Spencer Reeve

Theme by:
Ron Grainer

Incidental Music By:
Albert Elms
(Episodes 2, 4, 6, 7, 9 to 17)

Music Editors:
Bob Dearberg (Episodes 1, 3, 5)
John S. Smith (Episode 7)
Eric Mival (All others)

Assistant Directors:
Gino Marotta (Episodes 1 to 11 and 16)
Ernie Morris (Episode 12)

Casting Director:
Rose Tobias Shaw

(Episodes 13, 14, 15 and 17)
Production personnel as above with the following changes

Production Manager:
Ronald Liles

Editors:
Eric Boyd-Perkins, Maureen Ackland

Assistant Directors:
Gino Marotta (All episodes)
Ernie Lewis (Episode 13)

An ITC Production by Everyman Films Ltd.
Made on location and at Metro Goldwyn Mayer Studios,
Borehamwood, England

THE PRISONER

A Concise History of the Prisoner Appreciation Society

FORMED IN DECEMBER 1976, so much has happened in the annals of *Six Of One* that to attempt to give a full description of events would take several pages. Ergo this potted history – with apologies to my good friend Simon Coward, who spent much of his leisure time putting together a five and a half-page document intended for that very purpose. (Sorry chum!)

Since the birth of *Six Of One* in January 1977 (prior to this date the society was distributing a Prisoner newsletter *The Tally Ho Special Edition*) several thousands of people have joined the network, each receiving a veritable wealth of professionally-produced colourful magazines, badges, maps of the Village, episode guides and music albums as well as merchandise such as T-shirts, stickers and postcards – all of a high standard. Conventions are held on an annual basis, with the highlight of the year being a weekend event at Portmeirion itself – although the gatherings do not stop there. Mini-conventions are regularly held elsewhere, the majority usually taking place with a visit to the sites that served as locations for the series: Beachy Head in Sussex, The Thatched Barn Hotel in Borehamwood (*Many Happy Returns* and *The Girl Who Was Death*), the disused railway tunnel at Mayfield, Sussex (*Fall Out*) and so on.

In addition to the regular quarterly magazines, other publications have been distributed: *The Prisoner Episode Guide*, *The Making of The Prisoner*, *The Prisoner of Portmeirion* – professionally produced publications of extremely high quality. *Think Tank* and its sequel *When In Rome* are immensely readable novels based on the series, written and produced by noted Prisoner authority Roger Langley. *Six Of One* has released a long-playing album of Prisoner music, an extended-play single and a flexi-disc containing an alternative (unused) version of the main theme by Ron Grainer.

In addition to these, the society has interviewed its Honorary President, Patrick McGoohan, producer David Tomblin, script editor George Markstein and actors and actresses who appeared in the series. In 1982 *The Prisoner Shop and Information Centre* was opened in Portmeirion. A film *By Public Demand* was produced and given a four-star rating in the *Movie Maker* magazine's 'Ten Best' competition. Members were asked to participate in the Channel 4 documentary *Six Into One: The Prisoner File*.

If all this sounds too good to be true, or strikes you as being far-removed from the average 'fan' organisation, it is hardly surprising. Take it from one who knows, there is nothing *average* about *Six Of One*. Since its inception, the society has signposted the path for others to follow. Wish to learn more? Drop a line to:–

P.O. Box 60, Harrogate, HG1 2TP

Anyone writing should include a stamped S.A.E. Overseas enquiries should contain an *unstamped* self-addressed envelope, together with International Reply Coupons (obtainable from post offices) to cover return postage.

Notes on the Author

Book by book, the author is becoming Britain's popular TV guru.

Born in Stoke-on-Trent, Staffordshire, Dave Rogers found himself thrust into becoming an author of books based on television and film by accident – literally. Having spent 25 years of his life as a house decorator, a tumble from a ladder caused injury to his vertebrae and left him encased in plaster of Paris for a period of 10 months, during which time he sought solace from his injuries by deciding to capitalise on his interest in television by writing a book based upon the hugely popular 60s cult TV series *The Avengers*, a volume that proved so popular that Dave was commissioned to write a second Avengers-related volume *The Avengers Anew* two years later by the same publisher.

The author's ongoing relationship with Boxtree Limited began in 1987 when he was commissioned to research and write *The ITV Encyclopedia of Adventure*. With over 3,200 entries and 5,400 episodes from 200 of the most popular British-produced TV series screened on independent television over the last thirty years, this is an essential unputdownable viewing companion that is destined to become the standard work on the subject.

This title was followed with the publication of *The Complete Avengers*, Dave's third book on the series, which provided for the first time in a single volume the definitive guide to the show.

Now Dave has used his encyclopedic knowledge of the world of television to produce this book. *The Prisoner/Danger Man* is the fully comprehensive account of the true story behind the series that held the nation spellbound during the late 60s. This title is based on the official archives and is fully endorsed by the Six-of-One Prisoner Appreciation Society.

What the critics had to say about:

The ITV Encyclopedia of Adventure
An absolute cracker (Swansea Gazette)
Provides endless enjoyment (Time Out)

The Complete Avengers
A glorious celebration of one of the most compelling action/adventure TV series ever devised (Swansea Gazette)
Recalling those fantastical plots has hijacked my mind (The Listener)

Prisoner Videos

All 17 episodes of *The Prisoner* starring Patrick McGoohan are available on video from:
PolyGram Video Limited.
Available from all good video stores.

Details are as follows

Episode 1 and 2: Arrival/The Chimes of Big Ben
Episode 3 and 4: A, B and C/Free For All
Episode 5 and 6: The Schizoid Man/The General
Episode 7 and 8: Many Happy Returns/Dance of the Dead
Episode 9 and 10: Checkmate/Hammer into Anvil
Episode 11 and 12: It's Your Funeral/A Change of Mind
Episode 13 and 14: Do Not Forsake Me Oh My Darling/Living In Harmony
Episode 15 and 16: The Girl Who Was Death/Once Upon a Time
Episode17: Fall Out

Danger Man Videos

6 episodes of *Danger Man* starring Patrick McGoohan are available on three volumes from:

ITC Home Video

Danger Man No. 1: 'Koroshi'/'Shinda Shima'
Danver Man No. 2: 'Colony Three'/'The Ubiquitous Mr Lovegrove'
Danger Man No. 3: 'I'm Afraid You Have The Wrong Number'/'Not So Jolly Roger'

Further bestsellers from
B⬚XTREE

THE INCREDIBLE WORLD OF 007

Lee Pfeiffer and Philip Lisa

Over one quarter of the world's population has seen a James Bond film, and this book sets out to investigate every aspect of the Bond phenomenon.

It reveals the minutiae of detail that every Bond fan craves: the television versions, rare memorabilia and merchandise, the film soundtracks, out-takes and bloopers, and all the ingenious gadgets – plus exclusive interviews with the actors who have played Bond.

THE INCREDIBLE WORLD OF 007 includes previously unpublished photographs from the Bond archives, and is a must for every Bond fan.

1 85283 141 3   £15.99 pb

THE JAMES BOND GIRLS

Graham Rye

The James Bond girls, like 007 himself, have become part of cinema legend . . . Ursula Andress's memorable emergence from the sea in *Dr. No*, Honor Blackman's judo-throwing pilot Pussy Galore in *Goldfinger*, and Diana Rigg's firey Tracey in *On Her Majesty's Secret Service* – the only woman to ever become Mrs James Bond.

Featuring over 100 colour photos, THE JAMES BOND GIRLS is the first book to examine fully the extraordinary women who grace the world of Ian Fleming's secret agent.

1 85283 267 3   £9.99 pb

THUNDERBIRDS ARE GO!

John Marriot
Published in association with ITC

Buckle your seatbelts and prepare for lift off – Thunderbirds are go! The unforgettable puppet heroes who first launched into action in 1964 are back. In this ideal gift book the history and background of the series are detailed, including interviews with the creator, Gerry Anderson, scriptwriters and production staff.

The biographies of Jeff Tracey, his five sons, Brains, Lady Penelope and her chauffeur, Parker, are all here. And careful attention has been paid to the functions and features of the five fabulous, futuristic, Thunderbird machines – not forgetting Lady Penelope's pink Rolls Royce!

1 85283 164 2   £9.99 pb

STINGRAY

Dave Rogers

It's 2065 and Captain Troy Tempest is in command of a super-submarine patrolling the seas for the World Aquanaut Security Patrol.

Another classic from the cult Supermarionation team, STINGRAY is returning to our television screens, and in this book fans can find details of all the characters and their adventures, plus background information on the series and its creators.

1 85283 191 X   £9.99 pb

THE BOXTREE ENCYCLOPEDIA OF TV DETECTIVES

Geoff Tibballs

This comprehensive volume brings together for the first time all the essential information on television detective programmes.

Covering more than 250 series, both British and international, this fascinating encyclopedia features all the police detectives, amateur sleuths and private investigators that have entertained us since television began. Entries include the working methods, style and characteristics of the detectives, descriptions of the series, cast lists and transmission dates.

1 85283 129 4   £17.99 pb

THE COMPLETE AVENGERS

Dave Rogers

The Avengers, first shown in 1961, has become a cult fantasy adventure series that is still shown regularly today. THE COMPLETE AVENGERS provides for the first time in a single volume a comprehensive guide to all the Avengers programmes including The New Avengers.

It features interviews with the Avengers' stars, including Patrick Macnee, Honor Blackman, Joanna Lumley and Gareth Hunt; it includes over 200 black and white photographs, never before published, plus much, much more.

1 85283 244 4   £12.99 pb